W9-CHQ-116

Neue Freunde

HBJ

Foreign Language Programs

GERMAN

- **Neue Freunde**
  Level 1
- **Wir, die Jugend**
  Level 2
- **Unsere Welt**
  Level 3

Neue Freunde

HBJ
HARCOURT BRACE JOVANOVICH, PUBLISHERS
Orlando San Diego Chicago Dallas

Printed in the United States of America
ISBN 0-15-383500-1

PHOTO CREDITS: All photos by George Winkler/Harbrace except: **1:** Horst Munzig/Anne Hamann; **2:** (tr circle)Hans Madej/Bilderberg; (c)Ossi Baumeister/Anne Hamann; (br)Hans Madej/Bilderberg; **3:** (insert)Ossi Baumeister/Anne Hamann; **4:** (c)Ossi Baumeister/Anne Hamann; (b)Walter Schmitz/Bilderberg;(insert)J. Messerschmidt/Stock Market; **5:** (t)R. Betzler/Anne Hamann; (bl)Margot Granitsas/Photo Researchers;(br)Guido Mangold/Anne Hamann; **6:** (t–insert)Andrej Reiser/Bilderberg; (c)Milan Horacek/Bilderberg; (b)Andrej Reiser/Bilderberg; (insert)Andrej Reiser/Bilderberg; **7:** (tl)Ossi Baumeister/Anne Hamann; (br)Alexas Urba/Stock Market; **8:** (t)Luis Villota/Stock Market; (t–insert)Guido Mangold/Anne Hamann; (b)Werner Müller/Peter Arnold; (b–insert)Werner Müller/Peter Arnold; **9:** (tl)Steve Vidler/Leo de Wys; (tr)G. Davies/Leo de Wys; (bl)Dagmar Fabricius/Stock Boston; (br)Steve Vidler/Leo de Wys; **10:** (tr)Ossi Baumeister/Anne Hamann; (br—2nd from bottom)Bob Krist/Leo de Wys; **11:** (tl)Culver; (tr)Bettmann Archive; (cl)Scala/Art Resource; (cr)Giraudon/Art Resource; (bl)Bettmann Archive; (bc)Ken Hawkins/Sygma; (br)Marburg/Art Resource; **12:** (tl)Culver; (tr)Bettmann Archive; (cl)Culver; (cr)Bettmann Archive; (bl)German Information Center; (br)Bettmann Archive; **13:** (tl insert)H. Newton/Sygma; (t)J.L. Atlan/Sygma; (bl)Sygma; (bc)H. Newton/Sygma; (br)Culver; **14:** (b)Adam Woolfitt/Woodfin Camp;

continued on page 391

Writer
George Winkler

Contributing Writer
Margrit Meinel Diehl

Editorial Advisors

Robert L. Baker
Middlebury College
Middlebury, VT

Pat Barr-Harrison
Prince George's County Schools
Landover, MD

Ellen N. Benson
Northwestern High School
Hyattsville, MD

Ann Beusch
Hood College
Frederick, MD

Guy Capelle
Université de Paris VIII
Paris, France

Inge D. Halpert
Columbia University
New York, NY

Charles R. Hancock
Ohio State University
Columbus, OH

William Jassey
Norwalk Board of Education
Norwalk, CT

Dora Kennedy
Prince George's County Schools
Landover, MD

Claire J. Kramsch
Massachusetts Institute of Technology
Cambridge, MA

Ilonka Schmidt Mackey
Université Laval
Québec, Canada

William F. Mackey
Université Laval
Québec, Canada

Consultants and Reviewers

Wolfgang M. Bauer
Loyola High School
Los Angeles, CA

Dorothea Bruschke
Parkway School District
Chesterfield, MO

Edeltraut Ehrlich
Markgräfler Gymnasium
Müllheim, FRG

Eileen Johannsen
Nicolet High School
Glendale, WI

Gisela Schwab
Ramapo High School
Franklin Lakes, NJ

Field-Test Teachers

Cecilia Brisentine,
Baltimore, MD

Dieter Dose
Accompsett Intermediate School
Smithtown, NY

Maureen Helinski
Andover Senior High School
Baltimore, MD

Barbara Hoess
Springfield High School
Erdenheim, PA

Carol Paezold Kochefko
Staples High School
Westport, CT

Robert K. Krebs
Smithtown High School West
Smithtown, NY

Rita Leonardi
Brian McMahon High School
South Norwalk, CT

Lynn Preston
Haddon Township High School
Westmont, NJ

Renate Wilson
Frederick High School
Frederick, MD

ACKNOWLEDGMENTS

We wish to express our thanks to the students pictured in this textbook and to the parents who allowed us to photograph these young people in their homes and in other places. We also thank the teachers and the families who helped us find these young people; the school administrators who allowed us to photograph the students in their schools; and the merchants who permitted us to photograph the students in their stores and other places of business.

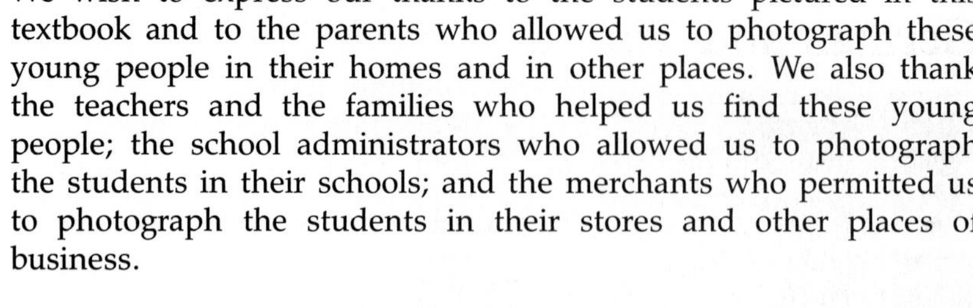

YOUNG PEOPLE
Christof Augenstein, Nadja Balawi, Jens Balcke, Anja Bayertz, Jutta Bolanz, Michael Böse, Bernhard Braun, Matthias Braun, Daniela Broghammer, Christine Cochius, Margit Dastl, Josef Eisenhofer, Hans-Georg Esser, Natalie Fiedler, Jörg Flechtner, Michael Gipp, Nicolas Golubvic, Olaf Günter, Anja Hauswirth, Herman Holst, Marina Hrusha, Mona Johannsen, Daniele Käser, Daniel Kehl, Katja Keiling, Josef Kerscher, Stefan Kiefer, Katja Kramer, Birte Kreuzer, Matthias Kroll, Eva Leonhardt, Michaela Mayer, Jörg Mast, Giuseppe Matano, Philipp Nedel, Wiebke Nedel, Meike Nimmermann, Sven Nipken, Gupse Özkan, Kathrin Pahulycz, Michael Pertsch, Christian Risch, Bruno Schmidlin, Ulrike Schwemmer, Tobias Steinhoff, Claudia Stromberger, Friederike Thyssen, Hendrik Wermier, Rita Werner, Christian Wild

TEACHERS AND FAMILIES
Fritz and Marianne Brunner, Dornbirn; Burkhardt and Edeltraut Ehrlich, Müllheim; Ernst and Christine Hofer, Wien; Hartmut and Sabine Nedel, Neuss; Karl-Uwe and Renate Sperling; Niebüll; Marianne Sperling, München

CONTENTS

INTRODUCTION
German and You 1

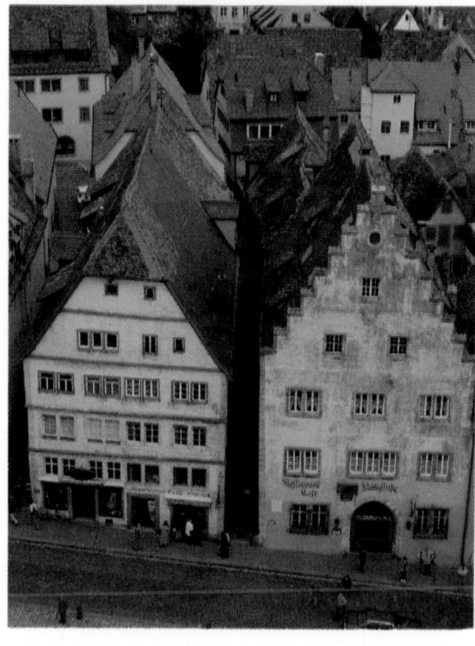

ERSTER TEIL

BASIC MATERIAL

COMMUNICATIVE FUNCTIONS	GRAMMAR	CULTURE
Socializing • Saying hello and goodbye • Greeting adults		Popular first names of boys and girls Meeting and greeting people
Exchanging information • Asking and giving names • Asking who someone is	The definite articles **der, die, das**	German family names and German names in the United States
Exchanging information • Asking someone's age and telling your age **Counting** • Learning the numbers from 0 to 20	The personal pronouns and the verb **sein**	How numerals are written and how they are signaled by hand
Exchanging information • Asking where someone else is from and telling where you're from **Socializing** • Saying you don't understand and asking for clarification	Asking and answering questions	A map of the German-speaking countries showing where our friends live Using the **Sie**-form
Recombining communicative functions, grammar, and vocabulary		Writing a letter in German to a pen pal
Reading for practice and pleasure		Geography of German-speaking countries Greetings on postcards

BASIC MATERIAL

KAPITEL 2
Schule 60

COMMUNICATIVE FUNCTIONS	GRAMMAR	CULTURE
Exchanging information • Telling how you get to school	The verb **kommen**	How students get to school
Exchanging information • Asking about prices of school supplies **Socializing** • Saying please, thank you, and you're welcome • Getting someone's attention	The definite articles **der, die, das** Noun plurals **Was kostet—was kosten** The pronouns **er, sie, es,** and **sie** (plural)	German currency and how to read prices The concept of grammatical gender
Exchanging information • Giving information about your class schedule • Telling time	The verb **haben**	System of scheduling classes Subjects taught in German schools
Exchanging information • Talking about homework and grades **Expressing feelings and emotions** • Responding to good news and to bad news		System of grading
Recombining communicative functions, grammar, and vocabulary		A German exchange student talks about himself
Reading for practice and pleasure		

BASIC MATERIAL

COMMUNICATIVE FUNCTIONS	GRAMMAR	CULTURE
Exchanging information • Asking someone about his or her interests	Using the **du**-form Using the **ihr**-form The present tense	Popular sports and hobbies Three ways of saying *you* in German
Exchanging information • Talking about when and how often you do your various sports and activities	Word order: verb in second place	How young people spend their free time
Expressing attitudes and opinions • Asking for an opinion; expressing enthusiasm or the lack of it • Expressing surprise, agreement, and disagreement **Expressing feelings and emotions** • Expressing likes, dislikes, and preferences	**gern, lieber, am liebsten, nicht gern**	Student survey: preferred sports activities
Recombining communicative functions, grammar, and vocabulary		Olympic sports symbols Pen-pal section from a magazine for young people
Reading for practice and pleasure		What young people read A computer hobbyist
Reviewing communicative functions, grammar, and vocabulary		Excerpts from a school newspaper

ZWEITER TEIL

BASIC MATERIAL

COMMUNICATIVE FUNCTIONS	GRAMMAR	CULTURE
Exchanging information • Saying what you need to take on a trip	The definite article, nominative and accusative case	Map of Germany, showing cities with airports Welcome aboard—information for air travelers
Exchanging information • Asking for information and giving directions • Giving distances from one city to another using a map	The **möchte-**forms	Arriving at a German airport—international signs and symbols The German post office and phone company Measuring distances in kilometers
Socializing • Exchanging money • Making a phone call **Exchanging information** • Reading a flight monitor • Expressing flight numbers, departure times, and gate numbers		German money; exchanging money The 24-hour system of telling time The German telephone system
Recombining communicative functions, grammar, and vocabulary		At the airport information counter; plane and train schedules
Reading for practice and pleasure		Landmarks of the city of Cologne

BASIC MATERIAL

KAPITEL 6
Bei den Nedels 166

COMMUNICATIVE FUNCTIONS	GRAMMAR	CULTURE
Socializing • Introducing someone, introducing yourself, and responding to an introduction	**ein** and **mein,** nominative case forms	Family members and close relatives
Exchanging information • Talking about your home **Socializing** • Complimenting someone and responding to a compliment • Saying thank you and you're welcome	Indefinite articles, accusative case The preposition **für**	Inside a German home How Germans respond to a compliment
Exchanging information • Talking about appearance and personal characteristics **Expressing attitudes and opinions** • Agreeing, disagreeing, and expressing surprise	The verb **aussehen** Third person pronouns, accusative case	
Recombining communicative functions, grammar, and vocabulary		Germany through the eyes of an American exchange student
Reading for practice and pleasure		Tradition of folklore

BASIC MATERIAL

COMMUNICATIVE FUNCTIONS	GRAMMAR	CULTURE
Exchanging information • Telling where you live and what kind of place it is • Pointing out landmarks • Asking for directions	The verb **wissen**	Some standard greetings States in the Federal Republic of Germany Landmarks of Munich
Exchanging information • Talking about shopping **Persuading** • Suggesting where to shop • Making requests	The verb **sollen**	Shopping for groceries Units of weight and liquid measure
Expressing feelings • Expressing annoyance **Expressing attitudes** • Asking and telling how something tastes **Socializing** • Saying you want or don't want more • Talking about the weather	The verb **essen** **noch ein,** another Making suggestions using command forms	Reading a menu with local specialties
Recombining communicative functions, grammar, and vocabulary		Conversations at the market
Reading for practice and pleasure		The city of Munich, culture and character
Reviewing communicative functions, grammar, and vocabulary		A train schedule A map of a train station Menu from a snack bar

DRITTER TEIL

BASIC MATERIAL

KAPITEL 9
Eine Party 238

COMMUNICATIVE FUNCTIONS	GRAMMAR	CULTURE
Socializing • Inviting someone to a party; accepting or declining an invitation	First and second person pronouns, accusative case The verbs **anrufen, einladen,** and **vorhaben**	Planning a party and inviting your friends
Exchanging information • Telling what there is to eat and drink		Some party foods and beverages
Socializing • Offering something to eat or drink; accepting or declining what is being offered **Exchanging information** • Making negative statements	**kein,** nominative and accusative case The verb **nehmen**	Accepting or declining something at a party
Persuading • Talking about things to do at a party; making suggestions and responding to ideas **Socializing** • Complimenting people and complimenting someone on food	Possessives, nominative and accusative case	What young people do at a party Polite small talk Responding to a compliment
Recombining communicative functions, grammar, and vocabulary		A party invitation
Reading for practice and pleasure		An American teenager in Germany comments on cultural differences A German recipe

KAPITEL 10
Gehen wir aus! 268

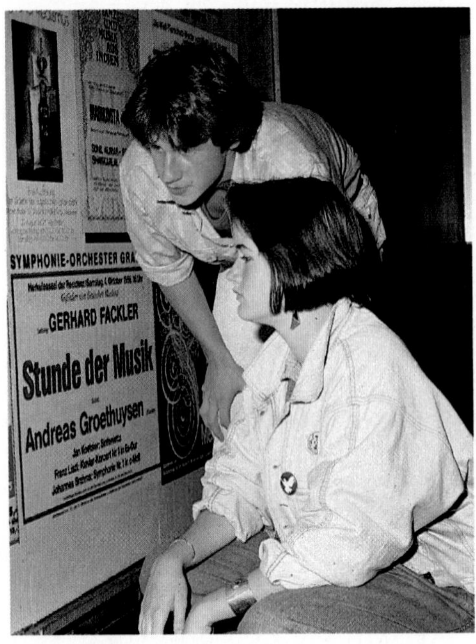

BASIC MATERIAL

COMMUNICATIVE FUNCTIONS	GRAMMAR	CULTURE
Exchanging information • Talking about what you do in your spare time **Socializing** • Asking and responding to "How are you?" **Persuading** • Making suggestions	The verbs **können** and **wollen** The verbs **fahren, radfahren,** and **ausgehen**	Young people going out
Expressing attitudes • Making choices about where to go • Discussing types of movies **Expressing feelings** • Expressing preference or indifference **Exchanging information** • Asking for information	The verb **anfangen** **welcher, welche, welches,** nominative and accusative case **was für ein?** Nominative and accusative case	Concerts and movies in Germany Going to the movies in Germany
Expressing feelings and emotions • Liking or disliking someone or something	The verb **mögen**	Movie and concert ads
Exchanging information • Talking about what you did	The conversational past tense	
Recombining communicative functions, grammar, and vocabulary		A young German writes to his American pen pal, who is coming to visit
Reading for practice and pleasure		Young people comment on their favorite stars and groups

BASIC MATERIAL

COMMUNICATIVE FUNCTIONS	GRAMMAR	CULTURE
Expressing attitudes and opinions • Wondering what to give as a present; asking for advice on what to give	Indirect objects; dative case forms of possessives The verb **geben**	Buying presents
Socializing • Getting someone's attention **Exchanging information** • Conversing with a salesperson; talking about colors	**dieser, jeder,** nominative and accusative case **der, die, das** used as demonstrative pronouns	Types of stores and store hours
Exchanging information • Saying the seasons and months • Giving the date **Socializing** • Expressing good wishes	Third person pronouns, dative case More past participles	Occasions for giving gifts; gifts to give a host or hostess
Recombining communicative functions, grammar, and vocabulary		Birthday cards and a thank-you note Birthday calendars
Reading for practice and pleasure		A man is talked into buying a pair of shoes
Reviewing communicative functions, grammar, and vocabulary		Vacation activities in Austria Travel brochure Menu from an Austrian café

FOR REFERENCE

MAPS

GETTING TO KNOW YOUR TEXTBOOK

WILLKOMMEN

Some of us are fortunate enough to be able to learn a new language by living in another country, but most of us are not. We begin learning the language and getting acquainted with the foreign culture in a classroom with the help of a teacher and a textbook. Your textbook can be a reliable guide if you know how to use it effectively. The following pages will help you get to know this book, **Neue Freunde** *(New Friends)*, and its various features.

INTRODUCTION

Who speaks German? Where is German spoken? Where did the language come from? Why should I learn it? How can I learn it well? You'll find the answers to these questions in English, illustrated with colorful photographs, in the Introduction, which begins on page 1.

INTRODUCTION

German and You

Welcome to the German-speaking world! During the coming year you will learn to understand, speak, read, and write German in a variety of situations. You will also learn more about the German-speaking world outside your classroom: daily life, customs, traditions, music, art, science, and history. As you begin your travels through the German-speaking world, here's wishing you . . .

Viel Glück!
Good luck!

In this introduction you will learn about:

1 Germany: a pictorial view

2 the German-speaking countries

3 German in the United States

4 German, English, and other languages

5 German and your future career

6 suggestions for studying German

1

ERSTER TEIL

ZWEITER TEIL

DRITTER TEIL

237

PART OPENER

There are twelve units in Neue Freunde, **grouped in three Parts. Each Part contains three units and a review unit based on them. At the beginning of each Part, you'll see an illustrated table of contents like the one shown here. It will tell you the number, title, and opening page of each unit** (Kapitel) **and give you a brief preview, in English, of each unit's theme and content.**

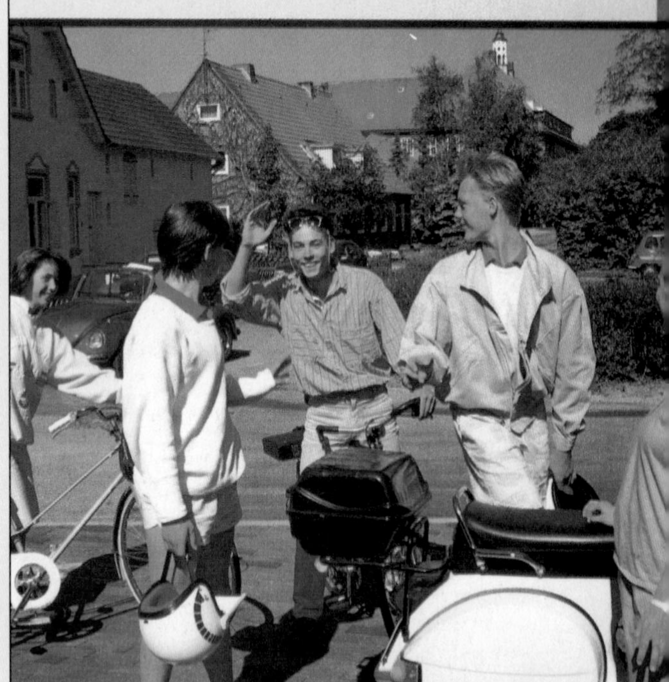

UNIT OPENER

Nine units in your textbook present new material. Each of these units opens the same way. Before you begin a unit, examine its two opening pages. First scan the photos—they'll give you an idea of what the unit is about. Next read the introductory paragraph—it sets the theme and provides information about the life and customs of German-speaking people. Finally, look at the outline of the unit. Read the objectives of each section carefully. They'll tell you specifically what you'll be learning to communicate.

REVIEW UNIT OPENER

Review is essential to learning a second language. It's good to stop now and then to ask yourself what you've learned and, more importantly, to practice your new skills in different situations. That's just what each review unit (Wiederholungskapitel) will help you do. There is one review unit at the end of each Part—three in the book. In the review unit you'll be introduced to a new theme and

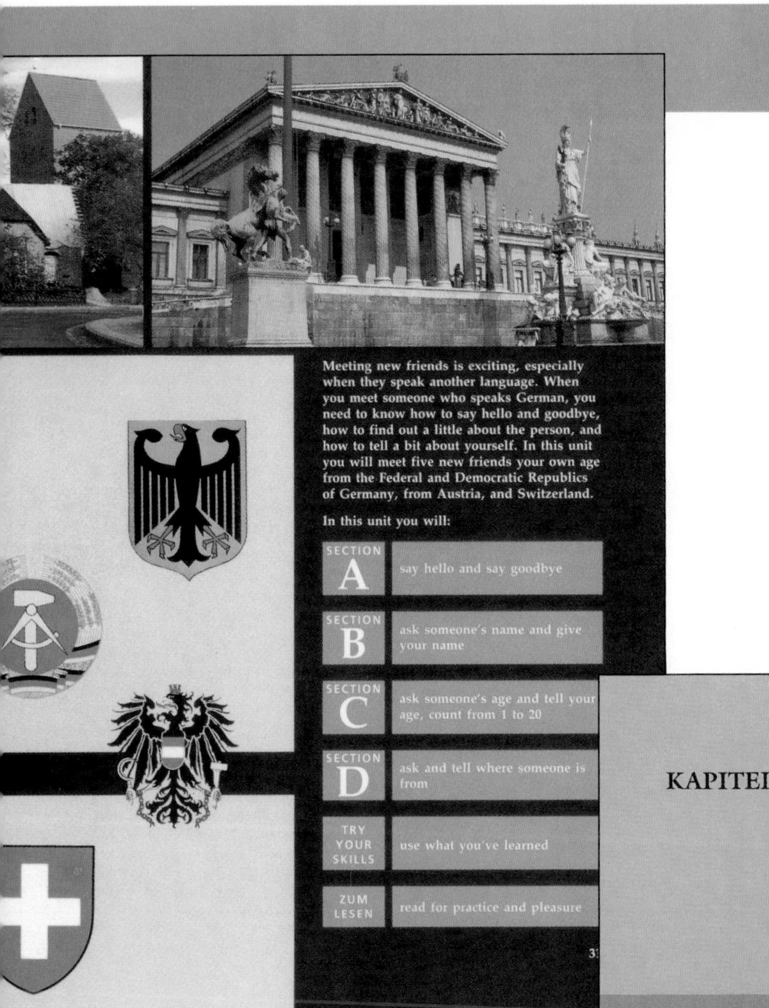

Meeting new friends is exciting, especially when they speak another language. When you meet someone who speaks German, you need to know how to say hello and goodbye, how to find out a little about the person, and how to tell a bit about yourself. In this unit you will meet five new friends your own age from the Federal and Democratic Republics of Germany, from Austria, and Switzerland.
In this unit you will:
SECTION A
say hello and say goodbye
SECTION B
ask someone's name and give your name
SECTION C
ask someone's age and tell your age, count from 1 to 20
SECTION D
ask and tell where someone is from
TRY YOUR SKILLS
use what you've learned
ZUM LESEN
read for practice and pleasure

KAPITEL 12
Ferien in Österreich
Wiederholungskapitel

setting, but you won't have to learn any new vocabulary, grammar, or communicative functions (language uses). Just concentrate on using what you've already studied in new and interesting ways.

SECTIONS

With the exception of the three review units, each unit is made up of three or four sections. The beginning of each section will remind you of your objective and introduce you briefly, in English, to the theme of the section. Read these introductions carefully—they'll give you pieces of information about German-speaking people and their way of life.

SECTION **D** asking and telling where you are from

Now you will meet some young people from the German-speaking countries.

D1 **Woher bist du?**

Ich heisse Jens Kröger. Ich bin sechzehn Jahre alt. Ich bin aus Niebüll, aus Deutschland.
Jens Kröger, 16
Niebüll, Deutschland
Ich bin die Wiebke Nedel. Ich bin fünfzehn. Ich bin auch aus Deutschland, aus Neuss.
Wiebke Nedel, 15
Neuss, Deutschland
Ich heisse Dastl, Margit Dastl. Ich bin vierzehn. Ich bin aus Wien, aus Österreich.
Margit Dastl, 14
Wien, Österreich
Ich heisse Bruno Schmidlin. Ich bin auch fünfzehn. Ich bin aus der Schweiz, aus Zimmerwald.
Bruno Schmidlin, 15
Zimmerwald, Schweiz
Ich bin Kurt Langer. Ich bin 15. Ich bin aus der DDR, aus Dresden.
Kurt Langer, 15
Dresden, DDR
Und woher bist du? Aus Kansas City? Aus Harrisburg? Aus Dallas? Ich bin aus ____.

Neue Freunde 45

C7 WIE SAGT MAN DAS?
Asking someone's age and telling yours

QUESTION	ANSWER
Wie alt bist du? How old are you?	**Ich bin dreizehn Jahre alt.** I'm thirteen years old.
Wie alt ist der Stefan? How old is Stefan?	**Er ist fünfzehn.** He is fifteen.
Wie alt ist die Sabine? How old is Sabine?	**Sie ist fünfzehn Jahre alt.** She's fifteen years old.
Wie alt sind Ulrike und Jochen? How old are Ulrike and Jochen?	**Sie sind auch fünfzehn.** They are also fifteen.

C8 ERKLÄRUNG *Explanation*
Personal Pronouns and the Verb sein

The phrases **ich bin, du bist, er ist, sie ist,** and **sie sind** each contain a subject pronoun corresponding to the English *I, you, he, she,* and *they,* plus a form of the verb **sein,** *to be: I am, you are, he/she/it is, they are.* **Sein** is one of the most frequently used verbs in German. The chart shows the plural forms **wir,** *we,* and **ihr,** *you* (plural), but you do not need to use them yet.

Singular			*Plural*		
Ich	**bin**		Wir	**sind**	
Du	**bist**		Ihr	**seid**	
Der Stefan / Er	**ist**	15 Jahre alt.	Stefan and Sabine / Sie	**sind**	15 Jahre alt.
Die Sabine / Sie	**ist**				

C9 Übung • Wie alt sind die Schüler? —Vierzehn.

Everyone in this group is 14 years old.

A: Wie alt ist der Fritz?
B: Er ist vierzehn.

1. Wie alt ist der Hans?
2. Wie alt ist die Monika?
3. Wie alt sind Hans und Monika?
4. Wie alt ist der Günter?
5. Wie alt ist die Ulrike?
6. Wie alt sind Günter and Ulrike?

Neue Freunde 43

COMMUNICATIVE FUNCTIONS

The material labeled **Wie sagt man das?** *(How do you say that?)* summarizes the sentences, phrases, and expressions you'll need in order to accomplish your purpose—that is, to express and react to requests, opinions, and emotions. Mastery of this material is the key to meeting the objective or objectives of the section.

GRAMMAR

In order to communicate effectively, you'll need to understand and use some grammatical forms. Look for these forms in the boxes with the heading **Erklärung** *(Explanation).* Once again, the color blue is a cue that the material in the box is to be mastered.

BASIC MATERIAL

The material in each section is numbered in sequence together with the letter of the section: A1, A2, A3, and so on. The first presentation is always new or basic material, signaled by a number and title in blue. In some sections new material may be introduced in two or three other places. Whenever you see a heading in blue, you'll know that there's something new to learn. The new material is a model of what to say in a situation. Its authentic language and pictures will acquaint you with the way German-speaking people live, think, and feel and familiarize you with the various settings in which German is spoken.

CULTURE NOTES

The head **Ein wenig Landeskunde** *(A little culture)* printed in green invites you to find out more about the life of German-speaking people. These culture notes in English provide additional information about the theme of the section to help you increase your cultural awareness.

ACTIVITIES

The headings of all the activities in the section begin with the word **Übung** in orange. This signals an opportunity to practice and work with new material—and sometimes old material—either orally or in writing. Many of the activities are designed so that you may work together with your classmates in pairs or in small groups.

LISTENING

Listening is an essential skill that requires practice to develop. Whenever you see this cassette symbol 🖭 after a heading, you'll know that the material is recorded, with pauses provided for your repetition or responses. A special listening comprehension activity in each section is headed **Hör gut zu!** *(Listen carefully).* In order to respond, you will need to listen as your teacher plays the cassette or reads the German to you.

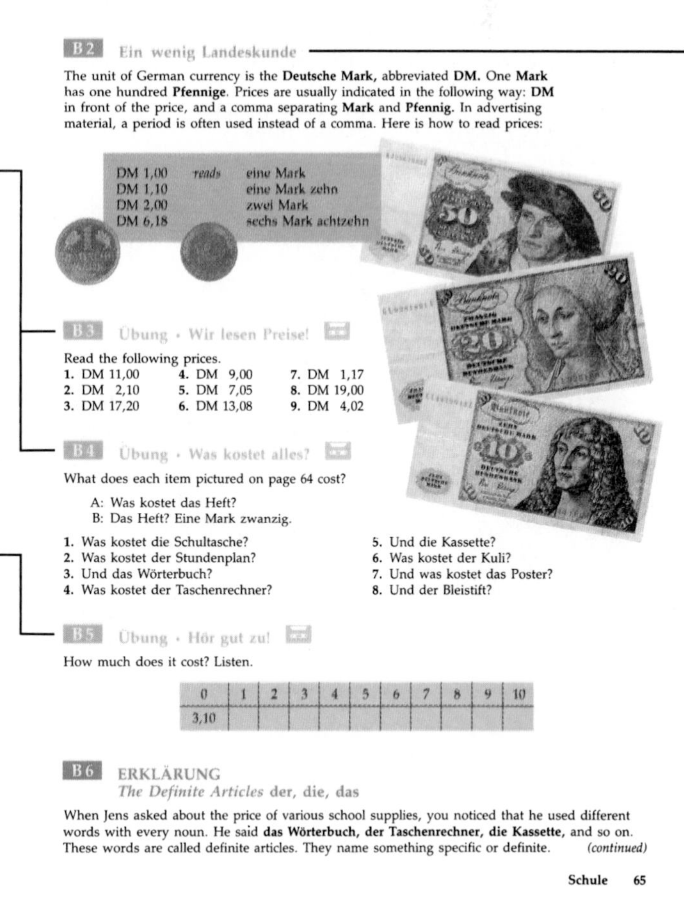

B2 Ein wenig Landeskunde

The unit of German currency is the **Deutsche Mark,** abbreviated **DM.** One **Mark** has one hundred **Pfennige**. Prices are usually indicated in the following way: **DM** in front of the price, and a comma separating **Mark** and **Pfennig.** In advertising material, a period is often used instead of a comma. Here is how to read prices:

DM 1,00	*reads*	eine Mark
DM 1,10		eine Mark zehn
DM 2,00		zwei Mark
DM 6,18		sechs Mark achtzehn

B3 Übung · Wir lesen Preise!

Read the following prices.

1. DM 11,00 **4.** DM 9,00 **7.** DM 1,17
2. DM 2,10 **5.** DM 7,05 **8.** DM 19,00
3. DM 17,20 **6.** DM 13,08 **9.** DM 4,02

B4 Übung · Was kostet alles?

What does each item pictured on page 64 cost?

A: Was kostet das Heft?
B: Das Heft? Eine Mark zwanzig.

1. Was kostet die Schultasche?
2. Was kostet der Stundenplan?
3. Und das Wörterbuch?
4. Was kostet der Taschenrechner?
5. Und die Kassette?
6. Was kostet der Kuli?
7. Und was kostet das Poster?
8. Und der Bleistift?

B5 Übung · Hör gut zu!

How much does it cost? Listen.

0	1	2	3	4	5	6	7	8	9	10
3,10										

B6 ERKLÄRUNG
The Definite Articles der, die, das

When Jens asked about the price of various school supplies, you noticed that he used different words with every noun. He said **das Wörterbuch, der Taschenrechner, die Kassette,** and so on. These words are called definite articles. They name something specific or definite. *(continued)*

Schule 65

TRY YOUR SKILLS

This section will let you experiment with the skills and knowledge you've gathered in the previous sections of the unit. Its variety of activities will give you many opportunities to practice communicating with others.

TRY YOUR SKILLS — using what you've learned

1 Gerd Ecker in den USA

Gerd Ecker, a student from Germany, introduces himself to your class.

Guten Tag! Ich heisse Gerd Ecker. Ich bin 16 Jahre alt. Ich bin aus Paderborn. Paderborn ist in der Bundesrepublik Deutschland. Ich gehe aufs Goerdeler Gymnasium. Ich komme mit dem Rad in die Schule, und die Klassenkameraden—ja, sie kommem mit dem Bus, mit dem Moped, mit dem Auto und auch zu Fuss.
Wir haben von Montag bis Freitag Schule. Wir haben Sonnabend frei. Die Schule beginnt um Viertel vor acht, und sie ist um ein Uhr aus.
Welche Fächer ich habe? Nun, ich habe Deutsch, Mathe, Englisch, Geschichte, Geographie, Sport und Kunst. Ich bin gut in Englisch und in Deutsch. Ich habe eine Eins in Englisch und eine Zwei in Deutsch. Englisch und Deutsch sind leicht. Ich bin nicht so gut in Mathe. Mathe ist schwer. Ich habe nur eine Vier.

2 Übung · Rollenspiel

A classmate plays the role of Gerd. You missed some of his presentation, so you ask him questions about himself. Then you take the role of Gerd, and your classmate asks you.

A: Wie heisst du?
B: Ich heisse. . .

3 Übung · Erzähl mal, was Gerd gesagt hat!

A friend of yours missed Gerd's presentation. You tell him or her what Gerd said.

Der Schüler aus Deutschland heisst. . .

4 Übung · Vortrag *Presentation*

You are visiting a class in Germany. Tell the class something about yourself and your school day.

82 Kapitel 2

WAS KANNST DU SCHON?

Let's review some important points that you have learned in this unit.

SECTION A

Can you greet young people and adults in German?
Say hello to the following people:

1. Katrin	**3.** Mr. Sperling	**5.** Mrs. Meier
2. Stefan	**4.** Miss Seifert	**6.** your teacher

Can you say goodbye in German?
Say goodbye to the same people.

SECTION B

Can you introduce yourself in German?

1. Say hello.
2. Give your name.
3. Ask a classmate his or her name.

Can you find out who someone is?

1. Ask a boy's name, then tell it to someone else.
2. Ask a girl's name, then tell it to someone else.
3. Ask who someone is and give the answer.

SECTION C

Can you ask someone's age and tell yours?
Write a question and answer about age for each of the following pronouns: ich, du, er, sie, sie (plural).

Do you know the numbers from 0 to 20?
Write out in German the numbers from 0 to 20.

Do you know the forms of the verb *sein*?
Complete the following sentences.

1. Das Mädchen ____ 15.	**5.** ____ du aus Deutschland?
2. Ich ____ 13.	**6.** Wer ____ das?
3. Der Junge ____ 16.	**7.** Jens und Wiebke ____ aus Deutschland.
4. Frl. Seifert ____ aus Wien.	**8.** Er ____ aus Österreich.

SECTION D

Can you say where you are from? Can you ask where others are from?
Say where you are from. Ask one of your classmates where he or she is from.

Can you ask questions anticipating a yes or no answer?
Make up three questions anticipating a yes or no answer.

Can you ask for information to be repeated?
What do you say if you don't understand part or all of the following statements?

1. Ich bin aus Deutschland.
2. Er heisst Jens Kröger.
3. Das Mädchen ist 15 Jahre alt.
4. Der Deutschlehrer heisst Sperling.

Can you address adults using the *Sie*-form?
Ask your teacher his or her name and where he or she is from.

54 Kapitel 1

SELF-CHECK

Each of the nine basic units ends with a one-page self-check called **Was kannst du schon?** *(What have you learned?)*. It includes a series of questions in English for you to ask yourself. Following the questions are short activities that will check your knowledge and skills. The questions and activities are grouped by section, so if you can't answer yes to a question or if the exercise shows that you need to review, you'll know which section to turn to.

WORTSCHATZ

SECTION A

armer Peter! *poor Peter!*
bei den Nedels *at the Nedels'*
der **Bruder, ⸚** *brother*
da: wir sind da *we're here*
das sind *these are*
dass *that*
die **Freundin, -nen** *girl friend*
die **Geschwister** (pl) *brothers and sisters*
die **Grosseltern** (pl) *grandparents*
der **Hund, -e** *dog*
kennenlernen: du lernst viele Leute kennen *you're going to meet a lot of people*
die **Klassenkameradin, -nen** *classmate* (f)
die **Kusine, -n** *cousin* (f)
die **Leute** (pl) *people*
mein, meine *my*
die **Oma, -s** *grandma*
der **Onkel, -** *uncle*
der **Opa, -s** *grandpa*
schlimm *bad*
schön *nice;* schön, dass du da bist *nice that you're here*
die **Schwester, -n** *sister*
so *so, well then*
die **Tante, -n** *aunt*
der **Vetter, -n** *cousin* (m)
viele *many*
von *of;* ein Freund von Wiebke *a friend of Wiebke's*
Willkommen in Neuss! *welcome to Neuss!*

SECTION B

der **Audi, -s** *Audi* (a German-made automobile)
auf *on*
auspacken: er packt den Rucksack aus *he unpacks his backpack*
aussehen *to look (like), appear,* (see p 179)
das **Auto, -s** *car*
das **Bad, ⸚er** *bathroom*
bekommen *to get, receive*
bitte schön *you're welcome*
das **Buch, ⸚er** *book*
Dank: vielen Dank! *thanks a lot!* tausend Dank! *thanks a million!*
danken *to thank;* nichts zu danken *don't mention it*
dein, deine *your*
das **Esszimmer, -** *dining room*
finden: findest du? *do you think so?*
die **Garage, -n** *garage*
der **Garten, ⸚** *garden*
das **Gästezimmer, -** *guest room*
gemütlich *cozy, comfortable*
gern: ja, gern *yes, I'd like that*
gross *big*
die **Halskette, -n** *necklace*
das **Haus, ⸚er** *house*
hell *light*
der **Keller, -** *basement, cellar*
klein *small*
komm! *come on!*
die **Küche, -n** *kitchen*
mehr *more*
Mensch! *boy! wow!*
modern *modern*
oben *upstairs*
die **Party, -s** *party*
der **Rucksack, ⸚e** *knapsack, backpack*
das **Schlafzimmer, -** *bedroom*
schön *pretty, beautiful*
sehen *to see*
sehr *very*
stehen: da steht noch mehr auf Peters Zettel *there's still more on Peter's slip*
tausend *thousand;* tausend Dank! *thanks a million!*
die **Toilette, -n** *toilet*
unten *downstairs*
wieviel? *how many?*
das **Wohnzimmer, -** *living room*
zeigen *to show;* ich zeig es dir *I'll show it to you*
der **Zettel, -** *note, slip of paper*
das **Zimmer, -** *room*

SECTION C

arrogant *arrogant*
attraktiv *attractive*
aussehen: gut aussehen *to look good; to be handsome, pretty, attractive*
blond *blond*
die **Brille, -n** *glasses*
brünett *brunette*
dunkel *dark*
dunkelblond *dark blond*
freundlich *friendly*
Geschmackssache: das ist Geschmackssache *that's a matter of taste*
gross *tall*
hübsch *pretty*
kennen *to know*
klein *short, small*
lustig *merry, funny*
meinen: meinst du? *do you think so?* meinst du nicht? *don't you think so?*
nett *nice*
nicht? *don't you thi*
recht haben *to be ri*
schlank *slim*
sympathisch *likeabl*
unsympathisch *unp* *not nice*
vollschlank *heavyse*

WORTSCHATZÜBUNGEN

1. Look at the Wortschatz and make a list of all singular nouns with their definite articles. Then write the nouns again with their indefinite articles.
2. Pick out all the adjectives and write them down. How many pairs of opposites can you find? Write them next to each other.

Bei den Ned

VOCABULARY

The German-English vocabulary list **(Wortschatz)** after the self-check contains the unit words and phrases you'll need to know. They're grouped according to the sections of the unit. A word-study exercise, **Wortschatzübung,** below the list will focus your attention on various aspects of the vocabulary and provide helpful ways to work with and learn the new words and phrases.

READING

A reading section, **Zum Lesen** *(To Read)*, concludes the unit. Here you'll find one or more reading selections related to the unit's theme. They include comic strips, postcards, interviews, opinion polls of German teenagers, factual selections, and stories. Most reading selections are followed by questions and activities designed to help you practice and develop your reading skills.

ZUM LESEN

Ein Gewohnheitsmensch

Herr Neuschuh ist ein netter Mann. Er ist höflich°, pünktlich, immer korrekt. Er ist auch immer gut angezogen°: er kauft seine Sachen in den besten Geschäften°. Aber er macht sich wenig aus der Mode°. „Die Mode", so sagt er, „ist nur für die Jugend." Herr Neuschuh liebt den klassischen Stil. Seine Anzüge° kommen aus England, seine Krawatten kommen aus Frankreich und seine Schuhe aus Italien. Jeden Morgen, bevor Herr Neuschuh zur Arbeit geht, bürstet er seinen Anzug und putzt° seine Schuhe. Er ist ein schicker Herr°.

Nun, eines Tages möchte Herr Neuschuh ein Paar neue Schuhe. Er geht in das Schuhgeschäft, wo er immer seine Schuhe kauft. Dort kennt er alle Verkäufer.

„Guten Tag, Herr Neuschuh! Was darf es heute sein?"

„Ist Frl. Seidel nicht da?"

„Frl. Seidel ist gestern in Urlaub gegangen°."

„Ach, so was! —Nun, das macht nichts°. Ich möchte ein Paar Schuhe."

„Welche Marke°?"

„Diese hier."

ein Gewohnheitsmensch *a creature of habit;* **höflich** *polite;* **gut angezogen** *well-dressed;* **das Geschäft** *store;* **er macht sich wenig aus der Mode** *he doesn't pay much attention to fashion, to what's in style;* **der Anzug** *suit;* **putzen** *to clean, polish;* **ein schicker Herr** *a smartly-dressed gentleman;* **in Urlaub gehen** *to go on vacation;* **das macht nichts** *it doesn't matter;* **die Marke** *make*

324 **Kapitel 11**

PHOTO ESSAYS

Following each of the three review units in the textbook, you'll find a cultural photo essay called **Landeskunde.** The three essays tell you more about the lives of the German-speaking people and the places where they live.

LANDESKUNDE 1

A Glimpse of the Federal Republic of Germany

Germany lies in the center of Europe. It is about six hundred miles long, bounded by the North Sea to the north and the Alps to the south. From east to west the country is narrow, seldom more than two hundred miles wide. Contained in this area is a surprising variety of landscapes. There are coastal regions and flatlands in northern Germany and gently rolling hills in the central and southwestern part of the country. South of the river Danube is a high plateau that reaches to the majestic Alpine range. It is surprising that in such a highly industrialized country more than half the area is farmland and another third is forest land.

❶ Promenadenkonzert auf der Nordseeinsel Sylt

❷ Kurort Badenweiler im Schwarzwald

❸ Die Zugspitze, Deutschlands höchster Berg, 2 963 m

125

LANDESKUNDE 2

Other German-speaking Countries and Regions

The German Democratic Republic

The German Democratic Republic (GDR) is located in Central Europe, with the Federal Republic to the west, Poland to the east, and Czechoslovakia to the south. The GDR is a socialist state, formed in 1949 from the Soviet-occupied zone of Germany, six months after the formation of the Federal Republic. In the GDR all decision making is in the hands of the communist party, officially known as the Socialist Unity Party (SED). Geographically, the northern and central parts of the GDR are a low-lying plain intersected by gentle ranges of hills. The southern part of the country is highland. Some of the chief cities are (East) Berlin, the capital; Leipzig, a center of printing and book trade and the site of trade fairs since 1100; Dresden, a baroque art city that has been carefully restored; and the port of Rostock on the Baltic Sea.

Die Deutsche Demokratische Republik feiert ihren 35. Geburtstag

LANDESKUNDE 3

Festivals and Holidays

It is said that in Germany festivals are as numerous as the days of the year. This is no exaggeration! Wherever you go, there is always something going on—a popular festival, a religious feast, a folk-dance, a historical or costume parade, or simply some occasion for public merry-making. The calendar of festivities begins with carnival, a season that starts on the seventh of January and lasts until Lent, 40 days before Easter. It is celebrated mostly in the Catholic areas. The Rhenish carnival turns Cologne, Düsseldorf, and Mainz upside down. During the famous "Fasching," its Bavarian counterpart, Munich celebrates. The Swabian "Fasnet" conjures up the ghosts and demons of old in the strange dance of bell-jingling masks.

❶ Fastnacht in Rottweil, Schwaben

❷ Lustige Maske

❸ Rosenmontag in Köln; keiner arbeitet, alle feiern Karneval auf der Strasse

❹ Kinderfasching

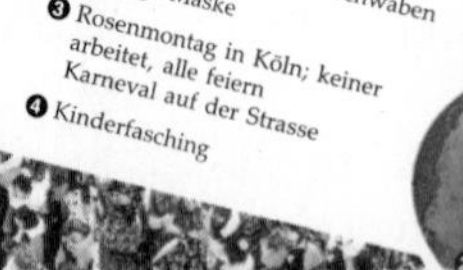

333

FOR REFERENCE

The reference section at the end of the textbook provides you with valuable aids. It is grouped into the following parts: Summary of Functions, Grammar Summary, Pronunciation, Numbers, English Equivalents, German-English Vocabulary, English-German Vocabulary, and Grammar Index.

SUMMARY OF FUNCTIONS

The Summary of Functions sums up the communicative functions you have learned and practiced in a variety of situations throughout this textbook. If you want to ask for directions, invite someone to a party, pay a compliment, or respond to a friend's good fortune, for example, you will find the appropriate phrases and sentences listed here, as well as the unit in which the particular function was introduced.

GRAMMAR SUMMARY

The grammar points that have been presented in the textbook are organized in tables for easy reference and review in the Grammar Summary.

GERMAN-ENGLISH VOCABULARY

The German-English Vocabulary includes almost all the words you will come across in this textbook. The numbers after each entry tell you in which unit the word first appeared. If the number is in heavy type, you are expected to know that word or phrase and be able to use it. In this Vocabulary, you can look up the English meanings of words and phrases, and you can check the gender of nouns as well as the plural forms.

BITTE SCHÖN!

There it is, a special textbook that will help you enlarge your view of the world and enable you to contribute to better understanding and communication among people. Now you're ready to begin an exciting, rewarding experience—learning another language and meeting new friends, Neue Freunde.

INTRODUCTION

German and You

Welcome to the German-speaking world! During the coming year you will learn to understand, speak, read, and write German in a variety of situations. You will also learn more about the German-speaking world outside your classroom: daily life, customs, traditions, music, art, science, and history. As you begin your travels through the German-speaking world, here's wishing you . . .

Viel Glück!
Good luck!

In this introduction you will learn about:

Germany: a pictorial view

the German-speaking countries

German in the United States

German, English, and other languages

German and your future career

suggestions for studying German

1 GERMANY: A PICTORIAL VIEW

What comes to mind when you think of Germany? Majestic castles along the Rhine? Quaint medieval villages? Fairy tales? The Black Forest? The Alps? Bavarian folk costume? Fast, elegant cars? Scientists? Modern technology? Beethoven? Goethe? Einstein?

Germany is all of these things—some of them just as you imagined, others quite different. But Germany is also images you may not have pictured. The following pages take you on an armchair tour of Germany. It's not the same as being there, of course, but see how these glimpses compare with your image of Germany.

Germany is a land of abundance . . .

and a land of contrasts—mountains and flatlands,

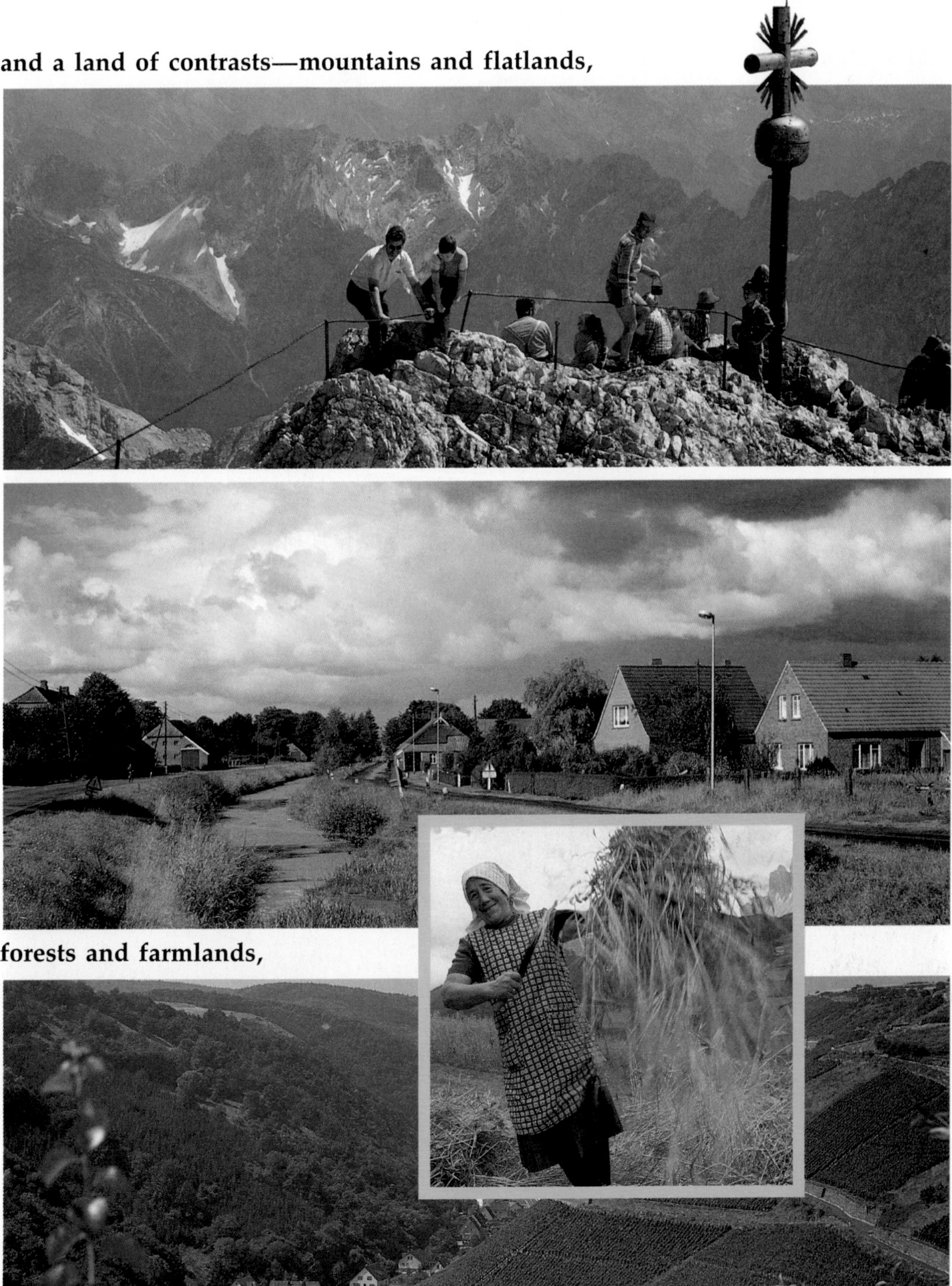

forests and farmlands,

seaports and overland routes.

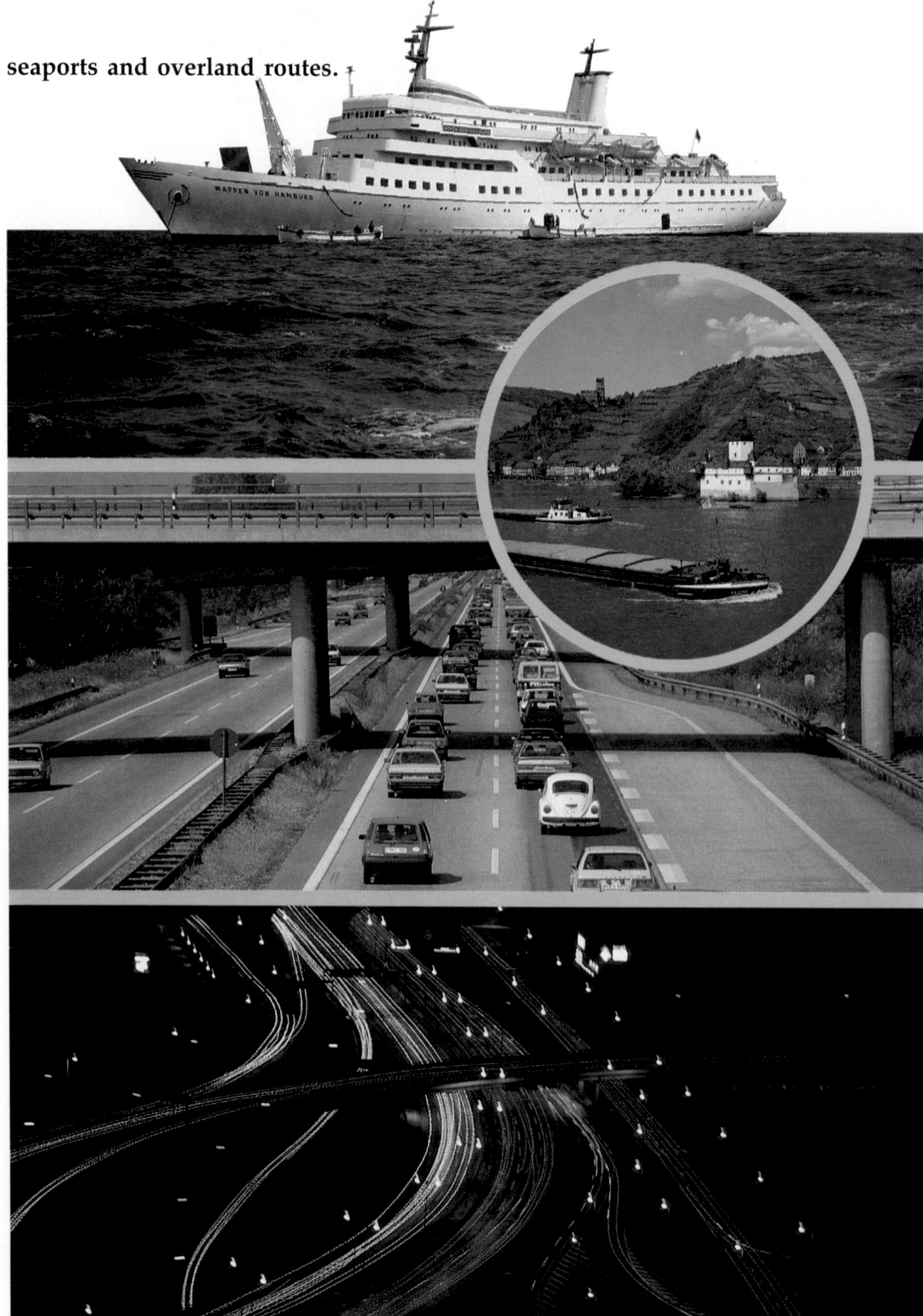

The country is strongly regional

and busily cosmopolitan,

highly industrialized

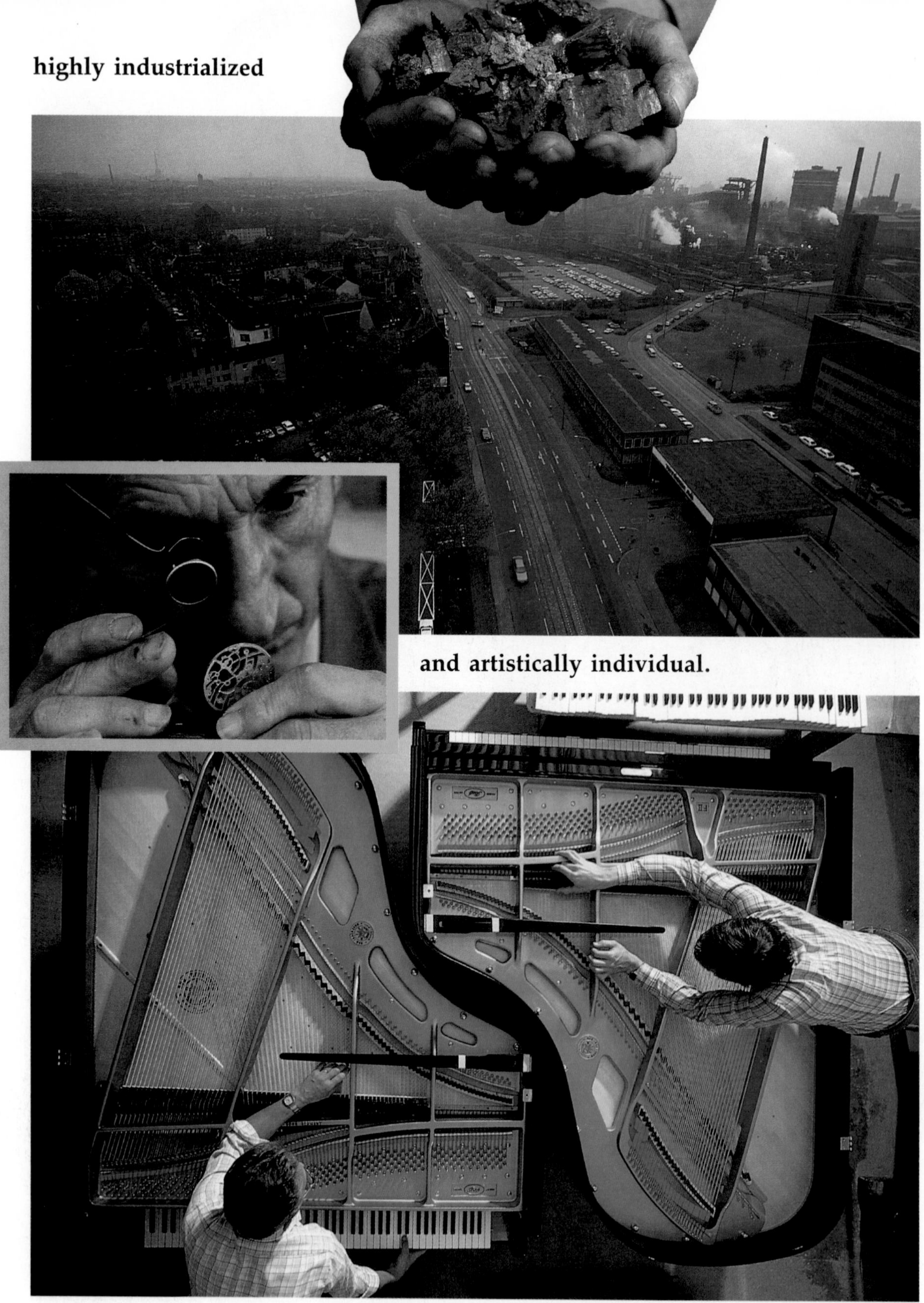

and artistically individual.

There are ordinary stores for everyday things

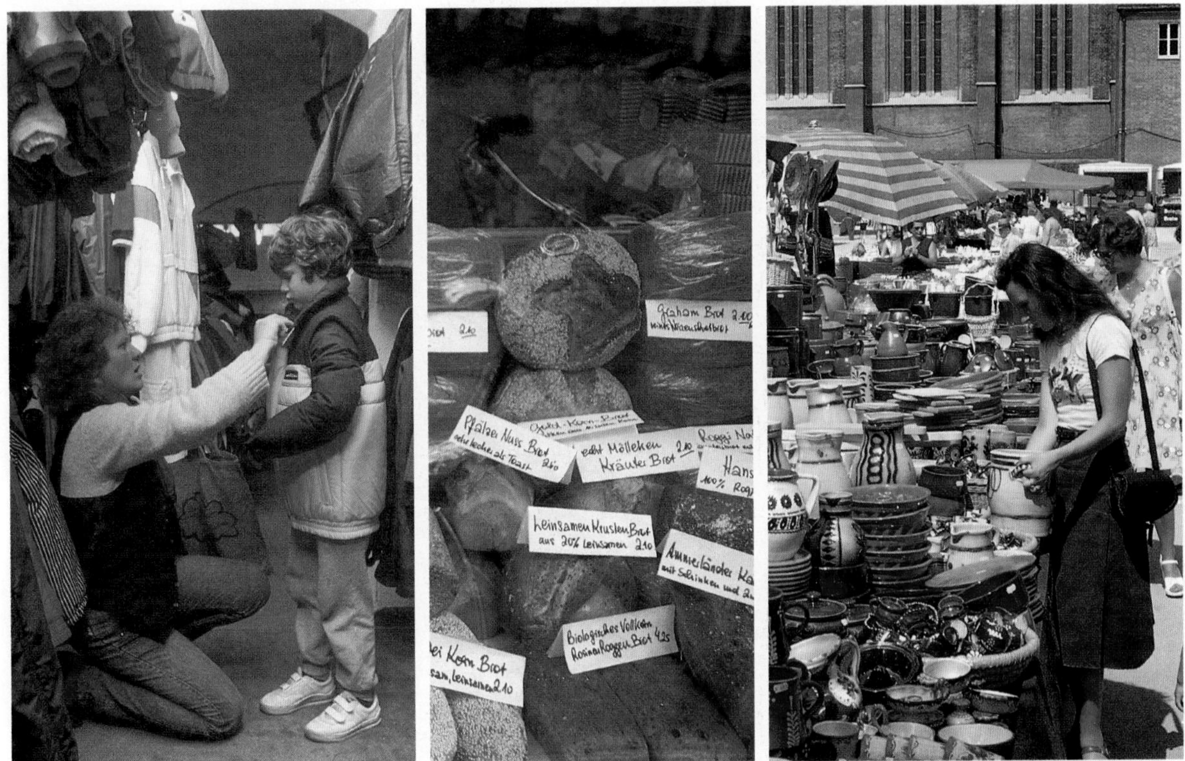

and elegant stores for luxuries.

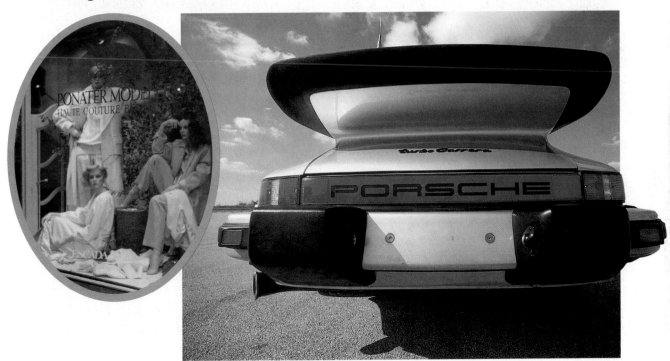

Germany is rich in tradition . . .

and rich in innovation.

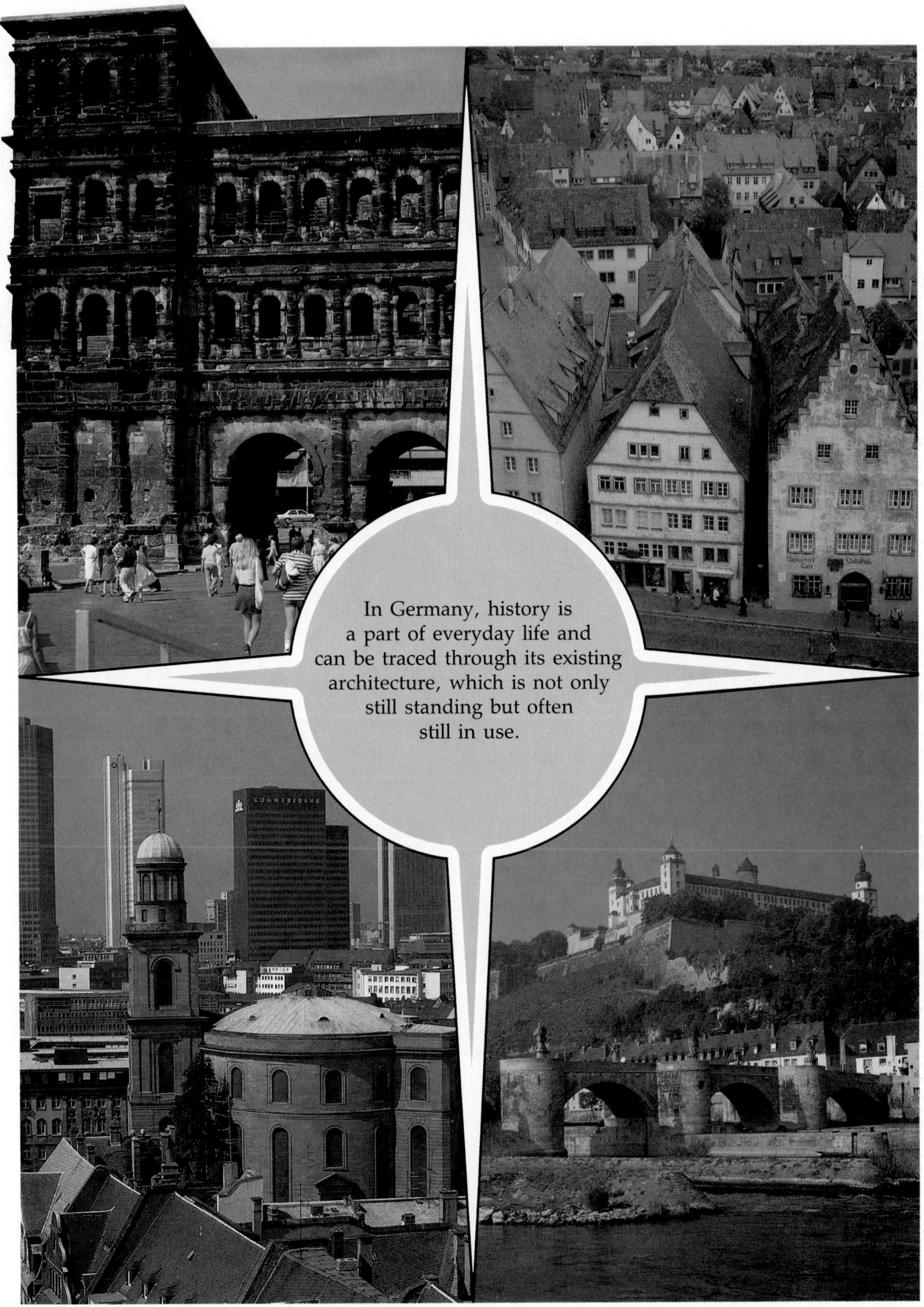

In Germany, history is a part of everyday life and can be traced through its existing architecture, which is not only still standing but often still in use.

Germany has elegant restaurants . . .

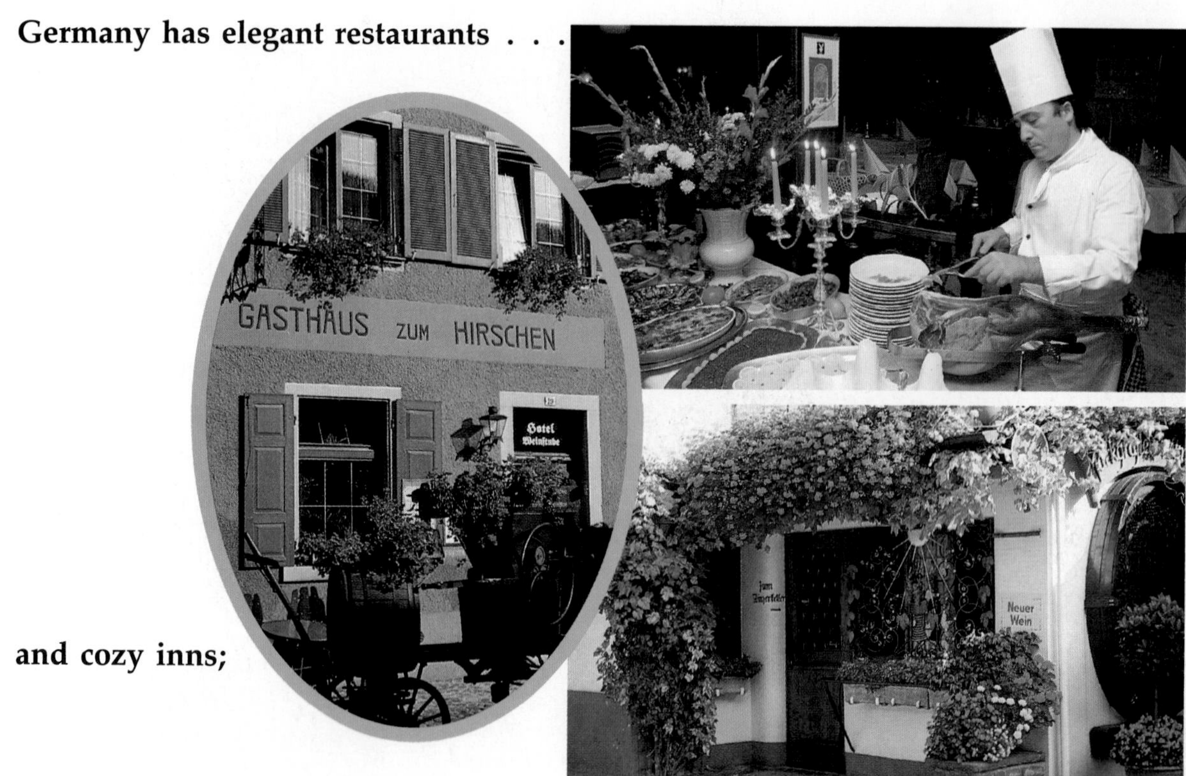

and cozy inns;

exciting theater, music, and art . . . both indoors

and outdoors.

And from Germany have come great composers,

J. S. Bach (1685–1750)

Beethoven (1770–1827)

great artists,

Kokoschka (1886–1980)

Dürer (1471–1528)

great poets and writers,

Hesse (1877–1963)

Gras (1927–)

Goethe (1749–1832)

great philosophers,

Kant (1724–1804)

Nietzsche (1844–1900)

great inventors,

Daimler (1834–1900)

Gutenberg (before 1400–1468)

great scientists,

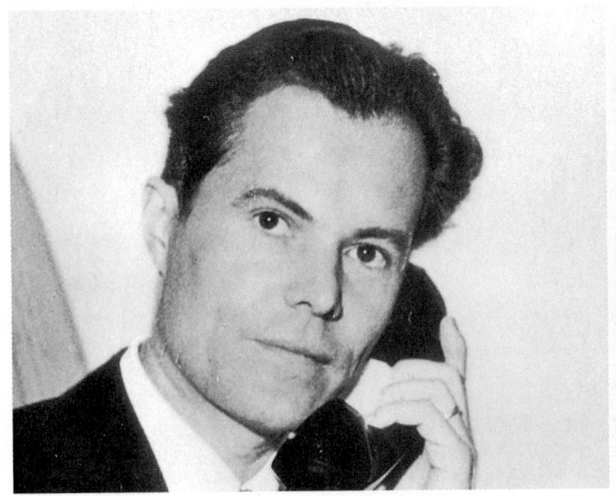

Mössbauer (1929)

Einstein (1879–1955)

great filmmakers

von Trotta

Herzog

as well as great stars.

Dietrich

Brandauer

Schygulla

2 THE GERMAN-SPEAKING COUNTRIES

German is the native language of more than 100 million people in Austria, East and West Germany, Liechtenstein, Switzerland, and parts of France and Italy. It is used as a second language by many others in Central Europe.

For a map of the German-speaking countries turn to page 57.

Bundesrepublik Deutschland

Area: 96,010 sq. mi.
Population: 60.7 million
Monetary unit:
Deutsche Mark
Capital: Bonn

The area of Central Europe historically regarded as Germany was split into two zones of occupation after World War II. The western part of Germany was occupied by Britain, France, and the United States and is known today as the Federal Republic of Germany.

Deutsche Demokratische Republik

Area: 41,767 sq. mi.
Population: 16.7 million
Monetary unit:
Mark of the Deutsche Demokratische Republik
Capital: Berlin (Ost)

The eastern part of Germany was occupied by the Soviet Union after World War II and is known today as the German Democratic Republic. The prewar capital of Germany—Berlin—was also divided into occupation zones after the war. East Berlin is now the capital of the German Democratic Republic; West Berlin is a part of the Federal Republic.

Österreich

Area: 32,375 sq. mi.
Population: 7.6 million
Monetary unit:
Schilling
Capital: Vienna

Austria is just a little larger than the state of South Carolina. Its beautiful mountain scenery, art, and music attract millions of tourists each year. One fifth of the population of Austria lives in the capital city of Vienna.

Schweiz / Suisse / Svizzera

Area: 15,941 sq. mi.
Population: 6.5 million
Monetary unit:
Swiss franc
Capital: Berne

Switzerland is the land of the Alps, famous for its spectacular scenery, luxurious ski resorts, and, of course, Swiss cheese. Switzerland has three official languages: French, Italian, and German. Seventy percent of the population speaks Swiss German or **Schwyzerdütsch.** A fourth language, spoken by about 1 percent of the total population, is called Romansh. It is closely related to Latin and is spoken only in the canton of Graubünden.

Liechtenstein

Area: 61 sq. mi.
Population: 28,000
Monetary unit:
Swiss franc
Capital: Vaduz

Liechtenstein is one of the smallest countries in the world. Its area is less than that of Washington, D.C. Nestled between Germany, Austria, and Switzerland, the principality of Liechtenstein has close ties with Switzerland. The two countries share similar customs. Swiss currency is used in Liechtenstein, and Switzerland operates Liechtenstein's postal, telegraph, and telephone systems. Switzerland also represents Liechtenstein in diplomatic and trade relations.

3 GERMAN IN THE UNITED STATES

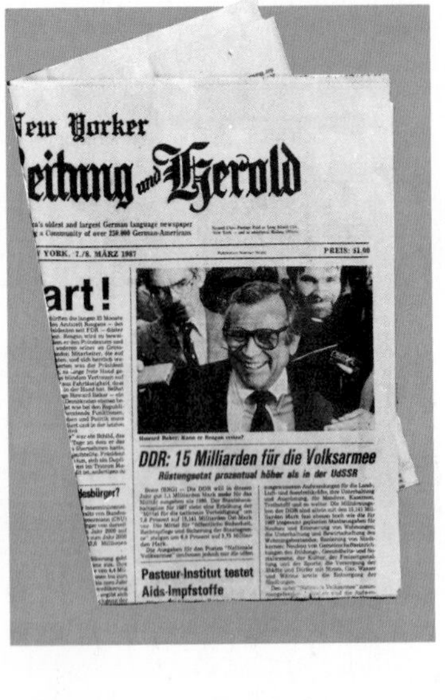

ew Yorker
eitung und Herold

art!

DDR: 15 Milliarden für die Volksarmee

Pasteur-Institut testet Aids-Impfstoffe

Can you guess how many Americans trace all or part of their ethnic background to the countries of Germany, Austria, or Switzerland?—5 million? 15 million? 25 million? 50 million? If you guessed 50 million, you are right! According to a recent survey published by the U.S. Census Bureau, 52 million people or 28.8 percent of the total population reported that they were at least partly of German ancestry.

Germans were among the earliest settlers in the United States. On October 6, 1683, a group arrived from Krefeld, Germany, on the *Concord*, a ship that has since been nicknamed the "German Mayflower." They settled in Pennsylvania and founded Germantown. These early settlers quickly established their own schools, print shops, and newspapers. It was a small German newspaper that gave the first report of the Declaration of Independence on July 5, 1776. In fact, German almost became the official language of the United States. The Continental Congress at one point thought of having a new language for this country, and German was considered a good choice for a number of reasons. When it came to a vote, however, English was chosen instead of German by the slim majority of one vote!

Since 1683 more than seven million immigrants from German-speaking regions of Europe have come to the shores of North America. These immigrants influenced the history and development of this country and over the years have made many contributions.

In many parts of the country there are reminders of the role Germans have played in the development of the United States. You can find names of towns and cities such as Hanover, Berlin, and Potsdam. Steubenville, Ohio, was named in honor of Friedrich Wilhelm von Steuben, the German officer who trained George Washington's army. The state where you live may have place names that are German in origin and would be interesting to research.

Baron von Steuben inspecting the squalid conditions at Valley Forge

The trial of John Peter Zenger in New York in 1735. The printer of the *New York Weekly Journal* was accused of criminal libel. He was acquitted, and this precedent established freedom of the press in this country.

German family names are also plentiful in the United States. There are last names such as Klein, Myer (or Meyer, Maier, Meier), and Schneider. Very often German family names indicate occupations (Bauer, *farmer*), places (Berlin or Berliner, *a citizen of Berlin*), or physical descriptions (Kraft, *strong*). If you are interested in tracing the origins of German family names, keep in mind that there may have been changes—for example, Schmidt may have become Smith; Mueller may have turned into Miller.

Many words and phrases contributed by the German immigrants have become part of our everyday language—pumpernickel, noodle, hausfrau, lager beer and bock beer, wienerwurst (often shortened to wiener or wienie), sauerbraten, schnitzel, dachshund, zwieback, delicatessen, kindergarten, and katzenjammer. And don't forget those "typically American" foods such as hamburgers, pretzels, liverwurst, and frankfurters with sauerkraut—all introduced by the Germans.

The Germans who came to the United States brought customs that have become part of our way of life. They introduced the Christmas tree (as well as many Christmas carols), the Easter bunny and Easter egg hunts, county fairs, and more recently, the folk march or Volksmarsch, which has made its appearance in many communities.

And there is a long list of individual Germans who have made invaluable contributions to this country in art and music, science and

Peter Lorre

John Jacob Astor

Levi Strauss

industry, education and politics. From John Peter Zenger to Levi Strauss, from Albert Einstein to Marlene Dietrich, German names appear throughout our history.

Activities

1. See how many German names you and your classmates can find in your local telephone book.
2. Get a map of your state and circle any German place names.
3. Visit your local historical society. Find out about any Germans who may have settled in your area. Historical societies often have documents, correspondence, and sometimes even pictures and memoirs of early settlers.
4. Choose a famous German-American to research in the library and give a short report to the class. As a class project, make a bulletin board display of famous German-Americans. Here are a few suggestions: John Peter Zenger, Friedrich Wilhelm von Steuben, John Jacob Astor, Carl Schurz, Levi Strauss, Leopold Damrosch, Maximilian Berlitz, Charles Steinmetz, Albert Einstein, Mies van der Rohe, Hannah Arendt, Wernher von Braun, Henry Kissinger.
5. As you study German this year, be aware of news about German-speaking countries. You may hear of visits by well-known Germans to the United States. Also, news about sports events, athletes, films, or new German cars may interest you. Keep track of current events in German-speaking countries. Keep a scrapbook with articles and information you find.

4 GERMAN, ENGLISH, AND OTHER LANGUAGES

Kristin ist 14 Jahre alt.

As you look at this German sentence, you may be able to guess its meaning because some words remind you of English. If you guessed "Kristin is fourteen years old," you are right. The verb *ist* is close to the English *is.* If you pronounce *Jahre,* it sounds something like the English *year,* and the German *alt* seems to be related to *old* in some way or other. The explanation for these similarities is that German and English belong to the same family tree. They are both Germanic languages, tracing their roots back to Germanic languages that began to appear in written form as early as the first century B.C.

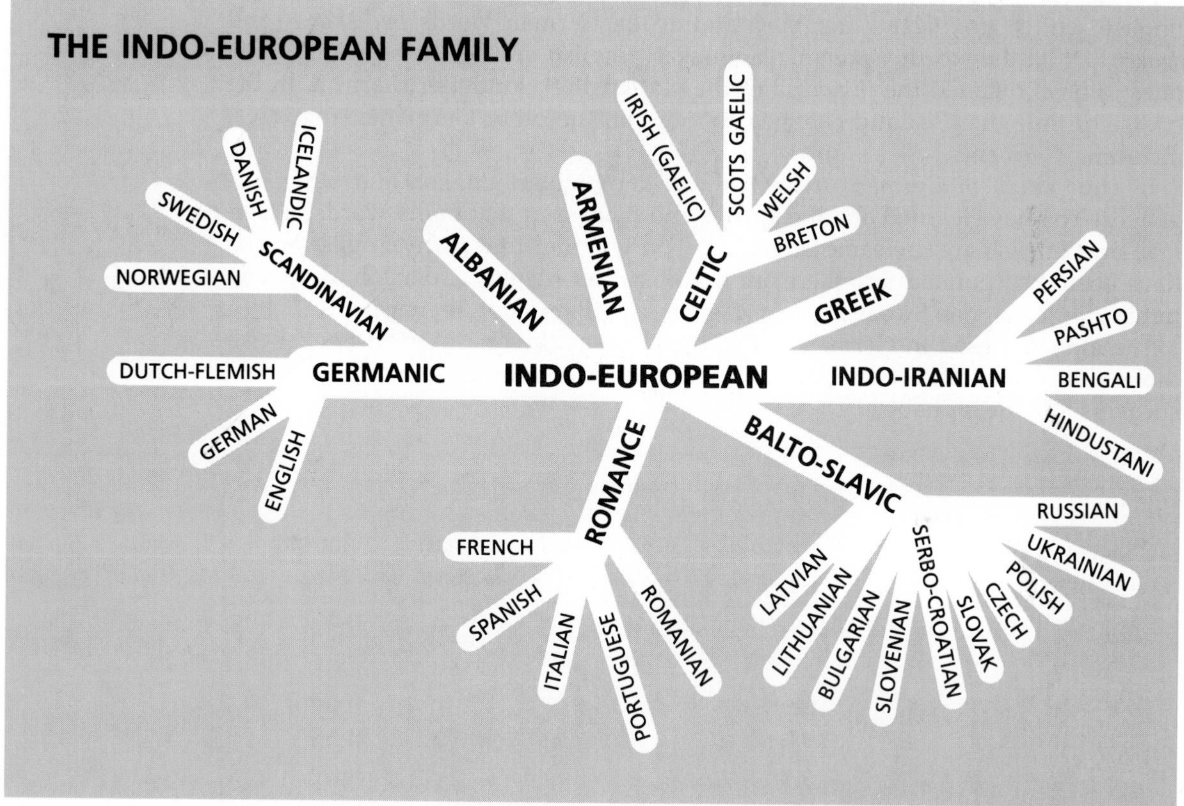

The Indo-European language family is divided into several groups, such as Germanic, Romance, and Balto-Slavic. About half of the people in the world speak a language belonging to this family.

About half the words in English are Germanic in origin. They are basic words in such categories as family, food, farming, parts of the body, and everyday living. See if you can guess the meaning of these German words: Vater, Mutter, Bruder, Milch, Apfel, Finger, Fuss, Hand. Easy! These look-alikes are called *cognates* and may help you particularly when you read German. But be careful of false cognates—words that look like English words but have totally different meanings. A **Teller** in German is a plate and not someone who works in a bank. **Gift** means poison in German, not a present!

German and English are also related to Dutch and to the Dutch-related languages of Flemish and Afrikaans, and also to Danish and the related languages of Norwegian and Swedish. They are all Germanic languages and have many words in common. Compare the following examples:

English	German	Dutch	Danish
bath	Bad	bad	bad
blind	blind	blind	blind
book	Buch	boek	bog
father	Vater	vader	fader
think	denken	denken	taenke

As you compare these words, you will notice something interesting. Look at the English words *bath, father,* and *think* and at the German words *Bad, Vater,* and *denken.* Of all the North Germanic languages, English and Icelandic are the only ones to have retained the *th* sound of the old Anglo-Saxon letter thorn, þ. In the course of time the *th* sound changed to *d* or *t* in the other Germanic languages, including German.

In your study of German, use what you know about English and other languages. You have learned about cognates and have seen that many words in German and English are the same or similar. You will find that many English words have been incorporated into German: der Boss, der Manager, der Job, der Computer, die Jeans, das Sweatshirt, das T-shirt, das Baby, der Teenager.

The alphabet used in German is also the same as the one used in English, although the names of the letters are pronounced differently. Here is how German-speakers say the alphabet:

German Letters	Roman Letters	German Name	German Letters	Roman Letters	German Name
𝔄 𝔞	A a	[ah]	𝔑 𝔫	N n	[en]
𝔅 𝔟	B b	[bay]	𝔒 𝔬	O o	[oh]
ℭ 𝔠	C c	[tsay]	𝔓 𝔭	P p	[pay]
𝔇 𝔡	D d	[day]	𝔔 𝔮	Q q	[koo]
𝔈 𝔢	E e	[ay]	ℜ 𝔯	R r	[air]
𝔉 𝔣	F f	[ef]	𝔖 𝔰	S s	[ess]
𝔊 𝔤	G g	[gay]	𝔗 𝔱	T t	[tay]
ℌ 𝔥	H h	[hah]	𝔘 𝔲	U u	[oo]
ℑ 𝔦	I i	[ee]	𝔙 𝔳	V v	[fow]
𝔍 𝔧	J j	[yot]	𝔚 𝔴	W w	[vay]
𝔎 𝔨	K k	[kah]	𝔛 𝔵	X x	[iks]
𝔏 𝔩	L l	[el]	𝔜 𝔶	Y y	[ipsilon]
𝔐 𝔪	M m	[em]	ℨ 𝔷	Z z	[tset]

As in English, German words can be grouped into word families. Look at the example below. Knowing the key word Zimmer, *room*, helps you to remember or to figure out the meaning of other words in the family.

Zimmer *room*	Badezimmer *bathroom*
Wohnzimmer *living room*	im Nebenzimmer *in the next room*
Schlafzimmer *bedroom*	Zimmerpflanze *houseplant*
Arbeitszimmer *workroom*	

You will find other similarities between German and English, and you will also find differences. You have probably noticed that all nouns in German are capitalized. You will discover that there are many more endings to verbs, articles, and adjectives in German than there are in English. And word order in German sentences can be quite different. If you try to render a German sentence word for word in English, the results would be quite amusing! As you learn more German, you will become aware of other differences. Comparing these differences with English will help you to understand how both languages operate.

Activities

1. Can you spell aloud—in German—these common acronyms and abbreviations that are used in Germany?

1. BMW
2. VW
3. dtv
4. ADAC
5. BRD
6. DDR
7. USA
8. GmbH

2. Here is a list, in German, of items you can find at home or at school. See how many you can identify just by guessing. You can check your answers in the German-English Vocabulary at the back of this textbook.

1. die Lampe
2. das Poster
3. das Sofa
4. die Banane
5. die Butter
6. die Tomate
7. der Joghurt
8. das Telefon
9. das Mathematikbuch
10. das Papier
11. die Schokolade
12. die Milch
13. die Waschmaschine
14. der Fotoapparat
15. der Kassetten-Recorder

3. Pennsylvania Dutch (Dutch = Deutsch, *German*) is still spoken in the state of Pennsylvania. How it got there in the first place is an interesting story. Track down the history of this German dialect and give a report to the class.

5 GERMAN AND YOUR FUTURE CAREER

Have you ever wondered what you will be doing ten, fifteen, or even twenty years from now? Where you will be living and working? What kind of job you will have? For many jobs it is very helpful to know a foreign language such as German, and for some it is essential. Teachers of German must be fluent in the language and also know a great deal about the culture of German-speaking countries. They travel and study abroad or sometimes teach for a year in schools in Germany, Austria, or Switzerland to expand their knowledge. In addition, they must keep up with advances in educational technology such as microcomputers.

Interpreters of German, Spanish, and French translate speeches at the United Nations and at large international conferences. Interpreters must be able to think quickly in two languages.

Translators have to know not only the German language, but also the culture. Translators of literature need to study the author's background and style. Translators are also needed to prepare the subtitles or dubbing in English for German films shown in the United States.

Translators and interpreters at the United Nations are required to know at least two foreign languages.

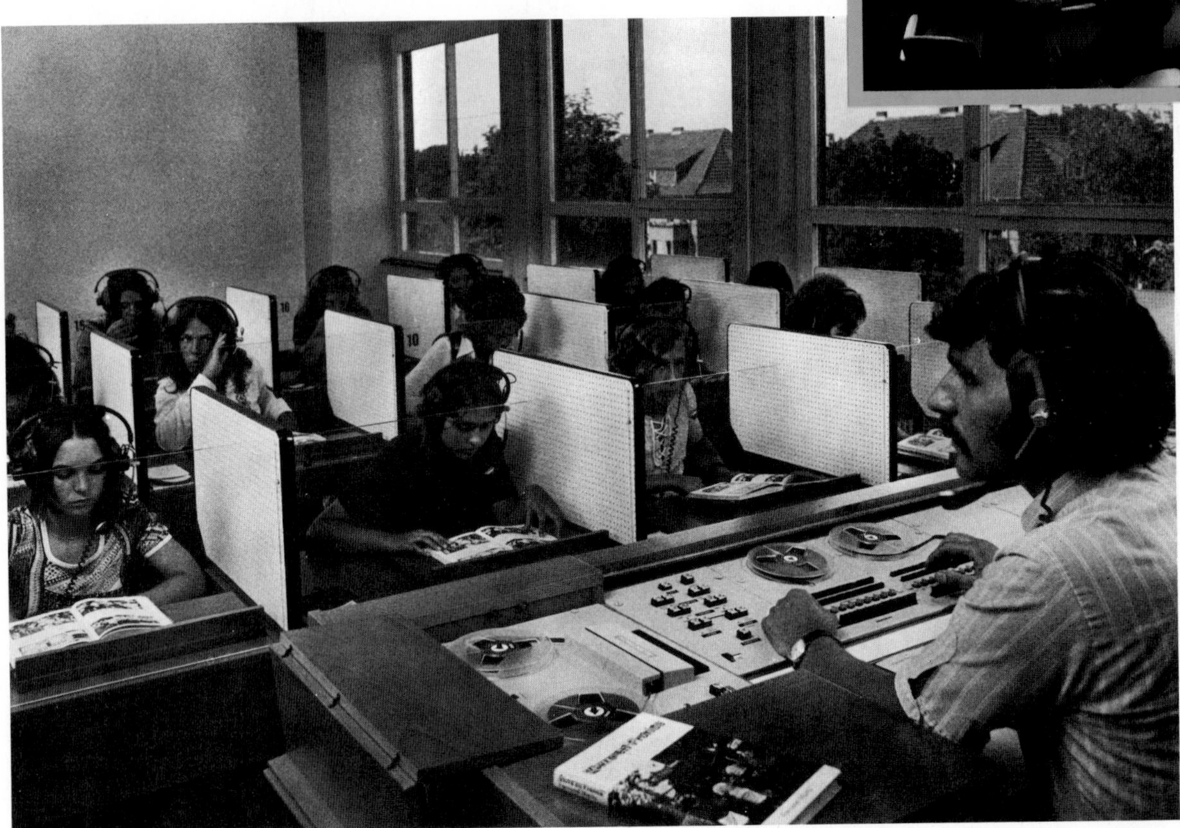

These students are learning German in a language lab.

Most libraries have a foreign language section, and the knowledge of a foreign language can be most useful for a librarian.

Librarians find it very useful to know more than one language. And in the field of publishing, writers and editors use foreign language skills to produce teaching materials and textbooks like this one.

A knowledge of German can be an asset in many occupations and professions. Interested in a career in business? Over 25,000 companies in the United States are engaged in the export business and hire managers, shipping clerks, and specialists in export traffic. In addition, there are more than 500 large American companies based abroad: large manufacturing firms, major petroleum companies, banks, and engineering firms. These businesses employ more than 100,000 Americans overseas. German is particularly useful in technological fields. Many high-tech companies name German as the language they would prefer prospective employees to have studied.

Many German companies now have branches in the United States. They hire managers and other employees who speak German. Many American firms deal with companies in the German-speaking countries and need personnel who know German.

Buyers for large department stores and small specialty shops travel abroad to select merchandise—from clothing to fine china, from sports equipment to toys. German is needed not only to do business in the foreign country, but also to read catalogues, correspondence, and other documents.

People who work in the food industry often have to travel to foreign countries, where they sample and buy local products and are in close contact with local merchants. Chefs may train abroad. Food and travel writers visit restaurants and collect recipes.

Many highly skilled professionals find foreign languages an asset. Economists sometimes deal with foreign countries. Financial experts may work in the international commodity and money markets. Lawyers and paralegals who specialize in international law or handle cases or conduct negotiations with companies in German-speaking countries must know German. Legal translators are also very much in demand.

Reporters, including sportswriters and sportscasters, can do a much better job if they can speak the language of the country where they are working and can also understand its culture.

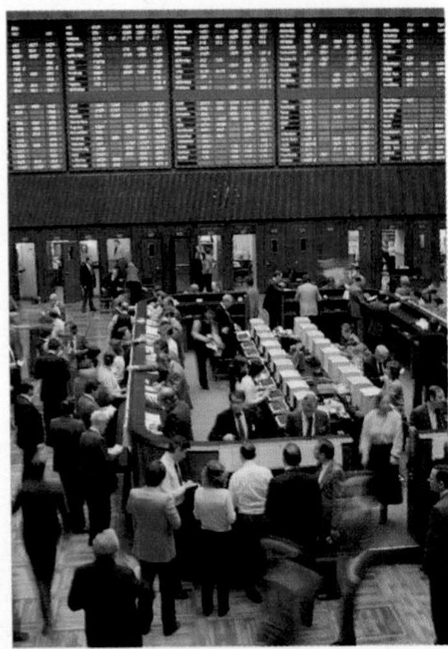

Knowledge of a foreign language can be of great advantage on the stock exchange.

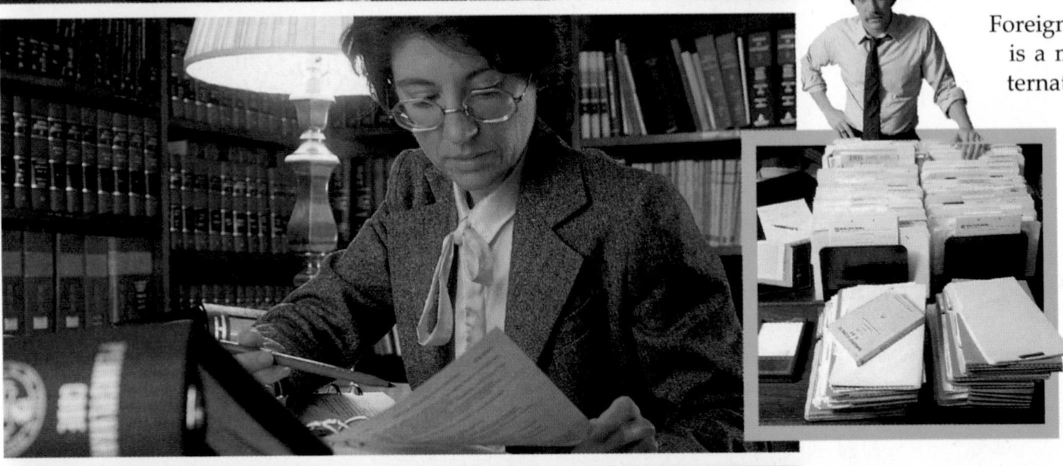

Foreign language is a must in international law.

Foreign correspondents need to know a foreign language to have first-hand knowledge about events.

Germany has many regional orchestras and opera companies, and young musicians often get experience playing and singing with them. A thorough knowledge of German and excellent pronunciation skills are essential for an opera singer who will sing roles in German.

A career with the U.S. government in the foreign service, with the diplomatic corps, or with the U.S. information services in foreign countries is an interesting way to use your foreign language ability.

Tourists from all over the world visit the United States. Travel agents, flight attendants, tour guides, salespeople in stores, desk clerks in hotels, waiters and waitresses in restaurants—anyone who deals with foreign travelers—should know more than one language.

To work in a foreign country you need to know the native language.

Opera singers sing roles in many languages.

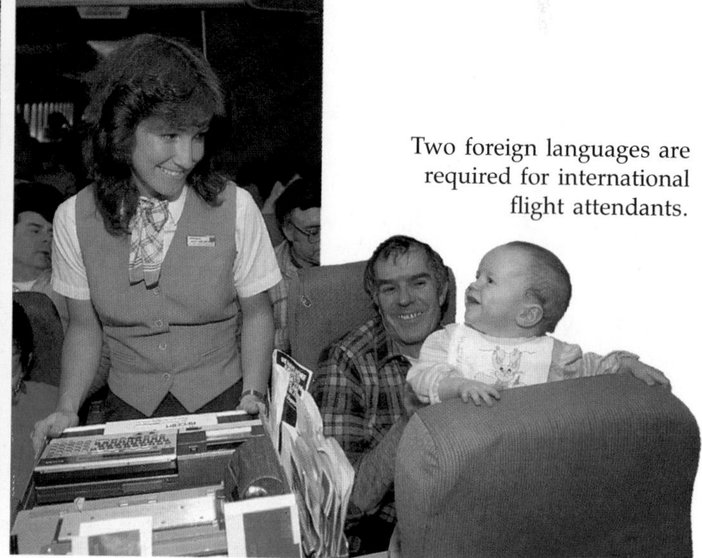

Two foreign languages are required for international flight attendants.

Activities

1. Before you make your career choice, it is wise to talk to as many people as you can about their jobs—what they actually do, and what they like and don't like about their work. Find some people in your family, school, or neighborhood who use German in their work. Interview them, asking them to describe their jobs and to answer the following questions and others you might think of.

1. What do you like best about your job? What do you like least about it?
2. How do you use German in your work?
3. How did you prepare for your job? What types of German courses did you take?
4. Do you travel as part of your job?

Write up the interview or record it to share with the class.

2. Who are the people listed below and why are they speaking German? Work in a group of two or three students. Think of as many reasons as you can why German would be useful in the jobs listed. Take notes on your ideas and report to the class. Write up your notes to post on the bulletin board. Write an imaginary interview with one of these people.

salesperson in a bookstore	museum director
soccer coach	radio announcer
auto mechanic	travel agent
pilot	waiter or waitress
aerospace engineer	librarian
research scientist	reporter

3. Choose an occupation that you might be interested in. Write a paragraph telling why you are interested in this particular occupation and how German might be of help to you in that field. Attach a picture of someone in that field if you can find one in a newspaper or magazine.

Help Wanted 2600
BILINGUAL FEE PAID

Interlangue

GERMAN

MUSIC To $35,000
Ability to work independently & attention to detail nec as exec secy for int'l div Pres. Skills in Engl. Benefits.

FINANCE $30-35
Office administrator for int'l ment concern. Skills in English. organizational abilities nec. Ben

CULTURAL $30
Asst SR exec at mjr int'l corp both, ability to prioritize. Proje

LEGAL To
Midtown/downtown locatior for legal secretayy. Skills in ly. Fantastic benefits, bonus

JOURNALISM $2
Bureau chief of major co cy. Diverse duties. Great involved in all aspects. Ex

INT'L BANK $
No steno necessary. To dept of major Europ train WP. Excellent ber

4 DAY WK
Export co sks admin V.P. Skills in Engl only

GERMAN-ENGL GUY-GAL
for smaller newspaper, full or time, W 72 St area. Call between 1 PM, 212-873-7400.

GERMAN/ENGL Fee Paid to $3
See our ad under "BILINGUAL
CALL 687-6335
William Harris Assoc 17 E 45 St. NY

German/Eng Secy $425
PRESTIGIOUS CO
PILOT, 198 Bway, rm 300 962-1430

BILINGUAL
GERMAN/ENGLISH RECEPTIONIST
To $18,000
Prestigious bank, located in midtn, needs to hire an expd recpt. Lite typing; excell benefits. For appt, please call / 212-682-5530.

GERMAN
Exec secy.CEO int'l co to $35,000
Personal private secy $30,000
Secy.Charming corp atty $28,600
Secy.US corp+ 13% bonus $27,000

Flight Attendants

SPRECHEN SIE DEUTSCH

Parlez-vous Français.

¿HABLA USTED ESPAÑOL

日本語ができる。*

*"Do you speak German, French, Spanish or Japanese" or do you know someone who speaks German, French, Spanish or Japanese?

American Airlines offers you the opportunity to be someone special while working for a company where excellence is the standard. If ensuring customer satisfaction and working varied schedules appeal to you, we have what you're looking for. We presently have Flight Attendant positions available. Listed below are our minimum qualifications.

American Airlines, Inc.
Flight Service Recruitment, Dept. NYT-0287
P.O. Box 619410, Mail Drop 908
Dallas/Fort Worth Airport, TX 75261-9410

AmericanAirlines
An Equal Opportunity Employer

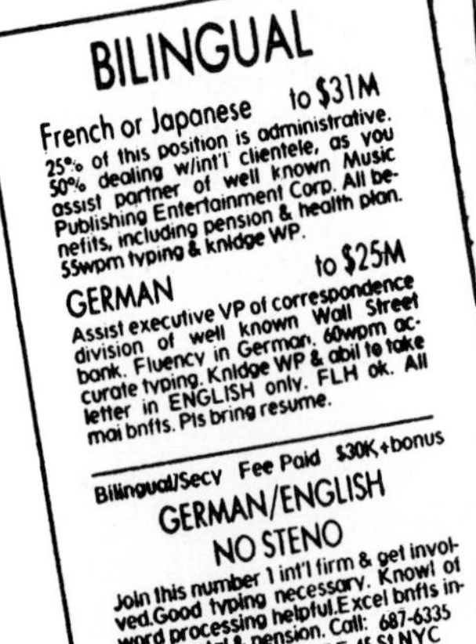

BILINGUAL

French or Japanese to $31M
25% of this position is administrative. 50% dealing w/int'l clientele, as you assist partner of well known Music Publishing Entertainment Corp. All benefits, including pension & health plan. 55wpm typing & knldge WP.

GERMAN to $25M
Assist executive VP of correspondence division of well known Wall Street bank. Fluency in German. 60wpm accurate typing. Knldge WP & abil to take letter in ENGLISH only. FLH ok. All maj bnfts. Pls bring resume.

Bilingual/Secy Fee Paid $30K+bonus
GERMAN/ENGLISH
NO STENO
Join this number 1 int'l firm & get involved. Good typing necessary. Knowl of word processing helpful. Excel bnfts include dental & pension. Call: 687-6335
William Harris Assoc 17 E 45 St NYC

ASSOCIATE SALES MANAGER
International Sales

Prominent periodical distribution organization offers a promising, challenging growth opportunity to an energetic, career-motivated sales achiever. Initial assignment will emphasize sales administration functions. The successful candidate will get involved in the planning, development and implementation of export distribution programs, preparation of new business proposals and travel to meet with our overseas wholesalers. We seek a candidate with proven sales ability, strong writing skills, and the desire to move ahead. Marketing degree preferred, knowledge of French or German an asset. Salary $21-$25,000 plus comprehensive company paid benefits package. Send resume including salary history in confidence to **T 7213 TIMES 10108.**

6 SUGGESTIONS FOR STUDYING GERMAN

LISTEN

Listening is particularly important at the beginning because you have to get used to a whole new set of sounds. Sometimes you will need to listen very carefully to understand what is being said to you, so that you can answer in German.

PRACTICE

Learning German—or any foreign language—is like learning to play a musical instrument. You have to practice speaking, listening, reading, and writing in order to make progress. You already have these skills in English. Now you have to apply them to a new language. Practice a little every day. Several short periods are more effective than one long, last-minute cramming session.

VISUALIZE

Remembering German vocabulary is easier if you visualize what a sentence, phrase, or word means as you're studying or practicing it, orally or in writing. For example, if you're practicing a sentence like *Die Kinder schwimmen,* try to picture children swimming as you say the sentence to yourself several times.

CONNECT

Make use of your English connections. Find cognates or near-cognates (schwimmen, *to swim;* Garten, *garden;* Wasser, *water*) to help you understand the meaning of a sentence or paragraph that you are reading. Also, group German words into families to help you remember—for example, Freund, *friend;* Freundschaft, *friendship;* freundlich, *friendly.*

ORGANIZE

Use memory devices. Look for ways to organize the material you have to learn. Invent a system to help you remember a word or concept. Group vocabulary in meaningful segments. Put words in context and learn phrases rather than isolated words. Your teacher will help you to recognize patterns and devices that will make learning easier.

EXPAND

Use German outside class. Speak German—perhaps on the phone—with friends who are also studying the language. Find people in your family or in the neighborhood who know some German and practice with them. Talk into your cassette recorder in German. If you have a shortwave radio, try to pick up German-language broadcasts. Look at German magazines, newspapers, and books—you may not understand much at first, but it will get easier.

ENJOY

You may want to choose a new name in German. Join the German Club and make new friends. If there are any German-speaking exchange students in the area, make a point of meeting them and making them feel welcome. Above all, don't be afraid to make mistakes in German! Concentrate on getting your message across and have fun doing it.

SOME CLASSROOM PHRASES

Your teacher will be using German to give routine directions in the classroom. Here are a few phrases that you should recognize.

Hör(t) zu, bitte!	*Please listen.*
Sprich (sprecht) nach!	*Repeat after me.*
Noch mal!	*Again! Say it again!*
Antworte(t), bitte!	*Please answer.*
Steh(t) auf!	*Get up.*
Setz dich! (to one person) Setzt euch! (to more than one person)	*Sit down.*
Nimm (nehmt) ein Blatt Papier!	*Take out a piece of paper.*
Ruhe, bitte!	*Quiet, please.*
Pass(t) auf!	*Pay attention.*
Das ist richtig.	*That's right.*
Gut! Prima!	*Good.*

KAPITEL 1

Neue Freunde

Meeting new friends is exciting, especially when they speak another language. When you meet someone who speaks German, you need to know how to say hello and goodbye, how to find out a little about the person, and how to tell a bit about yourself. In this unit you will meet five new friends your own age from the Federal and Democratic Republics of Germany, from Austria, and Switzerland.

In this unit you will:

SECTION A	say hello and say goodbye
SECTION B	ask someone's name and give your name
SECTION C	ask someone's age and tell your age, count from 1 to 20
SECTION D	ask and tell where someone is from
TRY YOUR SKILLS	use what you've learned
ZUM LESEN	read for practice and pleasure

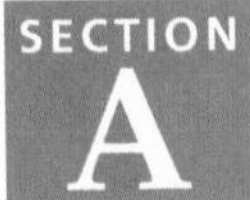

saying hello and saying goodbye

School begins. Students meet and greet one another on their way to class. Let's hear what they're saying.

A1 Guten Tag! Auf Wiedersehen!

[1] **Tschau!** is the German spelling of the Italian **ciao.**

A2 Übung • *Exercise*

Make a name tag for yourself, with your own name or one chosen from those shown in A4. Practice saying hello and goodbye to your classmates, using the names on the tags.

A3 WIE SAGT MAN DAS? *How do you say that?*
Saying hello and goodbye

Here are some ways of saying hello and goodbye. **Guten Morgen!, Guten Tag!,** and **Auf Wiedersehen!** are standard. They can be used in almost any situation. You can also use the abbreviated forms **Morgen!, Tag!,** and **Wiedersehen!** The phrases **Hallo!, Grüss dich!, Tschüs!, Tschau!,** and **Bis dann!** are more casual.

SAYING HELLO		SAYING GOODBYE	
Guten Morgen! Morgen!	Good morning! Morning.	Auf Wiedersehen! Wiedersehen!	Goodbye! Bye!
Guten Tag! Tag!	Hello! Hi!		
Grüss dich! Hallo!	Hi!	Tschüs! Tschau!	Bye! So long!
		Bis dann!	See you later.

A4 Ein wenig Landeskunde *A little culture*

These are popular first names of German boys and girls today.

Vornamen für Jungen	Vornamen für Mädchen
Frank, Markus, Jörg, Mark, Stefan, Sven, Dirk, Christof, Holger, Andreas, Michael, Matthias	Antje, Ulrike, Monika, Katja, Daniele, Claudia, Natalie, Marina, Kirsten, Nicole, Silke, Michaela

A5 HERR, FRAU, FRÄULEIN

As the students enter their classrooms, they greet their teachers.

Guten Morgen, Herr Sperling!
Tag, Antje!

Guten Tag, Frau Meier!
Grüss dich, Michael!

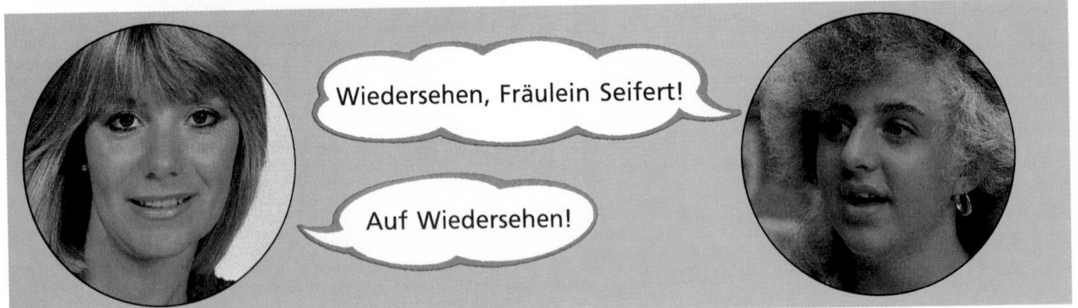

Wiedersehen, Fräulein Seifert!
Auf Wiedersehen!

A6 Übung • Jetzt bist du dran *Now it's your turn*

Greet each of the people pictured below. Then say goodbye to each one.

Lars Uschi Frl.[1] Müller

Herr Braun

Frau Binder

[1] **Frl.** is the abbreviation of **Fräulein.**

A7 WIE SAGT MAN DAS? *How do you say that?*
Greeting adults

In German, you use **Herr** for *Mister (Mr.)*, **Frau** for *Mrs.*, and **Fräulein** for *Miss*.

Guten Tag, Herr Sperling!	Hello, Mr. Sperling.
Tag, Frau Meier!	Hi, Mrs. Meier.
Guten Morgen, Fräulein Seifert!	Good morning, Miss Seifert.

A8 Ein wenig Landeskunde *A little culture*

When you greet someone, you shake hands and make eye contact. When you greet adults, it's polite to also nod your head slightly.

A9 Übung • Hör gut zu! *Listen carefully*

Do you say this to a teacher or to a student? Listen.

	0	1	2	3	4	5	6	7	8	9
a male teacher										
a female teacher	✓									
a student										

A10 Übung • Jetzt bist du dran *Now it's your turn*

1. Greet your teacher.
2. Tell the class how you greet each of your teachers.

A11 Schreibübung *Writing practice*

Write how you would greet and say good-bye to the following people:

1. your friend Peter
2. your German teacher
3. your principal

SECTION B introducing yourself

Now that you know how to say hello, let's find out how you introduce yourself.

B1 Wie heisst du?

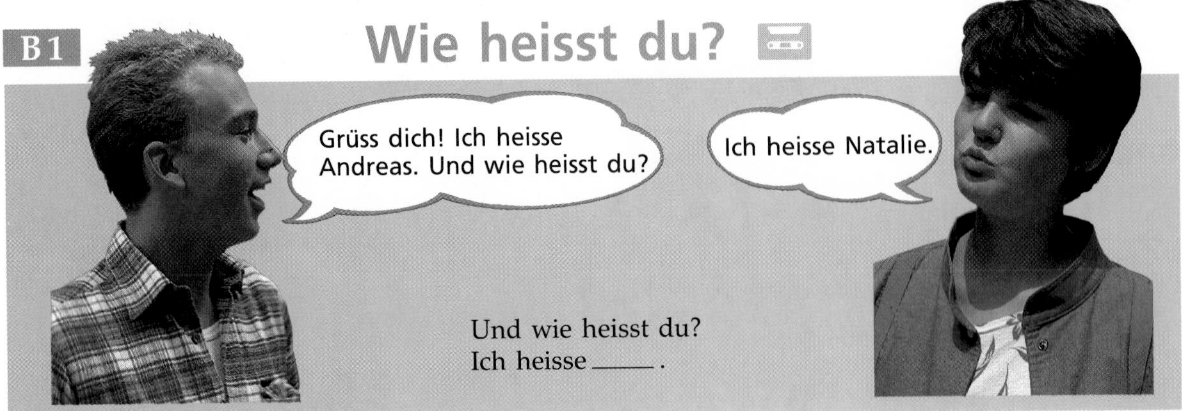
Grüss dich! Ich heisse Andreas. Und wie heisst du?
Ich heisse Natalie.

Und wie heisst du?
Ich heisse ____ .

B2 Übung • Jetzt bist du dran

1. With a classmate, practice reading this short dialog aloud, filling in your own names. Then try saying the dialog without looking at the printed words.

   A: Hallo! Ich heisse ____ . Und wie heisst du?
   B: Ich heisse ____ .

2. Now practice with other classmates.

B3 WIE HEISST DER JUNGE? WIE HEISST DAS MÄDCHEN? 

Because you still do not know many of the boys and girls in your class, you ask someone to tell you their names.

Wie heisst der Junge?
Er heisst Stefan.

Und das Mädchen? Wie heisst sie?
Sie heisst Sabine.

B4 Übung • Wie heisst er? Wie heisst sie? 

1. Ulrike

2. Lars

3. Natalie

4. Andreas

B5 WIE SAGT MAN DAS?
Asking and giving names

QUESTION	ANSWER
Wie heisst du? What's your name?	Ich heisse Andreas. My name is Andreas.
Wie heisst der Junge? What's the boy's name?	Er heisst Stefan. His name is Stefan.
Wie heisst das Mädchen? What's the girl's name?	Sie heisst Sabine. Her name is Sabine.

B6 Übung • Partnerarbeit *Teamwork*

Team up with a classmate. Ask each other the names of several other students in your class.

B7 Schreibübung • Wie heissen deine Mitschüler?

You are new in the class and want to find out the names of your new classmates. Rewrite each dialog, filling in the missing words.

A: Wie ____ du?
B: ____ ____ Andreas.

A: ____ heisst der Junge?
B: Er ____ Stefan.

A: Und das Mädchen? Wie ____ sie?
B: Sie ____ Ulrike.

A: Wie heisst ____?
B: Ich ____ ____.

B8 WER IST DAS?

Here is another way of finding out who someone is.

Wer ist das?

Das ist der Stefan.

Und wer ist das?

Das ist Herr Sperling, der Lehrer.

Wer ist das?

Das ist die Sabine.

Und das ist Frau Meier, die Lehrerin.

Herr Sperling, der Deutschlehrer

Frau Meier, die Deutschlehrerin

B9 WIE SAGT MAN DAS?
Asking who someone is

QUESTION	ANSWER
	Das ist der Stefan. Das ist die Sabine. That's Stefan. That's Sabine.
Wer ist das? Who is that?	Das ist Herr Sperling, der Deutschlehrer. That's Mr. Sperling, the German teacher.
	Das ist Frau Meier, die Deutschlehrerin. That's Mrs. Meier, the German teacher.

In everyday speech, the articles **der** and **die** are often used together with proper names when referring to other people, especially if you know the people well.

B10 Übung • Jetzt bist du dran

Ask a classmate to identify various people in your class, including your teacher.

A: Wer ist das?
B: Das ist . . .

B11 ERKLÄRUNG *Explanation*
The Definite Articles der, die, das

German has three words for *the:* **der, die,** and **das,** called the definite articles. These words tell us which class (or gender) a German noun belongs to. For example, **der Junge,** *the boy,* belongs to a class called "masculine"; **die Lehrerin,** *the female teacher,* to a class called "feminine"; and **das Mädchen,** *the girl,* to a class called "neuter." You will learn more about this in Unit 2.

Masculine Nouns	*Feminine Nouns*	*Neuter Nouns*
der Junge		**das Mädchen**
der Lehrer	**die Lehrerin**	
der Deutschlehrer	**die Deutschlehrerin**	

B12 Schreibübung *Writing practice*

Rewrite the sentences, filling in the missing words.

1. Wie heisst ____ Junge?
2. ____ Lehrerin heisst Meier.
3. Das ist ____ Lehrer.
4. ____ Mädchen heisst Sabine.
5. Wie heisst ____ Deutschlehrerin?
6. Und ____ Deutschlehrer?

B13 Übung • Ein Spiel *A game*

Do you know everyone in your class? Divide the class into two teams. The first student on Team A identifies himself or herself, saying **Ich heisse . . .** and then points to a student on the same team, asking **Wer ist das?** The first student on Team B must give the correct name. If the answer is correct, the student stays in the game. If it is incorrect, the student is out. Continue in this way, alternating teams.

B14 Übung • Hör gut zu! *Listen carefully*

Are you referring to a girl or a boy? To a woman or a man?

	0	1	2	3	4	5	6	7	8
refers to a girl or a woman									
refers to a boy or a man	✓								

B 15 Übung • Ratespiel: Wer ist das? *Guessing game*

Bring in pictures of well-known people and ask the class to identify them.

A: Wer ist das? *or* A: Wie heisst er? Wie heisst sie?
B: Das ist . . . B: Er heisst . . . Sie heisst . . .

B 16 Ein wenig Landeskunde *A little culture*

In German, as in English, many family names reflect the occupation or characteristics of ancestors. Many family names were given to help identify people at a time when only first names were customary.

Wie heisst er? Er heisst

1. Fritz. . .

2. Herman. . .

3. Hans. . .

4. Gerhard. . .

5. Paul. . .

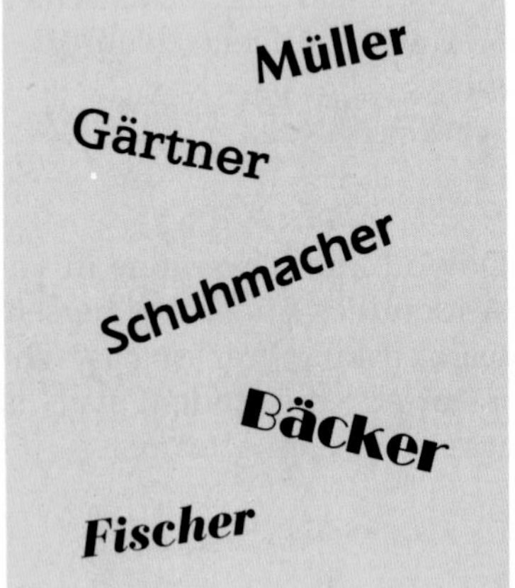

Do you know someone with a German name? The United States' census of 1980 revealed that 27.4 percent of the population of the United States can claim German ancestry. It is therefore not surprising to find German family names in all parts of the United States, and there may be a number of students with a German name in your class. What German names do you know? In Germany today, the most common last name is **Müller.**

SECTION C asking someone's age and telling your age

How old are your friends? How old are you?

C1 Wie alt bist du?

Wie alt bist du?
Ich bin dreizehn Jahre alt.
Wie alt ist die Sabine?
Die Sabine ist fünfzehn.
Und wie alt ist der Stefan?
Der Stefan ist auch fünfzehn.
Wie alt sind Ulrike und Jochen?
Sie sind auch fünfzehn Jahre alt.
Jochen
Ulrike
Und wie alt bist du?
Ich bin ____ .

C2 Übung • Wie alt sind die Jungen und Mädchen?

1. Wie alt ist der Stefan?
2. Wie alt ist die Sabine?
3. Wie alt ist der Jochen?
4. Und die Ulrike?
5. Wie alt sind Stefan und Jochen?
6. Und wie alt bist du?

C3 DIE ZAHLEN VON NULL BIS ZWANZIG

0	1	2	3	4	5	6	7	8	9	10
null	eins	zwei	drei	vier	fünf	sechs	sieben	acht	neun	zehn

11	12	13	14	15	16	17	18	19	20
elf	zwölf	dreizehn	vierzehn	fünfzehn	sechzehn	siebzehn	achtzehn	neunzehn	zwanzig

C4 Ein wenig Landeskunde

Notice in C3 how the numerals are written in German. Pay particular attention to the numerals 1 and 7.

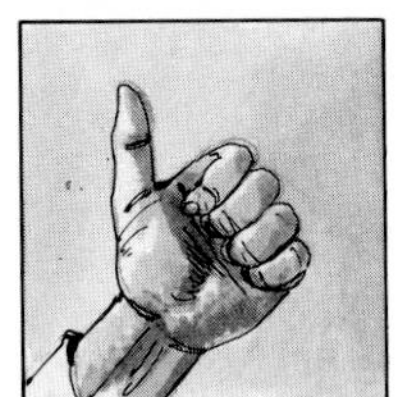

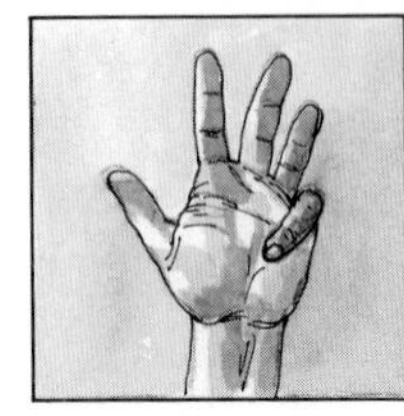
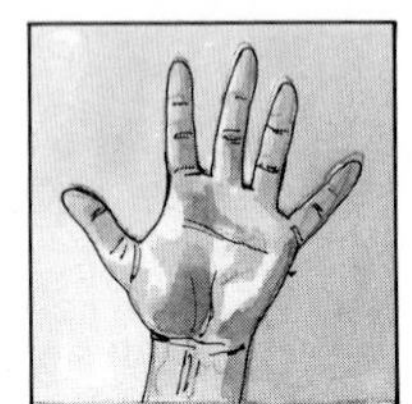

When using hand signals to indicate numbers, you use the thumb to indicate one, the thumb and the index finger to indicate two, and so on.

C5 Übung • Wir üben mit Zahlen

1. Count off in sequence: first student, **eins,** second student, **zwei,** etc.
2. Choose one student to count aloud all the boys and all the girls.
3. Complete each sequence of numbers. Say the numbers aloud in German.

   3, 4, 5, ____ drei, vier, fünf, sechs

   1. 9, 10, 11, ____
   2. 16, 17, 18, ____
   3. 1, 2, 3, ____
   4. 11, 12, 13, ____
   5. 2, 4, 6, ____
   6. 12, 14, 16, ____
   7. 6, 8, 10, ____
   8. 14, 16, 18, ____
   9. 5, 4, 3, ____
   10. 10, 9, 8, ____
   11. 20, 19, 18, ____
   12. 6, 5, 4, ____

4. Tell the class your phone number in German. Your classmates should write it down as you say it.

   Meine Telefonnummer ist . . .

C6 Übung • Zahlenlotto *Number Lotto*

Draw a rectangle and divide it into twenty squares as shown. Number the squares from 1 to 20 in any order you choose. Use each number only once. One student calls numbers from 1 to 20 in random order. As you hear each number, mark the corresponding square. The winner is the first one to fill in a horizontal line.

8	2	5	13	14
7	1	6	4	15
9	10	3	19	17
18	11	16	12	20

C7 WIE SAGT MAN DAS?
Asking someone's age and telling yours

QUESTION	ANSWER
Wie alt bist du? How old are you?	Ich bin dreizehn Jahre alt. I'm thirteen years old.
Wie alt ist der Stefan? How old is Stefan?	Er ist fünfzehn. He is fifteen.
Wie alt ist die Sabine? How old is Sabine?	Sie ist fünfzehn Jahre alt. She's fifteen years old.
Wie alt sind Ulrike und Jochen? How old are Ulrike and Jochen?	Sie sind auch fünfzehn. They are also fifteen.

C8 ERKLÄRUNG *Explanation*
Personal Pronouns and the Verb **sein**

The phrases **ich bin, du bist, er ist, sie ist,** and **sie sind** each contain a subject pronoun corresponding to the English *I, you, he, she,* and *they,* plus a form of the verb **sein,** *to be: I am, you are, he/she/it is, they are.* **Sein** is one of the most frequently used verbs in German. The chart shows the plural forms **wir,** *we,* and **ihr,** *you* (plural), but you do not need to use them yet.

Singular			*Plural*		
Ich	**bin**	15 Jahre alt.	Wir	**sind**	15 Jahre alt.
Du	**bist**		Ihr	**seid**	
Der Stefan / Er	**ist**		Stefan and Sabine / Sie	**sind**	
Die Sabine / Sie	**ist**				

C9 Übung • Wie alt sind die Schüler? —Vierzehn. 

Everyone in this group is 14 years old.

A: Wie alt ist der Fritz?
B: Er ist vierzehn.

1. Wie alt ist der Hans?
2. Wie alt ist die Monika?
3. Wie alt sind Hans und Monika?
4. Wie alt ist der Günter?
5. Wie alt ist die Ulrike?
6. Wie alt sind Günter and Ulrike?

C10 Übung • Und wie alt sind diese Schüler?

The young people in each pair are the same age.

A: Der Jochen ist fünfzehn. Und die Ulrike?
B: Sie ist auch fünfzehn.

1. Die Sabine ist 15. Und der Stefan?
2. Der Andreas ist 11. Und die Erika?
3. Dieter and Petra sind 16. Und Peter und Monika?
4. Die Katrin ist 15. Und der Kurt?
5. Der Michael ist 17. Und die Helga?
6. Die Karin und der Bernd sind 13. Und der Hans und die Sabine?

C11 Übung • Hör gut zu!

Which sentences refer to a girl and which to a boy? Listen.

	0	1	2	3	4	5	6	7	8
Junge	✓								
Mädchen									

C12 Übung • Jetzt bist du dran

Your teacher has asked you to introduce three students to the class, giving their names and ages. First ask each of the three students, and then introduce them to the class.

A: Wie heisst du? Wie alt bist du?
B: Ich heisse . . . Ich bin . . .
A: Das ist . . . Er ist . . . Sie ist . . .

C13 Schreibübung

1. Which verb form is missing?
   1. Wer _____ das?
   2. Das _____ Sabine.
   3. Sie _____ 14 Jahre alt.
   4. Wie alt _____ du?
   5. Peter und Ulrike _____ vierzehn.
   6. Ich _____ . . .
2. Write the numbers.
   1. Write your phone number, using German numerals.
   2. In German, dictate your phone number to a classmate. Have him or her write it down and read it back to you. Reverse roles.
   3. Now do the same thing with your zip code.

asking and telling where you are from

Now you will meet some young people from the German-speaking countries.

D1 Woher bist du?

Ich heisse Jens Kröger. Ich bin sechzehn Jahre alt. Ich bin aus Niebüll, aus Deutschland.

Jens Kröger, 16
Niebüll, Deutschland

Ich bin die Wiebke Nedel. Ich bin fünfzehn. Ich bin auch aus Deutschland, aus Neuss.

Wiebke Nedel, 15
Neuss, Deutschland

Ich heisse Dastl, Margit Dastl. Ich bin vierzehn. Ich bin aus Wien, aus Österreich.

Margit Dastl, 14
Wien, Österreich

Ich heisse Bruno Schmidlin. Ich bin auch fünfzehn. Ich bin aus der Schweiz, aus Zimmerwald.

Bruno Schmidlin, 15
Zimmerwald, Schweiz

Ich bin Kurt Langer. Ich bin 15. Ich bin aus der DDR, aus Dresden.

Kurt Langer, 15
Dresden, DDR

Und woher bist du? Aus Kansas City? Aus Harrisburg? Aus Dallas? Ich bin aus ____.

D2 Übung • Woher sind unsere Freunde?

Take a look at the map, and locate where our friends live. Say where each one is from.

D3 Übung • Schau auf die Karte! Woher ist . . .?

Look at the map and pictures on the preceding page and ask a classmate where the different young people are from.

A: Woher ist Jens?
B: Er ist aus Niebüll.

A: Wer ist aus Wien?
B: Margit Dastl ist aus Wien.

D4 WIE SAGT MAN DAS?
Talking about where you are from

QUESTION	ANSWER
Jens, woher bist du? Jens, where are you from?	Ich bin aus Deutschland. Aus Niebüll. I'm from Germany. From Niebüll.
Woher ist Wiebke? Woher ist Margit? Woher ist Bruno? Woher ist Kurt?	Sie ist aus Deutschland. Margit ist aus Österreich. Er ist aus der Schweiz. Er ist aus der DDR.

D5 Übung • Jetzt bist du dran

1. Say hello to a classmate you haven't met yet. Ask his or her name and age and where he or she is from.
2. Introduce your new friend to the class. Give his or her name and age, and tell where he or she is from.
3. Talk about the girl or boy in each picture, telling the name and age and where she or he is from.

1. 
2. 
3. 
4. 
5. 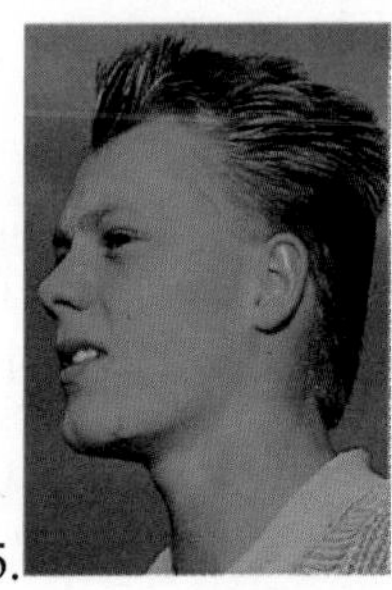

4. Now introduce yourself, giving your name and age and where you are from.

D6 Übung • Etwas über deine Freunde, etwas über dich

1. Pick two of the new friends you met in D1 and write a few sentences about each one, telling the name and age and where he or she is from.
2. Write a few sentences about yourself.

   Ich heisse . . .

D7 JA ODER NEIN?

Let's listen to how our friends answer the following questions.

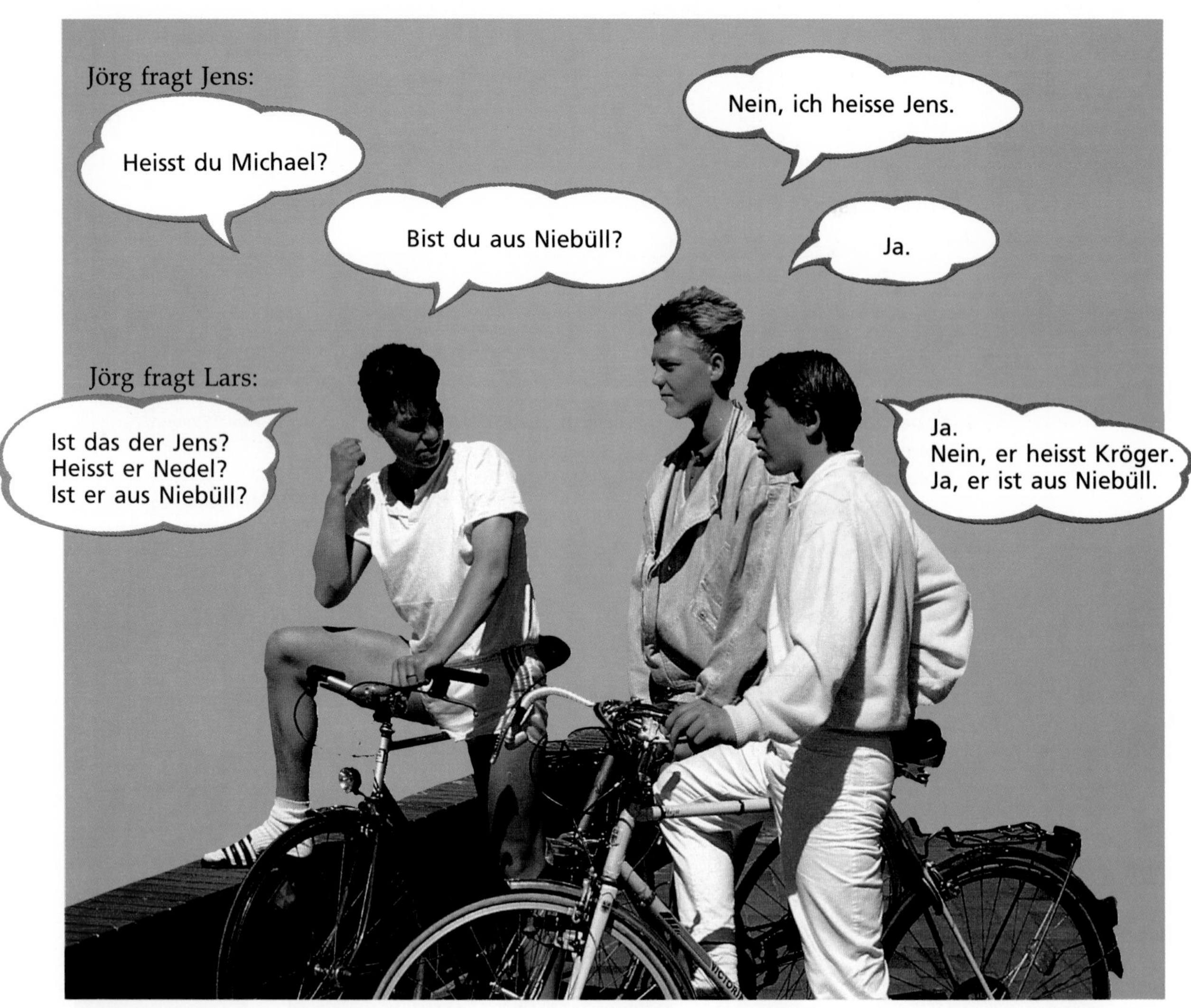

Jörg fragt Jens:
Heisst du Michael?
Nein, ich heisse Jens.
Bist du aus Niebüll?
Ja.
Jörg fragt Lars:
Ist das der Jens?
Heisst er Nedel?
Ist er aus Niebüll?
Ja.
Nein, er heisst Kröger.
Ja, er ist aus Niebüll.

D8 ERKLÄRUNG
Asking and Answering Questions

1. There are questions that begin with a question word like **wer?**, *who?*, **wie?**, *how?*, and **woher?**, *from where?*

Questions beginning with a question word	*Answers*
Wer ist das?	Das ist Jens.
Wie alt ist er?	Er ist sechzehn.
Woher ist er?	Er ist aus Deutschland.

2. There are also questions that begin with verbs. Such questions anticipate answers that start with **ja,** *yes,* or **nein,** *no.*

Questions beginning with a verb	*Answer*
Heisst du Michael?	Nein.
	Nein, ich heisse Jens.
Bist du aus Niebüll?	Ja.
	Ja, ich bin aus Niebüll.
Ist er 16 Jahre alt?	Ja, er ist 16.

D9 Übung • Jetzt bist du dran

Ask different classmates questions about themselves, anticipating *yes* or *no* answers.

Heisst du . . .? Bist du fünfzehn? Bist du aus . . .?

D10 Übung • Wer ist dein Partner?

Write an age from 13 to 15 and the name of one of the cities in a German-speaking country on an index card and put the card in your pocket. Mingle with your classmates and try to find a partner whose card has information that matches your own. Be sure to ask and answer in German.

D11 Übung • Hör gut zu!

Questions and answers. Which ones go together? Listen.

	Ex.	Sie ist aus Deutschland.	3		Sie ist fünfzehn.
1		Ich bin vierzehn.	4		Das ist Jens Kröger.
2		Er heisst Michael.	5		Ich bin aus der Schweiz.

D12 Übung • Was sagt er? Was sagt sie?

Rewrite each dialog, supplying appropriate lines.

SCHÜLER 1 Guten Morgen!
SCHÜLER 2 ____________
SCHÜLER 1 Wer ist das?
SCHÜLER 2 ____________
SCHÜLER 1 Woher ist er/sie?
SCHÜLER 2 ____________

FRAU MEIER ____________
SCHÜLER Guten Tag, Frau Meier!
FRAU MEIER ____________
SCHÜLER Das ist die Wiebke Nedel.
FRAU MEIER ____________
SCHÜLER Sie ist aus Neuss.

D13 WIE BITTE?

Sometimes you do not quite hear or understand what someone has said and need the information repeated. How do you do this?

D14 WIE SAGT MAN DAS?
What to say if you don't understand

If you have not heard or understood what someone has said, you ask for the information to be repeated. In German, this is generally done with **Wie bitte?** or more specifically, with a word such as **wer?**, *who?* or **woher?**, *from where?*, or by repeating the key word. Make sure to raise the tone of your voice.

You did not understand what was said and ask for the entire statement to be repeated.	Der Stefan ist aus Oberpfaffenhofen.	Wie bitte?	I beg your pardon?
You did not understand part of what was said and ask only for a part to be repeated.	Er ist aus Wien. Das ist der Lehrer. Wie alt ist der Stefan? Wie heisst du?	Woher? Wer ist das? Der Stefan? Ich?	From where? Who is that? Stefan? Me?

D 15 Übung • Jetzt bist du dran

A classmate makes a statement or asks a question, and you ask that person to repeat the information that you did not understand. Your classmate then gives an appropriate response.

A: Sabine ist 15 Jahre alt.
B: Wer? *or* Wie alt? *or* Wie bitte?
A: Sabine. *or* Fünfzehn. *or* Sabine ist 15 Jahre alt.

D 16 WIE HEISSEN SIE? WOHER SIND SIE?

How do you ask your teacher some of the questions you have been asking your classmates? When you talk to your teacher and to most other adults outside your family, you use the **Sie**-form.

D 17 Übung • Frag deinen Lehrer! *Ask your teacher!*

1. Wie heissen Sie?
2. Woher sind Sie? Sind Sie aus Deutschland?

D 18 Übung • Guten Tag! Ich heisse . . .

Pick a German first and last name for yourself. Then select a city in one of the German-speaking countries as your home town. Tell the class who you are now.

TRY YOUR SKILLS

using what you've learned

Now you know how to greet people, to talk a little about yourself, and to ask others about themselves. Here are some more opportunities to use what you have learned.

1

Zwei Briefe

It is fun to have a pen pal. As you continue your study of German, perhaps you, too, will have a pen pal. Imagine that these letters are for you.

Lieber Eric!

Ich heisse Petra Schmitt. Ich bin aus Salzburg. Das ist in Österreich. Ich bin 15 Jahre alt.
Woher bist Du? Wie alt bist Du? Bitte schreib mir!

Viele Grüsse
Petra

Liebe Mary!

Ich heisse Günter Weiss. Ich bin aus Frankfurt. Frankfurt ist in Deutschland. Ich bin 14 Jahre alt.
Woher bist Du? Wie alt bist Du?

Viele Grüsse
Günter

Look at these letters. How do they start? Why do you think the greetings are spelled differently? How is the word **Du** spelled?

2

Übung • Woher ist das Mädchen? Wer ist der Junge?

1. Wie heisst das Mädchen?
2. Woher ist sie?
3. Wie alt ist sie?
4. Wie heisst der Junge?
5. Woher ist er?
6. Wie alt ist er?

3 Übung • Brieffreunde *Pen Pals*

You choose a pen pal and a pen pal chooses you!

1. Write a letter like one of the sample letters, introducing yourself in German to a pen pal in a German-speaking country.
2. Write a letter that one of our friends from abroad (p. 45) might have written to you.

4 Übung • Du triffst neue Freunde. Was sagst du? *You meet new friends. What do you say?*

Imagine that you are staying at a youth hostel in Germany. A youth hostel is an inexpensive hotel for young people. While there, you meet several of our young German-speaking friends pictured on page 45. Exchange greetings and tell one another something about yourselves—for example, your name and age and where you are from.

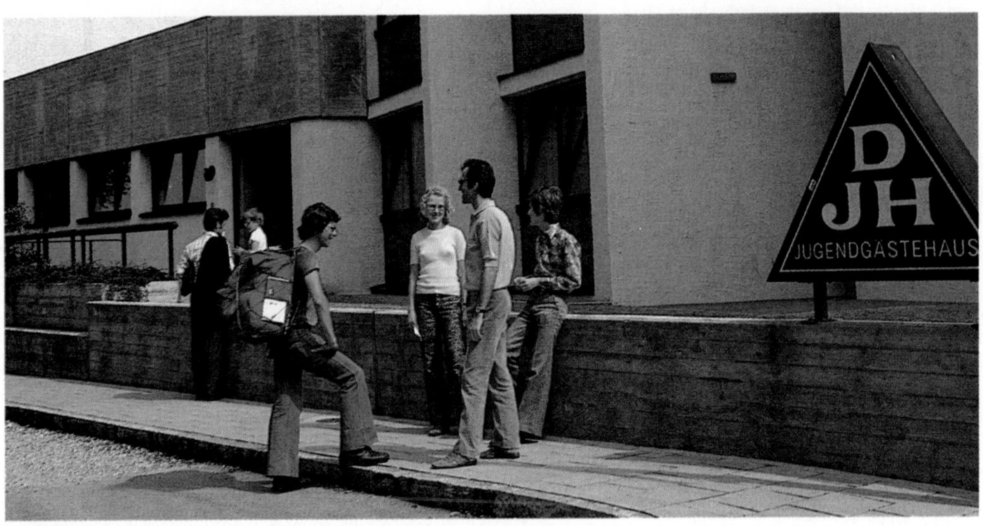

5 Übung • Unsere Freunde

Write a brief paragraph about the five friends from abroad. Write their names and ages and where they are from.

6 Aussprache-, Lese- und Schreibübungen *Pronunciation, Reading, and Writing Exercises*

1. Listen carefully and repeat what you hear.
2. Listen, then read aloud.
   ich, acht, dich, auch; alt, elf, null; wie, wer, Wien, wir, wo, woher, Wiedersehen; Zahl, zwei, zehn, Schweiz
3. Copy the following sentences to prepare yourself to write them from dictation.
   1. Wo ist Wien?
   2. Wie alt ist Michael?
   3. Zehn und zwei ist zwölf.
   4. Ich bin auch elf.

WAS KANNST DU SCHON?

Let's review some important points that you have learned in this unit.

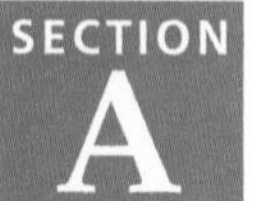

Can you greet young people and adults in German?
Say hello to the following people:

1. Katrin
2. Stefan
3. Mr. Sperling
4. Miss Seifert
5. Mrs. Meier
6. your teacher

Can you say goodbye in German?
Say goodbye to the same people.

Can you introduce yourself in German?

1. Say hello.
2. Give your name.
3. Ask a classmate his or her name.

Can you find out who someone is?

1. Ask a boy's name, then tell it to someone else.
2. Ask a girl's name, then tell it to someone else.
3. Ask who someone is and give the answer.

Can you ask someone's age and tell yours?
Write a question and answer about age for each of the following pronouns: ich, du, er, sie, sie (plural).

Do you know the numbers from 0 to 20?
Write out in German the numbers from 0 to 20.

Do you know the forms of the verb *sein?*
Complete the following sentences.

1. Das Mädchen _____ 15.
2. Ich _____ 13.
3. Der Junge _____ 16.
4. Frl. Seifert _____ aus Wien.
5. _____ du aus Deutschland?
6. Wer _____ das?
7. Jens und Wiebke _____ aus Deutschland.
8. Er _____ aus Österreich.

Can you say where you are from? Can you ask where others are from?
Say where you are from. Ask one of your classmates where he or she is from.

Can you ask questions anticipating a yes or no answer?
Make up three questions anticipating a yes or no answer.

Can you ask for information to be repeated?
What do you say if you don't understand part or all of the following statements?

1. Ich bin aus Deutschland.
2. Er heisst Jens Kröger.
3. Das Mädchen ist 15 Jahre alt.
4. Der Deutschlehrer heisst Sperling.

Can you address adults using the *Sie*-form?
Ask your teacher his or her name and where he or she is from.

WORTSCHATZ *Vocabulary*

SECTION A

auf Wiedersehen! *goodbye!*
bis dann! *see you later!*
Frau *Mrs.*
Fräulein *Miss*
Frl. = Fräulein *Miss*
grüss dich! *hi!*
guten Morgen! *good morning!*
guten Tag! *hello!*
hallo! *hello! hi!*
Herr *Mr.*
Morgen! *morning!*
Tag! *hello! hi!*
tschau! *bye! so long!*
tschüs! *bye, so long!*
Wiedersehen! *bye!*

SECTION B

das *the; that*
das ist . . . *that's . . .*
der *the*
der **Deutschlehrer** *the German teacher* (m)
die **Deutschlehrerin** *the German teacher* (f)
die *the*
er heisst *his name is*
ich heisse *my name is*
der **Junge** *the boy*
der **Lehrer** *the teacher* (m)
die **Lehrerin** *the teacher* (f)
das **Mädchen** *the girl*
sie heisst *her name is*
und *and*
wer? *who?*
wer ist das? *who's that?*
wie heisst das Mädchen? *what's the girl's name?*
wie heisst der Junge? *what's the boy's name?*
wie heisst du? *what's your name?*
wie heisst er? *what's his name?*
wie heisst sie? *what's her name?*

SECTION C

alt *old*
auch *also*
du bist *you are*
er ist *he is*
ich bin *I am*
ich bin dreizehn. *I am thirteen.*
ich bin sechzehn Jahre alt. *I am sixteen years old.*
sie ist *she is*
sie sind *they are*
wie? *how?*
wie alt bist du? *how old are you?*
die **Zahlen** *the numbers*
die **Zahlen von null bis zwanzig** *the numbers from zero to twenty*, see page 42

SECTION D

aus *from*
aus der Schweiz *from Switzerland*
DDR = Deutsche Demokratische Republik *German Democratic Republic*[1]
Deutschland *Germany*
fragt *asks*
heissen Sie Müller? *is your name Müller?*
heisst du Michael? *is your name Michael?*
ich? *me?*
ich bin aus *I'm from*
ja *yes*
der **Mathematiklehrer** *the math teacher*
München *Munich*
nein *no*
oder *or*
Österreich *Austria*
Schweiz *Switzerland*
wie bitte? *I beg your pardon?*
wie heissen Sie? *what's your name?*
Wien *Vienna*
woher? *from where?*
woher bist du? *where are you from?*
woher sind . . .? *where are . . . from?*
woher sind Sie? *where are you from?*

[1]German words are usually stressed on the first syllable. When this is not the case, it will be indicated on the vocabulary list so you will know how to pronounce the word. The stress will be marked by an underscore or a dot. In addition to stress, the underscore will signify a long vowel; the dot will signify a short vowel.

WORTSCHATZÜBUNGEN *Vocabulary Activities*

1. All German nouns begin with a capital letter. Look at the **Wortschatz** and pick out all the nouns.
2. German has several letters that do not exist in English: **ä, ö, ü,** and **äu.** The marking ¨ is called an umlaut. Look at the **Wortschatz** above. Pick out all the words that have an umlaut, write them down, and say them.

ZUM LESEN

Wo ist Deutschland?

Deutschland ist in Europa. Deutschland: das sind zwei Länder°, die Bundesrepublik Deutschland (BRD) and die Deutsche Demokratische Republik (DDR).

Die Bundesrepublik Deutschland hat° neun Nachbarn°: die Deutsche Demokratische Republik, die Tschechoslowakei, Österreich, die Schweiz, Frankreich, Luxemburg, Belgien, die Niederlande und Dänemark.

Wo ist Dänemark?—Dänemark ist nördlich von° Deutschland. Die Deutsche Demokratische Republik und die Tschechoslowakei sind östlich°, Österreich und die Schweiz sind südlich°, und Frankreich, Luxemburg, Belgien und die Niederlande sind westlich von° Deutschland.

Margit Dastl ist aus Wien. Wien ist die Hauptstadt° von Österreich. Die Hauptstadt der Bundesrepublik Deutschland ist Bonn. Berlin (Ost) ist die Hauptstadt der Deutschen Demokratischen Republik, und Bern ist die Hauptstadt der Schweiz.

Man spricht Deutsch° in Deutschland: in der Bundesrepublik und in der Deutschen Demokratischen Republik. Man spricht Deutsch auch in Österreich, in der Schweiz, in Liechtenstein (zwischen° Österreich und der Schweiz), auch in einem Teil von° Luxemburg und in Norditalien (in Südtirol).

Think about what you have read. What information could you give to someone who asked you "Where is Germany?" What else could you tell him or her?

Übung • Beantworte die Fragen! *Answer the questions.*

1. Wo ist Deutschland?
2. Wie heissen die Nachbarn?
3. Wo ist Österreich? Und Frankreich?
4. Welche° Nachbarn sind westlich der Bundesrepublik? Und östlich? Südlich?
5. Was ist Wien? Berlin (Ost)? Bern? Bonn?
6. Wo spricht man Deutsch?
7. Wo spricht man Deutsch in den Vereinigten Staaten°?
8. Wie heissen unsere Nachbarn?
9. Und wie heisst unsere Hauptstadt?

---

wo *where;* **Länder** *countries;* **hat** *has;* **Nachbarn** *neighbors;* **nördlich von** *north of;* **östlich** *east (of);* **südlich** *south (of);* **westlich von** *west of;* **die Hauptstadt** *the capital;* **man spricht Deutsch** *German is spoken;* **zwischen** *between;* **in einem Teil von** *in a part of;* **welche** *which;* **in den Vereinigten Staaten** *in the United States*

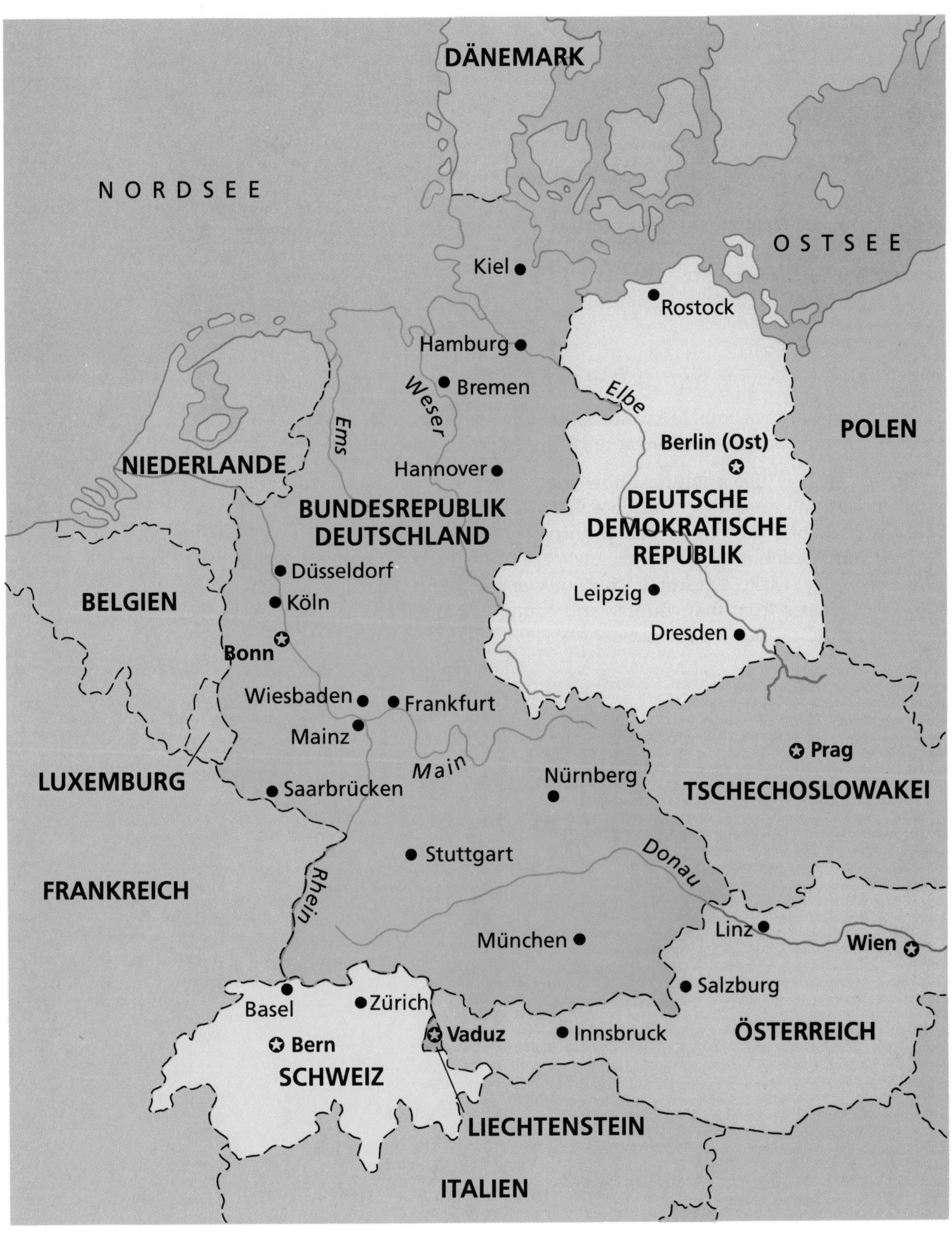
DÄNEMARK
NORDSEE
OSTSEE
Kiel
Rostock
Hamburg
Bremen
Weser
Elbe
Ems
POLEN
Berlin (Ost)
NIEDERLANDE
Hannover
BUNDESREPUBLIK
DEUTSCHLAND
DEUTSCHE
DEMOKRATISCHE
REPUBLIK
Düsseldorf
Köln
BELGIEN
Leipzig
Dresden
Bonn
Wiesbaden
Frankfurt
Mainz
Prag
Main
LUXEMBURG
Nürnberg
Saarbrücken
TSCHECHOSLOWAKEI
Stuttgart
Donau
Rhein
FRANKREICH
Linz
München
Wien
Salzburg
Basel
Zürich
Bern
Vaduz
Innsbruck
ÖSTERREICH
SCHWEIZ
LIECHTENSTEIN
ITALIEN

Übung • Stimmt oder stimmt nicht? *True or not true?*

Read the following statements. If a statement is true, say **Stimmt!** If a statement is false, say **Stimmt nicht!** Then correct it.

1. England ist mitten in Europa.
2. Wien ist die Hauptstadt Österreichs.
3. Dänemark liegt nördlich von Deutschland.
4. Die Hauptstadt der DDR ist Bern.
5. Die Schweiz liegt östlich von Österreich.
6. In der DDR spricht man Deutsch.
7. Österreich ist Frankreichs Nachbar.
8. Liechtenstein ist zwischen Österreich und der Schweiz.

Übung • Klassenprojekt *Class project*

Divide into groups of four to six students. Choose a country where German is the official language and do one or more of the following projects:

1. Draw a map of that country. Show the capital, the principal cities, the major rivers and mountains, and the boundaries.
2. Draw and color the flag of that country.
3. Try to find some magazine and newspaper articles and photos pertaining to that country. Make a cultural scrapbook or a bulletin board.
4. Collect recipes from that country and compile a cookbook. If possible, prepare some of the recipes for the class.

Postkarten

Our new friends are traveling. Here are some postcards they sent to their friends.

Schweiz . Suisse . Svizzera
Bern - Hauptstadt der Schweiz

Herzliche Grüsse
aus der Schweiz.
Ich bin in
Bern.
Wiebke

Frl. Katja Hauser
Haupts... 17
7840 ...

Wien . Vienna
Parlament

Grüss dich!
Ich bin in
Österreich,
in Wien!
Tschüs, Bruno

Herrn Michael Pertsch
Bahnhofstrasse 38
4790 Paderborn

Übung • Jetzt bist du dran!

Now write in German a postcard to a friend back home from one or all of the following places: Wien, Dresden, Hamburg, Innsbruck.

KAPITEL 2

Schule

In this unit you will meet some high school students from German-speaking countries. About 35 percent of the young people between the ages of 10 and 19 attend academic high schools, and many, though not all, will continue on to a university or to another school of higher learning.

In this unit you will:

SECTION A	tell how you get to school
SECTION B	talk about school supplies and how much they cost
SECTION C	talk about your class schedule, tell time
SECTION D	talk about homework and grades
TRY YOUR SKILLS	use what you've learned
ZUM LESEN	read for practice and pleasure

SECTION A

telling how you get to school

These are the ways some of our friends from abroad get to school. Let's see if they are different from the way you get to school.

A1 Wie kommst du in die Schule?

A: Schau, da kommt der Jens mit dem Moped!
B: Toll!
A: Wie kommst du in die Schule?
B: Ich? Ich komme mit dem Bus. Und du?
A: Zu Fuss.

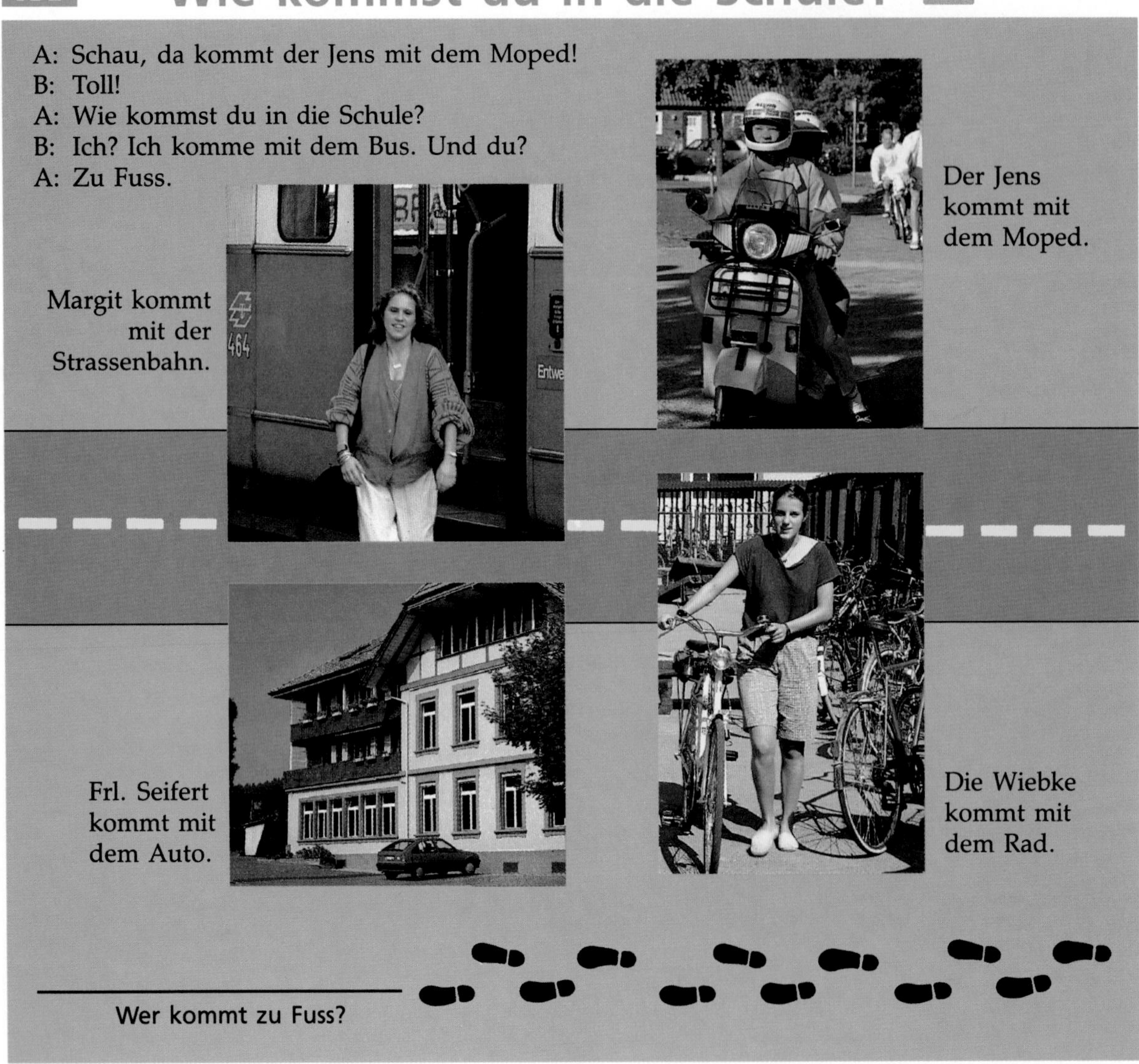

Margit kommt mit der Strassenbahn.

Der Jens kommt mit dem Moped.

Frl. Seifert kommt mit dem Auto.

Die Wiebke kommt mit dem Rad.

Wer kommt zu Fuss?

A2 Übung • Beantworte die Fragen! *Answer the questions.*

1. Wie kommt Jens in die Schule?
2. Wie kommt Margit in die Schule?
3. Und Wiebke?
4. Wie kommt Frl. Seifert in die Schule?
5. Wer kommt mit dem Moped?

A3 WIE SAGT MAN DAS?
Saying how you get to school

The verb **kommen** can have different meanings.

Schau, da kommt der Jens mit dem Moped.	Look, here comes Jens on his moped.
Wie kommt Margit in die Schule?	How does Margit get to school?
Margit kommt mit der Strassenbahn.	Margit comes by streetcar.
Wer kommt zu Fuss?	Who walks?

A4 Übung • Und du? Wie steht's mit dir? *And what about you?*

1. Wie kommst du in die Schule?
2. Wer kommt mit dem Rad?
3. Wer kommt mit dem Bus?
4. Wer kommt zu Fuss?

A5 ERKLÄRUNG
The Verb **kommen**

The verb **kommen** has the following forms. You do not have to use **wir,** *we,* and **ihr,** *you* (plural) yet.

Singular			*Plural*		
Ich	**komme**	mit dem Rad.	Wir	**kommen**	mit dem Rad.
Du	**kommst**		Ihr	**kommt**	
Jens (er) Karin (sie)	**kommt** **kommt**		Jens und Karin (sie)	**kommen**	

A6 Übung • Jetzt bist du dran

1. You are conducting a survey for your teacher. Go around the class and find out how everyone gets to school.

   A: Wie kommst du in die Schule?
   B: Ich komme . . .

2. Now tell your teacher how everybody gets to school.

   Der Peter kommt . . . Die Barbara kommt . . .
   Der Paul, der Martin, die Mary und die Heidi kommen . . .

A7 Übung • Wie kommen alle in die Schule?

1. Pick four classmates and one of your teachers and write sentences telling how each one gets to school.
2. Make a chart showing how your classmates get to school. Report your findings to the class.

Mit dem Bus:	10
Mit . . .	

SECTION B

asking about prices of school supplies

At the beginning of the school year, everyone has to buy school supplies. Jens goes to a store where school supplies are displayed in the window. He goes inside and asks about prices. —What supplies do you need for school?

B1

Schulsachen

Wörterbuch
DM 13,00

Schultasche
DM 20,00

Bleistift
DM 1,00

Kuli
DM 4,00

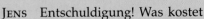

Heft
DM 1,20

Taschenrechner
DM 18,00

Poster
DM 5,00

Kassette
DM 6,00

Stundenplan
DM 1,10

JENS: Entschuldigung! Was kostet das Wörterbuch, bitte?
VERKÄUFERIN: Das Wörterbuch? —Dreizehn Mark.
JENS: Und was kostet der Taschenrechner?
VERKÄUFERIN: Achtzehn Mark.
JENS: Wie bitte?
VERKÄUFERIN: Achtzehn Mark.
JENS: Prima, nur achtzehn Mark! Und was kostet die Kassette?
VERKÄUFERIN: Sechs Mark.
JENS: Danke!
VERKÄUFERIN: Bitte!

B2 Ein wenig Landeskunde

The unit of German currency is the **Deutsche Mark,** abbreviated **DM.** One **Mark** has one hundred **Pfennige**. Prices are usually indicated in the following way: **DM** in front of the price, and a comma separating **Mark** and **Pfennig.** In advertising material, a period is often used instead of a comma. Here is how to read prices:

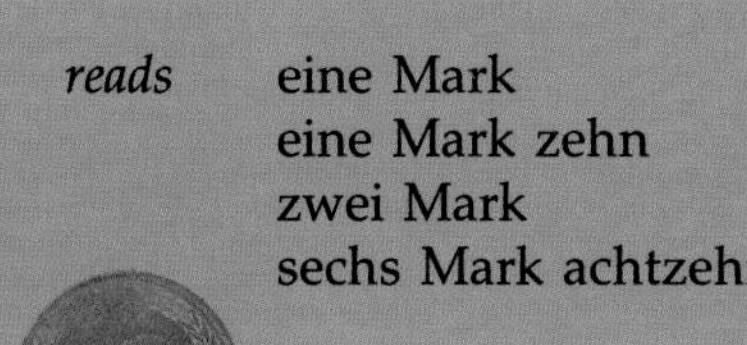

DM 1,00	*reads*	eine Mark
DM 1,10		eine Mark zehn
DM 2,00		zwei Mark
DM 6,18		sechs Mark achtzehn

B3 Übung • Wir lesen Preise!

Read the following prices.

1. DM 11,00
2. DM 2,10
3. DM 17,20
4. DM 9,00
5. DM 7,05
6. DM 13,08
7. DM 1,17
8. DM 19,00
9. DM 4,02

B4 Übung • Was kostet alles? 

What does each item pictured on page 64 cost?

A: Was kostet das Heft?
B: Das Heft? Eine Mark zwanzig.

1. Was kostet die Schultasche?
2. Was kostet der Stundenplan?
3. Und das Wörterbuch?
4. Was kostet der Taschenrechner?
5. Und die Kassette?
6. Was kostet der Kuli?
7. Und was kostet das Poster?
8. Und der Bleistift?

B5 Übung • Hör gut zu! 

How much does it cost? Listen.

0	1	2	3	4	5	6	7	8	9	10
3,10										

B6 ERKLÄRUNG
The Definite Articles der, die, das

When Jens asked about the price of various school supplies, you noticed that he used different words with every noun. He said **das Wörterbuch, der Taschenrechner, die Kassette,** and so on. These words are called definite articles. They name something specific or definite. *(continued)*

There are three genders of German nouns: masculine, feminine, and neuter. The definite articles **der, die,** and **das** tell you the gender—they are gender markers. The gender marker **der** tells you **der Bleistift,** *the pencil,* is masculine; **die** tells you **die Schultasche,** *the schoolbag,* is feminine; **das** tells you **das Heft,** *the notebook,* is neuter. Since usually there is no other way of telling the gender of a noun, you must remember each noun with its gender marker, the definite article.

Nouns for people are generally masculine for males **(der Junge)** and feminine for females **(die Lehrerin).** There are a few exceptions, such as **das Mädchen,** *the girl,* which is neuter because of its ending **-chen.** All nouns with the ending **-chen** are neuter.

Here is a list of the nouns that you have learned so far. Study them with their gender markers.

Masculine	*Feminine*	*Neuter*
der Lehrer	**die Frau**	**das Mädchen**
der Junge	**die Lehrerin**	**das Heft**
der Kuli	**die Verkäuferin**	**das Poster**
der Bleistift	**die Zahl**	**das Wörterbuch**
der Stundenplan	**die Schule**	
der Taschenrechner	**die Schultasche**	
	die Kassette	

B7 Übung • Was kostet . . .?

Your friend wants to know what each item costs. Tell him or her.

1. Das Heft kostet DM 1,20. **2.** Der Taschenrechner . . .

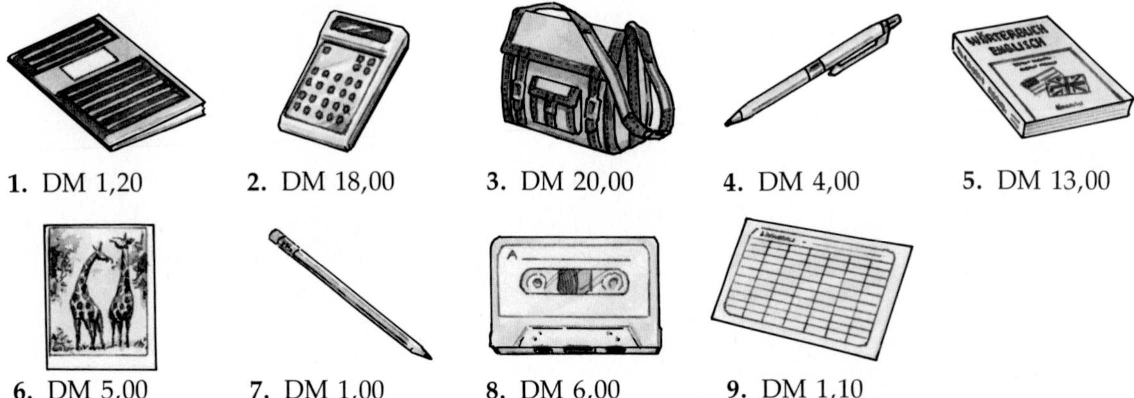

1. DM 1,20 **2.** DM 18,00 **3.** DM 20,00 **4.** DM 4,00 **5.** DM 13,00

6. DM 5,00 **7.** DM 1,00 **8.** DM 6,00 **9.** DM 1,10

B8 WIE SAGT MAN DAS?
Saying please, thank you, and you're welcome

The word **bitte** means both *please* and *you're welcome.*

Das Poster, bitte!	The poster, please.
Danke!	Thank you.
Bitte!	You're welcome.

B9 Übung • Rollenspiel *Role playing*

Lay out various school supplies (a pen, a notebook, and so on) on a table. Make a price tag for each item and turn it face down. Take turns with classmates playing salesperson and customer. Practice polite exchanges: the customer asks the price of an item, the salesperson looks it up and answers. Don't forget to say please, thank you, and you're welcome.

A: Was kostet das Poster, bitte?
B: Das Poster kostet sieben Mark.
A: Danke!
B: Bitte!

B10 Übung • Hör gut zu! 

Is the noun masculine, feminine, or neuter? Listen.

	0	1	2	3	4	5	6	7	8	9	10
masculine											
feminine	✓										
neuter											

B11 Schreibübung • Im Laden *In the store*

You want to buy a dictionary, a schoolbag, and a pocket calculator. You are asking the salesperson for prices. Write out your conversation. Be polite!

B12 WAS KOSTEN DIE SCHULSACHEN?

B13 Übung • Was kostet alles?

1. Was kosten die Kassetten?
2. Was kosten die Poster?
3. Und die Bücher?
4. Was kosten die Taschenrechner?
5. Was kosten die Bleistifte?
6. Und was kosten die Kulis?

B14 ERKLÄRUNG
Noun Plurals

1. There is no gender distinction in the plural. The definite article used with all plural nouns is **die.**

Singular	*Plural*
der Kuli	Kulis
die Kassette → **die** –	Kassetten
das Poster	Poster

2. The plural form of most German nouns is not predictable from the singular form and must be learned for each noun. The following list shows you the plural forms of the German nouns that you have learned so far. Each noun is listed with its definite article and its plural form.

Singular	*Plural*		*Singular*	*Plural*	
der Bleistift das Heft	die Bleistifte die Hefte	**-e** **-e**	das Buch das Wörterbuch	die Bücher die Wörterbücher	**¨er** **¨er**
der Stundenplan	die Stundenpläne	**¨e**	der Kuli	die Kulis	**-s**
der Junge die Kassette die Schule die Schultasche	die Jungen die Kassetten die Schulen die Schultaschen	**-n** **-n** **-n** **-n**	der Lehrer das Mädchen das Poster der Taschenrechner	die Lehrer die Mädchen die Poster die Taschenrechner	**-** **-** **-** **-**
die Zahl die Lehrerin die Verkäuferin	die Zahlen die Lehrerinnen die Verkäuferinnen	**-en** **-nen** **-nen**			

B15 Übung • Singular und Plural 

Say the article and the plural form for each of the following nouns.

A: Heft
B: das Heft, die Hefte

1. Bleistift
2. Lehrerin
3. Poster
4. Wörterbuch
5. Kuli
6. Mädchen
7. Schultasche
8. Junge
9. Buch
10. Kassette
11. Taschenrechner
12. Zahl
13. Lehrer
14. Schule
15. Verkäuferin

B 16 ERKLÄRUNG
Was kostet—was kosten

asking for one item	Was **kostet** die Kassette?	*How much is the cassette?*
asking for more than one item	Was **kosten** die Bleistifte?	*How much are the pencils?*

B 17 Übung • Jetzt bist du dran

You are in the store and are asking about prices.

das Poster Was kostet das Poster?
die Bleistifte Was kosten die Bleistifte?

1. die Schultasche
2. der Taschenrechner
3. die Kassetten
4. das Buch
5. die Bleistifte
6. das Wörterbuch
7. der Kuli
8. das Heft

B 18 Übung • Hör gut zu!

Singular or plural? Listen.

	0	1	2	3	4	5	6	7	8	9	10
singular	✓										
plural											

B 19 Schreibübung

1. Write the plural form of each of the following nouns.

der Junge die Jungen

1. das Mädchen
2. das Poster
3. das Wörterbuch
4. der Kuli
5. die Verkäuferin
6. der Bleistift
7. der Stundenplan
8. der Taschenrechner

2. Write each of the following questions in the plural.

Was kostet das Poster? Was kosten die Poster?

1. Was kostet das Heft?
2. Was kostet die Schultasche?
3. Was kostet das Buch?
4. Was kostet die Kassette?
5. Was kostet der Bleistift?
6. Was kostet der Taschenrechner?
7. Was kostet das Wörterbuch?
8. Was kostet der Stundenplan?

3. Write a dialogue that takes place in a **Schreibwarengeschäft.**

Get the salesperson's attention and ask for the prices of the following items: pens, pencils, posters, cassettes, notebooks, calculators, schoolbags, and dictionaries.

B 20 DU, WO IST DAS WÖRTERBUCH? 

Du, Jens, wo ist das Wörterbuch?

Es ist dort drüben. Schau, Kristin, dort!

Du, Kristin, der Taschenrechner ist weg.

Unsinn! Er ist da.

Jens, wo ist die Kassette?

Ist sie nicht da?—Schau mal, Kristin! Hier ist sie.

Entschuldigung, Frau Meier! Wo sind die Poster, bitte?

Ich weiss nicht. Sind sie nicht da?

Nein, sie sind weg.

Weg? Schau mal, sie sind da drüben!

B 21 Übung • Wo ist . . .?

You are looking for the following items. Ask your teacher.

SCHÜLER Wo ist die Schultasche?
LEHRER Schau, sie ist hier. *or* Sie ist da. *or* Sie ist dort drüben.

1. Wo ist das Wörterbuch?
2. Wo sind die Poster?
3. Wo ist der Kuli?
4. Wo ist die Kassette?
5. Wo ist der Jens?
6. Wo ist die Kristin?

B 22 ERKLÄRUNG
The Pronouns er, sie, es, *and* sie *(plural)*

You can refer to noun phrases such as **der Taschenrechner, die Kassette, das Wörterbuch, die Poster,** using the words **er, sie,** and **es.** These words are called pronouns. The pronoun **er** refers to a masculine noun; **sie** refers to a feminine noun or a plural noun, and **es** refers to a neuter noun. Notice that **er, sie,** and **es**—when referring to things in the singular—all mean *it.*

		Noun Phrase	*Pronoun*	
Singular	*Masculine*	Wo ist **der Taschenrechner?**	**Er** ist dort drüben.	*It is . . .*
	Feminine	Wo ist **die Kassette?**	**Sie** ist dort drüben.	
	Neuter	Wo ist **das Wörterbuch?**	**Es** ist dort drüben.	
Plural	*(no gender)*	Wo sind **die Poster?**	**Sie** sind dort drüben.	*They are . . .*

B 23 Übung • So eine Unordnung!

What a mess! You and your friend can't find anything. Help each other out.

A: Die Schultasche ist weg!
B: Unsinn! Sie ist hier!

1. Der Stundenplan ist weg!
2. Die Bleistifte sind weg!
3. Das Wörterbuch ist weg!
4. Die Kassette ist weg!
5. Die Hefte sind weg!
6. Der Kuli ist weg!
7. Das Poster ist weg!
8. Der Taschenrechner ist weg!

B 24 Übung • Die Schule beginnt. Wo ist . . .?

When you get to school, you ask a friend where the following people are.

A: Wo ist Herr Sperling?
B: Ist er nicht da?

1. Wo ist der Jens?
2. Wo sind Jens und Kristin?
3. Wo ist Frl. Seifert?
4. Wo ist der Deutschlehrer?
5. Wo ist das Mädchen[1]?
6. Wo ist der Junge?

[1]The pronoun **sie** is used to refer to **das Mädchen.**

B 25 WIE SAGT MAN DAS?
Getting someone's attention

Here are some expressions you can use to get someone's attention.

Entschuldigung!	Excuse me.
Du, Jens, . . .	Hey, Jens, . . .
Schau!	Look!
Schau, Jens!	Look, Jens!
Schau mal!	Take a look!
Schau mal, Kristin!	Take a look, Kristin!

B 26 Übung • Partnerarbeit

1.

Wörterbuch
Kassetten
Taschenrechner
Bleistifte
Kuli
Schultasche
Heft

Here is a list of school supplies that have been misplaced. A classmate is asking you about each of these items. You tell where they are, or you may say that you don't know. Vary your answers, using the words and phrases given on the right.

A: Du, Paul, wo ist das Wörterbuch?
B: Schau mal! Es ist hier.
A: Prima!

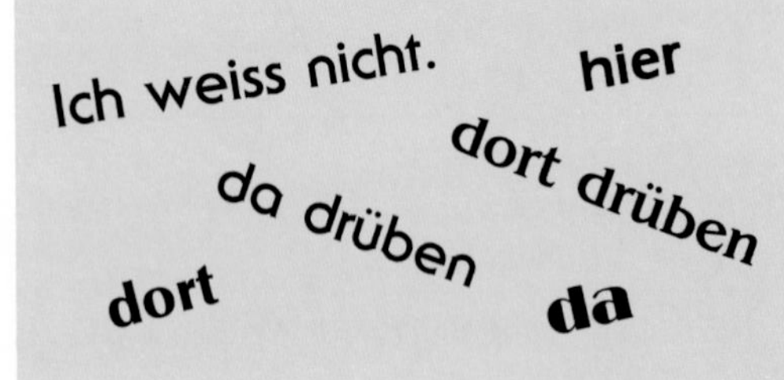

Ich weiss nicht.
hier
dort drüben
da drüben
dort
da

2. You are looking at school supplies with a friend. Practice the following dialog, substituting the words given on the right. Give a price or say you don't know.

A: Schau mal, Jens! Der Taschenrechner ist prima!
B: Du, was kostet er?
A: . . .

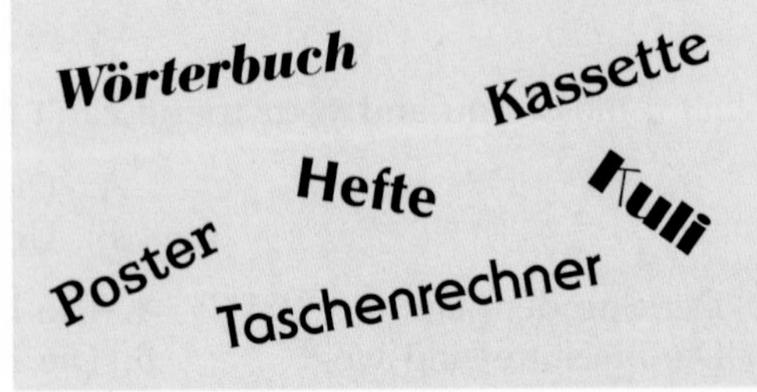

3. You are asking for someone's name. Practice the following dialog, substituting a person listed on the right. Make up a name for each person.

A: Entschuldigung! Wie heisst der Deutschlehrer?
B: Er heisst Sperling.
A: Ach ja, Sperling.

die Verkäuferin
der Junge
die Deutschlehrerin
das Mädchen
der Lehrer

B 27 Übung • Hör gut zu!

Er, sie, or **es?** Listen.

	0	1	2	3	4	5	6	7	8	9	10	11	12
er													
sie	✔												
es													

B 28 Schreibübung • Entschuldigung! Was kostet . . .?

Write a dialog that takes place in a store. The customer gets the salesperson's attention and asks about the price of various school supplies. The salesperson tells the prices, using pronouns to refer to the items. The customer thanks the salesperson and he or she responds. Practice your dialog with a classmate.

SECTION
C giving information about your class schedule

German high school students in the upper grades must take a number of core subjects, and they are limited in their choice of minor subjects. Take a look at Jens' schedule, a typical ninth grade schedule, and compare it with your own.

C1 Welche Fächer hast du heute?

FRAU KRÖGER Welche Fächer hast du heute?
JENS Ich habe Mathe, Geschichte, Moment mal! Schau, hier ist der Stundenplan. Heute ist Dienstag?
FRAU KRÖGER Ja.
JENS Ich habe um acht Uhr Deutsch, um Viertel vor neun Mathe.
Ich habe dann Englisch und Geschichte.

Wann hast du Physik?
Am Freitag.

Jens geht auf die Oberschule in Niebüll. Er hat von Montag bis Freitag Schule. Jens hat sonnabends frei. Die Schule beginnt um acht Uhr, und sie ist um ein Uhr aus.

Welche Fächer hat er? Hier ist Jens' Stundenplan.

Stundenplan für Jens Kröger 9a

Zeit	Montag	Dienstag	Mittwoch	Donnerstag	Freitag	Samstag
8.00-8.40	Deutsch	Deutsch	Mathe	—	Physik	
8.45-9.30	Deutsch	Mathe	Deutsch	Physik	Mathe	
9.30-9.45	—	—	Pause	—		frei
9.45-10.30	Religion	Englisch	Englisch	Biologie	Deutsch	
10.30-11.15	Biologie	Englisch	Latein	Englisch	Latein	
11.15-11.30	—	—	Pause	—		
11.30-12.15	Latein	Geschichte	Sport	Geschichte	Kunst	
12.15-13.00	Musik	—	Sport	Geographie		

C2 Ein wenig Landeskunde

Jens is in a high school that emphasizes science subjects: mathematics, physics, biology, and chemistry, a subject that Jens will start in the tenth grade. At the same time, Jens is required to take two foreign languages, English and Latin. As you can see, his class schedule varies from day to day, and he takes more subjects than you do. He does not have the same subject at the same time every day, nor does he always have the same subjects every day. Jens and his classmates stay together for all their classes, and for the most part, they stay in the same classroom, unless they go to the science lab, the art room, or the gym. In German schools, the teachers move from room to room. German students generally spend less time in school than American students. There are no study halls or lunch periods. After school there are few school-sponsored sports, clubs, or social activities.

C3 Übung • Stimmt oder stimmt nicht?

Check each of the following statements against Jens' class schedule. If a statement is true, say **Stimmt;** if it is not true, say **Stimmt nicht!**

1. Jens hat am Montag Latein.
2. Er hat am Dienstag Geographie.
3. Jens hat am Donnerstag Deutsch.
4. Er hat sonnabends frei.
5. Er hat am Dienstag um acht Uhr Deutsch, dann Latein und Sport.

C4 Übung • Jens' Stundenplan

1. Auf welche Schule geht Jens?
2. Wann hat Jens Schule?
3. Welche Fächer hat er am Montag?
4. Was hat er am Dienstag?
5. Welche Fächer hat er am Mittwoch?
6. Was hat er am Donnerstag?
7. Welche Fächer hat er am Freitag?
8. Was hat er sonnabends?
9. Wann beginnt die Schule?
10. Wann ist sie aus?

C5 Übung • Und du? Wie steht's mit dir?

1. Auf welche Schule gehst du?
2. Welche Fächer hast du?
3. Welche Fächer hast du am Montag?
4. Was hast du am Dienstag?
5. Wann hast du Deutsch?
6. Wann hast du frei?
7. Wann beginnt die Schule?
8. Wann ist sie aus?

C6 ZAHLEN

Let's count by fives.

5	10	15	20	25	30
fünf	zehn	fünfzehn	zwanzig	fünfundzwanzig	dreissig
35	40	45	50	55	60
fünfunddreissig	vierzig	fünfundvierzig	fünfzig	fünfundfünfzig	sechzig

C7 WANN HAT JENS MATHE? 

um ein Uhr
um eins

um zwei Uhr
um zwei

Wie spät ist es? Es ist . . .

neun Uhr

neun Uhr fünf
fünf nach neun

neun Uhr zehn
zehn nach neun

neun Uhr fünfzehn
Viertel nach neun

neun Uhr zwanzig
zwanzig nach neun

neun Uhr fünfundzwanzig
fünfundzwanzig nach neun

neun Uhr dreissig
halb zehn

neun Uhr fünf-
unddreissig

neun Uhr vierzig

neun Uhr fünfundvierzig
Viertel vor zehn

neun Uhr fünfzig
zehn vor zehn

neun Uhr fünf-
undfünfzig
fünf vor zehn

C8 Übung • Wie spät ist es? 

See if you can express the following times in two different ways.

Es ist . . . oder . . .

1. 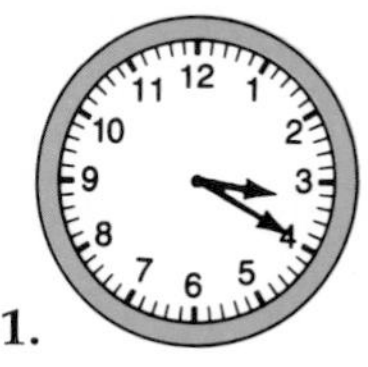
2. 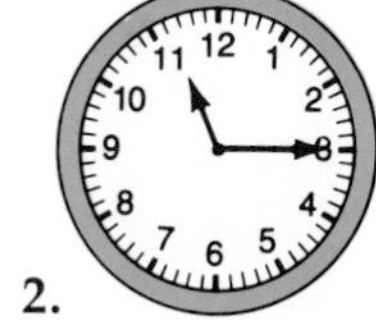
3. 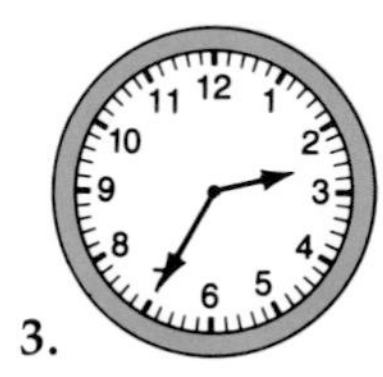
4. 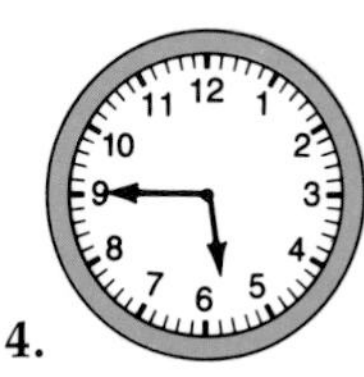
5. 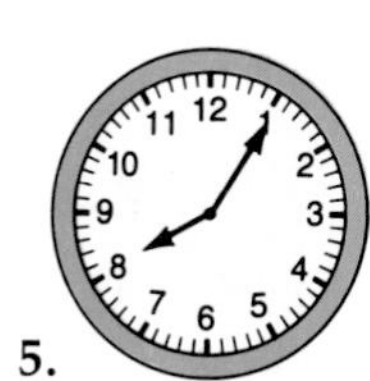
6. 

C9 Übung • Rollenspiel

Pretend you are Jens. Practice the following dialog with a classmate.

Montag um 10.30?

MITSCHÜLER Was hast du am Montag um halb elf?
JENS Um halb elf? Moment mal! —Ich habe Biologie um halb elf.

1. Dienstag um 8.45?
2. Um 11.15?
3. Mittwoch um 11.30?
4. Montag um 11.45?
5. Freitag um 9.45?
6. Montag um 8.00?

C10 WAS HABT IHR JETZT?

Was habt ihr jetzt?
Wir haben jetzt Bio. Und ihr?
Mathe. Wir haben eine Klassenarbeit.
Na, dann viel Glück!

Jörg und Kristin sind Klassenkameraden. Sie gehen in die neunte Klasse, die 9a.

Mona und Lars sind auch Klassenkameraden. Sie gehen auch in die neunte Klasse, in die Parallelklasse, die 9b.

C11 Übung • Beantworte die Fragen!

1. Wer sind Lars und Mona?
2. In welche Klasse gehen sie?
3. Welches Fach haben sie jetzt?
4. Und Jörg und Kristin? Was haben sie jetzt?

C12 ERKLÄRUNG
The Verb haben

The verb **haben,** *to have,* has the following forms.

Ich	**habe**	Deutsch.	Wir	**haben**	Deutsch.
Du	**hast**		Ihr	**habt**	
Jens (er)	**hat**		Jens und Kristin (sie)	**haben**	
Kristin (sie)	**hat**				

C13 Übung • Wer hat heute Deutsch?

Do all these students have German today? They do!

Jens? Ja, er hat heute Deutsch.

1. Kristin?
2. Jörg und Kristin?
3. Du?
4. Der Junge?
5. Ihr?
6. Ich?
7. Das Mädchen?
8. Wir?

C14 Übung • Was haben die Schüler heute? 

What courses do the students have? Use a different course in each answer.

Jörg? Er hat Geschichte.

1. Ich?
2. Das Mädchen?
3. Der Junge?
4. Wir?
5. Lars und Mona?
6. Kristin?

C15 Übung • Hör gut zu! 

What time is it?

							1		
6.50	12.30	9.35	1.10	10.40	11.45	4.15	7.20	2.25	8.45

C16 Übung • Partnerarbeit

Practice the following activities with a classmate.

1. Ask what time it is, and after he or she responds, say thank you. Begin by saying:
   Wie spät ist es?
2. Tell what subjects you have and when you have them. Here are some additional subjects that you might have. Not all of them are taught in German high schools: Chemie, Sozialkunde *(social studies)*, Naturwissenschaft *(science)*, Algebra, Geometrie, Französisch, Spanisch, Zeichnen *(drawing)*, Hauswirtschaftskunde *(home economics)*, Werken *(industrial arts)*, Musik, Schulorchester, Schulkapelle *(band)*, Schulchor, Fahrunterricht *(driver's education)*, Schreibmaschineschreiben *(typing)*.

C17 Schreibübung

1. Rewrite each sentence, filling in the correct form of **haben.**
   1. Ich ____ heute Deutsch.
   2. Was ____ du heute?
   3. Der Jens ____ jetzt Mathe.
   4. Wir ____ jetzt auch Mathe.
   5. Was ____ ihr dann?
   6. Jens und Kristin ____ Biologie.
2. Write out what time it is.

   5.10 Es ist fünf Uhr zehn (zehn nach fünf).

   1. 2.30 2. 3.45 3. 7.10 4. 6.15 5. 9.30 6. 8.50
3. Write out your own class schedule, using German words for your subjects. How well do you know your schedule? Exchange schedules with a classmate and ask each other questions.
   Wann hast du Geschichte? Was hast du am Dienstag um . . .?

talking about homework and grades

Homework takes up a large part of a student's afternoon. There is homework in many subjects, and students have to work hard to get good grades to stay in school.

D1 Hausaufgaben und Noten

Jens macht Hausaufgaben. Er macht Mathe. In Mathe ist Jens nicht so gut. Welche Noten hat er in Mathe? Eine Vier, eine Drei, eine Vier.

Zensuren-spiegel

Fächer	Noten	Halbj.-zeugn.	Noten	Jahres-zeugn.
Deutsch	2 2 1 2			
Englisch	1 1 2 1 1			
Mathematik	4 3 4			
~~Franz.~~ Latein	3 1 2 2			
Physik	3 2 2 1			
Chemie				
Biologie	1 2 2			
Erdkunde	3 3			
Geschichte	4 1 2			
Musik	1 1			
Kunst	2 1			
Religion	1 2			

Hier sind Jens' Noten.

Was hast du?
Eine Eins!
Toll!
Prima!
Schade!
Blöd!

KRISTIN Du, Jens, was hast du in Deutsch?
JENS Eine Zwei.
KRISTIN Das ist prima! Eine Zwei in Deutsch. Phantastisch!
JENS Ja, das ist gut. Aber ich habe nur eine Vier in Mathe. Blöd!
KRISTIN Ja, das ist schlecht. Schade!

D2 Ein wenig Landeskunde

In German schools, grades range from 1 to 6: 1 (sehr gut, *excellent*), 2 (gut, *good*), 3 (befriedigend, *satisfactory*), 4 (ausreichend, *just passing*), 5 (mangelhaft, *almost failing*), and 6 (ungenügend, *failing*)—corresponding to A, B, C, D, and F in American schools. On report cards, German students also receive grades in Betragen, *conduct*, Fleiss, *diligence*, Aufmerksamkeit, *attentiveness*, and Ordnung, *neatness*.

D3 Übung • Beantworte die Fragen!

1. Was macht Jens?
2. Ist er gut in Mathe?
3. Welche Noten hat er in Mathe?
4. Welche Noten hat er in Latein?

D4 Übung • Und du? Wie steht's mit dir?

1. Bist du gut in Mathe?
2. Was hast du in Mathe?
3. Welche Noten hast du in Deutsch?
4. Was hast du in Englisch?

D5 WIE SAGT MAN DAS?

Some ways of responding to good news and to bad news

good news	Gut! Prima! Phantastisch! Toll!	Good! Terrific! Fantastic! Great!
bad news	Blöd! Das ist nicht so gut. Das ist schlecht. Schade!	Too dumb! That's not so good. That's bad! Too bad!

D6 Übung • Jetzt bist du dran

Now ask your classmates what their grades are in different subjects and react to the good news or bad news. Then have a classmate ask you the same questions.

A: Was hast du in Biologie?
B: Ich habe eine. . .
A: . . . *or* . . .

D7 IST BIO SCHWER?

D8 Übung • Jetzt bist du dran

A: Wie ist Bio? Schwer? Leicht?

Geschichte
Bio
Physik
Deutsch
Latein
Geografie
Englisch
Mathe
Musik

B: Bio ist nicht schwer. Bio ist . . .

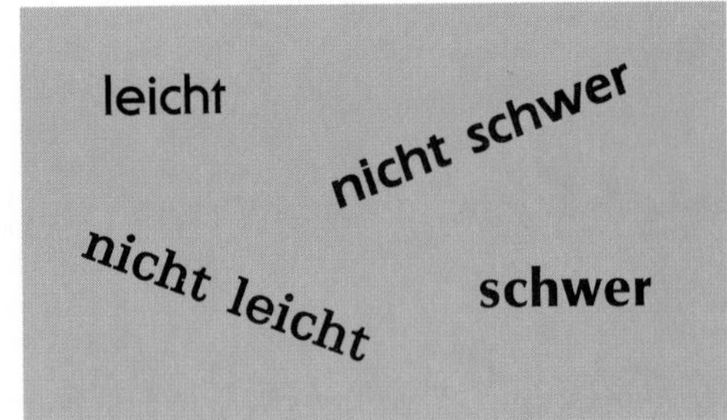

D9 Übung • Gut oder schlecht? 

Choose a partner. React to each of the following statements made by your partner. Use different expressions as you respond to good news or bad news.

A: Ich habe eine Zwei in Deutsch.
B: Das ist prima!

1. Ich habe eine Fünf in Physik.
2. Ich habe eine Drei in Mathe.
3. Ich habe eine Eins in Biologie.
4. Ich habe eine Vier in Geschichte.
5. Ich habe eine Sechs in Algebra.
6. Ich habe eine Zwei in Erdkunde.

D 10 Übung • Hör gut zu!

Is it good news or bad news? Listen.

	0	1	2	3	4	5	6	7	8	9	10
good news											
bad news	✓										

D 11 Schreibübung • Was meinst du? *What do you think?*

1. Write four short dialogs, asking friends about their grades and reacting to the good or bad news.

Peter, Geschichte, Vier

A: Was hat Peter in Geschichte?
B: Er hat eine Vier.
A: Das ist schade!

1. du, Deutsch, Eins
2. Barbara, Englisch, Fünf
3. Peter, Erdkunde, Sechs
4. Jens und Kristin, Latein, Zwei

2. Write sentences agreeing or disagreeing with each of the following statements.

A: Algebra ist schwer.
B: Ja, Algebra ist schwer. *or* Nein, Algebra ist nicht schwer.
or Nein, Algebra ist leicht.

1. Biologie ist leicht.
2. Kunst ist nicht leicht.
3. Deutsch ist toll.
4. Englisch ist schwer.
5. Geschichte ist nicht schwer.
6. Die Hausaufgaben sind schwer.

D 12 Übung • Wer hat gute Augen? *Who has good eyes?*

Was ist alles auf diesem Bild?

Und was fehlt hier?

TRY YOUR SKILLS

using what you've learned

1 Gerd Ecker in den USA

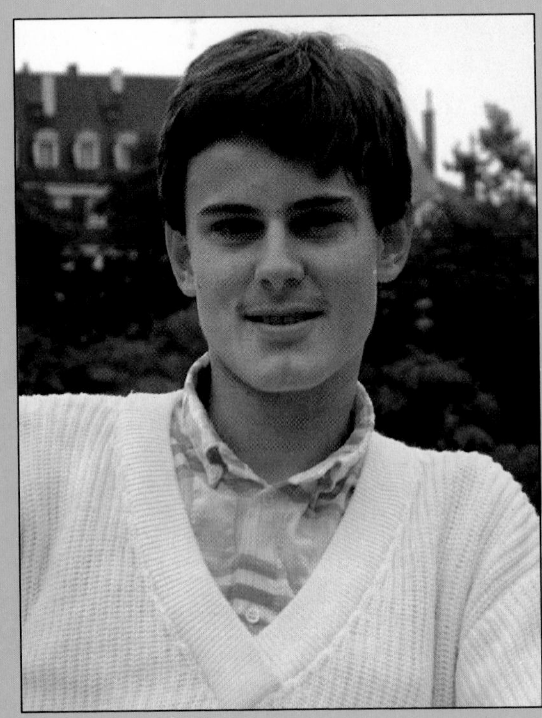

Gerd Ecker, a student from Germany, introduces himself to your class.

Guten Tag! Ich heisse Gerd Ecker. Ich bin 16 Jahre alt. Ich bin aus Paderborn. Paderborn ist in der Bundesrepublik Deutschland. Ich gehe aufs Goerdeler Gymnasium. Ich komme mit dem Rad in die Schule, und die Klassenkameraden—ja, sie kommem mit dem Bus, mit dem Moped, mit dem Auto und auch zu Fuss.

Wir haben von Montag bis Freitag Schule. Wir haben Sonnabend frei. Die Schule beginnt um Viertel vor acht, und sie ist um ein Uhr aus.

Welche Fächer ich habe? Nun, ich habe Deutsch, Mathe, Englisch, Geschichte, Geographie, Sport und Kunst. Ich bin gut in Englisch und in Deutsch. Ich habe eine Eins in Englisch und eine Zwei in Deutsch. Englisch und Deutsch sind leicht. Ich bin nicht so gut in Mathe. Mathe ist schwer. Ich habe nur eine Vier.

2 Übung • Rollenspiel

A classmate plays the role of Gerd. You missed some of his presentation, so you ask him questions about himself. Then you take the role of Gerd, and your classmate asks you.

A: Wie heisst du?
B: Ich heisse. . .

3 Übung • Erzähl mal, was Gerd gesagt hat!

A friend of yours missed Gerd's presentation. You tell him or her what Gerd said.

Der Schüler aus Deutschland heisst. . .

4 Übung • Vortrag *Presentation*

You are visiting a class in Germany. Tell the class something about yourself and your school day.

5 Schreibübung • Ein Artikel für die Schülerzeitung

The school newspaper in the German school you are visiting would like to write an article about you. Write up the presentation you gave to the class for the school newspaper. Include a picture of yourself.

6 Übung • Immer diese Schule! *School, school, school!*

Practice the following dialogs with a classmate. Try to come up with as many variations as possible and see how long you can keep each conversation going.

1. You talk about how to get to school.
A: Wie kommst du in die Schule?
B: Ich komme mit. . .

2. You are in a store and want to know what different school items cost.
A: Entschuldigung! Was kostet der Kuli?
B: Er kostet vier Mark.
A: Danke!
B: Bitte!

3. You ask your classmate what subjects he or she has on certain days.
A: Was hast du am Montag?
B: Ich habe. . .

4. You ask your classmate when he or she has certain subjects.
A: Wann hast du Deutsch?
B: Um Viertel vor zehn.

5. You ask your classmates what their grades are in different subjects.
A: Du, was hast du in Bio?
B: Ich habe eine Zwei.
A: Das ist prima!

6. You talk about how easy or difficult certain subjects are.
A: Mathe ist schwer.
B: Nein. Mathe ist leicht.

7 Schreibübung • Was passt zusammen? *What goes together?*

Write the pairs.

1. Auf welche Schule gehst du?
2. Wo ist sie?
3. Wie kommst du in die Schule?
4. Was kostet das Wörterbuch?
5. Wie spät ist es?
6. Ich habe um neun Uhr Deutsch.
7. Wann hast du Mathe?
8. Ich habe eine Zwei in Mathe.
9. Du hast eine Eins in Geschichte?
10. Entschuldigung, ist das Herr Meier?

a. Und wann hast du Englisch?
b. Ich habe nur eine Drei.
c. Ja, was hast du?
d. Mit dem Rad.
e. Ja, das ist er.
f. Zwölf Mark sechzig.
g. Um zehn Uhr zwanzig.
h. Es ist acht Uhr.
i. In Westbury.
j. Ich gehe auf die Kennedy Schule.

8 Übung • Was sagen sie?

9 Übung • Reklame in der Zeitung *Ads in the paper*

Look at the following ad and write out what each of the items costs.

Die Bleistifte kosten. . .

10 Aussprache-, Lese- und Schreibübungen

1. Listen carefully and repeat what you hear.

2. Listen, then read aloud.

1. da, sag, Rad, Tag, schade, Zahl; dem, zehn; wir, prima, sie, wie, vier, sieben, hier, Wien; wo, Montag, Moped; du, Schule, Kuli, Fuss, gut, nur, Uhr
2. für, grüss, drüben; fünf, München, Niebüll, Glück, Tschüs; blöd, Kröger, Österreich, Wörterbuch
3. und, sind, Rad, blöd, Deutschland, Sonnabend, Klassenkamerad
4. sag, Tag, Montag, Dienstag, Donnerstag, Freitag, Samstag, Sonntag, weg
5. zwanzig, dreissig, vierzig, fünfzig, sechzig

3. Copy the following sentences to prepare yourself to write them from dictation.

1. Die Zahl sieben.
2. Um vier Uhr.
3. Sie sind in Wien.
4. Mit dem Rad.

WAS KANNST DU SCHON?

Let's review some important points that you have learned in this unit.

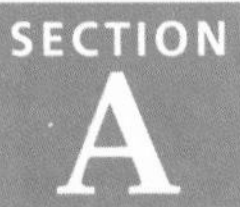

Can you say how to get to school?
Using the verb **kommen,** make complete sentences saying how each person comes to school. Vary the means of transportation.

1. Kristin 2. er 3. du 4. Peter und Barbara 5. ich

Can you name some school supplies?
Say the definite article and the plural form of:

Heft, Wörterbuch, Kuli, Bleistift, Schultasche, Taschenrechner, Kassette, Stundenplan

Can you buy things in a store, asking for prices and saying thank you and you're welcome?
Ask how much these items cost and give an answer. Say thank you and you're welcome.

Kuli, Heft, Schultasche, Kassetten

Can you use the right pronoun for people and things?
For each of these nouns, use the pronoun that correctly refers to it:

Schultasche, Lehrer, Mädchen, Taschenrechner, Karin, Bleistifte, Frl. Seifert, Jens, Wörterbuch, Heft

Can you talk about your class schedule?
Say what subjects you have on each day of the week.

Say the names of the days of the week.

Do you know the forms of the verb *haben?*
Write the forms of **haben** that go with these subjects:

1. ich 2. er 3. Sabine und Peter 4. Sabine 5. du
6. Peter 7. sie 8. wir 9. ihr

Can you tell time?
Say what time it is: 7.30; 9.45; 12.50; 1.30; 5.20; 8.15

Can you talk about grades?
What would you say if you got an A? an F?

Can you say whether or not a subject is easy or difficult?
Respond to the following questions:

Du hast eine Eins in Bio? Eine Fünf in Mathe?

WORTSCHATZ

SECTION A

da *there; here*
kommen *to come*
mit dem Auto *by car*
mit dem Bus *by bus*
mit dem Moped *by moped*
mit dem Rad *by bicycle*
mit der Strassenbahn *by streetcar*
schau! *look!*
die **Schule, -n** *school*
toll! *great!*
wie kommst du in die Schule? *how do you get to school?*
zu Fuss *on foot*

SECTION B

bitte *please; you're welcome*
der **Bleistift, -e** *pencil*
da drüben *over there*
danke *thank you, thanks*
DM = Deutsche Mark *German mark*
dort *there*
dort drüben *over there*
du, . . . *hey, . . .*
Entschuldigung! *excuse me!*
er *he; it*
es *it; she*
das **Heft, -e** *notebook*
hier *here*
die **Kassette, -n** *cassette*
der **Kuli, -s** *ballpoint pen*
die **Mark, -** *mark* (German monetary unit); eine Mark *one mark*
nicht *not*
nur *only*
das **Poster, -** *poster*
prima! *great!*
schau mal! *look!*
die **Schulsachen** (pl) *school supplies*
die **Schultasche, -n** *schoolbag*
sie *she; it; they*
der **Stundenplan, ¨-e** *class schedule*
der **Taschenrechner, -** *pocket calculator*
Unsinn! *nonsense!*
die **Verkäuferin** *salesperson*
was? *what?*
was kosten? *how much are?*
was kostet? *how much is?*
weg *gone*
weiss: ich weiss nicht *I don't know*
wo? *where?*
das **Wörterbuch, ¨-er** *dictionary*

SECTION C

am Freitag *on Friday*
aus *out, over*
beginnt *begins*
Bio *short for* Biologie
Biologie *biology*
dann *then*
Deutsch *German*
der **Dienstag** *Tuesday*
der **Donnerstag** *Thursday*
ein, eine *a, an*
Englisch *English*
das **Fach, ¨-er** *subject*
frei *off;* er hat frei *he has off, he has no school*
der **Freitag** *Friday*
gehen: sie gehen in die neunte Klasse *they're in the ninth grade*
Geographie *geography*
Geschichte *history*
haben *to have*
halb: halb zehn *nine thirty*
heute *today*
ihr *you* (pl)
in *in*
jetzt *now*
die **Klasse, -n** *class; grade*
die **Klassenarbeit, -en** *test*
der **Klassenkamerad, -en** *classmate*
Kunst *art*
Latein *Latin*
Mathe *math*
der **Mittwoch** *Wednesday*
Moment mal! *wait a minute!*
der **Montag** *Monday*
Musik *music*
na *well*
nach *after, past*
der **Name, -n** *name*
die **Oberschule, -n** *high school;* er geht auf die Oberschule *he goes to high school*
die **Parallelklasse, -n** *class of the same grade*
die **Pause, -n** *break, recess*
Physik *physics*
Religion *religion*
der **Sonnabend** *Saturday*
sonnabends *(on) Saturdays*
spät: wie spät ist es? *what time is it?* (see page 75)
um *at;* um acht Uhr *at eight o'clock;* um eins *at one*
viel Glück! *good luck!*
Viertel nach neun *a quarter after nine*
vor *before, of*
wann? *when?*
welche? *which, what?*
wir *we*
die **Zahlen von 5 bis 60** *the numbers from 5 to 60* (p. 74)
die **Zeit** *time*

SECTION D

aber *but*
Algebra *algebra*
blöd *stupid, dumb*
eine **Eins** *a one* (see page 79)
gut *good*
die **Hausaufgaben** (pl) *homework*
leicht *easy*
macht: er macht Mathe *he's doing math*
die **Note, -n** *grade, mark*
phantastisch *fantastic, great*
schade! *too bad!*
schlecht *bad*
schwer *difficult*
so *so*

WORTSCHATZÜBUNGEN

1. Look at the nouns in the **Wortschatz** above and note how the plural forms are indicated. Then write out each noun in the plural.
2. Make a list of all the words that are similar to English, writing both the German and the English. Compare the spelling and meaning of the words in each pair.

ZUM LESEN

Hausaufgabenlied

Endlich° ist die Schule aus,
und ich gehe jetzt nach Haus',
pack' alles aus der Tasche aus.

Bleistift, Kuli und Papier,
Hefte, Bücher—zwei, drei, vier.
Taschenrechner? Ja, alles hier.

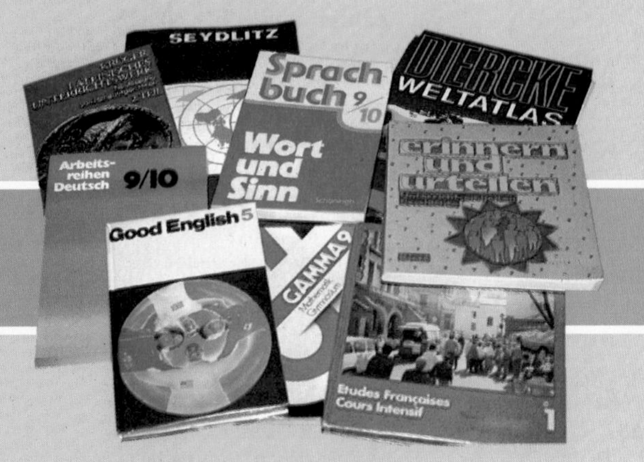

Mathe, Deutsch, Biologie,
Englisch, Kunst, Geographie,
Latein, Geschichte und Chemie.

Hausaufgaben muss ich machen°,
Hausaufgaben, nichts zu lachen°!
Hausaufgaben—viel° zu schwer!
Hausaufgaben—danke sehr°!

Übung • Beantworte die Fragen!

1. Was ist aus?
2. Wohin geht der Schüler?
3. Was macht er?
4. Was packt er aus der Tasche?
5. Welche Fächer hat er?
6. Was macht er jetzt?
7. Sind die Hausaufgaben leicht?

Hausaufgabenlied *homework song* **endlich** *finally* **muss ich machen** *I have to do* **nichts zu lachen** *no laughing matter* **viel** *much* **danke sehr** *thank you very much—you can have them*

Der Traum

Übung • Stimmt oder stimmt nicht?

According to Paul's dream, are these statements true or not true?

1. Es ist Montag.
2. Paul kommt zu spät in die Schule.
3. Paul kommt mit dem Bus in die Schule.
4. Pauls Freunde kommen auch zu spät.
5. Paul hat die Hausaufgaben.
6. Was?! Es ist Sonnabend.

---

der Traum *dream* **schnell!** *hurry up!* **ich komme zu spät** *I'll be late* **warten!** *wait!* **endlich** *finally* **zu Hause** *at home* **Gott sei Dank!** *Thank heavens!* **Sonntag** *Sunday*

KAPITEL 3

Freizeit

Young people in German-speaking countries like to do many of the same things you do in your free time. Their free time, however, is often limited. Many teenagers are in apprenticeship programs. They work full-time most of the week and attend trade school one or two days. Young people who attend high school are required to put a great deal of time into their studies.

In this unit you will:

SECTION A	talk about your favorite sports and activities
SECTION B	say when and how often you do these activities
SECTION C	express an opinion, agree or disagree, and say what you like, dislike, or prefer
TRY YOUR SKILLS	use what you've learned
ZUM LESEN	read for practice and pleasure

SECTION A

asking someone about his or her interests

What do young Germans do in their free time? They participate in sports, play games, and have hobbies. They enjoy music and like to get together with their friends. How do you spend your free time?

A1 Freizeit: Sport und Hobbys

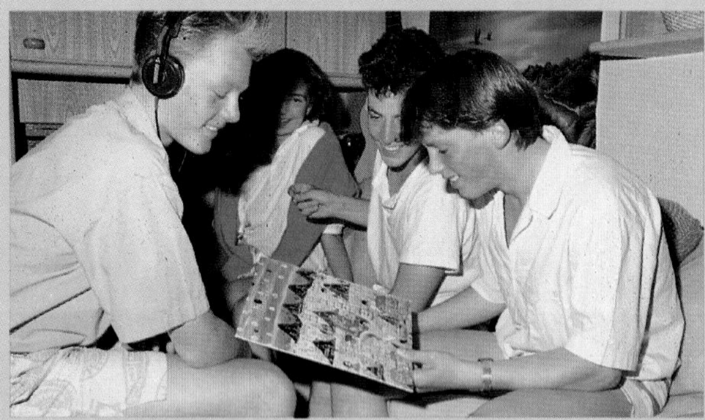

Jens besucht Freunde. Sie hören Musikkassetten.

INTERVIEWER Wie heisst du?
JENS Ich heisse Jens.
INTERVIEWER Wie alt bist du?
JENS Sechzehn.
INTERVIEWER Was machst du in deiner Freizeit?
JENS Tja, ich besuche Freunde, ich höre Musikkassetten, ich. . .

Jens schwimmt, und er spielt Tennis.

INTERVIEWER Machst du Sport?
JENS Ja. Ich schwimme, und ich spiele Tennis.

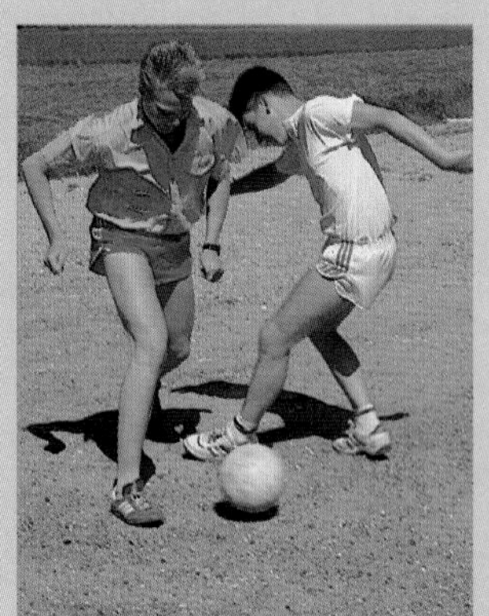

Jens spielt auch Fussball.

INTERVIEWER Spielst du auch Fussball?
JENS Na klar!

INTERVIEWER Spielst du ein Instrument?
JENS Ja, ich spiele Gitarre.

Er spielt Gitarre.

Jens sammelt Briefmarken.

INTERVIEWER Hast du auch Hobbys?
JENS Ich sammle Briefmarken, und ich spiele Schach.

A2 Übung • Mix-Match: Was macht Jens?

1. Jens besucht . . .	Briefmarken.
2. Er hört . . .	Freunde.
3. Jens spielt auch . . .	Musikkassetten.
4. Und er . . .	schwimmt.
5. Er sammelt . . .	Tennis.

A3 Übung • Bilder-Quiz: Was macht Jens? Er . . .

1. 
2. 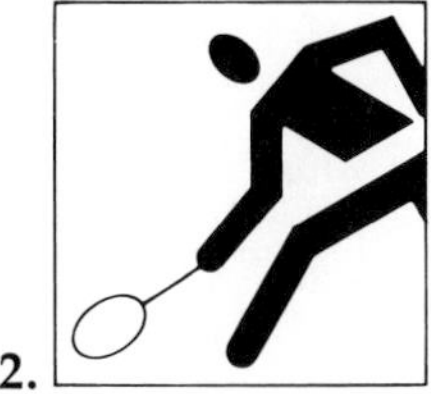
3. 
4. 
5. 

A4 ERKLÄRUNG
Addressing Someone Using the du-*form*

When you talk to a friend in German, use **du** with the verb form ending in **-st: du bist, du hast, du spielst.** When someone addresses you, respond using **ich** with the verb form ending in **-e: ich habe, ich spiele.** The form **ich bin** is an exception.

du-*form*	ich-*form*
Wie **heisst du?**	**Ich heisse** Jens.
Wie alt **bist du?**	**Ich bin** fünfzehn.
Hast du Hobbys?	Ja, **ich habe** auch Hobbys.
Spielst du Tennis?	Nein, **ich spiele** Fussball.
Sammelst du Briefmarken?	Ja, **ich sammle** Briefmarken.

A5 Übung • Jetzt bist du dran 

The interviewer asks and you answer yes to all the questions.

A: Machst du Sport?
B: Ja, ich mache Sport.

1. Spielst du Gitarre?
2. Hast du Hobbys?
3. Sammelst du Briefmarken?
4. Besuchst du Freunde?
5. Hörst du Musikkassetten?
6. Schwimmst du auch?

A6 Übung • Frag deinen Mitschüler! 

Ask your classmate if he or she has the same interests as Jens does.

A: Jens spielt Schach.
B: Spielst du auch Schach?

1. Jens besucht Freunde.
2. Jens hat Musikkassetten.
3. Jens sammelt Briefmarken.
4. Jens spielt Fussball.
5. Jens schwimmt.
6. Jens spielt Gitarre.

A7 WIE SAGT MAN DAS?
Asking about someone's interests

Here are some phrases that you can use to ask a friend about his or her interests.

Was machst du?	What are you doing?
Was machst du in deiner Freizeit?	What do you do in your spare time?
Machst du Sport?	Do you participate in sports?
Spielst du Fussball?	Do you play soccer?
Hast du Hobbys?	Do you have hobbies?

A8 Übung • Partnerarbeit 

Now ask your classmates what they do in their spare time.
Then have a classmate ask you.

A: Was machst du in deiner Freizeit?
B: Ich . . .

1.  2.  3.  4.

5.  6.  7.  8.

A 9 Neu im Sport

Drachenfliegen, Eistanzen, Gymnastik, Aerobics und Windsurfen sind heute sehr populär.

A 10 Übung • Und du? Wie steht's mit dir?

1. Was machst du in deiner Freizeit?
2. Machst du Sport?
3. Spielst du auch Tennis?
4. Hast du Hobbys?

A 11 UND WAS MACHT IHR?

INTERVIEWER Und was macht ihr? Macht ihr auch Sport?
GÜNTER Wir spielen Basketball.

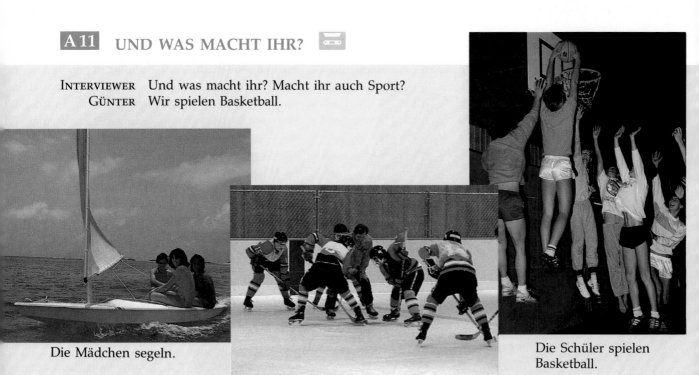

Die Mädchen segeln.

Die Jungen spielen Hockey.

Die Schüler spielen Basketball.

INTERVIEWER Habt ihr Hobbys?
GÜNTER Ja, ich sammle Münzen.
INTERVIEWER Und du, Kurt?
KURT Ich auch.

Günter und Kurt sammeln Münzen.

Die vier Klassenkameraden spielen Karten. Das Spiel heisst Mau-Mau.

INTERVIEWER Was spielt ihr?
KRISTIN Mau-Mau[1].
INTERVIEWER Wirklich? Wer gewinnt?
KRISTIN Der Jens und der Jörg.
JENS Wie immer.
KRISTIN Aber ihr mogelt. Wie immer.
JENS Was?! Wir mogeln nicht. Ihr verliert, und ihr seid sauer. Haha!

[1]**Mau-Mau** is a card game similar to crazy eights.

A12 Übung • Mix-Match: Was machen die Jungen und Mädchen?

1. Günter und Kurt . . .
2. Sie sammeln auch . . .
3. Die Mädchen . . .
4. Die Jungen . . .
5. Die vier Klassenkameraden . . .
6. Das Spiel heisst . . .
7. Wer gewinnt . . .
8. Jens und Jörg . . .
9. Mogeln . . .
10. Nein, sie mogeln . . .

das Spiel?
die Jungen?
gewinnen.
Mau-Mau.
Münzen.
nicht.
segeln.
spielen Basketball.
spielen Hockey.
spielen Karten.

A13 Übung • Bilder-Quiz: Was machen die Jungen und Mädchen?

Sie segeln. Sie . . .

1. 2. 3. 4.

5. 6. 7. 8.

A14 Übung • Der Sport- und Hobbymuffel!

This boy doesn't do anything! When you ask him if he does the activities pictured in A13, he always answers no!

Segelst du? Nein, ich segle nicht.
Spielst du . . .?

A 15 ERKLÄRUNG
Addressing People Using the ihr-*form*

When you talk to two friends in German, use **ihr** with the verb form ending in **-t: ihr macht, ihr spielt, ihr habt.** When you answer for yourself and somebody else, use **wir** and the verb form ending in **-en** or only in **-n.** The forms **ihr seid** and **wir sind** are exceptions.

ihr-*form*	wir-*form*
Was **macht ihr?**	**Wir machen** Sport.
Habt ihr Hobbys?	Ja, **wir haben** Hobbys.
Spielt ihr Tennis?	**Wir spielen** Fussball.
Segelt ihr?	Ja, **wir segeln.**
Seid ihr sauer?	Ja, **wir sind** sauer.

A 16 Übung • Interview

The interviewer is asking you and your friends what you do. You speak for everyone and answer yes.

A: Macht ihr Sport?
B: Ja, wir machen Sport.

1. Spielt ihr Basketball?
2. Segelt ihr?
3. Sammelt ihr Münzen?
4. Spielt ihr Schach?
5. Verliert ihr?
6. Seid ihr sauer?

A 17 Übung • Was macht ihr?

The interviewer is surprised at your answers. What does he say?

A: Wir spielen Karten.
B: Wirklich? Ihr spielt Karten?

1. Wir spielen Basketball.
2. Wir spielen Gitarre.
3. Wir sammeln Münzen.
4. Wir spielen Mau-Mau.
5. Wir gewinnen.
6. Wir sind sauer.

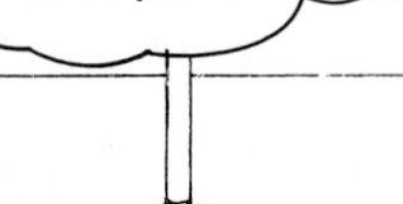

A 18 Übung • Lücken-Dialog

Practice the following dialog with a classmate, supplying the missing words.

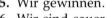

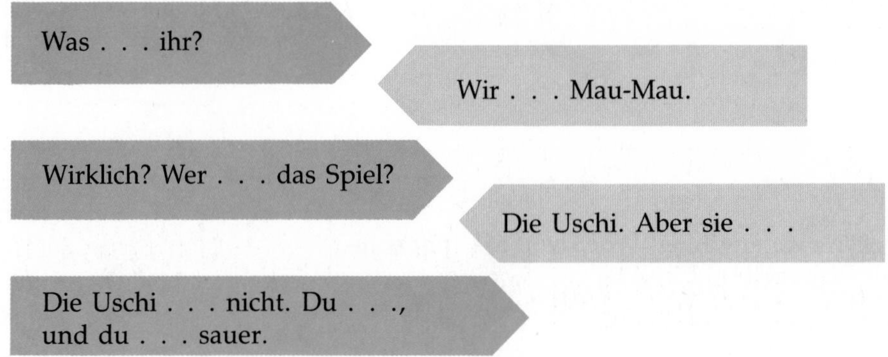

Was . . . ihr?
Wir . . . Mau-Mau.
Wirklich? Wer . . . das Spiel?
Die Uschi. Aber sie . . .
Die Uschi . . . nicht. Du . . .,
und du . . . sauer.

A 19 ERKLÄRUNG
The Present Tense

1. The statements and questions that you have been practicing all refer to present time. Therefore, the verbs in these statements and questions are in the present tense.

   Was **machst** du? Ich **spiele** Tennis.

2. Present tense verb forms have endings. The ending you use depends upon the noun **(Jens, Ursel, Jens und Ursel)** or the pronoun **(ich, du, er, sie, es, wir, ihr, sie)** used with the verb.

3. The following chart summarizes the different verb forms, using **spielen** as a model.

Singular			*Plural*		
Ich	spiel**e**	Tennis.	Wir	spiel**en**	Tennis.
Du	spiel**st**		Ihr	spiel**t**	
Jens (er)	spiel**t**		Jens und Ursel (sie)	spiel**en**	
Ursel (sie)	spiel**t**				

4. When speaking to adults such as your teacher, salespeople, or any adults who are not family members or relatives, you must use the formal form of address: **Sie. Sie** is used with the verb form ending in **-en,** the same verb form used with **wir** and **sie** (plural).

   Wie **heissen Sie?** Was **machen Sie?**
   Woher **sind Sie,** Herr Huber? **Spielen Sie** Tennis?

5. All verbs have a base form, the form appearing in your wordlist **(Wortschatz)** or in a dictionary. This form is called the infinitive. The infinitive of most German verbs has the ending **-en,** as in **spielen,** *to play.* Some verbs end in **-n,** such as **segeln,** *to sail,* **mogeln,** *to cheat,* **sammeln,** *to collect.* The **ich**-form of these verbs is: **ich segle, ich mogle, ich sammle.**

A 20 Übung • Bilder-Quiz: Was machen die Schüler? 

Say what everyone does, using the words and pictures as cues.

Wir . . .

Jens . . .

Ihr . . .

Ich . . .

Die Mädchen . . .

Du . . .

Die Jungen . . .

Wir . . .

Er . . .

Du . . .?

A 21 Übung • Frag mal deinen Lehrer!

Now ask your teacher about his or her sports and hobbies. Use the following questions and the pictures in A20 as a guide.

1. Was . . . Sie? **2.** Spiel- . . .?

A 22 Übung • Versteckte Sätze *Hidden sentences*

Look for sentences. How many can you make?

Ich spiele Karten.

ich	**besuchen**	**das Spiel**
du	**hört**	**Freunde**
Jens	**ist**	**immer**
wir	**mogelt**	**Karten**
ihr	**sammelst**	**Münzen**
die Jungen	**spiele**	**Musik**
Ursel	**verlieren**	**sauer**

A 23 Übung • Hör gut zu!

Are you talking to one friend, several friends, or an adult? Listen.

	0	1	2	3	4	5	6	7	8	9	10
addressing one student											
addressing several students	✓										
addressing an adult											

A 24 Schreibübung

1. Rewrite the following questions and statements, supplying the appropriate verb endings.

1. Was mach__ du? Ich spiel__ Karten.
2. Was mach__ Jens? Er spiel__ Tennis.
3. Die Jungen spiel__ Mau-Mau. Mogel__ der Jens?
4. Mach__ ihr Sport? Ja, wir schwimm__.
5. Spiel__ Sie Schach, Herr Huber?

2. You have met two young people and would like to know more about them. What questions would you ask? Think of at least eight questions and write them down. Remember to use the **ihr**-form.

SECTION **B**

talking about when and how often you do your various sports and activities

Young people pursue sports and activities after school and on the weekend. They take tennis and music lessons, they belong to sports and computer clubs. When do you have your activities? Do you take any lessons? Do you belong to a club?

B1

Wann machst du Sport?

Was macht ihr im Sommer? Im Herbst? Im Winter? Im Frühjahr?

Ursel
Im Sommer spiele ich Tennis, und ich schwimme.

Peter
Im Herbst spiele ich Fussball.

Hans
Im Winter spiele ich Eishockey, und ich laufe Schi.

Karin
Im Frühjahr spiele ich Basketball.

Jörg, was machst du am Wochenende?

Am Wochenende spiele ich Fussball.

JULI 7 SONNTAG	JULI 13 SONNAB./SAMST.	JULI 14 SONNTAG
am Sonntag	am Wochenende	

B2 Übung • Und du? Wie steht's mit dir?

1. Was machst du im Sommer?
   Ich . . .
2. Was machst du im Winter?
   Ich . . .
3. Was machst du im Frühjahr?
   Ich . . .
4. Was machst du im Herbst?
   Ich . . .

B3 WIE OFT MACHT IHR SPORT?

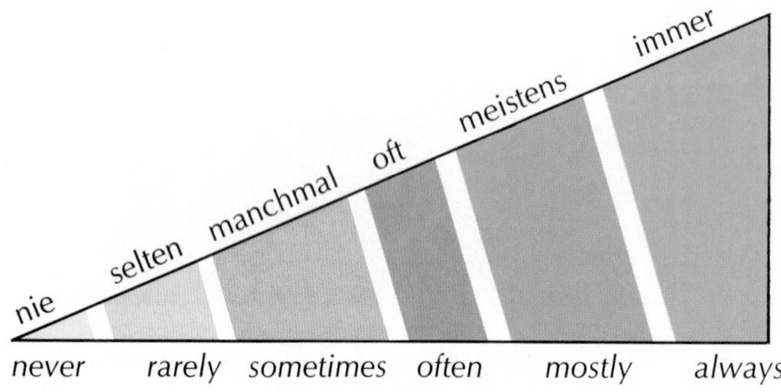

x	einmal	am Tag
xx	zweimal	in der Woche
xxx	dreimal	im Monat
xxxx	viermal	im Jahr (im Sommer)

PETRA:
„Ich spiele selten Tennis. Ja, manchmal im Sommer. Im Winter spiele ich oft Basketball."

MICHAEL:
„Ich mache Sport viermal in der Woche. Einmal, meistens am Mittwoch, spiele ich Tennis. Am Wochenende spiele ich Fussball, und ich schwimme zweimal in der Woche."

B4 Übung • Was sagt Michael? Was sagt Petra? Erzähl mal! 

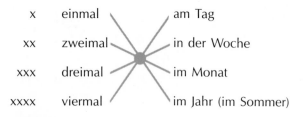

Report what these students just told you about how often they have their activities.

1. Michael sagt, er macht . . .
2. Petra sagt, sie spielt . . .

B5 Ein wenig Landeskunde

How much free time do young Germans actually have? Many teenagers are learning a trade and are required to be at work all day. They may have one day a week of classes at a **Berufsschule,** *vocational school.* Their free time is limited to evenings and weekends.

Teenagers who attend high schools have more free time. The school day is over by 1:00 P.M., and though some states in Germany have school on Saturday twice a month, most do not. Many students belong to **Sportvereine,** *sport clubs,* outside of school. Students have **Sport,** *gym,* as part of the curriculum, but there are few intramural sports and school teams. Musical activities are usually not part of school. There are many orchestras, choirs, and music clubs as well as other types of clubs for people of all ages in the community.

High school students usually do not have part-time jobs, though some may do things like distributing flyers for a local store or babysitting.

B6 ERKLÄRUNG
Word Order: Verb in Second Place

If you listen to what these students are saying, you will notice that most of the statements do not begin with **ich,** but with some other phrase, such as **im Sommer, am Wochenende,** etc. The verb, however, always remains in second place.

	Verb in second place		
Ich	**spiele**	am Wochenende	Fussball.
Am Wochenende	**spiele**	ich	Fussball.
Ich	**spiele**	im Winter	Basketball.
Im Winter	**spiele**	ich	Basketball.

B7 Übung • Frag deine Mitschüler! Frag deinen Lehrer!

Ask your classmates what they do in various seasons of the year and on various days of the week. Ask them how often they do their sports and hobbies. First ask one classmate, then ask a few at once, and then ask your teacher.

A: Was machst du im Winter?
B: Im Winter . . .

A: Was machst du am Wochenende?
B: Am Wochenende . . .

A: Wie oft machst du Sport?
B: Zweimal in der Woche . . .

A: Wie oft spielst du Tennis?
B: Tennis . . .

B8 Übung • Hör gut zu! 

When or how often? Listen.

	0	1	2	3	4	5	6	7	8	9	10
wann											
wie oft?	✓										

B9 Schreibübung • Sport ist prima!

Rewrite the following paragraph, varying word order.

Sport ist prima! Ich spiele am Dienstag und am Freitag Tennis. Ich spiele am Samstag Fussball. Ich spiele auch Fussball im Sommer. Fussball ist toll! Wir sind gut. Wir gewinnen meistens; wir verlieren selten. Ich laufe im Winter Schi, und ich spiele Hockey. Ich habe einmal in der Woche Musik. Ich spiele Gitarre. Ich besuche oft Freunde, und wir hören Kassetten. Das ist auch toll!

asking about someone's likes, dislikes, and preferences and expressing your own

Young people like to sit around and discuss their opinions and talk about their interests. What do you like to do? What are your favorite activities?

C1 Fussball ist Klasse!

INTERVIEWER Was machst du, Margit? Machst du Sport?
MARGIT Ich mache Gymnastik.
INTERVIEWER Wirklich?
MARGIT Ja, Gymnastik macht Spass!

INTERVIEWER Jörg, du spielst Fussball?
JÖRG Ja, Fussball ist Klasse.
INTERVIEWER Spielst du auch Tennis?
JÖRG Nein. Ich finde Tennis langweilig.

INTERVIEWER Wiebke, was machst du in deiner Freizeit?
WIEBKE Ich lese viel.
INTERVIEWER Das ist interessant. Was liest du?
WIEBKE Romane, Sportbücher, Fantasy-Bücher . . . sie sind Spitze!
INTERVIEWER Wie findest du Comics?
WIEBKE Blöd!

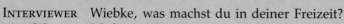

C2 Übung • Mix-Match: Was machen die drei Schüler?

1. Die Margit macht . . .
2. Das macht . . .
3. Der Jörg sagt, Fussball . . .
4. Er spielt nicht . . .
5. Er findet Tennis . . .
6. Wiebke sagt: Ich . . .
7. Ich lese . . .
8. Die Comics . . .

Romane.
Gymnastik.
ist Klasse.
langweilig.
lese viel.
sind blöd.
Spass.
Tennis.

C3 WIE SAGT MAN DAS?

Asking for an opinion, expressing enthusiasm or lack of it

You already know some expressions for good news **(Das ist gut, prima, phantastisch, toll!)** and for bad news **(Das ist blöd!).** You can also use them to express your opinion about activities you like and dislike. Here are some more words and expressions.

asking for an opinion	Wie findest du Fussball?	What do you think of soccer?
expressing enthusiasm	Ich finde Fussball interessant! Fussball ist Klasse! Das ist Spitze! Fussball macht Spass!	I think soccer is interesting! Soccer is terrific! That's great! Soccer is fun!
lack of enthusiasm	Ich finde Fussball blöd. Fussball ist langweilig.	I think soccer is dumb. Soccer is boring.

C4 Übung • Was meint dein Freund? *What does your friend think?* 

You tell your friend what you think and he or she agrees.

A: Hockey ist toll!
B: Ich finde Hockey auch toll!

1. Fussball ist Spitze.
2. Tennis ist Klasse.
3. Sammeln ist interessant.
4. Kartenspielen ist blöd.
5. Mau-Mau ist langweilig.
6. Gymnastik ist prima.

C5 Übung • Jetzt bist du dran

Ask your classmates how they like the sports and activities shown below.

A: Wie findest du . . . *or* Wie findet ihr . . . ?
B: Ich finde Fussball . . . *or* Fussball ist . . .

Mau-Mau **Fussball** ***Hockey*** Tennis Segeln
Lesen Briefmarkensammeln **Sport** Schach ***Musik***
Basketball Gymnastik Kartenspielen Schwimmen

Spitze!
super!
Klasse!
toll!
prima!
phantastisch!
interessant!
macht Spass!

langweilig!
blöd!

C6 STIMMT! STIMMT NICHT! 

A: Fussball ist Klasse!
B: Stimmt!

A: Wie findest du die Kassette?
B: Super! Sie ist Spitze!
A: Wirklich? Ich finde sie blöd.

A: Du sammelst Briefmarken?
B: Ja. Sammeln macht Spass.
A: Was? Das finde ich nicht.

A: Kartenspielen ist langweilig.
B: Das finde ich auch.

A: Segeln ist auch langweilig.
B: Stimmt nicht! Segeln ist prima!

C7 WIE SAGT MAN DAS?

Expressing surprise, agreement, disagreement

surprise	Was? Wirklich?	What? Really?
agreement	Stimmt! Das finde ich auch.	True! That's right! I think so, too.
disagreement	Stimmt nicht! Das finde ich nicht.	Not true! That's not so. I don't think so.

C8 Übung • Partnerarbeit 

Team up with a classmate. Express an opinion about some sport or activity. Your classmate should agree with your opinion or express surprise and disagree. Then reverse roles.

A: Kartenspielen ist langweilig.
B: Stimmt! *or* Das finde ich auch.

A: Ich finde Hockey prima.
B: Wirklich? Das finde ich nicht.

C9 Übung • Und du? Wie steht's mit dir? 

Agree or disagree with the following statements.

1. Segeln ist Klasse!
2. Kartenspielen ist langweilig.
3. Deutsch ist interessant.
4. Eine Zwei in Deutsch ist prima.
5. Wir haben am Samstag Schule.
6. Die Hausaufgaben sind leicht.
7. Briefmarkensammeln ist blöd!
8. Comics sind Spitze!

C10 WAS MACHST DU GERN?

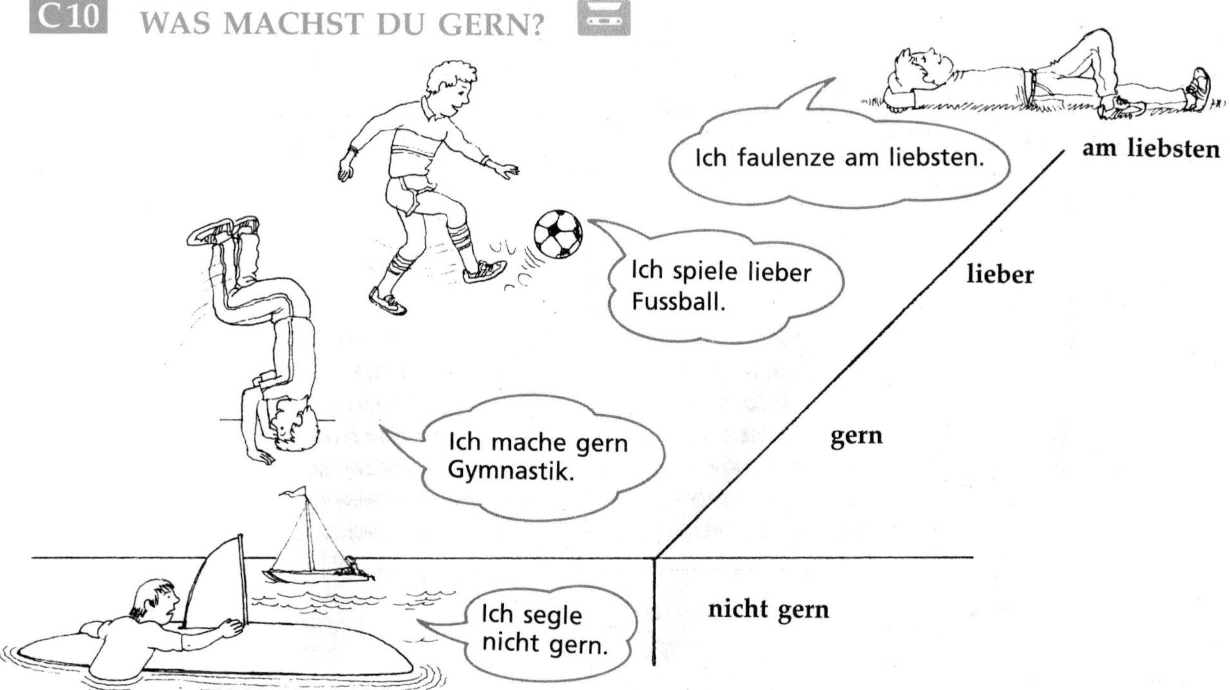

C11 WIE SAGT MAN DAS?
Expressing likes, dislikes, and preferences

Use the word **gern** together with a verb to express the idea of liking something and **nicht gern** to express disliking something.

liking	Ich spiele **gern** Karten.	I like to play cards.
disliking	Ich spiele **nicht gern** Karten.	I don't like to play cards.

Use the word **lieber** together with a verb to express preference. Use **am liebsten** to express what you like best of all.

preference	Ich spiele **lieber** Fussball.	I prefer playing soccer.
strong preference	Ich spiele **am liebsten** Tennis.	I like tennis best of all.

C12 Übung • Und du? Wie steht's mit dir? 

1. Tell which of the following you like and which you don't like.

   Ich spiele gern Tennis.
   Ich . . . gern . . .

   Ich spiele nicht gern Schach.
   Ich . . . nicht gern . . .

2. Tell what you prefer.

   Ich lese nicht gern Comics. Ich lese lieber . . .

3. Now tell what you like to do best of all.

   Ich mache am liebsten . . .

4. Ask your classmates what they like and what they don't like to do. Ask them what they prefer and what they like most of all.

C13 Übung • Der Sport- und Hobbyfreund: Was macht er denn alles?

C14 Übung • Hör gut zu!

Do you like this activity or don't you? What do you prefer? What do you like best of all? Listen.

	0	1	2	3	4	5	6	7	8	9	10
likes											
does not like											
prefers	✓										
likes most of all											

C15 Schreibübung • Was machen die Schüler gern? Und du?

1. Write what each student likes and doesn't like to do. Use the following cues.

	gern	am liebsten	nicht gern
1. Paul:	Gymnastik	schwimmen	Basketball
2. Sabine:	Karten	Mau-Mau	Schach
3. Monika und Anke:	Kassetten	Sport	sammeln

1. Paul macht gern Gymnastik. Er . . .
2. Sabine . . .

2. Write a paragraph about what you like and don't like to do.

C16 Übung • Umfrage: Was machst du in deiner Freizeit?

The survey sheet below was given to a German 9th-grade class. The students were asked to rank their sports activities, putting their favorite sport at the top of the list. Read the survey sheet and discuss it in class. Tell what this student likes and dislikes, what he prefers, and when and how often he does the various activities listed.

Name: *Markus Walden*

	Was?	Wann?					Wie oft?								
		im Frühjahr	im Sommer	im Herbst	im Winter	am Wochenende	nie	selten	manchmal	oft	immer	am Tag	in der Woche	im Monat	im Jahr
am liebsten	*Fussball*		✓	✓		✓				✓			2x		
	Basketball	✓			✓						✓		1x		
lieber	*Windsurfen*		✓			✓			✓					4x	
	Segeln		✓	✓					✓					1x	
gern	*Volleyball*	✓								✓			1x		
	Gymnastik				✓					✓			3x		
nicht gern	*Handball*				✓			✓						1x	
	Golf			✓				✓							1x

C17 Übung • Klassenprojekt

Do a similar survey in your class and discuss the results.

TRY YOUR SKILLS

using what you've learned

Friends do not always have the same opinion about sports and activities.

1 Stimmt nicht! Du bist nur sauer! 

HELMUT Hast du ein Hobby?
JENS Ja, Schach.
HELMUT Was? Schach ist so langweilig.
JENS Das finde ich nicht. Schach ist interessant. Es macht Spass! Spielst du auch Schach?
HELMUT Ja, aber nicht oft.
JENS Bist du gut? Gewinnst du oft?
HELMUT Nein, ich verliere meistens.
JENS Ach so! Du verlierst immer, und du bist sauer.

Aber Lars, Jörg und Jens spielen gern Schach.

2 Übung • Deine Meinung—meine Meinung *Your opinion—my opinion* 

Ask a classmate to tell you five things that he or she likes to do. After each response, give your own opinion. If you like the same thing, say why. If you don't like it, say that you prefer something else. Your conversation might go like this:

A: Was machst du gern?
B: Ich spiele gern Hockey.
A: Ich auch. Hockey ist toll! *or* Ich nicht. Ich laufe lieber Schi.

3 Übung • Stimmt!—Stimmt nicht! 

Some of your classmates have definite opinions when it comes to certain sports and activities. Listen to what they say and agree or disagree. One classmate might begin by saying:

A: Ach, Hockey ist so langweilig!
B: Das finde ich nicht. *or* Stimmt!

4 Übung • Sport und Spiel

The following are pictorial symbols you can see in stadiums where sports events take place.

1. Identify each symbol:
   1. Fussball
   2. . . .

2. Look at the activities depicted and answer these questions.
   Was machst du gern?
   Was machst du nicht gern?
   Was machst du am liebsten?
3. Now give an opinion on each of the activities shown.
   Ich finde . . .

5 Übung • Wann spielen sie was?

These German friends participate in different sports during different seasons. According to the diagram, who does what and when?

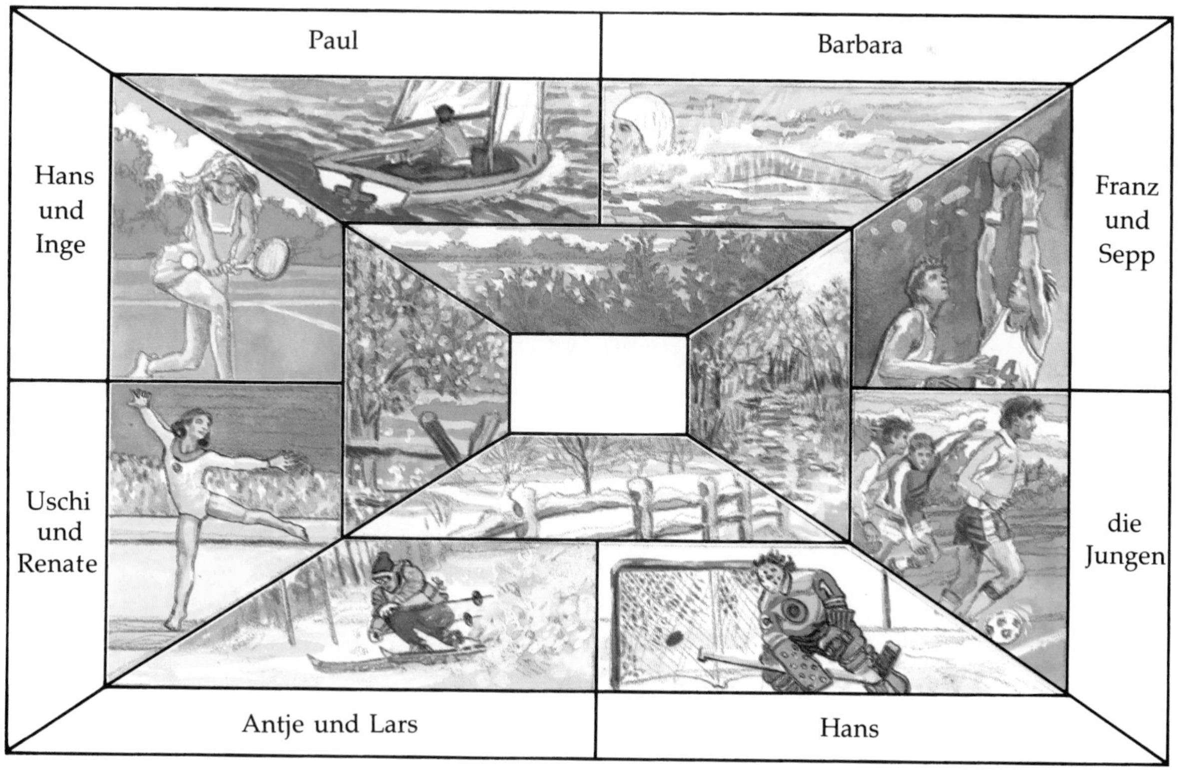

6 Übung • Hallo! Wer schreibt uns?

The following excerpts are from a special report, „Hallo! Wer schreibt uns? Wir antworten!", which appeared in a magazine for young people. Report to a classmate or to your teacher what these two ads say. Use complete sentences.

Vorname: Bettina
Nachname: Schilling
Alter: 14
Strasse: Schulstrasse 17
Stadt: D - 7900 Ulm
Hobbys/Interessen: schwimmen, segeln, Basketball spielen

Vorname: Markus
Nachname: Wallner
Alter: 15
Strasse: Hebbelstrasse 8
Stadt: D - 6100 Darmstadt
Hobbys/Interessen: Fussball, Gymnastik, Briefmarken sammeln

7 Schreibübung • Interview und Anzeige

1. Pretend that you would like to place a similar ad in this magazine in order to find a pen pal, and you are giving information about yourself over the phone.

   INTERVIEWER Wie heisst du?
   DU . . .

2. Write down the phone conversation you had with a person from this magazine.
3. Write how your ad would appear in the column.

8 Übung • Ein Brief an Markus Wallner

Here is a letter that was written in response to Markus Wallner's ad. Read the letter.

Lieber Markus!

Ich heisse Martin Obermeyer. Ich bin 14 Jahre alt und wohne in Regensburg (D-8400) Bahnhofstasse 17. Meine Interessen sind Musik und Sport. Ich höre gern Musikgruppen aus England. Ich schwimme gern, ich spiele Squash, und am liebsten spiele ich Fussball.

Was machst Du? Bitte schreib mir!

Dein
Martin

9 Schreibübung • Jetzt bist du dran

Now write a letter of your own, similar to the one on the preceding page. Answer either Markus Wallner's ad or Bettina Schilling's.

10 Schreibübung • Klassenprojekt

After your class has written ads to appear in the pen pal column „Hallo! Wer schreibt uns?", exchange ads with another German class. Pick a pen pal and write a letter in response to the ad.

11 Übung • Dialog-Mischmasch

With the help of a classmate, unscramble the following dialog. Start with 1. Write down your dialog and read it aloud together.

Bist du gut? Gewinnst du oft?

Ach, ich verliere oft.

Na klar! Ich spiele Tennis.

1. Machst du Sport?

Ich gewinne meistens. Und du?

Tennis? Ich finde Tennis langweilig.

Soso. Du bist nur sauer.

Wirklich? Ich spiele gern, und ich finde Tennis Spitze.

12 Aussprache-, Lese- und Schreibübungen

1. Listen carefully and repeat what you hear.

2. Listen, then read aloud.
1. frei, Frau, Freund, drei, dreimal, prima, hören, Karte, Roman, Rad
2. ihr, vier, hier, wir, er, der, schwer
3. aber, oder, lieber, immer, Sommer, Winter, sauer, Schüler, Lehrer, super
4. ein, eine, eins, einmal, heisse, Latein
5. Mau-Mau, sauer, schau, aus, auch
6. neun, heute, Freund, neunzehn; Fräulein, Verkäuferin
7. Schule, Schi, schwer, schlecht
8. spielen, Sport, Spitze, spät; Stundenplan, Bleistift

3. Copy the following sentences to prepare yourself to write them from dictation.
1. Wir haben immer frei.
2. Fräulein Meier spielt heute.
3. Meine Freundin heisst Winter.
4. Die Schule ist schwer.

WAS KANNST DU SCHON?

Let's review some important points that you have learned in this unit.

SECTION A

Can you address a person using the *du*-form?
Ask a friend questions about his or her interests using the following verbs:
machen, spielen, sammeln, schwimmen, besuchen

Give a reply for each question.

Can you address a group of people using the *ihr*-form?
Approach a group of people and ask them what they are doing. Give an appropriate response.

Do you know how to address adults?
Ask your teacher about his or her activities.

SECTION B

Can you say when and how often you do various sports and activities?
Mention four activities. Tell when you do them (in what season or on what day) and how often.

Mention activities that you rarely or never do, as well as ones you do sometimes, often, and always.

SECTION C

Can you ask about someone's interests?
Ask a friend what he or she thinks of the following:
Tennis, Fussball, Gymnastik, Kartenspielen, Briefmarkensammeln

Do you know how to express enthusiasm or lack of enthusiasm?
Give your opinion about five different sports and activities.

Can you express surprise and also say that you agree or disagree with something?
Respond to each of the following statements, expressing surprise, agreement or disagreement.

1. Deutsch ist leicht.
2. Schach ist interessant.
3. Comics sind super.
4. Tennis ist schwer.
5. Briefmarkensammeln ist blöd.

Can you talk about your likes, dislikes, and preferences?
Tell what you like to do, what you prefer to do, and what you like to do most of all. Tell what you don't like to do.

Now ask a friend about his or her likes and dislikes.

WORTSCHATZ

SECTION A

auch: ich auch *me too*
Basketball *basketball*
besuchen *to visit*
die **Briefmarke, -n** *stamp*
ein *a, an*
die **Freizeit** *free time;* in deiner Freizeit *in your free time*
der **Freund, -e** *friend*
Fussball *soccer*
gewinnen *to win*
die **Gitarre, -n** *guitar*
haha! *ha ha!*
das **Hobby, -s** *hobby*
Hockey *hockey*
hören *to listen (to)*
das **Instrument, -e** *instrument*
der **Interviewer, -** *interviewer*
die **Karten** (pl) *cards*
machen *to do;* was machst du? *what are you doing? what do you do?*
Mau-Mau (card game similar to crazy eights)
mogeln *to cheat*
die **Münze, -n** *coin*
die **Musikkassette, -n** *music cassette*
na klar! *of course!*
sammeln *to collect*
sauer *sore*
Schach *chess*
der **Schüler, -** *student, pupil*
schwimmen *to swim*
segeln *to sail*
Sie *you* (formal)
das **Spiel, -e** *game*
spielen *to play*
der **Sport** *sport; sports;* Sport machen *to participate in a sport, to do sports*
Tennis *tennis*
tja *hm*
verlieren *to lose*
was!? *what!?*
wie immer *as always*
wirklich? *really?*

SECTION B

am Sonntag *on Sunday*
am Tag *(times) a day*
am Wochenende *on the weekend*
dreimal *three times*
einmal *once*
Eishockey *ice hockey*
im Frühjahr *in the spring*
im Herbst *in the fall*
im Jahr *(times) a year*
im Monat *(times) a month*
im Sommer *in the summer*
im Winter *in the winter*
immer *always*
in der Woche *(times) a week*
manchmal *sometimes*
meistens *mostly*
nie *never*
oft *often*
Samstag *Saturday*
Schi: ich laufe Schi *I go skiing*
selten *seldom*
Sonntag *Sunday*
viermal *four times*
wie oft? *how often?*
zweimal *twice*

SECTION C

am liebsten (machen) *to like (to do) most of all*
Comics (pl) *comics*
das **Fantasy-Buch, ¨er** *fantasy book*
faulenzen *to lie around, be lazy*
finden *to find, think (have the opinion about something);* das finde ich nicht *I don't think so;* wie findest du . . .? *how do you like . . .? what do you think of . . .?*
gern (machen) *to like (to do)*
Gymnastik *gymnastics;* Gymnastik machen *to do gymnastics*
interessant *interesting*
Kartenspielen *playing cards*
Klasse! *great!*
langweilig *boring*
lesen *to read*
lieber (machen) *to prefer (to do);* ich spiele lieber Fussball *I rather play soccer*
liest: was liest du? *what do you read?*
nicht gern (machen) *to not like (to do)*
der **Roman, -e** *novel*
Sammeln *collecting*
Segeln *sailing*
Spass *fun;* Gymnastik macht Spass *gymnastics are fun*
Spitze! *terrific!*
das **Sportbuch, ¨er** *book about sports*
stimmt! *that's right! true!*
stimmt nicht! *not true! that's not so!*
super! *super! terrific!*
viel *much, a lot*

WORTSCHATZÜBUNGEN

1. Look at the **Wortschatz** and make a list of all the verbs. What do most verbs end in? (Look at the last two or three letters.) Now put a slash between the verb infinitive stem and the ending.
2. Pick out the words that are listed twice. What is the difference in spelling? What is the difference in meaning?
3. Make a list of all the words that are similar to English, writing them both in German and English. Compare the spelling and the meaning of each pair of words.

ZUM LESEN

Keine Freizeitmuffel!

Was machen Jungen und Mädchen in der Freizeit?—Sie machen Sport, sie gehen ins Kino, ins Konzert, zu Sportveranstaltungen. Sie hören Musik, diskutieren und philosophieren. Was machen sie noch? Fragen wir sie mal!

Lest ihr gern, oder seht ihr nur fern°?

Frage an Jungen und Mädchen: Wie oft lest ihr in Büchern?	**1968**	**1986**
—täglich°:	10%	12%
—2–3 mal in der Woche:	19%	21%
—einmal in der Woche:	13%	11%
—gar nicht:	32%	28%

Was lest ihr? Lest ihr auch Bücher, oder seid ihr Büchermuffel?

„Ich lese viel. Ich lese Zeitschriften°, Hobbybücher—am liebsten lese ich Comics."

Zeitschriften

seht ihr nur fern *watch T.V.* **täglich** *daily*
Zeitschriften *magazines*

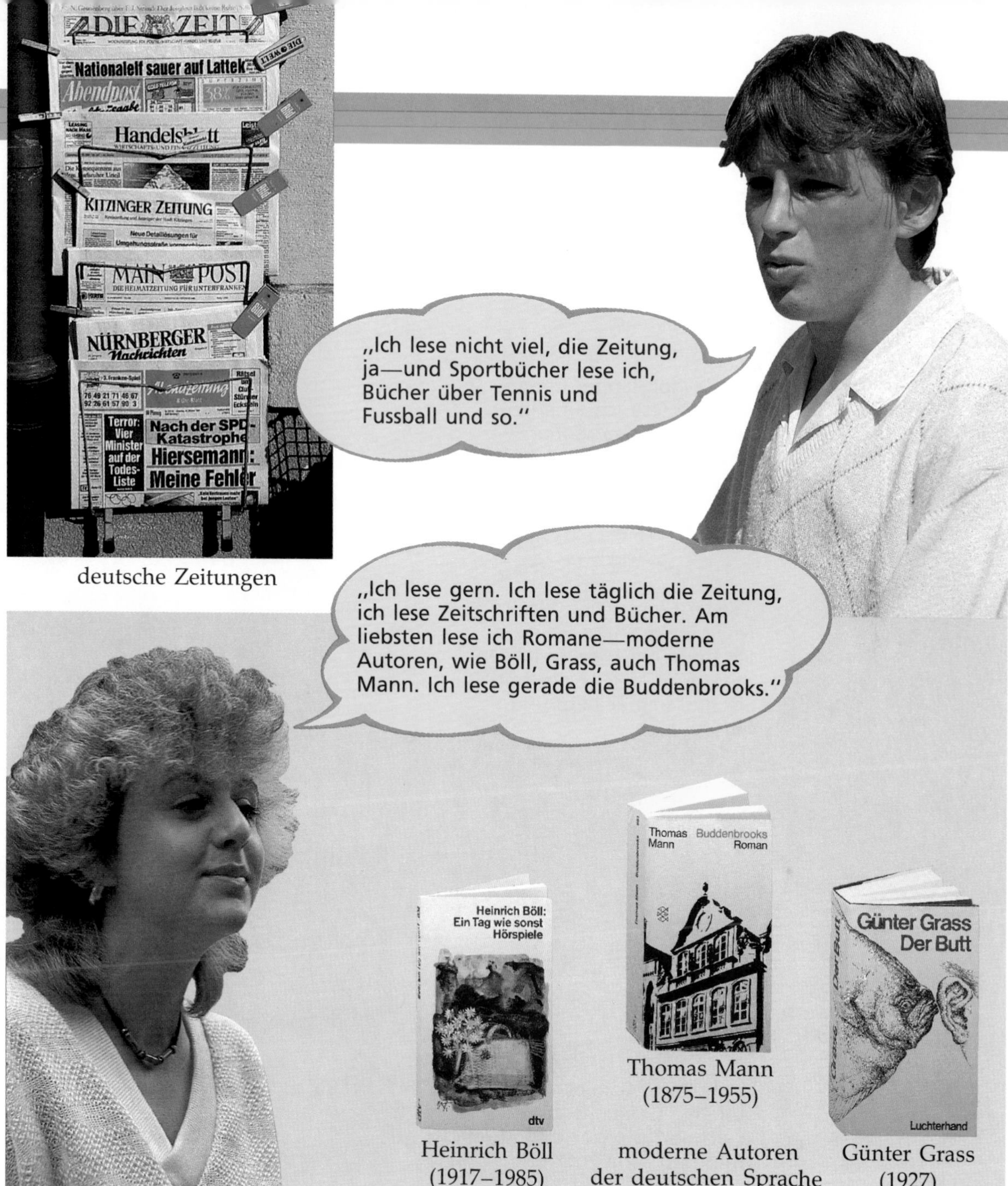

deutsche Zeitungen

Thomas Mann (1875–1955)

Heinrich Böll (1917–1985)

moderne Autoren der deutschen Sprache

Günter Grass (1927)

Übung • Sprechen wir darüber! *Let's talk about it!*

1. Was machst du in der Freizeit?
2. Was liest du?
3. Wie oft liest du Bücher? Oder bist du ein Büchermuffel?
4. Was liest du gern? Am liebsten?
5. Welche Autoren liest du?
6. Wie heissen einige deutsche Zeitschriften?
7. Wie heissen einige deutsche Zeitungen?
8. Wie heissen einige Autoren?
9. Die *Buddenbrooks* sind von . . .?
10. Und *Der Butt?*

Wie findet ihr Comics?

„Ich lese schon lange° Comics. Am liebsten lese ich amerikanische Superhelden°-Comics. Manchmal lese ich sie im Original."

„Es gibt auch deutsche Comics. Sie sind nicht so gut. Ich finde Matthias Schultheiss und amerikanische Comics toll."

„Viele° Comics sind blöd. Nur Moebius lese ich gern. Ich finde die Frauen° in den meisten° Comics nicht gut. Sie sind immer blöd und hilflos°."

Andrea

Michael

Kristin

Natalie

Kurt

„Ich liebe° Comics, und ich sammle Comics-Hefte. Die Zeichner° Mercier und Moebius finde ich sehr gut."

„Ich lese Comics selten. Mein Interesse ist Kunst. Aber für mich sind Comics auch Kunst. Am liebsten lese ich MAD."

---

lange *for a long time* **der Superheld** *super hero* **viele** *many* **die Frau** *woman* **die meisten** *most* **hilflos** *helpless*
lieben *to love* **der Zeichner** *artist*

Welche° Figuren kennen° die deutschen Jungen und Mädchen?

Übung • Und du? Wie steht's mit dir?

1. Welche Comics kennst du?
2. Welche Zeichner findest du gut?
3. Welche Comics gibt es?
4. Welche Figuren kennst du?
5. Sammelst du Comics-Hefte?

Neue Hobbys 

„Mein Hobby ist der Homecomputer. Ich mache Computerspiele , ich spiele ‚Hangman', und jetzt lerne ich Schach. Schach mit dem Computer! Das ist toll, das macht Spass!"

---

welche *which* **kennen** *to know*

KAPITEL **4**

Aus einer Schülerzeitung

Wiederholungskapitel

1

Schüler aus der 9c

Wir sind Schüler aus der 9c in der List Realschule in München. Wir sind diesen Monat in unserer Schülerzeitung, im List-Käfer. Warum? Wir korrespondieren mit englischen und amerikanischen Schülern.

Das sind unsere „Steckbriefe."

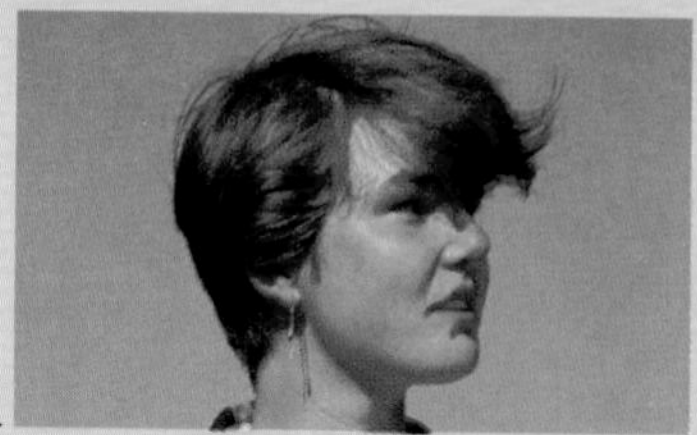

1
Name: Natalie Fiedler
Alter: 15 J.
Hobby: Gymnastik, Tanzen, Windsurfen, Schwimmen
Lieblingsfächer: Ek[1], Mu, E
Schulweg: Rad

2
Name: Nicolas Kraindl
Alter: 15 J.
Hobby: Squash, Musik (Gitarre spielen)
Lieblingsfächer: Mu, E
Schulweg: Strassenbahn

3
Name: Steffi Huber
Alter: 15 J.
Hobby: Gymnastik, Volleyball, Schi laufen
Lieblingsfächer: M, G
Schulweg: U-Bahn

4
Name: Michael Strasser
Alter: 16 J.
Hobby: Hockey, Judo, Schach
Lieblingsfächer: Ku, Ch
Schulweg: U-Bahn

5
Name: Monika Schönfeld
Alter: 16 J.
Hobby: Klavier, Schwimmen, Windsurfen, Tennis
Lieblingsfächer: Mu, E, D
Schulweg: Rad/zu Fuss

6
Name: Andreas Reichel
Alter: 16 J.
Hobby: Tennis, Fussball, Briefmarken
Lieblingsfächer: D, Bio
Schulweg: Moped

7
Name: Marina Welzel
Alter: 16 J.
Hobby: Musik (Klavier), Segeln, Schi laufen
Lieblingsfächer: Mu, E, D
Schulweg: zu Fuss

8
Name: Stefan Knötzinger
Alter: 15 J.
Hobby: Schach, Tennis, Basketball
Lieblingsfächer: M, E, Ek
Schulweg: Bus

9
Name: Matthias Blick
Alter: 15 J.
Hobby: Fussball, Schwimmen, Schi laufen, Münzen
Lieblingsfächer: D, E
Schulweg: Rad

[1] Abkürzungen: Ek = Erdkunde; Mu = Musik; E = Englisch; M = Mathematik; G = Geographie; Ku = Kunst; Ch = Chemie; D = Deutsch; Bio = Biologie; **Schi laufen: sie läuft Schi** *she skis;* **U-Bahn: mit der U-Bahn** *by subway;* **Klavier** *piano*

2 Übung • Beantworte die Fragen!

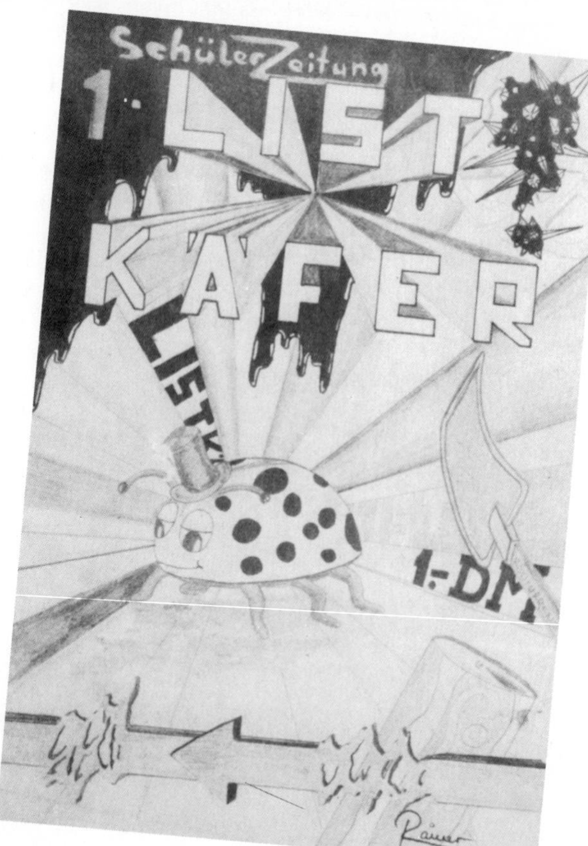

1. In welche Klasse gehen die Schüler?
2. Wie heisst ihre Schule?
3. Warum sind sie in der Schülerzeitung?
4. Wie heissen die Schüler?
5. Lies die neun Steckbriefe!
6. Identifiziere die Schüler! (Sag, wie sie heissen, wie alt sie sind, was für Hobbys sie haben, was ihre Lieblingsfächer sind und wie sie in die Schule kommen!)
7. Wer ist 15 Jahre alt? Wer ist 16?
8. Wer kommt mit dem Rad in die Schule?
9. Wer kommt mit der Strassenbahn? Und mit der U-Bahn?
10. Wie kommen die andern in die Schule?

3 Übung • Jetzt bist du dran

Your German class is going to be featured in the **List-Käfer.** Interview your classmates and write a **Steckbrief** for each one.

4 Schreibübung • Partnerarbeit

You and your partner are going to interview one of the students shown on page 121. Look back through Units 1, 2, and 3 and make a list of questions you could ask the student.

5 Schreibübung • Interview

Pretend that you are interviewing one of the students on page 121. Write out your interview. Then you and your partner take the roles of the interviewer and the student and present it to the class. Your classmates may have other questions to ask.

6 Schreibübung • Ein Freund aus der List-Schule

Now you and your partner take the interview you have written and rewrite it as a newspaper article.

7 Übung • Klassenprojekt

Collect the articles written by your classmates and make a scrapbook or a bulletin board titled **Unsere Freunde aus der List-Schule.**

Ruth Maier BUCHHANDLUNG AM RATHAUS

STARNBERG • HAUPTSTRASSE 14 • TELEFON 7341

Bücher, Schallplatten, Schreibwaren & Posters

Bücher—und alles für die Schule
Ruth Maier hat's!

Schulsachen

Schultaschen	DM 15,00
Taschenrechner	22,00
Kulis	2,10
Hefte	1,20

Wörterbücher

Wörterbuch D/E—E/D nur DM 12,00!

Bleistifte (10 St.) DM 3,50

Poster ab DM 4,00

Musik

Platten	ab DM	7,00
Kassetten	ab	6,80
Video-Kassetten	ab	12,00

Spiele

Computerspiele DM 23,00

Bücher ab DM 6,00

9 Übung • Beantworte die Fragen!

1. Was hat die Buchhandlung am Rathaus alles?
2. Was kostet alles? Was kostet . . .? Was kosten . . .?

10 Schreibübung • In der Buchhandlung

You go into Ruth Maier's bookstore and want to know the prices of four items. Write out a dialog and practice it with a classmate. Don't forget to be polite.

11 Übung • Aus dem List-Käfer

So sehen die Schüler der List-Schule ihre Schulwoche—Und du?
Wie steht's mit dir? Wie siehst du deine Schulwoche?

LANDESKUNDE 1

A Glimpse of the Federal Republic of Germany

Germany lies in the center of Europe. It is about six hundred miles long, bounded by the North Sea to the north and the Alps to the south. From east to west the country is narrow, seldom more than two hundred miles wide. Contained in this area is a surprising variety of landscapes. There are coastal regions and flatlands in northern Germany and gently rolling hills in the central and southwestern part of the country. South of the river Danube is a high plateau that reaches to the majestic Alpine range. It is surprising that in such a highly industrialized country more than half the area is farmland and another third is forest land.

❶ Promenadenkonzert auf der Nordseeinsel Sylt

❷ Kurort Badenweiler im Schwarzwald

❸ Die Zugspitze, Deutschlands höchster Berg, 2 963 m

The North

The North abounds in architectural and artistic treasures and is the area of Germany most influenced by the sea. There are several historic Hanseatic cities, including the great port cities of Hamburg, Bremen, Kiel, and Lübeck. The coasts of the Baltic Sea and the North Sea are dotted with fishing villages. Many have become popular summer resorts, but fishing is still an important industry. Inland is a rich agricultural area that supports a thriving dairy industry. There are many towns with red brick buildings that are characteristic of the north, and villages that still have windmills and thatched-roof houses.

Lieber Gast!
Bitte keine Halme (Reêt) rausziehen. Wenn jeder einen Halm nehmen würde, hätte ich bald kein Dach mehr über dem Kopf.
Der Eigentümer

❶ Ausflugsschiffe vor der Insel Helgoland

❷ Nordfriesenhaus mit Reetdach auf der Insel Föhr

❸ Tracht auf der Insel Föhr

❹ Fischerhafen Bensersiel in Ostfriesland

❺ Das Rathaus von Bremen

❻ Lübeck mit Blick auf das Holstentor (1477)

❼ Schaffner vor dem Lübecker Rathaus

❽ Lüneburger Heide: Schäfer mit Hund und Heidschnucken

❾ Hamburg, grösste Stadt der Bundesrepublik

❿ Berlin: Ruine und Neubau der Kaiser-Wilhelm Gedächtniskirche

Central Germany

The central part of Germany is highly diversified in both geography and character. The busy Moselle River flows through Trier, the oldest city in Germany. The famous Rhine River cuts a scenic path through terraced vineyards, past romantic castles and the rock upon which the fabled Lorelei sat, through the great cities of Cologne, Düsseldorf, and Bonn, the capital of the Federal Republic of Germany. The state of North Rhine–Westphalia, its rolling hills sprinkled with old castles, is called the forge of Germany because of its highly industrialized Ruhr area with such cities as Essen and Dortmund. The second largest industrialized area of the Rhine-Main region is Hessia, but it is also known as the land of healing springs because of its many spas. Located in Hessia is the city of Frankfurt, the business and banking capital of the Federal Republic.

1. Fachwerkhäuser in Paderborn, Westfalen
2. Der Wormser Dom aus dem 11. und 12. Jahrhundert
3. Weinberge in Bacherach am Rhein
4. Trier, die älteste Stadt, mit der Porta Nigra aus der Zeit der Römer

❺ Braunkohlenwerk in der Nähe von Jülich, im Rheinland

❻ Arbeiter im Ruhrgebiet

❼ Der Rhein in der Nähe von Duisburg

❽ Frankfurt am Main, Finanzzentrum der Bundesrepublik

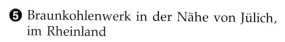

The South

The South, a beautiful and historic region, begins at the River Main and stretches all the way to Switzerland, Lake Constance, and the Alps. In this area are found the old university cities of Heidelberg, Tübingen, and Freiburg; historic art cities such as Würzburg, Nürnberg, and Bamberg; perfectly preserved medieval towns such as Rothenburg, Dinkelsbühl, and Nördlingen; wine-growing regions in the southwest; and spas that pre-date Roman times. Munich, the capital of Bavaria, is in the southeast, a center of art and culture, and the city in which sixty-nine percent of all Germans would like to live. The area around Munich offers both natural and man-made wonders, baroque churches, monasteries, and King Ludwig's castles. The Alps themselves offer magnificent scenery, dotted with lakes, forests, flower-filled meadows, and charming Alpine villages that are year-round resorts.

❶ Blumenfrau auf dem Marktplatz in Freiburg

❷ Gasthaus zur Sonne

❸ Schwarzwälder Schinken und Bauernbrot

❹ Heidelberg am Neckar, Universitätsstadt seit 1386

❺ Rathausfassade von Staufen an der Badener Weinstrasse

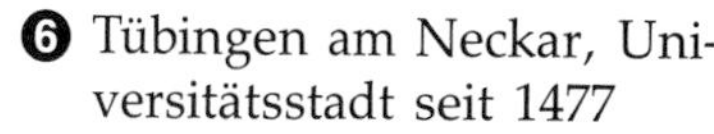

❻ Tübingen am Neckar, Universitätsstadt seit 1477

❼ Treppenhaus in der Würzburger Residenz mit dem in der Welt grössten Deckenfresko von Tiepolo

❽ Das Rathaus von Ulm mit Fresken von 1540

❾ Landshut an der Isar, mit Giebelhäusern aus dem 15. und 16. Jahrhundert

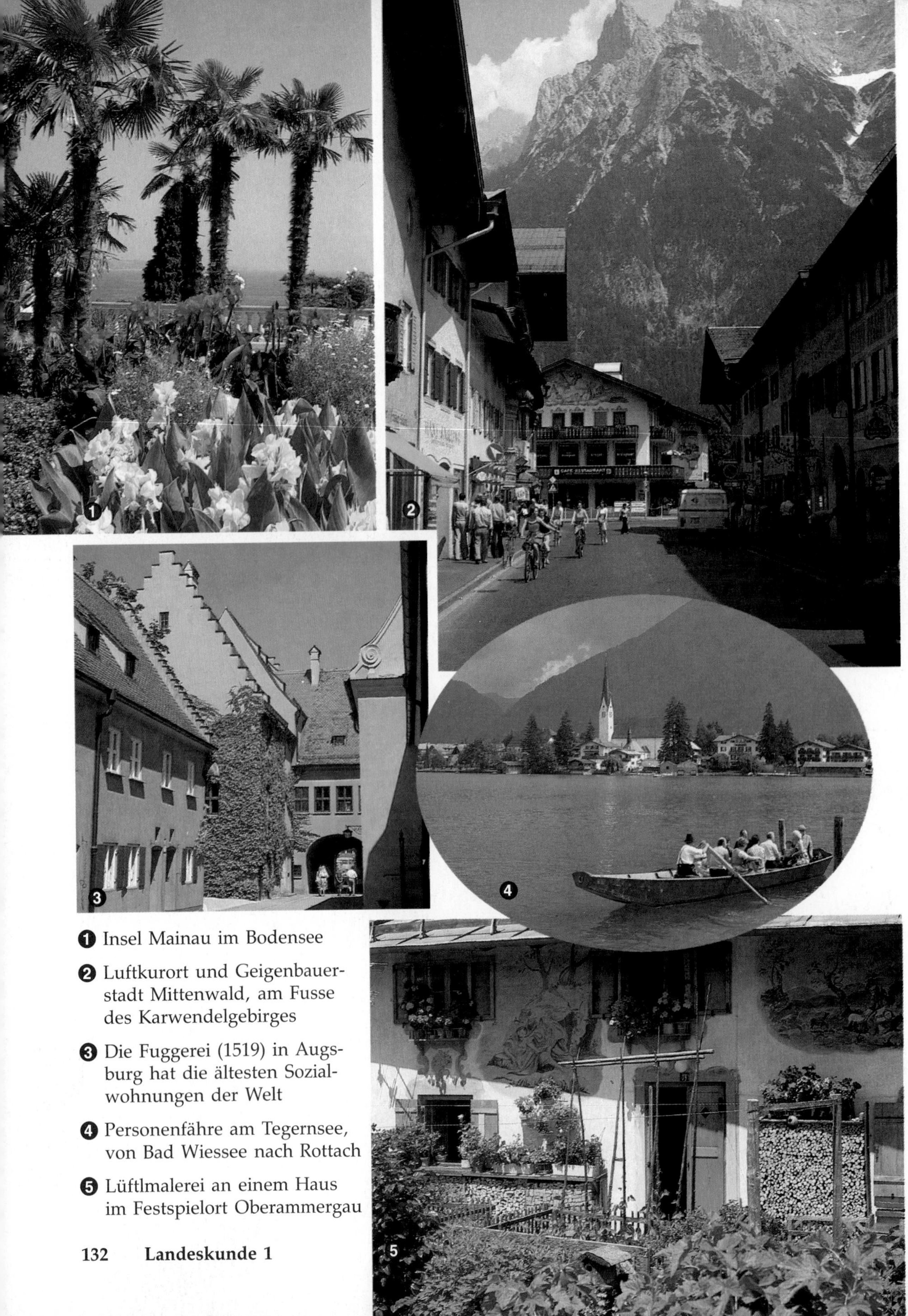

❶ Insel Mainau im Bodensee

❷ Luftkurort und Geigenbauerstadt Mittenwald, am Fusse des Karwendelgebirges

❸ Die Fuggerei (1519) in Augsburg hat die ältesten Sozialwohnungen der Welt

❹ Personenfähre am Tegernsee, von Bad Wiessee nach Rottach

❺ Lüftlmalerei an einem Haus im Festspielort Oberammergau

KAPITEL 5

Auf nach Köln!

It is interesting and fun to travel to a foreign country, especially if you have been learning the language of that country. In Europe, traveling is easy because the countries are so close together. Young Europeans often spend their vacations with families in different countries. There are also many student exchanges between the United States and European countries. Young people participate in exchanges between schools, they travel privately or with groups, sometimes with their families, visiting friends and relatives abroad.

In this unit you will:

SECTION A	talk about going to Germany and what you need to take
SECTION B	ask for information and give directions
SECTION C	exchange money, make a phone call, tell official time
TRY YOUR SKILLS	use what you've learned
ZUM LESEN	read for practice and pleasure

SECTION A — talking about going to Germany; what to take on the trip

Many young people, Americans and Germans alike, travel abroad, especially in the summer. They may be in an exchange program, or they may be visiting friends and relatives abroad. Where do they go? What do they take on the trip?

A1 Auf nach Deutschland!

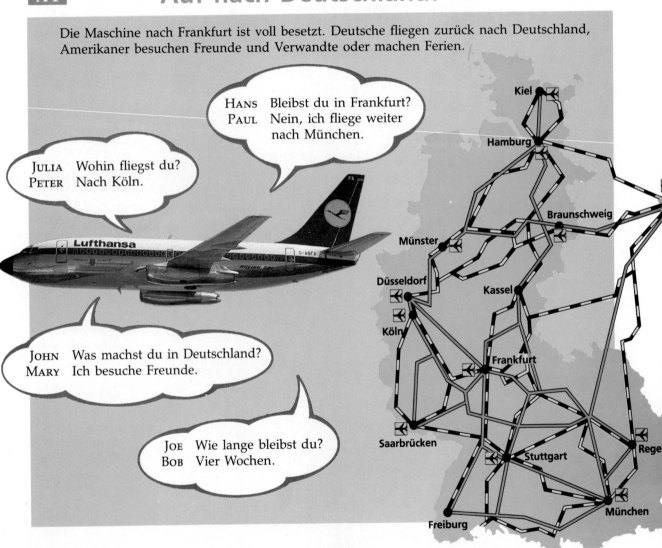

Die Maschine nach Frankfurt ist voll besetzt. Deutsche fliegen zurück nach Deutschland, Amerikaner besuchen Freunde und Verwandte oder machen Ferien.

HANS Bleibst du in Frankfurt?
PAUL Nein, ich fliege weiter nach München.

JULIA Wohin fliegst du?
PETER Nach Köln.

JOHN Was machst du in Deutschland?
MARY Ich besuche Freunde.

JOE Wie lange bleibst du?
BOB Vier Wochen.

Kiel
Hamburg
Braunschweig
Münster
Düsseldorf
Kassel
Köln
Frankfurt
Saarbrücken
Stuttgart
Reger
München
Freiburg

A2 Übung • Stimmt! Stimmt nicht!

1. Die Maschine fliegt nach Köln.
2. Die Maschine ist voll besetzt.
3. Deutsche fliegen zurück nach Amerika.
4. Amerikaner machen Ferien.
5. Mary fliegt weiter nach Köln.
6. Paul besucht Freunde.
7. Bob bleibt fünf Wochen.
8. Peter fliegt nach Köln.

A3 Übung • Wohin fliegen die Schüler? 

Köln

Peter . . .

München

Paul . . .

Berlin

Julia . . .

Hamburg

Mary . . .

Wien

Joe . . .

A4 Übung • Wohin fliegst du? 

Schau auf die Karte auf Seite 136. Welche Städte möchtest du sehen und welche nicht?

A: Wohin fliegst du?
B: Ich fliege nach . . .
A: Prima! . . . ist toll!

A: Fliegst du auch nach Hamburg?
B: Nein, ich fliege nicht nach Hamburg.
A: Schade.

A5 Übung • Bleibst du hier oder fliegst du weiter? 

A: Wohin fliegst du?
B: Ich fliege nach Frankfurt.
A: Bleibst du in Frankfurt?
B: Nein, ich fliege weiter nach München.

Frankfurt / München
1. Frankfurt / Berlin
2. München / Wien
3. Köln / Hamburg

A6 Übung • Und du? Wie steht's mit dir?

1. Hast du Freunde oder Verwandte in Deutschland?
2. Wo in Deutschland?
3. Besuchst du deine Freunde manchmal?
4. Wie oft besuchst du sie?
5. Wie lange bleibst du?
6. Wohin fliegst du manchmal?
7. Was machst du dort?

A7 WAS BRAUCHT PETER FÜR DIE REISE? 

Peter Seber, a young American, is getting everything ready for his trip to Germany. What are some of the things he needs? What do you need when you take a trip?

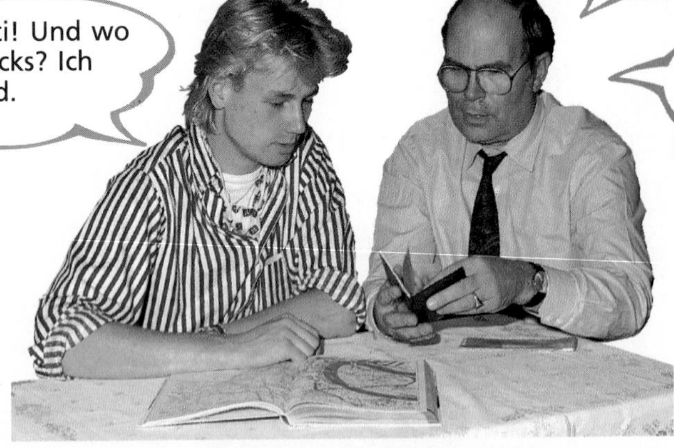

Vati, wo ist das Flugticket? Und der Reiseführer?
Peter, hier hab' ich den Pass, das Flugticket und den Reiseführer.
Prima! Danke, Vati! Und wo sind die Reiseschecks? Ich brauche auch Geld.
Stimmt. Hier sind die Reiseschecks. Hast du jetzt alles? Was brauchst du noch?

Wer ist Peter?

Peter Seber ist Amerikaner. Er ist 15 Jahre alt und wohnt in New York. Peters Vater ist aus Österreich, die Mutter aus Kalifornien.

Die Sebers haben Freunde in Deutschland, die Familie Nedel in Neuss. Peter besucht die Nedels. Er fliegt morgen nach Frankfurt und von dort weiter nach Köln.

A 8 Übung • Peter plant seine Reise

Peters Vater fragt:
Wo ist (sind) . . .?

Peter schaut nach, ob er alles hat:
Ich habe . . .

der Pass, das Flugticket, die Reiseschecks, die Spielkarten, die Kamera, die Musikkassetten, der Walkman, das Wörterbuch, der Film, der Reiseführer, das Adressbuch	die Kamera, den Walkman, den Pass, das Flugticket, den Film, die Spielkarten, das Wörterbuch, den Reiseführer, die Musikkassetten, das Adressbuch, die Reiseschecks

A 9 Übung • Etwas über Peter Seber

1. Wohin fliegt Peter Seber?
2. Was macht er in Deutschland?
3. Woher sind Peters Vater und Mutter?

A 10 WAS SUCHST DU? WEN FRAGST DU?

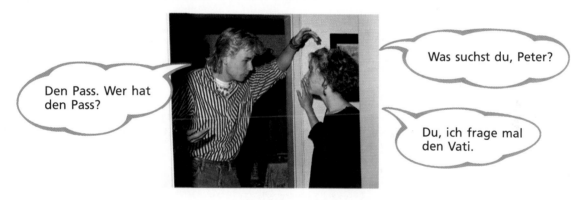

Was suchst du, Peter?
Den Pass. Wer hat den Pass?
Du, ich frage mal den Vati.

A 11 Übung • Wer hat was?

A: Wer hat . . .?

B: Du, ich frage mal . . .

Wörterbuch, Kamera, Adressbuch, Film, Walkman, Reiseschecks, Reiseführer, Flugticket	die Barbara, Frau Weiss, die Katja, den Vati, Herrn Hausmann, den Michael, den Lehrer, die Jungen

A 12 ERKLÄRUNG
The Definite Article, Nominative and Accusative Case

1. Peter asks his father **Wo ist das Flugticket? Und der Reiseführer?** The noun phrases **das Flugticket** and **der Reiseführer** function as subjects and are in the nominative case.
2. Peter's father responds **Hier hab' ich den Pass, das Flugticket und den Reiseführer.** In this sentence, the noun phrases function as direct objects and are in the accusative case.

	Noun Phrase as Subject (Nominative Case)			*Noun Phrase as Direct Object (Accusative Case)*		
Masculine		**der**	Pass?		**den**	Pass.
Feminine	Wo ist	**die**	Kamera?	Ich brauche	**die**	Kamera.
Neuter		**das**	Flugticket?		**das**	Flugticket.
Plural	Wo sind	**die**	Reiseschecks?	Ich brauche	**die**	Reiseschecks.

3. From this chart you can see that subject and direct object are clearly signaled only when the noun is masculine. The noun phrases that contain a feminine, a neuter, or a plural noun are identical when they function as subject or direct object.
4. There are a few masculine nouns that add the ending **-n** or **-en** when used in the accusative case. You have learned **der Herr, der Junge, der Klassenkamerad.**

   Ich frage Herr**n** Sperling. Er fragt den Junge**n.** Sie fragt den Klassenkamerad**en.**

5. There are many verbs that can take a direct object in the accusative case. You have learned the following: **besuchen, brauchen, finden, fragen, gewinnen, haben, hören, machen, sammeln, spielen, suchen, verlieren.**
6. You have been using the interrogative **wer?** and **was?** The accusative forms are **wen?** and **was?**

	Referring to people (one or many)	*Referring to things (one or many)*
Nominative	**wer?** *who?*	**was?** *what?*
Accusative	**wen?** *whom?*	**was?** *what?*

Peter fragt **den Vati.** **Wen** fragt er?
Peter sucht **den Pass.** **Was** sucht er?

A 13 Übung

Frag mal einen Mitschüler!

A: Was suchst du?
B: Den Pass.
A: Ach so!

A: Ich brauche den Pass.
B: Hier ist er.
A: Danke!

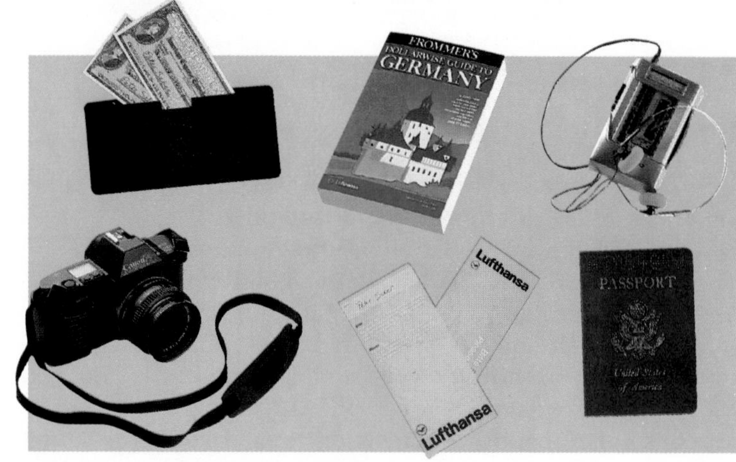

A 14 Übung • Wo hast du deine Sachen?

Frag mal eine Mitschülerin!

A: Wo hast du den Reiseführer?
B: Schau, er ist da!
A: Gut!

A: Du, wie findest du den Reiseführer?
B: Er ist prima.
A: Das finde ich auch.

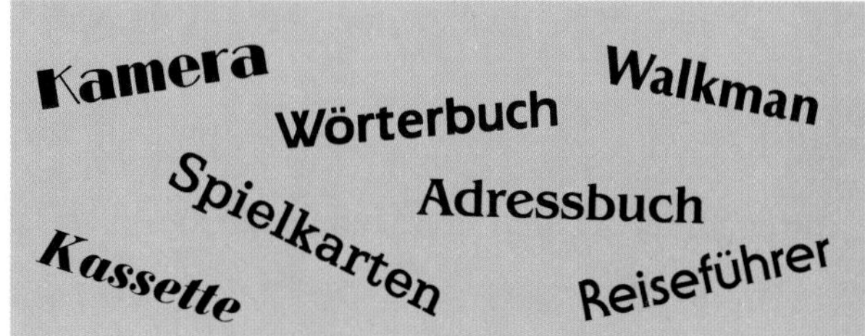

A 15 Übung • Wen suchst du?

A: Wen suchst du?
B: Ich suche Herrn Hausmann.

1. Herr Seber **2.** Frau Meier **3.** Jens **4.** Kristin 5. der Junge

A 16 Übung • Wen? oder Was?

A: Peter fragt die Inge.
B: Wie bitte? Wen fragt er?

A: Peter sucht den Pass.
B: Wie bitte? Was sucht er?

1. Peter sucht den Vater.
2. Peter sucht das Wörterbuch.
3. Peter braucht den Film.
4. Peter braucht den Lehrer.
5. Peter hat die Kamera.
6. Peter besucht die Nedels.
7. Peter fragt Frau Maier.
8. Peter sucht den Walkman.

A 17 Übung • Merkspiel *Memory Game*

Das Merkspiel heisst: Reisetasche packen

PETER In die Reisetasche packe ich: das Wörterbuch.
INGE In die Reisetasche packe ich: das Wörterbuch und den Reiseführer.
KATJA In die Reisetasche packe ich: das Wörterbuch, den Reiseführer und den Pass.
DU . . .

A 18 Übung • Beim Packen

Peter packt den Rucksack und die Reisetasche.

Was packt er in den Rucksack? Was packt er in die Reisetasche?

Film Adressbuch Reiseführer Spielkarten Kamera Walkman Kassetten Kuli Flugticket Taschenrechner Reiseschecks Wörterbuch D-Mark

A 19 Übung • Hör gut zu!

Is it the subject or the direct object? Listen.

	0	1	2	3	4	5	6	7	8	9	10
subject											
direct object	✓										

A 20 Übung • Im Flughafen

Du sprichst mit einem deutschen Schüler. Frag ihn oder sie:

1. woher er/sie ist
2. wohin er/sie fliegt
3. wann er/sie in . . . ist
4. was er/sie dort macht
5. wie lange er/sie dort bleibt
6. wann er/sie zurück nach Deutschland fliegt

A 21 Schreibübung • Gespräch im Flugzeug

Peter sitzt im Flugzeug. Er spricht mit einem deutschen Schüler. Was fragt der Schüler? Schreib den Dialog!

SCHÜLER . . .?
PETER Nach Frankfurt.
SCHÜLER . . .?
PETER Nein, ich fliege weiter nach Köln.
SCHÜLER . . .?
PETER Ich besuche Freunde in Neuss.
SCHÜLER . . .?
PETER Mit dem Auto.
SCHÜLER . . .?
PETER Um neun Uhr sind wir in Frankfurt.

Information für junge Reisende

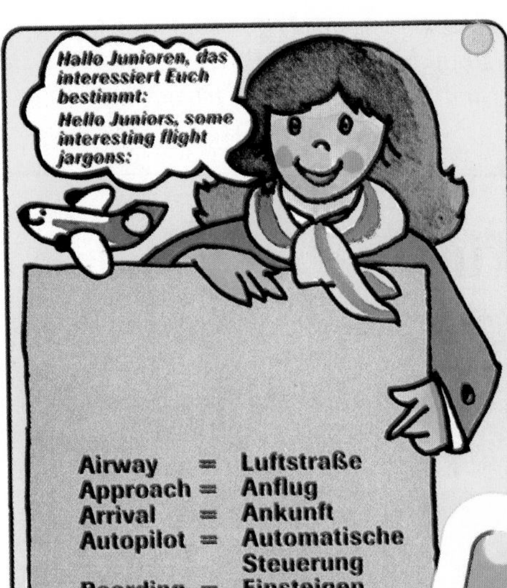

Hallo Junioren, das interessiert Euch bestimmt:
Hello Juniors, some interesting flight jargons:
Airway = Luftstraße
Approach = Anflug
Arrival = Ankunft
Autopilot = Automatische Steuerung
Boarding = Einsteigen
Cargo = Luftfracht
Climb = Steigflug
Duty free = Zollfrei
Exit = Ausgang
Purser = Chefsteward
Terminal = Abfertigungsgebäude

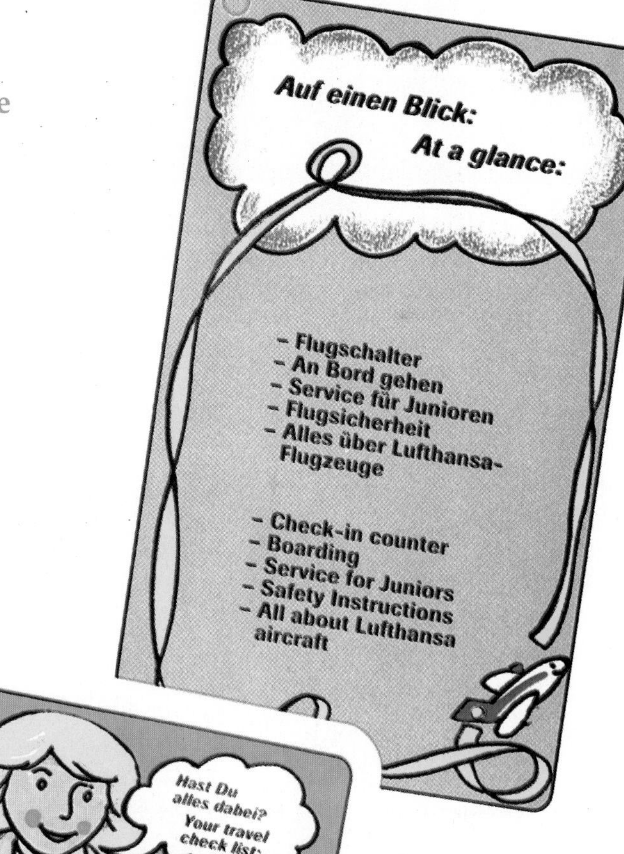

Auf einen Blick:
At a glance:
- Flugschalter
- An Bord gehen
- Service für Junioren
- Flugsicherheit
- Alles über Lufthansa-Flugzeuge
- Check-in counter
- Boarding
- Service for Juniors
- Safety Instructions
- All about Lufthansa aircraft

Hast Du alles dabei?
Your travel check list:
Paß, Flugticket, Gel
Kamera und Filme,
alles zum Anziehen,
Schuhe, Jacke, Mant
Sport-und Badesache
Passport, Ticket,
Money, Camera and
Films,
Clothing, Shoes, Jacket,
Coat and Sport and
Swimming gear.

Sicherheit Safety
Bei Start und Landung gilt: „Anschnallen" und „Nicht Rauchen". During take-off and landing please fasten your seat-belt and observe the No-smoking sign.

Airport Frankfurt
Frankfurt Main
Lufthansa
Die Lufthansa-Crew wünscht Dir einen guten Flug.
Lufthansa crew wishes you an enjoyable flight.
18 Millionen Fluggäste und 220 000 Starts und Landungen jährlich
Größter deutscher Flughafen
18 Million passengers and 220,000 take-offs and arrivals yearly
Largest german airport.

asking for information, giving directions

When you arrive abroad, you'll have to go through passport control, get your luggage, and go through customs. But even at an airport as big as Frankfurt's, it is easy to get around. There are signs that help you find most airport facilities, and if you don't find what you are looking for—well, you simply ask.

B1 Peter in Frankfurt

Das Flugzeug landet in Frankfurt. Die Reisenden gehen durch die Passkontrolle, sie holen das Gepäck und gehen durch den Zoll.

Ankunft / Arrivals
Nur für Fluggäste / Passengers only
Gepäckausgabe / Baggage Claim

BEAMTER	Den Pass, bitte!
PETER	Bitte!
BEAMTER	Wie lange bleiben Sie?
PETER	Vier Wochen.
BEAMTER	Gut. Und schöne Ferien!
PETER	Danke!

JULIA	Hast du alles?
PETER	Die Reisetasche fehlt.
JULIA	Schau, da ist sie!
PETER	Gott sei Dank!

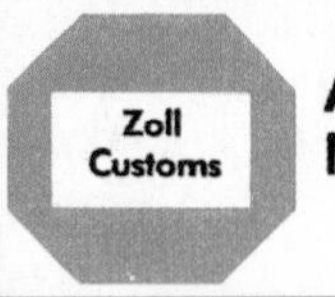

Anmeldefreie Waren
Nothing to declare

Anmeldepflichtige Waren
Goods to declare

Peter hat nichts zu verzollen. Er geht bei Grün durch.

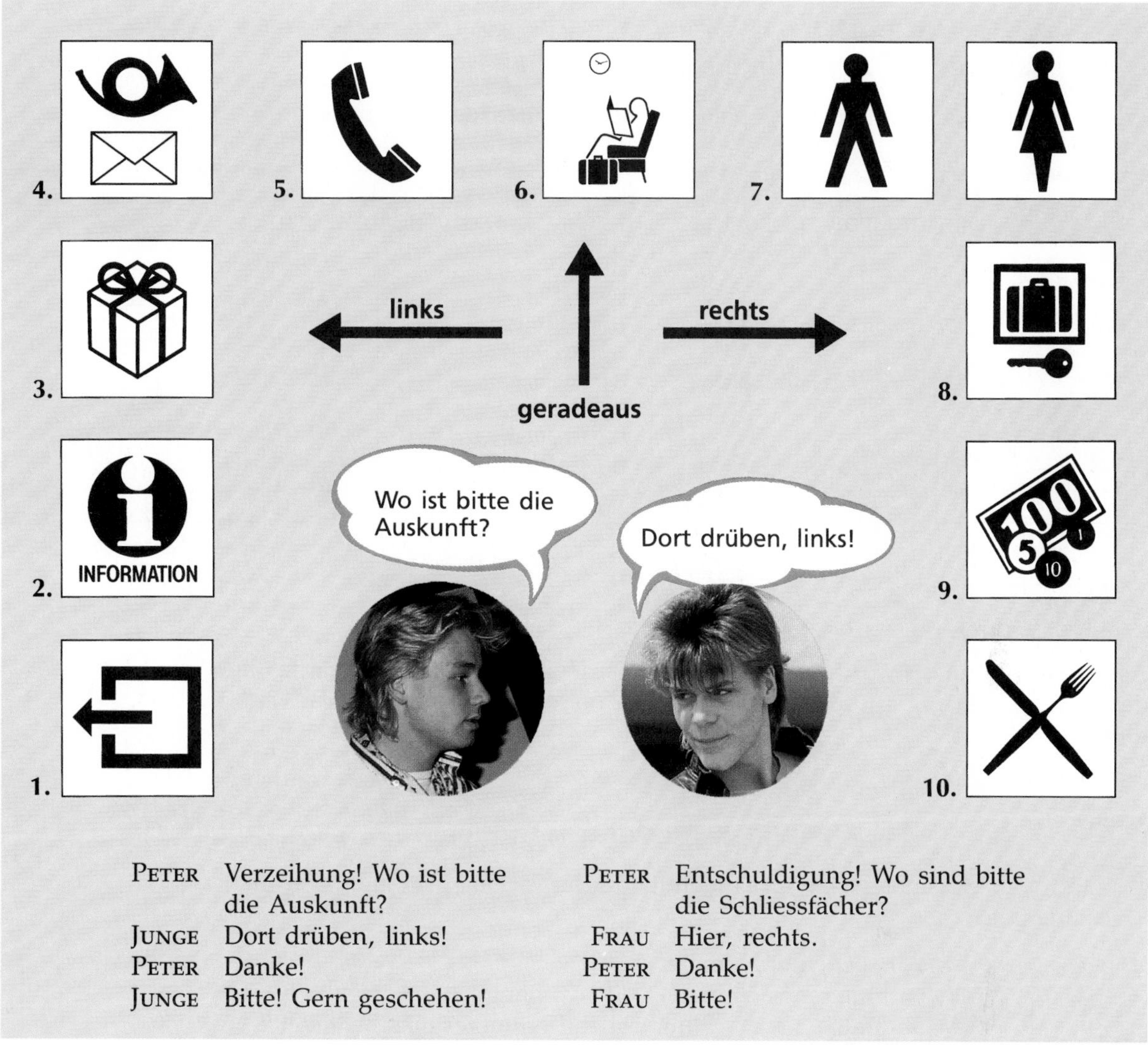

PETER	Verzeihung! Wo ist bitte die Auskunft?
JUNGE	Dort drüben, links!
PETER	Danke!
JUNGE	Bitte! Gern geschehen!

PETER	Entschuldigung! Wo sind bitte die Schliessfächer?
FRAU	Hier, rechts.
PETER	Danke!
FRAU	Bitte!

B2 Übung • Partnerarbeit

Team up with a classmate and practice asking and giving directions. Use the dialogs above and the words and phrases shown below.

was?

die Auskunft
die Toilette
das Telefon
der Ausgang
die Schliessfächer (pl)
die Wartehalle
die Post
das Restaurant
der Geschenkladen
die Bank

wo?

Da drüben.
Links.
Hier, rechts.
Dort drüben, links.
Da.
Hier.
Geradeaus.

B3 WIE SAGT MAN DAS?
Asking for and giving directions

When you ask for directions, it is polite to include **bitte** in the question.

ASKING FOR DIRECTIONS	GIVING DIRECTIONS	
	Hier!	Here!
	Da.	There.
Wo ist bitte das Telefon?	Hier, rechts!	Here, on the right!
	Da, links.	There, to the left.
Wo ist das Telefon, bitte?	Geradeaus.	Straight ahead.
	Da drüben. Dort drüben.	Over there.
	Dort drüben, rechts.	Over there, to the right.

B4 Übung • Wo ist . . .?

As you read off each word or phrase in the list in B3, a classmate indicates the direction by pointing appropriately. Then you point as your partner reads the direction word(s).

B5 Übung • Was bedeuten die Piktogramme?

You and your classmates take turns identifying the various pictograms on the preceding page.

A: Was bedeutet Nummer eins?
B: Nummer eins bedeutet „der Ausgang".
A: Stimmt! *or* Stimmt nicht! Nummer eins bedeutet . . .

B6 Übung • Was suchst du?

Referring to the pictograms on the preceding page, practice the following dialog with a classmate. Vary the directions.

A: Was suchst du?
B: Ich suche den Ausgang.
A: Dort drüben ist der Ausgang.
B: Danke!

B7 Übung • Rollenspiel

Turn your classroom into an airport. Draw pictograms on poster paper. Several students stand in different parts of the classroom, each holding up a pictogram. One student stands behind the information counter. Other students are travelers coming into the airport and asking directions.

B8 WAS SAGEN DIE REISENDEN? 

Ich suche die Auskunft.
Ich möchte etwas fragen.

Ich suche das Restaurant.
Ich möchte etwas essen und trinken.

Ich suche die Post. Ich möchte telefonieren und Briefmarken kaufen.

Ich suche die Bank. Ich möchte Geld wechseln.

Ich suche den Geschenkladen. Ich möchte ein Geschenk kaufen.

B9 Ein wenig Landeskunde

In Germany, the post office is also the telephone company. For this reason, telephones are located in all post offices, both inside and outside. You will recognize a post office by a plaque with the word **Postamt** printed below either a black eagle or a black posthorn, with a yellow background. All mail boxes and postal vehicles are painted yellow, the postal color. In Germany, the postal service as well as the railroad are owned and operated by the federal government.

B10 Übung • Was suchst du? 

Using the following dialog as a model and the signs above as cues, ask different classmates what they are looking for.

A: Was suchst du?
B: Die Post. Ich möchte telefonieren.
A: Schau! Dort drüben ist die Post.

B 11 ERKLÄRUNG
The möchte-*forms*

1. The **möchte**-forms express a wish, conveying the idea of "would like (to)."
2. **Möchte** has the following forms:

ich **möchte**	wir **möchten**
du **möchtest**	ihr **möchtet**
er, sie, es **möchte**	sie, Sie **möchten**

3. The **möchte**-forms are often used with another verb. In such sentences there are two verbs:
   a. The inflected verb, that is the verb form whose ending changes to match the subject. The inflected verb is always in the second position.
   b. The infinitive, which is always in last position.

	2nd Position		*Last Position*
Subject	*Inflected Verb*		*Infinitive*
Peter	**möchte**	Geld	**wechseln.**
Du	**möchtest**	ein Geschenk	**kaufen?**

B 12 Übung • Was möchten diese Leute machen?

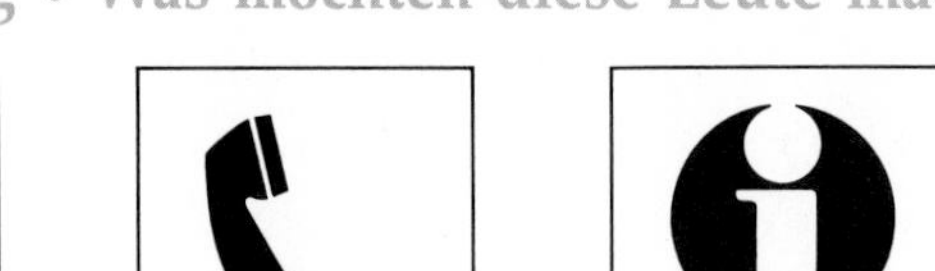

1. Wir . . .

2. Peter . . .

3. Die Jungen . . .

4. Ich . . .

5. . . . du . . .?

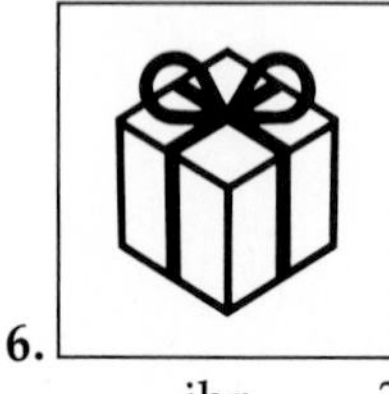
6. . . . ihr . . .?

7. Kristin . . .

8. Ich . . .

9. Wir . . .

10. . . . Sie . . .?

B 13 Übung • Hör gut zu!

What is each person looking for? Listen.

					INFORMATION			
A						1		
B						1		

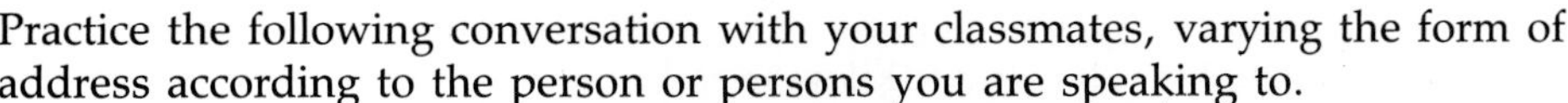

B 14 Schreibübung • Wo ist die Post?

Practice the following conversation with your classmates, varying the form of address according to the person or persons you are speaking to.

A: Peter! Was suchst du?
B: Ich suche die Post.
A: Möchtest du Briefmarken kaufen?
B: Nein, ich möchte telefonieren.

1. You are talking to Mrs. Meier.
2. Sabine and Antje are looking for the post office.
3. You are talking to your friend Paul.

Write dialogs modeled on the one above. First address your teacher; then address two friends of yours.

B 15 WIE KOMMT PETER NACH NEUSS?

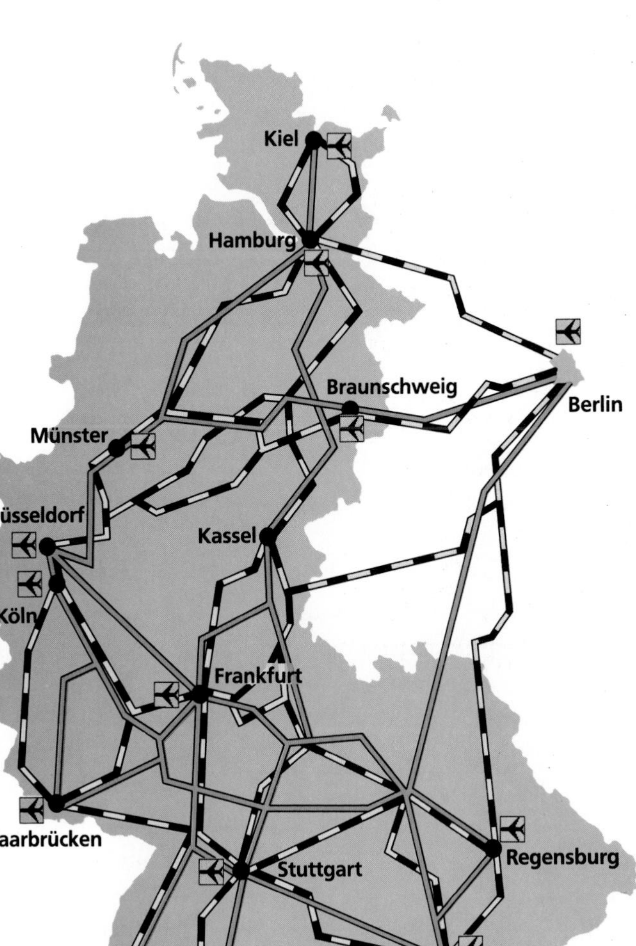

JULIA Wie kommst du nach Neuss, Peter?
PETER Von Frankfurt nach Köln mit dem Flugzeug und von Köln nach Neuss mit dem Auto.
JULIA Wie weit ist es von Frankfurt nach Köln?
PETER Moment mal! — Schau, 189 Kilometer! Das sind ungefähr 120 Meilen.

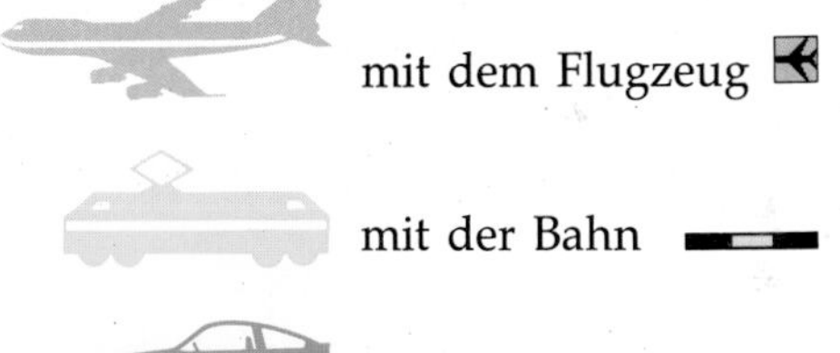

mit dem Flugzeug
mit der Bahn
mit dem Auto

Berlin	Düsseldorf	Frankfurt/M.	Hamburg	Kiel	Köln	München	Münster	Regensburg	Saarbrücken	Stuttgart	Kilometer
	572	555	289	370	569	584	466	499	745	624	**Berlin**
572		232	427	520	47	621	135	558	332	419	**Düsseldorf**
555	232		495	588	189	395	326	332	202	217	**Frankfurt/M.**
289	427	495		93	422	782	271	719	685	700	**Hamburg**
370	520	588	93		515	875	364	812	778	793	**Kiel**
569	47	189	422	515		578	150	515	289	376	**Köln**
584	621	395	782	875	578		715	120	431	220	**München**
466	135	326	271	364	150	715		652	426	513	**Münster**
499	558	332	719	812	515	120	652		505	289	**Regensburg**
795	332	202	685	778	289	431	426	505		226	**Saarbrücken**
624	419	217	700	793	376	220	513	289	226		**Stuttgart**

B 16 Ein wenig Landeskunde

In German-speaking countries, the metric system is used to measure distances. One measure of distance is the kilometer. To convert kilometers to miles, you divide the number of kilometers by 1.6.

eine Meile = 1,6 Kilometer
ein Kilometer = 0,62 Meilen

B 17 DIE ZAHLEN VON 20 BIS 1 000 

20 zwanzig	21 einundzwanzig	22 zweiundzwanzig	23 dreiundzwanzig	24 vierundzwanzig	
30 dreissig	31 einundreissig	40 vierzig	50 fünfzig	60 sechzig	70 siebzig
80 achtzig	90 neunzig	100 hundert	101 hunderteins	102 hundertzwei	103 hundertdrei
200 zweihundert	201 zweihunderteins	300 dreihundert	400 vierhundert	1000 tausend	

B 18 Übung • Lies die Zahlen!

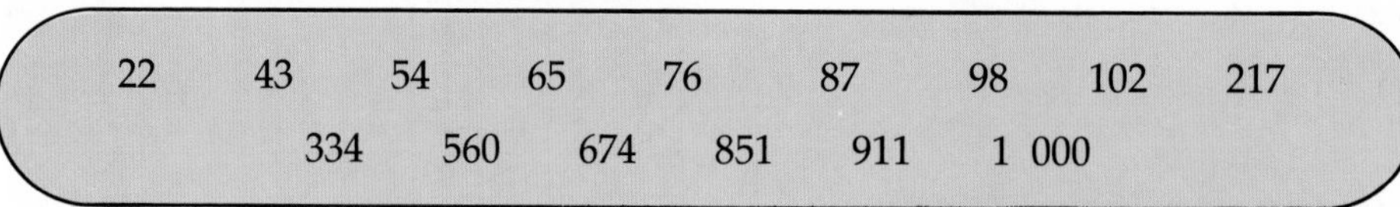

22 43 54 65 76 87 98 102 217

334 560 674 851 911 1 000

B 19 Übung • Jetzt bist du dran

1. Schau auf die Karte auf Seite 149! Wie kommst du zum Beispiel von Frankfurt nach Saarbrücken? Jetzt schau auf die Tabelle! Wie weit ist es von Frankfurt nach Saarbrücken?
2. Deine Klassenkameraden besuchen Freunde und Verwandte in anderen Städten. Wie kommen sie dorthin? Wie weit ist es? Frag sie mal!

SECTION C — exchanging money, making a phone call, and telling official time

Exchanging money, making a phone call—simple things can be a problem in a foreign country unless you know the procedures and have some knowledge of the language. Peter finds out what to do.

C1 Peter wechselt Geld

PETER Ich möchte 50 Dollar wechseln.
BANKANGESTELLTER Wieviel bitte?
PETER 50 Dollar.
BANKANGESTELLTER In D-Mark?
PETER Ja, bitte!
BANKANGESTELLTER Der Kurs ist heute DM 2,34.
PETER Nicht schlecht.
BANKANGESTELLTER Das sind 117 Mark.
PETER Danke!
BANKANGESTELLTER Bitte! Und schöne Ferien!
PETER Danke!

C2 DAS DEUTSCHE GELD

Es gibt Scheine:

ein 10-Mark-Schein

ein 20-Mark-Schein

ein 50-Mark-Schein

ein 100-Mark-Schein

und es gibt Münzen:

ein Pfennig

fünf Pfennig

ein Mark-Stück

ein 5-Mark-Stück

C3 Ein wenig Landeskunde

The German bank notes shown in C2 are the most common in circulation. There are also 500-Mark notes and 1000-Mark notes. The bills have different sizes and colors. When you exchange money, the amount of German marks you receive in exchange for your dollars depends on **der Kurs,** *the rate of exchange,* an amount that is fixed daily. For example, the exchange rate on a certain day may be DM 2,40—that means you will get 2 **Mark** and 40 **Pfennig** for each dollar you exchange. Before you exchange money, you can always check the exchange rate on boards posted at the entrance of every bank that has an exchange office. You can also check the rate of exchange in most newspapers.

USA

42-013/19 186

Devisenkurse

1,– US $ = DM 2,40 DM 1,– = 0,42 US $

US $	DM	US $	DM	DM	US $
0,05	0,12	30,–	72,–	0,10	0,04
0,10	0,24	40,–	96,–	0,20	0,08
0,15	0,36	45,–	108,–	0,50	0,21
0,25	0,60	80,–	192,–	1,–	0,42
0,50	1,20	95,–	228,–	2,–	0,83
1,–	2,40	120,–	288,–	5,–	2,08
1,50	3,60	150,–	360,–	10,–	4,17
2,–	4,80	180,–	432,–	20,–	8,33
2,50	6,–	200,–	480,–	50,–	20,84
3,–	7,20	230,–	552,–	100,–	41,67
4,–	9,60	400,–	960,–	150,–	62,51
5,–	12,–	450,–	1.080,–	200,–	83,34
7,50	18,–	800,–	1.920,–	250,–	104,18
10,–	24,–	1.000,–	2.400,–	300,–	125,01
20,–	48,–	5.000,–	12.000,–	400,–	166,68

Bitte berücksichtigen Sie, daß sich die Kurse kurzfristig ändern können.

Deutsche Bank

C4 Übung • Rollenspiel

You are the teller at the exchange window. Count out the money as you give it to each customer.

DM 132,00 Das sind zwei 50-Mark-Scheine, ein 20-Mark-Schein, ein 10-Mark-Schein, ein 2-Mark-Stück.

1. DM 78,60
2. DM 136,75
3. DM 286,94
4. DM 365,47

C5 Schreibübung • In der Bank

You want to exchange $100. Write out your conversation with the bank teller.

C6 TELEFONIEREN IST NICHT SCHWER

Telefonieren in Deutschland ist wirklich nicht schwer!
Du hebst den Hörer ab, steckst Münzen in den Apparat und wählst die Nummer. Das ist alles.

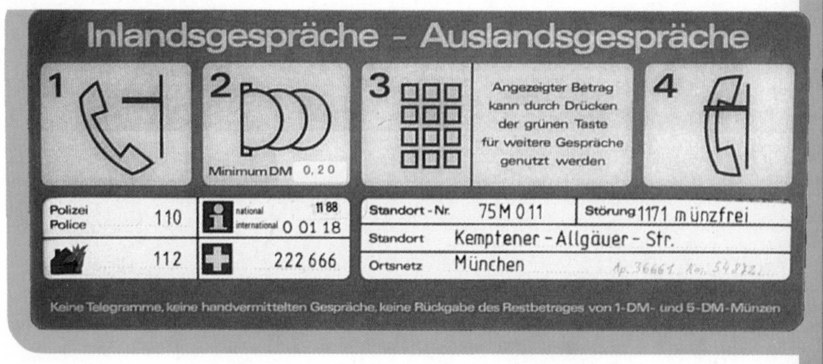

Aber manchmal . . .
sind alle Telefonzellen besetzt . . .

oder der Apparat
geht nicht

Endlich! Aber . . .

Peter versucht es noch einmal. (tüt, tüt, tüt)

PETER	0 3 4 3 1 6 4 2 3
FRAU NEDEL	Hier Nedel.
PETER	Ja, hier Peter Seber.
FRAU NEDEL	Du bist's, Peter! Wo bist du denn?
PETER	In Frankfurt. Im Flughafen.
FRAU NEDEL	Ach so! Und du bist um 13 Uhr 10 in Köln?
PETER	Ja, wie verabredet. Ich habe den Flug LH 368.
FRAU NEDEL	Gut! Wir sind pünktlich da. Bis gleich! Tschüs!
PETER	Auf Wiedersehen!
FRAU NEDEL	Auf Wiederhören!

C7 Übung • Stimmt! Stimmt nicht!

1. Peter ist in Köln.
2. Er ist im Flughafen.
3. Er telefoniert mit Wiebke Nedel.
4. Peter ist um zehn nach eins in Köln.

C8 Ein wenig Landeskunde

In German-speaking countries and in many other places in the world, the 24-hour system of telling time is used on official schedules. When you travel, it is important to know this system. The 24-hour system is based on 24 hours, starting with 1 A.M. One o'clock in the afternoon is **13 Uhr,** 2 P.M. is **14 Uhr,** 12 P.M. (midnight) is **24 Uhr.** For example, a plane departing at 19.30 **(neunzehn Uhr dreissig)** leaves at 7:30 P.M.

C9 Übung • Wann fliegst du?

Ask different classmates when their planes leave. Practice giving the time both ways.

A: Wann fliegst du?
B: Um halb sieben. *or*
Um achtzehn Uhr dreissig.

1. 

2. 

3. 

4. 

5. 

6. 15:50

7. 

8. 14:40

C10 Ein wenig Landeskunde

The German telephone system is fully automated, and it is very easy to make a telephone call from any public booth. Most public booths carry the sign **Inland/ Ausland,** *National/International,* and from here you can call all over the world. All you need is your access code for a particular country, the area code, and the phone number—and lots of coins because you have to "feed" the telephone. When calling within Germany, you need **die Vorwahlnummer,** *the area code,* of the city or area you are calling. Here are some area codes for big cities:

Berlin	030	Frankfurt	069	Köln	0221
Düsseldorf	0211	Hamburg	040	München	089

If you want to call the United States from Germany, you must dial the access code for the United States, your area code, and your phone number. The access code for the United States is 001.

C11 WIE SAGT MAN DAS?
Making a phone call

Here are some ways of beginning and ending a phone conversation:

the person who answers says	Nedel. Hier Nedel.
the person who is calling responds with	Hier Peter Seber. Hier ist Peter.
the conversation may end with	Auf Wiederhören! Tschüs! Bis gleich!

C12 Übung • Am Telefon

Ein Freund ruft an und sagt, wann er kommt.
Du hebst den Hörer ab und sagst:

A: Hier . . .
B: Ja, hier ist . . .
A: Du bist's . . .! Wann bist du in Chicago?
B: Um 14 Uhr 10.
A: Prima! Bis gleich! Tschüs!
B: Tschüs!

Du wohnst 1. in Chicago

2. in St. Louis

3. in Los Angeles

C13 WANN GEHT DER FLUG NACH KÖLN? 

Das ist der Monitor.

PETER Wann geht der Flug nach Köln? Ich habe Flugnummer LH 368.
AUSKUNFT Flug LH 368 nach Köln um 12 Uhr 40. Ausgang B 10.
PETER Danke!
AUSKUNFT Bitte sehr! Guten Flug!

C14 Übung • Rollenspiel

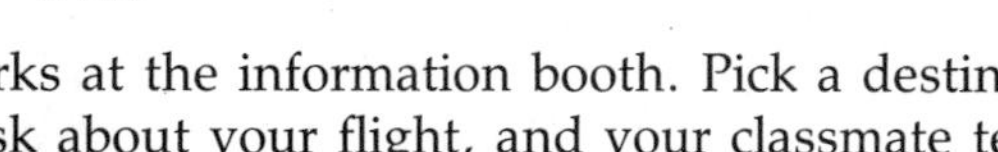

You are a traveler. A classmate works at the information booth. Pick a destination and a flight off the monitor. You ask about your flight, and your classmate tells you the time and the gate number.

C15 Übung • Hör gut zu! 

Which gate do you go to? Listen.

	17:10	18:30	15:15	16:45	16:05	17:45
Hamburg						
New York	A17					
Madrid						
Brüssel						
Paris						
Tel Aviv						

TRY YOUR SKILLS

using what you've learned

1 An der Auskunft

Ich heisse Silvia Friedrich. Ich bin hier in der Flughafen-Auskunft von Montag bis Freitag, von acht bis siebzehn Uhr. Manchmal bin ich auch am Wochenende da; dann habe ich ein oder zwei Tage in der Woche frei. Ich spreche Englisch und Französisch—ja, und ich beantworte viele Fragen. Manchmal sind die Fragen auch langweilig und blöd! Aber ich finde meine Arbeit gut.

Information
Ist heute Montag oder Dienstag?
Bin ich hier in Frankfurt oder in Stuttgart?
Ich heisse Meier. Und Sie?
Wie weit ist es von Frankfurt nach Stuttgart?
Ich brauche ein Taxi!
Wann geht der Flug nach Hamburg?

2 Übung • Rollenspiel

You are a clerk at the information desk. Your classmates are travelers. Respond to the following statements and questions. Then you and your classmates make up some questions and answers of your own.

—Ich möchte etwas essen.

—Ich möchte ein Geschenk kaufen.

—Wie weit ist es nach Hamburg?

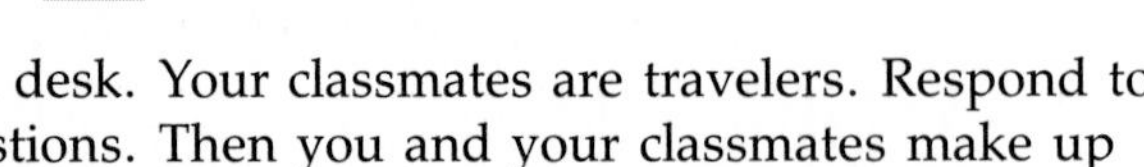
—Wann geht der Flug nach München?

—Wo ist die Toilette?

—Wie komme ich nach Hannover?

3 Übung • Geld wechseln

You are a clerk at the currency exchange window at the airport. Your classmates are tourists. Armed with a calculator and referring to the conversion table, you change money for them. The tourists are from different countries, so they will have different kinds of currency.

ANGESTELLTER	Wieviel Geld möchten Sie wechseln?
TOURIST	Hundert Dollar, bitte!
ANGESTELLTER	Hundert Dollar . . . das sind . . . Mark.

4 Übung • Am Telefon 

You arrive in Frankfurt and are going on to a different city. Check the train and plane schedules and call your friends to tell them how and when you will arrive.

A: Hier . . .
B: Hier ist . . .! Guten Tag!
A: Du bist's, . . .! Grüss dich! Wo bist du?
B: In Frankfurt.
A: Prima! Wann bist du in Stuttgart?
B: Ich komme mit dem Zug um . . . *or* Der Flug geht um . . . Uhr.
Ich bin um . . . in Stuttgart. Ich bin um . . . Uhr in Stuttgart.

Fahrplan 

von Frankfurt

nach	Hamburg	München	Stuttgart
ab an	10.24 14.56	10.21 14.03	10.45 12.51
ab an	11.24 15.56	10.50 15.10	11.03 13.27
ab an	12.24 16.56	11.21 15.24	11.45 13.51
ab an	12.41 17.46	12.21 16.03	12.45 14.51

Flugplan 

nach Hamburg

10.15–11.20	LH 764	727	Nonstop
10.40–11.40	PA 314	737	Nonstop
11.15–12.20	LH 763	727	Nonstop

nach München

10.40–11.35	LH 312	727	Nonstop
11.05–12.05	TW 164	737	Nonstop
11.40–12.35	LH 451	AB	Nonstop

nach Stuttgart

11.50–12.30	PA 328	727	Nonstop
12.40–13.25	LH 906	737	Nonstop
13.20–14.00	LH 455	AB	Nonstop

5 Schreibübung • An Bord

With a classmate, make up a conversation between two travelers on a flight to Germany. Then write down your dialog and act it out in front of the class.

6 Übung • Ach du Schreck!

While waiting for your connecting flight, you suddenly panic. Do you have everything? You had better check!

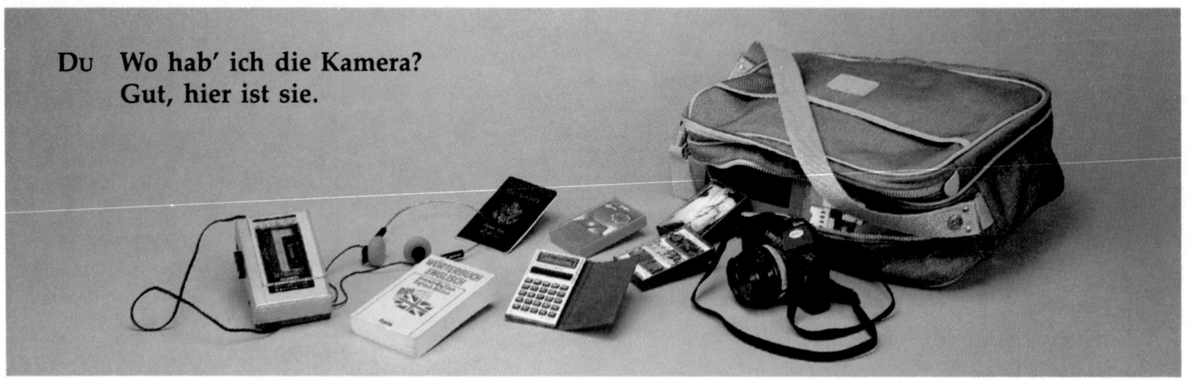

DU **Wo hab' ich die Kamera?**
Gut, hier ist sie.

7 Übung • Was passt zusammen?

1. Hast du alles?
2. Wann bist du in Köln?
3. Ich möchte Briefmarken kaufen.
4. Hier Schmidt.
5. Guten Flug!
6. Wann geht der Flug nach Köln?
7. Ich möchte Geld wechseln.
8. Bis gleich!
9. Wo bist du?

a. Auf Wiedersehen!
b. Danke!
c. Der Kurs ist heute gut.
d. Dort drüben ist die Post.
e. Im Flughafen.
f. Ja, hier Karin Braun.
g. Du, wo ist der Pass?
h. Morgen um 9.
i. Schau, da ist der Monitor!

8 Übung • Hör gut zu!

Where is each conversation taking place? Listen.

	0	1	2	3	4	5
im Flugzeug	✓					
an der Passkontrolle						
am Telefon						
an der Auskunft						
in der Bank						
im Geschenkladen						

9 Schreibübung • Ich möchte . . .

For each pictogram, write an exchange modeled on the one below.

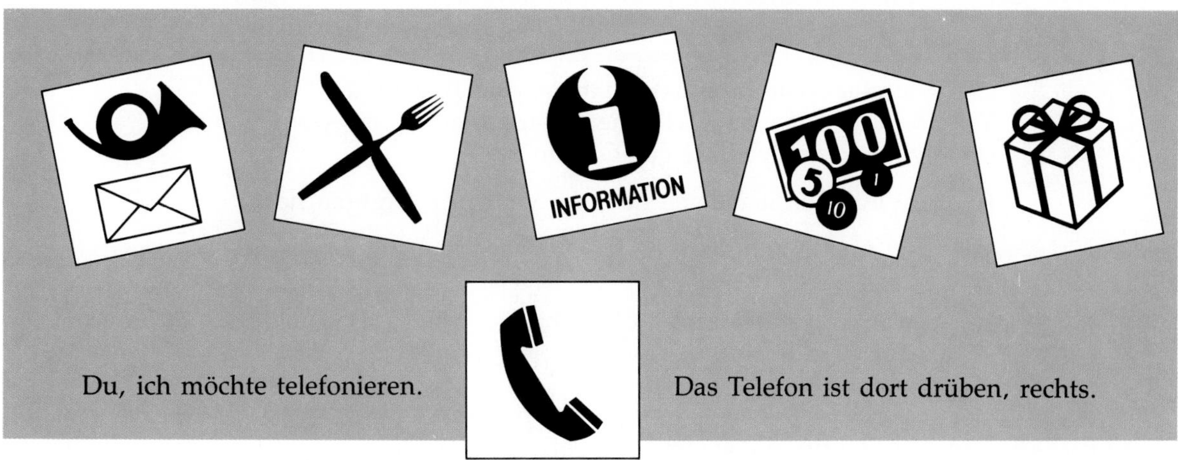

INFORMATION
100
5
10
Du, ich möchte telefonieren.
Das Telefon ist dort drüben, rechts.

10 Schreibübung • Was fragen die Leute?

You overheard the following responses. Now write an appropriate question for each one.

Nein, ich fliege weiter nach Wien.

Ich besuche Freunde.

Nach Hannover.

Vier Wochen.

Mit der Bahn.

Von Frankfurt nach Köln mit dem Flugzeug.

Nach Köln: 14.20, Ausgang B.

Nein, ich möchte Briefmarken kaufen.

Der Reiseführer ist prima.

Nach Hamburg sind es 220 Kilometer.

Dort drüben ist die Post.

Schau, da ist die Reisetasche!

Um halb neun.

11 Aussprache-, Lese- und Schreibübungen 

1. Listen carefully and repeat what you hear.

2. Listen, then read aloud.
1. schlecht, Fach, nichts, Woche, durch, Buch, manchmal, leicht, auch, möchte, nach
2. Junge, lange, Ausgang, Inge
3. ja, Jahr, Jens, jetzt, Junge
4. aus, Ausgang, Post, alles, nichts, etwas; Pass, essen, Schliessfach
5. sagen, suchen, seine, sieben, segeln, selten; Reise, besetzt, besuchen, lesen
6. vier, vor, von, viel, voll, Vati, Vater, Verwandte, verlieren

3. Copy the following sentences to prepare yourself to write them from dictation.
1. Der Junge ist sieben Jahre.
2. Ich besuche sie jetzt.
3. Jens und Inge lesen selten.
4. Suchst du auch den Ausgang?

WAS KANNST DU SCHON?

Let's review some important points you have learned in this unit.

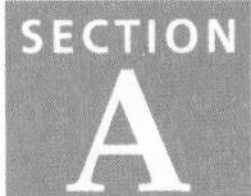

Can you give some information about your travel plans?
You are planning a trip. Tell where you are going, how long you are staying, and what you are going to do there.

Name at least ten items you need for your trip. Ich brauche . . .

You can't find any of these items. Ask the following people. Ich frage mal . . .

1. Vati **2.** Mutter **3.** Lehrer **4.** Herr Schmidt **5.** Junge **6.** Barbara

Can you identify pictograms in public places?
Ask directions to eight facilities in the airport.

Wo ist bitte die Auskunft? Wo ist . . .

Now give directions for finding each facility you named. Use different directions.

Die Auskunft ist dort drüben, rechts.

Can you use *möchten*?
Write the forms of **möchten** that go with the following subjects:

1. wir **2.** ich **3.** Peter **4.** ihr **5.** du **6.** Sie

Say that you would like to do five different things at the airport. Use the **möchte**-forms.

Can you say how you get from one place in Germany to another and give the distance?
Say you are going from Frankfurt to Stuttgart by plane, from Stuttgart to Munich by train, and from Munich to Regensburg by car. Tell how far it is.

Can you identify German money and exchange your dollars?
Name the German bills and coins: Es gibt . . .

Exchange $100. Write the conversation at the exchange window.

Can you answer the phone and say goodbye on the phone?
What do you say when you answer the phone? How do you say goodbye at the end of a phone conversation?

Do you know the two ways of expressing time?
Say what time it is in two ways:

1. 21.30 **2.** 23.15 **3.** 17.45 **4.** 16.05 **5.** 14.50

Do you know how to ask for flight information?
You are on flight number LH 348 to Cologne. Ask when it leaves.

WORTSCHATZ

SECTION A

das **Adressbuch, ⸚er** *address book*
alles *everything*
der **Amerikaner, -** *American* (person); er ist Amerikaner *he's an American*
auf nach . . . *off to . . .*
besetzt *occupied*
bleiben *to stay*
brauchen *to need*
der **Deutsche, -n** *German* (person)
die **Familie, -n** *family*
die **Ferien** (pl) *vacation;* Ferien machen *to go on vacation*
der **Film, -e** *(camera) film*
fliegen *to fly*
das **Flugticket, -s** *plane ticket*
fragen *to ask*
für *for*
das **Geld** *money*
Kalifornien *California*
die **Kamera, -s** *camera*
Köln *Cologne*
mal: ich frag' mal den Vati *I'll just ask Dad*
die **Maschine, -n** *plane*
morgen *tomorrow*
die **Mutter, ⸚** *mother*
nach *to*
noch *still*
ob *if, whether*
der **Pass, ⸚e** *passport*
planen *to plan*
die **Reise, -n** *trip*
der **Reiseführer, -** *travel guide*
der **Reisescheck, -s** *traveler's check*
schauen *to look;* Peter schaut nach *Peter checks*
seine *his*
die **Spielkarten** (pl) *cards*
suchen *to look for*
der **Vater, ⸚** *father*
der **Vati, -s** *dad*
der **Verwandte, -n** *relative*
voll *full*
von *from*
der **Walkman** *Walkman*
weiter *further, on*
wen? *whom?*
wie lange? *how long?*
die **Woche, -n** *week*
wohin? *to where?*
wohnen *to live*
zurück *back*

SECTION B

der **Ausgang, ⸚e** *exit*
die **Auskunft** *information*
die **Bahn: mit der Bahn** *by train*
die **Bank** *bank*
der **Beamte, -n** *official*
bei Grün *by the green symbol*
bitte! *here you are!*
das sind *that comes to*
durch *through*
essen *to eat*
etwas *something*
fehlen *to be missing*
das **Flugzeug, -e** *airplane*
gehen *to go*
das **Gepäck** *baggage*
geradeaus *straight ahead*
gern geschehen! *my pleasure!*
das **Geschenk, -e** *present*
der **Geschenkladen, ⸚** *gift shop*
Gott sei Dank! *thank God!*
gut *ok, good*
holen *to get, pick up*
kaufen *to buy*
der **Kilometer, -** *kilometer*
kommen nach *to get to*
landen *to land*
links *left, on the left*
die **Meile, -n** *mile*
möchten *would like to*
nichts *nothing*
die **Passkontrolle** *passport check*
die **Post** *post office*
rechts *right, on the right*
der **Reisende, -n** *traveler*
die **Reisetasche, -n** *travel bag*
das **Restaurant, -s** *restaurant*
sagen *to say*
das **Schliessfach, ⸚er** *locker*
schöne Ferien! *have a nice vacation!*
das **Telefon, -e** *telephone*
telefonieren *to telephone*
die **Toilette, -n** *restroom*
trinken *to drink*
ungefähr *approximately*
Verzeihung! *excuse me!*
verzollen *to declare at customs*
die **Wartehalle, -n** *waiting room*
wechseln *to exchange*
weit *far*
die **Zahlen von 20 bis 1000** see p 150
der **Zoll** *customs*
zu *to*

SECTION C

ach so! *oh, I see!*
alle *all*
alles *all*
der **Apparat, -e** *phone*
auf Wiederhören! *good-bye*
der **Bankangestellte, -n** *bank teller*
besetzt *busy* (a phone)
bis gleich *see you soon*
bitte sehr! *you're welcome!*
da: wir sind da *we'll be there*
die **D-Mark = Deutsche Mark** German monetary unit
denn: wo bist du denn? *where are you?*
das **deutsche Geld** *German money*
der **Dollar, -** *dollar*
du bist's *it's you*
endlich *finally*
es gibt *there is, there are*
der **Flug, ⸚e** *flight;* guten Flug! *have a good flight!*
der **Flughafen, ⸚** *airport*
gehen: der Apparat geht nicht *the phone is out of order*
heben: du hebst den Hörer ab *you lift the receiver*
hier Nedel *Nedel speaking*
der **Hörer, -** *telephone receiver*
im = in dem *in the*
in *into*
der **Kurs** *rate of exchange*
noch einmal *again, once more*
der **Pfennig, -** *penny*
pünktlich *on time, punctual*
der **Schein, -e** *bill* (money)
stecken *to stick, put*
das **Stück: ein 5-Mark-Stück** *a five-mark piece*
Telefonieren *telephoning*
die **Telefonzelle, -n** *phone booth*
verabredet: wie verabredet *as planned*
versuchen *to try*
wählen *to dial*
wie *as, like*
wieviel? *how much?*
wirklich *really*

ZUM LESEN

Köln am Rhein

Nedels holen den Peter am Flughafen in Köln ab°. „Jetzt fahren wir über den Rhein, Peter! Siehst du die Schiffe da unten°?"

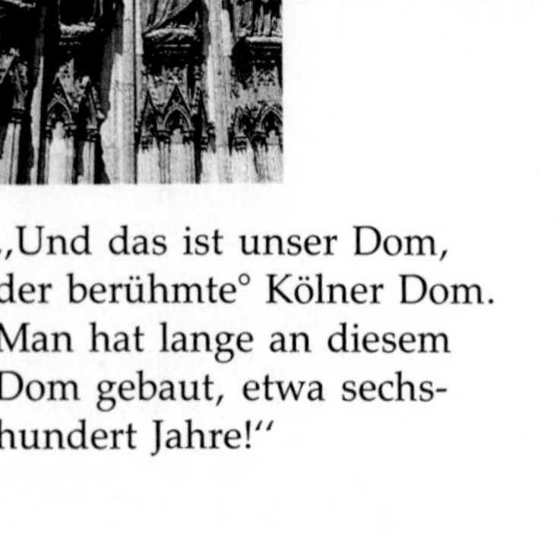

„Und das ist unser Dom, der berühmte° Kölner Dom. Man hat lange an diesem Dom gebaut, etwa sechshundert Jahre!"

„Was ist das?"

„Das ist Gross St. Martin, eine Kirche; sehr alt, um 1172."

---

holen ab *pick up* **da unten** *down there* **berühmt** *famous*

DAS RÖMISCHE NORDTOR
ERBAUT BEI GRÜNDUNG
DER COLONIE
50 nach CHR.
Der mittlere Torbogen trug
auf der Feldseite den Stadtnamen
C. C. A. A.
Colonia Claudia Ara Agrippinensium
Von den Seitenbögen ist einer 1971
hier wieder über den sichtbar
erhaltenen Resten von Tor und Mauer
aufgebaut worden.

„Siehst du das alte Tor dort drüben? Das haben die Römer gebaut, schon um 50 nach Christo°!"

„Und hier ist die Hohe Strasse—die Geschäftsstrasse° Kölns."

„Und dort rechts ist das Römisch-Germanische Museum! Da gehen wir mal hin!"

„Ja, Peter, Köln ist eine alte Stadt, zwei tausend Jahre alt. Köln hat heute fast° eine Million Einwohner°—es ist die viert grösste° Stadt in der Bundesrepublik, und es ist die grösste Stadt am Rhein."

---

nach Christo *A.D.* **Geschäftsstrasse** *shopping street* **fast** *almost* **Einwohner** *inhabitant* **viert grösste** *fourth biggest*

Ein kleines Missverständnis

Gabi Sauer is going to the airport to meet an American exchange student. Look at the title of the story. What do you think happens? Here is a clue: the word **Verständnis** comes from **verstehen,** *to understand*. The prefix **Miss-** is the same as *mis-* in English. Read the story and see how much you understand.

Heute nachmittag wollen Bärbel Wegener und Gabi Sauer zum Flughafen fahren. Die Wegeners erwarten einen jungen Amerikaner, einen Brieffreund von Bärbels Bruder Werner. Aber um halb eins klingelt bei Gabi das Telefon.

„Gabi, hier ist die Bärbel. Grüss dich!"

„Grüss dich, Bärbel! Was gibt's?"

„Du, Gabi, kannst du allein zum Flugplatz fahren? Ich kann nicht, ich bin krank."

„Was? Ich?—Der Amerikaner kommt zu euch! Und ich weiss nicht, wie der junge Mann aussieht."

„Du, das ist einfach: er ist gross, er hat schwarzes Haar. Er schreibt, er kommt mit einem roten Rucksack."

„O.K. Und wie heisst er?"

„Will Baden. Er ist aus Denver. Du, und die Maschine ist um 14.30 in München."

„Na, gut, Bärbel. Ich finde deinen Amerikaner schon. Tschüs!"

„Ja, bis später!"

Gabi ist im Flugplatz. Es ist Viertel nach zwei. Sie wartet dort, wo die Reisenden durch den Zoll kommen.—Ah! Da ist er. Ein grosser Junge, der Will Baden. Ja, das ist er—der grosse, rote Rucksack!

„Will Baden?"

„Ja. Guten Tag!"

„Grüss dich! Ich bin die Gabi. Ich bin Bärbels Freundin. Die Bärbel kann nicht kommen, und der Werner ist auch nicht da."

„Das ist schade. Aber prima, dass du da bist!—Du, ich möchte Geld wechseln. Ich brauche D-Mark."

„Komm, ich habe Geld. Dein Geld kannst du später wechseln. Dort drüben ist ein Taxi!"

Die beiden sitzen im Taxi. Der junge Amerikaner ist sehr nett, denkt Gabi.

„Denver ist eine schöne Stadt."
„Denver? Ja, ich weiss nicht."
„Du kommst doch aus Denver, ja?"
„Ich? Nein, ich komme aus Chicago."
„Chicago? Aber die Bärbel sagt, du kommst aus Denver."
„Wer ist Bärbel?"
„Die Bärbel Wegener. Du besuchst doch die Familie Wegener."
„Ich weiss nicht, wer die Familie Wegener ist."
„Ja, sag, bist du denn der Will Baden?"
„Nein. Ich heisse Bill Barton. Und ich komme aus Chicago und besuche die Familie Krause hier in München."
„Ach, du meine Güte!—Fahren Sie bitte zurück zum Flugplatz!"

In der Wartehalle steht ein grosser Junge: schwarze Haare, Brille—und da ist ein grosser, roter Rucksack! Der Junge hat ein Schild in der Hand: Will Baden. Im selben Augenblick hört man über den Lautsprecher: „Bill Barton bitte zur Auskunft kommen. Ein Fräulein Krause wartet hier auf Sie!"

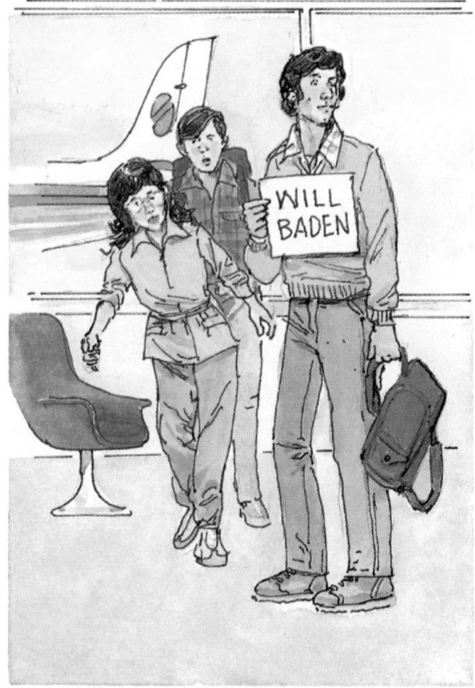

Ende gut, alles gut!

Übung • Hast du die Geschichte verstanden?

1. Whom is Gabi supposed to meet? Will Baden or Bill Barton?
2. What is the point of this story—Gabi goes to the wrong airport or Gabi thinks that Bill Barton is Will Baden?
3. Why is the last line „Ende gut, alles gut"? Is it because Gabi returns to the airport and finds her friend's real pen pal or because Bill Barton's pen pal is named Bärbel Wegener?
4. Which passages in the story give you clues that there might be a misunderstanding?

Übung • Stimmt! Stimmt nicht!

1. Die Deutschen sprechen Will Baden aus wie Bill Barton.
2. Die beiden Jungen sind gross und blond.
3. Die zwei sind Amerikaner.
4. Die beiden kommen aus Denver.
5. Sie besuchen deutsche Familien.

Übung • Wer ist wer?

Who's who in this story? Identify these people and say a little about each one.

1. Gabi   2. Bärbel   3. Will Baden   4. Bill Barton

KAPITEL 6

Bei den Nedels

The arrival of an exchange student from the United States is a big occasion. Germans are very interested in other countries and cultures and they love to travel. The United States has an especially great influence on Germany. It is most obvious in the language, dress, music, and television programs. Many people are critical of this influence. What influence has Germany had on the United States? What about the influence of other cultures on the United States?

In this unit you will:

SECTION A	introduce someone, introduce yourself and members of your family
SECTION B	talk about the rooms in your home
SECTION C	discuss appearance and personal characteristics
TRY YOUR SKILLS	use what you've learned
ZUM LESEN	read for practice and pleasure

introducing someone, introducing yourself

When you visit new places, you also meet new people. How are you introduced and what do you say? How do you introduce yourself? When Peter arrives in Neuss, many of the Nedels' family and friends are waiting to meet him.

A1 Freunde und Verwandte

HERR NEDEL So, Peter, wir sind da. Jetzt lernst du viele Leute kennen. Armer Peter!
PETER Ach, das ist nicht so schlimm.

WIEBKE Peter, das sind meine Grosseltern—Herr und Frau Graf—mein Opa, meine Oma.
PETER Guten Tag, Frau Graf! Guten Tag, Herr Graf!
HERR GRAF Willkommen in Neuss!
PETER Danke!

WIEBKE Mein Onkel und meine Tante, Jürgen und Christa Wolf.
PETER Guten Tag!

WIEBKE Das sind meine Geschwister—mein Bruder Philipp und meine Schwester Ulrike.
PETER Hallo, Philipp! Wie geht's?
PHILIPP Schön, dass du da bist.

Und das ist mein Hund, der Beppo.

WIEBKE Das ist mein Vetter Julian.
PETER Tag, Julian!

WIEBKE Und meine Kusine Alice, die Ali.
PETER Guten Tag, Ali!

A2 Übung • Wer ist wer?

1. Jürgen Wolf ist	der Julian.
2. Herr und Frau Graf	der Hund.
3. Wiebkes Bruder	ein Klassenkamerad.
4. Beppo, so heisst	ein Onkel von Wiebke.
5. Philipp und Ulrike sind	eine Klassenkameradin.
6. Wiebkes Vetter ist	heisst Monika.
7. Jochen ist	heisst Philipp.
8. Wiebkes Freundin	sind die Grosseltern.
9. Markus ist ein Freund	von Wiebke.
10. Und die Antje ist	Wiebkes Geschwister.

A3 WIE SAGT MAN DAS?
Introducing someone, introducing yourself

These are some informal ways of introducing someone, and of introducing yourself. When being introduced, you respond by saying hello.

introducing someone	Peter, das ist mein Onkel, Herr Wolf.
introducing yourself	Ich heisse Markus. Ich bin ein Freund von Wiebke. Ich bin die Alice, Wiebkes Kusine.
responding to an introduction	Guten Tag, Frau Graf! Hallo, Philipp! Grüss dich, Antje! Wie geht's?

A4 Übung • Wer ist das?

1. Tell who is who in Wiebke's family. Tell how each of the following people are related to Wiebke: Herr Nedel, Frau Nedel, Alice, Christa Wolf, Julian, Herr und Frau Graf, Jürgen Wolf, Philipp, Ulrike.

   Herr Nedel ist der Vater von Wiebke.
   Frau Nedel ist . . .

2. Introduce Wiebke's friends and mention if they are classmates, friends, or both.

   Das ist Jochen. Er ist . . .

A5 Übung • Jetzt bist du dran

1. Introduce yourself to some of your classmates. Say that you are a friend or a classmate of some other student.

   A: Ich heisse . . .; ich bin ein/eine . . . von . . .
   B: Tag, . . .! Wie geht's?

2. Introduce different classmates to each other and mention whose friend or classmate he or she is.

   A: Das ist . . ., ein Freund/eine Freundin von . . .
   B: Grüss dich, . . .!

A6 ERKLÄRUNG
ein *and* mein, *Nominative Case Forms*

1. The word **ein,** *a, an,* is called the indefinite article. The indefinite articles corresponding to **der, die,** and **das** are **ein, eine,** and **ein.** Before a masculine and a neuter noun, the form is **ein;** before a feminine noun, **eine.** There is no plural form of **ein.**

Masculine	Markus ist	**der** / **ein**	Freund von Wiebke.
Feminine	Antje ist	**die** / **eine**	Klassenkameradin.
Neuter	Monika ist	**das** / **ein**	Mädchen aus Köln.
Plural	Antje und Jochen sind	**die** / —	Klassenkameraden von Wiebke.

2. The words **mein** and **meine,** *my,* are called possessives. Their endings are the same as those of the indefinite articles. The possessives, however, have plural forms. You will learn other possessives later.

Masculine	**der**	**ein**	**mein**
Feminine	**die**	**eine**	**meine**
Neuter	**das**	**ein**	**mein**
Plural	**die**	—	**meine**

A7 Übung • Kennst du Wiebkes Klassenkameraden?

A: Wer ist der Jochen?
B: Der Jochen ist ein Klassenkamerad von Wiebke.

1. Wer ist die Antje?
2. Wer sind Antje und Jochen?
3. Wer ist der Jochen?
4. Wer ist die Monika?
5. Wer sind Monika und Markus?

A8 Übung • Wiebke stellt ihre Familie und Freunde vor

A: Wer ist Frau Nedel?
B: Das ist meine Mutter.

1. Wer ist Herr Nedel?
2. Wer sind Herr und Frau Graf?
3. Wer ist Ali?
4. Wer ist Julian?
5. Wer ist Philipp?
6. Wer ist Jürgen Wolf?
7. Wer ist Ulrike?
8. Wer ist Christa Wolf?

A9 Übung • Deine Familie

Draw a sketch depicting the members of your immediate family. Now introduce each family member to the class, pointing to the corresponding figure.

Das ist meine Mutter, Frau . . .; Das ist mein Bruder.
Er heisst . . . Er ist . . . Jahre alt.

A10 Schreibübung • Meine Klassenkameraden

Pick ten people in your class and write a sentence introducing each one:

Das ist . . ., ein Freund von . . .,
or ein Junge/ein Mädchen aus . . .

SECTION B

talking about your home

Wiebke shows Peter around the house. How does Peter like it? What does he say? How do you like the Nedels' home?

B1 Peter findet das Haus toll!

PETER Du, Wiebke, ich finde das Haus toll!
WIEBKE Ja, wirklich?
PETER Es ist gross, modern . . . Wieviel Zimmer habt ihr?
WIEBKE Möchtest du das Haus sehen?
PETER Ja, gern.
WIEBKE Komm! Ich zeig es dir.

WIEBKE Wir haben sechs Zimmer, eine Küche, . . .
PETER Wie modern sie ist!

WIEBKE Ein Wohnzimmer . . .
PETER Es sieht so gemütlich aus!
WIEBKE Findest du?
PETER Ja, sehr gemütlich!

WIEBKE Ein Esszimmer, . . .

WIEBKE Ein Bad und zwei Toiletten, eine unten und eine oben.
PETER So gross und hell!

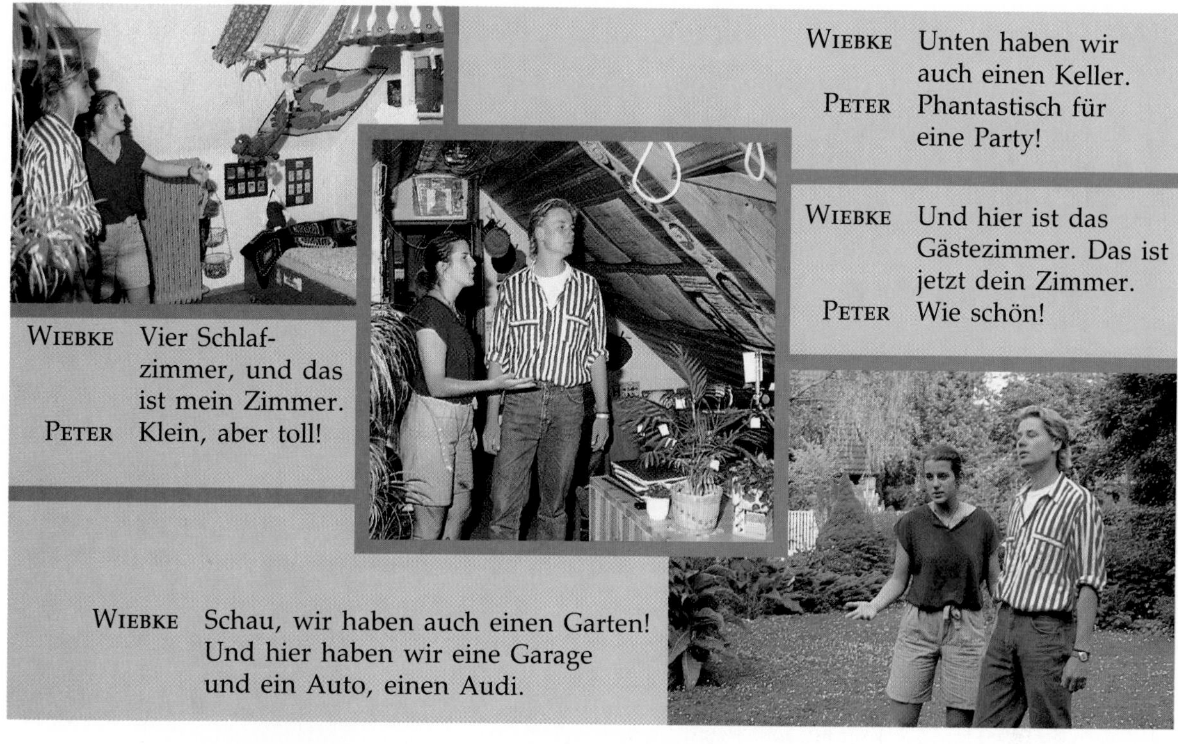

WIEBKE Unten haben wir auch einen Keller.
PETER Phantastisch für eine Party!
WIEBKE Vier Schlafzimmer, und das ist mein Zimmer.
PETER Klein, aber toll!
WIEBKE Und hier ist das Gästezimmer. Das ist jetzt dein Zimmer.
PETER Wie schön!
WIEBKE Schau, wir haben auch einen Garten! Und hier haben wir eine Garage und ein Auto, einen Audi.

B2 Übung • Wie sieht Nedels Haus aus?

Wieviel Zimmer hat das Haus? Was sagt Wiebke?

B3 WIE SAGT MAN DAS?

Complimenting and responding to a compliment

complimenting	Ich finde das Haus toll! Das Wohnzimmer sieht gemütlich aus.	I think your house is great! The living room looks cozy!
responding to compliments	Ja, wirklich? Findest du?	Really? (You think so?) You think so?

How would you compliment someone in English? How would you respond to a compliment?

B4 Ein wenig Landeskunde

When somebody compliments you, you usually say thank you. In German-speaking countries the reaction to a compliment is quite different. German-speakers will either respond with another question—**Findest du?** or **Meinst du?**—or they will downplay the compliment. For example, a typical German response to the comment "I find this room very cozy" would be "Yes, but it really needs new wallpaper."

B5 Übung • Rollenspiel—Partnerarbeit

You are Wiebke and your classmate is Peter. Wiebke shows Peter around the house.

A: Hier ist die Küche.
B: Wie schön!
A: Ja, wirklich?

A: Wir haben eine Küche.
B: So gross und hell!
A: Findest du?

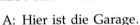

Wie modern! Klasse! *Wie schön (sie) ist!* Toll! So gemütlich. Phantastisch für eine Party. Prima! Wie gross (sie) ist! So gross und so hell.

B6 ERKLÄRUNG
Indefinite Articles, Accusative Case

On page 170 you learned the nominative forms of the indefinite article. You use nominative forms when the noun phrase functions as the subject of a sentence. Listed below are the accusative forms of the indefinite article. You use accusative forms when the noun phrase functions as the direct object of a sentence.

		Nominative		*Accusative*
Masculine *Feminine* *Neuter*	Da ist	**ein** Garten. **eine** Küche **ein** Bad.	Wir haben	**einen** Garten. **eine** Küche. **ein** Bad.
Plural	Da sind	vier Zimmer.	Wir haben	vier Zimmer.

B7 Übung • Und was habt ihr?

A: Hier ist die Garage.
B: Wir haben auch eine Garage.

1. Hier ist der Garten.
2. Hier ist das Esszimmer.
3. Hier ist der Keller.
4. Hier ist die Garage.
5. Hier ist das Auto.
6. Hier ist der Audi.

B8 Übung • Schüler erzählen

Draw a simple floor plan of your house or apartment, or make up a floor plan. With the help of your drawing, explain to a classmate what rooms you have. For example:

„Wir haben ein Haus. Es hat vier Zimmer. Wir haben ein Wohnzimmer, ein Esszimmer, eine Küche, zwei Schlafzimmer, ein Bad, eine Toilette, einen Keller und eine Garage. Das Wohnzimmer ist gross und gemütlich, die Schlafzimmer sind klein, die Küche ist hell und modern und . . ."

B 9 Übung • Und du? Wie steht's mit dir?

Was habt ihr? Erzähl mal!

wir haben eine Wohnung ein Haus	Schlafzimmer Wohnzimmer Esszimmer Küche Bad Toilette Keller Garten Garage Auto	. . . ist schön gross, klein hell modern gemütlich nicht (gross) toll! prima! Klasse!

B 10 Schreibübung

Write a paragraph describing where you live, or describing some other place you know. What kind of house or apartment is it? How many rooms are there? What are they? What are they like? You may refer to the list above and the narration in B8.

B 11 PETER HAT FÜR ALLE NEDELS EIN GESCHENK 

Peter packt den Rucksack aus. Alle Nedels bekommen ein Geschenk.

PETER Hier ist eine Halskette für die Wiebke.
WIEBKE Toll! Vielen Dank, Peter!
PETER Nichts zu danken!

PETER Und hier hab' ich einen Taschenrechner für den Philipp.
PHILIPP Mensch, prima! Tausend Dank!

PETER Und da ist ein Buch für die Ulrike.
ULRIKE Danke, Peter!
PETER Bitte schön!

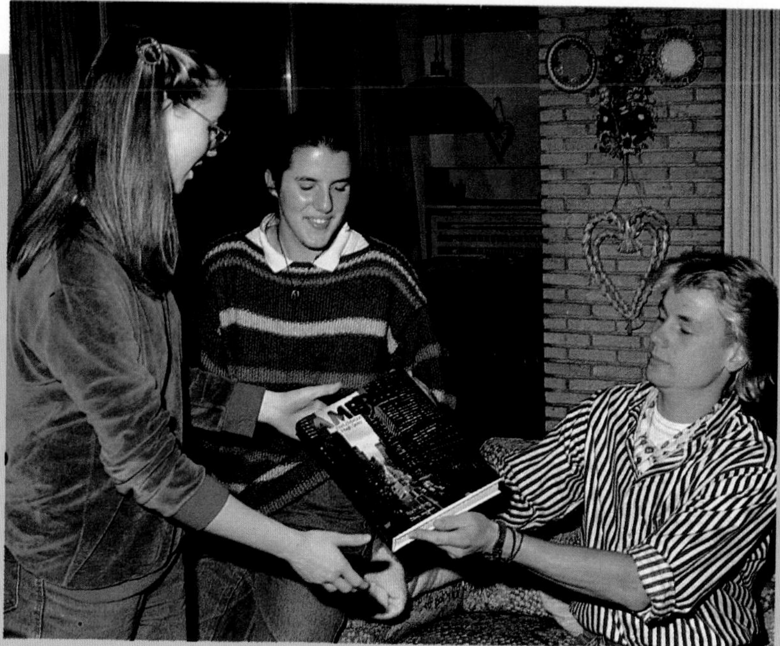

Da steht noch mehr auf Peters Zettel!

B 12 Übung • Mix-Match

1. Peter packt	Dank!
2. Alle Nedels bekommen	den Rucksack aus.
3. Da ist eine Halskette	ein Buch.
4. Und für den Philipp	ein Geschenk.
5. Die Ulrike bekommt	ein Taschenrechner.
6. Peter, tausend	für die Wiebke.
7. Bitte	schön!
8. Nichts	zu danken.

B 13 ERKLÄRUNG
The Preposition für

The preposition **für** is always followed by accusative case forms.

		Accusative	
Masculine *Feminine* *Neuter* *Plural*	Das Geschenk ist für	**den** Philipp. **die** Wiebke. **das** Mädchen. **die** Grosseltern.	
	Für	**wen**	ist das Geschenk?

B 14 Übung • Peter hat noch mehr Geschenke 

Hier ist Peters Zettel. Wer bekommt was?

Kassette / Sabine
Buch / Herr Graf
Münze / Ali
Briefmarken / Hartmut
Kuli / Wiebke
Spielkarten / Philipp

Hier ist eine Kassette für die Sabine.
Hier ist . . .

B 15 Schreibübung • Was sagt Peters Mutter?

Peter's mother gave him the note above to remind him who all the presents were for. Write what she said as she handed him the note.

Die Kassette ist für die . . .

B 16 WIE SAGT MAN DAS?
Saying thank you and you're welcome

You have learned to say thank you and you're welcome when shopping and when asking for information—for example, when asking for directions. Here are some more ways of expressing gratitude. These are appropriate to use when you receive a present.

saying thank you	Danke! Tausend Dank! Vielen Dank!	Thanks. Thanks a million. Thanks a lot.
responding to a thank you	Bitte schön! Nichts zu danken.	You're welcome. Don't mention it.

B 17 Übung • Für wen sind die Geschenke?

Du hast auch Geschenke für die Nedels. Für wen sind sie?

A: Hier ist ein Buch für die Ulrike.
B: Vielen Dank!
A: Bitte schön!

or

A: Hier hab' ich eine Kassette für den Philipp.
B: Tausend Dank!
A: Nichts zu danken.

B 18 Übung • Hör gut zu!

Which conversation are you overhearing? Listen.

	0	1	2	3	4	5	6
Wiebke showing Peter the house							
Peter distributing gifts	✓						

SECTION C

talking about appearance and personal characteristics

At the gathering for Peter, Wiebke and her friends are talking. Do you agree with their opinions? What do you think?

C1 Kennst du Wiebkes Freunde?

Die Antje ist klein, blond, schlank. Sie ist sehr hübsch.

MARKUS Die Antje ist so attraktiv.
JOCHEN Das ist Geschmackssache. Ich finde sie nicht unsympathisch.
MARKUS Wirklich?

Das ist der Markus. Er ist gross, dunkel, er hat eine Brille.

ALI Der Markus sieht gut aus, nicht?
ANTJE Ja, das stimmt. Und er ist auch gar nicht arrogant.
ALI Meinst du?

Der Jochen ist dunkelblond.

ANTJE Mensch, ist der Jochen langweilig!
WIEBKE Was?! Das finde ich nicht. Ich finde ihn nett.
ANTJE Nett, ja—aber langweilig!
WIEBKE Das stimmt nicht!

Die Monika ist brünett.

PHILIPP Die Monika ist sehr freundlich, meinst du nicht?
JOCHEN Du hast recht. Sie ist lustig, und ich finde sie sehr sympathisch.
PHILIPP Ich auch.

C2 Übung • Wer sind Wiebkes Freunde? Wie sehen sie aus?

1. Wer ist Markus? Wie sieht er aus?
2. Wer ist Antje? Wie sieht sie aus?
3. Und wie sieht die Monika aus?
4. Und der Jochen?

C3 WIE SAGT MAN DAS?
Talking about appearance

To describe how someone looks, you can use the verb **aussehen,** *to look, to look like.*

Wie sieht er aus?	What does he look like?
Er sieht gut aus.	He is good-looking.
Er ist gross und schlank.	He is tall and slim.

C4 Übung • Und du?

1. Wie heissen deine Freunde?
2. Wie alt sind sie?
3. Wie sehen sie aus?

C5 ERKLÄRUNG
The Verb aussehen

The verb **aussehen,** *to look (like),* is a verb with a prefix. The prefix **aus-** is often separated from the verb and is placed at the end of the sentence. The verb **aussehen** also has a vowel change in the **du-** and **er/sie-**forms.

Singular				*Plural*			
Ich	**sehe**	gut	**aus.**	Wir	**sehen**	gut	**aus.**
Du	**siehst**			Ihr	**seht**		
Markus (er)	**sieht**			Die Geschwister (sie)	**sehen**		
Antje (sie)	**sieht**						
Sie	**sehen**			Sie	**sehen**		

C6 Übung • Frag, wie alle aussehen!

A: Kennst du den Thomas?
B: Wie sieht er aus?

1. Kennst du die Wiebke?
2. Kennst du Jochen und Ursel?
3. Kennst du Wiebkes Eltern?
4. Kennst du Wiebkes Bruder?
5. Kennst du Wiebkes Kusine?
6. Kennst du Wiebkes Grossvater?

C7 Übung • Wiebkes Familie sieht nett aus!

A: Wie sieht Wiebkes Vater aus?
B: Er sieht nett aus.

1. Wie sieht Philipp aus?
2. Wie sehen Wiebkes Grosseltern aus?
3. Wie sieht Wiebkes Onkel aus?
4. Wie sieht die Alice aus?

C8 Übung • Ratespiel: Wer ist das?

Play these guessing games with your classmates.

1. You think of someone and give a brief description of that person. Your classmates have to guess who it is. (Sie ist gross und schlank, blond, 16 Jahre alt. Sie spielt Tennis. Sie sammelt Briefmarken. Sie ist aus . . . —Wer ist das?)
2. You think of someone and your classmates ask questions to find out who it is. (Ist sie gross? Ist sie dunkel? Ist sie schon 16? Hat sie eine Schwester? etc.)

C9 WIE SAGT MAN DAS?
Agreeing, disagreeing, expressing surprise

You already know some phrases for expressing agreement, disagreement, and surprise. Some other expressions have been added to this list.

agreeing	Das stimmt. Du hast recht. Das finde ich auch. Ich auch.	That's right./That's true. You're right. I think so, too. Me, too.
disagreeing	Das stimmt nicht. Das finde ich nicht. Das ist Geschmackssache.	That's not so. I don't think so. That's a matter of taste.
expressing surprise	Wirklich? Was?! Meinst du?	Really? Do you think so? What?! Do you think so?

C10 Übung • Wie findest du Wiebkes Freunde?

Somebody expresses an opinion about one of Wiebke's friends or relatives. Agree with that opinion or express surprise and disagree.

A: Ich finde den Jochen lustig.
B: Ich auch. *or* Was? Ich finde den Jochen langweilig.

C11 ERKLÄRUNG
Third Person Pronouns, Accusative Case

In Unit 2, you learned the pronouns **er, sie, es,** and **sie.** These pronouns refer to both people and things. You use them to refer to noun phrases that are in the nominative case.

The pronouns **ihn, sie, es,** and **sie** also refer to both people and things, but you use them to refer to noun phrases that are in the accusative case. **Ihn** refers to a masculine noun phrase, **es** to a neuter noun phrase, and **sie** to a feminine or plural noun phrase.

		Accusative		*Accusative*	
Masculine *Feminine* *Neuter*	Wie findest du	**den Jungen? den Garten?** **die Oma? die Küche?** **das Mädchen? das Poster?**	Ich finde	**ihn** **sie** **es**	nett.
Plural		**die Kinder? die Zimmer?**		**sie**	

C12 Übung • Wie findest du . . .?

A: Ist der Thomas nett?
B: Ja, ich finde ihn nett.

1. Ist die Antje lustig?
2. Ist die Küche gemütlich?
3. Ist der Markus arrogant?
4. Sind die Zimmer gross?
5. Ist der Audi toll?
6. Sind die Kinder nett?
7. Ist die Ali sympathisch?
8. Ist der Jochen freundlich?
9. Ist das Haus schön?

C13 Übung • Der Miesmacher

Kennst du den Miesmacher? Er sagt nie etwas Nettes!

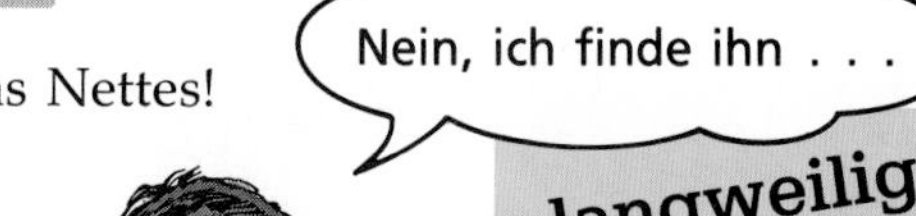

1. Findest du den Markus nett?
2. Findest du die Antje hübsch?
3. Findest du die Ali interessant?
4. Findest du den Jochen freundlich?
5. Findest du den Philipp sympathisch?

C14 Übung • Hör gut zu!

Who or what is being talked about? Listen.

	0	1	2	3	4	5	6	7	8	9	10
ein Junge											
ein Mädchen	✓										
das Haus											
zwei Schulfreunde											

C15 Übung • Wie sind diese Leute?

Wie sehen sie aus? Wie findest du sie?

Hans

Herr Krauss

Gerda

Frau Hagen

Fritz

er/sie ist	**gross, klein** **schlank, vollschlank** **hübsch, sehr hübsch** **dunkel, blond, dunkelblond, brünett** **nett**
er/sie sieht . . . aus	**gut, nicht gut** **hübsch, sehr hübsch, nett** **toll, prima** **alt, interessant**
er/sie	**hat eine Brille**
ich finde ihn/sie	**(sehr) nett, attraktiv, freundlich, lustig, sympathisch, hübsch, unsympathisch, arrogant, unfreundlich, langweilig, blöd**

Was kannst du auch sagen?	
Er/sie ist:	Er/sie sieht . . . aus.
intelligent	dumm
sportlich	ordentlich
musikalisch	schlampig

Du erzählst: Das ist Fritz. Er ist gross, vollschlank, blond. Er sieht nett und intelligent aus. Er hat eine Brille. Ich finde ihn sehr sympathisch.

C16 Übung • Hör gut zu!

Who fits the description?

C17 Schreibübung • Kennst du . . . ?

1. Petra has just come to the gathering at the Nedels. She does not know many people, so Jochen is pointing out who some of them are. For each person Jochen notices, write the conversation he and Petra might have.

JOCHEN Kennst du den Frank, den Freund von Wiebke?

PETRA Nein, ich kenne ihn nicht. *or* Ja, ich kenne ihn.

1. Monika, eine Schwester von Thomas
2. Philipp, der Bruder von Wiebke
3. Elke, eine Freundin von Monika
4. Ursel, eine Kusine aus Wien
5. Peter, ein Freund aus Amerika

2. Write a logical answer to each question, using the word or words in parentheses.

Ist er gross? (klein) Nein, er ist klein.
Macht sie Sport? (Tennis) Ja, sie spielt Tennis.

1. Ist sie blond? (brünett)
2. Hat er einen Bruder? (eine Schwester)
3. Ist sie hübsch? (sehr hübsch)
4. Ist er 15 Jahre alt? (16)
5. Ist er blond? (dunkelblond)
6. Sieht er gut aus? (toll)
7. Sieht sie nett aus? (sehr nett)
8. Hat sie Geschwister? (drei Geschwister: einen Bruder und zwei Schwestern)

3. Pick three photos of relatives or friends, or find pictures in a magazine and write a description of each person pictured. You may want to start by describing the students pictured below.

TRY YOUR SKILLS

using what you've learned

An American exchange student writes home to his German teacher.

---

1 Ein Brief aus Deutschland

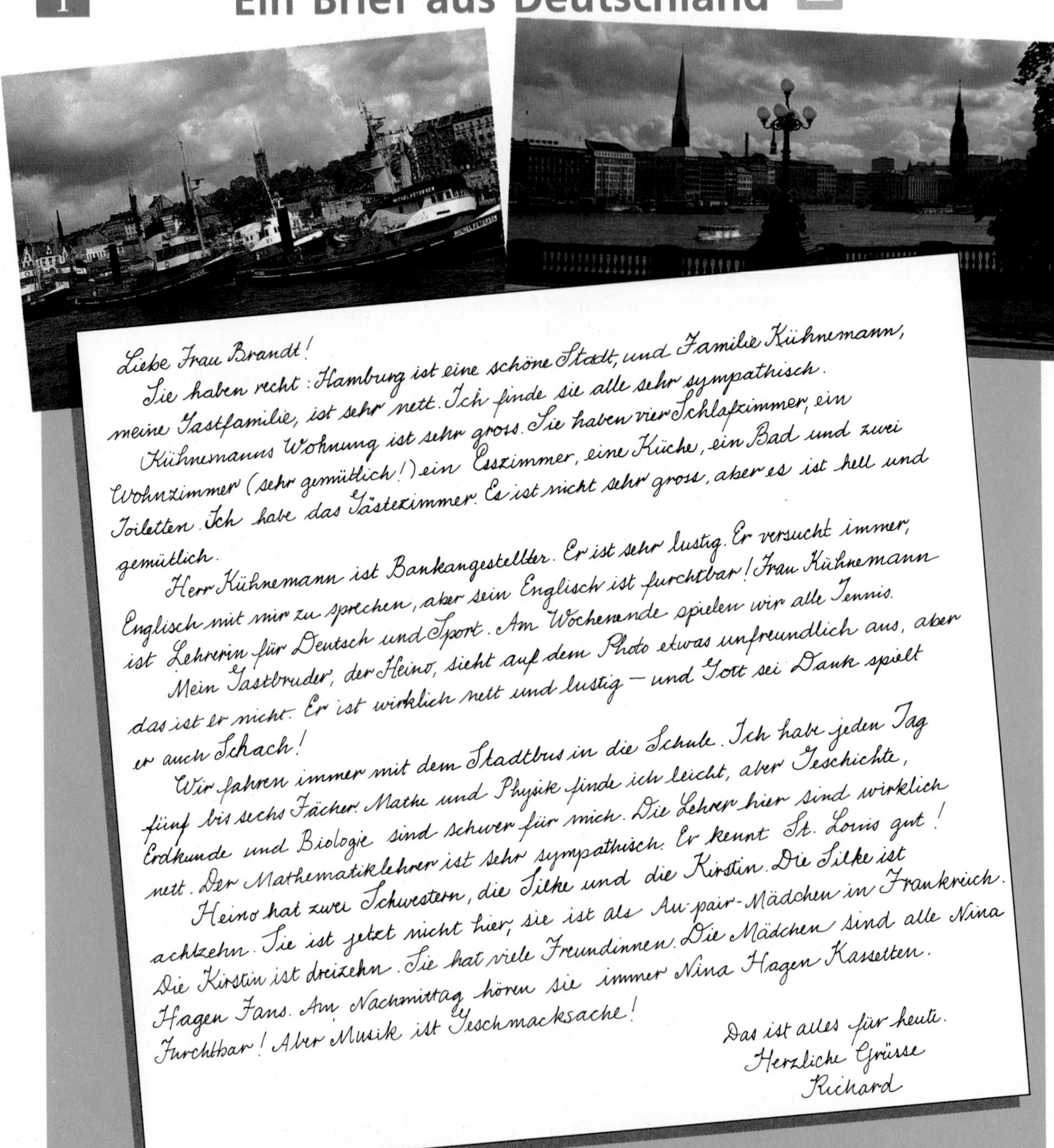

Liebe Frau Brandt!

Sie haben recht: Hamburg ist eine schöne Stadt, und Familie Kühnemann, meine Gastfamilie, ist sehr nett. Ich finde sie alle sehr sympathisch.

Kühnemanns Wohnung ist sehr gross. Sie haben vier Schlafzimmer, ein Wohnzimmer (sehr gemütlich!) ein Esszimmer, eine Küche, ein Bad und zwei Toiletten. Ich habe das Gästezimmer. Es ist nicht sehr gross, aber es ist hell und gemütlich.

Herr Kühnemann ist Bankangestellter. Er ist sehr lustig. Er versucht immer, Englisch mit mir zu sprechen, aber sein Englisch ist furchtbar! Frau Kühnemann ist Lehrerin für Deutsch und Sport. Am Wochenende spielen wir alle Tennis.

Mein Gastbruder, der Heino, sieht auf dem Photo etwas unfreundlich aus, aber das ist er nicht. Er ist wirklich nett und lustig — und Gott sei Dank spielt er auch Schach!

Wir fahren immer mit dem Stadtbus in die Schule. Ich habe jeden Tag fünf bis sechs Fächer. Mathe und Physik finde ich leicht, aber Geschichte, Erdkunde und Biologie sind schwer für mich. Die Lehrer hier sind wirklich nett. Der Mathematiklehrer ist sehr sympathisch. Er kennt St. Louis gut!

Heino hat zwei Schwestern, die Silke und die Kirstin. Die Silke ist achtzehn. Sie ist jetzt nicht hier; sie ist als Au-pair-Mädchen in Frankreich. Die Kirstin ist dreizehn. Sie hat viele Freundinnen. Die Mädchen sind alle Nina Hagen Fans. Am Nachmittag hören sie immer Nina Hagen Kassetten. Furchtbar! Aber Musik ist Geschmacksache!

Das ist alles für heute.
Herzliche Grüsse
Richard

2 Übung • Was schreibt Richard?

Was schreibt Richard über seine Gastfamilie? über die Wohnung? über die Schule?

3 Schreibübung • Ein Brief von Peter aus Neuss

Du bist jetzt Peter. Schreib einen Brief an deine Eltern. Beschreibe die Familie Nedel und Nedels Haus in Neuss!

> Liebe Eltern!
> Grüsse aus Neuss! Ich bin schon eine Woche hier, und es ist sehr schön. Die Nedels sind . . .

4 Übung • Deine Meinung—meine Meinung

Bring in pictures of well-known people and discuss each person with your classmates. Express your opinion and agree or disagree with the various comments.

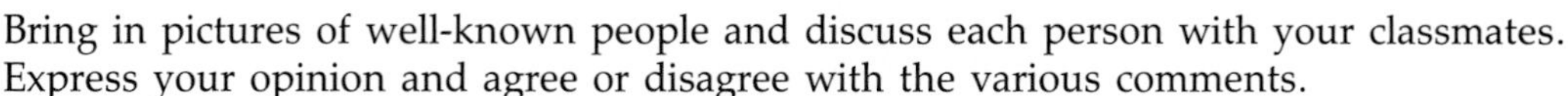

A: Wie findest du . . .?

B: Ich finde sie arrogant.	*or*	B: Ich finde sie sehr nett.
A: Wirklich? Ich finde sie nett.		A: Meinst du? Ich finde sie unsympathisch.

5 Übung • Geschenke für die Nedels

Peter kauft Geschenke für die Familie Nedel. Seine Mutter fragt, was er für jeden hat.

MUTTER Was hast du für den Philipp?
PETER Für ihn habe ich eine Musikkassette.
MUTTER Gut.
PETER Schau! Wie findest du die Kassette?
MUTTER Du, ich finde sie prima!

Philipp

Ulrike

Hartmut

Wiebke

Opa

Oma

6 Übung • Danke!—Bitte schön! 

Die Nedels danken Peter für die Geschenke.

PHILIPP Danke für die Musikkassette.
PETER Nichts zu danken!

ULRIKE . . .
PETER . . .

7 Schreibübung • Wie heisst die Frage?

Ich finde den Markus arrogant.

Wiebkes Geschwister heissen Philipp und Ulrike.

Sie ist gross, blond, schlank.

Nein, ich kenne Herrn Graf nicht.

Wir haben fünf Zimmer.

Ich bin ein Klassenkamerad von Markus.

Ja, einen Audi.

8 Übung • Ein Wohnungsplan

1. Beschreibe die Wohnung! Was ist rechts? Was ist links?
2. Jemand zeigt dir die Wohnung. Was sagst du?

   A: Hier ist das Wohnzimmer.
   B: Es ist sehr hell. Ich finde es sehr schön.

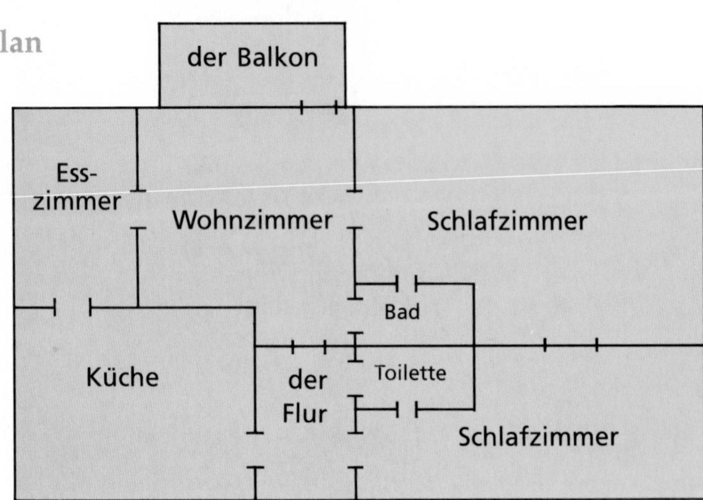

9 Schreibübung • Wir wohnen in Wien

Rewrite the following selection, replacing each underlined noun phrase with a pronoun.

Wir haben ein Haus in Wien. Wir finden <u>das Haus</u> toll! Wir haben einen Garten. <u>Der Garten</u> ist sehr gross und schön, und wir finden <u>den Garten</u> prima.

Meine Grosseltern wohnen auch in Wien. Wir sehen <u>meine Grosseltern</u> oft. Sie haben eine Wohnung. <u>Die Wohnung</u> ist sehr gemütlich. Mein Grossvater und ich spielen immer Schach. Ich finde <u>das Spiel</u> interessant. Mein Bruder Fritz findet Schach langweilig. Ich finde <u>den Fritz</u> blöd.

10 Übung • Hör gut zu!

Does the statement express agreement, disagreement, surprise, or gratitude? Listen.

	0	1	2	3	4	5	6	7	8	9	10
agreement	✓										
disagreement											
surprise											
gratitude											

11 Übung • Was sagen sie?

Hier ist das Wohnzimmer.
Das ist mein Freund Kurt.
Die Antje sieht toll aus!
Nichts zu danken!
Eine Halskette! Vielen Dank, Peter!
Das ist Geschmackssache.
Wie gemütlich!
Grüss dich!

12 Aussprache-, Lese- und Schreibübungen

1. Listen carefully and repeat what you hear.

2. Listen, then read aloud.
1. trinken, Brille, drei, Freund, mehr, Vater, gross, sehr, brauchen, Zimmer
2. Väter, wählen, Bäder, Flughäfen, ungefähr; Pässe, Gepäck, Gästezimmer
3. ob, halb, abheben, verabredet, Wiebke
4. gebe, gibst, gebt; bleibe, bleibst, bleibt; sage, sagst, sagt; frage, fragst, fragt
5. hab'—habe, bleib'—bleibe, Freund—Freunde, Hund—Hunde, frag'—frage

3. Copy the following sentences to prepare yourself to write them from dictation.
1. Ich hab' einen Freund.
2. Wie spät ist es, bitte?
3. Bleib bitte hier!
4. Die Flughäfen sind sehr gross.

WAS KANNST DU SCHON?

Let's review some important points that you have learned in this unit.

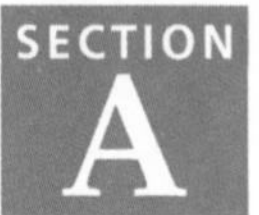

Can you introduce someone and introduce yourself?
Introduce the following people to a classmate:

your father, your mother, a sister, a brother, an uncle, an aunt, your grandparents

Introduce yourself to a classmate and say you are a friend of another classmate.

Can you describe your home or an imaginary home?
Say how many rooms you have and what they are.

Can you comment on someone else's home?
Someone is showing you his or her home. Make some appropriate comments.

Can you specify that something is for someone?
You have brought gifts to the Nedel family. Say that you have the following gifts for each person:

Poster / Wiebke   Ich habe ein Poster für die Wiebke.

1. Kassette / Ulrike
2. Taschenrechner / Philipp
3. Buch / Oma
4. Briefmarken / Hartmut

Do you know how to say thank you when you receive a present?
You have just received a book as a present. Give three ways of saying thank you.

Say you're welcome.

Do you know how to describe someone?
Describe three people in your class, using the verb **aussehen.**

Do you know how to express an opinion?
Describe someone you like and someone you don't like.

Do you know how to agree or disagree with someone else's opinion?
Respond to the following statements, first agreeing, then disagreeing.

1. Ich finde die Antje nett.
2. Philipp ist lustig.
3. Wiebke ist hübsch.

WORTSCHATZ

SECTION A

armer Peter! *poor Peter!*
bei den Nedels *at the Nedels'*
der **Bruder, ¨** *brother*
da: wir sind da *we're here*
das sind *these are*
dass *that*
die **Freundin, -nen** *girl friend*
die **Geschwister** (pl) *brothers and sisters*
die **Grosseltern** (pl) *grandparents*
der **Hund, -e** *dog*
kennenlernen: du lernst viele Leute kennen *you're going to meet a lot of people*
die **Klassenkameradin, -nen** *classmate* (f)
die **Kusine, -n** *cousin* (f)
die **Leute** (pl) *people*
mein, meine *my*
die **Oma, -s** *grandma*
der **Onkel, -** *uncle*
der **Opa, -s** *grandpa*
schlimm *bad*
schön *nice;* schön, dass du da bist *nice that you're here*
die **Schwester, -n** *sister*
so *so, well then*
die **Tante, -n** *aunt*
der **Vetter, -n** *cousin* (m)
viele *many*
von *of;* ein Freund von Wiebke *a friend of Wiebke's*
Willkommen in Neuss! *welcome to Neuss!*

SECTION B

der **Audi, -s** *Audi* (a German-made automobile)
auf *on*
auspacken: er packt den Rucksack aus *he unpacks his backpack*
aussehen *to look (like), appear,* (see p 179)
das **Auto, -s** *car*
das **Bad, ¨er** *bathroom*
bekommen *to get, receive*
bitte schön *you're welcome*
das **Buch, ¨er** *book*
Dank: vielen Dank! *thanks a lot!* tausend Dank! *thanks a million!*
danken *to thank;* nichts zu danken *don't mention it*
dein, deine *your*
das **Esszimmer, -** *dining room*
finden: findest du? *do you think so?*
die **Garage, -n** *garage*
der **Garten, ¨** *garden*
das **Gästezimmer, -** *guest room*
gemütlich *cozy, comfortable*
gern: ja, gern *yes, I'd like that*
gross *big*
die **Halskette, -n** *necklace*
das **Haus, ¨er** *house*
hell *light*
der **Keller, -** *basement, cellar*
klein *small*
komm! *come on!*
die **Küche, -n** *kitchen*
mehr *more*
Mensch! *boy! wow!*
modern *modern*
oben *upstairs*
die **Party, -s** *party*
der **Rucksack, ¨e** *knapsack, backpack*
das **Schlafzimmer, -** *bedroom*
schön *pretty, beautiful*
sehen *to see*
sehr *very*
stehen: da steht noch mehr auf Peters Zettel *there's still more on Peter's slip*
tausend *thousand;* tausend Dank! *thanks a million!*
die **Toilette, -n** *toilet*
unten *downstairs*
wieviel? *how many?*
das **Wohnzimmer, -** *living room*
zeigen *to show;* ich zeig es dir *I'll show it to you*
der **Zettel, -** *note, slip of paper*
das **Zimmer, -** *room*

SECTION C

arrogant *arrogant*
attraktiv *attractive*
aussehen: gut aussehen *to look good; to be handsome, pretty, attractive*
blond *blond*
die **Brille, -n** *glasses*
brünett *brunette*
dunkel *dark*
dunkelblond *dark blond*
freundlich *friendly*
Geschmackssache: das ist Geschmackssache *that's a matter of taste*
gross *tall*
hübsch *pretty*
kennen *to know*
klein *short, small*
lustig *merry, funny*
meinen: meinst du? *do you think so?* meinst du nicht? *don't you think so?*
nett *nice*
nicht? *don't you think so?*
recht haben *to be right*
schlank *slim*
sympathisch *likeable, nice*
unsympathisch *unpleasant, not nice*
vollschlank *heavyset*

WORTSCHATZÜBUNGEN

1. Look at the Wortschatz and make a list of all singular nouns with their definite articles. Then write the nouns again with their indefinite articles.
2. Pick out all the adjectives and write them down. How many pairs of opposites can you find? Write them next to each other.

ZUM LESEN

Märchen

Sind Märchen° wieder „in"? 

We're asking teenagers how they feel about fairy tales. What do they say?

Die klassischen Märchen wie „Schneewittchen", „Rotkäppchen", „Rumpelstilzchen" waren lange Zeit nicht mehr „in". Viele Eltern und Erzieher° sagten, die Märchen haben heute mit uns nichts zu tun°, sie sind unwahr°, sie zeigen den Kindern eine Welt° mit einem König° an der Spitze°, eine Welt, wo nur Männer regieren.

Heute erkennt man, dass° Märchen nicht nur für Kinder sind. Die Märchensymbole sind für jung und alt. Die Symbole sind stark°, klar, einfach°: Apfel und Gürtel° sind Symbole für Liebe°, Zepter und Krone sind Symbole für Macht°, Hexe, Wolf und Wald° sind Symbole für die bösen Mächte° in der Welt. Diese Symbole haben eine Beziehung° zu der Welt heute; sie haben eine Bedeutung° für uns. Vielleicht° sind deshalb° die Märchen auch heute noch bei Kindern und Erwachsenen° so beliebt°.

Märchen sind nicht nur für kleine Kinder; sie können uns viel über das Leben° heute sagen.

Ich lese zum Beispiel Märchen lieber als Comics. Ich finde Comics blöd: der Superman ist für mich sehr unrealistisch.

Märchen sind für mich immer aktuell°. Märchen zeigen oft Konflikte in der Familie.

Ich finde Märchen prima. Sie sind manchmal ein bisschen brutal, aber es gibt doch immer ein „Happy End".

Märchen *fairy tales;* **Erzieher** *educators;* **tun** *to do;* **unwahr** *untrue;* **eine Welt** *a world;* **der König** *king;* **an der Spitze** *at the top;* **heute erkennt man, dass** *today people recognize that;* **stark** *strong;* **einfach** *simple;* **der Gürtel** *belt;* **die Liebe** *love;* **die Macht** *power, force;* **der Wald** *forest;* **die bösen Mächte** *bad influences, evil forces;* **die Beziehung** *connection;* **die Bedeutung** *meaning;* **vielleicht** *maybe;* **deshalb** *therefore;* **Erwachsene** *adults;* **beliebt** *popular;* **das Leben** *life;* **aktuell** *current, up-to-date*

Die Brüder Grimm

Diesen Namen kennt ihr von „Grimm's Fairy Tales". Die Brüder heissen Jakob und Wilhelm Grimm. Ihr zweihundertster Geburtstag war 1985/86. In der hessischen Stadt Kassel ist das Brüder Grimm Museum. Hier können Besucher die Bücher und Manuskripte der Brüder Grimm sehen.

Die Märchen der Brüder Grimm waren schon im 19. Jahrhundert ein grosser Erfolg°. Nur die Bibel wurde noch öfter gedruckt°. Und heute leben° die Märchen noch! Es gab noch nie so viele Märchenbücher, Märchenkassetten und Märchenfilme wie heute!

---

der Erfolg *success;* **. . . gedruckt** *only the Bible had more printings;* **leben** *to live*

Übung • Was sagst du?

1. Wie findest du Märchen?
2. Welche Märchen liest du am liebsten? Welche Märchen hast du nicht gern? Warum?

Übung • Sprechen wir darüber!

1. How do fairy tales reflect problems in our society today?
2. Discuss some of the symbols found in popular fairy tales. What could the symbols stand for in our contemporary world?

Übung • Klassenprojekte

1. Write a report on the Brothers Grimm and present it to the class.
2. Find illustrated editions of Grimms' "Kinder- und Hausmärchen" in German and in English. Compare the titles of various tales in both languages.
3. Choose one of the fairy tales and write a modern version in English. As a class project, write one of the stories in dialog form in German and act it out for the class.

Kennt ihr diese Märchen?

Könnt ihr raten, wie die Märchen heissen?

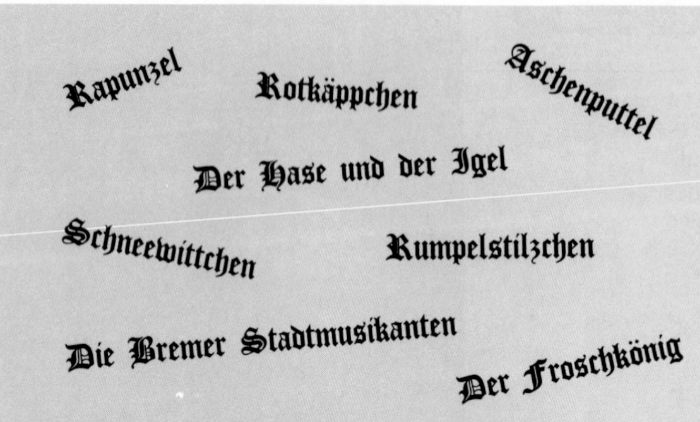

Dieses Mädchen hat eine Stiefmutter und zwei böse Schwestern. Sie muss hart arbeiten. Sie geht auf einen Ball . . . Sie tanzt mit dem Prinzen, sie verliert einen Schuh . . .

Eine Königstochter spielt mit ihrem goldenen Ball. Der Ball fällt in den Brunnen. Hier wohnt der hässliche Frosch. Aber ist er wirklich ein Frosch? Muss die Königstochter ihn küssen?

Herr Langohr ist arrogant. Der kleine Dicke ist intelligent. Sie machen eine Wette. Der kleine Dicke gewinnt die Wette . . . Wer ist jetzt der Dummkopf?

Die vier Freunde wandern zu einer grossen Stadt in Norddeutschland. Sie wollen Musik machen. Im Wald wohnen Räuber in einem Haus. Die vier Freunde wollen in dem Haus schlafen . . .

Die Königstochter hat eine böse Stiefmutter. Die schaut immer in den Spiegel und fragt: „Spieglein, Spieglein an der Wand, wer ist die schönste im ganzen Land?" Die sieben Zwerge helfen der Königstochter . . .

Kennt ihr diesen kleinen Mann? Er spinnt Stroh zu Gold für die Müllerstochter. Dann will er ihr erstes Kind haben . . . Aber wie heisst er?

Warum sitzt das schöne Mädchen ganz allein im Turm? Warum hängt ihr langes goldenes Haar herunter? Wer besucht sie in der Nacht? Wie kommt der Königssohn in den Turm?

„Grossmutter, was hast du für grosse Augen!"
„Damit ich dich besser sehen kann!"

KAPITEL 7

Wo wohnen sie?

Where do Germans live? About 45 percent live in large cities such as Hamburg, Frankfurt, Berlin, and Munich. About 45 percent live in small cities and towns. The remaining 10 percent live in rural areas. Although society has become more mobile, many people live near the place where they were born. Big cities are made up of many different sections, each one almost like a small town. Just as in a small town, people know one another; they regularly shop at the same local stores and patronize local businesses and restaurants.

In this unit you will:

SECTION A	tell where you live, show somebody your town, ask for directions
SECTION B	shop for groceries in local stores and make suggestions about where to shop
SECTION C	talk about the weather, order food, talk about how something tastes and if you want more
TRY YOUR SKILLS	use what you've learned
ZUM LESEN	read for practice and pleasure

SECTION
A telling where you live, showing somebody your town, and asking for directions

The German-speaking countries are small in area, with many people living in apartments or in homes on relatively small plots of land.

A1 Wo wohnen unsere Freunde?

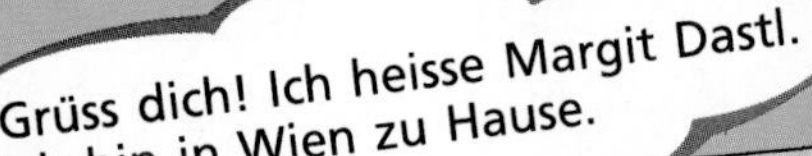

Grüss dich! Ich heisse Margit Dastl.
Ich bin in Wien zu Hause.

Wien, die Hauptstadt von Österreich, hat 1,5 Millionen Einwohner.

Hallo! Ich bin der Jens. Ich wohne in Niebüll.

Niebüll ist eine Stadt in Schleswig-Holstein. Niebüll hat 7 000 Einwohner.

Ich wohne in Neuss.

Neuss, eine Stadt in Nordrhein-Westfalen. Neuss hat 200 000 Einwohner.

Gruetzi! Ich bin der Bruno Schmidlin. Ich wohne in Zimmerwald in der Schweiz.

Die Schmidlins wohnen in Zimmerwald. Zimmerwald ist ein Dorf, ein Vorort von Bern. Bern ist die Hauptstadt der Schweiz.

Grüss Gott! Ich bin die Steffi Huber. Ich bin 15 Jahre alt, und ich wohne hier in München.

München ist die Hauptstadt von Bayern. München ist eine Grossstadt; sie hat 1,3 Millionen Einwohner.

A2 Ein wenig Landeskunde

You know some standard greetings, such as **Hallo!, Guten Tag!, Grüss dich!** There are also many regional greetings used in different parts of the German-speaking countries. For example, in southern Germany people say: **Grüss Gott!** and in Switzerland they say: **Gruetzi!** How do you greet your friends? Would you use a different greeting if you lived in another part of the country?

A3 Übung • Mix-Match

1. Niebüll ist eine Stadt	eine Stadt in Nordrhein-Westfalen.
2. Neuss ist	in Schleswig-Holstein.
3. Wien ist die Hauptstadt	von Bern.
4. Zimmerwald ist ein Vorort	von Bayern.
5. München ist die Hauptstadt	von Österreich.

A4 Übung • Und du?

1. Wo wohnst du?
2. Was ist . . .?
3. Wie gross ist . . .?
4. Wo wohnen deine Grosseltern?

Dorf Grossstadt Stadt Hauptstadt Vorort

A5 Ein wenig Landeskunde

The Federal Republic is a federation of eleven states, called **Länder,** each one with its own state capital. The capital of the Federal Republic is Bonn. The cities of Hamburg and Bremen are states as well as cities. The city of Berlin (West) is also a state of the Federal Republic, but its status is somewhat different from that of the other states. The Federal Republic has roughly 61.5 million inhabitants.

A6 Übung • Die Bundesrepublik und ihre Länder

1. Die Bundesrepublik hat elf Länder. Wie heissen sie?
2. Jedes Land hat eine Landeshauptstadt. Wie heissen sie?
   Die Landeshauptstadt von Schleswig-Holstein ist . . .
   Düsseldorf ist die Landeshauptstadt von . . .
3. Wieviel Einwohner hat Hessen?
4. Wie heisst die Hauptstadt der BRD?
5. Die Hauptstadt der DDR ist . . .
6. Wie heisst die Hauptstadt von Österreich?
7. Die Hauptstadt der Schweiz ist . . .
8. Wo ist München? Und Stuttgart?
9. Was ist Stuttgart?

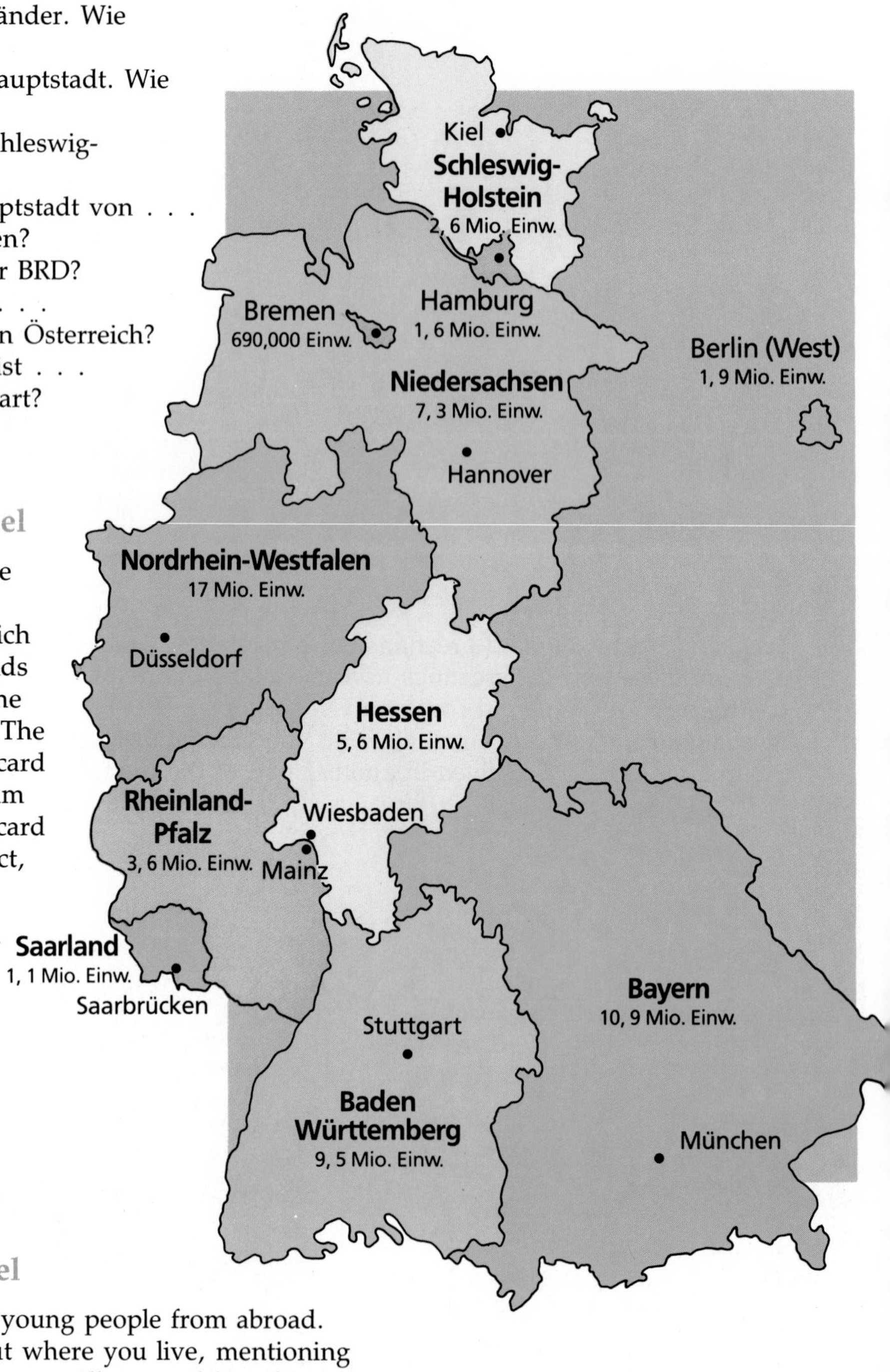

A7 Übung • Länderspiel

On cards, write the names of the cities and towns shown on the map. Also write the state in which each is located. One student holds all the cards and keeps score. The other students form two teams. The first student on team A picks a card and asks the first student on team B where the city named on the card is located. If the answer is correct, team B gets one point. If the answer is incorrect, the questioner gives the correct answer and the card is put at the bottom of the stack. Then the student on team B picks a card and asks the student on team A where the city named on the card is located. The team with the highest score wins.

A8 Übung • Rollenspiel

Pretend that you are one of the young people from abroad. Introduce yourself and talk about where you live, mentioning whether that place is a city, town, or village, and how big it is. Use an appropriate greeting.

A9 Schreibübung • Unsere Freunde

Write a paragraph about each of the young people from abroad.

A 10 IN MÜNCHEN

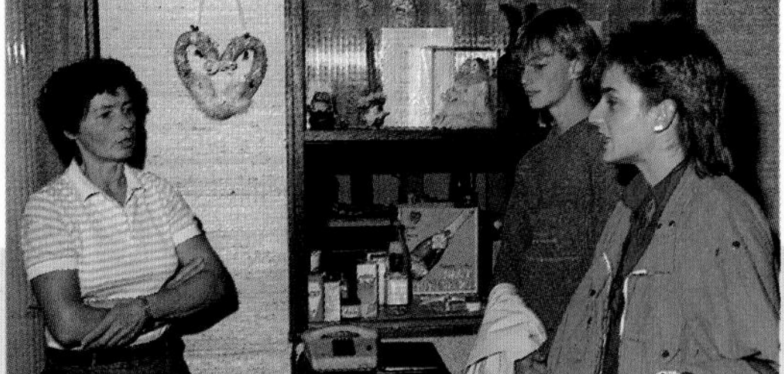

Frau Huber und ihre Tochter, die Steffi

Die Hubers wohnen in München. Sie haben eine Wohnung im Lehel.

Hubers haben Besuch, einen Jungen aus Freiburg. Der Florian kennt die Stadt nicht, und die Steffi zeigt ihm die Sehenswürdigkeiten Münchens.

Wer möchte nicht München besuchen? München ist die „heimliche Hauptstadt" Deutschlands, und jedes Jahr kommen Millionen von Besuchern aus aller Welt in das „Millionendorf" an der Isar.

Das Münchner Kindl, offizielles Wappen Münchens

Der „Alte Peter", die Peterskirche, ein Wahrzeichen Münchens

Schau, Flori! Das ist der Marienplatz und das Neue Rathaus.

GLOCKENSPIEL
CARILLON
TURM-LIFT
SAMSTAG, SONNTAG
& AN FEIERTAGEN

Schau, dort oben ist das Glockenspiel!

Die Fussgängerzone. Die Innenstadt ist nur für Fussgänger da. Und hier ist der Dom. Er hat zwei Türme.

Hier ist das Nationaltheater. Möchtest du vielleicht in die Oper gehen?

Und das ist das Schloss Nymphenburg.

Das ist die Theatinerkirche.

Die Alte Pinakothek, ein Museum.

Und das ist der Chinesische Turm im Englischen Garten.

A 11 Übung • Mix-Match: Die Stadt München

1. Die Stadt München heisst auch	im Rathaus am Marienplatz.
2. Das Glockenspiel ist	das offizielle Wappen.
3. Hier ist der Marienplatz	die „heimliche Hauptstadt" Deutschlands.
4. Die Innenstadt ist nur	die Oper Münchens.
5. Das Nationaltheater ist	ein Museum.
6. Der Chinesische Turm ist	ein Schloss in München.
7. Die Alte Pinakothek ist	ein Wahrzeichen Münchens.
8. Nymphenburg heisst	für Fussgänger da.
9. Der Alte Peter ist	im Englischen Garten.
10. Das Münchner Kindl ist	und das Rathaus.

A 12 Ein wenig Landeskunde

Munich, the capital city of Bavaria, has over one million inhabitants and is the most popular city in Germany among both foreign visitors and native Germans.

Munich owes its origins to **Herzog Heinrich der Löwe,** *Duke Henry the Lion,* who built a bridge over the river Isar and established a customs station there in 1158. The city got its name from the monastery which was built nearby—the bridge was **bei den Mönchen.** The **Münchner Kindl,** the coat of arms of Munich, shows a monk with a stein of beer because it was the monks who started the brewery business.

Often called **das Millionendorf,** *Village of Millions,* and **Weltstadt mit Herz,** *Metropolis with Heart,* Munich has many attractive features: its location at the foot of the Alps and the Alpine lakes; its position as a capital of European art, music, theater, publishing, and fashion; its great university and its beautiful Baroque palaces and churches; its reputation for friendliness; and its beer festival—the biggest in the world—the **Oktoberfest!**

A 13 ENTSCHULDIGUNG, WO IST BITTE . . .?

Florian ist allein in der Stadt. Er möchte das Nationalmuseum sehen, aber er weiss nicht, wo es ist. Er fragt:

FLORIAN Entschuldigung! Wo ist bitte das Nationalmuseum?
MANN Keine Ahnung! Ich bin nicht von hier.

* * *

FLORIAN Verzeihung! Weisst du vielleicht, wo das Nationalmuseum ist?
JUNGE Nein, ich weiss es leider nicht.

* * *

FLORIAN Entschuldigung! Wissen Sie, wo das Nationalmuseum ist?
FRAU Moment mal, das Nationalmuseum—ja, das ist in der Prinzregentenstrasse.

A 14 WIE SAGT MAN DAS?
Asking for directions, saying you don't know

You have used **„Wo ist bitte . . .“** to ask for directions. Here are some additional ways of asking for directions and some expressions that you can use when someone asks you and you don't know the answer.

asking for directions	Wo ist bitte . . .? Wissen Sie, wo . . . ist? Weisst du vielleicht, wo . . . ist?	Where is . . ., please? Do you know where . . . is? Perhaps you can tell me where . . . is?
saying you don't know	Ich weiss es nicht. Ich weiss es leider nicht. Keine Ahnung! Ich bin nicht von hier.	I don't know. I'm sorry, I don't know. I have no idea! I'm not from here.

A 15 Übung • Wo ist . . .? 

A: Verzeihung! Wo ist bitte das Rathaus?
B: Ich weiss es leider nicht.

* * *

A: Entschuldigung! Weisst du vielleicht, wo das Rathaus ist?
B: Keine Ahnung, ich bin nicht von hier.

der	die
Dom Englische Garten Marienplatz	Alte Pinakothek Oper Theatinerkirche
das	
Nationalmuseum Nationaltheater	Rathaus Schloss Nymphenburg

A 16 ERKLÄRUNG
The Verb **wissen**

1. The verb **wissen,** *to know (a fact, information, etc.),* has these forms in the present tense:

ich **weiss**	wir **wissen**
du **weisst**	ihr **wisst**
er, sie, es **weiss**	sie, Sie **wissen**

2. The verb **wissen** is commonly used with the direct object **es.**

Wo ist bitte der Dom? Ich weiss **es** nicht.

3. Wissen can be followed by an entire clause. In such clauses, the verb is in last position.

Weiss Florian, wo der Dom **ist?** Er weiss es nicht.

Wer weiss, wo der Dom **ist?** < Ich weiss es. / Ich weiss, wo der Dom **ist.**

4. In response to a comment, the **ich**-form **ich weiss** can be used without **es.**

Niebüll hat 7 000 Einwohner. Ich weiss.

A 17 Übung • Wer weiss es?

Ich weiss, wo der Dom ist. Wir . . .

Ich . . .

Wir . . .

Florian . . .

Du . . .

Ihr . . .

A 18 Übung • Wissen Sie, wo . . .?

Du kennst München nicht, und du fragst verschiedene Passanten, wo folgende Sehenswürdigkeiten sind. Schau auf den Stadtplan!

A: Verzeihung! Wissen Sie, wo das Nationalmuseum ist?

B: Ich weiss es nicht. *or* Moment mal! Das Nationalmuseum ist in der . . .strasse.

Theatinerkirche
Nationaltheater
Alte Pinakothek
Ludwigskirche
Nationalmuseum

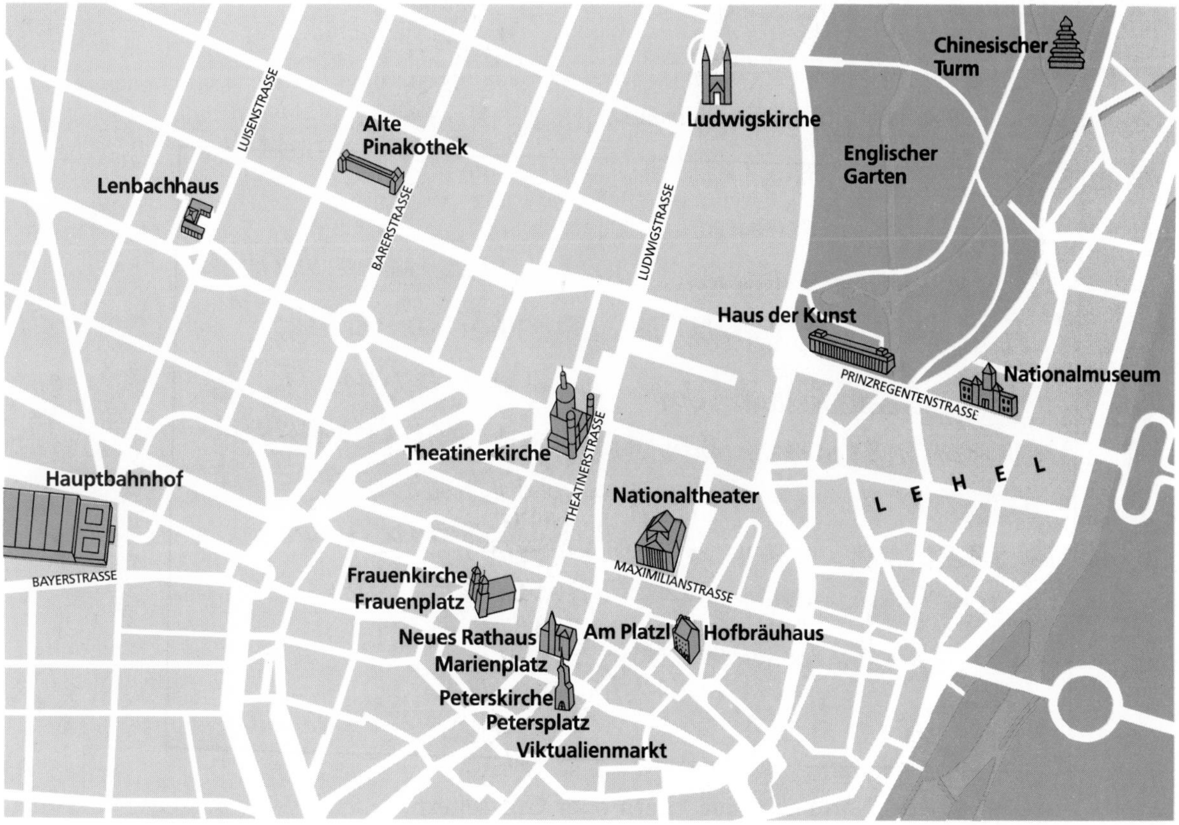

Chinesischer Turm
Ludwigskirche
Englischer Garten
Alte Pinakothek
Lenbachhaus
LUISENSTRASSE
BARERSTRASSE
LUDWIGSTRASSE
Haus der Kunst
Nationalmuseum
PRINZREGENTENSTRASSE
Theatinerkirche
THEATINERSTRASSE
Hauptbahnhof
Nationaltheater
LEHEL
BAYERSTRASSE
MAXIMILIANSTRASSE
Frauenkirche
Frauenplatz
Neues Rathaus
Am Platzl
Hofbräuhaus
Marienplatz
Peterskirche
Petersplatz
Viktualienmarkt

A 19 Übung • Hör gut zu! 

Über was spricht die Steffi?

1.  ______

2.  ______

3.  ______

4.  ______

5.  ______

6.  ______

7.  ______

8. 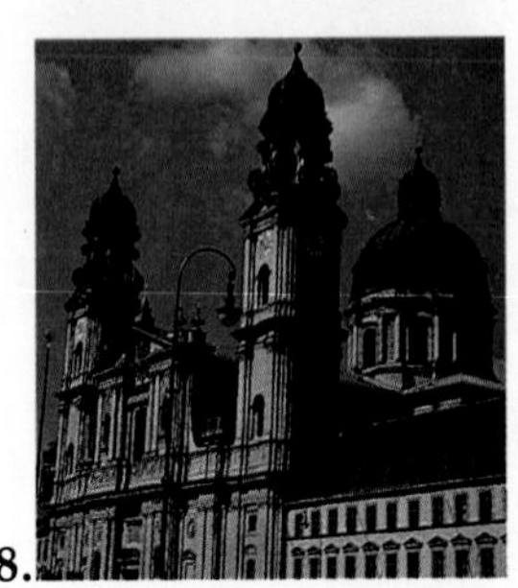 ______

A 20 Lese– und Schreibübung • Florian schreibt nach Hause

1. Was schreibt er? Kannst du die Karte lesen?

Liebe Eltern!
Grüsse aus München! Die heimliche [illegible]stadt Deutchlands ist toll! Es [illegible] hier so viele [illegible]würdigkeiten! Ich kenne jetzt das National[illegible], das [illegible]haus, den Englischen [illegible], etc. [illegible] ihr, wo der Chinesische [illegible] ist? – Die Hubers [illegible] so nett, und ich [illegible] immer mit Steffi in die Stadt.
Herzliche [illegible],
Flori

2. Jetzt schreibst du eine Karte an deine Eltern oder Grosseltern.

SECTION **B** shopping for groceries, making suggestions about where to shop

Steffi has to go shopping for her mother. Where does she go? What does she buy?

B1

Steffi geht einkaufen

Steffis Einkaufszettel:

1 Pfd. Hackfleisch
200 g Aufschnitt
1 Brot
6 Semmeln
1 Salat
1 kg Tomaten
1 Pfd. Kirschen
1 Gurke
1 l Milch
10 Eier
1/2 Pfd. Butter
Käse, 100 g
1 Pfd. Kaffee
2 Pfd. Zucker
4 Joghurt
2 Fl. Mineralwasser

FRAU HUBER Du, Steffi, geh doch bitte mal für mich einkaufen!

STEFFI O.K. Was brauchst du denn?

FRAU HUBER Schau, ich habe hier einen Zettel für dich. Aber kauf nicht alles im Supermarkt!

STEFFI Wo soll ich das Hackfleisch kaufen?

FRAU HUBER Kauf das Fleisch und die Wurst beim Metzger und hol das Obst und das Gemüse beim Gemüsehändler! Und kauf die Semmeln beim Bäcker! Dort sind sie immer frisch. Alles andere kaufst du im Supermarkt.

STEFFI Gut. Ich brauche aber Geld.

FRAU HUBER Hier sind hundert Mark. Pass bitte auf, und verlier das Geld nicht!

STEFFI Keine Sorge! Ich pass schon auf, Mutti. Tschüs!

Was kauft Steffi beim Metzger?

ein Pfund Hackfleisch

200 Gramm Wurst, Aufschnitt

Beim Bäcker kauft sie:

ein Brot

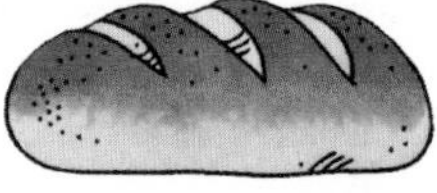

und sechs Semmeln

Was kauft sie beim Gemüsehändler? Und wieviel?

1 Kilo Tomaten

1 Pfund Kirschen

einen Kopf Salat

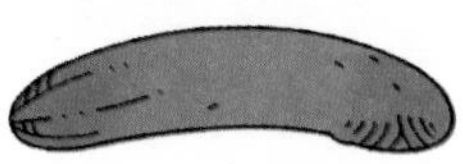

eine Gurke

Im Supermarkt kauft Steffi:

zehn Eier

einen Liter Milch

zwei Pfund Zucker

zwei Flaschen Mineralwasser

ein Pfund Kaffee

ein halbes Pfund Butter

vier Joghurt

100 Gramm Käse

B2 Übung • Mix-Match: Steffi geht einkaufen

1. Steffi geht für ihre Mutter
2. Sie kauft nicht alles
3. Das Fleisch kauft sie
4. Die Brötchen kauft sie
5. Beim Gemüsehändler kauft sie
6. Im Supermarkt holt sie

alles andere.
beim Bäcker.
beim Metzger.
die Tomaten.
einkaufen.
im Supermarkt.

B3 Übung • Und du?

1. Wo kaufst du das Fleisch?
2. Wo kaufst du die Milch?
3. Was kaufst du im Supermarkt?

B4 WIE SAGT MAN DAS?
Making requests

One common way of making requests is to use the verb stem without the verb ending. Requests made in this way are informal and can be used with people you address with **du.** The words **doch, mal,** and **bitte** are often included.

Geh doch bitte mal einkaufen!	Please go shopping.
Kauf bitte nicht alles im Supermarkt!	Please don't buy everything in the supermarket!
Hol doch das Obst beim Gemüsehändler!	Do get the fruit at the greengrocer's.
Pass bitte auf!	Please watch out!
Verlier das Geld nicht!	Don't lose the money!

B5 Übung • Wo soll ich alles kaufen?

STEFFI Wo soll ich das Fleisch kaufen?
MUTTER Kauf bitte das Fleisch beim Metzger!

* * *

STEFFI Und wo soll ich das Gemüse holen?
MUTTER Hol doch bitte das Gemüse beim Gemüsehändler!

beim Metzger
beim Bäcker
beim Gemüsehändler
im Supermarkt

der	die	das	die
Aufschnitt, Salat, Käse, Kaffee, Zucker, Joghurt	Wurst, Semmel, Gurke, Tomate, Kirsche, Milch, Butter	Hackfleisch, Brot, Ei, Mineralwasser, Obst	Semmeln, Gurken Tomaten, Kirschen Eier, Brote

B6 ERKLÄRUNG
The Verb sollen

1. The verb **sollen,** *supposed to, should,* has these forms in the present tense:

ich **soll**	wir **sollen**
du **sollst**	ihr **sollt**
er, sie, es **soll**	sie, Sie **sollen**

2. **Sollen** is usually used with an infinitive that comes at the end of the sentence:

   Wo **soll** ich das Brot **kaufen?**

3. In English there are many ways of expressing **sollen.** For example:

   Wo soll ich das Brot kaufen? { *Where am I supposed to buy the bread?* / *Where should I buy the bread?* / *Where do you want me to buy the bread?* }

B7 Übung • Was soll ich kaufen? 

Ich soll das Brot beim Bäcker kaufen. Wir . . .

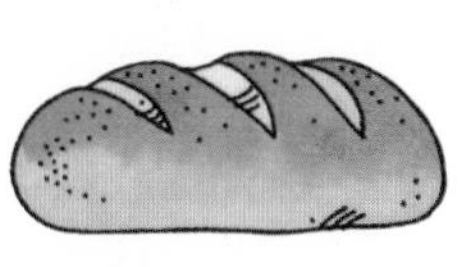

Ich . . .

Wir . . .

Steffi . . .

beim Bäcker
beim Metzger
beim Gemüsehändler
im Supermarkt

Ihr . . .

Du . . .

Die Kinder . . .

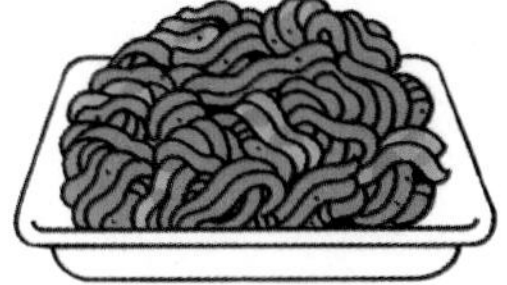

Er . . .

B 8 Ein wenig Landeskunde

In German-speaking countries, the **Kilo** is the unit of weight. One **Kilo** has **1 000 Gramm** and is the equivalent of 2.2 American pounds. In colloquial use, the word **Pfund** is also used when referring to weight. One **Pfund** has **500 Gramm,** half a **Kilogram.** The unit of liquid measure is the **Liter.** One **Liter** also contains **1 000 Gramm** and is a little more than a quart.

B 9 Leseübung • Wie schwer ist ein Pfund?

1 kg (ein Kilogramm) = 2,2 lb.
(zwei Komma zwei
amerikanische Pfund)

Das amerikanische Pfund hat nur 453 Gramm.

Das deutsche Pfund hat 500 Gramm.

1 Pfd.	(ein Pfund)	hat	500 g (Gramm)
1/2 Pfd.	(ein halbes Pfund)	hat	250 g
1/4 Pfd.	(ein viertel Pfund)	hat	125 g
3/4 Pfd.	(drei viertel Pfund)	sind	375 g
2 Pfd.	(zwei Pfund)	sind	1 000 g oder 1 kg (ein Kilogramm)

B 10 Übung • Geh mal für mich einkaufen!

A: Was brauchen wir?
B: Tomaten.
A: Und wieviel?
B: Ein Kilo.

1 kg Tomaten
250 g Kaffee
125 g Butter
1 l Milch
375 g Aufschnitt
500 g Hackfleisch

Für Ihren Campingurlaub

Aufschnitt
100 g nur **1.29**

Holzofenbrot
ca. 2000 g nur **2.89**

Original Alt-Münchner Leberkäs gebacken
100 g **–,79**

Deutscher Kopfsalat	Stck.	**–.39**
Spanische Tomaten	1 kg	**4.00**
Hohes C Orangensaft	0,7 l	**1.69**
Jakobs Kaffee	500 g	**10,60**
Deutsche Markenbutter	250 g	**2,20**
Joghurt, natur	150 g	**–,49**
Deutscher Tilsiter	100 g	**–,79**

B 11 Übung • Preisinformation

A: Du, was kostet der Kaffee im Supermarkt?
B: Ein Pfund Kaffee kostet DM 10,60.
A: Das ist preiswert!

* * *

A: Was soll ich kaufen?
B: Kauf doch bitte . . .!
A: Gut.

B 12 Übung • Was hat die Steffi alles im Netz? Rate mal!

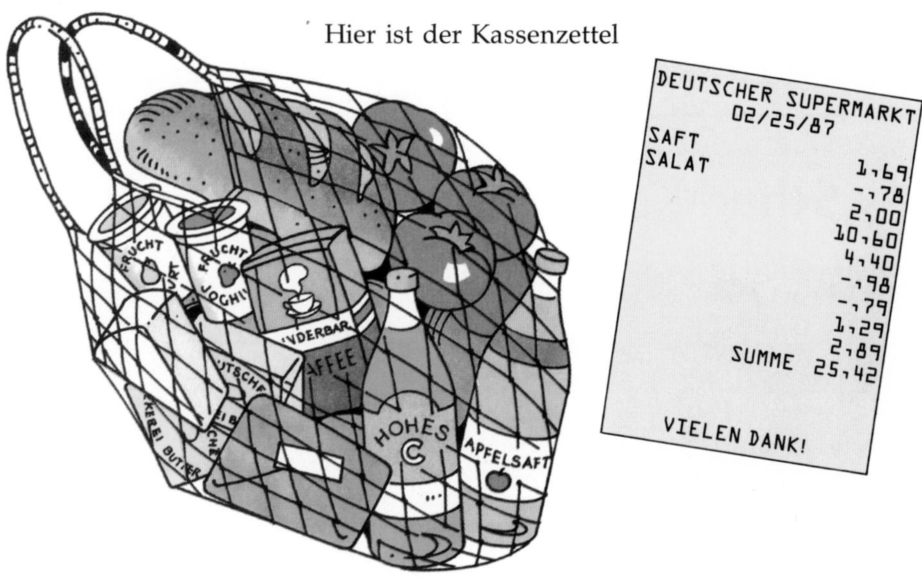

DEUTSCHER SUPERMARKT
02/25/87
SAFT
SALAT

	1,69
	-,78
	2,00
	10,60
	4,40
	-,98
	-,79
	1,29
	2,89
SUMME	25,42

VIELEN DANK!

B 13 Übung • Hör gut zu!

Wo kauft die Steffi ein?

	0	1	2	3	4	5	6	7	8	9	10
beim Bäcker											
beim Metzger											
beim Gemüsehändler											
im Supermarkt	✓										

B 14 Übung • Wo soll ich das kaufen?

Draw the grocery items mentioned in this unit on big cards—or bring in pictures of each item. One student holds up a card and asks where to buy the item pictured. Practice the following dialog with each item.

A: Wo soll ich die Tomaten kaufen?
B: Kauf sie bitte beim Gemüsehändler!
A: Wieviel Tomaten soll ich kaufen?
B: Kauf doch ein Pfund!

B 15 Schreibübung • Dein Einkaufszettel

Jetzt schreibst du einen Einkaufszettel! Du sollst acht Sachen kaufen, aber nicht alles im Supermarkt! Deine Mutter sagt dir, was du holen sollst. Schreib das Gespräch auf! Was sagt deine Mutter? Was sagst du?

SECTION C

talking about the weather, ordering in a restaurant, talking about how something tastes and if you want more

The weather doesn't look too good, but Steffi and Florian want to go into town anyway.

C1

Schade, es regnet.

FLORIAN	Steffi! Was ist los? Du siehst so traurig aus.
STEFFI	Ich bin sauer. —Schau, Flori, es regnet.
FLORIAN	Das ist blöd! Was sollen wir jetzt machen?
FRAU HUBER	Bleibt lieber zu Hause! Spielt Karten oder . . .
STEFFI	Ach, Mutti!
FLORIAN	Was sagt der Wetterbericht?
FRAU HUBER	Es bleibt bewölkt, und es soll ab und zu regnen.
STEFFI	Ach, komm, Flori! Gehen wir!
FRAU HUBER	Hast du einen Regenmantel, Flori? Es ist kühl.
FLORIAN	Ja, ich hole ihn schnell.
FRAU HUBER	Hier sind zwei Regenschirme für euch. Und kommt nicht so spät nach Hause!
STEFFI	Wir sind um 9 Uhr wieder da.
FRAU HUBER	Dann viel Spass!

FLORIAN	Danke!
STEFFI	Tschüs, Mutti!

Was sagt der Wetterbericht?

Heute bewölkt und kühl, ab und zu Regen.

Es regnet. Es ist kalt.

Heiter und warm.

Die Sonne scheint.

Das Wetter bleibt schön.

Es ist sonnig und heiss.

C2 Übung • Fragen

1. Warum ist Steffi sauer?
2. Was sollen Steffi und Flori machen? Was sagt Frau Huber?
3. Was sagt der Wetterbericht?
4. Warum holt Flori den Regenmantel?
5. Wann sind Steffi und Flori wieder da?

Wie ist das Wetter in Deutschland?

C3 Übung • Jetzt bist du dran

1. Wie ist jetzt das Wetter?
2. Was sagt der Wetterbericht?

C4 WIE SAGT MAN DAS?
Expressing annoyance

You know many ways of expressing approval or enthusiasm, such as **toll!**, **prima!**, and so on. Here are some ways of expressing annoyance.

annoyance	Das ist (zu) blöd!	That's (really) too bad!
	Das ist (zu) dumm!	That's (really) too bad!
	Ich bin sauer.	I am annoyed.

C5 Übung • Wie ist das Wetter?

A: Wie ist das Wetter?
B: Es (ist) . . .
A: Das ist blöd!

A: Was sagt der Wetterbericht?
B: Es . . .
A: Toll! Prima!

es regnet	es bleibt schön
kühl	es ist sonnig
bewölkt	es ist heiss
kalt	es bleibt warm
es soll regnen	

C6 Übung • Hör gut zu!

Wie ist das Wetter, gut oder schlecht?

	0	1	2	3	4	5	6
gut	✓						
schlecht							

C7 DER FLORI HAT HUNGER

FLORIAN Mensch, Steffi. Ich hab' Hunger.
STEFFI Ich auch.
FLORIAN Was möchtest du essen? Ein Eis? Ein Hähnchen?
STEFFI Dort drüben ist eine Imbiss-Stube.
FLORIAN Prima!

Probieren Sie mal den Leberkäs!
Leberkäs mit Senf 3.50
Bratwurst 2.80
Weisswurst 3.00
Wurstbrot 2.40
Fischbrot 3.50
Pizza 6.00
Mineralwasser 1.80
Kaffee 2.40
Cola 2.60

FLORIAN Was soll ich essen? Alles sieht so gut aus.
STEFFI Probier doch mal den Leberkäs[1]! Leberkäs mit Senf ist gut.
FLORIAN Und was isst du?
STEFFI Ich esse eine Bratwurst, und ich trinke ein Mineralwasser.
FLORIAN Na gut, ich probier' mal den Leberkäs, und ich trinke auch ein Wasser.

---

[1] **Leberkäs** is a southern German sausage specialty. It is made of beef or pork liver, pork, bacon, onion, and spices. It is baked in a loaf pan and is usually served cut in thick slices.

C8 Übung • Was soll ich essen? Was soll ich trinken? 

A: Was soll ich essen?
B: Ich esse den Leberkäs.
A: Ich auch.

der/ein	die/eine	das/ein
Leberkäs	Bratwurst	Hähnchen
Kaffee	Weisswurst	Wurstbrot
	Pizza	Mineralwasser
	Cola	Fischbrot
		Eis

C9 ERKLÄRUNG
The Verb essen

The verb **essen,** *to eat,* has the following forms in the present tense:

ich **esse**	wir **essen**
du **isst**	ihr **esst**
er, sie, es **isst**	sie, Sie **essen**

C10 Übung • Und du?

1. Was möchtest du mal probieren?
2. Was trinkst du? Was trinkst du gern?
3. Frag deine Klassenkameraden, was sie essen und trinken! Erzähl, was sie sagen!

C11 WIE SCHMECKT'S? 

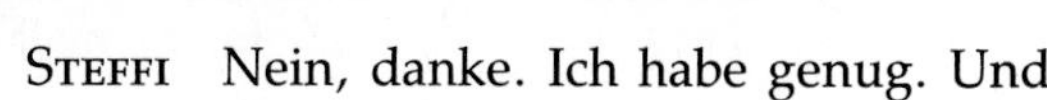

FLORIAN Wie schmeckt die Bratwurst, Steffi?
STEFFI Hm, prima! Sie schmeckt sehr gut. —Und wie ist der Leberkäs?
FLORIAN Auch gut. —Isst du noch eine Bratwurst?
STEFFI Nein, danke. Ich habe genug. Und du? Noch einen Leberkäs?
FLORIAN Nein, danke. Ich bin satt.

C12 WIE SAGT MAN DAS?
Asking and telling how something tastes

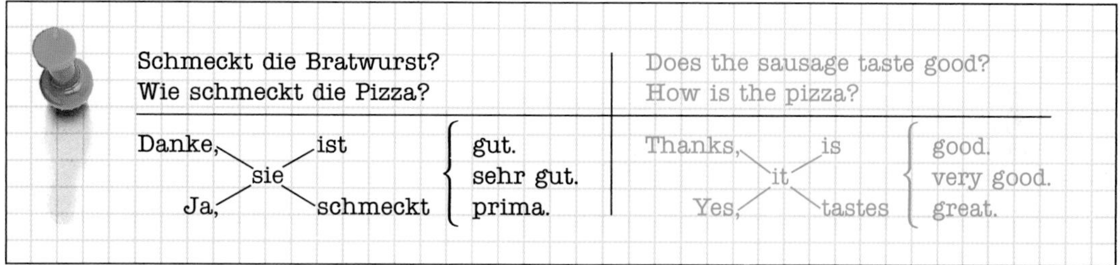

Schmeckt die Bratwurst?	Does the sausage taste good?
Wie schmeckt die Pizza?	How is the pizza?
Danke, sie ist / Ja, sie schmeckt { gut. / sehr gut. / prima.	Thanks, it is / Yes, it tastes { good. / very good. / great.

C13 Übung • Wie schmeckt's? 

A: Wie schmeckt das Hähnchen?
B: Es ist gut.

C14 ERKLÄRUNG
noch ein, *another*

The phrase **noch ein,** *another,* has the same endings as **ein.**

	Masculine	*Feminine*	*Neuter*
Nominative	**noch ein**	**noch eine**	**noch ein**
Accusative	**noch einen**		

C15 Übung • Möchtest du noch ein . . .?

A: Der Leberkäs schmeckt gut.
B: Möchtest du noch einen Leberkäs?

1. Das Wurstbrot schmeckt gut.
2. Die Bratwurst ist sehr gut.
3. Das Eis schmeckt toll.
4. Die Pizza ist phantastisch.
5. Das Hähnchen ist Klasse!
6. Der Kaffee ist prima.

C16 WIE SAGT MAN DAS?
Saying you want more or you don't want more

	Möchtest du noch ein Eis?	Would you like another ice cream?
saying yes	Danke, gern. Ja, bitte!	Thank you, I would (like more). Yes, please.
saying no	Nein, danke. Danke, ich bin satt. Nein, danke. Ich habe genug.	No, thank you. Thanks, I'm full. No thanks. I have enough.

C17 Übung • Partnerarbeit

Ask a classmate if he or she would like more to eat or drink. Refer to the chart in exercise C8 on page 212. Your classmate should make appropriate responses.

C18 ERKLÄRUNG
Making Suggestions Using Command Forms

One way of making a suggestion is to use the command form of the verb.

1. When suggesting something to a person you address with **du**, use the **du**-form of the verb without the ending **-st.**

Verb Form	*Command Form*	*Suggestion*
du kaufst	**kauf**	**Kauf** das Fleisch bitte beim Metzger!
du probierst	**probier**	**Probier** doch den Leberkäs!
du isst	**iss**	**Iss** doch eine Bratwurst!

2. When suggesting something to two people you address with **ihr,** use the **ihr**-form of the verb.

Verb Form	*Command Form*	*Suggestion*
ihr bleibt	**bleibt**	**Bleibt** doch zu Hause!
ihr spielt	**spielt**	**Spielt** doch Karten!
ihr esst	**esst**	**Esst** doch etwas!

3. When suggesting something to people you would address with **Sie,** use the **Sie**-form of the verb. The pronoun **Sie** is used and follows the verb.

Verb Form	*Command Form*	*Suggestion*
Sie probieren	**probieren Sie**	**Probieren Sie** mal den Leberkäs!
Sie holen	**holen Sie**	**Holen Sie** das Brot beim Bäcker!
Sie essen	**essen Sie**	**Essen Sie** doch das Hähnchen!

C19 Übung • Was passt?

1. Steffi, . . . mal für mich einkaufen!
2. Steffi und Flori, . . . nicht zu spät nach Hause!
3. Frau Huber, . . . Sie mal den Leberkäs!
4. Steffi, . . . doch eine Bratwurst!
5. Flori, . . . doch ein Mineralwasser!
6. Steffi und Flori, . . . bitte das Geld nicht!
7. Steffi, . . . doch bitte das Brot beim Bäcker!
8. Florian, . . . doch mal die Hubers!
9. Frau Huber, . . . Sie mal die Steffi!
10. Steffi, . . . doch mal den Regenschirm!
11. Steffi und Flori, . . . heute nicht Tennis!

essen
gehen
kaufen
kommen
probieren
trinken
verlieren
besuchen
fragen
suchen
spielen

C20 Übung • Was sagst du zu . . .? 

Was sollen sie tun? Sie sollen: eine Zeitung holen

Hol bitte eine Zeitung!

Holt bitte eine Zeitung!

Holen Sie bitte eine Zeitung!

1. einkaufen gehen
2. das Brot beim Bäcker holen
3. den Leberkäs probieren
4. die Bratwurst essen
5. lieber zu Hause bleiben
6. das Nationalmuseum besuchen

C21 Übung • Hör gut zu! 

Mit wem sprichst du? Mit Steffi? Mit Steffi und Flori? Mit Frau Huber?

	0	1	2	3	4	5	6	7	8	9	10
Steffi											
Steffi und Flori	✓										
Frau Huber											

C22 Schreibübung • Im Restaurant

Make up a menu and write it on poster board. Then write a dialog that takes place in a restaurant and practice it with a classmate. Use some of the following phrases.

Kellner/in	Gast 1	Gast 2
Was möchten Sie? Probieren Sie mal den . . .! Sie möchten den . . .? Möchten Sie noch einen . . .? Ist das alles? / Gut! Ja. / Nein.	Was soll ich essen? Ist der . . . gut? Ich esse . . . Haben Sie auch . . .?	Probier mal den . . .! . . . schmeckt . . .! Wie ist . . .? Und ich möchte . . .

TRY YOUR SKILLS

using what you've learned

1 Steffi geht mit Florian einkaufen 

Steffi geht für ihre Mutter einkaufen, und Flori geht mit. Zuerst kaufen sie beim Bäcker ein.

—Tag, Steffi!
—Guten Tag, Frau Schmitt! Frau Schmitt, das ist der Florian Schneider, Besuch aus Freiburg.
—Soso, aus Freiburg! In Freiburg soll das Wetter immer schön sein. Stimmt das?
—Nein. Es regnet auch in Freiburg, vielleicht nicht so oft wie in München.

Steffi kauft ein Brot und acht Semmeln, und dann kaufen die beiden Obst und Gemüse beim Gemüsehändler.

—So, Steffi, was möchtest du heute?
—Eine Gurke, einen Kopf Salat und ein Pfund Kirschen.
—Hier, probier mal eine Kirsche! Ist das dein Freund, Steffi?
—Das ist Florian Schneider. Der Flori ist der Sohn von Muttis Schulfreundin.
—Woher bist du?
—Aus Freiburg.
—Und du besuchst jetzt unser schönes München. Du, da hast du eine prima Fremdenführerin. Die Steffi kennt München gut.
—Ja, das weiss ich.

Dann gehen die beiden in den Supermarkt. Hier soll Steffi ein halbes Pfund Butter und einen Liter Milch kaufen. Zuletzt gehen die beiden in den Zeitungsladen. Der Vati möchte die Abendzeitung lesen.

2 Übung • Stimmt! Stimmt nicht!

1. Der Florian geht für seine Mutter einkaufen.
2. Die Steffi und der Flori kaufen zuerst beim Bäcker ein.
3. Die Bäckersfrau heisst Schmitt.
4. Sie möchte wissen, wie das Wetter in Freiburg ist.
5. In Freiburg regnet es so oft wie in München.
6. Im Supermarkt kaufen sie Obst und Gemüse.
7. Florians Mutter ist eine Schulfreundin von Steffis Mutter.
8. Steffi ist die Fremdenführerin—sie zeigt Florian die Stadt München.
9. Zuletzt kaufen die beiden eine Abendzeitung im Supermarkt.

3 Übung • Steffi geht einkaufen

Steffi geht einkaufen. Sie muss folgende Sachen holen: Brötchen, Aufschnitt, Tomaten, Salat, Milch, Kaffee, Zucker und Joghurt. Beschreib Steffis Einkaufsrunde.

Steffi geht zuerst zum . . . und kauft . . . Dann geht sie . . .

4 Übung • Ratespiel: Wo ist . . . ?

Practice this dialog using different cities in German-speaking countries. Then practice it using cities and towns you are familiar with in the United States.

A: Weisst du, wo Niebüll ist?
B: Na klar! Niebüll ist in Schleswig-Holstein. Niebüll ist eine Stadt; sie hat 7 000 Einwohner. *or* Ich weiss es leider nicht. *or* Keine Ahnung. *or* Frag doch mal deinen . . .

5 Übung • Werners Einkaufszettel

Was bringt Werner nach Hause?

1. Was soll Werner alles kaufen?
2. Was kauft er nicht?
3. Was bringt er nach Hause?

6 Übung • Rollenspiel: In der Imbiss-Stube

Du bist in der Imbiss-Stube und möchtest etwas essen.
Ein Mitschüler ist der Kellner oder die Kellnerin.

KELLNER/IN Probieren Sie doch mal den Leberkäs!
GAST Ist er heute gut?
KELLNER/IN Ja, sehr gut!
GAST Gut, dann esse ich einen Leberkäs.

Pizza
Bratwurst
Hähnchen
Fischbrot

7 Aussprache-, Lese- und Schreibübungen

1. Listen carefully and repeat what you hear.
2. Listen, then read aloud.
   1. allein, Bayern, Leute, Haus, Häuser
   2. holen, Dom, Oper, Obst, Brot, Tomate; Sonne, sollen, Schloss, wolkig, sonnig
   3. zum, zu Hause, Zimmer, Zoll, Verzeihung, Wahrzeichen, Einkaufszettel
   4. Wurst, wissen, Wien, Wasser, Weisswurst, Wetterbericht, warm, wieder, bewölkt
3. Copy the following sentences to prepare yourself to write them from dictation.
   1. Wir holen Wurst und Brot. 2. In Wien gehen die Leute oft in die Oper.

WAS KANNST DU SCHON?

Let's review some important points you have learned in this unit.

Can you talk about where some of our friends live?
Name three of the places where our friends live and say whether each place is a city, a town, or a suburb.

Tell where you live and what it is.

Can you identify landmarks in the city of Munich and ask for directions to get there?
Ask how to get to three landmarks in Munich.

What would you say if someone asked you directions and you did not know?

Do you know how to go shopping for groceries?
Name two items you would buy:

1. at the bakery **2.** at the greengrocer **3.** at the supermarket

Ask your friend to buy, in the appropriate store, each of these items you named. Use command forms.

Give the form of **sollen** that goes with each of the following subjects:

1. ich **2.** ihr **3.** Steffi **4.** wir **5.** du **6.** Steffi und Flori

Can you describe the weather?
Describe how the weather is today.

Say that the weather is bad and express annoyance.

Can you discuss items on a menu and talk about what you would like to order?
You are in a restaurant with a friend. Suggest three things to eat.

Your friend has ordered three different things. Ask how he or she likes each one. Ask your friend if he or she would like more. What would your friend say if:

1. he or she wanted more **2.** he or she didn't want more

Can you suggest that someone do something?
Suggest to the following people that they try a pizza, eat another sausage, and buy a yogurt:

1. your mother **2.** your brother and sister **3.** your teacher

WORTSCHATZ

SECTION A

die **Ahnung: keine Ahnung!** *I have no idea!*
allein *alone*
die **Alte Pinakothek** (see p 200)
Bayern *Bavaria*
der **Besuch** *company*
der **Besucher, -** *visitor*
der **Chinesische Turm** (see p 200)
der **Dom, -e** *cathedral*
das **Dorf, ⸚er** *village*
der **Einwohner, -** *inhabitant*
der **Englische Garten** (see p 200)
der **Fussgänger, -** *pedestrian*
die **Fussgängerzone, -n** *pedestrian mall*
das **Glockenspiel, -e** (see p 199)
die **Grossstadt, ⸚e** *big city*
Gruetzi! *hello!* (Swiss)
die **Hauptstadt, ⸚e** *capital city*
in der Prinzregentenstrasse *on Prinzregenten Street*
die **Innenstadt, ⸚e** *city center*
das **Jahr, -e** *year*
kennen *to know, be familiar with a place*
die **Kirche, -n** *church*
leider *unfortunately;* ich weiss es leider nicht *I'm sorry, I don't know*
der **Marienplatz** (see p 199)
die **Million, -en** *million*
das **Münchner Kindl** (see p 199)
das **Museum, Museen** *museum*
das **Nationaltheater** (see p 200)
das **Neue Rathaus** (see p 199)
oben: dort oben *up there*
die **Oper, -n** *opera;* in die Oper gehen *to go to the opera*
die **Peterskirche** (see p 199)
das **Schloss, ⸚er** *castle*
Schweiz: in der Schweiz *in Switzerland*
die **Sehenswürdigkeit, -en** *sight, place of interest*
die **Stadt, ⸚e** *city; town*
die **Tochter, ⸚** *daughter*
der **Turm, ⸚e** *tower*
vielleicht *maybe*
der **Vorort, -e** *suburb*
das **Wahrzeichen, -** *landmark*
das **Wappen, -** *coat of arms*
wissen *to know* (see p 202)
die **Wohnung, -en** *apartment*
zu Hause: ich bin in Wien zu Hause *I live in Vienna*

SECTION B

alles andere *everything else*
aufpassen: ich pass schon auf *I'll be careful;* pass bitte auf! please be careful!
der **Aufschnitt** *cold cuts*
der **Bäcker, -** *baker*
beim Bäcker *at the baker's*
das **Brot, -e** *bread*
die **Butter** *butter*
das **Ei, -er** *egg*
einkaufen gehen *to go shopping*
der **Einkaufszettel, -** *shopping list*
die **Flasche, -n** *bottle;* eine Flasche Mineralwasser *a bottle of mineral water*
das **Fleisch** *meat*
frisch *fresh*
das **Gemüse** *vegetable*
der **Gemüsehändler** *greengrocer*
das **Gramm** *gram;* 200 g Aufschnitt *200 grams of cold cuts*
die **Gurke, -n** *cucumber*
gut *okay, fine*
das **Hackfleisch** *chopped meat*
halb: ein halbes Pfund Butter *a half a pound of butter*
holen *to get, buy*
der **Joghurt, -** *yogurt*
der **Kaffee** *coffee*
der **Käse** *cheese*
das **Kilo = Kilogramm** *kilogram;* 1 kg Tomaten *1 kilogram of tomatoes*
die **Kirsche, -n** *cherry*
der **Kopf, ⸚e** *head;* ein Kopf Salat *a head of lettuce*
der **Liter** *liter;* ein Liter Milch *a liter of milk*
der **Metzger, -** *butcher*
die **Milch** *milk*
das **Mineralwasser** *mineral water*
die **Mutti, -s** *mom*
das **Obst** *fruit*
das **Pfund** *pound;* zwei Pfund Zucker *two pounds of sugar*
der **Salat, -e** *lettuce*
die **Semmel, -n** *roll*
sollen *should, supposed to*
die **Sorge: keine Sorge** *don't worry*
der **Supermarkt, ⸚e** *supermarket*
die **Tomate, -n** *tomato*
die **Wurst, ⸚e** *sausage; cold cuts*
der **Zucker** *sugar*

SECTION C

ab und zu *now and then*
bewölkt *cloudy, overcast*
blöd *too bad!*
die **Bratwurst, ⸚e** *fried sausage*
die **Cola, -s** *cola*
das **Eis** *ice cream*
essen *to eat* (see p 212)
das **Fischbrot, -e** *fish sandwich*
genug *enough*
das **Hähnchen, -** *chicken*
heiss *hot*
heiter *fair (weather)*
Hunger haben *to be hungry*
die **Imbiss-Stube, -n** *snack bar*
kalt *cold*
kühl *cool*
der **Leberkäs** see fn p 212
los: was ist los? *what's the matter?*
mit *with*
na gut *well, okay*
nach Hause kommen *to come home*
noch ein *another*
die **Pizza, -s** *pizza*
probieren *to try;* probier mal *why don't you try*
der **Regen** *rain*
der **Regenmantel, ⸚** *raincoat*
der **Regenschirm, -e** *umbrella*
regnen: es regnet *it's raining*
satt: ich bin satt *I'm full*
scheinen *to shine*
schmecken *to taste;* wie schmeckt's? *how does it taste?*
schnell *fast, quick*
der **Senf** *mustard*
die **Sonne** *sun*
sonnig *sunny*
der **Spass: viel Spass!** *have fun!*
traurig *sad*
warm *warm*
die **Weisswurst, ⸚e** *type of sausage*
das **Wetter** *weather*
der **Wetterbericht, -e** *weather report*
wieder *again;* wir sind um 9 wieder da *we'll be back at 9*
das **Wurstbrot, -e** *sandwich made with cold cuts*
zu Hause: bleibt lieber zu Hause! *you'd better stay home!*

ZUM LESEN

The city of Munich attracts people from all over Germany and from all over the world. What makes Munich so special?

„München mag man". Was ist diese Stadt für den Besucher? Hofbräuhaus—Oktoberfest—Theater, Oper, Kunst—„Gemütlichkeit"—oder einfach Bayern?

München ist nicht nur „deutsch", München hat auch einen südlichen Charakter: griechische Säulen, italienische Renaissance-Fassaden, barocke Kirchen.

München ist gemütlich. Wer kennt nicht den Marienplatz, „die gute Stube" Münchens?

München hat seinen Viktualienmarkt. Hier gibt es alles, was Herz und Magen begehren.

Wie wär's mit einer bayrischen Brotzeit?

Viktualienmarkt

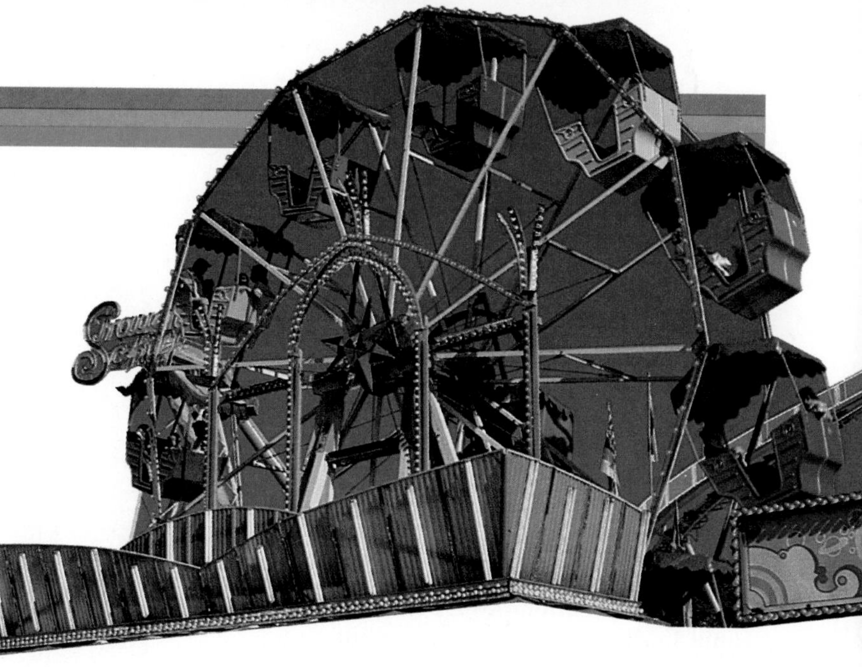

Eine der berühmtesten Attraktionen Münchens ist das Oktoberfest. Rund sieben Millionen Besucher gehen Jahr für Jahr auf die „Wies'n", um hier echte Oktoberfeststimmung „live" zu erleben.

Das Oktoberfest hat heute seine Freunde überall in der Welt. Aber das Oktoberfest ist noch immer ein echtes bayrisches Traditionsfest.

Mehr als die Hälfte der Besucher sind Münchner und weitere dreissig Prozent sind Nachbarn aus dem bayrischen Umland.

Wenn man schon in München ist, so besucht man auch ein König-Ludwig-Schloss.

Neuschwanstein ist das berühmteste Schloss. Es ist im gotischen Stil nachgebaut—und ist das Muster für das Märchenschloss in Disneyland.

Schloss Herrenchiemsee steht auf einer Insel im Chiemsee. Es ist im Stil von Schloss Versailles gebaut.

Linderhof, im Rokokostil gebaut, ist das kleinste und charmanteste Schloss. Hier hat König Ludwig am liebsten gewohnt.

Übung • Sprich darüber!

1. München hat viel für seine Besucher.
2. Die Stadt hat einen südlichen Charakter.
3. Das Oktoberfest ist weltberühmt.
4. Das Fest ist noch immer ein echt bayrisches Traditionsfest.
5. Viele Touristen besuchen die Königsschlösser—und jedes Schloss ist anders.

KAPITEL 8

Auf nach München!

Wiederholungskapitel

1

Am Bahnhof

Florian Schneider wohnt in Freiburg. Er ist mit seiner Mutter auf dem Bahnhof—er fährt heute mit dem Zug nach München. Dort besucht er die Hubers. Florian kennt München nicht.

FRAU SCHNEIDER	Wann bist du in München, Flori?
FLORIAN	Um Viertel nach zwei.
FRAU SCHNEIDER	Hast du alles?
FLORIAN	Ja, Mutti!
FRAU SCHNEIDER	Auch den Pass?
FLORIAN	Ich fahre nach München, Mutti!
FRAU SCHNEIDER	Hast du den Regenmantel?
FLORIAN	Warum? Das Wetter ist prima!
FRAU SCHNEIDER	Aber in München regnet es oft!
FLORIAN	Dann kaufe ich einen Regenschirm!
FRAU SCHNEIDER	Ja, und viele Grüsse an die Hubers.
FLORIAN	Mutti, hier kommt der Zug!
FRAU SCHNEIDER	Und telefoniere bitte und schreib eine Karte!
FLORIAN	Ja, ja! Tschüs, Mutti!
FRAU SCHNEIDER	Tschüs! Gute Reise!

2 Übung • Stimmt? Stimmt nicht?

1. Florian besucht die Schneiders in Freiburg.
2. Sein Vater bringt ihn zum Bahnhof.
3. Florian kennt München nicht.
4. Um Viertel nach zwei ist er in München.
5. Es regnet in Freiburg.
6. Er hat einen Regenschirm.
7. Florian soll eine Karte schreiben.
8. Er soll nicht telefonieren.

3 Übung • Und du? Wie steht's mit dir?

1. Hast du Freunde oder Verwandte in Deutschland, in Österreich, in der Schweiz oder in einem anderen Staat in den USA?
2. Wer sind diese Leute? Verwandte? —Wie heissen sie?
3. Wo wohnen sie, und wo ist das?
4. Haben sie eine Wohnung? ein Haus? Wieviel Zimmer haben sie?
5. Wie findest du die Wohnung? das Haus?
6. Wie ist das Wetter dort?
7. Besuchst du sie oft? Wie oft?
8. Wie lange bleibst du dort?
9. Wie kommst du dorthin?

4 Schreibübung

Was brauchst du für die Reise? Schreib auf, was du brauchst! Ein Klassenkamerad liest von seiner Liste und fragt dich, was du für die Reise hast. Du liest von deiner Liste und fragst ihn, was er hat.

A: Hast du den Reiseführer?
B: Ja. Und hast du den Regenmantel?
A: Ja . . .

5 Übung • Wo hast du alles?

A: Sag mal, hast du den Reiseführer?
B: Ja, er ist im Rucksack.
A: Gut. Aber pass auf und verlier ihn nicht!
B: Keine Sorge! Ich pass schon auf.

Reiseführer
Geld
Regenschirm
Kamera
Fahrkarte
Walkman
Adressbuch
Regenmantel
Reiseführer
Taschenrechner

6 Übung • Wann geht der Zug?

Du weisst nicht, wann der Zug geht. Du telefonierst.

A: Bahnhof Freiburg, Auskunft. Guten Tag!
B: Ich möchte nach München fahren. Wann geht da ein Zug?
A: Wann möchten Sie in München sein?
B: So um 16 Uhr.
A: O.K. Da haben wir einen Zug um 10.55. Er ist um 16.08 in München.
B: Ja, das passt prima. Vielen Dank!
A: Bitte schön! Gute Reise!

Fahrplanauszug
Sommer 1986
DB

01. Juni 1986 bis 27. September 1986

Freiburg/Breisg. → München 464 km

Verkehrszeiten über Stuttgart–Karlsruhe	ab	Zug	an	Gleis	Umsteigen in	an	ab	Zug
täglich	1.15	D 200	6.30	15	Karlsruhe	2.31	2.51	D 1163
Mo bis Sa	5.41	IC 593	10.08	18				
täglich	5.46	D 1270	11.08	18	Karlsruhe Stuttgart	7.01 8.31	7.25 8.57	D 893 IC 595
täglich	5.46	D 1270	11.20	14	Karlsruhe	7.01	7.25	D 893
täglich	6.58	E 3080	12.08	18	Stuttgart	9.46	9.57	IC 611
Mo bis Sa	7.55	IC 576	12.59	14	Karlsruhe Stuttgart	8.57 10.14	9.07 10.25	D 2751 D 795
täglich, ab Karlsruhe Kurswagen D 2753	8.55	IC 78	14.37	15	Karlsruhe	9.57	10.45	FD 211
Sonntag, ab Karlsruhe Kurswagen D 2753	9.12	D 1206	14.37	15	Karlsruhe	10.27	10.45	FD 211
täglich, ab Stuttgart nur 1.Klasse, Sonderzuschlag	10.55	IC 574	15.44	11	Karlsruhe Stuttgart	11.57 13.22	12.07 13.37	E 3009 TEE 17
täglich	10.55	IC 574	16.08	14	Karlsruhe Stuttgart	11.57 13.22	12.07 13.57	E 3009 IC 693
täglich	11.55	IC 76	16.34	19	Karlsruhe	12.57	13.05	FD 265

Angaben ohne Gewähr. Änderungen vorbehalten. Tarifangaben Stand 1.1.86

Anschlüsse von ab → nach an

1.Klasse –> 137,00 DM <–>274,00 DM Vorzugskarte <–> 220,00 DM IC Zuschlag 5,00 DM
2.Klasse –> 91,00 DM <–>182,00 DM Vorzugskarte <–> 146,00 DM IC Zuschl...

– 3 – Zugauskunft München Hbf

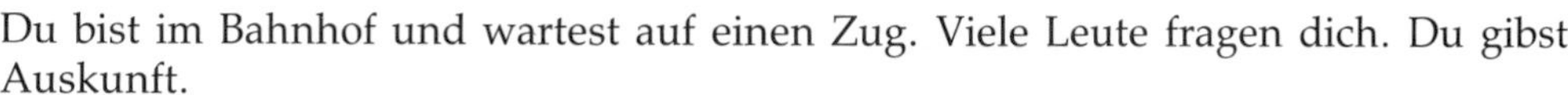

7 Übung • Entschuldigung! Ich bin nicht von hier.

Du bist im Bahnhof und wartest auf einen Zug. Viele Leute fragen dich. Du gibst Auskunft.

A: Ich brauche ein Taxi. Weisst du vielleicht, wo die Taxis sind?
B: Die Taxis sind . . .
A: Danke!
B: Bitte! Gern geschehen.

Wo ist . . . ?
Wann geht der Bus zum Flughafen?
Wo sind . . . ?
Ich möchte Geld wechseln.
Wissen Sie, . . . ?
Ich brauche eine . . .

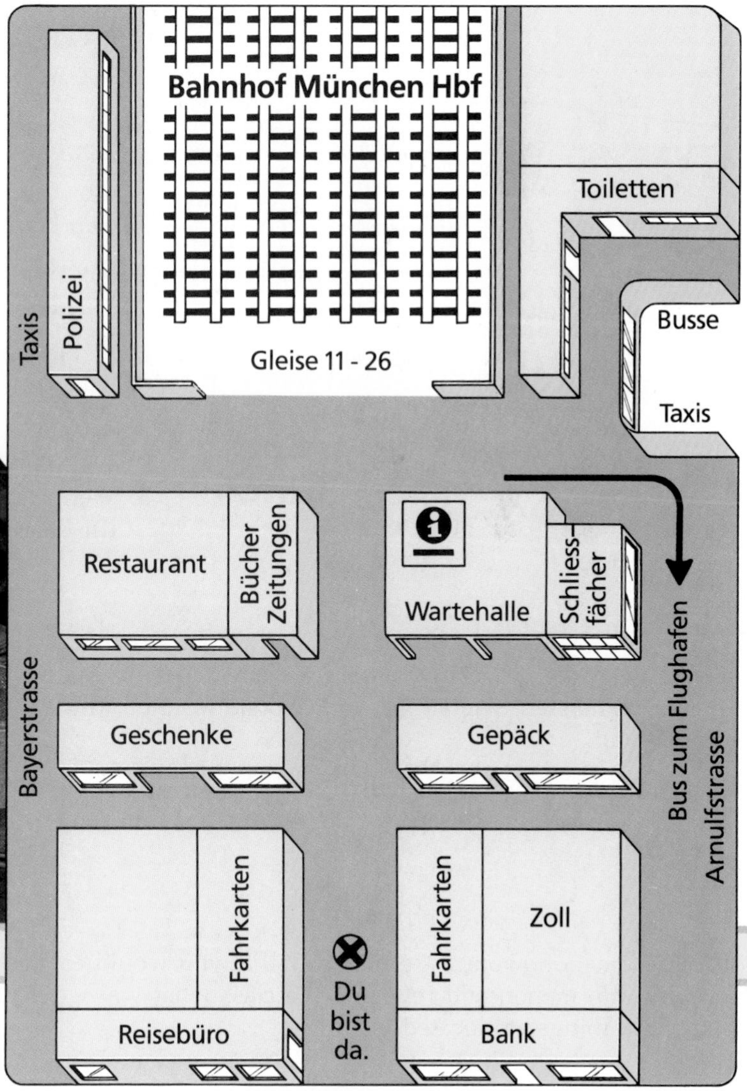

Bahnhof München Hbf
Gleise 11 - 26
Taxis
Polizei
Toiletten
Busse
Taxis
Restaurant
Bücher Zeitungen
Wartehalle
Schliessfächer
Bus zum Flughafen
Bayerstrasse
Arnulfstrasse
Geschenke
Gepäck
Fahrkarten
Reisebüro
Du bist da.
Fahrkarten
Zoll
Bank

8 Übung

Du hast Hunger, und du möchtest auch etwas trinken. Im Bahnhof gibt es alles—auch einen Bäcker und einen Metzger. Da ist auch ein Restaurant, aber du gehst lieber in die Imbiss-Stube.

A: Ja, bitte?
B: Eine Bockwurst mit Senf.
A: Etwas zu trinken?
B: Einen Apfelsaft, bitte.
A: Das macht vier Mark sechzig!

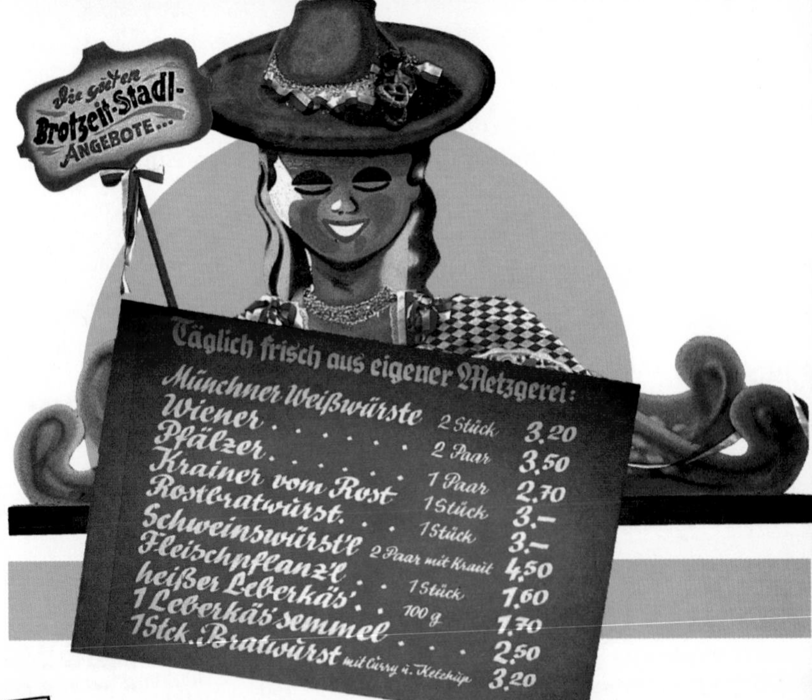

Opa - Briefmarken
Oma - Pulli
Onkel Kurt - Kassette
Tante Ella - Buch
Steffi - Taschenrechner

9 Übung • Geschenke für alle

Florian kauft für alle ein Geschenk.

1. Sag, was er für alle hat!
   Für den Opa . . .
2. Er gibt jedem ein Geschenk!
   A: Opa, hier sind Briefmarken für dich!
   B: Vielen Dank!
   A: Nichts zu danken.
3. Wenn du eine Reise machst, was kaufst du für deine Familie? Was sagst du?

10 Schreibübung • Wer ist wer?

Wer sind deine Verwandten? Schreib auf einen Zettel, was für Verwandte du hast, wie sie heissen, wie alt sie sind, wo sie wohnen und wie sie mit dir verwandt sind.

Ich habe einen Onkel. Er heisst John.
Er ist . . . alt. Er wohnt in . . . John ist Muttis Bruder.

11 Übung • Klassenprojekt

Collect information about a German city that you would especially like to visit. Study this information and report to the class what you would like to see and where these things are located.

Die Sehenswürdigkeiten Kölns sind . . .

LANDESKUNDE 2

Other German-speaking Countries and Regions

The German Democratic Republic

The German Democratic Republic (GDR) is located in Central Europe, with the Federal Republic to the west, Poland to the east, and Czechoslovakia to the south. The GDR is a socialist state, formed in 1949 from the Soviet-occupied zone of Germany, six months after the formation of the Federal Republic. In the GDR all decision making is in the hands of the communist party, officially known as the Socialist Unity Party (SED). Geographically, the northern and central parts of the GDR are a low-lying plain intersected by gentle ranges of hills. The southern part of the country is highland. Some of the chief cities are (East) Berlin, the capital; Leipzig, a center of printing and book trade and the site of trade fairs since 1100; Dresden, a baroque art city that has been carefully restored; and the port of Rostock on the Baltic Sea.

Die Deutsche Demokratische Republik feiert ihren 35. Geburtstag

❶ Strassengymnastik in Berlin (Ost)

❷ Vor dem Hauptbahnhof in Erfurt

❸ Freundschaftsbrunnen auf dem Alexanderplatz in Berlin (Ost)

❹ Reisende warten auf den Zug

❺ Kriegerdenkmal in Berlin (Ost)

❻ Der Zwinger in Dresden, im Barockstil gebaut, ist heute ein Kunstmuseum

❼ Die Parkanlagen des Zwingers. Besucher aus aller Welt kommen hierher, um sich die wertvolle Kunstsammlung anzusehen

❽ Kriegerdenkmal in Halle

❾ Stolberg im Harz

❿ Fussgänger in Leipzig

Austria

Austria is one of the smaller countries in Central Europe, mostly famous for its beautiful scenery, its music, and its culture. Two thirds of Austria is covered by the Alps, where skiing is the most popular sport. This country, with its beautiful mountains, lakes, historic cities, and picturesque villages, is a vacationer's dream. There are ancient abbeys, fairytale castles, and beautiful churches. Under the Habsburg rulers, Austria was the heart of a vast empire that included many different ethnic groups and nationalities. Their influence is still felt in Austria, especially in Vienna, Austria's capital.

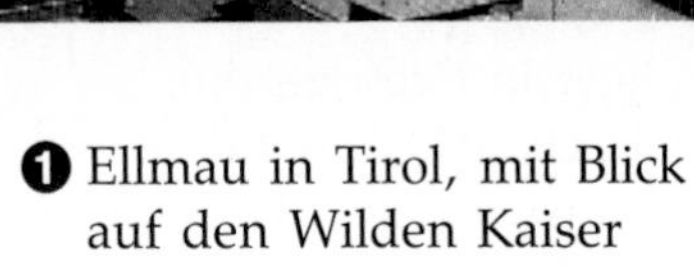

❶ Ellmau in Tirol, mit Blick auf den Wilden Kaiser

❷ Blick auf Salzburg mit Festung Hohensalzburg

❸ Das Geburtshaus von Mozart (1756–1791) in Salzburg

❹ Schilaufen in Hintertux

❺ Trachtengruppe aus der Wachau

❻ Opernball in Wien

❼ Die Wiener Sängerknaben

❽ Dressur eines Lipizzaners in der Spanischen Hofreitschule in Wien

❾ Café Central in Wien, ehemaliger Treffpunkt der Wiener literarischen Gesellschaft

❿ Sacher Hotel, Heimat der weltberühmten Sachertorte

Switzerland

Switzerland, with its beautiful scenery, is the most mountainous country in Europe. Besides its scenery, it is also famous for its watches and clocks, electrical equipment, precision machinery, banks, cheese, and milk chocolate. Switzerland is one of the oldest republics in the world, making democracy work in local government for seven hundred years. For more than one hundred years Switzerland has been neutral amid the wars that its neighbors fought and has been a place of safety for refugees of wars and revolutions.

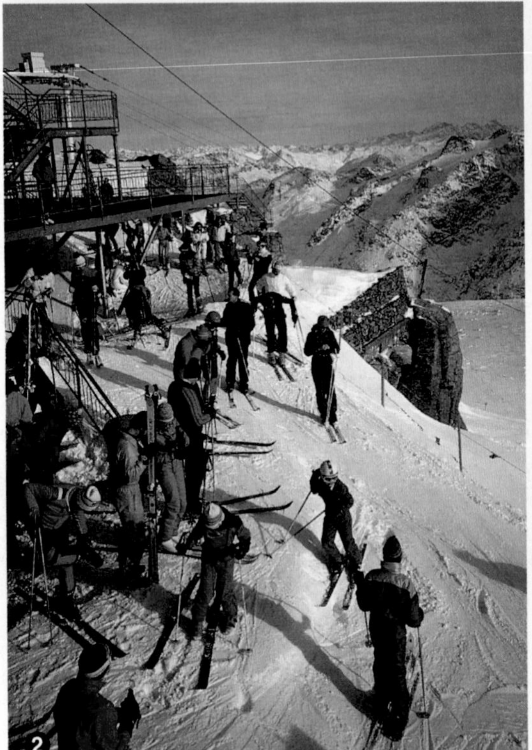

❶ Alphornbläser mit der Jungfrau (4 158 m) im Hintergrund

❷ Schilaufen in St. Moritz

❸ Bergsteigen im Berner Oberland

❹ Blick auf Zürich, grösste Stadt der Schweiz

❺ Die Bahnhofstrasse in Zürich: Banken und elegante Geschäfte

❻ Uhrmacher bei der Arbeit

❼ Bank Leu in Zürich

❽ Bankangestellte in der Schweizer Kreditbank

❾ Confiserie Sprüngli

Liechtenstein, Alsace, South Tyrol

The German-speaking Principality of Liechtenstein, wedged between Switzerland and Austria, is the fourth-smallest country in the world. It is one of the most industrialized countries, and it is among those with the highest per capita income.

German is also spoken in the Alsace, a region in northeastern France at the French-German border. For hundreds of years the inhabitants have been part French and part German, and the area has long been a prize in the wars between France and Germany. The Alsace is famous for its wine and cuisine, and for its quaint medieval cities and villages.

The South Tyrol extends south of Austria to the northern Italian provinces. In 1919, South Tyrol was taken from Austria and given to Italy. Today, both Italian and German are the official languages. This Alpine area is a year-round playground for people of many countries.

❶ Schloss Vaduz, seit 1712 Wohnsitz der Prinzen von Liechtenstein

❷ Colmar mit den schönsten Fachwerkhäusern des Elsass und seiner exzellenten Küche—hier: Choucroute garnie

❸ Viehabtrieb in Südtirol

Karin Haupt is having a party. She invites her friends. Some accept and others decline the invitation. Karin offers her friends various things to eat and drink. They compliment her mother. At the party Karin and her friends have a good time. They listen to music, dance, tell jokes, and gossip a bit.

Your German friends like to go out. They go visiting, ride bikes, play tennis, and go into town. They go to the movies and to concerts. Sabine and Stefan want to go out together. They check the movie and concert listings and discuss what they would like to do. They talk about their favorite music groups and what kinds of films they like.

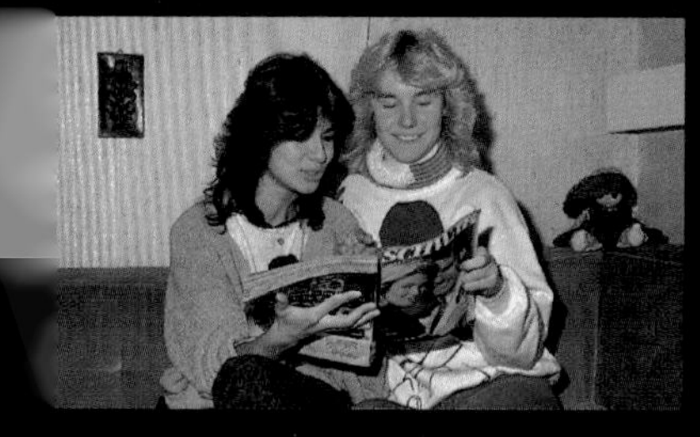

Your friends Andrea and Monika are shopping for presents—there are many birthdays and other occasions coming up. The girls go into a gift shop and also go to a clothing store where Monika buys a sweater on sale. You read some ads suggesting presents for various occasions and learn how to express good wishes on these occasions.

Natalie and her friend Uschi are going to Austria for a few days. The villages of Fieberbrunn and St. Ulrich are popular vacation spots and offer many things to do.

KAPITEL 9

Eine Party

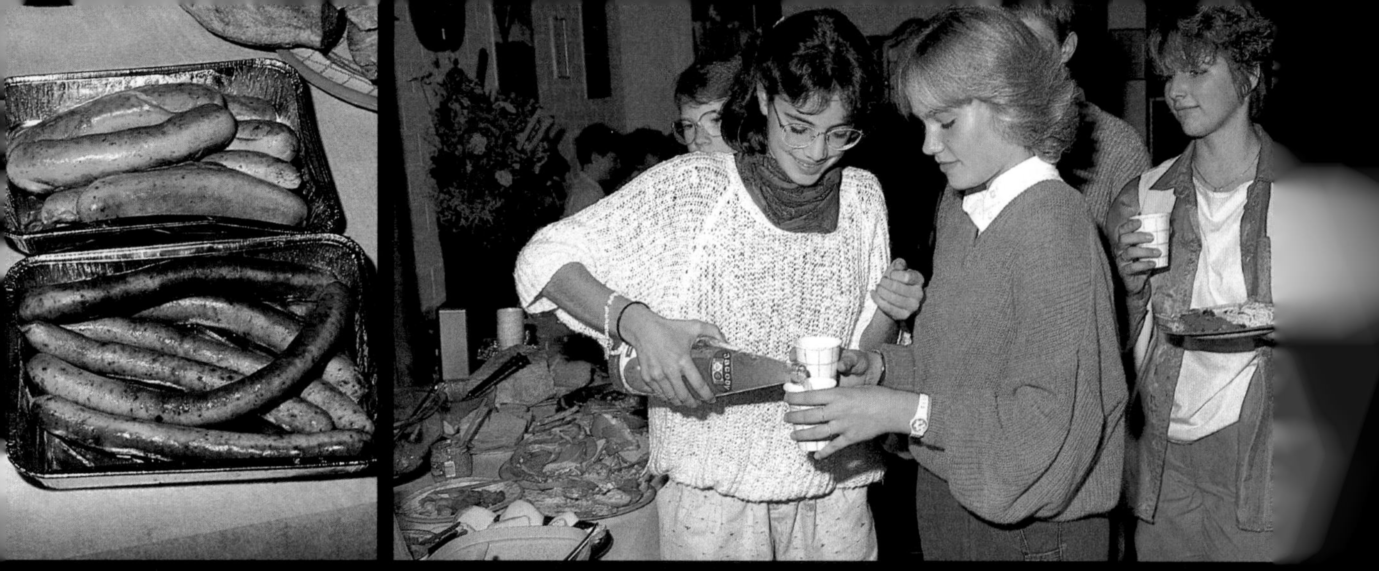

Parties are fun to give and fun to go to. Young people are always ready for an impromptu get-together, but a really good party takes planning. Whom do you invite? What do you serve to eat and drink? What kind of activities should you plan?

In this unit you will:

SECTION A	invite someone to a party and accept or decline an invitation
SECTION B	tell about what there is to eat and drink
SECTION C	offer someone something to eat and drink and accept or decline what is being offered
SECTION D	talk about things to do at a party and pay compliments
TRY YOUR SKILLS	use what you've learned
ZUM LESEN	read for practice and pleasure

SECTION A inviting someone to a party; accepting or declining an invitation

Karin is having a party. She has made her guest list and is calling her friends. What does she say? How do her friends respond? What would you say if you were invited?

A1 Karin hat eine Party

KARIN: Drei—fünf—neun—null—eins—vier. (Es klingelt.)

FRAU BERGER: Berger. Ja, hallo! Ich höre Sie, aber ich verstehe Sie nicht. Hallo, wer ist denn da?

(Klick.) (Es klingelt wieder.)

FRAU BERGER: Hier Berger.

KARIN: Guten Tag, Frau Berger! Hier ist die Karin. Ist die Christine da?

FRAU BERGER: Ach, du bist's Karin! Jetzt verstehe ich dich gut. Moment mal! . . . Christine! Die Karin möchte dich sprechen!

CHRISTINE: Grüss dich, Karin! Wie geht's? Was gibt's?

KARIN: Du, hör zu! Ich hab' am Samstag eine Party, und ich möchte dich einladen. Kommst du?

CHRISTINE: Ja, gern! Am Samstag hab' ich nichts vor. Um wieviel Uhr?

KARIN: Um sieben.

CHRISTINE: Das ist prima! Wen lädst du denn noch ein?

KARIN: Die Michaela, den Bernd, . . .

CHRISTINE: Wirklich? Du, ich bringe meine Musikkassetten, ja?

KARIN: Toll! Dann bis Samstag. Tschüs!

CHRISTINE: Tschüs! Und vielen Dank!

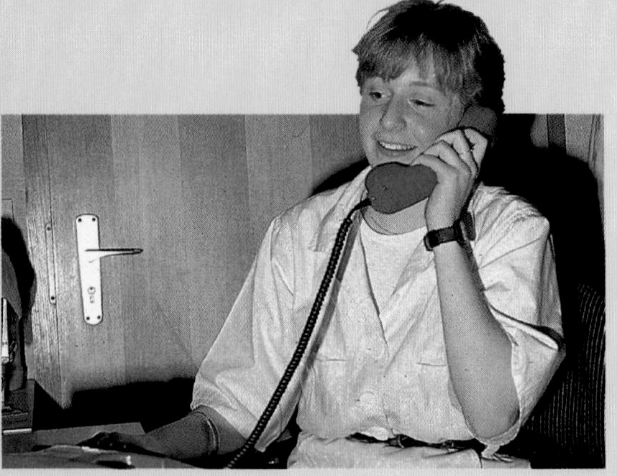

Karin ruft jetzt ihre Freunde und Freundinnen an. Wer kommt? Wer kommt nicht?

Michaela, eine Schulfreundin

Uwe, ein Klassenkamerad

Was? Du hast eine Party, und du lädst mich ein? Toll!

Hans-Peter, Michaelas Freund

Du, es geht leider nicht. Samstag hab' ich schon etwas vor.

Brigitte, eine Klassenkameradin

Um sieben. Uhr geht's nicht. Aber wir kommen etwas später, so um halb neun, O.K.?

Lisa und Heidi, Karins Kusinen

Na, klar! Samstag habe ich nichts vor, das passt prima!

Bernd, ihr Tennispartner

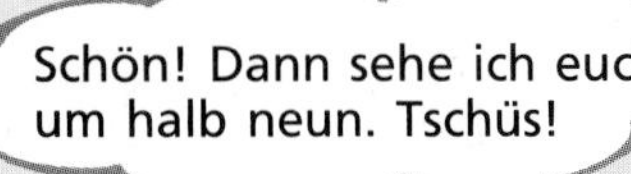

Schön! Dann sehe ich euch um halb neun. Tschüs!

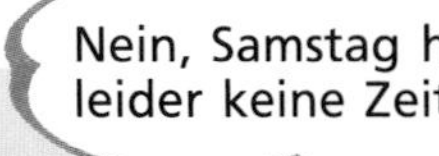

Nein, Samstag hab' ich leider keine Zeit. Schade!

Klaus, ein Klassenkamerad

A2 Übung • Wer hat eine Party?

1. Wer hat eine Party? Was sagt sie?
2. Wer kommt? Was sagen sie?
3. Wer kommt nicht? Was sagen sie?

A3 WIE SAGT MAN DAS?
Accepting and declining an invitation

accepting an invitation	Ja, gern! Ja, ich komme gern! Na, klar! Das passt prima!	Sure, I'd love to! Yes, I'd love to come! Well, of course! That suits me fine!
declining an invitation	Es geht nicht. Samstag geht es nicht.	I can't. I can't on Saturday.
regrets	Das ist schade! Es geht leider nicht.	That's too bad! I'm sorry, I can't.
excuses	Ich habe schon etwas vor. Ich habe keine Zeit.	I already have something planned. I have no time.

A4 Übung • Ich lade dich ein!

Invite six classmates to your party on Saturday. Which classmates accept, which ones decline your invitation? What does each one say?

A: Ich habe am Samstag eine Party. Kommst du?
B: Ja, . . . *or* Nein, . . .

A5 ERKLÄRUNG
First and Second Person Pronouns, Accusative Case

1. You know the subject pronouns **ich** and **wir, du** and **ihr** and **Sie.** Since these are subject pronouns, they are in the nominative case.
2. Each of these pronouns has an accusative case form you use when the pronoun functions as a direct object or as an object of a preposition such as **für.**

Pronoun as Subject (Nominative Case)			*Pronoun as Direct Object (Accusative Case)*		
Ich **Du**	rufe rufst	Bernd an.	Bernd ruft	**mich** **dich**	an.
Wir **Ihr**	rufen ruft			**uns** **euch**	
Sie	rufen			**Sie**	

A6 Übung • Jetzt bist du dran 

Du sprichst zuerst mit einem Freund, dann mit zwei Klassenkameraden, mit deiner Deutschlehrerin und mit zwei Lehrern.

Du möchtest ihn oder sie etwas fragen.
Was sagst du?
Ich möchte dich etwas fragen.
Ich möchte euch etwas fragen.
Ich möchte Sie etwas fragen.
Ich möchte Sie etwas fragen.

ein Freund

zwei Klassenkameraden

1. Du verstehst ihn oder sie nicht.
2. Du möchtest ihn oder sie einladen.
3. Du möchtest ihn oder sie morgen anrufen.
4. Du kennst ihn oder sie gut.
5. Du findest ihn oder sie prima!

die Deutschlehrerin

zwei Lehrer

A7 ERKLÄRUNG
The Verbs anrufen, einladen, vorhaben

1. The verbs **anrufen,** *to call on the telephone,* **einladen,** *to invite,* and **vorhaben,** *to plan to do,* belong to a group of verbs that have a separable prefix: **an**rufen, **ein**laden, **vor**haben. In the present tense, the prefix is separated from the verb and used at the end of the sentence. In addition, the verb **einladen** changes its stem vowel from **a** to **ä** in the **du-**form and in the **er/sie-**form.

anrufen				einladen				vorhaben			
Ich	**rufe**		**an.**	Ich	**lade**		**ein.**	Ich	**habe**		**vor.**
Du	**rufst**		**an.**	Du	**lädst**		**ein.**	Du	**hast**		**vor.**
Er, Sie	**ruft**	Bernd	**an.**	Er, Sie	**lädt**	Karin	**ein.**	Er, Sie	**hat**	was	**vor.**
Wir	**rufen**		**an.**	Wir	**laden**		**ein.**	Wir	**haben**		**vor.**
Ihr	**ruft**		**an.**	Ihr	**ladet**		**ein.**	Ihr	**habt**		**vor.**
Sie	**rufen**		**an.**	Sie	**laden**		**ein.**	Sie	**haben**		**vor.**

2. The verb **einladen** does not change the stem vowel in the command form.

Du, Karin, **lad** doch die Christine **ein!**

A8 Übung • Wen rufst du an? 

A: Rufst du den Bernd an?
B: Ja, ich rufe ihn an.

A: Und Bernds Freundin?
B: Ja, ich rufe sie auch an.

1. Und den Amerikaner aus New York?
2. Und mich?
3. Und uns?
4. Und Christines Freund?

A 9 Übung • Und wen lädst du ein?

A: Lädst du die Michaela ein?
B: Ja, ich lade sie ein.

A: Und Michaelas Freund?
B: Ja, ich lade ihn auch ein.

1. Und den Amerikaner aus New York?
2. Und uns?
3. Und mich?
4. Und Karins Freundin?

A 10 Übung • Alle haben etwas vor!

A: Hast du etwas vor?
B: Ja, ich habe leider etwas vor.

1. Hat Bernd etwas vor?
2. Und Bernds Schwester?
3. Und die Eltern?
4. Und ihr?

A 11 Übung • Partnerarbeit

Du fragst einen Mitschüler, was du machen sollst!

A: Was soll ich machen? Soll ich . . .
B: Ja, lad doch die Michaela ein!

die Michaela einladen?
den Leberkäs probieren?
den Lehrer einladen?
das Eis holen?
zu Karins Party gehen?
meine Mutter fragen?
eine Limo trinken?
den Bernd anrufen?
die Musikkassetten bringen?

A 12 Übung • Hör gut zu!

Sagen deine Freunde ja oder nein?

	0	1	2	3	4	5	6	7	8
accepting	✓								
declining									

A 13 Übung • Du möchtest eine Party haben

Deine Party ist am Samstag. Ruf die folgenden Leute an und lad sie ein: einen Freund, zwei Klassenkameradinnen, deinen Deutschlehrer. Schreib die Gespräche auf!

A: Ich habe am Samstag eine Party, und ich lade . . . ein. Kommst . . .?
B: . . .
A: . . .

SECTION B

telling what there is to eat and drink

Karin's friends are arriving at the party. They are hungry and already asking about the food! Let's hear and see what Karin and her mother have prepared for the guests to eat and drink. Think about what you would offer your guests at a party at your house.

B1 Was gibt es alles?

HEIDI Du, Karin! Wir haben Hunger. Wann essen wir?
KARIN Gleich!
HEIDI Was gibt es überhaupt?
KARIN Es gibt eine Suppe—eine Gulaschsuppe—Kartoffelsalat, Hamburger, Bratwurst, Wurstbrote und Käsebrote . . . und natürlich auch Kuchen.
HEIDI Und zu trinken?
KARIN Schau! Wir haben Erdbeerbowle[1], Limonade, Fanta, Cola, Mineralwasser, . . . äh . . . Apfelsaft, und die Mutti macht auch einen Kaffee.
HEIDI Prima! Wann geht's endlich los? Ich habe einen Bärenhunger!

Für dich? Einen Apfelsaft.
Was hast du für mich?

Was gibt's zu essen? Wer hat Hunger?

Suppe Hamburger Käsebrote BRATWURST Kartoffelsalat Kuchen Wurstbrote

Und was gibt's zu trinken? Wer hat Durst?

Mineralwasser Fanta Apfelsaft Limonade Erdbeerbowle Cola Kaffee

B2 Übung • Was gibt es zu essen und zu trinken?

A: Was gibt's zu essen?
B: Es gibt . . .
A: Toll! Wann geht's los!

A: Und was gibt's zu trinken?
B: Wir haben . . .
A: Du, ich hab' Durst!

[1]Karin made a strawberry punch for her friends with fresh strawberries, raspberry syrup, and lemon flavored soda.

B3 WIE SAGT MAN DAS?
Saying what there is to eat and drink

Was gibt's zu essen?	What's there to eat?
Was gibt's zu trinken?	What's there to drink?
Es gibt . . .	There is / There are . . .
Wir haben . . .	We have . . .

B4 HANS-PETER ISST ALLES GERN!

Hans-Peter is always hungry and he likes everything! What do you like to eat and drink?

KARIN Was isst du? Einen Hamburger?
HANS-PETER Natürlich! Ich esse Hamburger gern.
KARIN Für wen ist die Limonade?
HANS-PETER Für mich.
KARIN Was, du trinkst Limo?
HANS-PETER Na und?! Ich trinke Limo gern.

B5 Übung • Und du?

1. Was isst du gern? Was trinkst du gern?
2. Was isst du nicht gern?
3. Was isst und trinkst du am liebsten?
4. Frag deine Klassenkameraden und deine Lehrerin oder deinen Lehrer, was sie gern essen und trinken!
5. Erzähl, was sie sagen!

B6 Übung • Partnerarbeit 

You and a classmate are at Karin's party. Practice the following dialogs, using the list on the right. Make necessary changes.

A: Isst du einen Hamburger?
B: Nein, ich esse Hamburger nicht gern.
A: Isst du lieber ein Wurstbrot?
B: Ja, Wurstbrote esse ich gern!

* * *

A: Ich habe Durst. Ich trinke einen Apfelsaft. Was trinkst du?
B: Ich trinke lieber Mineralwasser.
A: Du trinkst immer nur Mineralwasser.
B: Na und? Mineralwasser schmeckt gut.

der / ein	die / eine	das / ein
Apfelsaft	Bratwurst	Käsebrot
Hamburger	Cola	Mineralwasser
Kaffee	Erdbeerbowle	Wurstbrot
Kartoffelsalat	Fanta	
	Limonade	
	Suppe	

B7 Übung • Auf der Party

Write what you like to eat and drink, choosing from the list on the preceding page. Then write what a friend of yours likes.

Ich esse gern . . . (Robert) isst gern . . .

B8 Übung • Wer bekommt was? 

A: Ist die Cola für den Bernd?
B: Ja, die Cola ist für ihn.

1. Ist der Apfelsaft für die Heidi?
2. Ist das Käsebrot für den Hans-Peter?
3. Ist die Limonade für die Kinder?
4. Ist der Hamburger für die Lisa?
5. Ist der Kartoffelsalat für die Karin?
6. Ist der Kaffee für die Eltern?

B9 Übung • Was möchtest du essen und trinken? 

Du hast eine Party. Deine Freunde haben Hunger und Durst. Was möchten deine Freunde und was möchte dein Lehrer essen und trinken? Was sagen sie? Was sagst du?

1. eine Klassenkameradin

Für mich einen Apfelsaft!

Hier, ein Apfelsaft für dich!

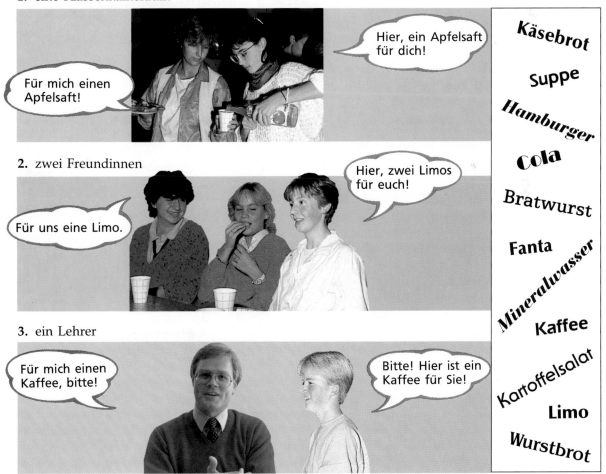

2. zwei Freundinnen

Für uns eine Limo.

Hier, zwei Limos für euch!

3. ein Lehrer

Für mich einen Kaffee, bitte!

Bitte! Hier ist ein Kaffee für Sie!

Käsebrot
Suppe
Hamburger
Cola
Bratwurst
Fanta
Mineralwasser
Kaffee
Kartoffelsalat
Limo
Wurstbrot

B 10 Übung • Hör gut zu!

Du bist auf einer Party. Was gibt es zu essen und zu trinken?

	0	1	2	3	4	5	6	7	8
zu essen	✓								
zu trinken									

B 11 Schreibübung • Auf der Party

1. Schreib einen Dialog!

Wir haben Hunger! Was gibt es zu essen?
Es gibt auch Kuchen.
Gleich!
Wir haben Durst! Was gibt es zu trinken?
Toll! Kuchen esse ich immer gern!
Prima!
Wann essen wir?
Es gibt Suppe, Bratwurst und Kartoffelsalat.
Wir haben Erdbeerbowle, Fanta und Limonade.

2. Karin und ihre Mutter bringen das Essen. Wer bekommt was? Schreib auf, was Karins Mutter fragt und was Karin antwortet!

der Bernd—die Bratwurst

Bekommt der Bernd die Bratwurst?
Ja, sie ist für ihn.

1. der Hans-Peter—das Käsebrot
2. die Heidi—den Apfelsaft
3. die Lisa—den Hamburger
4. die Kinder—die Limonade
5. der Bernd—den Kartoffelsalat

B 12 Schreibübung • Projekt

1. Plan a class party.
2. Design and draw a decorative menu for your party.
3. Make a shopping list.

SECTION C

offering someone something to eat and drink, accepting or declining what is being offered

Karin is offering her friends various things to eat and drink. Let's hear what everyone would like to have. What about you? What would you like?

C1 Was möchtest du? Einen Hamburger?

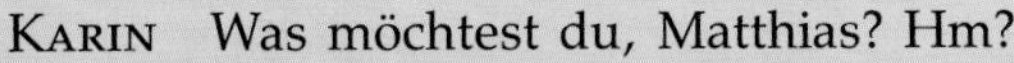

KARIN Was möchtest du, Matthias? Hm? Eine Gulaschsuppe? Einen Hamburger?
MATTHIAS Nein, keine Suppe, bitte! Und keinen Hamburger. Ich . . . äh . . . esse eine Bratwurst.

KARIN Und was nimmst du, Christine? Ein Wurstbrot, vielleicht?
CHRISTINE Ja, bitte!
KARIN Und eine Cola?
CHRISTINE Du, keine Cola, bitte. Ich nehme Mineralwasser.

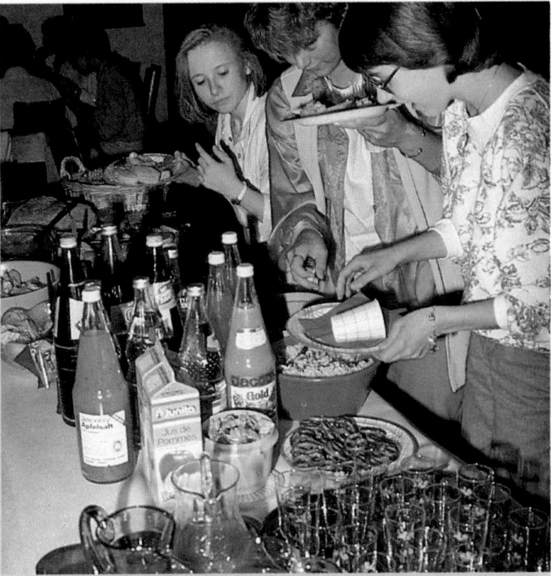

HANS-PETER Und ich nehme einen Hamburger, eine Bratwurst, ein Wurstbrot . . .
KARIN Noch was?
HANS-PETER Nein, danke!
KARIN Na, dann guten Appetit!

MICHAELA Herr Haupt, was trinken Sie? Eine Limo? Eine Fanta? Erdbeerbowle?
HERR HAUPT Keine Fanta. Hm, ich trinke einen Kaffee.

C2 Übung • Und du? Wie steht's mit dir?

1. Was möchtest du? Eine Suppe?
2. Möchtest du einen Hamburger?
3. Oder möchtest du eine Limo?
4. Was isst du gern?
5. Und was trinkst du?

C3 WIE SAGT MAN DAS?
Accepting or declining something to eat or drink

accepting	Ja, bitte! Ja, gern!	Yes, please. Yes, I'd love some.
declining	Nein, danke! Keinen Kaffee für mich, danke!	No thanks. No coffee for me, thanks.

C4 Übung • Du hast eine Party! 

Was möchten deine Gäste essen und trinken? Was sagen sie?

A: Möchtest du eine Limonade?
B: . . . *or* . . .

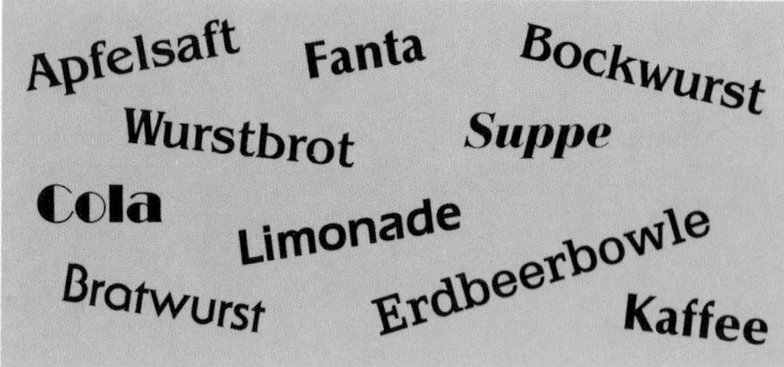

Apfelsaft
Fanta
Bockwurst
Wurstbrot
Suppe
Cola
Limonade
Erdbeerbowle
Bratwurst
Kaffee

C5 WIE SAGT MAN DAS?
Making negative statements

You already know that **nicht** is used to make negative statements. To negate a noun, use the word **kein.**

negating the entire statement	Ich esse die Suppe nicht. Ich trinke die Cola nicht.	I am not eating the soup. I am not drinking the cola.
negating noun phrases	Ich esse keine Suppe. Ich trinke keinen Kaffee.	I do not eat soup. I do not drink coffee.

Kein can have slightly different meanings in a sentence. What do you notice about the following examples?

Ich trinke keinen Kaffee. — *I do not drink coffee.*
Ich esse kein Wurstbrot, ich esse ein Käsebrot. — *I am not eating a sandwich with cold cuts; I am eating a cheese sandwich.*

ERKLÄRUNG
kein, *Nominative and Accusative Case*

1. The word **kein** has the same endings as **ein.**

	Nominative			*Accusative*		
Masculine	Ist das Das ist	**ein** **kein**	Hamburger? Hamburger.	Ich esse Ich esse	**einen** **keinen**	Hamburger. Hamburger.
Feminine	Ist das Das ist	**eine** **keine**	Erdbeerbowle? Erdbeerbowle.	Ich trinke Ich trinke	**eine** **keine**	Erdbeerbowle. Erdbeerbowle.
Neuter	Ist das Das ist	**ein** **kein**	Käsebrot? Käsebrot.	Ich esse Ich esse	**ein** **kein**	Käsebrot. Käsebrot.
Plural	Sind das Das sind	 **keine**	Bratwürste? Bratwürste.	Ich esse Ich esse	 **keine**	Bratwürste. Bratwürste.

2. **Kein** is also used before some nouns that have no determiner in the corresponding positive phrase.

Sie hat Durst.	Sie hat keinen Durst.	*She's not thirsty.*
Ich habe Hunger.	Ich habe keinen Hunger.	*I'm not hungry.*
Das macht Spass.	Das macht keinen Spass.	*That's no fun.*
Hast du Zeit?	Nein, ich habe keine Zeit.	*No, I don't have time.*

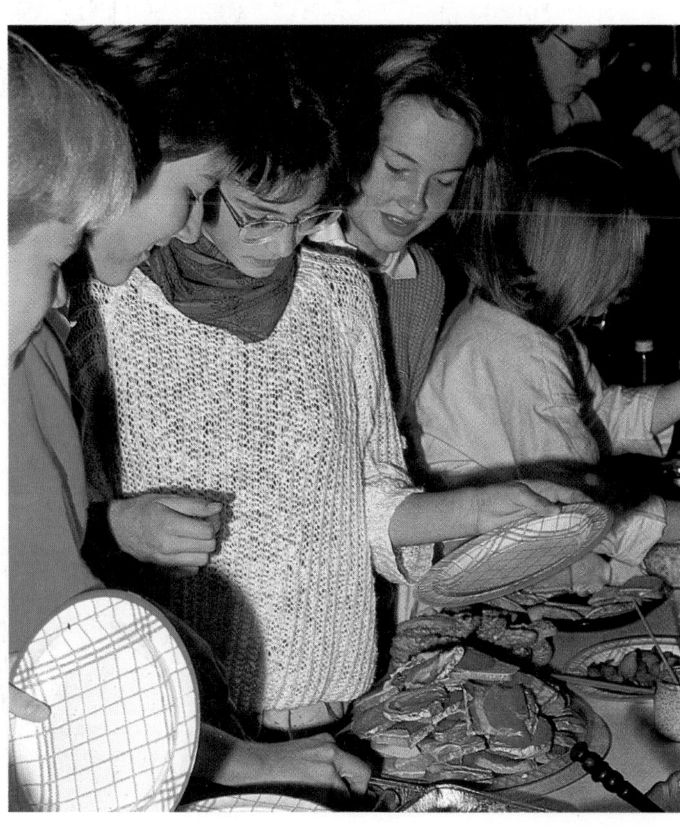

Übung

Du isst ja überhaupt nichts!

A: Was möchtest du? Eine Suppe?
B: Nein, keine Suppe, bitte!

1. einen Hamburger?
2. ein Käsebrot?
3. Bratwürste?
4. Kartoffelsalat?
5. ein Wurstbrot?
6. eine Gulaschsuppe?

Übung

Du trinkst ja nichts!

A: Was trinkst du? Eine Cola?
B: Danke, nein, keine Cola!

1. einen Kaffee?
2. eine Fanta?
3. ein Mineralwasser?
4. einen Apfelsaft?
5. eine Limonade?

C9 ERKLÄRUNG
The Verb nehmen

The verb **nehmen,** *to take,* has the following forms in the present tense:

ich **nehme**	wir **nehmen**
du **nimmst**	ihr **nehmt**
er, sie, es **nimmt**	sie, Sie **nehmen**

C10 Übung • Jetzt bist du dran

1. You're having a party. Ask various classmates what they would like to eat or drink and make suggestions. Your classmates do not care for what you suggest but would like something else.
   A: Was nimmst du? Eine Bratwurst vielleicht?
   B: Nein, danke! Keine Bratwurst. Ich nehme ein Käsebrot.
2. Now practice offering something to two classmates.
3. Offer your teacher something to eat or drink.

C11 Übung • Der Partymuffel

Was sagt der Partymuffel? Was sagen seine Freunde?

Ich komme nicht.
Ich esse keine Bratwurst.
Ich trinke keine Cola.
Ich möchte den Kuchen nicht probieren.
Ich tanze nicht.
Ich gehe jetzt.

Komm doch!
. . . . . . !

C12 Übung • Hör gut zu!

Was möchten deine Freunde essen und trinken? Was möchten sie nicht essen und trinken?

	0	1	2	3	4	5	6	7	8	9	10
accepting											
declining	✓										

C13 Schreibübung • Du planst eine Party

Write a paragraph telling about a party you are planning. Tell the day and time, whom you are inviting, and what you are going to have to eat and drink.

Ich habe am Samstag um . . .

talking about things to do at a party, paying compliments

What are our friends doing at their party? What would you like to do if you were there?

D1 So, was machen wir jetzt?

So, was machen wir jetzt? Wer hat eine Idee?

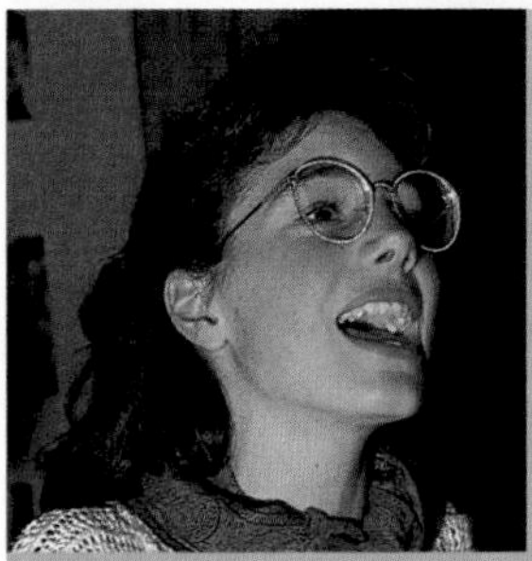

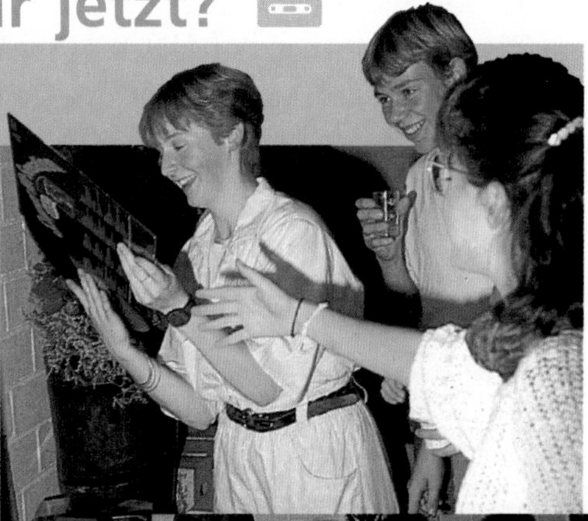

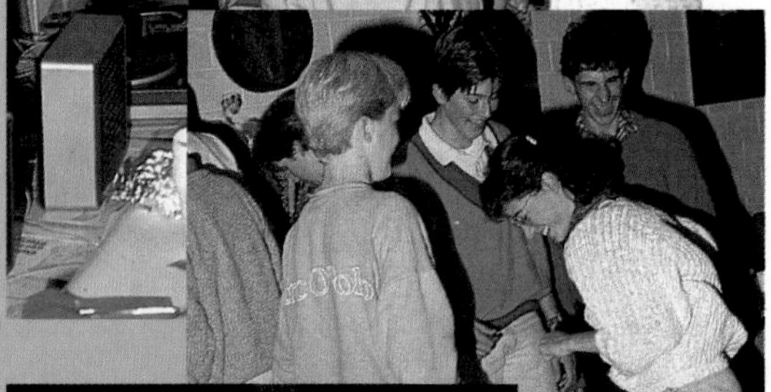

MICHAELA	Ich möchte Hans-Peters Kassette hören. —Wo habt ihr euren Kassetten-Recorder?
CHRISTINE	Karin, wo hast du deinen Plattenspieler? Ich möchte eine Platte hören.
HANS-PETER	Wo ist die Musik? Ich möchte tanzen.
UWE	Ich möchte einen Film sehen. —Habt ihr einen Video-Recorder?
BERND	Einen Film sehen? Du spinnst! —Möchtet ihr lieber einen Witz hören?

Ruhe! Der Bernd erzählt einen Witz!
Mensch, Bernd! Deine Witze sind blöd!

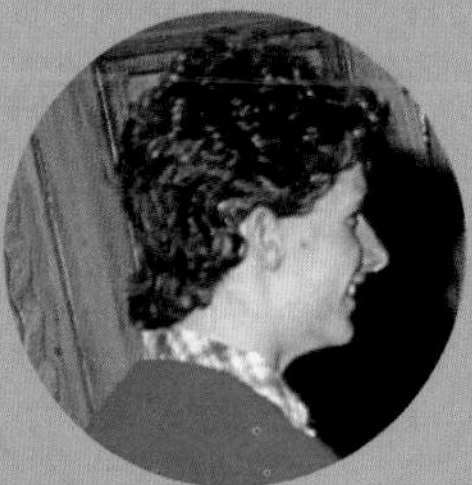

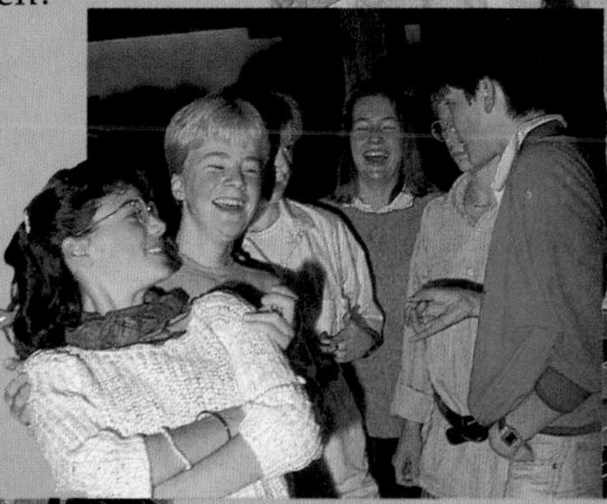

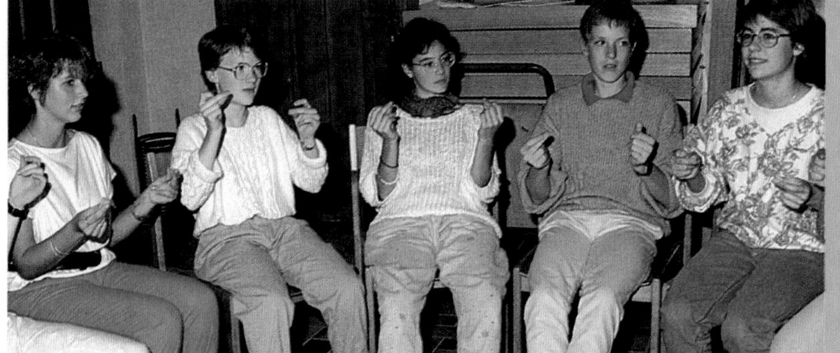

HEIDI	Ich habe eine Idee: wir spielen jetzt ein Ratespiel!
LISA	Ein Ratespiel? Ich möchte lieber diskutieren.

D2 Übung • Und du? Wie steht's mit dir?

1. Was machst du, wenn du eine Party hast?
2. Frage deine Klassenkameraden, was sie machen!
3. Jetzt fragst du deinen Lehrer oder deine Lehrerin!
4. Was machst du gern? Was machst du am liebsten?
5. Was machst du nicht? Warum nicht?
6. Hast du einen Video-Recorder?
7. Hast du Video-Filme oder mietest du sie?
8. Kennst du einen Witz? Möchtest du ihn erzählen?

Kassetten hören
tanzen
Musik hören
Witze erzählen
einen Film sehen
diskutieren
Ratespiel spielen
essen und trinken

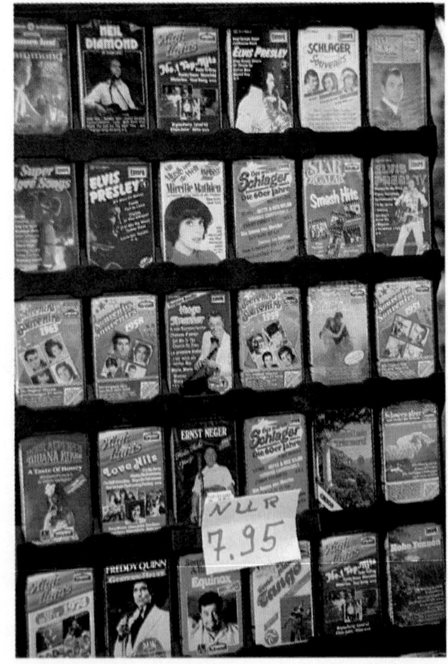

D3 WIE IST DIE PARTY?

Karin, deine Eltern sind so nett!

He, Bernd! Deine Kassette ist furchtbar!

Ich finde euer Haus so gemütlich.

Klasse Party!

Das Essen ist Spitze!

Lecker!

Ist das die Michaela? Wer ist denn ihr Tanzpartner? Uwe? Er tanzt wirklich toll!
Die Michaela sieht phantastisch aus!
Tolle Musik!
BOSS

Michaela und Hans-Peter finden das Essen prima. Was sagen sie?

HANS-PETER Frau Haupt, Ihr Kartoffelsalat schmeckt ausgezeichnet.
FRAU HAUPT Wirklich? Ist er gut?
HANS-PETER Ganz prima!
FRAU HAUPT Da bin ich aber froh.

MICHAELA Ihre Wurstbrote sehen lecker aus.
FRAU HAUPT Ja, schmecken sie auch?
MICHAELA Und wie!
FRAU HAUPT Das freut mich.

D4 ERKLÄRUNG
Possessives, Nominative and Accusative Case

The words **mein, dein, sein, unser, euer, ihr** are called possessives. They have the same endings as the indefinite article **ein** and are often called **ein**-words.

The following is a summary chart of the possessives showing all nominative and accusative forms used before masculine, feminine, neuter, and plural nouns.

	before a masculine noun		*before a neuter noun*	*before feminine & plural nouns*
	Nominative	*Accusative*	*Nominative & Accusative*	*Nominative & Accusative*
my	**mein**	**meinen**	**mein**	**meine**
your	**dein**	**deinen**	**dein**	**deine**
his	**sein**	**seinen**	**sein**	**seine**
her	**ihr**	**ihren**	**ihr**	**ihre**
our	**unser**	**unseren**	**unser**	**unsere**
your	**euer**	**eueren**	**euer**	**euere**
their	**ihr**	**ihren**	**ihr**	**ihre**
your	**Ihr**	**Ihren**	**Ihr**	**Ihre**

D5 Übung • Auf der Party gehört

Wie ist die Bratwurst, Bernd?
Frau Haupt, Ihre Bratwurst schmeckt ausgezeichnet!
der Kartoffelsalat? die Wurstbrote?
der Kaffee? die Limonade?
der Apfelsaft? die Gulaschsuppe?
Du, wie findest du meine Schwester?
Wie findest du Karins Party?
Ich finde ihre Party Klasse!
Ich finde deine Schwester sehr nett.

meinen Bruder? meine Kusine?
meine Eltern? meinen Freund?
meine Lehrerin? meine Geschwister?

Musik? Platten?
Tanzpartner? Video-Recorder?
Freunde?

D6 WIE SAGT MAN DAS?
Complimenting people, complimenting someone on food

In Unit 6 you learned how to pay a compliment and to respond to a compliment. Here are some more ways of complimenting.

complimenting people	Du siehst gut aus. Er tanzt wirklich toll. Deine Eltern sind so nett.	You look good. He really dances well. Your parents are so nice.
complimenting someone on food	Ihr Kuchen ist ausgezeichnet. Die Suppe schmeckt lecker. Ich finde Ihren Kaffee gut.	Your cake is excellent. The soup tastes delicious. I think your coffee is good.

Look at the dialogs on page 255. How does Frau Haupt respond to the compliments? What would you say if someone complimented you?

D7 Übung • Mach doch mal ein Kompliment! 

Du siehst, dass die Karin gut tanzt. Was sagst du? Und was sagt Karin?

A: Karin, du tanzt wirklich toll!
B: Meinst du?

1. Der Bernd erzählt gute Witze.
2. Frau Haupts Kartoffelsalat ist sehr gut.
3. Karins Zimmer ist gemütlich.
4. Christines Kassetten sind gut.
5. Michaela sieht sehr hübsch aus.
6. Der Hans-Peter hat eine gute Idee.
7. Karins Freunde sind lustig.
8. Karins Erdbeerbowle schmeckt gut.
9. Karins Eltern sind sehr nett.

ausgezeichnet
nett
Spitze!
gut
tanzt gut
gemütlich
prima
sieht hübsch aus
Klasse!
lustig
toll

Hast du sie gern?
Findest du?
Ja? Ist sie gut?
Ja, wirklich?
Schmeckt er auch?
Meinst du?

D8 Übung • Hör gut zu!

Listen to the statement. Is the one that follows appropriate or not?

	0	1	2	3	4	5	6	7	8	9	10
appropriate	✓										
not appropriate											

D9 Schreibübung • Wie ist die Party?

Pretend you are at a party at a classmate's house. Write a paragraph commenting on the party. Mention the food, company, music, and anything else that comes to mind.

TRY YOUR SKILLS

using what you've learned

1 Bernd schreibt eine Einladungskarte

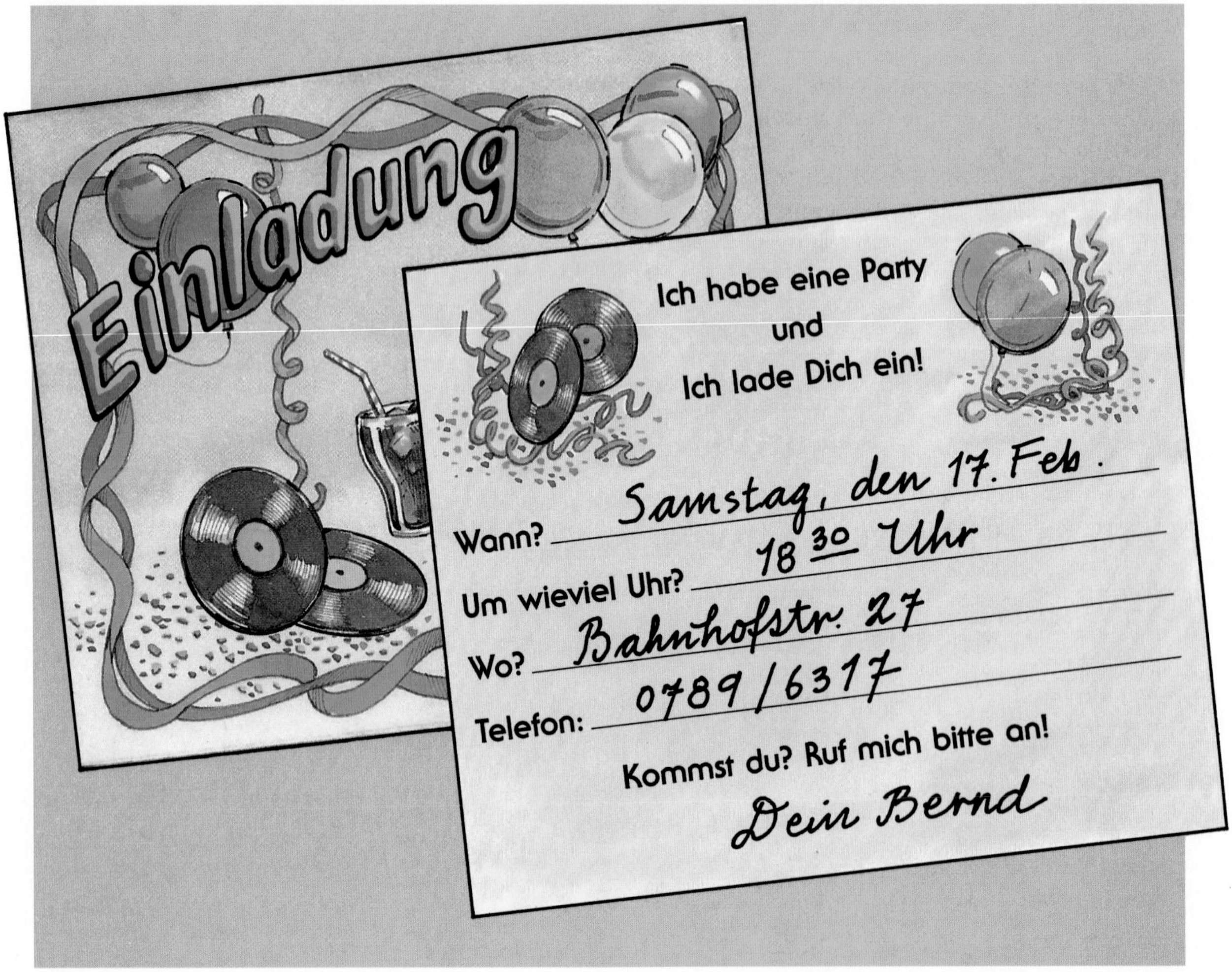

Einladung

Ich habe eine Party
und
Ich lade Dich ein!

Wann? Samstag, den 17. Feb.

Um wieviel Uhr? 18 30 Uhr

Wo? Bahnhofstr. 27

Telefon: 0789/6317

Kommst du? Ruf mich bitte an!

Dein Bernd

2 Übung • Du rufst den Bernd an. Gehst du oder gehst du nicht? 

DU Hallo, Bernd! Du hast eine Party und lädst mich ein! Toll!
BERND Na klar! Kommst du?
DU Ja, . . . *or* Nein, . . .

3 Schreibübung • Wann ist deine Party?

Du hast auch eine Party. Schreib eine Einladungskarte! Wen lädst du ein? Schreib eine Gästeliste! Was gibt es alles zu essen und zu trinken? Schreib eine Einkaufsliste! Was kann man alles auf einer Party tun? Schreib eine Liste mit Ideen!

4 Leseübung • Karins Party ist toll!

Karins Partys sind immer toll. Sie lädt nette Jungen und Mädchen ein. Leider kommt ihre Freundin Katja nicht, sie hat schon etwas vor. Das ist schade, denn sie ist die beste Tänzerin. Karins Mutter macht wieder ihren guten Kartoffelsalat, und Karin macht ihre Erdbeerbowle. Das Essen und die Getränke sind wirklich lecker. Karin hat einen neuen Plattenspieler. Ihr Freund Bernd bringt seine „tollen" Platten mit, aber Karin findet seine Musik furchtbar.

5 Übung • Meine Partys sind auch toll!

1. The preceding passage describes Karin's party in the third person. After you have read the text carefully, pretend that this is your party and that you are talking about it.
   Meine Partys sind immer . . .
2. Make up questions about the passage on Karin's party and ask a classmate to answer them.
   Wie sind Karins Partys? Wen . . .

6 Leseübung • Ein Durcheinander 

BERND	Mensch, Karin! Wo ist mein Hamburger?
KARIN	Ich glaube, der Hans-Peter isst deinen Hamburger.
HANS-PETER	Was? Ich . . . ich esse seinen Hamburger? —Nein!!!

HANS-PETER	Mensch, Christine, wo ist meine Fanta?
CHRISTINE	Deine Fanta? —Die Michaela trinkt deine Fanta.
MICHAELA	Was? Ich? Ich trinke seine Fanta? —Nein!!!

7 Übung • Rollenspiel 

You and your classmates take the roles of Bernd, Karin, Hans-Peter, Christine, and Michaela. Practice the dialogs above, substituting the following items:

Wurstbrot, Apfelsaft, Gulaschsuppe, Limonade
Kartoffelsalat, Mineralwasser, Bratwurst, Kaffee

8 Übung • Was gehört zusammen?

Match the statements on the left with appropriate responses on the right.

1. Was möchtest du, einen Hamburger?
2. Ich habe eine Party, und ich lade dich ein. Kommst du?
3. Wen lädst du noch ein?
4. Ich habe Durst.
5. Was gibt es zu essen?
6. Kommt ihr?
7. Ihr Kartoffelsalat ist ausgezeichnet, Frau Haupt.
8. Was gibt es zu trinken?
9. Christine! Hier ist die Karin!

a. Das geht leider nicht. Wir haben was vor.
b. Es gibt Apfelsaft, Fanta, Cola und Mineralwasser.
c. Möchtest du eine Cola?
d. Grüss dich, Karin! Was gibt's?
e. Ja, ich komme gern.
f. Den Bernd, die Michaela und die Heidi.
g. Wir haben Bratwurst, Käsebrote und Wurstbrote.
h. Nein, danke. Ich habe keinen Hunger.
i. Dann bin ich aber froh.

9 Übung • Mix-Match

Wieviel Sätze kannst du machen?

Karin lädt meine Kusine am Wochenende ein.

wer?		wen?	wann? wie oft?	
ich wir Karin	lade rufe laden rufen lädt ruft	dich euch meine Kusine meinen Freund ihre Freundin	am Wochenende einmal in der Woche um sieben Uhr immer	an ein

10 Übung • Karin geht für die Party einkaufen

Karin braucht noch ein paar Sachen für die Party. Schau auf den Einkaufszettel!

Für den Kuchen braucht sie . . .
Für den Kartoffelsalat braucht sie . . .
Für die Hamburger braucht sie . . .
Für die Wurst- und Käsebrote braucht sie . . .

Karins Mutter sagt ihr, wo sie alles kaufen soll:

Kauf die Kartoffeln beim . . .!
Hol . . .!

Karins Einkaufszettel:

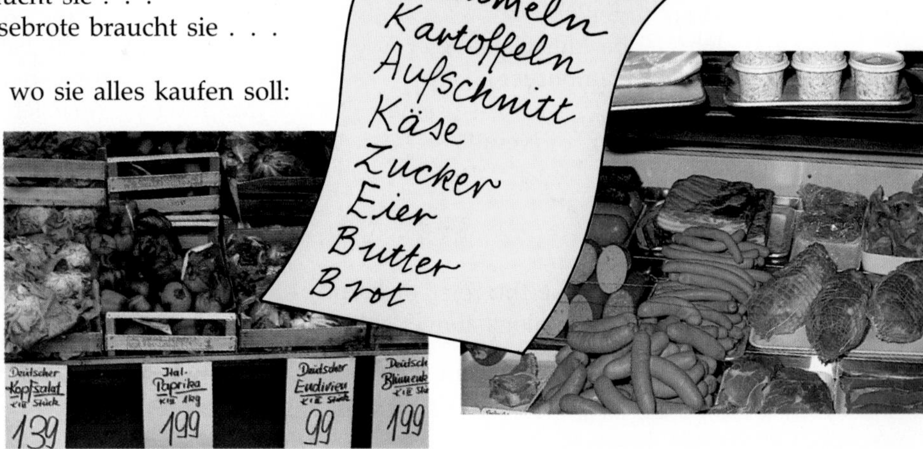

11 Übung • Im Lokal

Du bist mit einem Klassenkameraden in der Stadt. Ihr habt Hunger und Durst und geht in eine Imbiss-Stube.

1. A: Du, was gibt's denn hier?
B: Schau, hier gibt's . . .
A: Prima!

2. A: Was nimmst du?
B: Eine Limo.
A: Gut. Eine Limo für dich und einen Apfelsaft für mich.

3. A: Fräulein!
FRÄULEIN: Ja, bitte?
A: Eine Limo und einen Apfelsaft, bitte.
FRÄULEIN: Noch etwas?
A: Nein, danke!

4. FRÄULEIN: Eine Limo für Sie und . . .
A: Nein, ich bekomme keine Limo, ich bekomme den Apfelsaft.
FRÄULEIN: Entschuldigung!

5. FRÄULEIN: So, wer bekommt den Apfelsaft?
A: Der Apfelsaft ist für mich, und mein Freund bekommt die Limo.

...auch zum Mitnehmen...

Pommes frites	Portion	1.70
Sauerkraut	"	1.20
Kartoffelsalat . . .	"	1.20
Bier-hell	0,5 l	2.30
Weißbier	0,5 l	2.50
Pils	0,33 l	2.–
Radlermaß	1 l	4.40
Cola, Fanta, Spezi, . .	0,33 l	1.60
Apollinares	0,33 l	1.60
Apfel-u. Orangen-Saft	0,2 l	1.60
Zitronenlimonade . .	0,5 l	2.–

12 Übung • Was sagen sie?

13 Aussprache-, Lese- und Schreibübungen

1. Listen carefully and repeat what you hear.

2. Listen, then read aloud.
1. schlecht, Kirche, möchte, vielleicht, traurig; nach, noch, Buch, auch; Fach—Fächer, Buch—Bücher
2. Salat, Suppe, sein, Käse, Musik, Apfelsaft
3. hier, dein, Wien, wieder, heiss, vier, fliegen, gleich, leider, Spiel, vielleicht
4. unser, euer, später, lecker, Hunger, Spieler, Partner, Recorder

3. Copy the following sentences to prepare yourself to write them from dictation.
1. Unser Salat ist wieder lecker.
2. Ich fliege auch gleich weiter.
3. Ich möchte auch drei Bücher.
4. Das Spiel ist leider wieder in Wien.

WAS KANNST DU SCHON?

Let's review some important points you have learned in this unit.

Can you invite someone to a party?
You are having a party on Saturday at 7 o'clock. Call the following people and invite them to the party:

1. a friend **2.** two classmates **3.** your teacher

Do you know how to accept or decline a party invitation?
A classmate has just invited you to a party.

1. Accept the invitation.
2. Decline the invitation.
3. Decline the invitation and make an excuse.

Can you tell someone what there is to eat and drink?
You are having a party. Tell your guests what you have to eat and drink.

Do you know how to offer someone something to eat and drink?
Offer a friend each of the following things:

eine Bratwurst, Erdbeerbowle, ein Wurstbrot, Mineralwasser

Do you know how to accept or decline something to eat and drink?
You have just been offered some cake. Give two ways of accepting and two ways of declining.

Can you make negative statements?
Make each of the following statements negative:

1. Er isst die Suppe.
2. Wir haben Zeit.
3. Er möchte einen Hamburger.
4. Ich habe Hunger.
5. Du bekommst Apfelsaft.
6. Das macht Spass.

Can you talk about things to do at a party?
Name six things you like to do at a party.

Can you pay someone a compliment?
Compliment your friend's mother on the following things:

Kartoffelsalat, Kuchen, Gulaschsuppe

Compliment Karin on her party.

WORTSCHATZ

SECTION A

anrufen *to call up* (see p 243)
bringen *to bring*
einladen *to invite* (see p 243)
etwas *something;* etwas später *a little later*
der **Freund, -e** *boyfriend*
gehen: es geht nicht *I can't*
gut *well*
hör zu! *listen!*
kein, keine *no, not any*
klingeln: es klingelt *the phone rings*
noch: wen lädst du noch ein? *who else are you inviting?*
passen: das passt prima *that suits me fine*
schon *already*
schön! *good! great!*
die **Schulfreundin, -nen** *friend from school* (f)
so um halb neun *around 8:30*
später *later*
sprechen: die Karin möchte dich sprechen *Karin would like to talk to you*
Uhr: um wieviel Uhr? *at what time?*
verstehen *to understand*
vorhaben *to have plans* (see p 243)
was gibt's? *what's up?*
wie geht's? *how are you?*

SECTION B

der **Apfelsaft, ⸚e** *apple juice*
der **Bärenhunger: ich habe einen Bärenhunger!** *I'm hungry as a bear!*
die **Erdbeerbowle, -n** *strawberry punch*
es gibt *there is . . .*
die **Fanta** *orange-flavored soda*
gleich *right away*
die **Gulaschsuppe, -n** *goulash soup*
der **Hamburger, -** *hamburger*
der **Kartoffelsalat, -e** *potato salad*
das **Käsebrot, -e** *cheese sandwich*
der **Kuchen, -** *cake*
die **Limonade** *flavored soda*
los: wann geht's endlich los? *when are we finally going to get going?*
na und?! *so what?*
natürlich *of course*
die **Suppe, -n** *soup*
überhaupt *in any case;* was gibt es überhaupt? *what are we having anyway?*
was gibt es alles? *what do you have?*

SECTION C

Appetit: guten Appetit! *enjoy your meal!*
die **Limo = Limonade** *lemon soda*
na, dann *well then*
nehmen *to take* (see p 252)

SECTION D

ausgezeichnet *excellent*
dein, deine *your* (sing)
diskutieren *to discuss*
die **Eltern** (pl) *parents*
erzählen *to tell*
euer, euere *your* (pl)
der **Film, -e** *film, movie*
freuen: das freut mich *I'm glad*
froh *happy, glad;* da bin ich aber froh! *I'm glad to hear that!*
furchtbar *terrible, awful*
ganz prima! *really great!*
die **Idee, -n** *idea*
ihr, ihre *her; their*
Ihr, Ihre *your* (formal)
der **Kassetten-Recorder, -** *cassette recorder*
lecker *delicious*
die **Musik** *music*
die **Platte, -n** *record*
der **Plattenspieler, -** *record player*
das **Ratespiel, -e** *guessing game*
Ruhe! *quiet!*
sein, seine *his; its*
spinnen: du spinnst! *you're crazy!*
tanzen *to dance*
der **Tanzpartner, -** *dance partner*
und wie! *and how!*
unser, unsere *our*
der **Video-Recorder, -** *video recorder*
der **Witz, -e** *joke*

WORTSCHATZÜBUNGEN

1. Make a list of all the verbs in the **Wortschatz.** Which ones have a separable prefix? Which ones have a vowel change in the second and third person?
2. Write down all words that are not stressed on the first syllable. Pronounce each one.
3. How many compound words can you find in the **Wortschatz?**

ZUM LESEN

Peter Seber über deutsche Sitten

Peter Seber, der junge Amerikaner aus New York, ist schon drei Wochen bei den Nedels in Neuss. Zwei Schüler interviewen den Peter heute für die Schülerzeitung in Wiebkes Schule.

Was für Probleme hast du hier? Was findest du anders als° in Amerika?
Wie findest du unsere Musik?

„Ach, du, das Händeschütteln ist manchmal ein Problem für mich. Ich weiss oft nicht, ob ich zuerst die Hand geben soll oder nicht°. Und meistens vergesse ich es ganz°.

Auch beim Siezen und Duzen° gibt es oft Probleme. Manchmal sage ich ‚du' zu einem Lehrer, und dann lacht die ganze Klasse. Und ich habe beim Essen Schwierigkeiten°. Warum halten alle Deutschen immer die Gabel° in der linken Hand? Das ist einfach noch zu schwer für mich. Aber ich übe°, und eines Tages kann ich auch so essen wie die meisten Deutschen: die Gabel in der linken Hand und das Messer° in der rechten."

---

die Sitte *custom;* **anders als** *different than;* **ob . . . nicht** *whether I should hold out my hand first or not;* **vergesse ich es ganz** *I forget it completely;* **beim Siezen und Duzen** *when saying* **Sie** *or* **du;** **Schwierigkeiten** *difficulties;* **die Gabel** *fork;* **üben** *to practice;* **das Messer** *knife*

„Das Essen ist hier auch anders. Die meisten Leute haben ein grosses, warmes Essen zu Mittag und essen dann kalt zu Abend°. Wir machen das umgekehrt°! Und alle grillen hier. Ich finde das Wort ‚Grillfest' lustig. Wiebkes Vater sagt, es kommt aus Amerika! Und hier gibt es so viele Wurstsorten°. Man sagt, über 1 400!"

„Ja, und ich finde es prima, dass die Leute hier viel tanzen. Die Schüler besuchen alle eine Tanzschule—das ist anders als bei uns. Hier lernt man nicht nur Disko-Tanzen, sondern man lernt auch die traditionellen Tänze, den Walzer, den Tango und so weiter°. Und das finde ich prima."

„Nur ist die Musik hier nicht viel anders als zu Hause. Ihr kennt hier alle unsere amerikanischen Gruppen, und ihr kennt die Texte oft besser als wir—und sogar° in englisch. Ich finde aber viele deutsche Gruppen und Sänger auch toll, die Spider Murphy Gang, den Maffay und besonders° die Nina Hagen."

„Und wenn man hier auf eine Party geht, bringt man immer etwas mit°, Blumen°, Schokolade. Wenn Wiebkes Eltern zu einer Party gehen, bringen sie oft eine Flasche Wein mit. Ich finde, dass die meisten Leute hier Blumen gern haben, und man kauft hier viel mehr Blumen als bei uns."

zu Abend *in the evening;* **umgekehrt** *the other way around;* **die Wurstsorten** *types of cold cuts and sausages;* **und so weiter** *and so forth;* **sogar** *even;* **besonders** *especially;* **mit** *along;* **die Blumen** *flowers*

Übung • Stimmt! Stimmt nicht!

1. Peter gibt immer zuerst die Hand.
2. Er muss „Sie“ zum Lehrer sagen.
3. Die Deutschen essen mit der Gabel in der rechten Hand.
4. Peter möchte nie lernen, wie die Deutschen essen.
5. Die Deutschen essen gern gegrillte Würste.
6. Die jungen Deutschen lernen die traditionellen Tänze nicht.
7. In Deutschland hört man viel amerikanische Musik.
8. Die jungen Deutschen kennen die Texte nicht.
9. Die Deutschen haben Blumen gern.
10. Wenn man eingeladen ist, bringt man immer etwas mit.

Ein Rezept:

Warmer Kartoffelsalat

(für 6–8 Personen)

Zutaten:
9 mittelgrosse Kartoffeln
½ Pfund Speck
1 Zwiebel

¼ Tasse Essig
¼ Tasse Wasser

½ Teelöffel Salz
¼ Teelöffel Pfeffer

1. Die Kartoffeln waschen und kochen.

2. Das Wasser abgiessen.

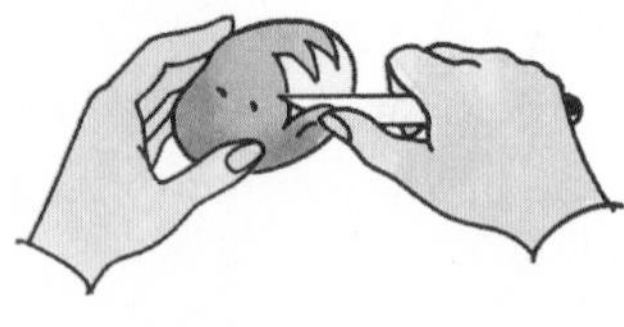

3. Die Kartoffeln schälen.

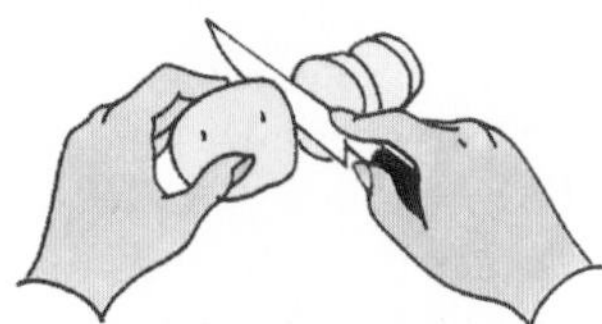

4. In Scheiben schneiden.

5. Die Kartoffelscheiben in eine Schüssel geben.

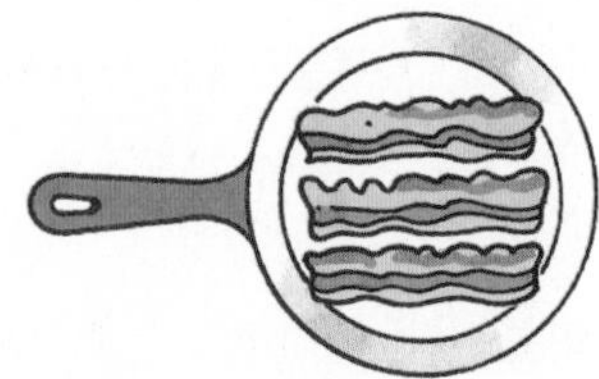

6. Den Speck bräunen.

7. Auf Papier legen.

8. In kleine Stücke schneiden.

9. Die Zwiebel in kleine Stücke schneiden.

10. Die Zwiebel im Fett vom Speck bräunen.

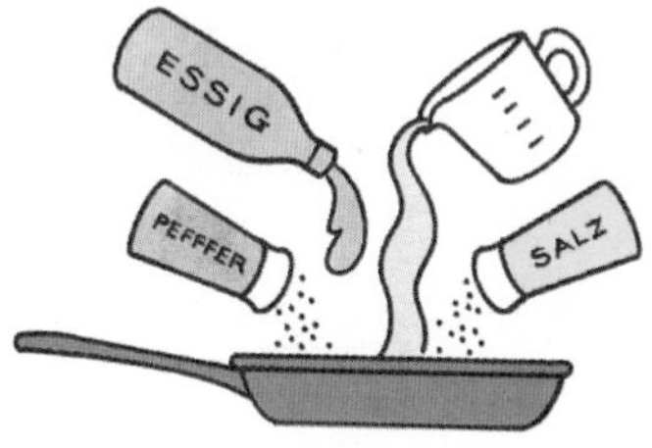

11. Essig, Wasser, Salz und Pfeffer zugeben. 1-2 Minuten rühren.

12. Die heisse Sosse über die Kartoffeln giessen.

13. Den Speck dazugeben.

14. Alles gut mischen.

Guten Appetit!

Übung • Jetzt bist du dran!

Before you attempt to make the German potato salad, make sure you can follow all the steps correctly. In this list, the steps are all mixed up. Place them in the proper order by referring to the pictures and captions.

Add the bacon pieces to the salad.
Drain the bacon on paper towels.
Peel the potatoes.
Wash and boil the potatoes.
Cut the onion into small pieces.
Brown the bacon.
Add vinegar, water, salt and pepper. Stir.
Brown the onions in bacon fat.
Put the potato slices in a bowl.
Cut the potatoes in slices.
Pour the hot sauce over the potatoes.
Cut the bacon in small pieces.
Mix everything.
Drain the potatoes.

KAPITEL **10**

Gehen wir aus!

There are many different activities to choose from when you go out. Should you go to a movie or a concert or a sports event? You discuss the choices, decide on an activity, and make your plans.

In this unit you will learn to:

SECTION A	discuss what you do in your free time, make and accept or reject suggestions for going out
SECTION B	make choices about where to go when you go out, express preference and indifference
SECTION C	express whether you like or dislike something or someone
SECTION D	talk about what you did
TRY YOUR SKILLS	use what you've learned
ZUM LESEN	read for practice and pleasure

SECTION
A

discussing what you do in your free time, making and accepting or rejecting suggestions for going out

Young people like to go out. Where do German teenagers go and what do they do? The following interview will tell you some of the things young Germans do in their free time. How does it compare with what you do?

A1 Was macht unsere Jugend?

Wie verbringst du deine Freizeit?

Unsere Jugendlichen: sie haben Geld, sie gehen aus, sie haben viele Interessen. Man sieht sie in Kinos, Konzerten und Sportveranstaltungen: sie sind keine Freizeitmuffel!—Was machen unsere Freunde? Wie verbringen sie ihre Freizeit? Wohin gehen sie? Was tun sie? Fragen wir mal!

Ja, ich gehe oft aus, zwei- oder dreimal in der Woche. Ich fahre in die Stadt, äh . . . ich gehe ins Kino, ins Theater, tja . . . und manchmal in ein Konzert. Oder ich besuche Freunde. Dann gehen wir zusammen aus.

KEINE FREIZEIT

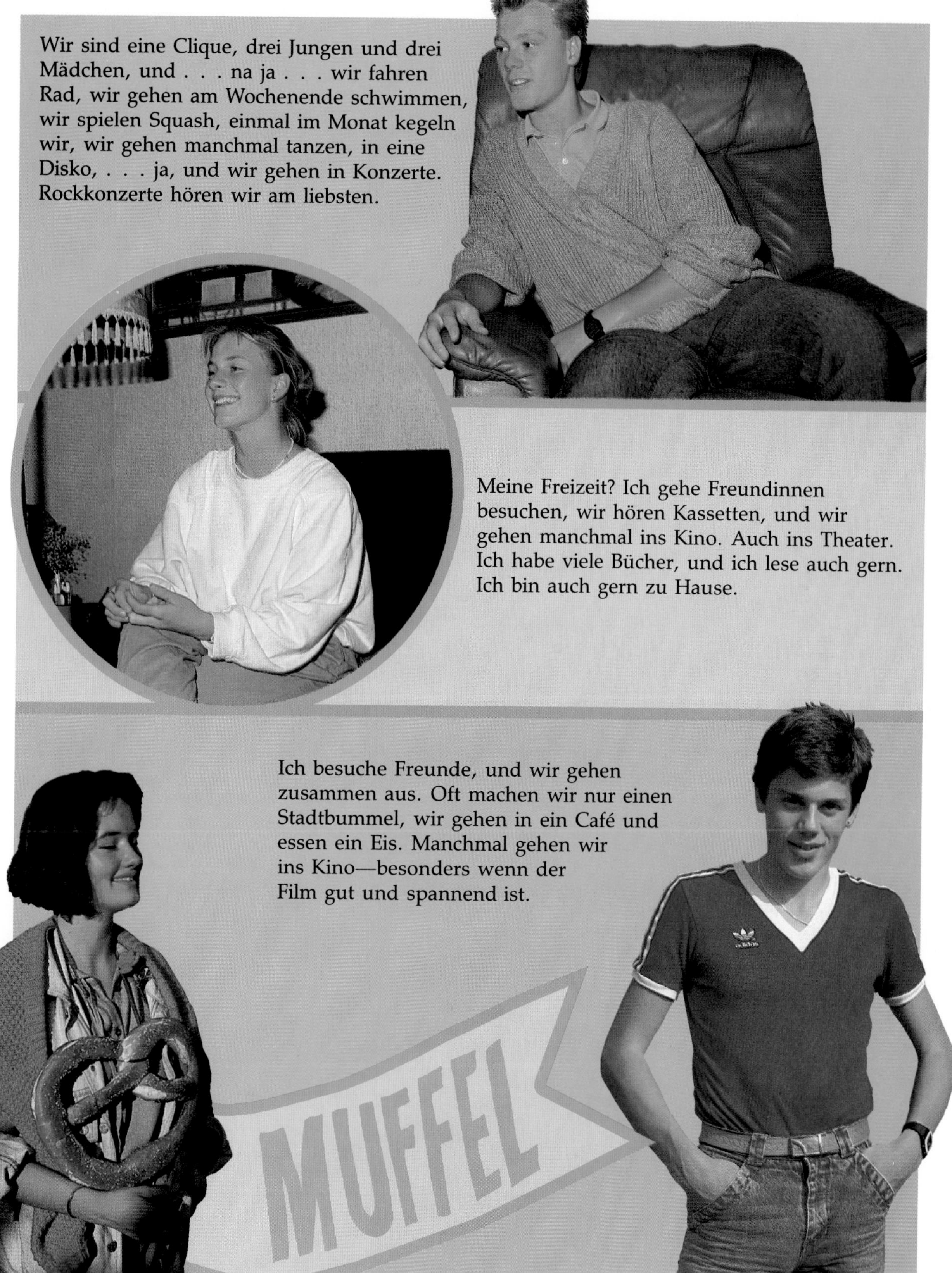

Wir sind eine Clique, drei Jungen und drei Mädchen, und . . . na ja . . . wir fahren Rad, wir gehen am Wochenende schwimmen, wir spielen Squash, einmal im Monat kegeln wir, wir gehen manchmal tanzen, in eine Disko, . . . ja, und wir gehen in Konzerte. Rockkonzerte hören wir am liebsten.

Meine Freizeit? Ich gehe Freundinnen besuchen, wir hören Kassetten, und wir gehen manchmal ins Kino. Auch ins Theater. Ich habe viele Bücher, und ich lese auch gern. Ich bin auch gern zu Hause.

Ich besuche Freunde, und wir gehen zusammen aus. Oft machen wir nur einen Stadtbummel, wir gehen in ein Café und essen ein Eis. Manchmal gehen wir ins Kino—besonders wenn der Film gut und spannend ist.

A2 Übung • Rollenspiel

Jetzt bist du ein Reporter oder eine Reporterin. Mitschüler übernehmen die Rollen von Margit, Jens, Kristin und Bruno. Du interviewst sie.

A3 Übung • Frag deine Klassenkameraden!

Wohin gehst du?
Was machst du?

Wie verbringst du deine Freizeit?

Wann gehst du aus?
Wie oft gehst du aus?

ins Kino gehen **ausgehen** **gern lesen** **schwimmen gehen** **Eis essen** **tanzen gehen** **Squash spielen** **kegeln** **Musik hören** **in ein Konzert gehen** **Freunde besuchen** **ins Theater gehen** **in die Stadt fahren** **gern zu Hause sein** **in ein Café gehen** **einen Stadtbummel machen** **in eine Disko gehen**	***einmal*** ***selten*** ***in der Woche*** ***nie*** ***manchmal*** ***im Monat*** ***dreimal*** ***meistens*** ***am Wochenende*** ***immer*** ***am Samstag*** ***oft*** ***am Sonntag*** ***zweimal***

A4 Übung • Und du? Wie steht's mit dir?

1. Wie verbringst du deine Freizeit?
2. Was machst du? Wohin gehst du?
3. Wann gehst du aus? Wie oft gehst du aus?

A5 Übung • Klasseninterview

Frag fünf Klassenkameraden, wohin sie gehen, was sie tun, wann oder wie oft sie ausgehen! Schreib die Antworten auf!

Name	wohin?	was?	wann?	wie oft?
1.				
2.				
3.				

A6 HAST DU ETWAS VOR, SABINE? 

Stefan runs into Sabine, a former classmate of his. They haven't seen each other in a while, and Stefan suggests that they do something together this afternoon or evening.

Das ist eine prima Idee!

STEFAN Sabine! Hallo!
SABINE Stefan! Ja, grüss dich! Wie geht's denn?
STEFAN Danke, prima! Mensch, das ist toll! Was machst du jetzt? Hast du etwas vor?
SABINE Nö[1]. Warum?
STEFAN Dann können wir zusammen etwas tun, ja?
SABINE Prima! —Also, was machen wir?
STEFAN Nun ja, wir können . . . wir können in die Stadt fahren und einen Stadtbummel machen. Oder willst du lieber in ein Café gehen? Eis essen?
SABINE Mensch, toll! Klasse!

Das find' ich blöd!

Gehen wir ins Kino! Es gibt einen prima Film im Roxi!

Oder möchtest du in ein Konzert gehen? In ein Rockkonzert?

A7 Übung • Jetzt fragst du!

Was möchten deine Klassenkameraden machen? Wie antworten sie?

1. Möchtest du . . .?
2. Willst du lieber . . .?
3. Wir können . . .
4. Gehen wir . . .!

[1] In casual German, **nö** is often used instead of **nein.**

A8 WIE GEHT'S?

Prima!	Gut, danke.	Nicht schlecht.	So lala.	Schlecht.	Miserabel!

A9 WIE SAGT MAN DAS?
Asking and responding to "how are you?"

Wie geht's? Wie geht's denn?	How are you? / How's it going? Say, how are things?
Ach, prima! Danke, gut! Nicht schlecht. So lala. Schlecht. Miserabel!	Oh, great! Fine, thanks. Not bad. So-so. Bad. Miserable!

A10 Übung • Grüss dich! Wie geht's? 

Begrüss deine Klassenkameraden und frag, wie es geht!

A: Grüss dich, Peter!
B: Tag, Monika! Wie geht's?
A: Danke, gut.

A11 WIE SAGT MAN DAS?
Making suggestions

How do you make suggestions? In Unit 5 you learned the **möchte-**forms. You can also use the forms of the verbs **wollen,** *to want to,* and **können,** *can,* expressing possibility. The **wir-**forms of most verbs, the *let's*-form, can also be used.

making suggestions	Möchtest du ins Kino gehen?	Would you like to go to the movies?
asking for someone's wishes	Willst du ins Kino gehen?	Do you want to go to the movies?
expressing possibility	Wir können ins Kino gehen.	We can go to the movies.
"let's" suggestion	Gehen wir doch ins Kino!	Let's go to the movies.

A 12 Übung • Und was willst du tun? 

1. You have the day off. Discuss with several classmates what you might do together. You make a suggestion, and a classmate either accepts or rejects your idea.

   A: Wir können in die Stadt fahren.
   B: . . .

2. After your classmate rejects your suggestion, he or she suggests something else. Now it's your turn to say whether or not you like the idea. Accept or reject your classmate's suggestion.

   A: Willst du einen Stadtbummel machen?
   B: Wie langweilig! Ich möchte heute lieber Tennis spielen.
   A: Mensch! Das ist eine prima Idee!

A 13 Übung • Ja, gehen wir . . . !

A: Möchtest du ins Kino gehen?
B: Ja, gehen wir ins Kino!

A 14 ERKLÄRUNG
The Verbs können *and* wollen

1. The verbs **können** and **wollen** have the following forms in the present tense:

können	wollen
ich **kann**	ich **will**
du **kannst**	du **willst**
er, sie, es **kann**	er, sie, es **will**
wir **können**	wir **wollen**
ihr **könnt**	ihr **wollt**
sie, Sie **können**	sie, Sie **wollen**

2. **Können** and **wollen** are usually used with an infinitive that comes at the end of the sentence. If the meaning of that infinitive is clear, it can be left out.

Wir können in die Stadt fahren.	*We can go to town.*
Du, ich kann heute nicht (in die Stadt fahren).	*I can't (go to town) today.*

A 15 Übung • Was willst du tun? Was kannst du machen?

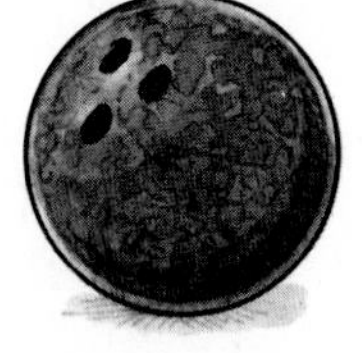

1. 1. Du willst ins Kino gehen. Du willst eine Kassette hören. Du . . .
2. Wir wollen ins Kino gehen. Wir wollen . . .
3. Ihr 4. Mein Vetter 5. Deine Freunde 6. Ich

2. 1. Du kannst ins Kino gehen. Du . . .
2. Wir können . . .
3. Ihr 4. Mein Bruder 5. Deine Freunde 6. Ich

A 16 Schreibübung • Versteckte Sätze

Wieviel Sätze kannst du machen? Schreib zehn Sätze!

Herbert will am Wochenende ins Kino gehen.

ich	kann	am Wochenende	einen Stadtbummel	besuchen
Katrin	können	am Samstag	Freunde	fahren
wir	möchte	einmal in der Woche	in die Stadt	gehen
Herbert	möchten	immer	in eine Disko	hören
die Jungen und Mädchen	will	manchmal	ins Kino	machen
	wollen	selten	Kassetten	spielen
du	willst	nie	Rad	
ihr	wollt	meistens	tanzen	
			Tennis	

A 17 ERKLÄRUNG
The Verbs fahren, radfahren, *and* ausgehen

1. The verbs **fahren,** *to go (by vehicle),* and **radfahren,** *to bicycle,* have a stem-vowel change in the **du-** and **er/sie-**forms. In addition, **radfahren** is a verb with a separable prefix. Note that **Rad** is capitalized when it is separated from **fahren.**

fahren			radfahren			
Ich Du Er, sie	**fahre** **fährst** **fährt**	in die Stadt.	Ich Du Er, sie	**fahre** **fährst** **fährt**	gern	**Rad.**

2. **Fahren** and **radfahren** do not have a stem-vowel change in the singular command form.

Fahr doch in die Stadt! **Fahr** mal **Rad!**

3. The verb **ausgehen,** *to go out,* is also a verb with a separable prefix.

Gehst du heute **aus?**
Ich **gehe** am Wochenende **aus.**

A 18 Übung • Was macht ihr jetzt?

A: Was macht ihr jetzt?
B: Wir fahren jetzt in die Stadt.

A: Und was macht Sabine?
B: Sie fährt jetzt auch in die Stadt.

1. Und du? **2.** Und deine Geschwister? **3.** Und der Stefan? **4.** Und ihr?

A 19 Übung • Was machst du jetzt?

A: Was machst du jetzt?
B: Ich fahre jetzt Rad.

A: Und Stefan?
B: Er fährt jetzt auch Rad.

1. Und ihr? **2.** Und Sabine? **3.** Und deine Geschwister? **4.** Und du?

A 20 Übung • Wann? Wie oft?

A: Wie oft geht Katrin aus? einmal in der Woche?
B: Ja, sie geht einmal in der Woche aus.

1. Und der Stefan? am Samstag?
2. Und du? am Wochenende?
3. Und deine Freunde? immer?
4. Und dein Bruder? zweimal im Monat?
5. Und ihr zwei? selten?

A 21 Übung • Was können wir tun?

You are bored and don't know what to do. Your brother makes some suggestions, first to you, then to you and a friend.

1. Geh doch ins Kino! Fahr . . .!
2. Geht doch ins Kino! Fahrt . . .!

A 22 Übung • Mix-Match

Discuss what you can do together with your classmates and with your teacher. Choose suggestions and responses from below.

Du, (Brian), willst du . . .?
Du, (Barbara), kannst du heute . . .?

Was macht ihr jetzt? Wollt ihr . . .?
(Frl. Seifert), können Sie heute . . .?

in die Stadt fahren	*Das find' ich blöd.*
ins Kino gehen	Ich habe schon was vor.
in ein Café gehen	*Nein, lieber nicht.*
einen Stadtbummel machen	Das ist eine prima Idee!
radfahren	*Ach, wie langweilig!*
Kassetten hören	Das geht jetzt nicht.
den (Jens) besuchen	*Mensch, toll!*
einen Film sehen	Ich kann leider nicht.
Karten spielen	*Ich habe heute keine Zeit.*
Tennis spielen	Super! Schade!
Windsurfen	*Nein, das macht keinen Spass.*

A 23 Übung • Was sagst du? Was sagen deine Mitschüler?

1. What would you say if someone asked you the following questions?

1. Wie geht's?
2. Hast du heute was vor?
3. Was machst du heute?
4. Können wir zusammen was tun?
5. So, was machen wir?
6. Wann fährst du in die Stadt?
7. Was machst du dort?
8. Machst du einen Stadtbummel?
9. Willst du radfahren?
10. Was machst du am liebsten?

2. Now ask some of your classmates the previous questions.

A 24 Übung • Partnerarbeit: Hast du was vor?

	FEBRUAR
	21 Mo
Fastnacht 15^{00} Party bei Sven	22 Di
Aschermittwoch	23 Mi
19^{00} Kegeln	24 Do
	25 Fr
Nachmittag: Stadtbummel mit Gitta	26 Sa
15^{00} Kino	27 So

Make a weekly planner. Write down what you are going to do on four different days. Indicate the activity and specific times. Don't let your classmates see your entries. Now select a partner. Call your partner up and invite him or her to the four activities. Your partner responds according to the entries on his or her calendar. If your partner is free, he or she accepts. If not, agree on another date. Then it is your partner's turn to invite you.

A 25 Übung • Hör gut zu! 

Listen to the statement. Is the one that follows appropriate or not?

	0	1	2	3	4	5	6	7	8	9	10
appropriate	✓										
not appropriate											

A 26 Schreibübung • Was macht Ulrike heute?

Ulrike tells you what she plans to do today. You repeat it to a friend. Write what you would say.

Ulrike: Ich fahre heute in die Stadt. Ich will einen Stadtbummel machen, und ich möchte meine Tante besuchen. Wir wollen zusammen einen Film sehen. Dann wollen wir in ein Café gehen. Am liebsten gehen wir ins Café Krone. Ich finde es dort sehr gemütlich. Um neun Uhr will ich wieder zu Hause sein.

Du erzählst: Ulrike fährt . . .

A 27 Schreibübung • Was hast du vor?

Using the suggestions and responses in Exercise A22, write five short conversations.

SECTION B

making choices about where to go when you go out, expressing preference and indifference

Stefan and Sabine cannot quite decide whether to go to a concert or a movie. The ads in the paper help them make up their minds.

B1 Konzert oder Kino?

STEFAN Du, Sabine, willst du ins Kino gehen oder lieber in ein Konzert?
SABINE Ach, Stefan, das ist mir gleich. Du, schauen wir doch mal in die Zeitung!
SABINE Hier, Konzerte!
STEFAN Wer singt?
SABINE Da ist der Falco . . . welchen Sänger hörst du gern?
STEFAN Ich habe viele gern. Schau, Sabine, die Gruppe ist toll!
SABINE Welche Gruppe?
STEFAN Die Scorpions. Hörst du die Gruppe gern?
SABINE Mensch, das ist meine Lieblingsgruppe! Was für Gruppen hast du am liebsten?
STEFAN Ich höre alle Rockgruppen gern.
SABINE Ich auch, aber die Scorpions höre ich besonders gern. Schade, die Konzerte fangen so spät an. Ich soll um 10 Uhr zu Hause sein.
STEFAN Dann gehen wir ins Kino, ja?
SABINE Gut!

KONZERTE „live"

JAZZ ROCK SOUL ACTION

Fr. 17.10. CIRCUS KRONE
SALSA FESTIVAL mit Eddie Palmieri Orchestra, Salsa Picante, und Celia Cruz & Tito Puente Orchestra 20.00

Fr. 17.10. ALABAMAHALLE
SCORPIONS Monsters of Rock, mit Ozzy Osbourne, Bon Jovi, Warlock 20.30

Fr. 17.10. OLYMPIAHALLE
QUEEN Die Englische Rockgruppe
VORGRUPPE: Craaft Eine deutsche Band auf dem Sprung in die US-Charts 20.00

Sa. 18.10. OLYMPIAHALLE
FALCO Der österreichische Popstar 20.00

Sa. 18.10. CIRCUS KRONE
REGGAE SUNSPLASH mit Black Uhuru, The Wailers, Dennis Brown & Guests 20.00

Sa. 18.10. ALABAMAHALLE
SUPERCHARGE Die sagenhafte Rhythm'n Blues Band 20.30

B2 Übung • Und du? Wie steht's mit dir?

1. Gehst du lieber ins Kino oder in ein Konzert?
2. Welchen Sänger oder welche Sängerin hörst du gern?
3. Wie heissen deine Lieblingssänger?
4. Welche Gruppe hörst du gern? Wie heisst deine Lieblingsgruppe?
5. Welche Gruppe möchtest du nicht hören? Warum nicht?
6. Wann fangen die Konzerte an?

B3 WAS FÜR FILME SIEHST DU GERN? 

Was für Filme siehst du gern?

Wie heisst dein Lieblingsstar?

SABINE Hm, *Zwölf Uhr mittags*—was für ein Film ist das?
STEFAN Das ist ein Western. Hast du Western gern?
SABINE Nicht besonders.
STEFAN Schau, *Piranha 2.* Ich glaube, das ist ein Naturfilm.
SABINE Ach, Quatsch! Das ist ein Action-Film und kein Naturfilm.

KINO KINO KINO

Mathäser–Filmpalast
16.00 und 18.45 Steve Martin
Der Mann mit 2 Gehirnen

Theatiner–Film
20.00 Gary Cooper
Zwölf Uhr mittags

Tivoli
17.00 u. 20.00 Sidney Pollack
Jenseits von Afrika

Royal-Filmpalast
13 / 15 / 17 / 19 Uhr
Piranha 2

Gloria
14.00 / 16.30 / 19.00
Das Boot

B4 Übung • Wie steht's mit dir?

1. Welchen Film möchtest du sehen? Warum?
2. Wo spielt der Film? (im . . .)
3. Wann fangen die Filme an?

B5 ERKLÄRUNG
The Verb anfangen

1. The verb **anfangen,** *to begin,* is a verb with a separable prefix. It also has a vowel change in the **du-** and **er/sie-**forms.

Ich Du Er, sie	**fange** **fängst** **fängt**	um 2 Uhr	**an.**	Wir Ihr Sie	**fangen** **fangt** **fangen**	um 2 Uhr	**an.**

2. The singular command form does not have a vowel change: **Fang** doch **an!**

B6 Übung • Frag deine Klassenkameraden!

1. Frag, wann die Filme und die Konzerte anfangen!
2. Frag deine Klassenkameraden, wann ihre (Mathestunden) anfangen!
3. Frag sie, wann sie ihre Hausaufgaben machen!

B7 WAS FÜR FILME SIND DAS?

A: Was für ein Film ist *Jenseits von Afrika?*
B: Ein Abenteuerfilm.
A: Kennst du die Schauspieler?
B: Na klar!

A: Was für ein Film ist . . .
B: . . . ist ein . . .

Jenseits von Afrika

ein Abenteuerfilm

Zwölf Uhr mittags

ein Western

Das Boot

ein Kriegsfilm

Der Mann mit 2 Gehirnen

eine Komödie

Werwolf in London

ein Horrorfilm

Piranha 2

ein Action-Film

Aliens

ein Science-fiction-Film

Liebesgeschichte

ein Liebesfilm

B8 Übung • Jetzt bist du dran

1. Was für Filme siehst du gern? Warum?
2. Was für ein Film ist *Das Boot?*
3. Und *Jenseits von Afrika?*
4. Welcher Film spielt im Mathäser? Was für ein Film ist das? etc. (Schau auf das Kinoplakat auf Seite 280!)

B9 Übung • Kennst du den Film?

Schreib den Titel von einem Film in grossen Buchstaben auf ein Blatt Papier! Zeig deinen Klassenkameraden den Titel und frag:

—Kennt ihr den Film?
—Was für ein Film ist das?
—Siehst du . . . filme gern?

B10 WIE SAGT MAN DAS?
Expressing preference and indifference

You already know the words **lieber** and **am liebsten.** Here are some other ways of expressing preference.

expressing preference	Ich höre Rock lieber. Ich sehe Western am liebsten. Ich höre Rockgruppen besonders gern. Das ist meine Lieblingsgruppe. Das ist mein Lieblingsstar.	I prefer rock. I like westerns best of all. I especially like to listen to rock groups. That's my favorite group. That's my favorite star.
expressing indifference	Das ist mir gleich.	It's all the same to me.

B11 Übung • Was willst du tun?

Now you and your friend are deciding what to do. You are standing in front of a **Plakatsäule.** Ask your friend what he or she prefers to do. Take turns making suggestions, accepting some, rejecting others, and then finally agreeing on something.

B12 Übung • Was hast du lieber?

In large letters, write the title of your favorite film on one sheet of paper and your favorite group on another sheet. Ask a classmate which one he or she would like to see or hear. After your classmate expresses an opinion, make an appropriate comment.

B13 WIE SAGT MAN DAS?
Asking for information

specific information	**Welcher Film spielt heute?** Which (What) film is playing today?	*Das Boot.*
categories of things	**Was für Filme siehst du gern?** What kind of films do you like to see?	Action-Filme.

B14 ERKLÄRUNG
welcher? welche? welches?, *Nominative and Accusative Case*

The interrogative **welcher? (welche?, welches?),** *which,* can be used in front of nouns: **welcher?** is used before a masculine noun, **welches?** before a neuter noun, and **welche?** before a feminine or plural noun.

Der Film ist toll. —Welcher Film ist toll?
Die Gruppe ist Spitze! —Welche Gruppe ist Spitze?
Das Konzert ist Klasse! —Welches Konzert ist Klasse?
Die Gruppen sind prima! —Welche Gruppen sind prima?

	Masculine	*Feminine*	*Neuter*	*Plural*
Nominative	**welcher?**	**welche?**	**welches?**	**welche?**
Accusative	**welchen?**			

B15 Schreibübung • Welche Form von welch-?

1. Im Gloria spielt *Das Boot.* ____ Film spielt im Gloria?
2. Ich sehe heute *Jenseits von Afrika.* ____ Film siehst du heute?
3. Wir hören heute das Salsa Festival. ____ Konzert hörst du?
4. Supercharge beginnt schon um 20 Uhr. ____ Konzert beginnt schon um 20 Uhr?
5. Ich höre die Gruppe Queen gern. ____ Gruppe hörst du gern?
6. Die Gruppe Reggae Sunsplash spielt heute. ____ Gruppe spielt heute?
7. Die Konzerte beginnen um 20 Uhr. ____ Konzerte beginnen um 20 Uhr?
8. Die Scorpions spielen in der Alabama-Halle. ____ Gruppe spielt in der Alabama-Halle?
9. Die Gruppe Queen ist aus England. ____ Gruppe ist aus England?
10. Das Falco Konzert beginnt um 19 Uhr. ____ Konzert beginnt um 19 Uhr?

B16 Schreibübung • Schreib Fragen!

Look at the ads on pages 279 and 280 and write eight questions similar to the ones you have been asking in Exercise B15. Begin each question with a form of **welcher.**

B 17 ERKLÄRUNG
was für ein?, *Nominative and Accusative Case*

The interrogative **was für ein?,** *what kind of (a)?,* introduces questions that ask about categories of things.

Was für ein Film ist das?	Ein Horrorfilm.
Was für eine Gruppe spielt?	Eine Gruppe aus England.
Was für ein Konzert ist das?	Ein Rockkonzert.
Was für Filme siehst du gern?	Naturfilme und Action-Filme.

<table>
<tr><th></th><th>Masculine</th><th>Feminine</th><th>Neuter</th><th>Plural</th></tr>
<tr><td>Nominative</td><td>was für ein?</td><td rowspan="2">was für eine?</td><td rowspan="2">was für ein?</td><td rowspan="2">was für?</td></tr>
<tr><td>Accusative</td><td>was für einen?</td></tr>
</table>

B 18 Schreibübung • Welche Form von was für ein?

1. *Zwölf Uhr mittags* ist ein Western. _____ Film ist *Zwölf Uhr mittags?*
2. Wir sehen heute einen Kriegsfilm. _____ Film seht ihr heute?
3. Ich höre am liebsten ein Rockkonzert. _____ Konzert hörst du am liebsten?
4. Ich sehe gern Western und Action-Filme. _____ Filme siehst du gern?
5. Ich höre am liebsten Pop- und Rockkonzerte. _____ Konzerte hörst du am liebsten?
6. Queen ist eine Rockgruppe. _____ Gruppe ist Queen?
7. *Piranha 2* ist ein Action-Film. _____ Film ist *Piranha 2?*

B 19 Schreibübung • Schreib Fragen!

1. Look at the ads on pages 279 and 280 and write five questions similar to the ones you have been asking in Exercise B18. Begin each question with a form of **was für ein?**

2. Schreib Fragen mit **welcher** oder **was für ein!**

   A: *Piranha 2* ist ein Abenteuerfilm.
   B: Was für ein Film ist *Piranha 2?*

   A: Ich sehe den Film *Jenseits von Afrika.*
   B: Welchen Film siehst du?

   1. Sunsplash ist eine Reggae Gruppe.
   2. Wir hören heute die Gruppe Queen.
   3. In der Olympiahalle gibt es ein Rockkonzert.
   4. Wir hören das Konzert in der Alabama-Halle.
   5. *Zwölf Uhr mittags* und *Rio Bravo* sind Western.
   6. Ich sehe den Western um 19 Uhr.

B 20 Ein wenig Landeskunde

American movies are very popular in Germany. Most movies are dubbed into German. However, larger cities usually have at least one movie theater that shows foreign movies with the original sound track.

All movies are rated, and movie ads give the ratings in the form of age limits: **ab 12 Jahre, ab 14 Jahre,** and so on.

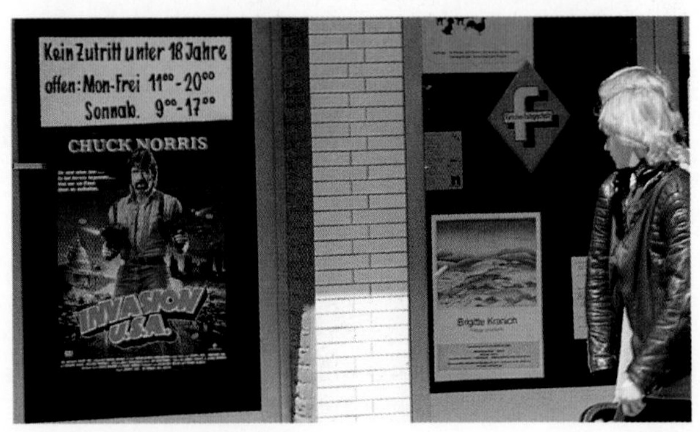

SECTION C

expressing whether you like or dislike someone or something, talking about what you did

Stefan is interviewing different people for his school paper. Let's hear what kind of movies these people like and dislike, and why. What are your likes and dislikes when it comes to movies?

C1 Was für Filme mögt ihr?

STEFAN Welchen Film möchtest du heute sehen?
SCHÜLER Moment mal, . . . wie heisst er denn? Der Film mit Steve Martin! —Ach, ja! *Der Mann mit zwei Gehirnen.*
STEFAN Der Film ist lustig. Magst du Steve Martin?
SCHÜLER Ich mag ihn gern.
STEFAN Ich auch.

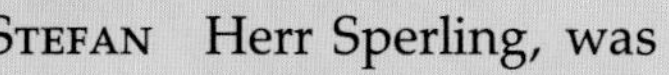

STEFAN Herr Sperling, was für Filme mögen Sie?
HERR SPERLING Ich? Am liebsten mag ich Science-fiction-Filme.
STEFAN Wirklich? Sie mögen Science-fiction-Filme?
HERR SPERLING Ja. Ich finde sie interessant und oft sehr spannend.

STEFAN Was für Filme mögt ihr zwei?
MÄDCHEN 1 Wir mögen Liebesfilme, Action-Filme—nur keine Kriegsfilme.
STEFAN Warum mögt ihr keine Kriegsfilme?
MÄDCHEN 2 Kriegsfilme finde ich grausam und traurig.
MÄDCHEN 1 Ich hasse sie.

C2 Übung • Beantworte die Fragen!

1. Welchen Film sieht der Schüler heute?
2. Wie ist der Film?
3. Magst du Steve Martin?
4. Was für Filme mag Herr Sperling?
5. Was für Filme mag er am liebsten? Warum?
6. Was für Filme mögen die beiden Mädchen?
7. Was für Filme finden sie grausam?

C3 WIE SAGT MAN DAS?
Saying you like or dislike someone or something

You have been expressing likes and dislikes using **gern** and **nicht gern** with various verbs. Here are some more ways of saying you like or dislike someone or something.

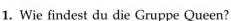

liking	Ich mag den Film. Ich mag Steve Martin.	Ich habe den Film gern. Ich mag Steve Martin gern.
disliking	Ich mag Kriegsfilme nicht. Ich mag den Schauspieler nicht.	Ich habe Kriegsfilme nicht gern. Ich mag den Schauspieler nicht gern.
strong disliking	Ich hasse Kriegsfilme. Ich hasse den Schauspieler.	

C4 Übung • Und du? 

1. Wie findest du die Gruppe Queen?
2. Wie findest du Falco?
3. Wie findest du den Film *Jenseits von Afrika?*
4. Wie findest du Robert Redford?
5. Wie findest du Abenteuerfilme?

C5 ERKLÄRUNG
The Verb mögen

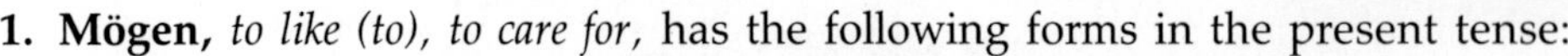

1. **Mögen,** *to like (to), to care for,* has the following forms in the present tense:

ich **mag**	wir **mögen**
du **magst**	ihr **mögt**
er, sie, es **mag**	sie, Sie **mögen**

2. An infinitive may also be used together with the **mag**-forms.

Welche Gruppe **magst** du nicht **hören?** *Which group don't you want to hear?*

C6 Übung • Alle mögen die Gruppe 

A: Warum hört ihr die Scorpions?
B: Wir mögen die Gruppe.

A: Und du?
B: Ich mag die Gruppe auch.

1. Und Sabine? **2.** Und die Schüler? **3.** Und ihr? **4.** Und Stefan?

C7 Übung • Keiner mag den Film 

A: Geht ihr in *Piranha 2?*
B: Nein, wir mögen den Film nicht.

A: Und Sabine?
B: Sabine mag den Film auch nicht.

1. Und die Schüler? **2.** Und Stefan? **3.** Und ihr? **4.** Und du?

C8 Übung • Versteckte Sätze

Wieviel Sätze kannst du machen?

Die Schüler mögen Horrorfilme nicht.

ich du Stefan Katrin ihr die Schüler	mögen mögt mag magst	die Gruppe aus England die Rockgruppe Horrorfilme Steve Martin	am liebsten besonders gern lieber nicht

C9 Übung • Was magst du am liebsten?

Rephrase each statement using **Lieblings-**. Then write a question.

Ich spiele Tennis am liebsten.
Tennis ist mein Lieblingsspiel. Welches Spiel magst du am liebsten?

1. Ich besuche die Stadt München am liebsten.
2. Ich höre die Gruppe Supercharge am liebsten.
3. Ich gehe am liebsten in das Café Krone.
4. Ich sehe Horrorfilme am liebsten.
5. Ich habe das Kartenspiel Mau-Mau am liebsten.

C10 Übung • Wie findest du die Gruppe? den Film? das Konzert?

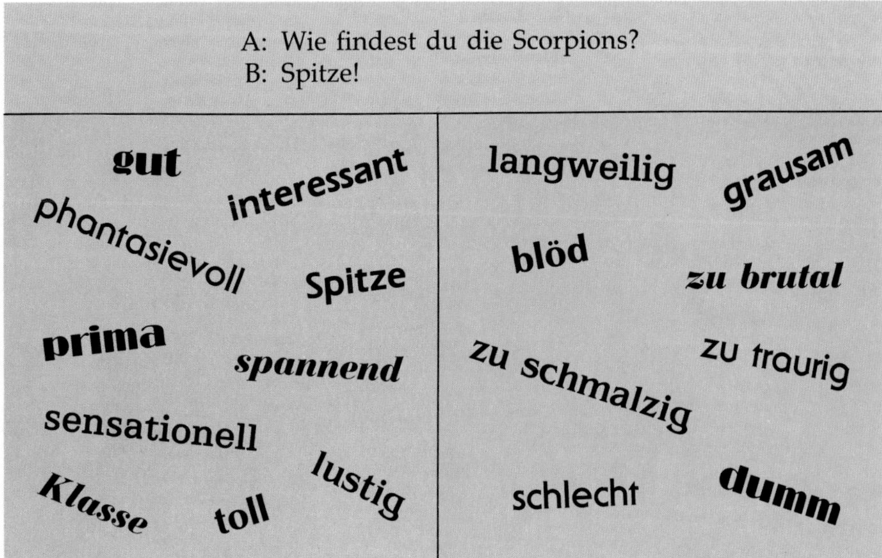

A: Wie findest du die Scorpions?
B: Spitze!
gut
interessant
phantasievoll
Spitze
prima
spannend
sensationell
lustig
Klasse
toll
langweilig
grausam
blöd
zu brutal
zu schmalzig
zu traurig
schlecht
dumm

C11 Übung • Umfrage

1. Mach eine Liste von Filmen und Musikgruppen, die du gern oder nicht gern hast! Frag deine Klassenkameraden, wie sie den Film oder die Gruppe finden!

2. Frag deine Mitschüler, was für Filme, Musikgruppen oder Konzerte sie mögen oder nicht mögen und warum! Frag auch deinen Lehrer!

C12 Übung • Hör gut zu!

Wer mag das? Wer mag das nicht?

	0	1	2	3	4	5	6	7	8	9	10
likes	✓										
dislikes											

C13 Schreibübung • Schreib zwei Dialoge!

1. Ein Freund fragt, ob du ins Kino gehen willst. Du sagst, dass du gern gehst. Du fragst, was er sehen möchte, und du sagst, dass du den Film auch gern siehst.
2. Ein Freund fragt, ob du ins Kino gehen möchtest. Du sagst, dass es geht, dass du Zeit hast. Du fragst, welchen Film er sehen möchte. Aber du hast den Film nicht gern, und du sagst, warum du ihn nicht sehen magst.

C14 Übung • Und du?

SECTION D

talking about what you did

D1 Was hast du gestern abend gemacht?

LEHRER Herbert, was hast du gestern abend gemacht?
HERBERT Ich bin ins Kino gegangen.
LEHRER Was hast du gesehen?
HERBERT *Jenseits von Afrika.* Ein prima Film!

LEHRER Und du, Karin? Was hast du gemacht?
KARIN Ich habe Freunde besucht, und wir haben Karten gespielt.

LEHRER Und du, Wiebke?
WIEBKE Ich bin zu Hause geblieben. Ich habe ein Buch gelesen.

D2 Übung • Mix-Match

1. Was hast du . . .?
2. Ich bin ins Kino . . .
3. Ich habe *Jenseits von Afrika* . . .
4. Ich habe Freunde . . .
5. Wir haben Karten . . .
6. Ich bin zu Hause . . .
7. Ich habe ein Buch . . .

besucht.
geblieben.
gegangen.
gelesen.
gemacht?
gesehen.
gespielt.

D3 ERKLÄRUNG
The Conversational Past Tense

1. In the conversational past tense, two verb forms are used: the present tense forms of the verbs **haben** or **sein** and a form of the main verb, called a past participle. The past participle is in last position.

	Helping Verb		*Past Participle*
Ich	**habe**	ein Buch	**gelesen.**
Er	**ist**	ins Kino	**gegangen.**

2. Here are some conversational past tense forms of verbs you have been using in this unit. Most past participles are used with the helping verb **haben.** Note especially those used with **sein.**

hat besucht	**hat gesehen**	**ist gegangen**
hat gemacht	**hat gelesen**	**ist geblieben**
hat gehört	**hat gegessen**	**ist gefahren**
hat gespielt	**hat getrunken**	

3. Can you name the infinitive forms of the past participles listed in this chart?

D4 Übung • Was hast du gestern abend gemacht? 

A: Was hast du gestern abend gemacht?
B: Ich habe . . . *or* Ich bin . . .

1. Ich . . . . . . gelesen.
2. Ich . . . . . . besucht.
3. Ich . . . . . . geblieben.
4. Ich . . . . . . gefahren.
5. Ich . . . . . . gegangen.
6. Ich . . . . . . gesehen.
7. Ich . . . . . . gehört.
8. Ich . . . . . . gemacht.

ein Buch
einen prima Film
einen Stadtbummel
Freunde
in die Stadt
ins Kino
Musik
zu Hause

D5 Übung • Wer hat was gemacht? 

Wir sind ins Kino gegangen.

1. Wir . . .

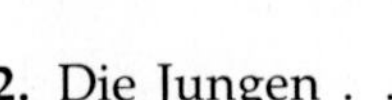

2. Die Jungen . . .

3. Hans . . .

4. Ich . . .

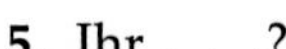

5. Ihr . . .?

6. Du . . .?

7. Karin . . .

8. Wir . . .

D6 Übung • Hör gut zu!

Is it in the present or is it in the conversational past?

	0	1	2	3	4	5	6	7	8	9	10
Present											
Convers. Past	✓										

D7 Übung • Und du? Wie steht's mit dir?

1. Was hast du gestern abend gemacht?
2. Was haben deine Freunde gemacht?
3. Was hat dein Klassenkamerad gemacht?

D8 Schreibübung • Was hast du gestern abend gemacht?

Schreib auf, was du letzte Woche an jedem Abend und am Wochenende gemacht hast:

Am Montag . . .

TRY YOUR SKILLS

using what you've learned

Having a pen pal in a foreign country can be a rewarding experience. Many students who have pen pals end up visiting them. Here, Ulli tells his American pen pal, John, about the different things they will be doing together when John comes to Germany. As you read Ulli's letter, think of what you would like to do and see, and where you would like to go in Munich.

1 Brief an einen Brieffreund

München, den 28. Mai

Lieber John!

Danke für Deinen Brief und die Briefmarken. Sie sind schön, und ich habe diese Marken noch nicht.

Ich schreibe heute, was wir machen können, wenn Du im Juli kommst. Im Juli haben wir ein Filmfest, ein internationales Filmfest. Da können wir viele interessante Filme sehen: Filme aus Frankreich, Ungarn, aus den USA natürlich, aus Deutschland, Italien, usw. Du gehst doch gern ins Kino, oder nicht? Ich gehe einmal in der Woche. Am liebsten mag ich Action-Filme. Und Du? Was für Filme magst Du am liebsten?

Meine Schwester, die Uschi, geht lieber in die Oper. Aber das ist nichts für mich. Ich finde Opern langweilig. Aber wir können auch ins Theater gehen. Sie spielen jetzt „Don Carlos", ein Stück von Schiller.

Im Sommer haben wir auch viele Gartenpartys. Diese Partys sind immer sehr lustig. Wir grillen, spielen tolle Musik und tanzen.

Und in der Nähe von uns ist eine Diskothek. Gehst Du gern in Diskotheken? Ich finde sie toll. Dort kannst Du Typen sehen - - und die Musik ist Klasse!

Es ist schade, dass Du nicht schon im Juni kommen kannst. Am 21. Juni, am längsten Tag im Sommer, haben wir in der Nähe immer ein grosses Johannisfeuer und ein ganz tolles Feuerwerk.

Meine Freunde und Freundinnen sind auch nett. Du hast sie bestimmt gern. Wir gehen oft zusammen aus: wir bummeln durch die Stadt, oder wir gehen in ein Café und diskutieren über alle möglichen Probleme.

Ich schicke Prospekte für die Rockkonzerte im Juli. Du kannst schon jetzt aussuchen, was Du hören willst. Und schreibe bald, dann kaufe ich schon die Karten. Viele Konzerte sind schnell ausverkauft. Wie Du siehst, spielen die meisten Gruppen in der Alabamahalle - - ja, wir haben eine Alabamahalle hier in München! Findest Du das nicht lustig?

Alles Gute und viele Grüsse, auch an Deine Eltern,

Dein Ulli

[1]**Johannisfeuer** is a huge bonfire in celebration of midsummer night.

2 Übung • Jetzt bist du dran

1. You have just received this letter from Ulli. In English, tell your friends who don't study German the gist of what he has written.
2. In German, tell a classmate what Ulli has written.
3. Pretend that you are about to visit Ulli in Germany. Tell your classmates what you and Ulli are going to do.

3 Schreibübung • Was schreibt Ulli? Was schreibst du?

1. Write a summary of Ulli's letter, using third person verb forms. Your letter may begin like this:

   Ulli dankt John für den Brief und die Briefmarken. Er hat diese Marken noch nicht. Ulli schreibt, was sie . . .

2. Now pretend the German student Ulli is coming to visit you. Tell him all about your friends and the things that you can do together when he comes to see you.

4 Übung • Telefongespräch

A student from Germany is visiting friends in your neighborhood. You have met this student at a party, and now you are inviting him or her to go out with you. You have not decided yet where to go and what to do, and you are discussing various possibilities, including:

—where you will go
—how to get there
—what time you will be there
—how much money you will need

5 Übung • Klassenprojekte

1. Choose a film that you have seen recently and design an ad for it in German.
2. Bring in a movie ad or a concert ad from your newspaper. Tell the class what kind of concert or film it is, why you like it, and when it begins.

6 Übung • Ratespiel

Amerikanische Filme in Deutschland haben meistens einen deutschen Titel. Der Titel ist oft ein wenig anders als der amerikanische. Rate mal: wie heissen diese Filme wohl auf englisch?

Zwölf Uhr mittags (mit Gary Cooper) ist . . .
Reise nach Indien
Der Mann mit 2 Gehirnen (mit Steve Martin)
Der weisse Hai
Odyssee im Weltraum
Für eine Handvoll Dollar (mit Clint Eastwood)
Nur Samstagnacht (mit John Travolta)
Der Herr der Ringe

7 Übung • Was sagen die Jungen und Mädchen?

Es ist Freitag. Die Schule ist aus. Die Jungen und Mädchen machen Pläne für das Wochenende. Was sagen sie?

In der Freizeit
wollen 10- bis 19jährige Jugendliche am liebsten

Sport treiben	46%
Lesen	31%
Musik hören	20%
Tanzen	8%
Fernsehen	9%
Kino gehen	1%
Basteln	8%
Wandern, spazierengehen	10%
Handarbeiten	5%

8 Übung • In der Freizeit

Eine Umfrage zeigt, wie die 10- bis 19jährigen Jugendlichen ihre Freizeit verbringen. Sprich darüber mit deinen Klassenkameraden, und mach eine ähnliche Umfrage in deiner Klasse und mit deinen Freunden! Vergleiche die beiden Umfragen!

9 Übung • Deine Eltern fragen Dich

Es ist Samstag abend. Du willst ausgehen, und du fragst deine Eltern.

Du: Ich möchte jetzt in die Stadt fahren.
Deine Eltern: Ja, (Peter), du gehst wieder aus?
Du: . . .
Deine Eltern: Wohin gehst du?
Du: . . .
Deine Eltern: Was machst du dort?
Du: . . .
Deine Eltern: Und wann kommst du nach Hause?
Du: . . .
Deine Eltern: Das ist sehr spät!
Du: . . .

10 Aussprache-, Lese- und Schreibübungen

1. Listen carefully and repeat what you hear.
2. Listen, then read aloud.
   Jugend, Jugendliche, jenseits; Konzert, Freizeit, Zeitung, schmalzig;
   singen, Sänger, anfangen, gegangen, verbringen, Zeitung, Lieblingsstar
3. Copy the following sentences to prepare yourself to write them from dictation.
   1. Jugendliche lesen auch die Zeitung.
   2. Wir sind ins Konzert gegangen.
   3. Der Sänger ist mein Lieblingsstar.
   4. Wie verbringen wir unsere Freizeit?

WAS KANNST DU SCHON?

Let's review some important points you have learned in this unit.

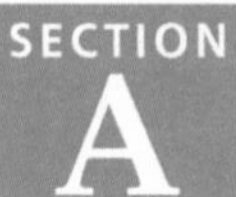

Can you tell what you do in your free time?
Mention six of your activities.

Can you suggest some things to do with a friend?
You and a friend want to do something together. Make six suggestions. Use **können, wollen,** and the *let's*-form.

Can you tell what kinds of movies you like and don't like?
Mention four kinds of movies and tell if you like or dislike each one. Tell which kind you prefer and which kind you like most of all. Give some reasons why.

Can you discuss which movie or concert you and a friend would like to go to?
Ask a friend which movie he or she would like to see.

Ask what kind of concert he or she would like to hear.

Can you say you like certain things or people and dislike others?
Name two movies and two movie stars you like and two you dislike. Use **mögen, nicht mögen,** and **gern haben.**

Can you talk about what you did?
Tell what you did yesterday evening.

Tell what the following people did:

1. your sister **2.** your parents **3.** you and your friend

WORTSCHATZ

SECTION A

also *well then*
ausgehen *to go out* (see p 276)
besonders *especially*
das **Café, -s** *café;* in ein Café gehen *to go to a café*
die **Clique, -n** *clique*
die **Disko, -s** *disco;* in eine Disko gehen *to go to a disco*
fahren *to go, drive, ride;* in die Stadt fahren *to go into town* (see p 276)
fragen wir mal! *let's ask*
die **Freizeit** *free time, leisure time*
der **Freizeitmuffel, -** *person who doesn't know what to do with free time*
gut, danke *fine, thanks*
das **Interesse, -n** *interest*
die **Jugend** *youth, young people*
die **Jugendlichen** (pl) *young people*
kegeln *to bowl*
das **Kino, -s** *movies;* ins Kino gehen *to go to the movies;* gehen wir ins Kino! *let's go to the movies!*
können *can, be able to* (see p 275)
das **Konzert, -e** *concert;* ins Konzert gehen *to go to a concert*
man *one, you (in general), people*
miserabel *miserable*
na ja *oh, well*
nö = nein *no* (casual)
nun ja *well, yes*
radfahren: wir fahren Rad *we go bike riding*
das **Rockkonzert, -e** *rock concert*
so lala *so-so*
spannend *exciting*
die **Sportveranstaltung, -en** *sports event*
Squash *squash*
der **Stadtbummel, -** *stroll through the city;* einen Stadtbummel machen *to take a stroll through the city*
das **Theater, -** *theater;* ins Theater gehen *to go to the theater*
tun *to do*
verbringen *to spend (time)*
wenn *when, if*
wollen *to want to* (see p 275)
zu Hause *at home*
zusammen *together*

SECTION B

der **Abenteuerfilm, -e** *adventure film*
der **Action-Film, -e** *action film*
anfangen *to start* (see p 280)
glauben *to think, believe*
gleich: das ist mir gleich *it's all the same to me*
die **Gruppe, -n** *group*
der **Horrorfilm, -e** *horror film*
ja? *okay?*
die **Komödie, -n** *comedy*
der **Kriegsfilm, -e** *war film*
der **Liebesfilm, -e** *love story*
Lieblings- *favorite*
die **Lieblingsgruppe, -n** *favorite group*
der **Lieblingsstar, -s** *favorite star*
der **Naturfilm, -e** *nature film*
Quatsch! *nonsense!*
der **Sänger, -** *singer*
schauen *to look;* in die Zeitung schauen *to look in the newspaper*
der **Schauspieler, -** *actor*
der **Science-fiction-Film, -e** *science fiction film*
singen *to sing*
was für *what kind of (a)*
welch- *which*
der **Western, -** *western*
die **Zeitung, -en** *newspaper*
zu *too*

SECTION C

brutal *brutal*
dumm *dumb, stupid*
grausam *cruel*
hassen *to hate*
heisst: wie heisst er denn? *what's it called again?*
mögen *to like;* gern mögen *to like* (see p 286)
phantasievoll *imaginative*
schmalzig *schmaltzy*
sensationell *sensational*
warum? *why?*

SECTION D

gestern abend *last night*

WORTSCHATZÜBUNGEN

1. Make a list of all the verbs in the **Wortschatz.** Which ones have a separable prefix? Which ones have a vowel change in the second and third person? Which ones change their forms in the first, second, and third person?
2. Write down all the nouns that contain the word **Film.**
3. **Lieblings-** is a noun prefix meaning *favorite.* Look at the **Wortschatz** and pick out all the nouns you can combine with it.
4. List all the words taken from English.

ZUM LESEN

Die Prominenten kommen auch nach Deutschland

Alle grossen Sänger und Musikgruppen aus dem Ausland kommen hierher—ihre Konzerte sind immer gleich ausverkauft°.

Die deutschen Jungen und Mädchen kennen die meisten Sänger und Gruppen aus dem Ausland. Die Hitliste zeigt euch, welche Sänger und Gruppen jetzt beliebt° sind.

Und ihr könnt auch einige Kommentare lesen. Junge Leute haben uns gesagt, wie sie einige Sänger und Musikgruppen finden. Was meint ihr? Habt ihr die gleiche Meinung° oder eine andere?

SUPERTRAMP

Ich finde diese Gruppe gut. Wenn man ihre Musik hört, kann man nachdenken°. Die Musik ist langsam°, und die Texte sind nicht so schwer zu verstehen.

(Annemarie Mai)

BOB MARLEY

Seine Texte sprechen von den Problemen in der Dritten Welt°. Ich finde es gut, wie er darüber singt. Seine Melodien habe ich gern.

(Klaus Holzer)

QUEEN

Man kann bei der Musik gut tanzen, und man kann auch gut nachdenken.

(Holger Sachs)

---

ausverkauft *sold out;* **beliebt** *popular;* **die gleiche Meinung** *the same opinion;* **nachdenken** *to think about* **langsam** *slow;* **in der Dritten Welt** *in the Third World*

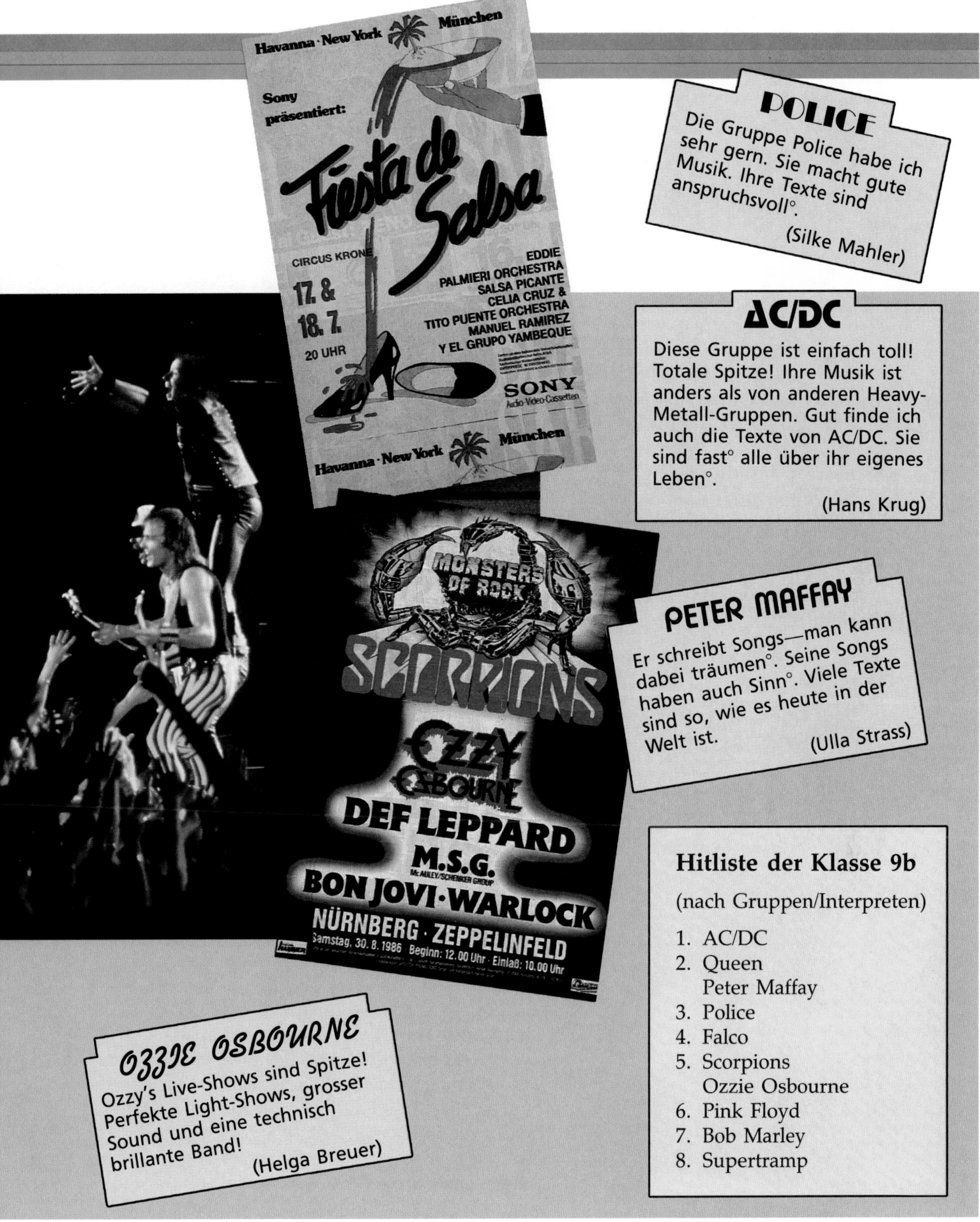

POLICE

Die Gruppe Police habe ich sehr gern. Sie macht gute Musik. Ihre Texte sind anspruchsvoll°.

(Silke Mahler)

AC/DC

Diese Gruppe ist einfach toll! Totale Spitze! Ihre Musik ist anders als von anderen Heavy-Metall-Gruppen. Gut finde ich auch die Texte von AC/DC. Sie sind fast° alle über ihr eigenes Leben°.

(Hans Krug)

PETER MAFFAY

Er schreibt Songs—man kann dabei träumen°. Seine Songs haben auch Sinn°. Viele Texte sind so, wie es heute in der Welt ist.

(Ulla Strass)

OZZIE OSBOURNE

Ozzy's Live-Shows sind Spitze! Perfekte Light-Shows, grosser Sound und eine technisch brillante Band!

(Helga Breuer)

Hitliste der Klasse 9b

(nach Gruppen/Interpreten)

1. AC/DC
2. Queen
   Peter Maffay
3. Police
4. Falco
5. Scorpions
   Ozzie Osbourne
6. Pink Floyd
7. Bob Marley
8. Supertramp

---

anspruchsvoll *stimulating;* **fast** *almost;* **über ihr eigenes Leben** *about their own life;* **träumen** *to dream;* **Sinn** *meaning*

Stars, die heute beliebt sind

Nina Hagen, eine deutsche Sängerin von Weltrang, kommt aus Berlin. Man nennt sie die Rocklady oder die Rock-Walküre. Nina gibt Konzerte in der ganzen Welt, in Italien, Frankreich, Österreich, Norwegen, Kanada, in den USA und in Südamerika.

Herbert Grönemeyer, „der Blonde aus Bochum", ist Pianist (er hatte seine erste Band schon mit zehn Jahren!), Schauspieler (er spielte den Leutnant Werner in dem Anti-Kriegsfilm „Das Boot"), Komponist, Musiker und Sänger. In seinen Kompositionen findet man viele Stilelemente: lateinamerikanische und karibische Rhythmen, Gospel, Soul, Calypso, Reggae, Rock. Grönemeyer singt mit kräftiger, harter Stimme; seine Konzerte sind immer ausverkauft.

In Deutschland ist er ein Super-Star, der Rocksänger Peter Maffay. Seine Konzerte sind immer ausverkauft, sein Publikum kommt aus allen Generationen: Oma, Opa, Mutter, Vater, Tochter und Sohn. Seine Musik und seine Texte sind für alle interessant.

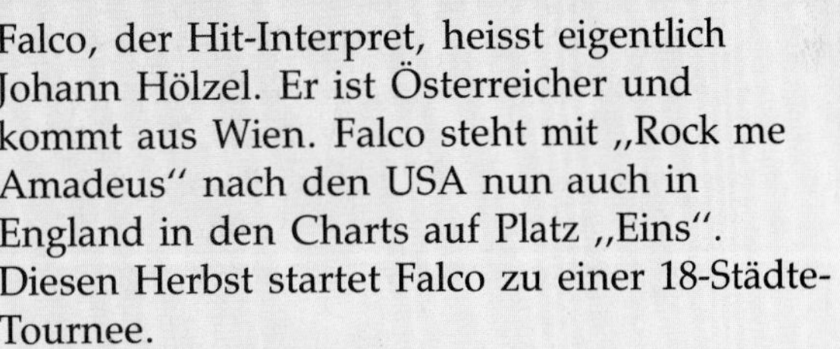

Falco, der Hit-Interpret, heisst eigentlich Johann Hölzel. Er ist Österreicher und kommt aus Wien. Falco steht mit „Rock me Amadeus" nach den USA nun auch in England in den Charts auf Platz „Eins". Diesen Herbst startet Falco zu einer 18-Städte-Tournee.

Übung • Jetzt bist du dran!

1. Welche Gruppen oder Sänger und Sängerinnen kennst du und welche kennst du nicht?
2. Welche Gruppen oder Interpreten hörst du gern? Welche hörst du nicht gern?
3. Wie heissen deine Lieblingsgruppen oder Lieblingssänger?

Übung • Umfrage

Welches ist eure Hitliste? Macht eine Umfrage in der Klasse:

Unsere Hitliste: Gruppen aus den USA
Unsere Hitliste: Gruppen aus anderen Ländern

Schreibübung • Klassenprojekt

Jeder von euch schreibt ein kurzes Resumé von einer Gruppe oder von einem Sänger oder einer Sängerin. Lest dann in der Klasse vor, was ihr geschrieben habt und besprecht eure Arbeiten!

KAPITEL 11
Geschenke kaufen

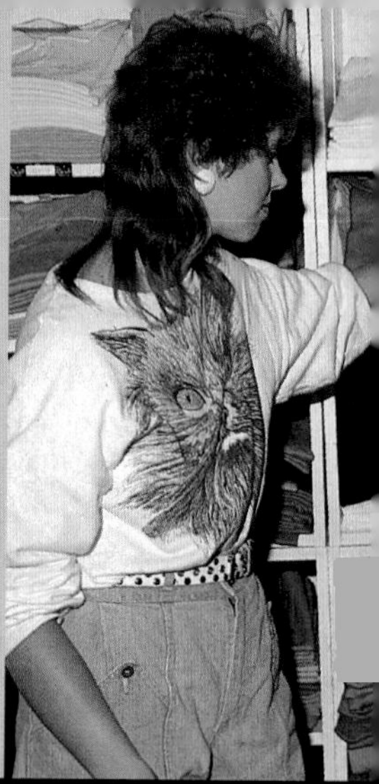

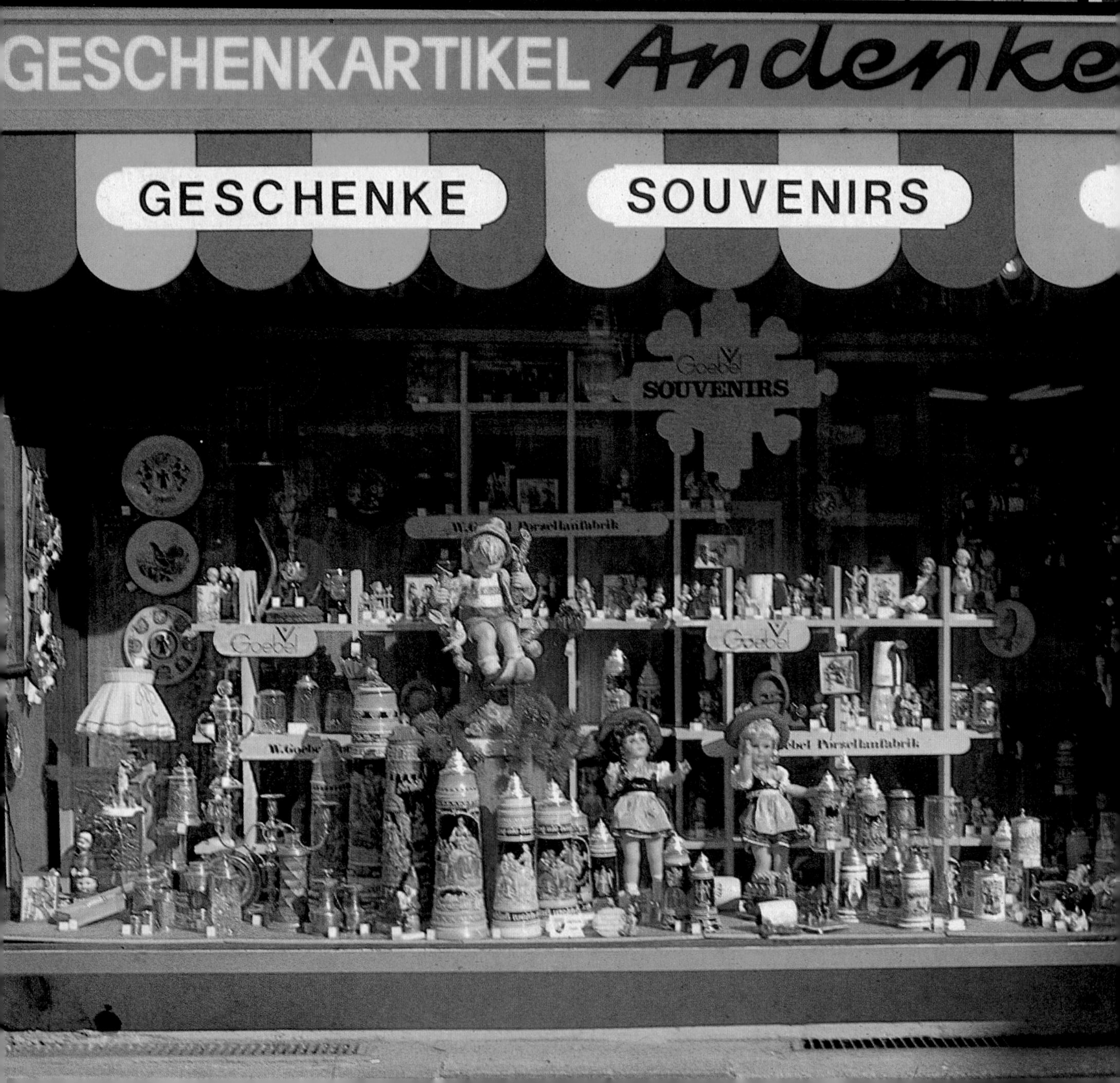

Birthdays and anniversaries, Christmas, and other holidays are occasions for buying gifts for family and friends. It is sometimes difficult, however, to find appropriate gifts, and the advice of friends is often appreciated. What do young people in the German-speaking countries buy and give as presents—the same type of things you do?

In this unit you will:

SECTION A	discuss buying presents for family and friends, ask for advice on what to give
SECTION B	get a salesperson's attention and ask about price and color of specific items
SECTION C	make suggestions for presents for special occasions and express good wishes
TRY YOUR SKILLS	use what you've learned
ZUM LESEN	read for practice and pleasure

SECTION A

buying presents for family and friends, thinking about what to give, and asking for advice

Special occasions are coming up and presents have to be bought. On a stroll down a popular shopping street, Andrea and Monika pass a store that sells presents and souvenirs.

A1 Geschenke für Freunde und Familie 

ANDREA Was schenke ich bloss meinem Vater? Er hat bald Geburtstag. Was meinst du? Hast du eine Idee? Was schenkst du gewöhnlich deinem Vater?

MONIKA Ach, ich kaufe meinem Vater meistens ein Buch. Er hat Reisebücher gern.

ANDREA Hm, der Vati hat schon so viele Bücher! — Du, und was gebe ich meinen Grosseltern? Sie haben bald goldene Hochzeit.

MONIKA Schau, Andrea, hier gibt es so viele Geschenke!

Was soll ich nur schenken?

DM 10,–

Eine Brieftasche?

DM 25,–

Ein Portemonnaie? Dieses Portemonnaie ist schick!

DM 40,–

Ein Radio, vielleicht?

DM 28,–

Parfüm? Dieses Parfüm ist toll!

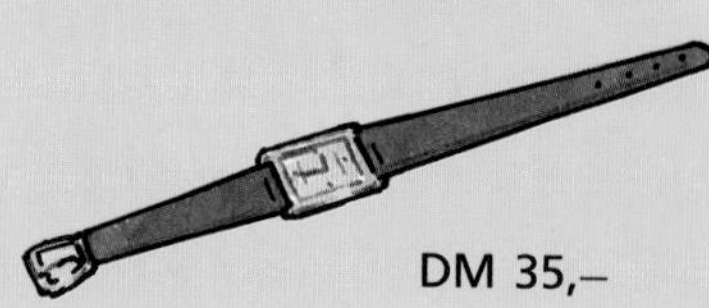

DM 35,–

Eine Armbanduhr, eine Quarzuhr?

DM 8,–

Einen Kalender?

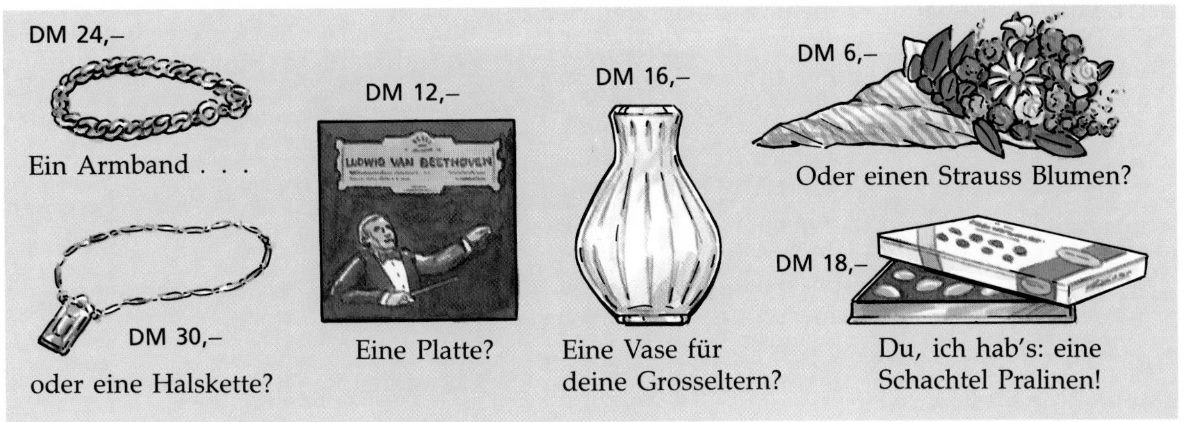

DM 24,–
Ein Armband . . .
DM 30,–
oder eine Halskette?
DM 12,–
LUDWIG VAN BEETHOVEN
Eine Platte?
DM 16,–
Eine Vase für
deine Grosseltern?
DM 6,–
Oder einen Strauss Blumen?
DM 18,–
Du, ich hab's: eine
Schachtel Pralinen!

A2 Übung • Im Schaufenster 

Let's take a look in the store window.

A: Was gibt es hier?
B: Hier gibt es Brieftaschen, . . .

A: Was kaufst du alles?
B: Ich kaufe eine Brieftasche, . . .

A: Was kostet das alles?
B: Die Brieftasche kostet zehn Mark, . . .

A3 Übung • Merkspiel: Was für Geschenke kaufst du?

MONIKA Ich kaufe ein Portemonnaie.
STEFAN Ich kaufe ein Portemonnaie und einen Kalender.
ANDREA Ich kaufe ein Portemonnaie, einen Kalender und ein . . .

A4 ERKLÄRUNG
Indirect Objects, Dative Case Forms of Possessives

1. The following sentences include a noun phrase you have not used up to now. This noun phrase signals the indirect object, which expresses the idea of "to someone" or "for someone." In German, the idea of "to someone" or "for someone" can be expressed by using dative case forms.

   Ich kaufe **meiner Schwester** eine Platte. < *I'm buying a record for my sister.* / *I'm buying my sister a record.*

   Ich gebe **meinen Brüdern** Bücher. < *I give my brothers books.* / *I give books to my brothers.*

2. In English, the indirect object is signaled by word order: I'm giving *my dad a wallet.* It can also be signaled by a prepositional phrase: I'm buying a record *for my sister.* In German, the indirect object is signaled by the form of the determiner **meinem, meiner, meinen,** etc. It is sometimes signaled by the noun itself:
   a. Nouns that add **-n** or **-en** in the accusative case (see page 140) also add these endings in the dative singular: **mein Klassenkamerad—meinem Klassenkameraden.**
   b. The dative plural of almost all nouns ends in **-n: seine Brüder—seinen Brüdern.** If the nominative plural form already ends in **-n,** there is no change in the dative plural form: **unsere Eltern—unseren Eltern.**

(continued)

3. The dative case forms of the possessives are listed below.

before masculine & neuter nouns	*before feminine nouns*	*before plural nouns*
meinem	**meiner**	**meinen**
deinem	**deiner**	**deinen**
seinem	**seiner**	**seinen**
ihrem	**ihrer**	**ihren**
unserem	**unserer**	**unseren**
euerem	**euerer**	**eueren**
ihrem	**ihrer**	**ihren**
Ihrem	**Ihrer**	**Ihren**

4. To ask the questions *to whom?* or *for whom?*, the dative form **wem?** is used.

Wem	kauft sie Pralinen?	*For whom is she buying fancy chocolates?*
Wem	schenkt sie ein Buch?	*To whom is she giving a book?*

A5 Übung • Was kauft Andrea für ihre Familie und Freunde?

A: Ihr Bruder bekommt ein Buch.
B: Wie bitte?
A: Sie kauft ihrem Bruder ein Buch.

1. Ihre Freundin bekommt Parfüm.
2. Ihr Vater bekommt ein Portemonnaie.
3. Ihre Geschwister bekommen Bücher.
4. Ihr Freund bekommt ein Poster.
5. Ihre Kusine bekommt eine Halskette.
6. Ihr Opa bekommt Pralinen.

A6 Übung • Was schenkst du alles?

A: Ich habe ein Buch für meinen Vater.
B: Vielleicht schenke ich meinem Vater auch ein Buch.

1. Ich habe eine Vase für meine Oma.
2. Ich habe eine Armbanduhr für meinen Freund.
3. Ich habe Pralinen für meine Eltern.
4. Ich habe ein Armband für meine Schwester.
5. Ich habe Kassetten für meine Freunde.
6. Ich habe eine Platte für meinen Vetter.

A7 ERKLÄRUNG
The Verb geben

The verb **geben** has the following forms in the present tense. Note the vowel change from **e** to **i** in the **du-** and **er/sie-**forms.

ich **gebe**	wir **geben**
du **gibst**	ihr **gebt**
er, sie, es **gibt**	sie, Sie **geben**

A8 Übung • Frag mal deine Klassenkameraden und deine Lehrer!

1. Was gibst du deinen Eltern?
2. Was gibst du deinen Geschwistern?
3. Was gebt ihr euern Grosseltern?
4. Frau (Meier), was geben Sie Ihren Kindern?

A 9 Übung • Mix-Match: Wem schenkst du was?

Ich kaufe meinem Vater gewöhnlich ein Buch.

ich	gebe	meinem Vater	gewöhnlich	ein Buch
wir	gibt	ihren Eltern	immer	eine Armbanduhr
Andrea	geben	seiner Schwester	meistens	Parfüm
Peter	kaufe	unseren Grosseltern	vielleicht	einen Strauss Blumen
die Kinder	kauft	seinem Opa		eine Schachtel Pralinen
	kaufen	seinen Eltern		eine Platte
	schenke	ihrer Tante		einen Kalender
	schenkt	ihren Geschwistern		eine Halskette
	schenken	meiner Mutter		ein Portmonnaie

A 10 Übung • Hör gut zu!

Does the sentence have an indirect object or not?

		0	1	2	3	4	5	6	7	8	9	10
sentence has an indirect object	ja	✓										
	nein											

A 11 Schreibübung • Deine Geschenkliste

Vati, vielen Dank für den Computer!

Make a list of your family members including some aunts, uncles, and cousins, and write what you might give each one as a present.

Ich schenke meiner Mutter . . .,
meinem Onkel (Fred) . . .

Now exchange lists with a classmate and take turns telling the class what is on your classmate's list.

(Bob) schenkt seiner Mutter . . .
Er schenkt seinem Vetter (David) . . .

A 12 WIE SAGT MAN DAS?

Wondering what to give, asking for advice

wondering what to give	Was schenke ich bloss meinem Vater? Was gebe ich nur meiner Mutter? Was soll ich kaufen?	What on earth should I give my father? What can I give to my mother? What should I buy?
asking for advice	Was meinst du? Hast du eine Idee?	What do you think? Do you have an idea?

A 13 Übung • Was soll ich bloss schenken?

You ask different classmates for advice on what to buy for various people.

A: Was schenk' ich bloss meiner Freundin? Was meinst du? Hast du eine Idee?
B: Hm. Ich kaufe meiner Freundin gewöhnlich ein Buch.
A: Ja! Vielleicht ein Buch!

* * *

A: Du, Peter!
B: Ja?
A: Was kann ich bloss meiner Kusine schenken?
B: Deiner Kusine? —Ich kaufe meiner Kusine meistens eine Platte. Sie hat Platten gern.
A: Ach, sie hat schon so viele Platten.

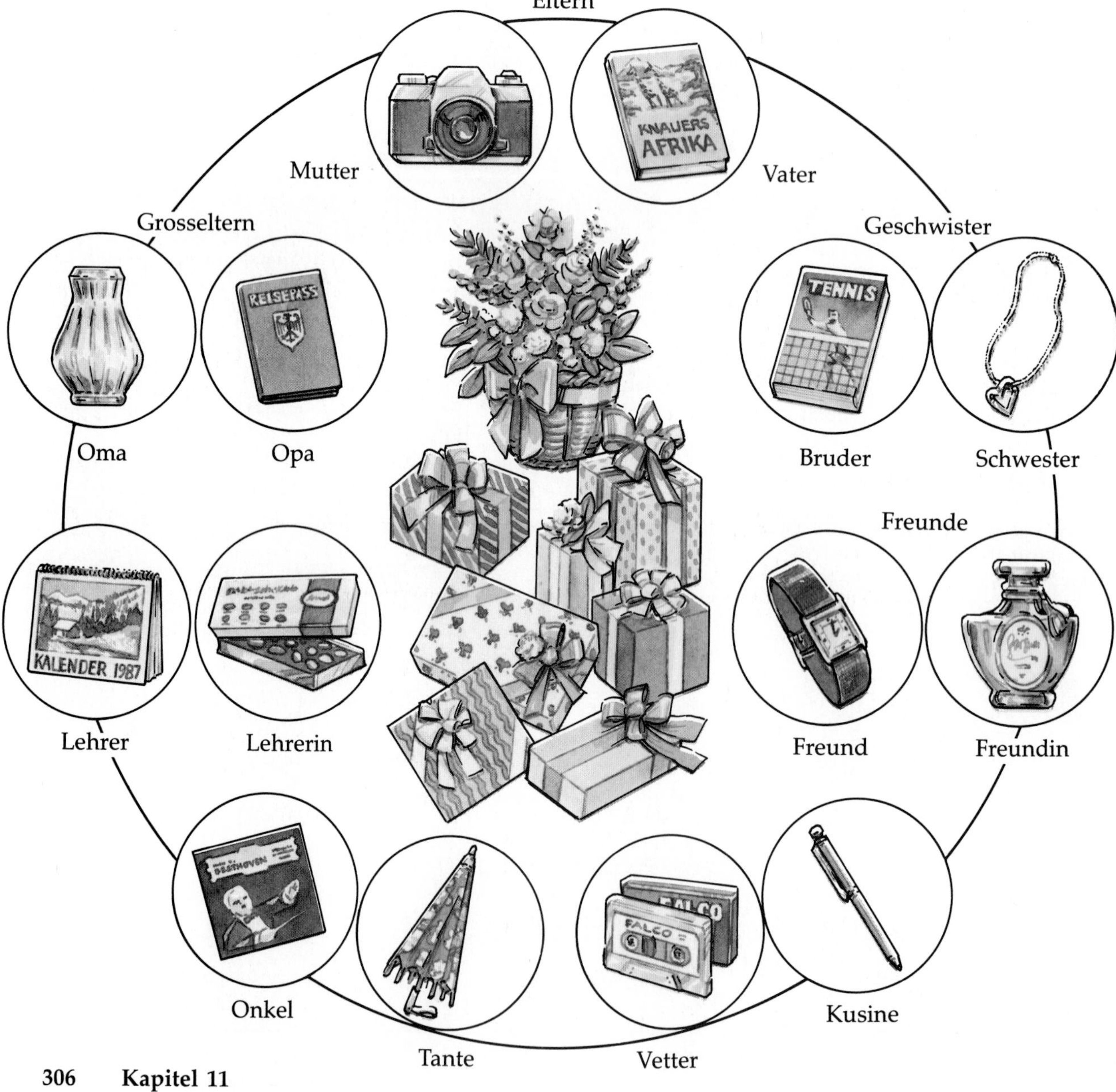

getting a salesperson's attention and asking about price and color of specific items

Andrea and Monika are in a department store. Some items don't have a price tag. Andrea asks the salesperson how much various items cost. Which items would you buy?

B1

Im Kaufhaus

ANDREA Fräulein!
VERKÄUFERIN Ja, bitte? Was darf es sein?
ANDREA Wie teuer ist dieser Pulli, bitte?
VERKÄUFERIN Die Pullis sind heute im Angebot. Jeder Pulli kostet achtzehn Mark.
ANDREA Danke!
VERKÄUFERIN Bitte schön!

Ich weiss noch nicht.

Nehmen Sie diesen Pulli?

Und dieses Hemd?

Diese Halstücher?

Diese Mütze?

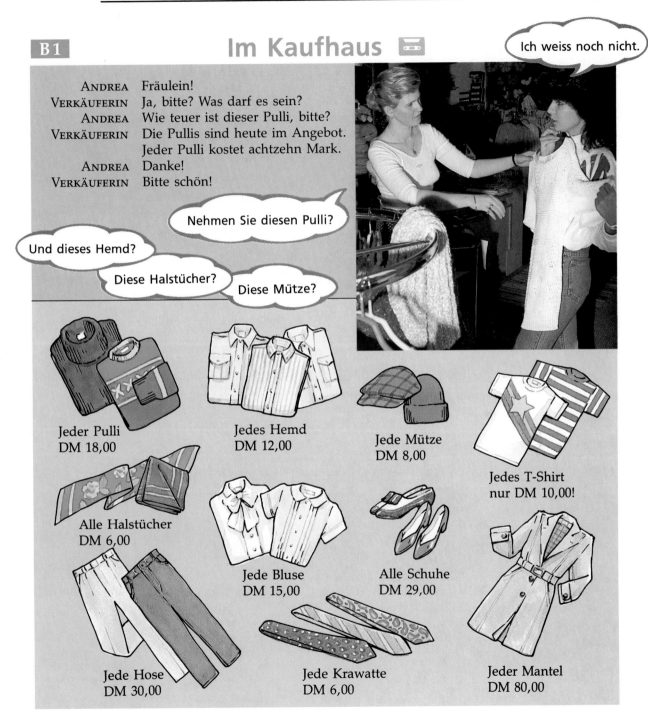

Jeder Pulli DM 18,00

Jedes Hemd DM 12,00

Jede Mütze DM 8,00

Jedes T-Shirt nur DM 10,00!

Alle Halstücher DM 6,00

Jede Bluse DM 15,00

Alle Schuhe DM 29,00

Jede Hose DM 30,00

Jede Krawatte DM 6,00

Jeder Mantel DM 80,00

B2 Übung • Was kaufst du?

1. Ich kaufe ein . . .
2. Wie teuer ist der . . .?
3. Sind die . . . im Angebot?
4. Ich möchte den . . .

der	die	das	die
Pulli Mantel	Mütze Bluse Hose Krawatte	Hemd Halstuch T-Shirt	Schuhe

B3 ERKLÄRUNG
dieser, jeder: *Nominative and Accusative Case*

1. **Dieser, diese, dieses,** *this, these,* are called demonstratives, because they are used to point to specific items.

   Wie teuer ist dieser Pulli? *How much is this sweater?*
   Diese Hemden sind teuer. *These shirts are expensive.*

   Dieser has the following forms in the nominative and the accusative cases:

	Masculine	*Feminine*	*Neuter*	*Plural*
Nominative	**dieser**	**diese**	**dieses**	**diese**
Accusative	**diesen**			

2. **Jeder, jede, jedes,** *each, every,* and the plural form **alle,** *all,* have the same endings as **dieser.**

   Jeder Mantel kostet DM 80. *Every coat costs 80 Marks.*
   Alle Mäntel kosten DM 80. *All coats cost 80 Marks.*

	Masculine	*Feminine*	*Neuter*	*Plural*
Nominative	**jeder**	**jede**	**jedes**	**alle**
Accusative	**jeden**			

B4 Übung • Im Kaufhaus 

Practice the conversations on the next page, using each item pictured.

1. DM 80,-

2. DM 18,-

3. DM 12,-

4. DM 8,-

5. DM 6,-

6. DM 15,-

7. DM 29,-

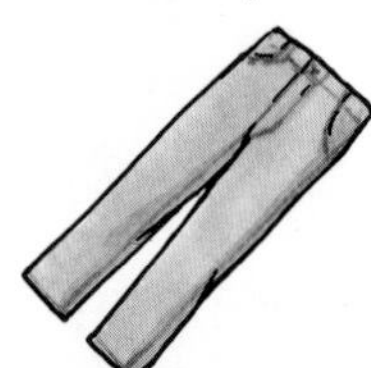

8. DM 30,-

9. DM 12,50

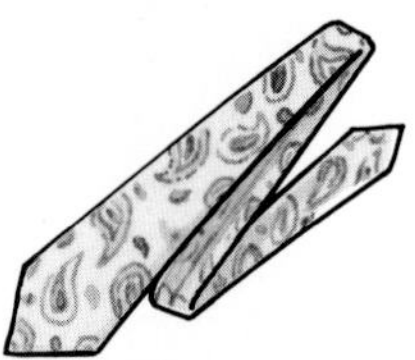

10. DM 6,-

1. A: Wie teuer ist dieser Mantel, bitte?
   B: Jeder Mantel kostet achtzig Mark.
   A: Das ist zu teuer!

2. A: Fräulein, was kostet dieser Mantel, bitte?
   B: Sie bekommen jeden Mantel für achtzig Mark.
   A: Ja, dann nehme ich ihn.

3. A: Der Mantel ist toll (prima, Spitze, schön)!
   B: Möchtest du diesen Mantel?
   A: Ich weiss noch nicht.

B5 Übung • Merkspiel

Wir gehen einkaufen.

MONIKA Ich möchte diesen Pulli.
STEFAN Ich möchte diesen Pulli und dieses T-Shirt.
ANDREA Ich möchte diesen Pulli, dieses T-Shirt und . . .

B6 WIE SAGT MAN DAS?
Getting someone's attention

The words **Entschuldigung!** and **Verzeihung!** can be used to get someone's attention. In a store you can also use **Fräulein** to get the attention of a saleswoman. The salesperson will usually respond with **Ja, bitte? Was darf es sein?** *May I help you?*

getting someone's attention in general	Entschuldigung! Verzeihung!	Excuse me!
getting the attention of a saleswoman	Fräulein!	Miss!
salesperson's response	Ja, bitte? Was darf es sein?	Yes, may I help you?

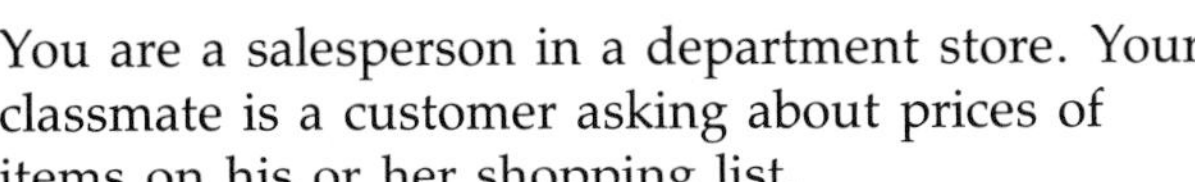

B7 Übung • Verkaufsgespräch

You are a salesperson in a department store. Your classmate is a customer asking about prices of items on his or her shopping list.

KUNDE Verzeihung!
VERKÄUFER/IN Ja, bitte?
KUNDE Wie teuer ist dieser Pulli, bitte?
VERKÄUFER/IN Jeder Pulli kostet zwanzig Mark.
KUNDE Danke!
VERKÄUFER/IN Bitte schön!

Pulli
Portemonnaie
Bluse
Armband
Halskette
Mütze
Kalender
Krawatte

B 8 Ein wenig Landeskunde

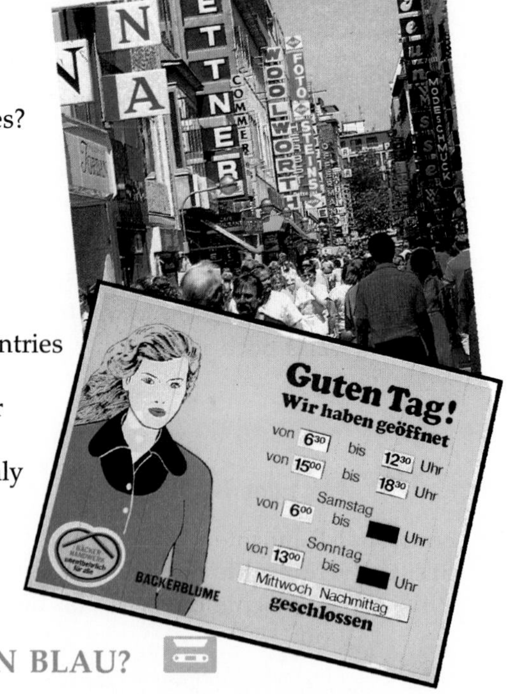

What kind of stores are there in German-speaking countries? There are smaller specialty stores—for example, **Bekleidungsgeschäfte,** *clothing stores,* **Plattenläden,** *record stores,* **Buchhandlungen,** *book stores,* and **Blumengeschäfte,** *florist shops.* There are large **Kaufhäuser,** *department stores,* and many areas now have a modern and attractive **Einkaufszentrum,** *shopping mall.*

Shopping hours are shorter in the German-speaking countries than in the United States. Small stores, except for those in downtown sections of cities, are usually closed for an hour or two at lunchtime. Almost all stores close by 6:30 P.M., including grocery stores. On Saturdays, stores are open only until 2 P.M., although once a month many cities have **„einen langen Samstag,"** *a long Saturday,* during which stores are open until 6. All stores are closed on Sundays.

B 9 HABEN SIE DEN PULLI VIELLEICHT IN BLAU?

VERKÄUFERIN Der Pulli ist hübsch, nicht?
MONIKA Ja, der ist sehr schön. Nur mag ich Rot nicht. Haben Sie den vielleicht in Blau? Blau ist meine Lieblingsfarbe.
VERKÄUFERIN Ich glaube, ja. —Hier ist dieser Pulli in Blau.
MONIKA Gut, den nehme ich. Das Blau ist toll.

Wir haben auch dieses Hemd in vielen Farben:

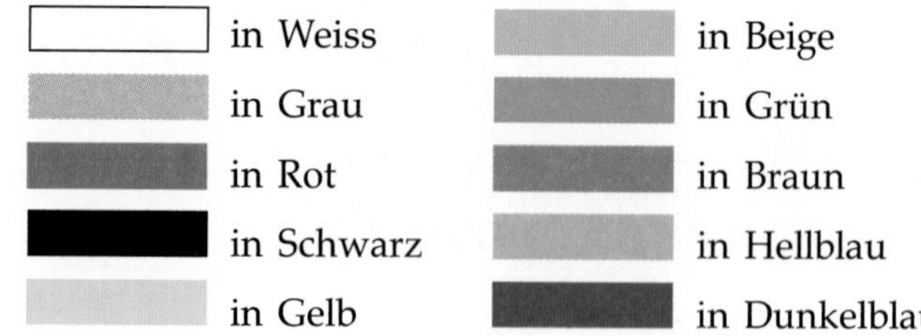

B 10 Übung • Und du? Wie steht's mit dir?

1. Welche Farben hast du gern?
2. Welche Farben hast du nicht gern?
3. Was ist deine Lieblingsfarbe?

B 11 ERKLÄRUNG
der, die, das *Used as Demonstrative Pronouns*

The definite articles are often used by themselves, that is, without a noun. When used this way, they are called demonstrative pronouns. They function as pronouns, but they have more emphasis than the personal pronouns **er, sie,** and **es.** When used as pronouns, the definite articles have the same forms as they have when used as definite articles.

	Masculine	*Feminine*	*Neuter*	*Plural*
Nominative	**der**	**die**	**das**	**die**
Accusative	**den**			

Dieser Pulli ist hübsch, nicht?	Ja, **der** ist sehr schön.
This sweater is pretty, isn't it?	*Yes, it is very nice.*
Möchten Sie **diesen Pulli?**	Ja, **den** nehme ich.
Would you like this sweater?	*Yes, that's the one I'll take.*

B12 Übung • Was sagt die Verkäuferin? Was sagst du?

A: Dieser Pulli ist hübsch, nicht?
B: Ja, der ist sehr schön.

1. diese Schuhe sind . . . ?
2. dieses Hemd?
3. dieser Mantel?
4. dieses T-Shirt?
5. diese Mütze?
6. dieses Halstuch?

B13 Übung • Was?! Du kaufst alles?

A: Möchten Sie diesen Mantel?
B: Ja, den nehme ich.

1. diese Bluse?
2. diese Schuhe?
3. dieses Hemd?
4. diesen Pulli?
5. diese Hose?
6. diesen Kalender?

B14 Übung • Hör gut zu!

Über was sprechen die beiden?

B15 Schreibübung • Was darf es sein, bitte?

Schreibe ein Verkaufsgespräch! Du bist in einem Kaufhaus, und du möchtest etwas kaufen, einen Mantel vielleicht. Du fragst die Verkäuferin, wie teuer die Mäntel sind und ob sie im Angebot sind. Die Verkäuferin zeigt dir einen Mantel. Du findest ihn schick, aber du möchtest eine andere Farbe. Übe dein Gespräch mit einem Klassenkameraden!

making suggestions for presents for special occasions and expressing good wishes on these occasions

There are many special occasions throughout the year when we buy presents, and ads in magazines can give us ideas for special gifts.

C1

Geschenkideen

Was schenken Sie ihm?
Was geben Sie ihr?

Zum Vatertag alles Gute!

Zum Muttertag? Schenken Sie ihr Parfüm!

Zum Vatertag? Kaufen Sie ihm ein Portemonnaie!

Alles Gute zum Muttertag!

Gute Wünsche zum Hochzeitstag!

Zum Hochzeitstag? Schenken Sie ihnen Blumen!

Herzliche Glückwünsche zum Geburtstag!

Zum Geburtstag? Geben Sie ihm ein T-Shirt!

Zu Weihnachten? Schenken Sie ihr eine Uhr!

Fröhliche Weihnachten!

C2 Ein wenig Landeskunde

Occasions for giving gifts in German-speaking countries are pretty much the same as in the United States: birthday, Christmas, anniversary, Mother's Day, and Father's Day, to mention a few. It is also customary to give a gift when visiting someone. Flowers, which Germans are especially fond of, are often given as a gift. Some flower shops even have a vending machine outside so that people can purchase a bouquet even if the store is closed—for example, on a Sunday. Many people buy a gift box of candy or a bottle of wine. It is also customary to bring a bar of chocolate for each child in the family.

C3 Was sagt die Reklame? 

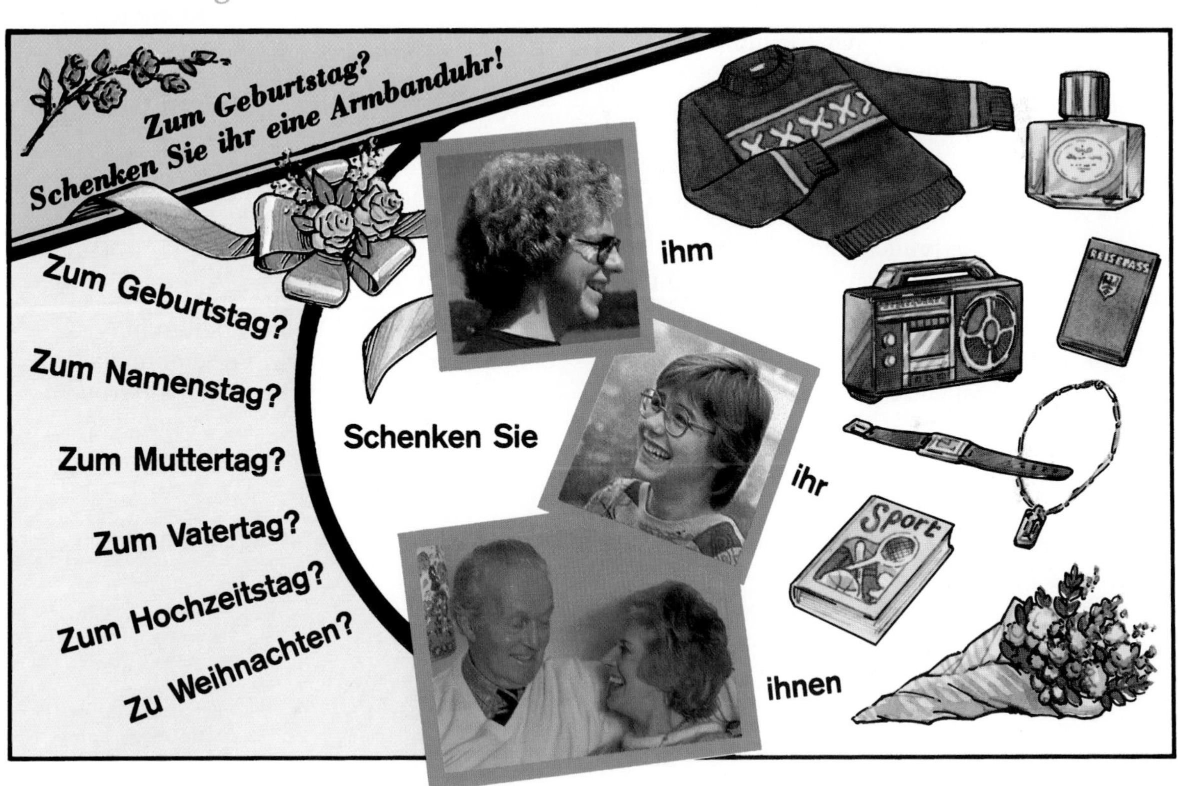

C4 Übung • Was schenkst du?

1. Zum Geburtstag schenke ich meinem Bruder ein T-Shirt.
2. Zum Namenstag schenke ich meiner Mutter ein Buch.
3. Zu . . .

C5 ERKLÄRUNG
Third Person Pronouns, Dative Case

The dative case forms of the third person pronouns are **ihm, ihr,** and **ihnen.** They refer to noun phrases in the dative case.

		Indirect Object: Dative Case		*Dative Pronoun*	
Masculine	Was schenkst du	**deinem Vater?**	Ich schenke	**ihm**	Blumen.
Feminine		**deiner Freundin?**		**ihr**	
Plural		**deinen Eltern?**		**ihnen**	

C6 Übung • Was soll ich bloss schenken? 

A: Was soll ich nur meinem Vater schenken?
B: Schenk ihm doch eine Krawatte!
A: Prima Idee. Er hat Krawatten gern.

* * *

A: Was gebe ich bloss meiner Freundin?
B: Gib ihr doch Parfüm!
A: Gut! Sie mag Parfüm.

Wem?	Eltern, Vater, Mutter, Freundin, Freund, Geschwister, Bruder, Schwester
Was?	Krawatte, Blumen, Schachtel Pralinen, Platte, Musikkassette, Halstuch, Buch

C7 Übung • Mutter hat für alle eine Geschenkidee

A: Die Monika braucht einen Pulli.
B: Gut, dann schenken wir ihr einen Pulli.

1. Der Stefan braucht ein T-Shirt.
2. Die Kinder brauchen Tennisschuhe.
3. Die Andrea braucht eine Bluse.
4. Der Vater braucht eine Brieftasche.
5. Die Ingrid braucht ein Portemonnaie.
6. Paul und Jörg brauchen ein Wörterbuch.

C8 Übung • Was schenkst du?

Was kann man diesen Personen zum Geburtstag schenken? Hast du eine Idee?

A: Die Monika hört gern Musik.
B: Die Monika hört gern Musik? Dann kannst du ihr eine Musikkassette schenken.

1. Frl. Seifert mag Blumen.
2. Die Kinder lesen gern.
3. Der Markus verliert immer sein Geld.
4. Die Monika fotografiert gern.
5. Der Jens ist schlecht in Mathe.

C9 WANN HAST DU GEBURTSTAG? 

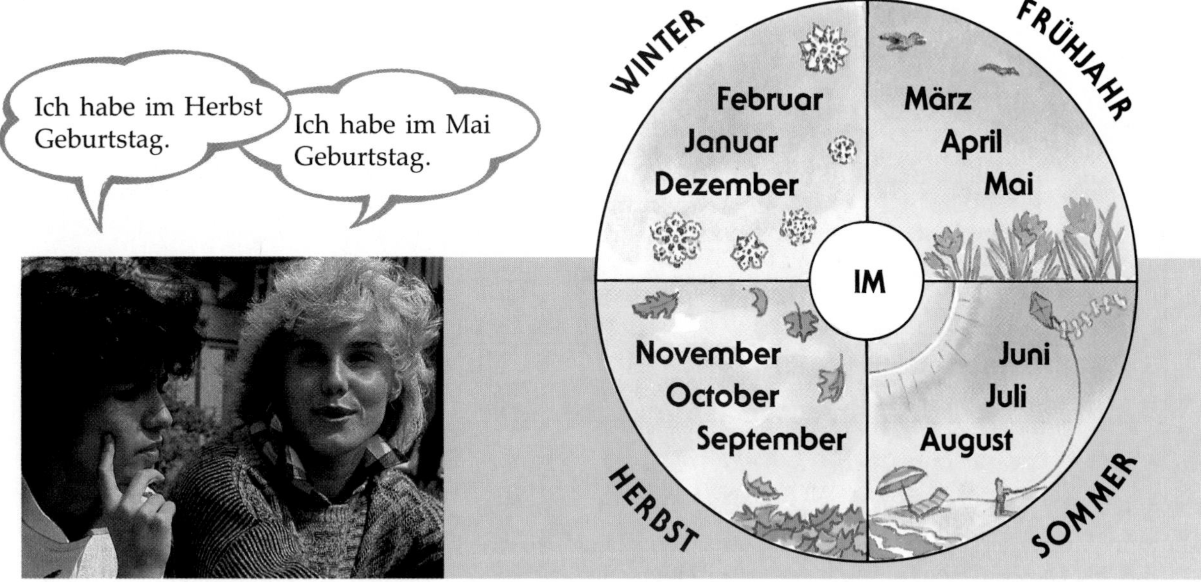

C10 WANN HAST DU GEBURTSTAG? ODER NAMENSTAG?

To say on what day your birthday is, you have to know some ordinal numbers, which are used in a phrase with **am.**

am 1. = am ersten
am 2. = am zweiten
am 3. = am dritten
am 4. = am vierten
am 5. = am fünften
am 6. = am sechsten
am 7. = am siebten
am 8. = am achten
am 9. = am neunten
am 10. = am zehnten
am 11. = am elften
am 12. = am . . .

am 20. = am zwanzigsten
am 21. = am einundzwanzigsten
am 22. = am zweiundzwanzigsten

Ich habe am vierten Mai Geburtstag.
Namenstage im Juli
10. Erich/Erika
13. Margarete
15. Heinrich
24. Christine
25. Jakob
26. Anne Marie
29. Martha
Gratulieren Sie mit Blumen

C11 Übung • Und du? Wie steht's mit dir?

1. Wann hast du Geburtstag?
2. Wann ist dein Namenstag?
3. Wann haben deine Eltern Geburtstag?
4. Und deine Geschwister?
5. Wann ist Muttertag?
6. Wann ist Vatertag?
7. Wann beginnen die Ferien?
8. Wann ist Weihnachten?
9. Wann haben deine Freunde Geburtstag?
10. Wann haben sie ihren Namenstag?

C12 WIE SAGT MAN DAS?
Expressing good wishes

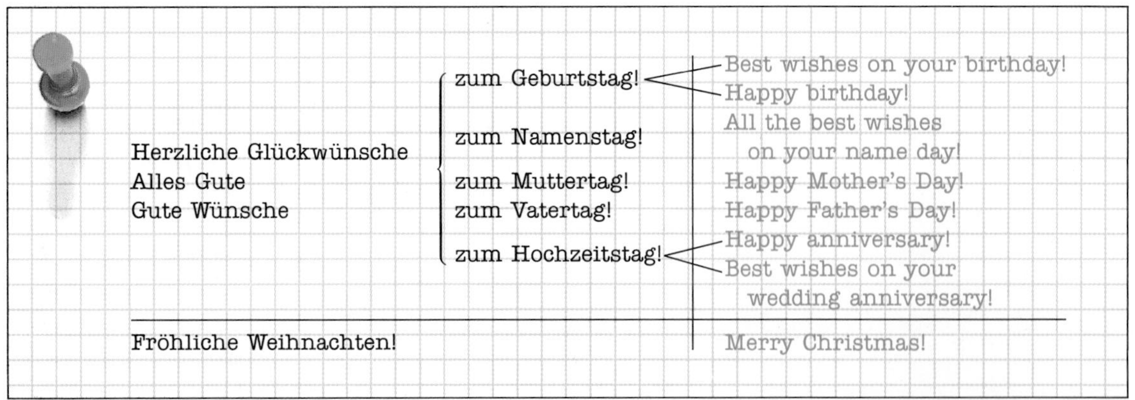

Herzliche Glückwünsche Alles Gute Gute Wünsche	zum Geburtstag!	Best wishes on your birthday! Happy birthday!
	zum Namenstag!	All the best wishes on your name day!
	zum Muttertag!	Happy Mother's Day!
	zum Vatertag!	Happy Father's Day!
	zum Hochzeitstag!	Happy anniversary! Best wishes on your wedding anniversary!
Fröhliche Weihnachten!		Merry Christmas!

C13 Übung • Was sagst du . . . 

1. zum Muttertag?
2. am 25. Dezember?
3. zum Geburtstag?
4. zum Hochzeitstag?
5. zum Vatertag?
6. zum Namenstag?

C14 Übung • Hör gut zu! 

Wem schenkst du was?

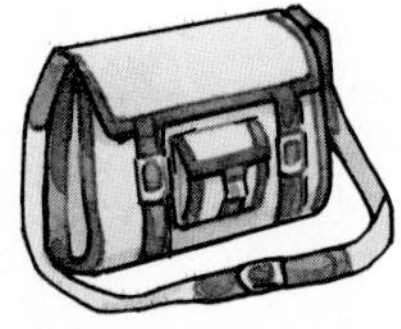

C15 Schreibübung • Wer hat Geburtstag?

1. Wer in der Klasse hat in diesem Monat Geburtstag? Du hast für jeden ein anderes Geschenk. Schreibe das Gespräch auf, und übe es mit einem Klassenkameraden!

   A: Der Fritz hat am achten Geburtstag. Was schenkst du ihm?
   B: Vielleicht ein T-Shirt.
   A: Was?! Du gibst ihm ein T-Shirt?
   B: Warum nicht?

2. Entwirf für jedes Geburtstagskind eine Geburtstagskarte!

C16 WAS HAST DU IHM GESCHENKT?

—Du, sag, wann hat dein Bruder Geburtstag gehabt?
—Am zweiten Mai.
—Was hast du ihm gekauft?
—Einen Pulli.

—Wann ist dein Namenstag gewesen?
—Am achten April.

—Was hast du deinen Eltern geschenkt?
—Ich habe ihnen eine Schachtel Pralinen gegeben.

C17 ERKLÄRUNG
More Past Participles

1. Here are the conversational past tense forms of some verbs you have been using in this unit.

hat gegeben	**ist gewesen**
hat gekauft	
hat geschenkt	
hat gehabt	

2. Can you name the infinitive forms of the past participles listed in this chart?

C18 Übung • Was haben alle gekauft?

Ich habe ein Portemonnaie gekauft.

1. Ich . . .

2. Die Mädchen . . .

3. Monika . . .

4. Wir . . .

5. Du . . . ?

C19 Übung • Und du? Wie steht's mit dir?

1. Hast du schon Geburtstag gehabt?
2. Wann ist dein Namenstag gewesen?
3. Was hast du deinen Freunden zum Geburtstag geschenkt?
4. Was hast du deinem Bruder gegeben? Und deinem Vater? Und . . .
5. Was hast du alles für die Ferien gekauft?

TRY YOUR SKILLS

using what you've learned

On special occasions it is nice to remember friends and family with gifts and cards. When somebody remembers you and sends a gift, you write a thank-you note.

1 Karin hat Geburtstag

Karin bekommt zum Geburtstag viele Geburtstagskarten.

Liebe Karin,
Zum Geburtstag alles Gute! Dein Oliver

Wir gehen am 23. Mai in ein Rockkonzert. Kommst du mit? Tschüs!

den 3. Mai
Liebe Karin!
Herzliche Glückwünsche zum Geburtstag und alles Gute,

Deine Tante Dora

P.S. Ein Geschenk ist unterwegs.

Liebe Karin!
Alles Gute zum Geburtstag!
Deine Kusine Annegret

Ich komme am 2. Juni mit Mutti nach Wien. Dann gehen wir zusammen aus ... ins Kino, Kaffee trinken ...

Karin schreibt an Tante Dora.

Wien, den 10 Mai
Liebe Tante Dora!
Vielen Dank für die Karte und die Geschenke zum Geburtstag. Die Quartzuhr ist toll! Ich brauche eine Uhr. Und die Musikkassette ist Spitze! Die Spider Murphy Gang ist meine Lieblingsgruppe.
Wie geht's? Wann besuchst Du uns? Viele Grüsse, auch an Onkel Heinz und an Babsie und Rolf.
Deine Karin

2 Übung • Beantworte die Fragen!

1. Wer hat Geburtstag?
2. Wer schickt eine Geburtstagskarte?
3. Was für Geschenke bekommt sie?
4. Wer sind Babsie und Rolf?

3 Schreibübung • Jetzt bist du dran

1. It is your best friend's birthday. Design and write a birthday card.
2. Your grandmother sent you a birthday card and a gift. Write a thank-you note. Comment on why you like the gift.

4 Übung • Probleme mit Geschenken!

Dein Vater, deine Freundin und deine Oma haben diesen Monat Geburtstag. Drei Geburtstage! Du brauchst drei Geschenke. Du hast aber nur vierzig Mark. Was kannst du kaufen? Du sprichst mit einem Freund darüber.

A: Du, ich brauche . . .
B: . . .

Ich habe nur vierzig Mark.
Was kann ich (ihm) kaufen?
Was meinst du?
Kauf (ihm) doch eine . . .
Was kostet . . .?
Nein, das ist zu teuer.
Hast du eine Idee?
Das ist eine prima Idee.
Was willst du (ihm) schenken?

12,-

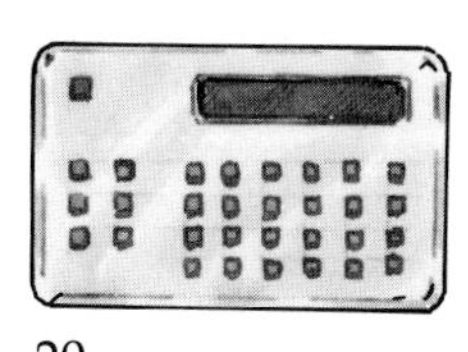
20,-

18,-

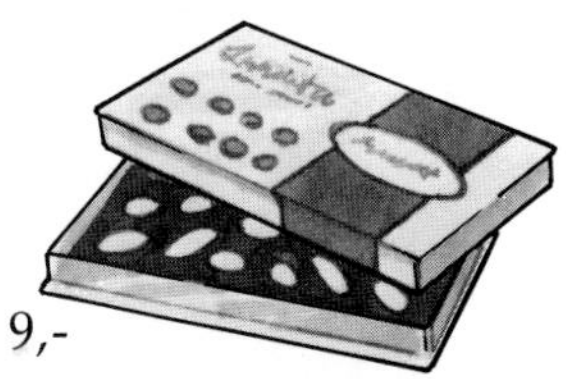
9,-

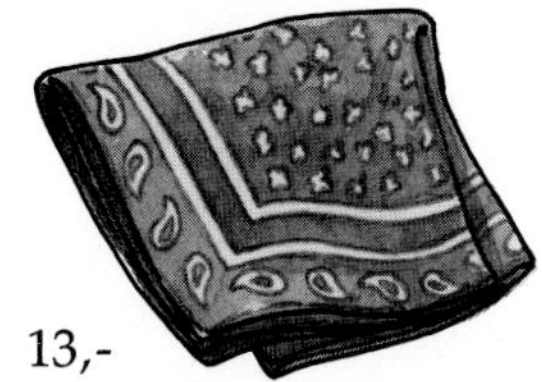
13,-

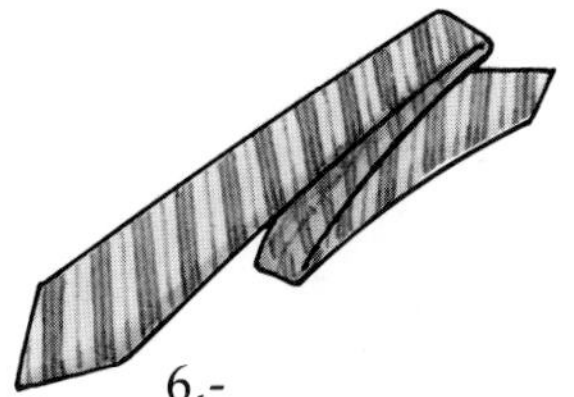
6,-

8,-

7,-

5 Übung • Farbenspiel: Ich seh' etwas, was du nicht siehst . . .

MONIKA Ich seh' etwas, was du nicht siehst, und es ist blau.
STEFAN Meinst du mein Hemd?
MONIKA Nein!
ULLI Peters T-Shirt?
MONIKA Nein!
JOCHEN Meinen Pulli?
MONIKA Jaaa! —So, Jochen, jetzt bist du dran!

6 Übung • Wenn ich Geld hätte . . .

Du hast viel Geld gewonnen und willst deinen Verwandten und Freunden schöne Geschenke kaufen. Was kaufst du? Was sagst du?

> Ich schenke meinem Bruder ein Sportrad. Er braucht ein Rad. *or* Er fährt gern Rad. *or* Er möchte ein Rad haben.

Ein Klassenkamerad erzählt, was du alles kaufst.

> Der Paul kauft seinem Bruder ein Sportrad. Sein Bruder braucht ein Rad. *or* Sein Bruder fährt gern Rad. *or* Sein Bruder möchte ein Rad haben.

7 Übung • Rollenspiel: Auf einer Auktion 

You and your classmate are at an auction. Each student should bring at least one item (or a picture of an item) to class. Take turns offering items for sale. Praise each item, using expressions such as **toll, Spitze, Klasse.**

AUKTIONÄR	Hier ist eine Halskette. Diese Halskette ist sehr alt. —Was bieten Sie°?
KÄUFER	Ich finde diese Halskette Spitze. Ich biete zwei Mark.
AUKTIONÄR	Zwei Mark. Wer bietet mehr?
KÄUFER	Drei Mark.
AUKTIONÄR	Zwei Mark, drei Mark für diese Halskette. Wer bietet mehr?
KÄUFER	Vier Mark.
AUKTIONÄR	Vier Mark! Zum ersten, zum zweiten—und zum dritten! Verkauft für vier Mark!

8 Übung • Wie passen die Sätze zusammen? 

1. Was schenke ich nur	achtzehn Mark.
2. Ich kaufe meinem Vater	auch in Grün?
3. Was schenkst du jetzt deiner Freundin	dein Parfüm?
4. Ich schenke der Monika eine Platte. Sie	gewöhnlich ein Buch.
5. Meine Grosseltern haben morgen	ihren Hochzeitstag.
6. Jeder Pulli kostet heute	im Oktober.
7. Haben Sie diesen Pulli	meine Lieblingsfarbe.
8. Du riechst so gut. Ist das	meinem Freund?
9. Das Blau ist schön. Blau ist	hört gern Musik.
10. Ich habe im Herbst Geburtstag,	zum Geburtstag?

Was bieten Sie? *What's your bid?*

9 Übung • Klassenprojekt: Ein Geburtstagskalender

Wer hat wann Geburtstag? Entwirf für deine Klasse einen Geburtstagskalender! Für jeden Monat frage deine Klassenkameraden: Wer hat im (Januar) Geburtstag? Alle, die in diesem Monat Geburtstag haben, sagen an welchem Tag, und du schreibst die Namen auf den Kalender.

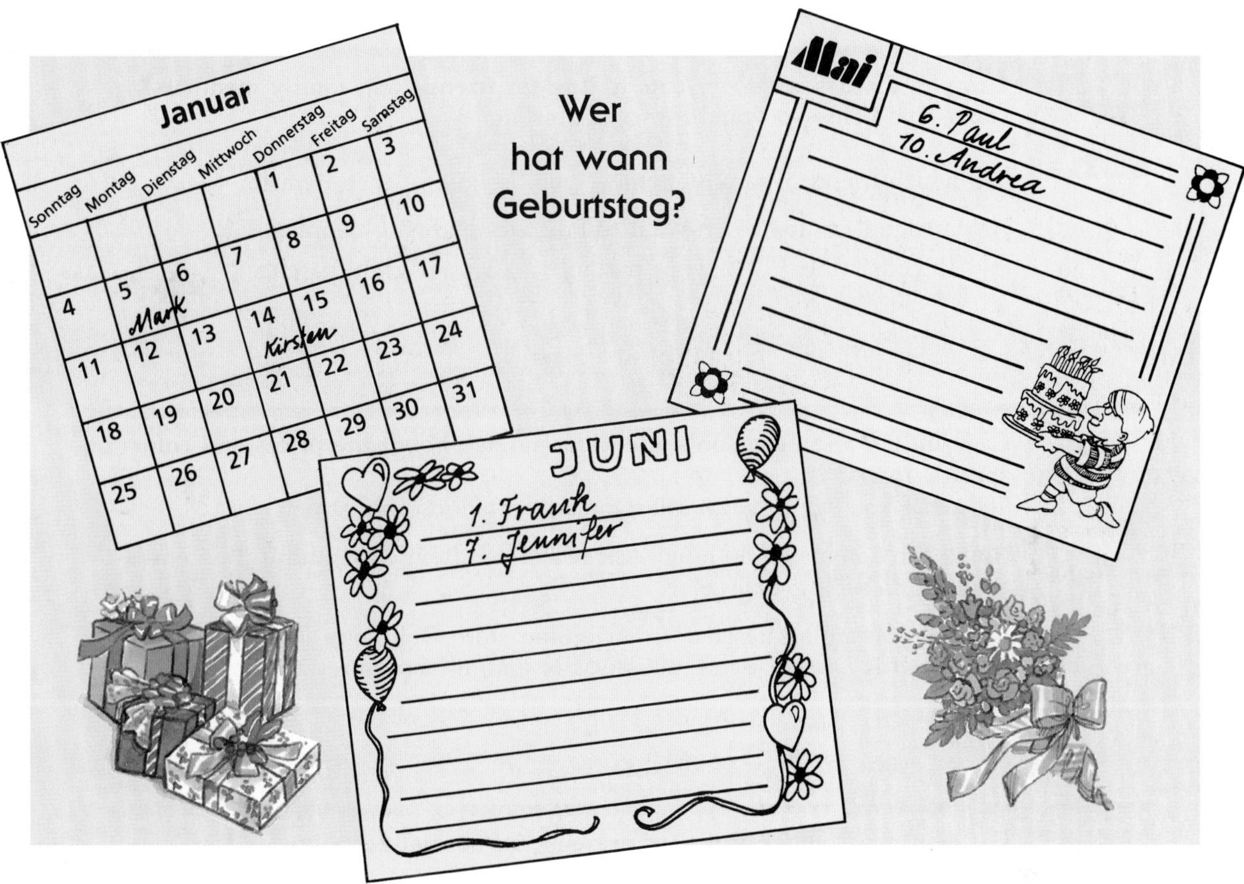

10 Aussprache-, Lese- und Schreibübungen

1. Listen carefully and repeat what you hear.
2. Listen, then read aloud.
   1. Armband, sag, ich glaub', Hemd, gelb, Vatertag, bald, gehabt
   2. Mütze, Hochzeit, schwarz, herzlich, zum
   3. Krawatte, Weihnachten, gewesen, gewöhnlich, weiss, schwarz, warum, Witz
   4. Halskette, Hose, diese, weiss, gewesen, bloss, Bluse, Vase, Strauss
   5. Vatertag, vielleicht, verbringen, verstehen, verlieren; Video, Vase
   6. braun, darf, Krawatte, teuer, nur, schwarz, Farbe, rot, Reisebuch, fröhlich, grün, Radio, dieser, Armbanduhr, Muttertag, Portemonnaie, Strauss, Uhr, herzlich, Kalender, grau, Geburtstag, Vatertag, jeder, Parfüm, Brieftasche, Pralinen, am dritten, am ersten, Quarzuhr
3. Copy the following sentences to prepare yourself to write them from dictation.
   1. Ich glaub', das Hemd ist gelb.
   2. Diese Hose ist zu teuer.
   3. Die Krawatte hab' ich zu Weihnachten bekommen.
   4. Herzliche Glückwünsche zum Geburtstag!

WAS KANNST DU SCHON?

Let's review some important points you have learned in this unit.

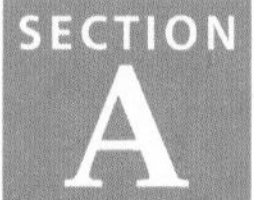

Can you discuss what presents to buy for friends and family members?
Name five items you might give as presents.

Tell which friend or family member you are giving each item to.

Ask a friend for advice on what to buy the following people:

1. your father **2.** your mother **3.** your grandparents

Can you get a salesperson's attention and ask about the prices and colors of specific items?
Tell what you say to get a saleswoman's attention in a store.

Name three items of clothing. Ask what each item costs and if the item is available in a particular color.

Pretend you are a salesclerk in a clothing store. Tell your customer that every coat is DM 80, every tie is DM 6, and all shoes are DM 20.

Can you make suggestions for presents for special occasions and express good wishes on those occasions?
Give the month and day of your mother's birthday, of your father's birthday, and of your grandparents' wedding anniversary. Say what you are going to give them.

How do you express good wishes on the following occasions?

1. birthday **2.** anniversary **3.** Christmas **4.** Mother's Day

A friend is asking for advice on what to give to his or her mother, brother, grandparents, and teacher for Christmas. Make suggestions for each one.

WORTSCHATZ

SECTION A

das **Armband, ¨er** *bracelet*
die **Armbanduhr, -en** *wristwatch*
bald *soon*
bloss: was schenke ich bloss meinem Vater? *what on earth should I give my father?*
die **Blume, -n** *flower*
die **Brieftasche, -n** *passport case*
dies- *this, these*
geben *to give* (see p 304)
der **Geburtstag, -e** *birthday;* er hat Geburtstag *it's his birthday*
gewöhnlich *usually*
die **Hochzeit: goldene Hochzeit** *golden wedding anniversary*
ich hab's! *I have it!*
der **Kalender, -** *calendar*
meinen *to think, be of the opinion;* was meinst du? *what do you think?*
nur: was soll ich nur schenken? *what should I give?*
das **Parfüm, -s** *perfume*
das **Portemonnaie, -s** *wallet*
die **Praline, -n** *fancy chocolate*
die **Quarzuhr, -en** *quartz clock, watch*
das **Radio, -s** *radio*
das **Reisebuch, ¨er** *travel book*
die **Schachtel, -n** *box;* eine Schachtel Pralinen *a box of fancy chocolates*
schenken *to give (as a gift)*
schick *chic*
der **Strauss, ¨e** *bouquet;* ein Strauss Blumen *a bouquet of flowers*
die **Vase, -n** *vase*

SECTION B

das **Angebot: im Angebot** *on sale*
das **Beige** *the color beige*
das **Blau** *the color blue;* in Blau *in blue*
die **Bluse, -n** *blouse*
das **Braun** *the color brown*
das **Dunkelblau** *the color dark blue*
die **Farbe, -n** *color;* in vielen Farben *in many colors*
das **Gelb** *the color yellow*
glauben: ich glaube, ja *I think so*
das **Grau** *the color grey*
das **Grün** *the color green*
das **Halstuch, ¨er** *scarf*
das **Hellblau** *the color light blue*
das **Hemd, -en** *shirt*
die **Hose, -n** *pants*
ja, bitte? *yes, may I help you?*
jed- *each, every*
das **Kaufhaus, ¨er** *department store;* im Kaufhaus *in the department store*
die **Krawatte, -n** *tie*
die **Lieblingsfarbe, -n** *favorite color*
der **Mantel, ¨** *coat*
die **Mütze, -n** *cap*
noch nicht *not yet;* ich weiss noch nicht *I don't know yet*
der **Pulli, -s** *sweater*
das **Rot** *the color red;* in Rot *in red*
der **Schuh, -e** *shoe*
das **Schwarz** *the color black*
teuer *expensive*
das **T-Shirt, -s** *t-shirt*
was darf es sein? *may I help you?*
das **Weiss** *the color white*
wie teuer ist *how much is*

SECTION C

alles Gute zum . . . *all the best wishes on . . .*
am ersten *on the first;* am ersten Mai *on May 1st* (see p 315)
April *April*
August *August*
Dezember *December*
Februar *February*
der **Geburtstag: herzliche Glückwünsche zum Geburtstag!** *happy birthday!* ich habe im Mai Geburtstag *my birthday is in May;* zum Geburtstag *for (your) birthday*
die **Geschenkidee, -n** *gift idea*
herzliche Glückwünsche zum . . . *happy . . .*
der **Hochzeitstag, -e** *wedding anniversary;* zum Hochzeitstag *for (your) anniversary*
Januar *January;* im Januar *in January*
Juli *July*
Juni *June*
Mai *May*
März *March*
der **Muttertag** *Mother's Day;* zum Muttertag *for Mother's Day*
der **Namenstag, -e** *name day;* zum Namenstag *for (your) name day*
November *November*
Oktober *October*
die **Reklame** *ad*
sag, . . . *say, . . .*
September *September*
die **Uhr, -en** *clock, watch*
der **Vatertag** *Father's Day;* zum Vatertag *for Father's Day*
Weihnachten *Christmas;* fröhliche Weihnachten! *merry Christmas!* zu Weihnachten *for Christmas*
der **Wunsch: gute Wünsche zum . . .** *best wishes on . . .*

WORTSCHATZÜBUNGEN

1. Make a list of all the compound nouns.
2. Which words are borrowed from other languages such as English and French?
3. The colors are listed in the **Wortschatz** as nouns and are therefore capitalized. When used as adjectives, they are spelled the same way but are not capitalized. Write the colors as nouns and as adjectives.

ZUM LESEN

Ein Gewohnheitsmensch

Herr Neuschuh ist ein netter Mann. Er ist höflich°, pünktlich, immer korrekt. Er ist auch immer gut angezogen°: er kauft seine Sachen in den besten Geschäften°. Aber er macht sich wenig aus der Mode°. „Die Mode", so sagt er, „ist nur für die Jugend." Herr Neuschuh liebt den klassischen Stil. Seine Anzüge° kommen aus England, seine Krawatten kommen aus Frankreich und seine Schuhe aus Italien. Jeden Morgen, bevor Herr Neuschuh zur Arbeit geht, bürstet er seinen Anzug und putzt° seine Schuhe. Er ist ein schicker Herr°.

Nun, eines Tages möchte Herr Neuschuh ein Paar neue Schuhe. Er geht in das Schuhgeschäft, wo er immer seine Schuhe kauft. Dort kennt er alle Verkäufer.

„Guten Tag, Herr Neuschuh! Was darf es heute sein?"

„Ist Frl. Seidel nicht da?"

„Frl. Seidel ist gestern in Urlaub gegangen°."

„Ach, so was! —Nun, das macht nichts°. Ich möchte ein Paar Schuhe."

„Welche Marke°?"

„Diese hier."

ein Gewohnheitsmensch *a creature of habit;* **höflich** *polite;* **gut angezogen** *well-dressed;* **das Geschäft** *store;* **er macht sich wenig aus der Mode** *he doesn't pay much attention to fashion, to what's in style;* **der Anzug** *suit;* **putzen** *to clean, polish;* **ein schicker Herr** *a smartly-dressed gentleman;* **in Urlaub gehen** *to go on vacation;* **das macht nichts** *it doesn't matter;* **die Marke** *make*

Herr Neuschuh zieht seine Schuhe aus°.
„Welche Grösse° haben Sie?"
„Dreiundvierzig."
„Diese Grösse haben wir, aber nicht in Schwarz."
„Nicht in Schwarz?"
„Nein, nur in Braun. Sie haben das letzte Paar in Schwarz. Dieses Modell gibt es jetzt nicht mehr."
„Warum nicht? Es ist doch ein perfektes Modell!"
„Ja, Sie haben recht, ein perfektes Modell. Aber die Mode ändert sich°."
„Ach, die Mode! Immer diese Mode!"
„Möchten Sie ein anderes° Modell anprobieren?"
„Nein, nie!"
„Wir haben aber sehr schöne Modelle. Möchten Sie sie nicht sehen?"
„Nein, kein Interesse."

Aber es ist zu spät. Die Verkäuferin ist schon weg, die Schuhe suchen. Herr Neuschuh wartet°, wütend°: „Ach, diese neue Verkäuferin! Warum ist Frl. Seidel ausgerechnet gestern° in Urlaub gegangen? —So, ich geh' jetzt. Hier bekomme ich doch nichts."
In diesem Moment kommt die Verkäuferin zurück.
„Herr Neuschuh, hier ist Ihr neues Modell!"
„Entschuldigung, mein Fräulein, aber ich habe jetzt keine Zeit."
„Nur eine Minute! Warten Sie doch!"
„Ich habe eine Verabredung°."
„Sehen Sie, das ist ganz genau° Ihre Marke."
„Na gut!"

Herr Neuschuh probiert die Schuhe an; rot, weich°, das neuste Modell. Und aus Italien. Wie immer.
„Laufen Sie doch ein wenig umher°! —Sie sehen prima aus. Ausgezeichnet!"
„Ich fühle mich lächerlich° in diesen Schuhen."

---

ausziehen *to take off;* **die Grösse** *size;* **die Mode ändert sich** *style changes;* **ein anderes** *another;* **warten** *to wait;* **wütend** *furious;* **ausgerechnet gestern** *yesterday of all days;* **die Verabredung** *appointment;* **ganz genau** *exactly;* **weich** *soft;* **laufen Sie doch ein wenig umher!** *why don't you walk around a little;* **ich fühle mich lächerlich** *I feel ridiculous*

„Zahlen° Sie bar° oder mit einem Euro-Scheck? Oder mit Kreditkarte?"

Hier steht nun Herr Neuschuh auf der Strasse mit seinen neuen Schuhen. Er betrachtet sich° in einem Schaufenster°. „Lächerlich! . . . Lächerlich!" Was mache ich jetzt bloss mit den Schuhen? Ach, ich hab's! Der Willibald hat bald Geburtstag—er hat auch Grösse 43."

Zwei Monate sind vergangen°, und Herr Neuschuh hat seinem Bruder die Schuhe noch immer nicht gegeben. Er hat seine alten Schuhe weggeworfen°, und er trägt° jetzt seine neuen Schuhe jeden Tag, auch in die Arbeit! Er hat sich an die Schuhe gewöhnt°. Jetzt ist er ein neuer Mann. Jetzt ist er ein Modemensch°!

„Ganz im Gegenteil°!" Diese Schuhe machen Sie jung!"

„Ich sehe grotesk aus."

„Nein, wunderbar!"

„Sie schmeicheln° mir, mein Fräulein."

„Wir haben dieses Modell auch in Grün, in Gelb, in . . ."

„Aber nicht in Schwarz?"

„Nein, Herr Neuschuh, nicht in Schwarz. Die Mode, wissen Sie. Das sind heute die Farben—diese Farben sind ‚in'".

„Nun, ich danke Ihnen. Ich komme nach meiner Verabredung zurück."

„Das macht zweihundertfünfundvierzig Mark."

„Aber ich will diese Schuhe nicht!"

„Soll ich die Schuhe in einen Karton packen, oder . . ."

„Nein, ich . . ."

---

ganz im Gegenteil *just the opposite;* **schmeicheln** *to flatter;* **zahlen** *to pay;* **bar** *cash;* **er betrachtet sich** *he looks at himself;* **das Schaufenster** *show window;* **vergangen** *past;* **wegwerfen** *to throw away;* **tragen** *to wear;* **er hat sich an die neuen Schuhe gewöhnt** *he got used to the new shoes;* **ein Modemensch** *a man of style*

Übung • Let's take a closer look

1. How can you tell what kind of a person Herr Neuschuh is? What words and phrases tell you?
2. There are quite a few words in this story that are very close to English in both spelling and meaning. Make a list of them with their English counterparts.
3. The saleswoman does not seem to hear what Herr Neuschuh says, or perhaps she just chooses to ignore him. Point out some examples of this—what does Herr Neuschuh say? How does the saleswoman respond?
4. How does Herr Neuschuh feel in the new shoes? How does he describe himself? What does the saleswoman say to convince him to buy the shoes?

Übung • Was meinst du?

1. Die Verkäuferin schmeichelt Herrn Neuschuh. Was sagt sie? Meinst du, sie glaubt das wirklich?
2. Warum kauft Herr Neuschuh die Schuhe?
3. Nach zwei Monaten hat Herr Neuschuh die Schuhe immer noch—und er trägt sie auch. Was meinst du? Hat er sich an die Schuhe gewöhnt? Mag er die Schuhe jetzt? Ist er irgendwie anders geworden?

Übung • Und du? Wie steht's mit dir?

1. Bist du ein „Modemensch", oder machst du dir wenig aus der Mode?
2. Wieso weisst du, was gerade Mode ist? Wie entscheidest du dich, wenn du etwas kaufst? Was ist für dich wichtig?
3. Wo kaufst du ein? Kaufst du gern in kleinen Geschäften ein oder in grossen Kaufhäusern? Lässt du dich gern von dem Verkäufer oder von der Verkäuferin beraten? Gehst du allein einkaufen, oder nimmst du gern jemanden mit? Wen am liebsten?

Übung • Klassenprojekte

1. Act out the scene in the shoe store as it is written. Then work out some other scenes—in teams or as a class—in which:
   a. Herr Neuschuh doesn't buy the shoes
   b. another salesclerk waits on him who isn't so assertive
   c. the salesclerk he usually goes to, Frl. Seidel, is there
2. Write a dialog between Herr Neuschuh and his brother as Herr Neuschuh presents the shoes to him on his birthday.
3. Pretend you are a friend of Herr Neuschuh's and you see him for the first time wearing his new shoes. What do you think? What do you say? What does he say? Write a dialog.

KAPITEL **12**

Ferien in Österreich

Wiederholungskapitel

1 Natalie macht Pläne für die Ferien

Die Ferien beginnen am 28. Juni. Natalie möchte gern wegfahren, nach Österreich. Aber sie weiss noch nicht, mit wem. Viele Freundinnen haben schon etwas vor. Da hat sie eine Idee. Sie ruft jetzt mal die Uschi an. Vielleicht kann sie mitfahren.

2 Übung • Ruf doch mal die Uschi an!

Natalie möchte gern am 11. oder am 18. Juli wegfahren und vier oder fünf Tage bleiben. Geht's? Kann die Uschi mitfahren? Was sagt Natalie? Was sagt Uschi? Hier ist Uschis Monatskalender:

JULI					
Sonntag	27	4	11 (Tenniskurs 11–13)	18 Stadtfest	25
Montag	28	5	12 Tenniskurs	19	26
Dienstag	29 Geburtstags-party f. Sabine	6	13	20 Vatis Geburtstag	27 Rockkonzert
Mittwoch	30	7	14	21	28
Donnerstag	1 Kino!	8	15 Grosseltern kommen	22	29 Ferien mit Eltern
Freitag	2	9	16	23	30 ↓
Samstag	3	10 Fussballspiel aus Mexiko	17	24 Sommerfest	31 ↓

3 Übung • Wohin?

Wohin wollt ihr fahren? Da sind zum Beispiel Fieberbrunn und St. Ulrich, zwei Feriendörfer in Tirol, in Österreich.

1. Wie kommt ihr nach Fieberbrunn? Nach St. Ulrich?
2. Was könnt ihr dort alles machen?
3. Wohin möchtest du lieber fahren?
4. Was ist dein Lieblingssport?

ÖSTERREICH
TIROL
St. Ulrich
835 m
Am Pillersee

FIEBERBRUNN
in den Kitzbüheler Alpen
AUSTRIA
TIROL

Und jetzt diskutiert, wohin ihr fahren wollt und warum!

A: Du, ich will lieber nach St. Ulrich fahren.
B: Warum?
A: Dort können wir . . .
B: Das stimmt. Aber im . . .

4 Übung • Was brauchst du noch? 

Du machst jetzt Ferien. Deine Mutter fragt dich, was du noch brauchst. Sie nennt sechs verschiedene Dinge. Du brauchst sie nicht. Was sagst du?

A: Brauchst du einen Regenschirm?
B: Nein, ich brauche keinen Regenschirm. Es . . .

5 Übung • Was macht ihr in der Freizeit? 

Natalie und Uschi spielen Minigolf. Und da spielt auch ein Junge. Er sieht nett aus. Er heisst Franz.

FRANZ	Ihr spielt aber nicht oft Minigolf!
USCHI	Das stimmt. Spielen wir so schlecht?
FRANZ	Das möchte ich nicht sagen!! Spielt ihr Tennis . . . was macht ihr denn gewöhnlich in der Freizeit?
NATALIE	Wir gehen schwimmen, wir wandern . . .
FRANZ	Geht ihr auch tanzen?
USCHI	Ja, manchmal.

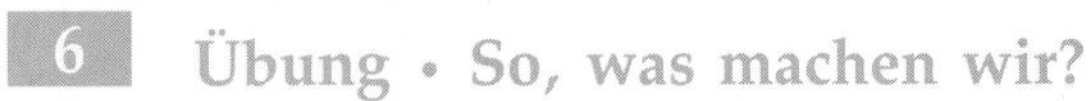

6 Übung • So, was machen wir? 

Franz lädt die Mädchen ein. Gehen sie mit oder nicht?

A: So, gehen wir zusammen in die Disko?
B: . . . *or* . . .

7 Übung • Im Geschenkladen

In St. Ulrich gibt es zwei Souvenirläden. Hier kannst du Geschenke für deine Eltern, Geschwister und Freunde kaufen.

A: Was kauf' ich bloss meiner Mutti?
B: Schau, die Blusen!
A: Die sind sehr schön, aber viel zu teuer.
B: Dann kauf ihr doch einen Kalender aus Österreich!
A: Du, das ist eine prima Idee!

* * *

A: Haben Sie dieses Halstuch auch in Blau?
B: Nein, leider nicht. Nur in Rot.
A: Schade. Blau ist meine Lieblingsfarbe.

8 Übung • Im Café Troger

Ihr habt einen Dorfbummel gemacht, und ihr möchtet jetzt etwas essen und trinken. Ihr geht ins Café Troger[1].

A: Was darf's sein, bitte?
B: Ein Eis für mich.
C: Und ein Wurstbrot für mich.
A: Ja, gern!

* * *

A: Für wen ist das Wurstbrot?
C: Für mich.
A: Guten Appetit!
C: Danke!

Zur Jause

SPEISEN

Gulaschsuppe mit Brot	ÖS 28,-
Lachsbrot mit Zwiebel	50,-
Schinken mit Brot	55,-
Schinken mit Ei	70,-
Wurstbrot	50,-
Wurstplatte mit Brot	65,-
Tiroler Speckplatte	75,-
Wurstsalat (in Essig und Öl)	45,-
Wiener mit Senf – 2 Paar	25,-
Käseplatte mit Brot	50,-
Pizza	35,-

GETRÄNKE

Tee	ÖS 25,-
Kaffee, Tasse	28,-
Mineralwasser	18,-
Limonade, Fanta	22,-

9 Schreibübung • Eine Karte

Schreib eine Karte nach Hause!

10 Übung • Wieder zu Hause

Eure Ferien sind zu Ende. Ihr seid wieder zu Hause. Du erzählst deinen Eltern, was du gesehen und gemacht hast.

[1]Note that the prices on the menu are in Austrian schillings. ÖS 50,- reads: fünfzig Schilling.

LANDESKUNDE 3

Festivals and Holidays

It is said that in Germany festivals are as numerous as the days of the year. This is no exaggeration! Wherever you go, there is always something going on—a popular festival, a religious feast, a folk-dance, a historical or costume parade, or simply some occasion for public merry-making. The calendar of festivities begins with carnival, a season that starts on the seventh of January and lasts until Lent, 40 days before Easter. It is celebrated mostly in the Catholic areas. The Rhenish carnival turns Cologne, Düsseldorf, and Mainz upside down. During the famous "Fasching," its Bavarian counterpart, Munich celebrates. The Swabian "Fasnet" conjures up the ghosts and demons of old in the strange dance of bell-jingling masks.

❶ Fastnacht in Rottweil, Schwaben

❷ Lustige Maske

❸ Rosenmontag in Köln; keiner arbeitet, alle feiern Karneval auf der Strasse

❹ Kinderfasching

The celebration of Easter week begins on Palm Sunday, seven days before Easter Sunday. Good Friday is a national holiday, and Easter week climaxes with Easter, a joyous celebration. Colorful Easter eggs and the Easter Bunny are part of the tradition for younger children.

❶ Palmsonntag-Umzug in Tirol

❷ Auferstehungsfeier an Ostersonntag in Wattens, Tirol

❸ Mädchen mit Ostereiern

❹ Ostereibrunnen in der Fränkischen Schweiz, Bayern

The advent of spring is celebrated in many different ways, depending upon the region. During springtime, one of the most impressive religious feasts in predominantly Catholic parts is Corpus Christi Day.

❺ Frühlingsanfang in Franken: der Winter wird offiziell verbrannt

❻ Am ersten Mai: Maibaumtanz im Westerwald

❼ Bergmesse in St. Jakob, Tirol

❽ Fronleichnamsprozession in einem bayrischen Dorf

During the summer and early fall there are innumerable local festivals throughout the country, festivals in which young and old participate and that uphold local and often century-old traditions.

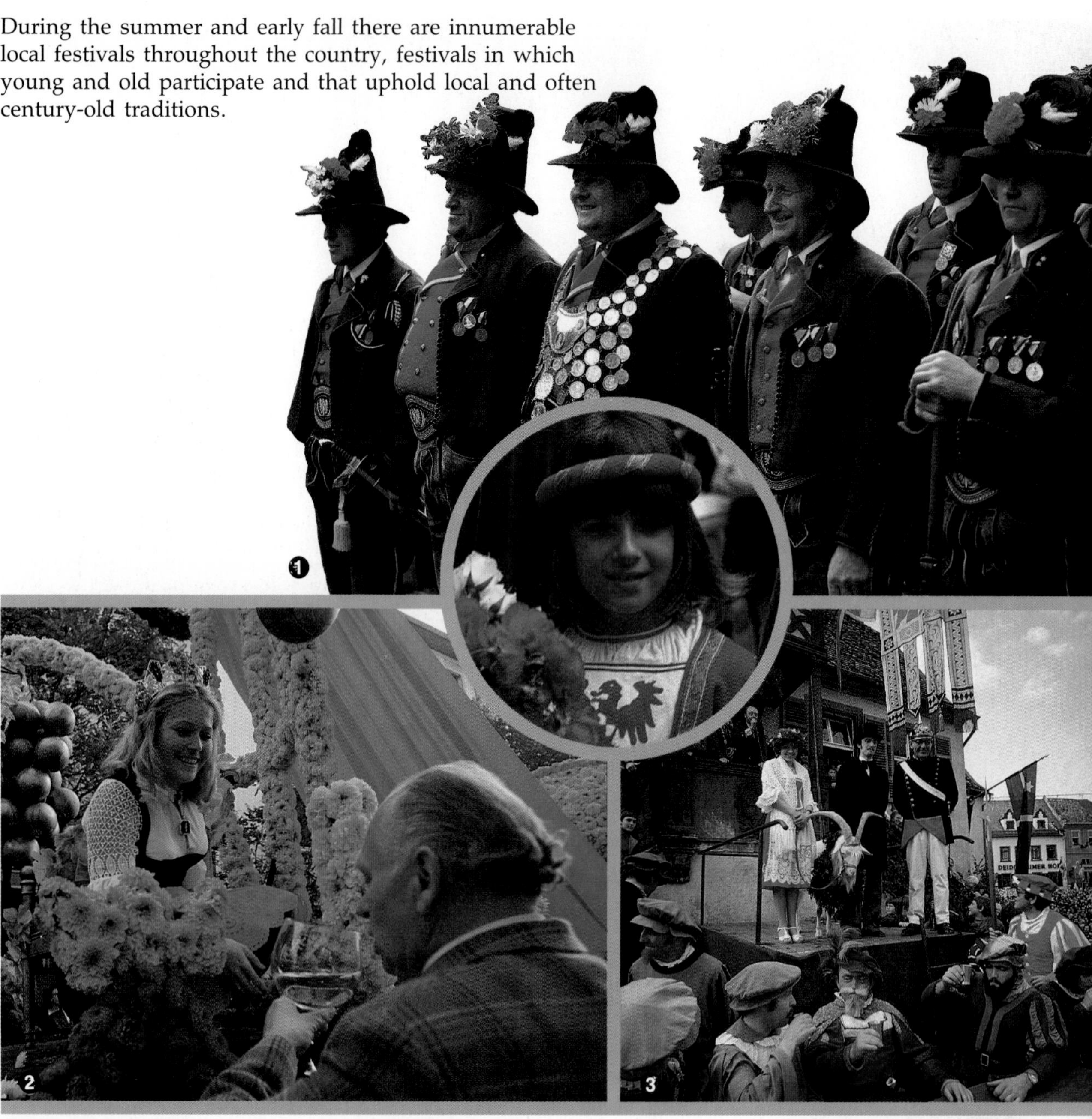

❶ Gebirgsschützen im Chiemgau, Bayern

❷ Die Deutsche Weinkönigin

❸ Weinfest in Deidesheim an der Deutschen Weinstrasse

❹ Landshuter Hochzeit: alle vier Jahre feiert Landshut die Fürstenhochzeit, die 1475 stattgefunden hat

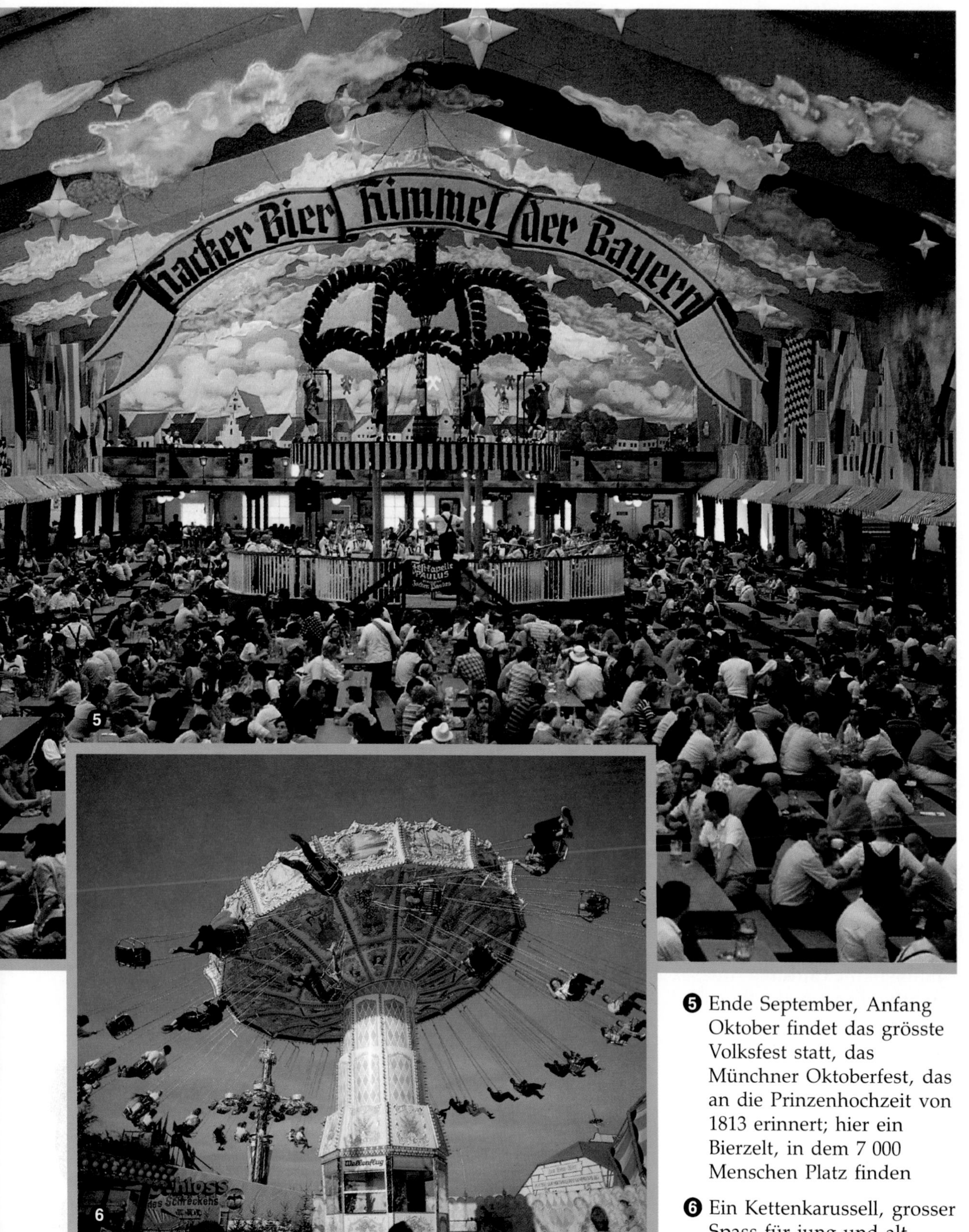

5 Ende September, Anfang Oktober findet das grösste Volksfest statt, das Münchner Oktoberfest, das an die Prinzenhochzeit von 1813 erinnert; hier ein Bierzelt, in dem 7 000 Menschen Platz finden

6 Ein Kettenkarussell, grosser Spass für jung und alt

Many of the world's most cherished Christmas traditions are of German or Austrian origin. It was in the Black Forest that evergreen trees were first decorated and used as a part of Christmas. The Christmas season begins on Advent, the fourth Sunday before Christmas. Many families display colorful Advent calendars with little windows, one for each day of the season. An evergreen wreath with four candles is made, and every Sunday until Christmas one more candle is lighted. Father Christmas, or St. Nicholas, brings gifts to the children on the sixth of December. During this joyous season many cities have colorful outdoor Christmas markets. Christmas Eve is celebrated by the lighting of the Christmas tree, exchanging gifts, and attending a midnight church service. New Year's Eve brings the holiday season to an exuberant end with fireworks and traditional balls.

1. Sankt Nikolaus
2. Christkindlmarkt auf dem Marienplatz in München
3. Weihnachtsbaum mit Kerzen
4. Bleigiessen an Sylvester bringt Glück!

Among all the public festivals and holidays there are many special occasions celebrated within the family, such as birthdays, baptisms, first communion, confirmation, graduations, weddings, and anniversaries.

❺ Eine Taufe

❻ Heilige Kommunion (im Klein-Walsertal, Österreich)

❼ Abiturklasse

❽ Kinder-Geburtstag

❾ Der Opa feiert seinen achtzigsten Geburtstag

1 Ein alter Hochzeitsbrauch: das junge Paar sägt Holz (Wernigerode, DDR)

2 Eine weisse Hochzeitskutsche

3 Gratulation zum 25jährigen Betriebsjubiläum

4 Sie gedenken der Toten—auf dem Friedhof in St. Jakob, Tirol

FOR REFERENCE

SUMMARY OF FUNCTIONS

The term *functions* can be defined as what you do with language—what your purpose is in speaking. As you use this textbook, you will find yourself in a number of situations—in a store, in a restaurant, at a party, at the airport, in a new city. How do you "function" in these situations? How do you ask about prices in a store, order a meal in a restaurant, compliment your host at a party, greet arriving friends at an airport, or ask for directions in an unfamiliar city? You need to know certain basic functional expressions.

Here is a list of functions accompanied by the expressions you have learned to communicate them. The number of the unit in which the expressions were introduced is followed by the section letter and number in parentheses.

SOCIALIZING

Saying hello

1 (A3) Guten Morgen!
Guten Tag!
short forms: Morgen!
Tag!
informal: Hallo!
regional: Grüss dich!

7 (A1) Grüss Gott!
Gruetzi!

Saying goodbye

1 (A3) Auf Wiedersehen!
short form: Wiedersehen!
informal: Tschüs!
Tschau!
Bis dann!

5 (C6) Bis gleich!

Addressing people

1 (A1) *first name*

1 (A7) Herr + *last name*
Frau + *last name*
Fräulein + *last name*

3 (A4) *with* du
(A15) *with* Ihr
(A19) *with* Sie

Introducing someone

6 (A3) Peter, das ist + *name*

Introducing yourself

6 (A3) Ich heisse . . .
Ich bin der / die + *first name*
Ich bin ein Freund von + *name*

Responding to an introduction

6 (A3) Guten Tag, + *name*
Hallo, + *first name*
Grüss dich, + *first name*. Wie geht's?

Asking "How are you?"

10 (A9) Wie geht's?
Wie geht's denn?

Responding to "How are you?"

10 (A9) Ach, prima!
Danke, gut!
Nicht schlecht.
So lala.
Schlecht.
Miserabel.

Welcoming people

6 (A1) Willkommen in . . .!
Schön, dass du hier bist!

Getting someone's attention

2 (B25) Du, (Jens), . . .
Schau!
Schau, (Jens)!
Schau mal!
Schau mal, (Jens)!
Entschuldigung!

5 (B1) Verzeihung!

11 (B6) Fräulein!

Greeting a customer in a store or restaurant

11 (B1) Ja, bitte? Was darf es sein?

Saying please
2 (B8) Bitte!

Saying thank you
2 (B8) Danke!
6 (B16) Tausend Dank!
Vielen Dank!

Responding to thank you
2 (B8) Bitte!
5 (B1) Gern geschehen!
5 (C13) Bitte sehr!
6 (B16) Bitte schön!
Nichts zu danken.

Making a phone call:
answering the phone
5 (C11) *last name*
Hier + *last name*

person calling
Hier + *name*
Hier ist + *name*

ending a phone conversation
Auf Wiederhören!
Tschüs!
Bis gleich!

Extending an invitation
9 (A1) Ich möchte dich einladen. Kommst du?

Accepting an invitation
9 (A3) Ja, gern!
Ja, ich komme gern.
Na, klar!
Das passt prima!

Declining an invitation
9 (A3) Es geht nicht.
(Samstag) geht es nicht.

Expressing regrets
9 (A3) Das ist schade!
Es geht leider nicht.

Making excuses
9 (A3) Ich habe schon was vor.
Ich habe keine Zeit.

Offering something to eat or drink
7 (C16) Möchtest du . . .?
9 (C1) Nimmst du . . .?
Essen Sie . . .?
(Ein Wurstbrot), vielleicht?

Accepting something to eat or drink
9 (C3) Ja, bitte!
Ja, gern!

Declining something to eat or drink
9 (C3) Nein, danke.
Keinen (Kaffee) für mich, danke!

Saying what you would like to eat or drink
9 (C1) Ich möchte . . .
Ich nehme . . .
Für mich einen . . .

Offering more or another
7 (C14) (Möchtest du) noch ein . . .?
Isst du noch ein . . .?
9 (C1) Nimmst du noch ein . . .?
10 (A6) Willst du noch ein . . .?

Accepting an offer
7 (C16) Danke, gern.
Ja, bitte!

Saying you don't want more to eat or drink
7 (C16) Nein, danke.
Danke, ich bin satt.
Nein, danke. Ich habe genug.

Complimenting someone
6 (B3) Ich finde (dein Zimmer) toll!
(Das Wohnzimmer) sieht gemütlich aus.
9 (D6) Du siehst (gut) aus.
(Du) tanzt wirklich (toll).
Deine Eltern sind (so nett).

Complimenting someone on food or drink
9 (D6) Ihr (Kuchen) ist ausgezeichnet.
(Die Suppe) schmeckt lecker.
Ich finde Ihren (Kaffee) gut.

Responding to compliments
6 (B3) Ja, wirklich?
Findest du?
6 (C1) Meinst du?
9 (D3) Da bin ich aber froh.
Das freut mich.

Expressing good wishes
2 (C10) Viel Glück!
5 (B1) Schöne Ferien!
5 (C13) Guten Flug!
7 (C1) Viel Spass!
9 (C1) Guten Appetit!
11 (C12) Herzliche Glückwünsche zum . . .!
Alles Gute zum . . .!
Gute Wünsche zum . . .!
Fröhliche Weihnachten!

Saying you don't understand
1 (D14) Wie bitte?
Woher?
Wer?
Der (Stefan)?
Ich?
9 (A1) Ich verstehe dich nicht.

EXCHANGING INFORMATION

Asking someone his or her name

1 (B5) Wie heisst du?

1 (D16) Wie heissen Sie?

and giving yours

1 (B5) Ich heisse . . .

Asking someone else's name

1 (B5) Wie heisst er / sie?

and giving it

Er / sie heisst . . .

Asking who someone is

1 (B9) Wer ist das?

Identifying people and places

1 (B9) Das ist . . .

7 (A10) Das ist . . . / Hier ist . . .

Asking someone his or her age

1 (C7) Wie alt bist du?

and giving yours

Ich bin (15).
Ich bin (15) Jahre alt.

telling someone else's age

Er / sie ist (15) Jahre alt.

Asking someone where he or she is from

1 (D4) Woher bist du?

and saying where you are from

Ich bin aus . . .

saying where someone else is from

Er / sie ist aus . . .

Asking someone about his or her interests

3 (A7) Was machst du?
Machst du (Sport)?
Spielst du (Fussball)?
Hast du Hobbys?

Saying where you live

7 (A1) Ich wohne in (Wien).
Ich bin in (Wien) zu Hause.

Answering questions

1 (D8) Ja, . . .
Nein, . . .

3 (A1) Na, klar!

9 (B4) Natürlich!

Asking for directions

5 (B3) Wo ist bitte . . .?
Wo ist . . . , bitte?

7 (A14) Weisst du, wo . . . ist?
Weisst du vielleicht, wo . . . ist?

Giving directions

5 (B3) . . . ist hier / da / hier rechts / da links!
Geradeaus!
Da drüben! / Dort drüben!
Dort drüben, rechts!

Saying you don't know

2 (B20) Ich weiss nicht.

7 (A14) Ich weiss es nicht.
Ich weiss es leider nicht.
Keine Ahnung!
Ich bin nicht von hier.

11 (B1) Ich weiss noch nicht.

Eliciting agreement, affirmation

6 (C1) Meinst du nicht?

9 (A1) Ja?

11 (B9) Nicht?

Asking about appearance

6 (C3) Wie sieht . . . aus?

describing appearance

. . . sieht (gut) aus.
. . . ist (gross, schlank).

Inquiring about prices

2 (B16) Was kostet . . .?

11 (B1) Wie teuer ist . . .?

Asking what there is (to eat)

9 (B3) Was gibt's zu (essen)?

and telling what there is

Es gibt . . .
Wir haben . . .

Asking for specific information

10 (B13) Welcher (Film) spielt heute?

Asking about categories of things

10 (B13) Was für (Filme) siehst du gern?

Saying that you don't do something in general or usually

3 (A14) Ich (segle) nicht.

(B3) Ich (spiele) nie (Fussball).

9 (C5) Ich (esse) keine (Suppe).

Saying you are not going to do something specifically or at the present time

9 (C5) Ich (esse) (die Suppe) nicht.

Talking about the past

10 (D1) Was hast du gemacht?
Gestern bin ich ins Kino gegangen.

EXPRESSING ATTITUDES AND OPINIONS

Expressing agreement

2 (D1) Ja, . . .
Ja, das ist (blöd).

3 (C7) Stimmt!
Das finde ich auch.

6 (C9) Du hast recht.
Ich auch.

7 (B1) Gut.
O.K.

7 (C7) Na, gut.

9 (A1) Schön!

11 (B9) Ich glaube, ja.

Expressing disagreement

3 (C7) Stimmt nicht!
Das finde ich nicht.

6 (C9) Das ist Geschmackssache.

Contradicting, correcting

2 (B20) Unsinn! Das ist . . .

10 (B3) Quatsch! Das ist kein . . .

Asking for an opinion

3 (C3) Wie findest du . . .?

11 (A12) Was meinst du?
Hast du eine Idee?

Giving an opinion

3 (C3) Ich finde . . . (toll).

Wondering what to give

11 (A12) Was schenke ich bloss meinem (Vater)?
Was gebe ich nur meiner (Mutter)?
Was soll ich kaufen?

Asking for advice

7 (C1) Was sollen wir machen?

11 (A12) Was meinst du?
Hast du eine Idee?

Giving advice

7 (C1) Bleibt lieber zu Hause!

11 (C1) Schenken Sie ihm ein . . .!

Asking about someone's wishes

9 (C1) Was möchtest du?
Was nimmst du?

10 (A11) Willst du (ins Kino gehen)?

Expressing wishes

5 (B11) Ich möchte (Briefmarken kaufen).

10 (A6) Ich will (in die Stadt fahren).

Expressing intention

5 (B11) Ich möchte . . .

9 (C1) Ich esse . . . / trinke . . . / nehme . . .

10 (A6) Ich will . . .

Asking how something tastes

7 (C12) Schmeckt (der, die, das) . . .?
Wie schmeckt (der, die, das) . . .?

9 (D5) Wie ist (der, die, das) . . .?

Telling how something tastes

7 (C12) Danke, (er, sie, es) ist . . .
Danke, (er, sie, es) schmeckt . . .

9 (D3) Und wie!

EXPRESSING FEELINGS AND EMOTIONS

Expressing surprise

3 (C7) Was?!
Wirklich?

6 (C9) Meinst du?

Expressing liking

3 (C11) Ich (spiele) gern (Gitarre).

10 (C3) Ich mag . . .
Ich mag . . . gern.
Ich habe . . . gern.

Expressing dislike

3 (C11) Ich (spiele) nicht gern (Fussball).

10 (C3) Ich habe . . . nicht gern.
Ich mag . . . nicht.
Ich mag . . . nicht gern.

Expressing strong dislike

10 (C3) Ich hasse . . .

Expressing preference

3 (C11) Ich (spiele) lieber . . .

10 (B10) Ich (höre) . . . lieber.
Ich (höre) . . . besonders gern.

Expressing strong preference

3 (C11) Ich (spiele) am liebsten . . .

10 (B10) Ich (sehe) . . . am liebsten.
Das ist mein(e) Lieblings . . .

Expressing indifference

9 (B4) Na und?!

10 (B10) Das ist mir gleich.

Responding to good news

2 (D5) Gut!
Prima!
Phantastisch!
Toll!

Responding to bad news

2 (D5) Blöd!
Das ist nicht so gut.
Das ist schlecht.
Schade!

Expressing enthusiasm

2 (A1) Toll!

3 (C1) Ich finde . . . interessant!
. . . ist Klasse / Spitze / super / prima / phantastisch / toll!
. . . macht Spass!

6 (B11) Mensch!

9 (A1) Schön!

9 (D3) Und wie!

Expressing lack of enthusiasm

3 (C1) Ich finde . . . blöd.
. . . ist langweilig.

10 (B3) Ich mag . . . nicht besonders.

Expressing annoyance

7 (C4) Das ist blöd / dumm!
Das ist zu blöd / dumm!
Ich bin sauer.

Expressing regret

9 (A3) Das ist schade.
Es geht leider nicht.

Expressing relief

5 (B1) Gott sei dank!

5 (C6) Endlich!

PERSUADING: GETTING SOMEONE TO DO SOMETHING

Making requests

7 (B4) Geh doch bitte mal (einkaufen)!
Kauf bitte nicht alles beim . . .!
Hol doch (das Obst) beim . . .!

Giving commands

7 (B4) Pass bitte auf!
Verlier das Geld nicht!

Making suggestions

7 (C7) Probier doch mal den . . .!

10 (A11) Möchtest du ins (Kino) gehen?
Willst du ins (Kino) gehen?
Gehen wir doch ins (Kino)!

11 (C1) Kaufen Sie . . .!
Schenken Sie ihm . . .!

Expressing possibility

10 (A11) Wir können ins (Kino) gehen.

Giving advice

7 (C1) Bleibt lieber zu Hause!

11 (C1) Kaufen Sie . . .!
Schenken Sie ihm . . .!

GRAMMAR SUMMARY

DETERMINERS

In German, nouns can be grouped into three classes or genders: masculine, feminine, and neuter. There are words that tell you the gender of a noun. One of these is called the definite article. In English there is one definite article: *the.* In German there are three, one for each gender: **der, die,** and **das.**

Gender:	MASCULINE		FEMININE		NEUTER	
Noun Phrase:	**der Junge** **der Ball**	*the boy* *the ball*	**die Mutter** **die Kassette**	*the mother* *the cassette*	**das Mädchen** **das Haus**	*the girl* *the house*

Other words can be used with a noun instead of the definite article. Examples of these words in English are *a, this, that, my,* and *every*. These words and the definite article are called determiners. They help to make clear, or determine, which person or thing you mean—for example, whether you are talking about *this book, my book,* or just any book. A determiner plus a noun is called a noun phrase.

DEFINITE ARTICLES

	NOMINATIVE	ACCUSATIVE
Masculine	**der**	**den**
Feminine	**die**	**die**
Neuter	**das**	**das**
Plural	**die**	**die**

DIESER–WORDS

The determiners **dieser, jeder, welcher,** and **alle** are called **dieser-**words because their endings are the same as those of **dieser.** Note that the endings of the **dieser-**words are very similar to those of the definite articles.

dieser	*this, that*
jeder	*each, every*
alle	*all*
welcher	*which, what*

	NOMINATIVE	ACCUSATIVE	NOMINATIVE	ACCUSATIVE	NOMINATIVE	ACCUSATIVE
Masculine	**dieser**	**diesen**	**jeder**	**jeden**	**welcher**	**welchen**
Feminine	**diese**	**diese**	**jede**	**jede**	**welche**	**welche**
Neuter	**dieses**	**dieses**	**jedes**	**jedes**	**welches**	**welches**
Plural	**diese**	**diese**	**alle**	**alle**	**welche**	**welche**

INDEFINITE ARTICLES

The determiner **ein,** *a, an,* is called an indefinite article. There is no plural form of **ein.** You must use words like **viele,** *many,* **einige,** *some,* **mehrere,** *several,* which you will learn later.

	Nominative	Accusative
Masculine	**ein**	**einen**
Feminine	**eine**	**eine**
Neuter	**ein**	**ein**
Plural	—	—

THE NEGATIVE DETERMINER *KEIN*

The negative determiner **kein,** *no, not, not any,* has the same endings as **ein.** Note that **kein** has a plural form.

	Nominative	Accusative
Masculine	**kein**	**keinen**
Feminine	**keine**	**keine**
Neuter	**kein**	**kein**
Plural	**keine**	**keine**

POSSESSIVES

	BEFORE MASCULINE NOUNS			BEFORE FEMININE NOUNS		BEFORE NEUTER NOUNS		BEFORE PLURAL NOUNS	
	Nom	Acc	Dat	Nom & Acc	Dat	Nom & Acc	Dat	Nom & Acc	Dat
my	mein	meinen	meinem	meine	meiner	mein	meinem	meine	meinen
your	dein	deinen	deinem	deine	deiner	dein	deinem	deine	deinen
his	sein	seinen	seinem	seine	seiner	sein	seinem	seine	seinen
her	ihr	ihren	ihrem	ihre	ihrer	ihr	ihrem	ihre	ihren
our	unser	unseren	unserem	unsere	unserer	unser	unserem	unsere	unseren
your	euer	eueren	euerem	euere	euerer	euer	euerem	euere	eueren
their	ihr	ihren	ihrem	ihre	ihrer	ihr	ihrem	ihre	ihren
your	Ihr	Ihren	Ihrem	Ihre	Ihrer	Ihr	Ihrem	Ihre	Ihren

Commonly used short forms for unseren: unsren *or* unsern *for* unsere: unsre
eueren: euren *or* euern euere: eure

for unserem: unsrem *or* unserm *for* unserer: unsrer
euerem: eurem *or* euerm euerer: eurer

NOUN PLURALS

Noun gender and plural forms are not always predictable. Therefore, you must learn each noun together with its article (**der, die, das**) and with its plural form. As you learn more nouns, however, you will discover certain patterns. Although there are always exceptions to these patterns, you may find them helpful in remembering the plural forms of many nouns.

Most German nouns form their plurals in one of five ways. Some nouns add endings in the plural; some add endings and/or change the sound of the stem vowel in the plural, indicating the sound change with the umlaut (¨). Only the vowels **a, o, u** and the diphthong **au** can take the umlaut. If a noun has an umlaut in the singular, it keeps the umlaut in the plural. Most German nouns fit into one of the following plural groups:

Group:	I	II	III	IV	V
Ending:	–	–e	–er	–(e)n	–s
Umlaut:	*sometimes*	*sometimes*	*always*	*never*	*never*

1. Nouns in Group I do not have any ending in the plural. Sometimes they take an umlaut. NOTE: There are only two feminine nouns in this group: **die Mutter** and **die Tochter.**

der Bruder, die Brüder
der Garten, die Gärten
der Lehrer, die Lehrer
der Mantel, die Mäntel
der Onkel, die Onkel
der Schüler, die Schüler
der Vater, die Väter

die Mutter, die Mütter
die Tochter, die Töchter

das Fräulein, die Fräulein
das Mädchen, die Mädchen
das Poster, die Poster
das Zimmer, die Zimmer

2. Nouns in Group II add the ending **-e** in the plural. Sometimes they take an umlaut. NOTE: There are many one-syllable words in this group.

der Bleistift, die Bleistifte
der Freund, die Freunde
der Pass, die Pässe
der Sohn, die Söhne
der Witz, die Witze

die Stadt, die Städte

das Jahr, die Jahre
das Spiel, die Spiele
das Stück, die Stücke

3. Nouns in Group III add the ending **-er** in the plural. They always take an umlaut wherever possible, that is when the noun contains the vowels **a, o,** or **u,** or the diphthong **au.** NOTE: There are no feminine nouns in this group. There are many one-syllable words in this group.

das Buch, die Bücher
das Dorf, die Dörfer
das Fach, die Fächer
das Haus, die Häuser
das Land, die Länder

4. Nouns in Group IV add the ending **-en** or **-n** in the plural. They never add an umlaut. NOTE: There are many feminine nouns in this group.

der Angestellte, die Angestellten
der Herr, die Herren
der Junge, die Jungen

der Kamerad, die Kameraden
der Name, die Namen
der Vetter, die Vettern

die Briefmarke, die Briefmarken
die Familie, die Familien
die Farbe, die Farben
die Frau, die Frauen
die Karte, die Karten
die Klasse, die Klassen

die Küche, die Küchen
die Schwester, die Schwestern
die Tante, die Tanten
die Wohnung, die Wohnungen
die Zahl, die Zahlen
die Zeitung, die Zeitungen

Feminine nouns ending in **-in** add the ending **-nen** in the plural.

die Freundin, die Freundinnen
die Lehrerin, die Lehrerinnen
die Verkäuferin, die Verkäuferinnen

5. Nouns in Group V add the ending **-s** in the plural. They never add an umlaut. NOTE: There are many words of foreign origin in this group.

der Kuli, die Kulis	das Auto, die Autos
die Kamera, die Kameras	das Hobby, die Hobbys

PRONOUNS

PERSONAL PRONOUNS

		Nominative	Accusative	Dative
Singular				
1st person		ich	mich	mir
2nd person		du	dich	dir
3rd person	*m.*	er	ihn	ihm
	f.	sie	sie	ihr
	n.	es	es	ihm
Plural				
1st person		wir	uns	uns
2nd person		ihr	euch	euch
3rd person		sie	sie	ihnen
Formal Address		Sie	Sie	Ihnen

DEFINITE ARTICLES AS DEMONSTRATIVE PRONOUNS

The definite articles can be used as demonstrative pronouns, giving more emphasis to the sentences than the personal pronouns **er, sie, es.** Note that the demonstrative pronouns have the same forms as the definite articles.

	Nominative	Accusative
Masculine	der	den
Feminine	die	die
Neuter	das	das
Plural	die	die

INTERROGATIVES

INTERROGATIVE PRONOUNS

Nominative	**wer?** *who?*	**was?** *what?*
Accusative	**wen?** *whom?*	**was?** *what?*
Dative	**wem?** *to, for whom?*	

SUMMARY OF INTERROGATIVES

wann?	*when?*	**wo?**	*where?*	**welche?**	*which? what?*
warum?	*why?*	**woher?**	*from where?*	**was für (ein)?**	*what kind of (a)?*
wie?	*how?*	**wohin?**	*to where?*		
wieviel?	*how much? how many?*				

WAS FÜR (EIN)?

	NOMINATIVE	ACCUSATIVE
Masculine *Feminine* *Neuter*	**Was für ein** Lehrer ist er? **Was für eine** Platte ist das? **Was für ein** Radio ist das?	**Was für einen** Lehrer hast du? **Was für eine** Platte kaufst du? **Was für ein** Radio hast du?
Plural	**Was für** Instrumente sind hier?	**Was für** Instrumente spielt ihr?

WORD ORDER

The verb is in first position in	*questions that do not begin with an interrogative:* Trinkst du Kaffee? Spielst du Fussball? *suggestions using command forms:* Geht doch ins Kino!
The verb is in second position in	*statements:* Wir spielen Tennis. Am Wochenende spiele ich Fussball. *questions that begin with an interrogative:* Wohin fahrt ihr? Was spielst du gern?
The verb is in last position in	*clauses following* **wissen:** Ich weiss, wo der Dom ist.

POSITION OF *NICHT* IN A SENTENCE

Er fragt seinen Vater		**nicht.**	*as near the end as possible to negate entire sentence*
Ich rufe ihn	**nicht**	an.	*before a separable prefix*
Er kommt	**nicht**	heute. (Er kommt morgen.)	*before any part of a sentence you want to negate, contrast, emphasize*
Ich wohne	**nicht**	in Berlin.	*before part of a sentence answering the question* wo?

VERBS

PRESENT TENSE VERB FORMS

INFINITIVES:		spiel -en	mogel -n	find -en	heiss -en
PRONOUNS		stem + ending	stem + ending	stem + ending	stem + ending
I	ich	spiel **-e**	mogl **-e**	find **-e**	heiss **-e**
you	du	spiel **-st**	mogel **-st**	find **-est**	heiss **-t**
he, she	er, sie	spiel **-t**	mogel **-t**	find **-et**	heiss **-t**
we	wir	spiel **-en**	mogel **-n**	find **-en**	heiss **-en**
you	ihr	spiel **-t**	mogel **-t**	find **-et**	heiss **-t**
they	sie	spiel **-en**	mogel **-n**	find **-en**	heiss **-en**
you (formal)	Sie	spiel **-en**	mogel **-n**	find **-en**	heiss **-en**

Note the following exceptions in the preceding chart:

a. Verbs ending in **-eln (mogeln, segeln)** drop the "**e**" of the ending **-eln** in the **ich-**form: **ich mogle,** and add only **-n** in the **wir-, sie-,** and **Sie-**form. These forms are always identical with the infinitive: **mogeln, wir mogeln, sie mogeln, Sie mogeln.**

b. Verbs with a stem ending in **-d** or in **-t,** such as **finden,** add **-est** in the **du-**form, and **-et** in the **er-** and **ihr-**forms: **du findest, er findet, ihr findet.**

c. All verbs with stems ending in an "**s**" sound **(heissen)** add only **-t** in the **du-**form: **du heisst.**

d. In speaking, the **ich-**form is often used without the ending **-e: ich spiel', ich frag'.** The omission of the **-e** is shown in writing by an apostrophe.

VERBS WITH A STEM–VOWEL CHANGE

There are a number of verbs in German that change their stem vowel in the **du-** and **er/sie-**form. Some verbs, such as **nehmen,** have a consonant change as well. There is no way to predict these verbs, so you must learn each one individually.

	e → i			e → ie		a → ä		
	essen	**geben**	**nehmen**	**lesen**	**sehen**	**anfangen**	**einladen**	**fahren**
ich	esse	gebe	nehme	lese	sehe	fange an	lade ein	fahre
du	**isst**	**gibst**	**nimmst**	**liest**	**siehst**	**fängst** an	**lädst** ein	**fährst**
er, sie	**isst**	**gibt**	**nimmt**	**liest**	**sieht**	**fängt** an	**lädt** ein	**fährt**
wir	essen	geben	nehmen	lesen	sehen	fangen an	laden ein	fahren
ihr	esst	gebt	nehmt	lest	seht	fangt an	ladet ein	fahrt
sie, Sie	essen	geben	nehmen	lesen	sehen	fangen an	laden ein	fahren

THE VERBS *HABEN, SEIN, WISSEN*

	haben	**sein**	**wissen**
ich	habe	bin	weiss
du	hast	bist	weisst
er, sie, es	hat	ist	weiss
wir	haben	sind	wissen
ihr	habt	seid	wisst
sie	haben	sind	wissen
Sie	haben	sind	wissen

SOME MODAL VERBS

The verbs **können, mögen** (and the **möchte-**forms), **sollen,** and **wollen** are usually used with an infinitive that comes at the end of the sentence. If the meaning of that infinitive is clear, it can be left out.

	können	**mögen**	**sollen**	**wollen**	**möchte-**forms
ich	kann	mag	soll	will	möchte
du	kannst	magst	sollst	willst	möchtest
er, sie, es	kann	mag	soll	will	möchte
wir	können	mögen	sollen	wollen	möchten
ihr	könnt	mögt	sollt	wollt	möchtet
sie	können	mögen	sollen	wollen	möchten
Sie	können	mögen	sollen	wollen	möchten

VERBS WITH SEPARABLE PREFIXES

Some verbs have separable prefixes. A separable prefix is a prefix that is sometimes separated from the main verb.

	INFINITIVE: **anfangen**
ich fange an	Ich **fange** jetzt **an.**
du fängst an	Wann **fängst** du **an?**
er, sie, es fängt an	**Fängt** er immer zuerst **an?**
wir fangen an	Wir **fangen** nicht zuerst **an.**
ihr fangt an	Warum **fangt** ihr nicht **an?**
sie fangen an	Sie **fangen** morgen nach der Schule wieder **an.**

Here is a list of verbs with separable prefixes and similar verbs.

abheben	auspacken	kennenlernen
anfangen	aussehen	radfahren
anrufen	einladen	
ausgehen	vorhaben	

COMMAND FORMS

Persons you address	**bleiben**	**essen**	**anfangen**
with **du** (*sing*)	bleib!	iss!	fang an!
with **ihr** (*pl*)	bleibt!	esst!	fangt an!
with **Sie** (*sing* & *pl*)	bleiben Sie!	essen Sie!	fangen Sie an!
let's form	bleiben wir!	essen wir!	fangen wir an!

Here are some other command forms you have learned:

anrufen	**ausgehen**	**einladen**	**erzählen**	**holen**	**kaufen**
ruf an!	geh aus!	lad ein!	erzähl!	hol!	kauf!
ruft an!	geht aus!	ladet ein!	erzählt!	holt!	kauft!
rufen Sie an!	gehen Sie aus!	laden Sie ein!	erzählen Sie!	holen Sie!	kaufen Sie!
rufen wir an!	gehen wir aus!	laden wir ein!	erzählen wir!	holen wir!	kaufen wir!

radfahren	schauen	schenken	verlieren	versuchen
fahr Rad! fahrt Rad! fahren Sie Rad! fahren wir Rad!	schau! schaut! schauen Sie! schauen wir!	schenk! schenkt! schenken Sie! schenken wir!	verlier! verliert! verlieren Sie! verlieren wir!	versuch! versucht! versuchen Sie! versuchen wir!

Verbs with stem vowel changes:

geben	nehmen	sehen
gib! gebt! geben Sie! geben wir!	nimm! nehmt! nehmen Sie! nehmen wir!	sieh! seht! sehen Sie! sehen wir!

THE CONVERSATIONAL PAST

German verbs are divided into two groups: weak verbs and strong verbs. Weak verbs usually follow a regular pattern, such as the English verb forms *play—played—has played.* Strong verbs usually have irregularities, like the English verb forms *run—ran—has run* or *go—went—has gone.*

The conversational past tense of weak and strong verbs consists of the present tense of **haben** or **sein** and a form called the past participle, which is usually in last position in the clause or sentence.

Die Schüler	**haben**	ihre Hausaufgaben schon	**gemacht.**
Sabine	**ist**	gestern zu Hause	**geblieben.**

Here is a list of past participles you have been using in this textbook. Note that:

1. The past participle of most weak verbs is formed by putting the prefix **ge-** before the present tense **er**-form, which ends in **-t.** The ending **-t** tells you that the verb is weak. (**gemacht, gehört, gekauft**)
2. Verbs with an inseparable prefix (a prefix never separated from the verb stem) do not add **ge-** in the past participle. (**besuchen, hat besucht**)
3. The past participle of many strong verbs is formed by putting the prefix **ge-** before the infinitive of the verb. However, the past participles of most strong verbs have a stem vowel different from the stem vowel of the infinitive. In addition, there may be consonant changes. Some strong verbs have special forms in the past participle, for example, the verb **sein.**

You have learned the following past participles:

Weak Verbs		Strong Verbs	
INFINITIVE	PAST PARTICIPLE	INFINITIVE	PAST PARTICIPLE
besuchen	hat **besucht**	bleiben	ist **geblieben**
hören	hat **gehört**	essen	hat **gegessen**
kaufen	hat **gekauft**	fahren	ist **gefahren**
machen	hat **gemacht**	geben	hat **gegeben**
schenken	hat **geschenkt**	gehen	ist **gegangen**
spielen	hat **gespielt**	haben	hat **gehabt**
		lesen	hat **gelesen**
		sehen	hat **gesehen**
		sein	ist **gewesen**
		trinken	hat **getrunken**

PRINCIPAL PARTS OF STRONG VERBS

This list includes all strong verbs listed in the **Wortschatz** sections of this textbook. Weak verbs with separable prefixes, stem vowel changes, or other irregularities are also listed. Past participles formed with **sein** are indicated. All other past participles on this list are formed with **haben.** Usually only one English meaning of the verb is given. Other meanings may be found in the German-English Vocabulary.

The past participles considered active, that is, the ones you learned in Units 10 and 11, are in heavy type.

INFINITIVE	PRESENT (stem vowel change and/or separable prefix)	PAST PARTICIPLE	MEANING
abheben	er hebt ab	abgehoben	*to lift (the receiver)*
anfangen	er fängt an	angefangen	*to start*
anrufen	er ruft an	angerufen	*to call up*
ausgehen	er geht aus	ist ausgegangen	*to go out*
aussehen	er sieht aus	ausgesehen	*to look, appear*
beginnen		begonnen	*to begin*
bekommen		bekommen	*to get, receive*
bleiben		**ist geblieben**	*to stay*
bringen		gebracht	*to bring*
einladen	er lädt ein	eingeladen	*to invite*
essen	er isst	**gegessen**	*to eat*
fahren	er fährt	**ist gefahren**	*to drive, ride*
finden		gefunden	*to find, think*
fliegen		ist geflogen	*to fly*
geben	er gibt	**gegeben**	*to give*
gehen		**ist gegangen**	*to go*
gewinnen		gewonnen	*to win*
haben	er hat	**gehabt**	*to have*
heissen		geheissen	*to be called*
kennen		gekannt	*to know*
kommen		ist gekommen	*to come*
können	er kann	gekonnt	*to be able to*
lesen	er liest	**gelesen**	*to read*
mögen	er mag	gemocht	*to like*
nehmen	er nimmt	genommen	*to take*
radfahren	er fährt Rad	ist radgefahren	*to go bike riding*
scheinen		geschienen	*to shine*
schwimmen		ist geschwommen	*to swim*
sehen	er sieht	**gesehen**	*to see*
sein	er ist	**ist gewesen**	*to be*
singen		gesungen	*to sing*
sprechen	er spricht	gesprochen	*to speak*
stehen		gestanden	*to stand*
trinken		**getrunken**	*to drink*
tun		getan	*to do*
verbringen		verbracht	*to spend (time)*
verlieren		verloren	*to lose*
verstehen		verstanden	*to understand*
vorhaben	er hat vor	vorgehabt	*to have planned*
wissen	er weiss	gewusst	*to know*
wollen	er will	gewollt	*to want*

PRONUNCIATION

Pronunciation and reading exercises are found in the Try Your Skills section of each unit, with the exception of the review units.

			as in:
Kapitel (p. 53)	1	The **ich**-Sound	ich, dich, Mädchen
		The **ach**-Sound	acht, achtzehn, auch
		The **l**-Sound	alt, elf, Lehrer
Kapitel (p. 85)	2	Long Vowels	da, dem, vier, du
		Short Vowels: The Sound **[ɔ]**	kosten, toll, von
		The **ü**-Sound	für, fünf, Glück
		The **ö**-Sound	blöd, Österreich, Wörterbuch
Kapitel (p. 113)	3	The Sounds **[R]** and Final **r**	frei, Rad, lieber
		The Diphthongs **[ai], [au], [ɔi]**	ein, sauer, neun
		The Sound **[ʃ]**	Schule, spät, Bleistift
Kapitel (p. 159)	5	The **l**-Sound (Review)	Köln, Zoll, Kilometer
		The **ich**-Sound (Review)	möchte, rechts, zwanzig
		The **ach**-Sound (Review)	nach, Schliessfach, besuchen
		The **ü**-Sound (Review)	Reiseführer, Münze, zurück
		The **ö**-Sound (Review)	Köln, möchte
Kapitel (p. 187)	6	Long Vowels (Review)	Bahn, gehen, wie, Oma, Flug
		The Sounds **[R]** and Final **r** (Review)	Bruder, Zimmer, Keller
		The Long **ä**-Sound	Mädchen, Bäder
		The Sound **[t]**	Mutter, bitte, Tante
Kapitel (p. 217)	7	The Diphthongs **[ei], [au], [ɔi]** (Review)	Eis, Hauptstadt, Leute
		The Sound **[ɔ]** (Review)	Dorf, Schloss, wolkig
		The Sound **[pf]**	Pfund, Pfennig
		The Sound **[ʃv]**	schwer, Schwester, Schweiz
Kapitel (p. 261)	9	The **ich**-Sound (Review)	gleich, mich, gemütlich
		The **ach**-Sound (Review)	Kuchen, Buch
		The **l**-Sound (Review)	Platte, einladen
		The Umlaute **ä, ö,** and **ü** (Review)	Käse, schön, hübsch
		The Sounds **[R]** and Final **r** (Review)	Ruhe, anrufen, leider
Kapitel (p. 293)	10	Long Vowels **[e:], [o:], [u:]** (Review)	gesehen, Kino, Jugend
		The **l**-Sound (Review)	also, wollen, miserabel
		The Sound **[ɔ]** (Review)	Sport, besonders, Konzert
Kapitel (p. 321)	11	Long Vowels **[a:], [e:], [o:], [u:],** and **[ü:]** (Review)	Vater, geben, Hose, Bluse, grün
		The Diphthongs **[ei], [au], [ɔi]** (Review)	weiss, glauben, Sträusse
		The **ich**-Sound (Review)	gewöhnlich, herzlich
		The **ach**-Sound (Review)	Schachtel, Weihnachten
		The **l**-Sound (Review)	Kalender, Blume, fröhlich

NUMBERS

0 null
1 eins
2 zwei
3 drei
4 vier
5 fünf
6 sechs
7 sieben
8 acht
9 neun
10 zehn
11 elf
12 zwölf
13 dreizehn
14 vierzehn
15 fünfzehn
16 sechzehn
17 siebzehn
18 achtzehn
19 neunzehn
20 zwanzig
21 einundzwanzig
22 zweiundzwanzig
23 dreiundzwanzig
24 vierundzwanzig
30 dreissig
31 einunddreissig
40 vierzig
50 fünfzig
60 sechzig
70 siebzig
80 achtzig
90 neunzig
100 hundert
101 hunderteins
102 hundertzwei
103 hundertdrei
200 zweihundert
201 zweihunderteins
300 dreihundert
400 vierhundert
1000 tausend

ENGLISH EQUIVALENTS

The following are the English equivalents of the basic material in each section of every unit, with the exception of review units. They are not literal translations, but represent what a speaker of English would say in the same situation.

1 NEW FRIENDS

A1 Hello! Goodbye!
Hi, Steffi!
Hi, Andreas!
Hi, Stefan!
Hello, Michael!
Morning, Natalie!
Good morning!
Bye!
Bye! So long!
See you later!
Goodbye!

A5 Mr., Mrs., Miss
Good morning, Mr. Sperling.
Hello, Antje.

Hello, Mrs. Meier.
Hi, Michael.

Bye, Miss Seifert.
Goodbye.

B1 What's your name?
Hi! My name is Andreas. What's your name?
My name is Natalie.

And what's your name? My name is ____.

B3 What's the boy's name? What's the girl's name?
What's the boy's name?
His name is Stefan.

And the girl? What's her name?
Her name is Sabine.

B8 Who is that?
Who is that?
That's Stefan.

And who is that?
That is Mr. Sperling, the teacher.

Who is that?
That's Sabine.
And that's Mrs. Meier, the teacher.

Mr. Sperling, the German teacher.
Mrs. Meier, the German teacher

C1 How old are you?
How old are you?
I'm thirteen years old.

How old is Sabine?
Sabine is fifteen.

And how old is Stefan?
Stefan is fifteen too.

How old are Ulrike and Michael?
They are also fifteen years old.

And how old are you? I'm ____.

D1 Where are you from?
My name is Jens Kröger. I am sixteen years old. I'm from Niebüll, from Germany.

I'm Wiebke Nedel. I'm fifteen. I am also from Germany, from Neuss.

My name is Dastl, Margit Dastl. I am fourteen. I'm from Vienna, from Austria.

My name is Bruno Schmidlin. I'm fifteen. I am from Switzerland, from Zimmerwald.

I am Kurt Langer. I'm fifteen too. I'm from the DDR, from Dresden.

And where are you from? From Kansas City? From Harrisburg? Dallas? I'm from ____.

D7 Yes or no?
Jörg asks Jens:
Is your name Michael?
No, my name is Jens.
Are you from Niebüll?
Yes.

Jörg asks Lars:
Is that Jens?
Yes.
Is his name Nedel?
No, his name is Kröger.
Is he from Niebüll?
Yes, he's from Niebüll.

D13 I beg your pardon?
I'm from Liechtenstein.
From where?

What's your name?

Me? My name is . . .

That's Hans-Helmut Kurtmeyer.
I beg your pardon? Who is that?

How old is Stefan?
Stefan? —He's fifteen.

D16 What is your name? Where are you from?
Are you the German teacher?
No, I'm the math teacher.

Is your name Müller?
My name is Fischer.

Where are you from?
From Munich.

2 SCHOOL

A1 How do you get to school?
A: Look, here comes Jens on his moped!
B: Great!
A: How do you get to school?
B: Me? I come by bus. And you?
A: On foot.

Margit comes by streetcar.
Jens comes by moped.
Miss Seifert comes by car.
Wiebke comes by bike.
Who walks?

B1 School Supplies

JENS	Excuse me! How much is the dictionary, please?
SALESWOMAN	The dictionary? —Thirteen marks.
JENS	And how much is the pocket calculator?
SALESWOMAN	Eighteen marks.
JENS	I beg your pardon?
SALESWOMAN	Eighteen marks.
JENS	Great, only eighteen marks! And how much is the cassette?
SALESWOMAN	Six marks.
JENS	Thank you.
SALESWOMAN	You're welcome.

B12 How much are the school supplies? They cost . . .
books, 8 marks; pocket calculators, 18 marks;
posters, 5 marks; pencils, 1 mark;
cassettes, 6 marks; ballpoint pens, 4 marks

B20 Hey, where is the dictionary?
Hey, Jens, where is the dictionary?
It's over there. Look, Kristin, there!

Hey, Kristin, the pocket calculator's gone.
Nonsense! It's there.

Jens, where is the cassette?
Isn't it there? —Take a look, Kristin! Here it is.

Excuse me, Mrs. Meier. Where are the posters, please?
I don't know. Aren't they there?
No, they're gone.
Gone? Take a look. They are over there.

C1 Which subjects do you have today?

MRS. KRÖGER	Which subjects do you have today?
JENS	I have math, history, —wait a minute! Look, here is my class schedule. Today is Tuesday?
MRS. KRÖGER	Yes.
JENS	I have German at eight o'clock, at a quarter to nine math. Then I have English and history.
MRS. KRÖGER	When do you have physics?
JENS	On Friday.

Jens goes to high school in Niebüll. He has school from Monday to Friday. Jens has Saturdays off. School begins at eight o'clock and is over at one.

What subjects does he have? Here is Jens' class schedule.

C7 When does Jens have math?
at one o'clock / at one
at two o'clock / at two
What time is it? It is . . .
nine o'clock
nine-oh-five / five after nine
nine-ten / ten after nine
nine-fifteen / a quarter after nine
nine-twenty
nine twenty-five
nine-thirty / half past nine
nine thirty-five
nine-forty
nine forty-five / a quarter of ten
nine-fifty / ten of ten
nine fifty-five / five of ten

C10 What do you have now?
What do you have now?
We have bio now. And you?
Math. We're having a test.
Well then, good luck!

Jörg and Kristin are classmates. They are in the ninth grade, the 9a.

Mona and Lars are also classmates. They are in the ninth grade too, in the other section, the 9b.

D1 Homework and grades

Jens is doing his homework. He's doing math. In math Jens is not so good. What marks does he have in math? A four, a three, and a four. Here are Jens' grades.

KRISTIN Hey, Jens, what do you have in German?
JENS A two.
KRISTIN That's great! A two in German. Fantastic!
JENS Yes, that's good, but I only have a four in math. Dumb!
KRISTIN Yes, that's bad. Too bad!

What do you have?
A one!
Great! Terrific!
Dumb! Too bad!

D7 Is bio hard?

Do you have a one in bio?
Yes, biology is easy.

You have algebra?
Yes.
Is algebra hard?
No, algebra isn't hard. It's easy.

3 LEISURE TIME

A1 Leisure Time: Sports and Hobbies

INTERVIEWER What's your name?
JENS My name is Jens.
INTERVIEWER How old are you?
JENS Sixteen.
INTERVIEWER What do you do in your free time?
JENS Well, I visit friends, I listen to music cassettes, I . . .

Jens visits friends. They listen to music cassettes.

INTERVIEWER Do you participate in sports?
JENS Yes. I swim and I play tennis.

Jens swims and he plays tennis.

INTERVIEWER Do you play soccer too?
JENS Of course!

Jens plays soccer too.

INTERVIEWER Do you play an instrument?
JENS Yes, I play guitar.

He plays guitar.

INTERVIEWER Do you also have hobbies?
JENS I collect stamps and I play chess.

Jens collects stamps.

A11 And what do you do?

INTERVIEWER And what do you do? Do you participate in sports too?
GÜNTER We play basketball.

The girls are sailing.
The boys are playing hockey.
The students are playing basketball.

INTERVIEWER Do you have hobbies?
GÜNTER Yes, I collect coins.
INTERVIEWER And you, Kurt?
KURT I do too.

Günter and Kurt collect coins.

The four classmates are playing cards. The game is called Mau-Mau.

INTERVIEWER What are you playing?
KRISTIN Mau-Mau.
INTERVIEWER Really? Who's winning?
KRISTIN Jens and Jörg.
JENS As always.
KRISTIN But you're cheating. As always.
JENS What?! We're not cheating. You're losing and you're sore. Ha ha!

B1 When do you participate in sports?

What do you do in the summer? In fall? In the winter? In the spring?

URSEL In the summer I play tennis and I swim.
PETER In the fall I play soccer.
HANS In the winter I play ice hockey and I ski.
KARIN In the spring I play basketball.

Jörg, what do you do on the weekend?
On the weekend I play soccer.

On Sunday
on the weekend

B3 How often do you do sports?

Petra: "I seldom play tennis. Well, sometimes in the summer. In the winter I often play basketball."

Michael: "I participate in sports four times a week. Once a week, usually on Wednesday, I play tennis. On the weekend I play soccer and I swim twice a week."

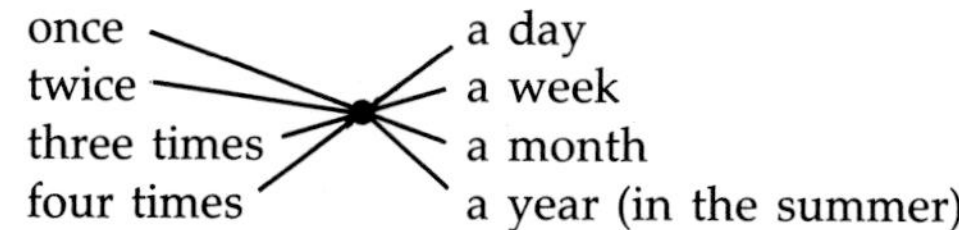

C1 Soccer is great!

INTERVIEWER What do you do, Margit? Do you participate in sports?
MARGIT I do gymnastics.
INTERVIEWER Really?
MARGIT Yes, gymnastics is fun!

INTERVIEWER Jörg, you play soccer?
JÖRG Yes, soccer is great.
INTERVIEWER Do you play tennis too?
JÖRG No. I think tennis is boring.

INTERVIEWER Wiebke, what do you do in your free time?
WIEBKE I read a lot.
INTERVIEWER That's interesting. What do you read?
WIEBKE Novels, books about sports, fantasy books . . . they're terrific!
INTERVIEWER What do you think of comics?
WIEBKE Dumb!

C6 True! Not true!

A: Soccer is great!
B: True!

A: How do you like the cassette?
B: Super! It's terrific!
A: Really? I think it's dumb.

A: You collect stamps?
B: Yes. Collecting is fun.
A: What? I don't think so.

A: Playing cards is boring.
B: I think so too.

A: Sailing is boring too.
B: That's not so! Sailing is great!

C10 What do you like to do?

I don't like to sail.
I like to do gymnastics.
I rather play soccer.
I like being lazy best of all.

5 OFF TO COLOGNE!

A1 Off to Germany!

The plane to Frankfurt is filled to capacity. Germans are flying back to Germany, Americans are visiting friends and relatives or going on vacation.

HANS Are you staying in Frankfurt?
PAUL No, I'm flying on to Munich.

JULIA Where are you going?
PETER To Cologne.

JOHN What are you going to do in Germany?
MARY I'm visiting friends.

JOE How long are you staying?
BOB Four weeks.

A7 What does Peter need for the trip?

PETER Dad, where's my flight ticket? And the travel guide?
VATI Peter, I have your passport, your flight ticket, and the travel guide here.
PETER Great! Thanks, Dad! And where are the traveler's checks? I need money too.
VATI That's right. Here are the traveler's checks. Do you have everything now? What else do you need?

I need the Walkman, the music cassettes, the address book, the dictionary, the camera, the film, and the playing cards.

Who is Peter?
Peter Seber is an American. He is 15 years old and lives in New York. Peter's father is from Austria, his mother is from California.

The Sebers have friends in Germany, the Nedel family in Neuss. Peter is going to visit the Nedels. Tomorrow he flies to Frankfurt and from there on to Cologne.

A10 What are you looking for? Whom do you ask?

What are you looking for, Peter?
My passport. Who has my passport?
Hey, I'll just ask Dad.

B1 Peter in Frankfurt

The plane lands in Frankfurt. The passengers go through the passport control, they get their luggage, and they go through customs.

OFFICIAL Passport, please.
PETER Here you are.
OFFICIAL How long are you staying?
PETER Four weeks.
OFFICIAL Good. And have a nice vacation!
PETER Thank you.

JULIA Do you have everything?
PETER My travel bag is missing!
JULIA Look, there it is!
PETER Thank God!

Peter has nothing to declare. He goes through by the green symbol.

left right straight ahead
Where is the information counter, please?
Over there, on the left.

PETER Excuse me! Where is the information counter, please?
BOY Over there, on the left.
PETER Thanks.
BOY You're welcome. My pleasure.

PETER Excuse me! Where are the lockers, please?
WOMAN Here, to your right.
PETER Thank you.
WOMAN You're welcome.

B8 What do the travelers say?

I'm looking for the information counter. I would like to ask something.

I'm looking for the restaurant. I would like something to eat and drink.

I'm looking for the post office. I would like to make a phone call and buy stamps.

I'm looking for the bank. I would like to exchange money.

I'm looking for the gift shop. I would like to buy a present.

B15 How does Peter get to Neuss?

JULIA How are you getting to Neuss, Peter?
PETER From Frankfurt to Cologne by plane and from Cologne to Neuss by car.
JULIA How far is it from Frankfurt to Cologne?
PETER Just a minute! —Look, 189 kilometers! That's about 120 miles.

by plane
by train
by car

C1 Peter changes money

PETER I would like to change 50 dollars.
BANK TELLER How much, please?
PETER 50 dollars.
BANK TELLER Into D-marks?
PETER Yes, please.
BANK TELLER The exchange rate today is DM 2,34.
PETER Not bad.
BANK TELLER That makes 117 marks.
PETER Thank you.
BANK TELLER You're welcome! And have a nice vacation!
PETER Thanks.

C2 German Money

There are bills:
a 10-mark bill, a 20-mark bill, a 50-mark bill, a 100-mark bill

there are coins:
a penny, five pennies, a one-mark piece, a 5-mark piece

C6 Telephoning is not hard

Telephoning in Germany is really not hard. You lift the receiver, put coins in the phone and dial the number. That's all.

but sometimes . . .
all the phone booths are occupied . . .
or the phone is out of order
Finally! But . . . Busy!
Peter tries once more. (sound you hear when making a call and it is ringing)

PETER 0 3 4 3 1 6 4 2 3
MRS. NEDEL Nedel speaking.
PETER Hello, Peter Seber speaking.
MRS. NEDEL It's you, Peter! Where are you?
PETER In Frankfurt. At the airport.
MRS. NEDEL Oh, I see. And you'll be in Cologne at 1:10?
PETER Yes, as planned. I'm on flight LH 368.
MRS. NEDEL Good! We'll be there on time. See you soon! Bye.
PETER Goodbye.
MRS. NEDEL Goodbye.

C13 When does the flight to Cologne leave?

This is the monitor.

PETER When does the flight to Cologne leave? I'm on Flight LH 368.
INFORMATION Flight LH 368 to Cologne at 12:40. Gate B 10.
PETER Thank you.
INFORMATION You're welcome. Have a good flight!

6 AT THE NEDELS'

A1 Friends and Relatives

MR. NEDEL So, Peter, we're here. Now you're going to meet a lot of people. Poor Peter!
PETER Oh, that's not so bad.

WIEBKE Peter, these are my grandparents—Mr. and Mrs. Graf—my grandpa, my grandma.
PETER Hello, Mrs. Graf. Hello, Mr. Graf.
MR. GRAF Welcome to Neuss!
PETER Thank you.

WIEBKE My uncle and my aunt, Jürgen and Christa Wolf.
PETER Hello!

WIEBKE This is my brother and my sister—my brother Philipp and my sister Ulrike.
PETER Hello, Philipp! How are you?
PHILIPP Nice that you're here.

WIEBKE And that's my dog Beppo.

WIEBKE This is my cousin Julian.
PETER Hi, Julian.

WIEBKE And my cousin Alice, Ali.
PETER Hello, Ali.

My name is Markus. I'm a friend of Wiebke's.
Hi, Markus.

My name is Monika. I'm a friend of Wiebke's.
Hello, Monika.

I'm Antje, a classmate.
Hello, Antje.

I'm a classmate of Wiebke's. My name is Jochen.
So, how are you?

B1 Peter thinks the house is great!

PETER Hey, Wiebke, I think your house is great!
WIEBKE Do you think so?
PETER It's big, modern . . . How many rooms do you have?
WIEBKE Would you like to see the house?
PETER Yes, I would like to.
WIEBKE Come on! I'll show it to you.

WIEBKE We have six rooms, a kitchen . . .
PETER How modern it is!

WIEBKE A living room . . .
PETER It looks so cozy!
WIEBKE You think so?
PETER Yes, very cozy.

WIEBKE A dining room, . . . A bathroom and two toilets, one downstairs and one upstairs.
PETER So big and bright!

WIEBKE Downstairs we have a basement too.
PETER Fantastic for a party!

WIEBKE And here is the guest room. This is your room now.
PETER How nice!

WIEBKE Four bedrooms, and this is my room.
PETER Small but great!

WIEBKE Look, we have a garden too. And here we have a garage and a car, an Audi.

B11 Peter has a present for all the Nedels

Peter unpacks his backpack. All the Nedels get a present.

PETER Here's a necklace for Wiebke.
WIEBKE Great! Thanks a lot, Peter!
PETER Don't mention it.

PETER And here I have a pocket calculator for Philipp.
PHILIPP Boy, terrific! Thanks a million!

PETER And here's a book for Ulrike.
ULRIKE Thanks, Peter.
PETER You're welcome.

There's still more on Peter's list.

C1 Do you know Wiebke's friends?

Antje is small, blond, and slim. She is very pretty.

MARKUS Antje is so attractive.
JOCHEN You think so? That's a matter of taste. I find her pretty.
MARKUS Really?

That's Markus. He's tall, dark, he wears glasses.

ALI Markus is good-looking, isn't he?
ANTJE Yes, that's true. I think he's intelligent.
ALI Do you think so?

Jochen has dark-blond hair.

ANTJE Boy, is Jochen ever boring!
WIEBKE What?! I don't think so. I think he's nice.
ANTJE Nice, yes—but boring!
WIEBKE That's not true!

Monika is brunette.

PHILIPP Monika is very friendly, don't you think so?
JOCHEN You're right. She's funny and I think she's very nice.
PHILIPP I do too.

7 WHERE DO THEY LIVE?

A1 Where do our friends live?

Hi! My name is Margit Dastl. I live in Vienna.

Vienna, the capital of Austria, has 1.5 million inhabitants.

Hello! I'm Jens. I live in Niebüll.
Niebüll is a town in Schleswig-Holstein.
Niebüll has 7,000 inhabitants.

Hello! I'm Wiebke Nedel. I live in Neuss.
Neuss, a city in Nordrhein-Westfalen.
Neuss has 200,000 inhabitants.

Hi! I'm Bruno Schmidlin. I live in Zimmerwald in Switzerland.
The Schmidlins live in Zimmerwald.
Zimmerwald is a village, a suburb of Bern.
Bern is the capital of Switzerland.

Hello! I'm Steffi Huber. I'm 15 years old, and I live here in Munich.
Munich is the capital of Bavaria. Munich is a big city: it has 1.3 million inhabitants.

A10 In Munich

Mrs. Huber and her daughter Steffi.

The Hubers live in Munich. They have an apartment in Lehel.

The Hubers have company, a boy from Freiburg. Florian doesn't know the city and Steffi shows him the places of interest in Munich.

Who wouldn't like to visit Munich?
Munich is the "secret capital" of Germany, and every year millions of visitors come from all over the world to the "village of millions" on the Isar River.

The "Münchner Kindl," official emblem of Munich

The "Alte Peter," St. Peter's Church, a Munich landmark

Look, Flori! That's the Marienplatz and the New City Hall.

Look, up there is the Glockenspiel!

The pedestrian mall. The inner city is only for pedestrians. And here is the cathedral. It has two towers.

Here is the National Theater. Would you perhaps like to go to the opera?

And that's Nymphenburg Castle.

That's the Theatinerkirche.

The Alte Pinakothek, a museum.

And that's the Chinese Tower in the English Garden.

A13 Excuse me. Where is . . . , please?

Florian is alone in the city. He would like to see the National Museum, but he doesn't know where it is. He asks:

FLORIAN Excuse me. Where is the National Museum, please?
MAN I have no idea! I'm not from here.
FLORIAN Excuse me. Perhaps you can tell me where the National Museum is?
BOY No, I'm sorry, I don't know.
FLORIAN Pardon me. Do you know where the National Museum is?
WOMAN Just a minute, the National Museum—oh, yes, that's on Prinzregenten Street.

B1 Steffi goes shopping

MRS. HUBER Steffi, would you please go shopping for me?
STEFFI Okay. What do you need?
MRS. HUBER Look, I have a list here for you. But don't buy everything at the supermarket.
STEFFI Where should I buy the chopped meat?
MRS. HUBER Buy the meat and the cold cuts at the butcher's and get the fruit and the vegetables at the greengrocer's. And buy the rolls at the bakery. They're always fresh there. Buy everything else at the supermarket.
STEFFI Okay. But I need money.
MRS. HUBER Here are 100 marks. Please be careful and don't lose the money!
STEFFI Don't worry! I'll be careful, Mom. Bye!

What does Steffi buy at the butcher's?
a pound of chopped meat
200 grams of cold cuts

At the bakery she buys:
a loaf of bread and six rolls

What does she buy at the greengrocer's?
And how much?
1 kilo of tomatoes, 1 pound of cherries, a head of lettuce, a cucumber

At the supermarket Steffi buys:
ten eggs, a liter of milk, two pounds of sugar, two bottles of mineral water, a pound of coffee, half a pound of butter, four yogurts, 100 grams of cheese

C1 Too bad, it's raining.

FLORIAN Steffi! What's the matter? You look so sad.

STEFFI I'm annoyed. —Look, Flori, it's raining.
FLORIAN That's too bad. What should we do now?
MRS. HUBER You'd better stay home. Play cards or . . .
STEFFI Oh, Mom!
FLORIAN What does the weather report say?
MRS. HUBER It's going to stay cloudy and it's supposed to rain now and then.
STEFFI Oh, come on, Flori! We'll go anyway.
MRS. HUBER Do you have a raincoat, Flori? It's cool.
FLORIAN Yes, I'll get it right away.
MRS. HUBER Here are two umbrellas for you. And don't come home so late.
STEFFI We'll be back at 9 o'clock.
MRS. HUBER Well then, have fun!
FLORIAN Thanks.
STEFFI Bye, Mom!

What does the weather report say?
Today cloudy and cool, occasional rain.
It's raining. It's cold.

Fair and warm.
The sun is shining.

The weather will stay nice.
It's sunny and hot.

C7 Flori is hungry

FLORIAN Boy, Steffi. I'm hungry.
STEFFI Me too.
FLORIAN What would you like to eat? An ice cream? A grilled chicken?
STEFFI Over there is a snack bar.
FLORIAN Great!

FLORIAN What should I eat? Everything looks so good.
STEFFI Why don't you try the Leberkäs? Leberkäs with mustard is good.
FLORIAN And what are you eating?
STEFFI I'm eating a Bratwurst and I'm drinking mineral water.
FLORIAN Okay, I'll try the Leberkäs and I'll drink mineral water too.

C11 How does it taste?

FLORIAN How's the Bratwurst, Steffi?
STEFFI Hm, great! It tastes very good. — And how's the Leberkäs?
FLORIAN It's good too. —Will you have another Bratwurst?
STEFFI No, thanks. I have enough. And you? Another Leberkäs?
FLORIAN No, thanks. I'm full.

9 A PARTY

A1 Karin has a party

KARIN Three—five—nine—zero—one—four. (It's ringing.)
MRS. BERGER Berger. Hello! I can hear you but I can't understand you. Hello, who's there?

(Click.) (It rings again.)

MRS. BERGER Here Berger.
KARIN Hello, Mrs. Berger. This is Karin. Is Christine there?
MRS. BERGER Oh, it's you, Karin! Now I can understand you well. Just a minute. . . . Christine! Karin would like to talk to you!
CHRISTINE Hi, Karin! How are you? What's up?
KARIN Listen! I'm having a party on Saturday and I would like to invite you. Can you come?
CHRISTINE I'd love to. I don't have anything planned for Saturday. What time?
KARIN At seven.
CHRISTINE That's great! Who else are you inviting?
KARIN Michaela, Bernd, . . .
CHRISTINE Really? Hey, I'll bring my cassettes, o.k.?
KARIN Great! Till Saturday, then. Bye!
CHRISTINE Bye! And thanks a lot.

Karin now calls up her friends. Who's coming? Who's not coming?

Yes, I'd love to come!
Michaela, a friend from school

Oh, that's too bad. Saturday I can't.
Uwe, a classmate

What? You're having a party and you're inviting me? Great!
Hans-Peter, Michaela's boyfriend

Oh, I can't. I already have something to do on Saturday.
Brigitte, a classmate

We can't at seven. But we can come a little later, around 8:30, okay?

Good! Then I'll see you at 8:30. Bye!
Lisa and Heidi, Karin's cousins

Well, of course! I am free on Saturday, that suits me fine!
Bernd, her tennis partner

No, Unfortunately I have no time on Saturday. Too bad!
Klaus, a classmate

B1 What's there to eat and drink?

HEIDI Hey, Karin! We're hungry. When are we going to eat?
KARIN Right away!
HEIDI What are we having anyway?
KARIN There's soup—a goulash soup—potato salad, hamburgers, bratwurst, sandwiches with cold cuts, and cheese sandwiches . . . and of course cake, too.
HEIDI And to drink?
KARIN Look! We have strawberry punch, lemonade, fanta, cola, mineral water, . . . uh . . . apple juice, and my mother's making coffee too.
HEIDI Great! When are we finally going to get started? I'm hungry as a bear!

What do you have for me?
For you? Apple juice.

What's there to eat? Who's hungry?
Soup, hamburgers, cheese sandwiches, bratwurst, potato salad, cake, and sandwiches with cold cuts.

And what's there to drink? Who's thirsty?
Mineral water, Fanta, apple juice, lemon soda, strawberry punch, cola, coffee

B4 Hans-Peter likes to eat everything!

KARIN What are you having to eat? A hamburger?
HANS-PETER Of course! I like hamburgers.
KARIN Who's the lemonade for?
HANS-PETER For me.
KARIN What, you're drinking lemonade?
HANS-PETER So what?! I like lemonade.

C1 What would you like? A hamburger?

KARIN What would you like, Matthias? Hm? Goulash soup? A hamburger?
MATTHIAS No, no soup, please. And no hamburger. I'll . . . ah . . . take a bratwurst.

KARIN And what are you having, Christine? A sandwich with cold cuts, maybe?
CHRISTINE Yes, please.
KARIN And a cola?
CHRISTINE No cola, please. I'll take mineral water.
HANS-PETER And I'll have a hamburger, a bratwurst, a sandwich with cold cuts . . .
KARIN Anything else?
HANS-PETER No, thanks.
KARIN Well, then, enjoy your meal!
MICHAELA Mr. Haupt, what would you like to drink? Lemon soda? Fanta?
MR. HAUPT Not fanta. Hm, I'll drink some coffee.

D1 So, what will we do now?

So, what will we do now? Who has an idea?

MICHAELA I would like to hear Hans-Peter's cassette. —Where do you have your cassette recorder?
CHRISTINE Karin, where do you have your record player? I would like to hear a record.
HANS-PETER Where's the music? I want to dance!
UWE I would like to see a film. —Do you have a video recorder?
BERND See a film? You're crazy! Would you rather hear a joke?

Quiet! Bernd is going to tell a joke!

Boy, Bernd! Your jokes are dumb!

HEIDI I have an idea: now we'll play a guessing game!
LISA A guessing game? I'd rather have a discussion.

D3 How's the party?

Karin, your parents are so nice!
Hey, Bernd! Your cassette is terrible!
I think your house is so cozy.
Great party!
The food is terrific!
Delicious!

Is that Michaela? Who is she dancing with?
Uwe? He really dances well!
Michaela looks fantastic!
Great music!

Michaela and Hans-Peter think the food is great. What do they say?

HANS-PETER Mrs. Haupt, your potato salad tastes excellent.

MRS. HAUPT Really? Is it good?
HANS-PETER Really great!
MRS. HAUPT Then I'm happy.
MICHAELA Your sandwiches with cold cuts look delicious.
MRS. HAUPT Oh, and do they also taste good?
MICHAELA And how!
MRS. HAUPT I'm glad.

10 LET'S GO OUT!

A1 What do our young people do?

Our young people: they have money, they go out, and they have many interests. You see them at the movies, at concerts, and at sports events: they know what to do with their free time! —What do our friends do? How do they spend their leisure time? Where do they go? What do they do? Let's ask!

Well, I go out a lot, two or three times a week. I go into the city, ah . . . I go to the movies, to the theater, . . . and sometimes to a concert. Or I visit friends. Then we go out together.

We're a clique, three boys and three girls, and . . . well . . . we ride bikes, we go swimming on the weekend, we play squash, once a month we bowl, sometimes we go dancing, to a disco, . . . well, and we go to concerts. We like rock concerts best.

My leisure time? I go to visit friends, we listen to cassettes, and sometimes we go to the movies. Also to the theater. I have lots of books, and I like to read too. I also enjoy staying at home.

I visit friends and we go out together. Often we just take a stroll through the city, we go to a café, and we eat some ice cream. Sometimes we go to the movies—especially if the film is good and exciting.

A6 Are you planning to do something, Sabine?

STEFAN Sabine! Hello!
SABINE Stefan! Well, hi! How are you?
STEFAN Thanks, terrific! Boy, this is great! What are you doing now? Are you doing anything?
SABINE No. Why?
STEFAN Then we can do something together, okay?
SABINE Great! —Well then, what should we do?
STEFAN Well, we can . . . we can go to the city and walk around. Or would you rather go to a café? Have some ice cream?
SABINE Boy, that's great! Terrific!

Let's go to the movies! There's a good film at the Roxi.

Or would you like to go to a concert? To a rock concert?

A8 How are you?

Great!
Fine, thanks.
Not bad.
So-so.
Bad.
Miserable! Terrible!

B1 Concert or Movie?

STEFAN Hey, Sabine, do you want to go to the movies or would you rather go to a concert?
SABINE Oh, Stefan, it's the same to me. Hey, let's take a look in the paper.
SABINE Here, concerts.
STEFAN Who's singing?
SABINE There's Falco . . . which singer do you like?
STEFAN I like a lot of them. Look, Sabine, this group is terrific!
SABINE Which group?
STEFAN The Scorpions. Do you like the group?
SABINE Wow, that's my favorite group! What groups do you like best?
STEFAN I like all rock groups.
SABINE Me too, but I especially like the Scorpions. Too bad that the concerts start so late. I'm supposed to be home at 10 o'clock.
STEFAN Then let's go to the movies, okay?
SABINE Good!

B3 What kind of films do you like to see?

SABINE What kind of films do you like to see?
STEFAN Who is your favorite star?
SABINE Hm, *High Noon*—what kind of a film is that?
STEFAN That's a western. Do you like westerns?
SABINE Not especially.
STEFAN Look, *Piranha 2*. I think that's a nature film.
SABINE Oh, don't be silly! That's an action film, not a nature film!

B7 What kind of films are they?

What kind of film is *Out of Africa?*
An adventure film.
Do you know the actors?
Of course!

What kind of film is . . . ?
. . . is a . . .

Out of Africa
an adventure film

High Noon
a western

The Boat
a war movie

The Man with Two Brains
a comedy

Werewolf in London
a horror movie

Piranha 2
an action film

Aliens
a science fiction movie

Liebesgeschichte
a romance

C1 What kind of films do you like?

STEFAN Which film would you like to see today?
STUDENT Just a minute . . . what's it called again? The film with Steve Martin. —Oh, yes! *The Man with Two Brains.*
STEFAN That film is funny. Do you like Steve Martin?
STUDENT I like him a lot.
STEFAN Me too.

STEFAN Mr. Sperling, what kind of movies do you like?
MR. SPERLING Me? I like science fiction movies best of all.
STEFAN Really? You like science fiction movies?
MR. SPERLING Yes. I think they're interesting and often very exciting.

STEFAN What kind of movies do you two like?
1ST GIRL We like love stories, action films—just no war movies.
STEFAN Why don't you like war movies?
2ND GIRL I think war movies are cruel and sad.
1ST GIRL I hate them.

D1 What did you do last night?

TEACHER Herbert, what did you do last night?
HERBERT I went to the movies.
TEACHER What did you see?
HERBERT *Out of Africa.* A terrific movie!

TEACHER And you, Karin? What did you do?
KARIN I visited friends and we played cards.

TEACHER And you, Wiebke?
WIEBKE I stayed home. I read a book.

11 BUYING PRESENTS

A1 Presents for Friends and Family

ANDREA What on earth should I give my father? He has a birthday soon. What do you think? Do you have an idea? What do you usually give your father?
MONIKA Oh, I buy my father a book most of the time. He likes travel books.
ANDREA Hm, Dad already has so many books. And what should I give my grandparents? Their golden wedding anniversary is coming up.
MONIKA Look, Andrea, there are so many presents.

What should I give?
A passport case?
A wallet? This wallet is chic.
A radio, perhaps?
Perfume? This perfume is great!
A wristwatch, a quartz watch?
A calendar?
A bracelet . . . or a necklace?
A record?
A vase for your grandparents?
Or a bouquet of flowers?
Hey, I have it: a box of fancy chocolates!

B1 In the Department Store

ANDREA Miss!
SALESPERSON Yes? May I help you?
ANDREA How much is this sweater, please?
SALESPERSON The sweaters are on sale today. Every sweater is 18 marks.
ANDREA Thank you!
SALESPERSON You're welcome.

Are you taking this sweater?
And this shirt? these scarves? this cap?
I don't know yet.

Every sweater, every shirt, every cap
Every T-shirt only 10 marks!
All scarves, every blouse, all shoes, every pair of pants, every tie, every coat

B9 Do you have this sweater in blue, perhaps?

SALESPERSON This sweater is pretty, isn't it?
MONIKA Yes, it's very nice. Only I don't like red. Do you perhaps have it in blue? Blue is my favorite color.
SALESPERSON I think so. Here is this sweater in blue.
MONIKA Good, I'll take it. The blue is great!

We also have this shirt in many colors:
in white, in grey, in red
in black, in yellow, in beige
in green, in brown
in light blue, in dark blue

C1 Gift Ideas

What are you going to give him?
What are you giving her?

For Mother's Day? Give her perfume.
Happy Mother's Day!

For Father's Day? Buy him a wallet.
Happy Father's Day!

For an anniversary? Give them flowers.
Best wishes on your anniversary!

For his birthday? Give him a T-shirt.
Happy Birthday!

For Christmas? Give her a watch.
Merry Christmas!

C9 When is your birthday?

My birthday is in the fall.
My birthday is in May.

C10 When is your birthday? Or your Name Day?

My birthday is on May 4.

C16 What did you give him?

—Hey, tell me, when was your brother's birthday?
—On May 2.
—What did you buy him?
—A sweater.

—When was your name day?
—On the eighth of April.

—What did you give your parents?
—I gave them a box of chocolates.

GERMAN-ENGLISH VOCABULARY

This vocabulary includes almost all words in this textbook, both active and passive. Active words and phrases are those introduced in basic material and listed in the **Wortschatz** sections of the units. You are expected to know and be able to use active vocabulary. All other words—those appearing in the Introduction, in exercises, in optional and visual material, in the Try Your Skills and **Zum Lesen** sections, in the review units, and in the pictorial **Landeskunde** sections—are considered passive. Passive vocabulary is for recognition only. The meaning of passive words and phrases can usually be understood from context or may be looked up in this vocabulary.

With some exceptions, the following are not included: most proper nouns, forms of verbs other than the infinitive, and forms of determiners other than the nominative.

Nouns are listed with definite article and plural form, when applicable. The numbers in the entries refer to the unit where the word or phrase first appears. A number in black, heavy type indicates that the word or phrase has been actively introduced in that unit. Passive vocabulary is followed by numerals in light type.

The following abbreviations are used in this vocabulary: adj (adjective), pl (plural), pp (past participle), sep (separable prefix), sing (singular), and s. th. (something).

A

ab *from, starting at,* **4;** *leaves, departs,* 5; ab und zu *now and then,* **7**
der **Abend:** zu Abend *in the evening,* 9
die **Abendzeitung, -en** *evening paper,* 7
der **Abenteuerfilm, -e** *adventure film,* **10**
aber *but,* **2**
abgiessen (sep) *to drain,* 9
abheben (sep) *to lift,* **5**
die **Abiturklasse, -n** *graduating class*
die **Abkürzung, -en** *abbreviation,* 4
ABR = Amtliches Bayrisches Reisebüro *Bavarian State Travel Bureau,* 8
ach: ach so! *oh, I see!* **5;** ach, Mutti! *oh, Mom!* **7**
acht *eight,* **1**
Achtung! *attention!* 2
achtzehn *eighteen,* **1**
achtzig *eighty,* **5**
der **Action-Film, -e** *action film,* **10**
ADAC = Allgemeiner Deutscher Automobil-Club *German Automobile Club*
das **Adressbuch, ⸚er** *address book,* **5**
ähnlich *similar,* 10
die **Ahnung:** keine Ahnung! *I have no idea!* **7**
Algebra *algebra,* **2**
alle *all; everyone,* **5;** alle drei Jahre *every three years*
allein *alone,* **7**
alles *everything; all,* **5;** alles andere *everything else,* **7;** alles Gute zum . . . *all the best wishes on . . .,* **11;** das ist alles *that's all,* **5**
der **Alphornbläser, -** *alpenhorn player*
als *than,* 7
also *well then,* **10**
alt *old,* **1**
der **Altar, ⸚e** *altar*
das **Alter** *age,* 3
ältest- *oldest*
am: am ersten *on the first,* **11;** am ersten Mai *on May first,* **11;** am Freitag *on Friday,* **2;** am Main *on the Main River;* am Sonntag *on Sunday,* **3;** am Tag *(times) a day,* **3;** am Wochenende *on the weekend,* **3**
der **Amerikaner, -** *American* (person), **5;** er ist Amerikaner *he's an American,* **5**
amerikanisch *American* (adj), 3
an *to,* 3; *arrives,* 5; an der Isar *on the Isar (River),* **7**
ander-: eine andere *another,* 10; in anderen Städten *in other cities,* 5; in einem anderen Staat *in another state,* 8
die **andern** *the others,* 4
ändern: sich ändern *to change,* 5
anders *different,* 7
der **Anfang, ⸚e** *beginning;* Anfang Oktober *beginning of October*
anfangen (sep) *to start,* **10**
das **Angebot:** im Angebot *on sale,* **11;** unser Schul-Spezial-Angebot *our school special offer,* 2
angezeigter: angezeigter Betrag *the amount shown,* 5
angezogen: gut angezogen *well-dressed,* 11
der **Ankauf** *purchase, buying,* 5
anprobieren (sep) *to try on,* 11
anrufen (sep) *to call up,* **9**
die **Anschlüsse** (pl) *connections,* 8
anspruchsvoll *stimulating,* 10
die **Antwort, -en** *answer,* 10
antworten *to answer,* 9
die **Anzeige, -n** *ad,* 3
der **Anzug, ⸚e** *(man's) suit,* 11
der **Apfel, ⸚** *apple,* 6
der **Apfelsaft, ⸚e** *apple juice,* **9**
Apollinaries *brand name of a mineral water,* 9
der **Apparat, -e** *phone,* **5**
Appetit: guten Appetit! *enjoy your meal!* **9**

der **April** *April,* **11**
die **Arbeit, -en** *work,* 5; bei der Arbeit *at work;* nach der Arbeit *after work*
arbeiten *to work,* 6
arm: armer Peter! *poor Peter!* **6**
das **Armband, ¨er** *bracelet,* **11**
die **Armbanduhr,-en** *wristwatch,* **11**
arrogant *arrogant,* **6**
der **Artikel, -** *article* (grammar), 1; *article for a newspaper or magazine,* 2
Aschenputtel *Cinderella,* 6
Aschermittwoch *Ash Wednesday,* 10
die **Attraktion, -en** *attraction,* 7
attraktiv *attractive,* **6**
auch *also,* **1;** ich auch *me too,* **3**
der **Audi, -s** *Audi* (a German-made car), **6**
auf *on,* **6;** *to,* 9; auf dem Marktplatz *at the market;* auf der Party *at the party,* 9; auf nach . . . *off to . . .,* **5;** auf Wiederhören! *goodbye* (on the phone), **5;** auf Wiedersehen! *goodbye!* **1;** schau auf die Karte! *look at the map,* 1
die **Auferstehungsfeier** *celebration of the Resurrection*
aufgebaut: ist aufgebaut worden *was built up,* 5
aufpassen: ich pass schon auf *I'll be careful,* **7;** pass bitte auf! *please be careful!* **7**
der **Aufschnitt** *cold cuts,* **7**
aufschreiben (sep) *to write down,* 8
der **Auftrag:** im Auftrag *commissioned by,* 7
das **Auge, -n** *eye,* 2
der **Augenblick:** im selben Augenblick *at the same moment,* 5
der **August** *August,* **11**
die **Auktion, -en** *auction,* 11
das **Au-pair-Mädchen, -** *mother's helper,* 6
aus *from,* **1;** *out, over,* **2;** *out of,* 4; aus der Schweiz *from Switzerland,* **1;** die Schule ist aus *school's out, over,* **1**
das **Ausflugsschiff, -e** *excursion boat*
der **Ausgang, ¨e** *exit,* **5**
ausgehen (sep) *to go out,* **10**
ausgezeichnet *excellent,* **9**
die **Auskunft** *information,* **5;** an der Auskunft *at the information desk,* 5
das **Ausland** *abroad, foreign country,* 10
das **Auslandsgespräch, -e** *telephone call to a foreign country,* 5
auspacken (sep) *to unpack,* 6; er packt den Rucksack aus *he unpacks his backpack,* **6**
aussehen (sep) *to look (like), appear,* **6;** gut aussehen *to look good; to be handsome, pretty, attractive,* **6**
die **Ausspracheübung, -en** *pronunciation exercise,* 1
aussprechen (sep) *to pronounce,* 6
aussuchen (sep) *to choose,* 10
ausverkauft *sold out,* 10
auswählen (sep) *to choose, select,* 2
ausziehen (sep) *to take off,* 11
das **Auto, -s** *car,* **6;** mit dem Auto *by car,* **2**
der **Autor, -en** *author,* 3

B

der **Bäcker, -** *baker,* 1, **7**
die **Bäckersfrau, -en** *baker's wife,* 7
das **Bad, ¨er** *bathroom,* **6**
die **Badener Weinstrasse** *scenic road winding through the wine-growing region of the state of Baden*
die **Bahn:** mit der Bahn *by train,* **5**
der **Bahnhof, ¨e** *railroad station,* 8; am Bahnhof *at the station,* 8; auf dem Bahnhof *at the station,* 8
die **Bahnhofsmission** *Traveler's Aid Society,* 8
die **Bahnpolizei** *railroad police,* 8
bald *soon,* **11**
der **Balkon, -s** *balcony,* 6
der **Ball, ¨e** *ball,* 6; sie geht auf einen Ball *she goes to a ball,* 6
die **Banane, -n** *banana*
die **Bank, -en** *bank,* **5**
der **Bankangestellte, -n** *bank teller,* **5**
bar *cash,* 11; zahlen Sie bar? *will you pay cash?* 11
der **Bärenhunger:** ich habe einen Bärenhunger! *I'm as hungry as a bear!* **9**
barock *Baroque,* 7
der **Bart, ¨e** *beard; mustache,* 5
Basel *Basel,* **1**
Basketball *basketball,* **3**
das **Basteln** *doing crafts and hobbies,* 10
der **Bau:** 1. Bau *first construction,* 7
das **Bauernbrot, -e** *dark peasant bread*
der **Baum, ¨e** *tree*
Bayern *Bavaria,* **7**
bayrisch *Bavarian* (adj), 7; das bayrische Umland *Bavarian countryside surrounding Munich,* 7
der **Beamte, -n** *official,* **5**
bedeuten *to mean,* 5
begehren *to desire,* 7
beginnen *to begin,* 10
beginnt *begins,* **2**
begrüssen *to greet*
bei *by, with,* 6; *at,* 9; bei den Nedels *at the Nedels',* **6;** bei Gabi *at Gabi's house,* 5; bei Grün *by the green* (symbol), **5;** bei uns *in our country, at home,* 9
die **beiden** *the two of them,* 5
das **Beige** *the color beige,* **11**
beim: beim Bäcker *at the baker's,* **7**
das **Beispiel, -e** *example,* 5; zum Beispiel *for example,* 5
bekommen *to get, receive,* **6**
Belgien *Belgium,* 1
beliebt *popular,* 10
beraten: sich beraten lassen *to get advice,* 11
der **Berg, -e** *mountain*
die **Bergmesse, -n** *mass celebrated on top of a mountain*
das **Bergsteigen** *mountain climbing*
Bern *Bern,* 1
berücksichtigen *to consider, take into consideration,* 5
berühmt *famous,* 7
beschreiben *to describe,* 6
die **Beschreibung, -en** *description,* 6
besetzt *occupied,* **5;** *busy* (a phone), **5**
besonders *especially,* **10**
besprechen *to discuss,* 10
besser *better,* 6
best- *best,* 9
bestimmt *surely,* 10
der **Besuch** *company,* **7**
besuchen *to visit,* **3;** Freunde besuchen *to visit friends,* **3**
der **Besucher, -** *visitor,* 7
betrachten *to look, observe,* 11; er betrachtet sich *he looks at himself,* 11
der **Betrag:** angezeigter Betrag *the amount shown,* 5
bevor *before,* 11
bewölkt *cloudy, overcast,* **7**
die **Bibel** *Bible,* 6
das **Bier** *beer,* 9
das **Bierzelt, -e** *tent at a beer festival or carnival where you drink beer and eat*
das **Bild, -er** *picture,* 2
das **Bilder-Quiz** *picture quiz,* 3
die **Bio** *short for* Biologie, **2**
die **Biologie** *biology,* **2**
bis *to,* 6; bis dann! *see you later,* **1;** bis gleich *see you soon,* **5;** von . . . bis *from . . . to,* **1**
bisher *until now,* 2
bisschen: ein bisschen *a little,* 6
bist: du bist *you are* **1;** du bist's *it's you,* **5**
bitte *please,* **2;** *you're welcome,* **2;** bitte! *here you are!* **5;** bitte schön! *you're welcome,* **6;** bitte sehr! *you're welcome,* **5**
bitten: darf ich mal bitten? *may I have this dance?* 9
das **Blatt, ¨er** *sheet (of paper),* 10
das **Blau** *the color blue,* **11;** in Blau *in blue,* **11**
bleiben *to stay,* **5**
das **Bleigiessen** *pouring lead* (a custom on New Year's Eve—the shape the lead takes tells you something about the new year)
der **Bleistift, -e** *pencil,* **2**
der **Blick, -e** *view;* mit Blick auf *with a view of*
blöd *stupid, dumb,* **2;** das ist blöd! *that's too bad!* **7**
blond *blond,* **6**

bloss: was schenke ich bloss meinem Vater? *what on earth should I give my father?* **11**
die **Blume, -n** *flower,* **11**
die **Blumenfrau, -en** *flower lady*
die **Bluse, -n** *blouse,* **11**
BMW = Bayerische Motorenwerke *Bavarian Motor Works* (BMW is a German-made car)
der **Bodensee** *Lake Constance*
Bord: an Bord *on board,* 5
böse *mean, bad, wicked,* 6
die **Bratwurst, ⸚e** *fried sausage,* **7**
brauchen *to need,* **5**
das **Braun** *the color brown,* **11**
bräunen *to brown,* 9
das **Braunkohlenwerk, -e** *brown-coal mine*
BRD = Bundesrepublik Deutschland *Federal Republic of Germany,* 1
die **Bremer-Stadtmusikanten** (pl) *The Bremen Town Musicians,* 6
der **Brief, -e** *letter,* 1
der **Briefeinwurf** *letter drop,* 5
der **Brieffreund, -e** *pen pal,* 1
die **Briefmarke, -n** *stamp,* **3**
das **Briefmarkensammeln** *stamp collecting,* 3
die **Brieftasche, -n** *passport case,* **11**
die **Brille, -n** *glasses,* **6**
bringen *to bring,* **9**
BRK = das Bayrische Rote Kreuz *Bavarian Red Cross,* 8
das **Brot, -e** *bread,* **7**
die **Brotzeit** *between-meal snack or light meal* (Bavarian), 7
der **Bruder, ⸚** *brother,* **6**
brünett *brunette,* **6**
der **Brunnen, -** *well,* 6
brutal *brutal,* **10**
das **Buch, ⸚er** *book,* **6**
der **Büchermuffel, -** *person who doesn't like books,* 3
die **Buchhandlung, -en** *book store,* 4
der **Buchstabe, -n** *letter* (of the alphabet), 10
bummeln *to stroll,* 10
die **Bundesrepublik** *Federal Republic,* 1
die **Bundesrepublik Deutschland** *Federal Republic of Germany,* 1
bürsten *to brush,* 11
der **Bus:** mit dem Bus *by bus,* **2**
der **Butt, -e** *flounder,* 3
die **Butter** *butter,* **7**

C

das **Café, -s** *café,* 10; in ein Café gehen *to go to a café,* **10**
der **Charakter** *character,* 7
charmanteste *most chaming,* 7
der **Chinesische Turm** *name of a well-known sight in Munich,* **7**
der **Christkindlmarkt** *Christmas market*
die **Clique, -n** *clique,* **10**
die **Cola, -s** *cola,* 7
die **Colonie, -n** *colony, settlement,* 5
die **Comics** (pl) *comics,* **3**
der **Computer, -** *computer,* 3
das **Computerspiel, -e** *computer game,* 3
die **Confiserie, -n** *candy shop*

D

da *there; here,* **2;** da drüben *over there,* **2;** da kommt *here comes,* **2;** wir sind da *we'll be there,* **5;** *we're here,* **6**
das **Dach, ⸚er** *roof*
damit *so that,* 6
Dänemark *Denmark,* 1
Dank: tausend Dank! *thanks a million!* **6;** vielen Dank! *thanks a lot!* **6**
danken *to thank,* **6;** danke! *thanks! thank you!* **2;** nichts zu danken *don't mention it,* **6**
dann *then,* **2**
darf: darf ich mal bitten? *may I have this dance?* 9; was darf es sein? *may I help you?* **11**
darüber: sprechen wir darüber! *let's talk about it,* 7, 10
das *the; that,* **1;** das ist *that is,* **1;** das sind *that makes, that comes to,* **5;** *these are,* **6**
dass *that,* **6**
dazugeben (sep) *to add to it,* 9
DDR = Deutsche Demokratische Republik *German Democratic Republic,* **1**
das **Deckenfresko, -ken** *ceiling fresco*
dein, deine *your* (sing), **6**
denken *to think,* 5
denn (particle), **5;** *because,* 9
der *the,* **1**
deutsch- *German* (adj), 9; das deutsche Geld *German money,* **5**
das **Deutsch** *German* (language), **2**
der **Deutsche, -n** *German* (person), **5**
die **Deutsche Demokratische Republik** *German Democratic Republic,* 1
Deutschland *Germany,* **1**
der **Deutschlehrer, -** *German teacher* (m), **1**
die **Deutschlehrerin, -nen** *German teacher* (f), **1**
der **Devisenkurs, -e** *rate of exchange,* 5
der **Dezember** *December,* **11**
der **Dialog, -e** *dialogue,* 5, 10
dich *you* (sing), 1, **9**
dick *fat,* 6
der **Dicke, -n** *fat one,* 6
die *the,* **1**
der **Dienstag, -e** *Tuesday,* **2**
dies- *this, these,* **11**
das **Ding, -e** *thing,* 12
dir *you* (sing), 7; wie steht's mit dir? *what about you?* 2
die **Disko, -s** *disco,* **10;** in eine Disko gehen *to go to a disco,* **10**
das **Disko-Tanzen** *disco dancing,* 9
die **Diskothek, -en** *discothèque,* 10
diskutieren *to discuss,* **9**
DM *abbreviation for Deutsche Mark,* **2**
die **D-Mark** = Deutsche Mark *German monetary unit,* **5**
doch (particle), 5; du kommst doch aus Denver, ja? *you do come from Denver, don't you?* 5
der **Dollar, -** *dollar,* **5**
der **Dom, -e** *cathedral,* **7**
die **Donau** *Danube River*
der **Donnerstag, -e** *Thursday,* **2**
das **Dorf, ⸚er** *village,* **7**
der **Dorfbummel** *stroll through the village,* 12
dort *there,* **2;** dort drüben *over there,* **2**
dorthin (to) there, 8; wie kommst du dorthin? *how do you get there?* 8
das **Drachenfliegen** *hang gliding,* 3
dran: jetzt bist du dran *now it's your turn,* 1
drei *three,* **1**
dreimal *three times,* **3**
dreissig *thirty,* 2, **5**
dreizehn *thirteen,* **1**
die **Dressur** *training*
dritt-: in der Dritten Welt *in the Third World,* 10; zum ersten, zum zweiten, zum dritten! *going, going, gone!* 11
drüben: da drüben *over there,* **2;** dort drüben *over there,* **2**
das **Drücken:** durch Drücken der grünen Taste *by pressing the green button,* 5
dtv = Deutscher Taschenbuch Verlag *German paperback publisher*
du *you* (sing), **1;** du, . . . *hey, . . .,* **2**
dumm *dumb, stupid,* 6, **10**
der **Dummkopf, ⸚e** *dummy,* 6
dunkel *dark,* **6**
das **Dunkelblau** *the color dark blue,* 11
dunkelblond *dark blond,* **6**
durch *through,* **5**
das **Durcheinander** *confusion, mix-up,* 9
das **Duzen** *addressing someone with* du, 9

E

echt *real, genuine,* 7
ehemalig *former*
das **Ei, -er** *egg,* **7**
eigen- *own,* 10; aus eigener Metzgerei *from our own butcher shop,* 7
eigentlich *actually,* 10
der **Eigentümer, -** *owner*
ein, eine *a, an,* **2, 3**
einfach *simple, easy,* 1; *simply,* 7

die **Einkaufsrunde** *shopping trip* (from store to store), 7

eingeladen *invited,* 9
einige *several, some,* 3
einkaufen (sep) *to shop,* 7; einkaufen gehen *to go shopping,* **7**
die **Einkaufsliste, -n** *shopping list,* 9
die **Einkaufsrunde** *shopping trip* (from store to store), 7
der **Einkaufszettel, -** *shopping list,* 7
einladen (sep) *to invite,* **9**
die **Einladungskarte, -n** *invitation,* 9
einmal *once,* **3;** *someday,* 9
eins *one,* **1;** eine Eins *a one* (see note, p 51), **2**
der **Einwohner, -** *inhabitant,* 7
das **Eis** *ice cream,* **7**
das **Eishockey** *ice hockey,* **3**
das **Eistanzen** *ice dancing,* 3
elf *eleven,* **1**
das **Elsass** *Alsace-Lorraine*
die **Eltern** (pl) *parents,* 6, **9**
das **Ende** *end;* Ende gut, alles gut! *all's well that ends well,* 5; Ende September *end of September;* zu Ende *over,* 12
endlich *finally,* **5**
englisch *English* (adj), 4
Englisch *English* (language), **2**
der **Englische Garten** *well-known public park in Munich,* **7**
entscheiden *to decide,* 11; wie entscheidest du dich? *how do you decide?* 11
Entschuldigung! *excuse me,* **2**
entwirf: entwirf eine Geburtstagskarte! *design a birthday card,* 11
er *he; it,* **2**
erbaut *built,* 5
die **Erdbeerbowle, -n** *strawberry punch,* 9
die **Erdkunde** *geography,* 4
erhalten *preserved,* 5
erinnern an *to commemorate*
die **Erklärung, -en** *explanation,* 1
erleben *to experience,* 7
erst: am ersten *on the first,* **11;** am ersten Mai *on May first* (see p 271), **11;** ihr erstes Kind *her first child,* 6; zum ersten, zum zweiten, zum dritten! *going, going, gone!* 11
erwarten *to expect,* 5
erzählen *to tell,* **9;** erzähl mal *tell,* 2
es *she; it,* **2;** es gibt *there is, there are,* **5**
essen *to eat,* **5, 7**
das **Essen** *food; eating; meal,* 9; beim Essen *while eating, at meals,* 9
der **Essig** *vinegar,* 9
das **Esszimmer, -** *dining room,* **6**
etwa *about, approximately,* 5
etwas *something,* **5;** etwas später *a little later,* **9;** etwas unfreundlich *a little unfriendly,* 6
euch *you* (pl), 5
euer, eure *your* (pl), **9**
Europa *Europe,* 1
der **Euro-Scheck, -s** *checking service providing members with checks that can be cashed in many European countries,* 11
die **Expressannahme** *express (baggage) check,* 8
die **Express-Ausgabe** *express pickup,* 8

F

das **Fach, ⸚er** *subject,* **2**
das **Fachwerkhaus, ⸚er** *half-timbered house*
fahren *to go, drive, ride,* **10;** in die Stadt fahren *to go into town,* **10**
der **Fahrplan, ⸚e** *(train) schedule, timetable,* 5
der **Fahrplanauszug, ⸚e** *excerpt from a train schedule,* 8
fällt *falls,* 6
die **Familie, -n** *family,* **5;** die Familie Nedel *the Nedel family,* **5**
die **Fanta** *orange-flavored soda,* **9**
das **Fantasy-Buch, ⸚er** *fantasy book,* **3**
die **Farbe, -n** *color,* **11;** in vielen Farben *in many colors,* **11**
das **Farbenspiel, -e** *color game,* 11
die **Fassade, -n** *front of a building,* 7
fast *almost,* 10
die **Fastnacht** *Shrove Tuesday,* 10
faulenzen *to lie around, be lazy,* **3**
der **Februar** *February,* **11**
fehlen *to be missing,* **5**
feiern *to celebrate*
der **Feiertag, -e** *holiday*
die **Ferien** (pl) *vacation,* **5;** Ferien machen *to go on vacation,* **5;** schöne Ferien! *have a nice vacation!* **5**
das **Feriendorf, ⸚er** *resort town,* 12
das **Fernsehen** *watching TV,* 10
das **Fest, -e** *festival,* 7
der **Festspielort, -e** *town having a festival or pageant*
die **Festung, -en** *fortress*
das **Fett** *fat,* 9
das **Feuerwerk** *fireworks,* 10
die **Figur, -en** *figure,* 3
der **Film, -e** *(camera) film,* **5;** *film (movie),* **9**
das **Filmfest, -e** *film festival,* 10
das **Finanzzentrum, -zentren** *financial center*
finden *to find, think, have the opinion about s.th.,* **3;** das finde ich nicht *I don't think so,* **3;** findest du? *do you think so?* **6;** ich finde mich nett *I think I'm nice,* 6; wie findest du . . .? *how do you like . . .? what do you think of . . .?* **3**
das **Fischbrot, -e** *fish sandwich,* **7**
der **Fischer, -** *fisherman,* 1
der **Fischerhafen, ⸚** *fishing port*
der **Fk-Schalter** = Fahrkartenschalter *ticket counter,* 8
Fl. = Flasche *bottle,* 7
die **Flasche, -n** *bottle,* **7;** eine Flasche Mineralwasser *a bottle of mineral water,* **7**
das **Fleisch** *meat,* **7**
fliegen *to fly,* **5**
fliessen *to flow*
der **Flug, ⸚e** *flight,* **5;** guten Flug! *have a good flight!* **5**
der **Flügelbahnhof, ⸚e** *wing of main train station, used for commuter trains,* 8
der **Flughafen, ⸚** *airport,* **5**
der **Flugplan, ⸚e** *flight schedule,* 5
der **Flugplatz, ⸚e** *airport,* 5
das **Flugticket, -s** *airplane ticket,* **5**
das **Flugzeug, -e** *airplane,* **5**
der **Flur, -e** *hall,* 6
der **Fluss, ⸚e** *river*
folgende *following,* 7
der **Fotoapparat, -e** *camera*
fotografieren *to photograph,* 11
die **Frage, -n** *question,* 10
fragen *to ask,* **5;** fragen wir mal *let's ask,* **10;** ich frag' mal . . . *I'll just ask . . .,* **5**
Franken *Franconia*
fränkisch: die Fränkische Schweiz *Franconian Switzerland (part of Franconia having many lakes)*
Frankreich *France,* 1
Französisch *French (language),* 5
die **Frau, -en** *Mrs.,* **1;** *woman,* 5
das **Fräulein, -** *Miss,* **1**
frei *off,* **2;** er hat frei *he has off, he has no school,* **2**
der **Freitag, -e** *Friday,* **2**
die **Freizeit** *free time, leisure time,* **10;** in deiner Freizeit *in your free time,* **3**
der **Freizeitmuffel, -** *person who doesn't know what to do with free time,* **10**
die **Fremdenführerin, -nen** *tour guide* (f), 7
das **Fresko, Fresken** *fresco*
freuen: das freut mich *I'm glad,* **9**
der **Freund, -e** *friend,* 3; *boyfriend,* **9**
die **Freundin, -nen** *girl friend,* **6**
freundlich *friendly,* **6**
frisch *fresh,* 7
Frl. = Fräulein *Miss,* **1**
froh *happy, glad,* **9;** da bin ich aber froh! *I'm glad to hear that!* **9**
fröhlich: fröhliche Weihnachten! *Merry Christmas!* **11**
die **Fronleichnamsprozession, -en** *Corpus Christi Day procession*
der **Frosch, ⸚e** *frog,* 6
der **Froschkönig** *The Frog Prince,* 6
das **Frühjahr** *spring,* 3; im Frühjahr *in the spring,* **3**
der **Frühlingsanfang** *beginning of spring*
die **Fuggerei** *trading company run by the Fugger family in the 16th century*
fühlen *to feel,* 11
das **Fundbüro, -s** *lost-and-found department,* 8

fünf *five,* **1**
fünfunddreissig *thirty-five,* **2**
fünfundfünfzig *fifty-five,* **2**
fünfundvierzig *forty-five,* **2**
fünfundzwanzig *twenty-five,* **2**
fünfzehn *fifteen,* **1**
fünfzig *fifty,* **2**
für *for,* **5**
furchtbar *terrible, awful,* **9**
die **Fürstenhochzeit, -en** *royal wedding*
der **Fuss:** am Fusse *at the foot of;* ich komme zu Fuss in die Schule *I walk to school,* **2;** zu Fuss *on foot,* **2**
Fussball *soccer,* **3**
der **Fussgänger, -** *pedestrian,* **7**
die **Fussgängerzone, -n** *pedestrian mall,* **7**

G

die **Gabel, -n** *fork,* 9
ganz *whole, entire,* 6; *completely, entirely,* 9; ganz allein *all alone,* 6; ganz genau *exactly,* 11; ganz prima! *really great!* **9;** im ganzen Land *in the whole country,* 6
gar: gar nicht *not at all,* 3
die **Garage, -n** *garage,* **6**
der **Garten, ⸚** *garden,* **6**
die **Gartenparty, -s** *garden party,* 10
der **Gärtner, -** *gardener,* 1
der **Gast, ⸚e** *guest,* 7
der **Gastbruder, ⸚** *host brother,* 6
die **Gästeliste, -n** *guest list,* 9
das **Gästezimmer, -** *guest room,* **6**
die **Gastfamilie, -n** *host family*
die **Gaststätte, -n** *restaurant,* 8
gebacken (pp) *baked,* 7
gebaut *built,* 7; man hat lange an diesem Dom gebaut *they worked on building this cathedral for a long time,* 5
geben *to give,* **11;** es gibt *there is, there are,* **5**
der **Gebirgsschütze, -n** *mountain marksman*
das **Geburtshaus, ⸚er** *house of birth*
der **Geburtstag, -e** *birthday,* **11;** er hat Geburtstag *it's his birthday,* **11;** ich habe im Mai Geburtstag *my birthday is in May,* **11;** herzliche Glückwünsche zum Geburtstag! *happy birthday!* **11;** zum Geburtstag *for (your) birthday,* **11**
der **Geburtstagskalender, -** *birthday calendar,* 11
die **Geburtstagskarte, -n** *birthday card,* 11
das **Geburtstagskind, -er** *birthday child,* 11
die **Gedächtniskirche, -n** *Memorial Church*
das **Gegenteil, -e** *opposite,* 11; ganz im Gegenteil *just the opposite,* 11
gegrillt *grilled, barbecued,* 9
gehen *to go,* **5;** der Apparat geht nicht *the phone is out of order,* **5;** es geht nicht *I can't,* **9;** geht's? *is it possible?* 12; sie gehen in die achte Klasse *they're in the eighth grade,* **2;** wann geht der Zug? *when does the train leave?* 8; wie geht's? *how are you?* **9**
das **Gehirn, -e** *brain,* 10
gehören: was gehört zusammen? *what belongs together?* 9
gehört: auf der Party gehört *heard at the party,* 9
die **Geigenbauerstadt, ⸚e** *town of violin makers*
das **Gelb** *the color yellow,* **11**
das **Geld** *money,* **5;** das deutsche Geld *German money,* **5**
das **Gemüse** *vegetable,* **7**
der **Gemüsehändler, -** *greengrocer,* **7**
gemütlich *cozy, comfortable,* **6**
die **Gemütlichkeit** *friendly, relaxed atmosphere,* 7
genau *exact,* 11; ganz genau *exactly,* 11
genug *enough,* **7**
genutzt: kann genutzt werden *can be used,* 5
die **Geographie** *geography,* **2**
das **Gepäck** *baggage,* **5**
die **Gepäckannahme** *baggage check,* 8
die **Gepäckausgabe** *baggage pickup,* 8
gerade *just now, at the moment,* 3
geradeaus *straight ahead,* **5**
gern *gladly,* 3; gern geschehen! *my pleasure!* **5;** gern (machen) *to like (to do),* **3;** ja, gern *yes, I'd like to,* **6;** nicht gern (machen) *to not like (to do),* **3**
gesagt: junge Leute haben uns gesagt *young people told us,* 10
die **Gesamtausgabe, -n** *complete edition,* 6
das **Geschäft, -e** *store,* 11
das **Geschenk, -e** *present,* **5**
die **Geschenkidee, -n** *gift idea,* **11**
der **Geschenkladen, ⸚** *gift shop,* **5**
die **Geschenkliste, -n** *gift list,* 11
die **Geschichte, -n** *history,* **2;** *story,* 5
geschlossen *closed,* 5, 12
die **Geschmackssache** *a matter of taste,* **6**
geschrieben (pp) *written,* 10
die **Geschwister** (pl) *brothers and sisters,* **6**
die **Gesellschaft, -en** *society*
das **Gespräch, -e** *conversation,* 5; *call,* 5; schreib das Gespräch auf! *write the conversation down,* 7
gestern abend *last night,* **10**
die **Getränke** (pl) *drinks,* 9
gewinnen *to win,* **3**
der **Gewohnheitsmensch, -en** *creature of habit,* 11
gewöhnlich *usually,* **11**
gewöhnt: er hat sich an die Schuhe gewöhnt *he got used to the shoes,* 11
gewonnen (pp) *won,* 11
gibt: es gibt *there is, there are,* **5;** was gibt's? *what's up?* **9**
das **Giebelhaus, ⸚er** *house with gables*
giessen *to pour,* 9
die **Gitarre, -n** *guitar,* **3**
glauben *to think, believe,* **10;** ich glaube, ja *I think so,* **11**
gleich *right away,* **9;** *same,* 10; es ist mir gleich *it's all the same to me,* **10**
das **Gleis, -e** *track,* 8
das **Glockenspiel, -e** *set of bells and mechanical figures often put in clock towers to play when the hour strikes,* **7**
das **Glück** *luck;* viel Glück *good luck!* **2**
die **Glückwünsche** (pl) *best wishes,* **11;** herzliche Glückwünsche zum . . . *best wishes on (your) . . ., happy . . .,* **11**
GmbH = Gesellschaft mit beschränkter Haftung *company with limited liability*
golden- *golden,* 6
gotisch *Gothic,* 7
der **Gott:** Gott bring mich durch diesen Tag! *God, let me survive this day!* 4; Gott sei Dank! *thank God!* **5**
g = Gramm *gram,* **7**
das **Gramm** *gram,* **7;** 200 g Aufschnitt *200 grams of cold cuts,* **7**
gratulieren *to congratulate,* 11
das **Grau** *the color grey,* **11**
grausam *cruel,* **10**
griechisch *Greek* (adj), 7
grillen *to barbecue,* 9
gross *big; tall,* **6**
die **Grösse, -n** *size,* 11
die **Grosseltern** (pl) *grandparents,* **6**
die **Grossmutter, ⸚** *grandmother,* 6
die **Grossstadt, ⸚e** *big city,* **7**
grösst- *biggest*
der **Grossvater, ⸚** *grandfather,* 6
grotesk *grotesque,* 11
Gruetzi! *hello!* (Swiss), **7**
das **Grün** *the color green,* **11**
die **Gründung:** bei Gründung der Colonie *at the founding of the colony,* 5
die **Gruppe, -n** *group,* **10**
der **Gruss, ⸚e** *greeting,* 6; viele Grüsse *best regards,* 1, 8; viele Grüsse an *best regards to,* 8
grüss dich! *hi!* **1**
die **Gulaschsuppe, -n** *goulash soup,* **9**
die **Gurke, -n** *cucumber,* 7
gut *good,* **2;** *okay,* **5;** *okay, fine,* **7;** *well,* **9;** gut, danke *fine, thanks,* **10;** guten Appetit! *enjoy your meal!* **9;** guten Flug! *have a good flight!* **5;** guten Morgen! *good morning!* **1;** guten Tag! *hello!* **1;** hör gut zu! *listen carefully,* 1
Gute: alles Gute zum . . . *all the best wishes for . . .,* **11**
Güte: ach, du meine Güte! *oh, for*

goodness' sake! 5
das **Gymnasium, Gymnasien** *type of German secondary school,* 2
die **Gymnastik:** Gymnastik machen *to do gymnastics,* **3**

H

das **Haar, -e** *hair,* 5
haben *to have,* **2;** ich hab's! *I have it!* **11**
das **Hackfleisch** *chopped meat,* **7**
haha! *ha ha!* 3
das **Hähnchen, -** *chicken,* **7**
der **Hai, -e** *shark,* 10
halb: ein halbes Pfund Butter *a half a pound of butter,* **7;** halb zehn *nine-thirty,* **2**
die **Hälfte** *half,* 7
hallo! *hi!* **1**
der **Halm, -e** *blade, piece*
die **Halskette, -n** *necklace,* **6**
das **Halstuch, ¨er** *scarf,* **11**
halten *to hold,* 9
der **Hamburger, -** *hamburger,* **9**
die **Hand, ¨e** *hand,* 5; in der Hand *in his hand,* 5
das **Handarbeiten** *doing needlework,* 10
das **Händeschütteln** *shaking hands,* 9
die **Handgepäckaufbewahrung** *carry-on luggage consignment,* 8
hängen: warum hängt ihr Haar herunter? *why is her hair hanging down?* 6
hart *hard,* 6, 10
der **Hase, -n** *hare,* 6
hassen *to hate,* **10**
hässlich *ugly,* 6
hatte *had,* 10
hätte *would have*
die **Hauptstadt, ¨e** *capital city,* **7**
das **Haus, ¨er** *house,* **6;** er schreibt nach Hause *he writes home,* **7;** nach Hause kommen *to come home,* **7;** zu Hause *at home,* 9
die **Hausaufgaben** (pl) *homework,* **2;** er macht Hausaufgaben *he's doing homework,* **2**
die **Hausfassade, -n** *house front*
Hbf = Hauptbahnhof *main train station,* 8
heben: du hebst den Hörer ab *you lift the receiver,* **5**
das **Heft, -e** *notebook,* **2**
die **Heide, -n** *heath, moor*
die **Heidschnucke, -n** *moorland sheep*
die **Heilige Kommunion** *Holy Communion*
die **Heimat** *home*
heimlich: die heimliche Hauptstadt Deutschlands *the secret capital of Germany,* **7**
heiss *hot,* **7**
heissen *to be called,* **1;** er heisst Jens *his name is Jens,* **1;** ich heisse *my name is,* **1;** wie heisst du? *what's your name?* **1;** wie heisst er denn? *what's it called again?* **10**
heiter *fair (weather),* **7**
helfen *to help,* 6
hell *light,* **6**
das **Hellblau** *the color light blue,* **11**
das **Hemd, -en** *shirt,* **11**
der **Herbst** *fall,* 3; im Herbst *in the fall,* **3**
Herr *Mr.,* **1**
herunterhängen (sep) *to hang down,* 6
das **Herz, -en** *heart,* 7
herzlich: herzliche Glückwünsche zum (Geburtstag) *best wishes on your (birthday), happy (birthday),* **11;** herzliche Grüsse *sincerely, best regards,* 6
hessisch *Hessian,* 6
heute *today,* **2**
die **Hexe, -n** *witch,* 6
hier *here,* **2;** hier Nedel *Nedel speaking,* **5**
hierherkommen (sep) *to come here,* 10
hin: da gehen wir mal hin *we'll go there sometime,* 5
der **Hintergrund** *background*
das **Hobby, -s** *hobby,* **3**
höchster: Deutschlands höchster Berg *Germany's highest mountain*
die **Hochzeit, -en** *wedding;* goldene Hochzeit *golden wedding anniversary,* **11**
der **Hochzeitstag, -e** *wedding anniversary,* **11;** zum Hochzeitstag *for (your) anniversary,* **11**
Hockey *hockey,* **3**
das **Hofbräuhaus** *a famous beer hall in Munich,* 7
höflich *polite,* 11
holen *to fetch, pick up,* **5;** *to get,* **7**
das **Holstentor** *Holsten Gate*
der **Holzschnitt, -e** *woodcut,* 6
hören *to listen,* **3;** *to hear,* 5; hör gut zu! *listen carefully!* 1; hör zu! *listen!* **9**
der **Hörer, -** *telephone receiver,* **5**
der **Horrorfilm, -e** *horror film,* **10**
das **Hörspiel, -e** *radio play*
die **Hose, -n** *pants,* **11**
hübsch *pretty,* **6**
der **Hubschrauber, -** *helicopter,* 2
der **Hund, -e** *dog,* **6**
hundert *hundred,* **5**
hunderteins *a hundred one,* **5**
der **Hunger:** Hunger haben *to be hungry,* **7**

I

ich *I,* **1;** ich? *me?* **1**
die **Idee, -n** *idea,* **9**
identifizieren *to identify,* 4
der **Igel, -** *hedgehog, porcupine,* 6
ihm *him,* 7
Ihnen *you,* 11
ihr *you* (pl), **2**
ihr, ihre *her; their,* **9**
Ihr, Ihre *your* (formal), **9**
im = in dem *in the,* **5**
die **Imbiss-Stube, -n** *snack bar,* **7**
immer *always,* **3;** noch immer nicht *still (did) not,* 11
in *in,* **2;** *into,* **5;** in der Prinzregentenstrasse *on Prinzregenten Street,* **7**
Indien *India,* 10
das **Inlandsgespräch, -e** *telephone call within the country,* 5
die **Innenstadt, ¨e** *center of the city,* **7**
die **Insel, -n** *island,* 7
das **Instrument, -e** *instrument,* **3**
interessant *interesting,* **3**
das **Interesse, -n** *interest,* **10**
der **Interpret, -en** *interpreter (of a song),* 10
das **Interview, -s** *interview,* 3
interviewen *to interview,* 9
der **Interviewer, -** *interviewer,* **3**
irgendwie *somehow,* 11
die **Isar** *Isar River,* 7
ist *is,* **1**
Italien *Italy,* 10
italienisch *Italian* (adj), 7

J

ja *yes,* **1;** ja? *okay?* **10;** ja, bitte? *yes, may I help you?* **11**
das **Jahr, -e** *year,* **7;** im Jahr *(times) a year,* **3;** Jahr für Jahr *year after year,* 7
das **Jahreszeugn.** = Jahreszeugnis, -se *report card,* 2
das **Jahrhundert, -e** *century*
jährig: die 10- bis 19jährigen *10- to 19-year-olds,* 10
der **Januar** *January,* **11;** im Januar *in January,* **11**
die **Jause, -n** *snack, small meal (Austrian),* 12
die **Jeans-Tasche, -n** *denim bag,* 2
jed- *each, every,* **11**
jemand *someone,* 6
jetzt *now,* **2**
der **Joghurt, -** *yogurt,* **7**
die **Jugend** *youth, young people,* **10**
die **Jugendlichen** (pl) *young people,* **10**
der **Juli** *July,* **11**
jung *young,* 5
der **Junge, -n** *boy,* **1**
der **Juni** *June,* **11**

K

der **Kaffee** *coffee,* **7**
der **Kaiser:** der Wilde Kaiser *mountain range in Tirol*
der **Kalender, -** *calendar,* **11**
Kalifornien *California,* **5**
kalt *cold,* **7**
die **Kamera, -s** *camera,* **5**
Kanada *Canada,* 10
das **Kapitel, -** *chapter,* 1
karibisch *Caribbean,* 10
der **Karneval, -e** *carnival, Mardi Gras*
die **Karte, -n** *map,* 1; *card,* **3;** *ticket,*

10; Karten spielen *to play cards,* **3**
das **Kartenspielen** *playing cards,* **3**
die **Kartoffel, -n** *potato,* 9
der **Kartoffelsalat, -e** *potato salad,* **9**
die **Kartoffelscheiben** (pl) *potato slices,* 9
der **Karton, -s** *carton, box,* 11
das **Karwendelgebirge** *Karwendel Mountains*
der **Käse** *cheese,* **7**
das **Käsebrot, -e** *cheese sandwich,* **9**
die **Käseplatte, -n** *platter with assorted cheeses,* 12
der **Kassenzettel, -** *cash register receipt,* 7
die **Kassette, -n** *cassette,* **2**
der **Kassetten-Recorder, -** *cassette recorder,* **9**
kaufen *to buy,* **5;** wo kauft Steffi ein? *where does Steffi shop?* 7
das **Kaufhaus, ⸚er** *department store,* **11;** im Kaufhaus *in the department store,* **11**
kegeln *to bowl,* **10**
kehrt: zurückkehren (sep) *to return,* 4
kein, keine *no, not any,* **9;** keine Sorge *don't worry,* **7**
keiner *no one,* 10
der **Keller, -** *basement, cellar,* **6**
der **Kellner, -** *waiter,* 7
die **Kellnerin, -nen** *waitress,* 7
kennen *to know,* **6;** *to know, be familiar with a place,* **7**
kennenlernen (sep) *to meet, get to know,* **6;** du lernst viele Leute kennen *you're going to meet a lot of people,* **6**
die **Kerze, -n** *candle*
kg = Kilogramm *kilogram,* **7**
das **Kilo** *short for* Kilogramm, **7;** 1 kg Tomaten *1 kilogram of tomatoes,* **7**
das **Kilogramm, -** *kilogram,* **7**
der **Kilometer, -** *kilometer,* **5**
das **Kind, -er** *child,* 6
der **Kinderfasching** *children's carnival, children's Mardi Gras*
das **Kino, -s** *movies,* **10;** gehen wir ins Kino! *let's go to the movies!* **10;** ins Kino gehen *to go to the movies,* **10**
das **Kinoplakat, -e** *movie poster,* 10
die **Kirche, -n** *church,* **7**
die **Kirsche, -n** *cherry,* **7**
klar *clear,* 6; na klar! *well, of course!* **3**
die **Klasse, -n** *class; grade,* **2;** Klasse! *great!* **3**
die **Klassenarbeit, -en** *test,* **2**
der **Klassenkamerad, -en** *classmate,* **2**
die **Klassenkameradin, -nen** *classmate* (f), **6**
das **Klassenprojekt, -e** *class project,* 1
klassisch *classical,* 6, 11
das **Klavier, -e** *piano,* 4
klein *small; short,* **6**
klick *click,* 9
klingeln: es klingelt *the phone rings,* **9**

kochen *to cook,* 9
Köln *Cologne,* **5**
das **Komma, -s** *comma,* 7
kommen *to come,* **2;** komm! *come on!* **6;** kommen nach *to get to,* **5;** wie kommt er in den Turm? *how does he get into the tower?* 6
der **Kommentar, -e** *commentary, remarks,* 10
die **Komödie, -n** *comedy,* **10**
das **Kompliment, -e** *compliment,* 9; ein Kompliment machen *to pay a compliment,* 9
der **Komponist, -en** *composer,* 10
die **Komposition, -en** *composition,* 10
der **Konflikt, -e** *conflict,* 6
der **König, -e** *king,* 7
das **König-Ludwig-Schloss, ⸚er** *castle built by King Ludwig of Bavaria,* 7
das **Königschloss, ⸚er** *royal castle,* 7
der **Königssohn, ⸚e** *king's son,* 6
die **Königstochter, ⸚** *princess, king's daughter,* 6
können *can, be able to,* **10**
das **Konzert, -e** *concert,* 10; ins Konzert gehen *to go to a concert,* **10**
der **Kopf, ⸚e** *head;* ein Kopf Salat *a head of lettuce,* **7**
korrekt *correct, proper,* 11
korrespondieren *to correspond,* 4
der **Körper, -** *body,* 4
kosten *to cost,* 2; was kosten? *how much are?* **2**
kostet: was kostet? *how much is?* **2**
kräftig *strong,* 10
krank *sick,* 5
die **Krawatte, -n** *tie,* **11**
die **Kreditbank** *bank*
die **Kreditkarte, -n** *credit card,* 11
der **Kriegsfilm, -e** *war film,* **10**
die **Krone, -n** *crown,* 6
die **Küche, -n** *kitchen,* **6**
der **Kuchen, -** *cake,* **9**
die **Kugel, -n** *ball,* 7
kühl *cool,* **7**
der **Kuli, -s** *ballpoint pen,* **2**
die **Kunst** *art,* 2
der **Kurort, -e** *health resort town*
der **Kurs, -e** *rate of exchange,* **5**
der **Kurswagen, -** *through car (of a train),* 8
kurz *short,* 10
kurzfristig *on short notice,* 5
die **Kusine, -n** *cousin* (f), **6**
küssen *to kiss,* 6

L

lachen *to laugh,* 9
das **Lachsbrot, -e** *smoked salmon (lox) sandwich,* 12
die **Ladeaufsicht** *loading supervisor,* 8
der **Laden, ⸚** *store,* 2
die **Lampe, -n** *lamp*
das **Land, ⸚er** *country,* 1; *state,* **6**
landen *to land,* **5**
das **Länderspiel, -e** *name-the-state game,* 7
die **Landeshauptstadt, ⸚e** *state capital,* 7
die **Landeskunde** *culture,* 1; ein wenig Landeskunde *a little culture,* 1
lange *long,* 5; *for a long time,* 5
langsam *slowly,* 4
längst: am längsten Tag *on the longest day,* 10
langweilig *boring,* **3**
lässt: lässt du dich gern von dem Verkäufer beraten? *do you like to get advice from the salesperson?* 11
Latein *Latin,* **2**
lateinamerikanisch *Latin American,* 10
laufend *continuously,* 7
der **Lautsprecher, -** *loudspeaker,* 5
das **Leben** *life,* 4; langsam kehrt Leben in meinen Körper zurück *slowly life is returning to my body,* 4
der **Leberkäs** (see fn p 212) **7**
lecker *delicious,* **9**
legen auf *to lay on,* 9
der **Lehrer, -** *teacher* (m), **1**
die **Lehrerin, -nen** *teacher* (f), **1**
leicht *easy,* **2**
leider *unfortunately,* **7;** ich weiss es leider nicht *I'm sorry, I don't know,* **7**
lernen *to learn,* 3
lesen *to read,* **3**
das **Lesen** *reading,* 3; zum Lesen *for reading,* 1
die **Leseübung, -en** *reading exercise,* 1
letzt- *last,* 10
die **Leute** (pl) *people,* **6**
der **Leutnant, -s** *second lieutenant,* 10
lieben *to love,* 11
lieber (machen) *to prefer (to do),* **3;** ich spiele lieber Fussball *I'd rather play soccer,* **3**
lieber (m), liebe (f) *dear,* 3
der **Liebesfilm, -e** *love story,* 10
Lieblings- (pref) *favorite,* **10**
das **Lieblingsfach, ⸚er** *favorite subject,* 4
die **Lieblingsfarbe, -n** *favorite color,* **11**
die **Lieblingsgruppe, -n** *favorite group,* **10**
der **Lieblingsstar, -s** *favorite star,* **10**
liebsten: am liebsten (machen) *to like (to do) most of all,* **3**
Liechtenstein *Liechtenstein,* 1
liegen *to lie,* 1
liest: was liest du? *what do you read?* **3**
lila *purple,* 10
die **Limo** = Limonade *lemon soda,* **9**
die **Limonade** *lemon soda,* **9**
link- *left,* 9; in der linken Hand *in the left hand,* 9
links *left, on the left,* **5**
der **Lipizzaner, -** *type of horse*
die **Liste, -n** *list,* 8
l = Liter *liter,* **7**
der **Liter, -** *liter,* **7;** ein Liter Milch *a liter of milk,* **7**

literarisch *literary*
das **Lokal, -e** *restaurant,* 9
los: wann geht's endlich los? *when are we finally going to get going?* **9;** was ist los? *what's the matter?* **7**
der **Lücken-Dialog, -e** *dialog with blanks to be filled in,* 3
der **Luftkurort, -e** *high-altitude or mountain resort*
die **Lüftlmalerei** *the tradition of painting scenes on houses*
lustig *merry, funny,* **6**

M

machen *to do,* **3;** er macht sich wenig aus *he doesn't care much about,* 11; was machst du? *what are you doing? what do you do?* **3**
macht: er macht Mathe *he's doing math,* **2**
das **Mädchen, -** *girl,* **1**
mag: München mag man *people like Munich,* 7
der **Magen, ¨** *stomach,* 7
der **Mai** *May,* **11**
der **Maibaumtanz** *dance around the Maypole*
mal (particle); ich frag' mal den Vati *I'll just ask Dad,* **5**
man *one, you (in general), people,* **10;** man spricht Deutsch *German is spoken,* 1; wie sagt man das? *how do you say that?* 1
manchmal *sometimes,* **3**
der **Mann, ¨er** *man,* 6, 7
der **Mantel, ¨** *coat,* **11**
das **Manuskript, -e** *manuscript,* 6
das **Märchen, -** *fairy tale,* 6
das **Märchenbuch, ¨er** *book of fairy tales,* 6
der **Märchenfilm, -e** *fairy-tale film,* 6
die **Märchenkassette, -n** *cassette recording of fairy tales,* 6
das **Märchenschloss, ¨er** *fairy-tale castle,* 7
das **Märchensymbol, -e** *symbol found in a fairy tale,* 6
der **Marienplatz** *square in front of the city hall in Munich,* **7**
die **Mark, -** *mark* (German monetary unit), **2;** eine Mark *one mark,* **2;** eine Mark zehn *one mark and 10 pennies,* **2;** zwei Mark *two marks,* 2
die **Marke, -n** *stamp,* 10; *make, brand,* 11
der **Marktplatz, ¨e** *marketplace*
der **März** *March,* **11**
die **Maschine, -n** *plane,* **5**
die **Maske, -n** *mask*
die **Mathe** *math,* **2**
das **Mathematikbuch, ¨er** *math book*
der **Mathematiklehrer, -** *math teacher,* **1**
die **Mathestunde, -n** *math class,* 10
die **Mauer, -n** *wall,* 5
Mau-Mau *card game similar to crazy eights,* **3**
mehr *more,* **6;** mehr als *more than,* 7
die **Meile, -n** *mile,* **5**
mein, meine *my,* **6**
meinen *to think, be of the opinion,* **11;** *to mean,* 11; meinst du? *do you think so?* **6;** meinst du mein Hemd? *do you mean my shirt?* 11; meinst du nicht? *don't you think so?* **6;** was meinst du? *what do you think?* 6
die **Meinung, -en** *opinion,* 3
die **meisten** *most,* 9
meistens *mostly,* **3;** *most of the time,* 9
die **Melodie, -n** *melody,* 10
der **Mensch, -en** *person;* Mensch! *boy! wow!* **6**
das **Merkspiel, -e** *memory game,* 5
das **Messer, -** *knife,* 9
der **Metzger, -** *butcher,* **7**
die **Metzgerei, -en** *butcher shop,* 7
der **Miesmacher, -** *grouch,* 6
mieten *to rent,* 9
die **Milch** *milk,* **7**
die **Million, -en** *million,* **7**
das **Millionendorf** *village of millions,* 7
das **Mineralwasser** *mineral water,* **7**
die **Minute, -n** *minute,* 9
mir: mit mir *with me,* 6
mischen *to mix,* 9
miserabel *miserable,* **10**
mit *with,* **7;** *along,* 7; mit dem Auto *by car,* **2;** mit dem Bus *by bus,* **2;** mit dem Moped *on (his) moped,* **2;** mit dem Rad *by bicycle,* **2;** mit der Strassenbahn *by streetcar,* **2;** mit zehn Jahren *at the age of 10,* 10
mitbringen (sep) *to bring along,* 9
mitfahren (sep) *to go along,* 12
mitgehen (sep) *to go along,* 7, 12
mitnehmen (sep) *to take along,* 9, 11; zum Mitnehmen *take-out,* 11
der **Mitschüler, -** *classmate (m),* 1
der **Mittag:** zu Mittag *at noon,* 9
mittelgross *medium-sized,* 9
mitten in *in the middle of,* 1
die **Mitternacht** *midnight,* 10
der **Mittwoch** *Wednesday,* **2**
möchten *would like to,* **5**
die **Mode** *fashion,* 11
das **Modell, -e** *model, style,* 11
der **Modemensch, -en** *person of style,* 11
modern *modern,* **6**
mogeln *to cheat,* **3**
mögen *to like,* **10;** gern mögen *to like a lot,* **11**
möglich *possible,* 10
der **Moment:** Moment mal! *wait a minute!* **2**
der **Monat, -e** *month,* 11; im Monat *(time) a month,* **3**
der **Monatskalender, -** *monthly calendar,* 12
der **Monitor, Monitoren** *monitor,* 5
der **Montag** *Monday,* **2**
das **Moped, -s** *moped,* 2; mit dem Moped *on (his) moped,* **2**
morgen *tomorrow,* **5**
der **Morgen, -** *morning,* 11; Morgen! *morning!* **1**
der **Müller, -** *miller,* 1
die **Müllerstochter, ¨** *miller's daughter,* 6
München *Munich,* **1**
der **Münchner, -** *person from Munich,* 7
das **Münchner Kindl** *official emblem of Munich,* **7**
die **Münze, -n** *coin,* **3**
das **Museum, Museen** *museum,* **7**
die **Musik** *music,* **2, 9**
musikalisch *musical,* 6
der **Musiker, -** *musician,* 10
die **Musikkassette, -n** *music cassette,* **3;** Musikkassetten hören *to listen to music cassettes,* **3**
müssen *must, have to,* **10**
das **Muster, -** *model,* 7
die **Mutter, ¨** *mother,* **5**
der **Muttertag** *Mother's Day,* **11;** zum Muttertag *for Mother's Day,* **11**
die **Mutti, -s** *mom,* **7**
die **Mütze, -n** *cap,* **11**

N

na *well,* **2;** na, dann *well then,* **9;** na gut *well, okay,* **7;** na ja *oh well,* **10;** na klar! *of course!* **3;** na und?! *so what?* **9**
nach *after, past,* **2;** to, **5;** *according to,* **10;** kommen nach *to get to,* **5;** nach Hause kommen *to come home,* 7
der **Nachbar, -n** *neighbor,* 1
nachdenken (sep) *to think about,* 10
nachgebaut *built in imitation of,* 7
der **Nachmittag, -e** *afternoon,* 5; am Nachmittag *in the afternoon,* 6; heute nachmittag *this afternoon,* 5
nachschauen (sep) *to check,* **5**
die **Nacht, ¨e** *night,* 6; in der Nacht *in the night,* 6
die **Nähe:** in der Nähe von uns *near where we live,* 10
der **Name, -n** *name,* **2**
der **Namenstag, -e** *name day,* **11;** zum Namenstag *for (your) name day,* **11**
das **Nationaltheater** *National Theater,* **7**
der **Naturfilm, -e** *nature film,* **10**
natürlich *of course,* **9**
nehmen *to take,* **9**
nein *no,* **1**
nennen *to call,* 10; *to name,* 12
nett *nice,* **6;** er sagt nie etwas Nettes *he never says anything nice,* 6
das **Netz, -e** *net shopping bag,* 7
neu *new,* 1; neue Freunde *new friends,* **1**

der **Neubau, -ten** *new building*
neun *nine,* **1**
neunzehn *nineteen,* **1**
neunzig *ninety,* **5**
neuste: das neuste Modell *the latest model,* 11
nicht *not,* **2;** nicht? *don't you think so?* **6**
nichts *nothing,* **5**
nie *never,* **3**
die **Niederlande** (pl) *the Netherlands,* 1
nö = nein *no* (casual), **10**
noch *still,* **5;** noch ein *another,* **7;** noch einmal *again, once more,* **5;** noch immer *still,* 7; noch mehr *still more,* 6; noch nicht *not yet,* **11;** noch nie *never yet,* 6; was brauchst du noch? *what else do you need?* **5;** was machen sie noch? *what else do they do?* 3; wen lädst du noch ein? *who else are you inviting?* **9**
Norddeutschland *Northern Germany,* 6
das **Nordfriesenhaus, ¨er** *North Frisian house*
Norditalien *Northern Italy,* 1
nördlich *north,* 1
Nördlicher Ladehof *north loading platform,* 8
Nordrhein-Westfalen *state in Germany,* **7**
die **Nordseeinsel, -n** *island in the North Sea*
das **Nordtor:** das Römische Nordtor *Roman North Gate,* 5
Norwegen *Norway,* 10
die **Note, -n** *grade, mark,* **2**
der **November** *November,* **11**
null *zero,* **1**
die **Nummer, -n** *number,* **5**
nun: nun ja *well, yes,* **10**
nur *only,* **2;** was soll ich nur schenken? *what on earth should I give?* **11**
nutzen *to use,* 5

O

ob *if, whether,* 5
oben *upstairs,* **6;** dort oben *up there,* **7**
das **Oberland** *highland*
die **Oberschule, -n** *high school,* **2;** er geht auf die Oberschule *he goes to high school,* **2**
das **Obst** *fruit,* **7**
oder *or,* **1**
offiziell *official,* 7
oft *often,* **3**
O. K. *okay,* **7**
der **Oktober** *October,* **11**
die **Oktoberfeststimmung** *mood, atmosphere of the Oktoberfest,* 7
das **Öl** *oil,* 12
die **Oma, -s** *grandma,* **6**
der **Onkel, -** *uncle,* **6**
der **Opa, -s** *grandpa,* **6**
die **Oper, -n** *opera,* **7;** in die Oper gehen *to go to the opera,* **7**
der **Opernball, ¨e** *opera benefit ball*
der **Orangensaft, ¨e** *orange juice,* 7
ordentlich *neat, orderly,* 6
das **Original:** im Original *in the original (language),* 3
Ost *East,* 1
das **Osterei, -er** *Easter egg*
der **Ostereibrunnen** *Easter egg well*
Österreich *Austria,* **1**
der **Österreicher, -** *Austrian* (person), 10
der **Ostersonntag** *Easter Sunday*
ostfriesisch *East Frisian*
Ostfriesland *East Frisia*
östlich *east,* 1

P

paar: ein paar *a few,* 9
das **Paar, -e** *pair,* 11; ein Paar Schuhe *a pair of shoes,* 11
packen *to pack,* 5
der **Palmsonntag** *Palm Sunday*
das **Papier** *paper,* 9
die **Parallelklasse, -n** *class of the same grade,* **2**
das **Parfüm, -s** *perfume,* **11**
der **Parkplatz, ¨e** *parking lot,* 8
der **Partner, -** *partner,* 1
die **Partnerarbeit** *teamwork,* 1
die **Party, -s** *party,* **6**
der **Pass, ¨e** *passport,* **5**
die **Passanten** (pl) *passers-by,* 7
passen *to fit,* 2; das passt prima! *that suits me fine!* **9**
die **Passkontrolle** *passport control,* **5**
die **Pause, -n** *break, recess,* **2**
perfekt *perfect,* 10
die **Person, -en** *person,* 9
die **Personenfähre, -n** *passenger ferry*
die **Peterskirche** *famous church in Munich,* 7
die **Pfarrkirche, -n** *parish church,* 7
Pfd. = Pfund *pound,* **7**
der **Pfeffer** *pepper,* 9
der **Pfennig, -e** *penny,* **5**
die **Pflanze, -n** *plant*
das **Pfund** *pound,* **7;** zwei Pfund Zucker *two pounds of sugar,* **7**
phantasievoll *imaginative,* **10**
phantastisch *fantastic, great,* **2**
philosophieren *to philosophize,* 3
das **Photo, -s** -Foto, 6
Physik *physics,* **2**
das **Piktogramm, -e** *pictogram,* 5
Pils *type of beer,* 9
die **Pinakothek:** Alte Pinakothek *name of a famous art museum in Munich,* **7**
die **Pizza, -s** *pizza,* **7**
die **Plakatsäule, -n** *large, round pillar with posters advertising various events,* 10
planen *to plan,* **5**
die **Platte, -n** *record,* **9**
der **Plattenspieler, -** *record player,* **9**
der **Platz, ¨e** *place, spot,* 10; Platz finden *to find a seat*
die **Pommes frites** (pl) *French fries,* 9
populär *popular,* 3
das **Portemonnaie, -s** *wallet,* **11**
die **Post** *post office,* 5
das **Postamt, ¨er** *post office,* **5**
das **Poster, -** *poster,* **2**
die **Postkarte, -n** *postcard,* 1
die **Praline, -n** *fancy chocolates,* **11;** eine Schachtel Pralinen *a box of fancy chocolates,* **11**
der **Preis, -e** *price,* 2
die **Preisinformation** *price information,* 7
preiswert *reasonable,* 7
prima! *great!* **2**
der **Prinz, -en** *prince,* 6
die **Prinzenhochzeit** *prince's wedding*
probieren *to try,* **7;** probier doch mal den . . . *why don't you try the . . .* **7**
das **Problem, -e** *problem,* 9
das **Promenadenkonzert, -e** *concert on a promenade*
der **Prominente, -n** *celebrity,* 10
der **Prospekt, -e** *flyer, ad,* 10
das **Prozent, -e** *percent,* 7
das **Publikum** *audience,* 10
der **Pulli, -s** *sweater (pullover),* **11**
pünktlich *on time, punctual,* **5**
putzen *to clean,* 11

Q

die **Quarzuhr, -en** *quartz clock,* **11**
Quatsch! *nonsense!* **10**

R

das **Rad;** mit dem Rad *by bike,* **2;** wir fahren Rad *we go bike riding,* **10**
das **Radio, -s** *radio,* **11**
die **Radlermass** *combination of beer and lemon soda,* 9
raten *to guess,* 1; rat mal! *take a guess!* 1
das **Ratespiel, -e** *guessing game,* 1, **9**
das **Rathaus, ¨er** *city hall,* 4; am Rathaus *next to the city hall,* 4; das Neue Rathaus *New City Hall,* **7**
die **Rathausfassade, -n** *front of the city hall*
der **Räuber, -** *robber,* 6
rausziehen (sep) *to pull out*
die **Realschule, -n** *type of German secondary school,* 4
recht- *right,* 9; in der rechten (Hand) *in the right (hand),* 9
recht haben *to be right,* **6**
rechts *right, on the right,* **5**
reduziert *reduced,* 2
das **Reetdach, ¨er** *thatched roof*
der **Regen** *rain,* **7**
der **Regenmantel, ¨** *raincoat,* **7**
der **Regenschirm, -e** *umbrella,* **7**

regieren *to reign, rule,* 6
regnen: es regnet *it's raining,* **7**
die **Reise, -n** *trip,* **5;** gute Reise! *have a good trip!* 8
das **Reisebuch, ⸚er** *travel book,* **11**
der **Reiseführer, -** *travel guide,* **5**
der **Reisende, -n** *traveler,* **5**
der **Reisescheck, -s** *traveler's check,* **5**
die **Reisetasche, -n** *travel bag,* **5**
die **Reitschule, -n** *riding school*
die **Reklame, -n** *ad,* 2, **11**
die **Religion** *religion,* **2**
der **Reporter, -** *reporter* (m), 10
die **Reporterin, -nen** *reporter* (f), 10
die **Residenz, -en** *(prince's) residence*
der **Rest, -e** *remains, ruins,* 5
das **Restaurant, -s** *restaurant,* **5**
das **Rezept, -e** *recipe,* 9
der **Rhein** *Rhine River,* 5; am Rhein *on the Rine,* 5
das **Rheinland** *Rhineland*
das **Rockkonzert, -e** *rock concert,* **10**
die **Rock-Walküre** *rock Valkyrie (Valykrie = figure from Norse mythology),* 10
der **Rokokostil** *Rococo style,* 7
das **Rollenspiel** *role-playing,* 2
der **Roman, -e** *novel,* **3**
der **Römer, -** *Roman* (person)
das **Römisch-Germanische Museum** *Roman-Germanic Museum,* 5
der **Rosenmontag** *Monday before Lent*
das **Rot** *the color red,* **11;** in Rot *in red,* **11**
Rotkäppchen *Little Red Riding Hood,* 6
der **Rucksack, ⸚e** *knapsack, backpack,* **6**
rufen: er ruft an *he calls up,* 5
die **Ruhe:** Ruhe! *quiet!* **9;** in Ruhe *not rushed,* 2
rühren *to stir,* 9
die **Ruine, -n** *ruin*
rund *around, about,* 7

S

die **Sache, -n** *thing, item,* 7
die **Sachertorte, -n** *special chocolate cake originated at the Hotel Sacher in Vienna*
sagen *to say,* **5;** sag, . . . *say, . . .,* **11;** sag mal, . . . *tell me, . . .,* 8
sagenhaft *sensational,* 10
der **Salat, -e** *lettuce,* **7**
das **Salz** *salt,* 9
sammeln *to collect,* **3**
das **Sammeln** *collecting,* **3**
der **Samstag** *Saturday,* **3**
der **Sänger, -** *singer,* **10**
die **Sängerin, -nen** *singer* (f), 10
der **Sängerknabe:** die Wiener Sängerknaben *Vienna Choir Boys*
satt: ich bin satt *I'm full,* **7**
der **Satz, ⸚e** *sentence,* 9
sauer *sore, annoyed,* **3**
die **Säule, -n** *pillar,* 7
die **S-Bahn** (Stadtbahn) *metropolitan rapid transit,* 8
der **Science-fiction-Film, -e** *science-fiction film,* **10**
Schach *chess,* **3**
die **Schachtel, -n** *box,* 11; eine Schachtel Pralinen *a box of fancy chocolates,* **11**
schade! *too bad!* **2**
der **Schäfer, -** *shepherd*
der **Schaffner, -** *guard*
schälen *to peel,* 9
die **Schallplatte, -n** *record,* 4
die **Schalterhalle, -n** *area where ticket counters are located,* 8
schauen *to look,* **10;** in die Zeitung schauen *to look in the newspaper,* **10;** Peter schaut nach *Peter checks,* **5;** schau! *look!* **2;** schau auf die Karte! *look at the map,* 1; schau mal! *look! take a look!* **2**
das **Schaufenster, -** *shop window,* 11
der **Schauspieler, -** *actor,* **10**
die **Scheibe, -n** *slice;* in Scheiben schneiden *to slice,* 9
der **Schein, -e** *bill,* **5;** ein 10-Mark-Schein *a ten-mark bill,* **5**
scheinen *to shine,* **7**
schenken *to give (as a gift),* **11**
Schi: ich laufe Schi *I go skiing,* **3**
schick *chic,* **11**
schicken *to send,* 10
das **Schiff, -e** *ship, boat,* 5
das **Schilaufen** *skiing*
das **Schild, -er** *sign,* 5
der **Schinken** *ham,* 12
schlafen *to sleep,* 6
das **Schlafzimmer, -** *bedroom,* **6**
schlampig *sloppy,* 6
schlank *slim,* **6**
schlecht *bad,* **2**
Schleswig-Holstein *state in Northern Germany,* **7**
das **Schliessfach, ⸚er** *locker,* **5**
schlimm *bad,* **6**
das **Schloss, ⸚er** *castle,* 6, **7;** Schloss Nymphenburg *Nymphenburg Castle,* **7**
schmalzig *schmaltzy,* **10**
schmecken *to taste,* **7;** wie schmeckt's? *how does it taste?* **7**
schmeicheln *to flatter,* 11
Schneewittchen *Snow White,* 6
schneiden *to cut,* 9
schnell *fast, quick,* **7**
die **Schokolade, -n** *chocolate,* 9
schon *already,* **9**
schön *nice; pretty, beautiful,* **6;** schön! *good! great!* **9;** schön, dass du da bist *nice that you're here,* **6;** schöne Ferien! *have a nice vacation!* **5**
die **schönste, -n** *most beautiful,* 6
Schreck: ach du Schreck! *horrors!* 5
schreiben *to write,* 1; bitte schreib mir! *please write to me,* 1; schreib das Gespräch auf! *write the conversation down,* 7; schreiben an *to write to,* 7; wer schreibt uns? *who will write to us?* 3
die **Schreibgeräte** (pl) *writing instruments,* 2
die **Schreibübung, -en** *writing exercise,* 1
die **Schreibwaren** (pl) *writing supplies,* 4
das **Schreibwarengeschäft, -e** *stationery store,* 2
der **Schuh, -e** *shoe,* **11**
das **Schuhgeschäft, -e** *shoe store,* 11
der **Schuhmacher, -** *shoemaker,* 1
der **Schulanfang** *beginning of school,* 2
die **Schule, -n** *school,* **2**
der **Schüler, -** *student, pupil,* **3**
die **Schülerzeitung, -en** *school newspaper,* 2
die **Schulfreundin, -nen** *friend from school* (f), **9**
die **Schulsachen** (pl) *school supplies,* **2**
die **Schultasche, -n** *school bag,* **2**
der **Schulweg** *way of getting to school,* 4
die **Schulwoche** *the school week,* 4
die **Schüssel, -n** *bowl,* 9; in eine Schüssel geben *to put in a bowl,* 9
Schwaben *Swabia*
das **Schwarz** *the color black,* **11**
der **Schwarzwald** *Black Forest*
Schwarzwälder: Schwarzwälder Schinken *Black Forest ham*
die **Schweiz** *Switzerland,* **1;** in der Schweiz *in Switzerland,* **7**
schwer *difficult,* **2;** *heavy,* 7
die **Schwester, -n** *sister,* **6**
die **Schwierigkeit, -en** *difficulty,* 9
schwimmen *to swim,* **3**
das **Schwimmen** *swimming,* 3
sechs *six,* **1**
sechzehn *sixteen,* **1**
sechzig *sixty,* **2**
segeln *to sail,* **3**
das **Segeln** *sailing,* **3**
sehen *to see,* **6**
die **Sehenswürdigkeit, -en** *place of interest, sight,* **7**
sehr *very,* **6**
sein, seine *his; its,* **5, 9**
seit *since*
die **Seite, -n** *page,* 5
selb-: im selben Augenblick *at the same moment,* 5
selten *seldom,* **3**
die **Semmel, -n** *roll,* **7**
der **Senf** *mustard,* **7**
sensationell *sensational,* **10**
der **September** *September,* **11**
sichtbar *visible,* 5
sie *she, it; they,* **2**
Sie *you* (formal), **1, 3**
sieben *seven,* **1**
siebzehn *seventeen,* **1**
siebzig *seventy,* **5**
das **Siezen** *addressing someone with* Sie, 10
singen *to sing,* **10**
der **Sinn** *meaning,* 10

die **Sitte, -n** *custom,* 9
sitzen *to sit,* 5
so *so,* **2;** *so, well then,* **6;** ach, so was! *well, of all things!* 11; so la la so-so, **10;** so um halb sechs *around 5:30,* **9**
das **Sofa, -s** *sofa*
sogar *even,* 9
der **Sohn, ¨e** *son,* 7
sollen *should, to be supposed to,* **7**
der **Sommer, -** *summer,* 3; im Sommer *in the summer,* **3**
sondern *but,* 9; nicht nur . . . sondern auch *not only . . . but also,* 9
der **Sonnabend** *Saturday,* **2**
sonnabends *Saturdays, on Saturdays,* **2**
die **Sonne** *sun,* **7**
sonnig *sunny,* **7**
der **Sonntag** *Sunday,* **3**
sonst: ein Tag wie sonst *a day like any other,* 3
die **Sorge:** keine Sorge *don't worry,* **7**
soso *well, well,* 7
die **Sosse, -n** *sauce,* 9
die **Sozialwohnung, -en** *government-supported housing*
spanisch *Spanish* (adj)
spannend *exciting,* **10**
der **Spass** *fun,* 3; Gymnastik macht Spass *gymnastics is fun,* **3;** viel Spass! *have fun!* **7**
spät *late,* 10; wie spät ist es? *what time is it?* **2;** später *later,* **9;** bis später *see you later,* 5
spazierengehen (sep) *to go for a walk,* 10
der **Speck** *bacon,* 9
die **Speckplatte:** Tiroler Speckplatte *plate of Tyrolean bacon,* 12
das **Spezi, -s** *combination of cola and lemon soda,* 9
die **Spezialität, -en** *specialty,* 7
der **Spiegel, -** *mirror,* 6; in den Spiegel schauen *to look in the mirror,* 6
das **Spieglein, -** *little mirror,* 6
das **Spiel, -e** *game,* **3**
spielen *to play,* **3**
die **Spielkarten** (pl) *playing cards,* **5**
spinnen *to spin,* 6; du spinnst! *you're crazy!* **9**
Spitze! *terrific!* **3**
der **Sport** *gym,* **2;** Sport machen *to participate in a sport, to do sports,* **3;** Sport treiben *to participate in sports,* 10
der **Sport- und Hobbyfreund, -e** *sport and hobby enthusiast,* 3
der **Sport- und Hobbymuffel, -** *person who doesn't like sports or hobbies,* 3
das **Sportbuch, ¨er** *book about sports,* **3**
sportlich *sporty,* 6
das **Sportrad, ¨er** *10-speed bike,* 11
die **Sportveranstaltung, -en** *sports event,* **10**
die **Sprache, -n** *language,* 3; der deutschen Sprache *of the German language,* 3
sprechen *to speak, talk,* 3; die Karin möchte dich sprechen *Karin would like to talk to you,* **9;** sie sprechen Will Baden aus wie Bill Barton *they pronounce Will Baden like Bill Barton,* 5; sprechen wir darüber! *let's talk about it,* 6
sprich: sprich darüber! *talk about it,* 10; sprich mich nicht an! *don't talk to me,* 4
sprichst: du sprichst mit *you are talking to,* 9
spricht: man spricht Deutsch *German is spoken,* 1; über was spricht Steffi? *what is Steffi talking about?* 7
Squash *squash,* **10**
der **Staat, -en** *state,* 8
die **Stadt, ¨e** *city; town,* **7**
der **Stadtbummel, -** *stroll through the city,* **10;** einen Stadtbummel machen *to take a stroll through the city,* **10**
der **Stadtbus, -se** *city bus,* 6
der **Stadtplan, ¨e** *city map,* 7
starten zu *to start on,* 10
stattfinden (sep) *to take place*
stattgefunden: hat stattgefunden *took place*
der **Steckbrief, -e** *resumé,* 4
stecken *to stick, put,* **5**
stehen *to stand,* 5; da steht noch mehr auf Peters Zettel *there's still more on Peter's list,* **6;** wie steht's? *how are things?* 9; wie steht's mit dir? *what about you?* 2
stellt: Wiebke stellt ihre Familie vor *Wiebke introduces her family,* 6
sterben *to die,* 4; lieber Gott, lass mich sterben! *dear God, let me die!* 4
die **Stiefmutter, ¨** *stepmother,* 6
der **Stil, -e** *style,* 7, 11
das **Stilelement, -e** *element of (one's) style,* 10
die **Stimme, -n** *voice,* 10
stimmt: stimmt! *that's right! true!* **3;** stimmt nicht! *that's not so! not true!* **3**
das **Stövchen, -** *candle warmer*
die **Strasse, -n** *street,* 3
die **Strassenbahn:** mit der Strassenbahn *by streetcar,* **2**
der **Strauss, ¨e** *bouquet,* 11; ein Strauss Blumen *a bouquet of flowers,* **11**
das **Stroh** *straw,* 6
die **Stube, -n** *room,* 7; die gute Stube *parlor, living room,* 7; Sacher Stube *Café Sacher*
St. = Stück *piece, item,* 4; Bleistifte (10 St.) *10 pencils,* 4
das **Stück, -e** *piece, item,* 2, 9; *play,* 10; ein Fünf-Mark-Stück *a five-mark piece,* **5**
der **Stundenplan, ¨e** *class schedule,* **2**
suchen *to look for,* **5**
Südamerika *South America,* 10
südlich *south,* 1; *southern,* 7
Südlicher Ladehof *south loading platform,* 8
Südtirol *South Tyrol,* 1
die **Summe** *sum, total,* 7
super! *super! terrific!* **3**
der **Supermarkt, ¨e** *supermarket,* **7;** im Supermarkt *in, at the supermarket,* **7**
die **Suppe, -n** *soup,* **9**
das **Sylvester** *New Year's Eve*
das **Symbol, -e** *symbol,* 6
sympathisch *likeable, nice,* **6**

T

die **Tabelle, -n** *table, chart,* 5
der **Tag, -e** *day,* 3; am Tag *(times) a day,* **3;** eines Tages *one day,* 11; guten Tag! *hello!* **1;** Tag! *hello! hi!* **1**
täglich *daily, every day,* 3, 10
die **Tante, -n** *aunt,* **6**
der **Tanz, ¨e** *dance,* 9
tanzen *to dance,* **9**
das **Tanzen** *dancing,* 4
die **Tänzerin, -nen** *dancer* (f), 9
der **Tanzpartner, -** *dance partner,* **9**
die **Tanzschule, -n** *dancing school,* 9
der **Taschenrechner, -** *pocket calculator,* **2**
die **Tasse, -n** *cup,* 9
die **Taste, -n** *(push) button,* 5
die **Taufe, -n** *baptism*
tausend *thousand,* **6;** tausend Dank! *thanks a million!* **6**
das **Taxi, -s** *taxi,* 5
technisch *technically,* 10
der **Tee** *tea,* 12
der **Teelöffel, -** *teaspoon,* 9
das **Teeservice, -** *tea set, service*
der **Teil, -e** *part,* 1
das **Telefon, -e** *telephone,* **5**
das **Telefongespräch, -e** *telephone conversation,* 10
telefonieren *to make a phone call,* **5**
das **Telefonieren** *telephoning,* **5**
die **Telefonnummer, -n** *telephone number,* 1
die **Telefonzelle, -n** *telephone booth,* **5**
das **Tennis** *tennis,* **3**
teuer *expensive,* **11;** wie teuer ist es? *how much is it?* **11**
der **Text, -e** *text, words (to a song),* 9
das **Theater, -** *theater,* **10;** ins Theater gehen *to go to the theater,* **10**
Tirol *Tyrol*
der **Titel, -** *title,* 10
tja *hm* **3**
die **Tochter, ¨** *daughter,* **7**
die **Toilette, -n** *toilet; bathroom,* **6;** *restroom,* **5**
toll! *great!* **2**
die **Tomate, -n** *tomato,* **7**

das **Tor, -e** *gate,* **5**
der **Tourist, -en** *tourist,* 7
die **Tournee, -s** *tour,* 10
die **Tracht, -en** *traditional costume*
die **Trachtengruppe, -n** *group in traditional costume*
traditionell *traditional,* 9
das **Traditionsfest, -e** *traditional festival,* 7
trägt *wears,* 11
träumen *to dream,* 10
die **Traumfabrik** *dream factory,* 10
traurig *sad,* **7**
der **Treffpunkt, -e** *meeting place*
treiben: Sport treiben *to participate in sports,* 10
das **Treppenhaus, ¨er** *staircase*
trinken *to drink,* **5**
tropisch *tropical*
trotzdem *anyway, in spite of,* **7**
tschau! *bye! so long!* **1**
die **Tschechoslowakei** *Czechoslovakia,* 1
tschüs! *bye! so long!* **1**
das **T-Shirt, -s** *T-shirt,* **11**
tun *to do,* **10**
der **Turm, ¨e** *tower,* **7**
tüt: tüt, tüt *sound heard when you make a call and it rings,* 5
der **Typ, -en** *character,* 10
typisch *typical*

U

die **U-Bahn** = Untergrundbahn *subway,* 4; mit der U-Bahn *by subway,* 4
üben *to practice,* 9
das **Üben** *practice, practicing,* 1
über *about,* 1; *over,* 5
überall *everywhere, all over,* 7
überhaupt *in any case,* **9;** du isst ja überhaupt nichts! *why, you're not eating anything at all!* 9; was gibt es überhaupt? *what are we having, anyway?* **9**
übernehmen *to take on,* 10
die **Übung, -en** *exercise, activity, practice,* 1
die **Uhr, -en** *clock, watch,* **1;** neun Uhr dreissig *nine-thirty,* **2;** neun Uhr fünf *nine-oh-five,* **2;** neun Uhr zehn *nine-ten,* **2;** um wieviel Uhr? *at what time?* **9**
der **Uhrmacher, -** *watchmaker*
um *at,* **2;** *in order to,* 7; so um *around, about,* 8; um acht Uhr *at eight o'clock,* **2;** um eins *at one,* **2;** um 1172 *around 1172,* 5
die **Umfrage, -n** *survey, poll,* 3
umgekehrt *the other way round,* 9
umherlaufen (sep) *to walk around,* 11
das **Umland** *surrounding area,* 7
umsteigen (sep) *to change (trains),* 8
der **Umzug, ¨e** *parade*
und *and,* **1;** und wie! *and how!* **9**
unfreundlich *unfriendly,* 6
Ungarn *Hungary,* 10
ungefähr *about, approximately,* **5**
die **Universitätsstadt, ¨e** *university town*
unmöglich *impossible,* 2
die **Unordnung** *mess, disorder,* 2; so eine Unordnung! *what a mess!* 2
unrealistisch *unrealistic,* 6
uns *us,* 3
unser, unsere *our,* **7, 9**
der **Unsinn:** Unsinn! *nonsense!* **2**
unsympathisch *unpleasant, not nice,* **6**
unten *downstairs,* **6**
unterwegs *on the way,* 11
der **Urlaub, -e** *vacation,* 11
usw. = und so weiter *etc., and so forth,* 8

V

die **Vase, -n** *vase,* **11**
der **Vater, ¨** *father,* **5**
der **Vatertag** *Father's Day,* **11;** zum Vatertag *for Father's Day,* **11**
der **Vati, -s** *dad,* **5**
verabredet: wie verabredet *as planned,* **5**
die **Verabredung, -en** *appointment,* 11
verbrannt *burned*
verbringen *to spend (time),* **10**
die **Vereinigten Staaten** (pl) *United States,* 1
vergangen *past (time),* 11
vergessen *to forget,* 9
vergleichen *to compare,* 10
der **Verkauf** *sale, selling,* 5
die **Verkäuferin, -nen** *salesperson,* **2**
das **Verkaufsgespräch, -e** *conversation with a salesperson,* 11
verkauft! *sold!* 11
verlieren *to lose,* **3**
verrückt *crazy,* 7
verschieden *different, various,* 7, 12
verstanden: hast du verstanden? *did you understand?* 5
versteckt: versteckte Sätze *hidden sentences,* 3
verstehen *to understand,* **9**
versuchen *to try,* **5**
verwandt *related,* 8; wie sind sie verwandt mit dir? *how are they related to you?* 8
der **Verwandte, -n** *relative,* **5**
Verzeihung! *excuse me!* **5**
verzollen *to declare at customs,* **5**
der **Vetter, -n** *cousin* (m), **6**
der **Video-Recorder, -** *video recorder,* **9**
der **Viehabtrieb** *driving cattle down from the mountain*
viel *much, a lot,* **3;** viel Glück! *good luck!* **2**
viele *many,* **6;** viele Grüsse *best regards,* 1
der **Vielfrass** *glutton,* 9
vielleicht *maybe,* **7**
vier *four,* **1**
viermal *four times,* **3**
das **Viertel:** Viertel nach neun *a quarter after nine,* **2**
vierzehn *fourteen,* **1**
vierzig *forty,* **2**
der **Viktualienmarkt** *colorful open market in Munich,* 7
das **Volksfest, -e** *fair, festival*
voll *full,* **5;** voll besetzt *completely occupied,* **5**
vollschlank *heavyset,* **6**
vom = von dem *from the,* 9
von *by,* 3; *from,* **5;** *of,* **6;** ein Freund von Wiebke *a friend of Wiebke's,* **6;** von . . . bis *from . . . to,* **1;** von dort *from there,* **5**
vor *before, of,* **2;** *in front of, outside of*
vorhaben (sep) *to have plans,* **9**
vorlesen (sep) *to read aloud,* 10
der **Vorname, -n** *first name,* 1
der **Vorort, -e** *suburb,* **7**
die **Vorschau** *preview,* 10
vorstellen (sep) *to introduce,* 6
der **Vortrag, ¨e** *presentation,* 2
VW = Volkswagen *a German-made car*

W

die **Wachau** *valley of the Danube in Austria*
wählen *to dial,* **5**
die **Währung, -en** *currency,* 5
das **Wahrzeichen, -** *landmark,* **7**
der **Wald, ¨er** *forest, woods,* 6
der **Walkman** *Walkman,* **5**
der **Walzer** *waltz,* 9
die **Wand, ¨e** *wall,* 6
wandern *to wander, hike,* 6
das **Wandern** *hiking,* 10
wann? *when?* **2**
das **Wappen, -** *coat of arms, emblem,* **7**
wär's: wie wär's mit *how about,* 7
warm *warm,* **7**
die **Wartehalle, -n** *waiting room,* **5**
warten *to wait,* 5; warten auf *to wait for,* 5, 8
der **Wartesaal, -säle** *waiting room,* 8
warum? *why?* **10**
was? *what?* **2;** was?! *what?!* **3;** ach, so was! *well, of all things!* 11; was darf es sein? *may I help you?* **11;** was für? *what kind of (a)?* **10;** was gibt's? *what's up?* **9;** was gibt es alles? *what's there to eat and drink?* **9;** was kosten? *how much are?* **2;** was kostet? *how much is?* **2;** was machst du? *what are you doing? what do you do?* **3**
waschen *to wash,* 9
die **Waschmaschine, -n** *washing machine*
das **Wasser** *water,* 9
das **Wasser** = Mineralwasser *mineral water,* **9**

wechseln *to change, exchange,* **5;** Geld wechseln *to exchange money from one currency to another,* **5**
die **Wechselstube, -n** *currency exchange office,* 8
weg *gone,* **2**
wegen *because of,* 5; wegen Störung geschlossen *closed—out of order,* 5
wegfahren (sep) *to go away,* 12
wegwerfen (sep) *to throw away,* 11
weich *soft,* 11
das **Weihnachten** *Christmas,* **11;** fröhliche Weihnachten *Merry Christmas,* **11;** zu Weihnachten *for Christmas,* **11**
der **Weihnachtsbaum, ¨e** *Christmas tree*
der **Wein, -e** *wine,* 9; eine Flasche Wein *a bottle of wine,* 9
der **Weinberg, -e** *vineyard*
das **Weinfest, -e** *wine festival*
die **Weinkönigin, -nen** *wine queen*
die **Weinstrasse, -n** *road through wine-growing villages*
weiss: ich weiss nicht *I don't know,* **2**
das **Weiss** *the color white,* **11**
das **Weissbier** *type of beer,* 9
die **Weisswurst, ¨e** *type of sausage,* **7**
weit *far,* **5**
weiter *further, on,* **5;** ich fliege weiter nach *I'm flying on to,* **5;** und so weiter *and so forth,* 9
weitere: für weitere Gespräche *for additional calls,* 5
welch- *which,* **10**
welche *which, what,* **2**
die **Welt** *world;* aus aller Welt *from all over the world,* 7
der **Weltatlas, -se** *world atlas,* 4
weltberühmt *world-famous,* 7
die **Weltmeisterschaft, -en** *world championship,* 10
der **Weltrang:** von Weltrang *world-class,* 10
der **Weltraum** *outer space,* 10
wem? *(to, for) whom?* 7
wen? *whom?* **5**
wenig: ein wenig *a little,* 1
wenn *when, if,* **10**
wer? *who?* **1**
werden: kann genutzt werden *can be used,* 5
der **Western, -** *western,* **10**
Westfalen *Westphalia*
westlich *west,* 1
die **Wette, -n** *bet,* 6
das **Wetter** *weather,* **7**
der **Wetterbericht, -e** *weather report,* **7**
wichtig *important,* 11
wie *such as,* 3; *as, like,* **5;** wie? *how?* **1;** wie bitte? *I beg your pardon?* **1;** wie geht's? *how are you?* **9;** wie heisst du? *what's your name?* **1;** wie immer *as always,* **3;** wie kommst du in die Schule? *how do you get to school?* **2;** wie lange? *how long?* **5;** wie oft? *how often?* **3;** wie spät ist es? *what time is it?* **2;** und wie! *and how!* **9**
wieder *again,* **7;** wir sind um 9 wieder da *we'll be back at 9,* **7**
das **Wiederholungskapitel, -** *review unit (chapter),* 4
das **Wiedersehen:** auf Wiedersehen! *goodbye!* **1;** Wiedersehen! *bye!* **1**
Wien *Vienna,* **1**
der **Wiener, -** *type of frankfurter sausage,* 12
Wies'n = Wiese *fairgrounds,* 7; auf die Wies'n gehen *to go to the* Oktoberfest, 7
wieso? *how?* 11
wieviel? *how much?* **5;** *how many?* **6**
Willkommen: Willkommen in Neuss! *welcome to Neuss!* **6**
das **Windsurfen** *wind surfing,* 3
der **Winter** *winter,* 3; im Winter *in the winter,* **3**
wir *we,* **2**
wird: wird offiziell verbrannt *is officially burned*
wirklich *really,* **5;** wirklich? *really?* **3**
wissen *to know (a fact, information),* **7**
der **Witz, -e** *joke,* **9**
wo? *where?* **2**
die **Woche, -n** *week,* **5;** in der Woche *(times) a week,* **3**
woher? *from where?* **1;** woher bist du? *where are you from?* **1**
wohin? *to where?* **5**
wohl *probably,* 10
wohnen *to live,* **5**
das **Wohnhaus, ¨er** *house*
der **Wohnsitz, -e** *residence*
die **Wohnung, -en** *apartment,* **7**
der **Wohnungsplan, ¨e** *floor plan of an apartment,* 6
das **Wohnzimmer, -** *living room,* **6**
der **Wolf, ¨e** *wolf,* 6
wollen *to want to,* **10**
das **Wort, ¨er** *word,* 9
das **Wörterbuch, ¨er** *dictionary,* **2**
der **Wortschatz** *vocabulary,* 1
die **Wortschatzübung, -en** *vocabulary exercise, practice,* 1
wunderbar *wonderful,* 11
der **Wunsch:** gute Wünsche zum *best wishes on,* **11**
würde *would*
die **Wurst, ¨e** *sausage; cold cuts,* **7**
das **Wurstbrot, -e** *sandwich made with cold cuts,* **7**
die **Wurstplatte, -n** *platter with an assortment of cold cuts,* 7
der **Wurstsalat, -e** *meat salad made with various cold cuts cut into strips and an oil and vinegar dressing,* 12
die **Wurstsorte, -n** *type of cold cuts or sausages,* 9
wütend *furious,* 11

Z

die **Zahl, -en** *number,* **1**
zahlen *to pay,* 11
zehn *ten,* **1**
zeigen *to show,* **6;** ich zeig es dir *I'll show it to you,* **6**
die **Zeit** *time,* **2**
die **Zeitschrift, -en** *magazine,* 3
die **Zeitung, -en** *newspaper,* **10**
der **Zeitungsladen, ¨** *paper store,* 7
der **Zensurenspiegel** *grade record,* 2
das **Zepter, -** *scepter,* 6
der **Zettel, -** *note, slip of paper, list,* **6**
das **Zimmer, -** *room,* **6**
die **Zitronenlimonade** *carbonated lemon drink,* 9
der **Zoll** *customs,* **5**
zu *to,* **5;** *too,* **10;** *for,* **11;** zu Fuss *on foot,* **2;** zu Hause *at home,* **10;** bleibt lieber zu Hause *you'd better stay home,* **7;** ich bin in Wien zu Hause *I live in Vienna,* **7;** zu Weihnachten *for Christmas,* **11**
der **Zucker** *sugar,* **7**
zuerst *first,* 7
die **Zugauskunft** *train information,* 8
zugeben (sep) *to add,* 9
zuletzt *last of all,* 7
zum: zum Bahnhof *to the station,* 8; zum Geburtstag *for (someone's) birthday,* **11;** alles Gute zum Geburtstag! *best wishes on (your) birthday!* **11;** herzliche Glückwünsche zum Geburtstag! *happy birthday!* **11**
Zürich *Zurich,* 1
zurück *back,* **5**
zurückkehren (sep) *to return,* 4
zusammen *together,* **10**
die **Zutaten** (pl) *ingredients,* 9
zwanzig *twenty,* **1**
zwei *two,* **1**
zweihundert *two hundred,* **5**
zweihunderteins *two hundred one,* **5**
zweimal *twice,* **3**
zweit-: zum ersten, zum zweiten, zum dritten! *going, going, gone!* 11
der **Zwerg, -e** *dwarf,* 6
die **Zwiebel, -n** *onion,* 9
zwischen *between,* 1
zwölf *twelve,* **1**

ENGLISH-GERMAN VOCABULARY

This vocabulary includes all the words in the **Wortschatz** sections of the units. These words are considered active—you are expected to know them.

Idioms are listed under the English word you would be most likely to look up. German nouns are listed with definite article and plural ending, when applicable. The number after each German word or phrase refers to the unit in which it is first introduced. To be sure of using the German words and phrases in correct context, refer to the units in which they appear.

A

a *eine,* 2; *ein,* 3
able: to be able to *können,* 10
about *ungefähr,* 5
action film *der Action-Film, -e,* 10
actor *der Schauspieler, -,* 10
address book *das Adressbuch, ¨er,* 5
adventure film *der Abenteuerfilm, -e,* 10
after *nach,* 2
again *wieder,* 7; *noch einmal,* 5
agree: as agreed on *wie verabredet,* 5
ahead: straight ahead *geradeaus,* 5
airplane *das Flugzeug, -e,* 5
airport *der Flughafen, ¨,* 5
algebra *Algebra,* 2
all *alle; alles,* 5
alone *allein,* 7
already *schon,* 9
also *auch,* 1
always *immer,* 3; as always *wie immer,* 3
am: I am *ich bin,* 1
American (person) *der Amerikaner, -,* 5; he's an American *er ist Amerikaner,* 5
an *ein,* 3; *eine,* 2
and *und,* 1
anniversary (wedding) *der Hochzeitstag, -e,* 11; for (your) anniversary *zum Hochzeitstag,* 11; golden wedding anniversary *goldene Hochzeit,* 11
another *noch ein,* 7
anyway *trotzdem,* 7; what are we having, anyway? *was gibt es überhaupt?* 9
apartment *die Wohnung, -en,* 7
appear *aussehen,* 6
apple juice *der Apfelsaft, ¨e,* 9
approximately *ungefähr,* 5
April *der April,* 11
are: you are *du bist,* 1; they are *sie sind,* 1
around *um,* 9; around 8:30 *so um halb neun,* 9
arrogant *arrogant,* 6
art *die Kunst,* 2
as *wie,* 5
ask *fragen,* 5
at *um,* 2; at eight o'clock *um acht Uhr,* 2; at one *um eins,* 2; at what time? *um wieviel Uhr?* 9
attractive *attraktiv,* 6
Audi (German car) *der Audi, -s,* 6
August *der August,* 11
aunt *die Tante, -n,* 6
Austria *Österreich,* 1
awful *furchtbar,* 9

B

back *zurück,* 5; we'll be back at 9 *wir sind um 9 wieder da,* 7
backpack *der Rucksack, ¨e,* 6
bad *schlecht,* 2; *schlimm,* 6; too bad! *schade!* 2; *blöd!* 7
bag: travel bag *die Reisetasche, -n,* 5
baggage *das Gepäck,* 5
baker *der Bäcker, -,* 7; at the baker's *beim Bäcker,* 7
ballpoint *der Kuli, -s,* 2
bank *die Bank, -en,* 5
bank teller *der Bankangestellte, -n,* 5
basement *der Keller, -,* 6
basketball *Basketball,* 3
bathroom *das Bad, ¨er,* 6; *die Toilette, -n,* 5
Bavaria *Bayern,* 7
beautiful *schön,* 6
bedroom *das Schlafzimmer, -,* 6
before *vor,* 2
begin *beginnen,* 2
beige *beige,* 11; the color beige *das Beige,* 11
believe *glauben,* 11
best: best wishes *alles Gute,* 11; best wishes on . . . *gute Wünsche zum . . .* 11; all the best wishes on *. . . alles Gute zum . . .* 11
bicycle *das Rad, ¨er,* 2; by bicycle *mit dem Rad,* 2; to go bicycle riding *radfahren,* 10; we go bike riding *wir fahren Rad,* 10
big *gross,* 6
bill *der Schein, -e,* 5; a 10-mark bill *ein 10-Mark-Schein,* 5
bio *Bio,* 2
biology *Biologie,* 2
birthday *der Geburtstag, -e,* 11; happy birthday! *herzliche Glückwünsche zum Geburtstag!* 11; my birthday is in May *ich habe im Mai Geburtstag,* 11; for (your) birthday *zum Geburtstag,* 11; it's his birthday *er hat Geburtstag,* 11
black *schwarz,* 11; the color black *das Schwarz,* 11
blond *blond,* 6
blouse *die Bluse, -n,* 11
blue *blau,* 11; the color blue *das Blau,* 11; in blue *in Blau,* 11; dark blue *dunkelblau,* 11; light blue *hellblau,* 11
book *das Buch, ¨er,* 6; address book *das Adressbuch, ¨er,* 5; book about sports *das Sportbuch, ¨er,* 3
booth: phone booth *die Telefonzelle, -n,* 5
boring *langweilig,* 3
bottle *die Flasche, -n,* 7; a bottle of mineral water *eine Flasche Mineralwasser,* 7
bouquet *der Strauss, ¨e,* 11; a bouquet of flowers *ein Strauss Blumen,* 11
bowl *kegeln,* 10
box *die Schachtel, -n,* 11; a box of fancy chocolates *eine Schachtel Pralinen,* 11
boy *der Junge, -n,* 1; boy! *Mensch!* 6
boyfriend *der Freund, -e,* 9
bracelet *das Armband, ¨er,* 11
bread *das Brot, -e,* 7
bring *bringen,* 9
brother *der Bruder, ¨,* 6; brothers and sisters *die Geschwister* (pl), 6
brown *braun,* 11; the color brown *das Braun,* 11
brunette *brünett,* 6
brutal *brutal,* 10
bus *der Bus, -se,* 2; by bus *mit dem Bus,* 2
busy (a phone) *besetzt,* 5
but *aber,* 2
butcher *der Metzger, -,* 7

butter *die Butter, 7*
buy *kaufen, 5*
by: by bicycle *mit dem Rad,* 2; by bus *mit dem Bus,* 2; by car *mit dem Auto,* 2; by moped *mit dem Moped,* 2; by streetcar *mit der Strassenbahn,* 2
bye! *tschau!* 1; *tschüs!* 1; *Wiedersehen!* 1

C

café *das Café, -s,* 10; to go to a café *in ein Café gehen,* 10
cake *der Kuchen, -,* 9
calculator: pocket calculator *der Taschenrechner, -,* 2
calendar *der Kalender, -,* 11
California *Kalifornien,* 5
call up *anrufen,* 9
called: what's it called again? *wie heisst er denn?* 10
camera *die Kamera, -s,* 5
can *können,* 10; I can't *es geht nicht,* 9
cap *die Mütze, -n,* 11
capital city *die Hauptstadt, ¨e,* 7
car *das Auto, -s,* 6; by car *mit dem Auto,* 2
cards *die Karten* (pl), 3; playing cards *die Spielkarten* (pl), 5
careful: I'll be careful *ich pass' schon auf,* 7; please be careful! *pass bitte auf!* 7
case: in any case *überhaupt,* 9
cassette *die Kassette, -n,* 2; music cassette *die Musikkassette, -n,* 3
cassette recorder *der Kassetten-Recorder, -,* 9
castle *das Schloss, ¨er,* 7
cathedral *der Dom, -e,* 7
center (of the city) *die Innenstadt, ¨e,* 7
change *wechseln,* 5
cheat *mogeln,* 3
check: traveler's check *der Reisescheck, -s,* 5; Peter checks *Peter schaut nach,* 5
cheese *der Käse,* 7; cheese sandwich *das Käsebrot, -e,* 9
cherry *die Kirsche, -n,* 7
chess *Schach,* 3
chic *schick,* 11
chicken *das Hähnchen, -,* 7
chocolates fancy chocolate candy *die Praline, -n,* 11; a box of fancy chocolates *eine Schachtel Pralinen,* 11
chopped meat *das Hackfleisch,* 7
Christmas *Weihnachten,* 11; for Christmas *zu Weihnachten,* 11; Merry Christmas! *fröhliche Weihnachten!* 11
church *die Kirche, -n,* 7
city *die Stadt, ¨e,* 7; big city *die Grossstadt, ¨e,* 7; capital city *die Hauptstadt, ¨e,* 7
class *die Klasse, -n,* 2; class of the same grade *die Parallelklasse, -n,* 2
classmate (m) *der Klassenkamerad, -en,* 2
classmate (f) *die Klassenkameradin, -nen,* 2
clique *die Clique, -n,* 10
clock *die Uhr, -en,* 11
cloudy *bewölkt,* 7
coat *der Mantel, ¨,* 11
coat of arms *das Wappen, -,* 7
coffee *der Kaffee,* 7
coin *die Münze, -n,* 3
cola *die (das) Cola, -s,* 7
cold *kalt,* 7
cold cuts *der Aufschnitt,* 7; *die Wurst, ¨e,* 7; sandwich made with cold cuts *das Wurstbrot, -e,* 7
collect *sammeln,* 3
collecting *Sammeln,* 3
Cologne *Köln,* 5
color *die Farbe, -n,* 11; in many colors *in vielen Farben,* 11
come *kommen,* 2; come on! *komm!* 6; that comes to *das sind,* 5
comedy *die Komödie, -n,* 10
comics *Comics* (pl), 3
company *der Besuch,* 7
concert *das Konzert, -e,* 10; to go to a concert *ins Konzert gehen,* 10
cool *kühl,* 7
cost *kosten,* 2
cousin (m) *der Vetter, -n,* 6
cousin (f) *die Kusine, -n,* 6
cozy *gemütlich,* 6
crazy: you're crazy! *du spinnst!* 9
cruel *grausam,* 10
cucumber *die Gurke, -n,* 7
customs *der Zoll,* 5; to declare at customs *verzollen,* 5

D

dad *der Vati, -s,* 5
dance *tanzen,* 9
dancing partner *der Tanzpartner, -,* 9
dark *dunkel,* 6; dark blond *dunkelblond,* 6
daughter *die Tochter, ¨,* 7
day *der Tag, -e,* 3; (times) a day *am Tag,* 3
December *der Dezember,* 11
declare (at customs) *verzollen,* 5
delicious *lecker,* 9
department store *das Kaufhaus, ¨er,* 11; in the department store *im Kaufhaus,* 11
dial *wählen,* 5
dictionary *das Wörterbuch, ¨er,* 2
difficult *schwer,* 2
dining room *das Esszimmer, -,* 6
disco *die Disko, -s,* 10; to go to a disco *in eine Disko gehen,* 10
discuss *diskutieren,* 9
do *machen,* 2, 3; *tun,* 10; he's doing math *er macht Mathe,* 2; what are you doing? *was machst du?* 3; what do you do? *was machst du?* 3
dog *der Hund, -e,* 6
dollar *der Dollar, -,* 5
downstairs *unten,* 6
drink *trinken,* 5
drive *fahren,* 10
dumb *blöd,* 2; *dumm,* 10

E

each *jed-,* 11
easy *leicht,* 2
eat *essen,* 5
egg *das Ei, -er,* 7
else: who else are you inviting?: *wen lädst du noch ein?* 9
emblem *das Wappen, -,* 7
English *Englisch,* 2
enjoy: enjoy your meal! *guten Appetit!* 9
enough *genug,* 7
especially *besonders,* 10
every *jeder (-e, -es),* 11
everything *alles,* 5; everything else *alles andere,* 7
excellent *ausgezeichnet,* 9
exchange *wechseln,* 5
exciting *spannend,* 10
excuse: excuse me! *Entschuldigung!* 2; *Verzeihung!* 5
exit *der Ausgang, ¨e,* 5
expensive *teuer,* 11

F

fair (weather) *heiter,* 7
fall *der Herbst,* 3; in the fall *im Herbst,* 3
familiar to be familiar with a place *kennen,* 7
family *die Familie, -n,* 5; the Nedel family *die Familie Nedel,* 5
fantastic *phantastisch,* 2
fantasy book *das Fantasy-Buch, ¨er,* 3
fast *schnell,* 7
father *der Vater, ¨,* 5
Father's Day *der Vatertag,* 11; for Father's Day *zum Vatertag,* 11
favorite *Lieblings-,* 10; favorite color *die Lieblingsfarbe, -n,* 11; favorite group *die Lieblingsgruppe, -n,* 10; favorite star *der Lieblingsstar, -s,* 10
February *der Februar,* 11
fetch *holen,* 5, 7
film *der Film, -e,* 5, 10
finally *endlich,* 5
find *finden,* 3
fine *gut,* 7; fine, thanks *gut, danke,* 10
first: on the first *am ersten,* 11; on May 1st *am ersten Mai,* 11
fish sandwich *das Fischbrot, -e,* 7
flight *der Flug, ¨e,* 5; have a good flight! *guten Flug!* 5
flower *die Blume, -n,* 11
fly *fliegen,* 5
foot: on foot *zu Fuss,* 2
for *für,* 5
four *vier;* four times *viermal,* 3
free time *die Freizeit,* 3; in your free time *in deiner Freizeit,* 3; person who does not know what to do with free time *der Freizeitmuffel, -,* 10

fresh *frisch*, 7
Friday *der Freitag*, 2; on Friday *am Freitag*, 2
friend *der Freund, -e*, 3; girlfriend *die Freundin, -nen*, 6; girlfriend from school *die Schulfreundin, -nen*, 9
friendly *freundlich*, 6
from *aus*, 1; *von*, 1, 5
fruit *das Obst*, 7
full *voll*, 5; I'm full *ich bin satt*, 7
fun *der Spass*, 3; gymnastics is fun *Gymnastik macht Spass*, 3; have fun! *viel Spass!* 7
funny *lustig*, 6
further *weiter*, 5

G

game *das Spiel, -e*, 3
garage *die Garage, -n*, 6
garden *der Garten, ⸚*, 6
geography *Geographie*, 2
German (language) *Deutsch*, 2
German (person) *der Deutsche, -n*, 2
German Democratic Republic *Deutsche Demokratische Republik (DDR)*, 1
Germany *Deutschland*, 1
get *bekommen*, 6; *holen*, 7; get to *kommen nach*, 5; how do you get to school? *wie kommst du in die Schule?* 2
gift *das Geschenk, -e*, 5
gift shop *der Geschenkladen, ⸚*, 5
girl *das Mädchen, -*, 1
girlfriend *die Freundin, -nen*, 6
give *geben*, 11; give as a gift *schenken*, 11; what should I give? *was soll ich nur schenken?* 11
glad *froh*, 9; I'm glad *das freut mich*, 9; I'm glad to hear that *da bin ich aber froh*, 9
glasses *die Brille, -n*, 6
go *gehen*, 5; when are we going to get going? *wann geht's los?* 9; *fahren*, 10; to go into the city *in die Stadt fahren*, 10; to go out *ausgehen*, 10
gone *weg*, 2
good *gut*, 2; good luck! *viel Glück!* 2; good! *schön!* 9
goodbye! *auf Wiedersehen!* 1; (on the phone) *auf Wiederhören!* 5
good morning! *good morning!* 1
goulasch soup *die Gulaschsuppe, -n*, 9
grade *die Note, -n*, 2; *die Klasse, -n*, 2
gram *das Gramm*, 7; 200 grams of cold cuts *200 Gramm Aufschnitt*, 7
grandma *die Oma, -s*, 6
grandpa *der Opa, -s*, 6
grandparents *die Grosseltern* (pl), 6
great! *prima!* 2; *toll!* 2; *Klasse!* 3; *schön!* 9
green *grün*, 11; the color green *das Grün*, 11; by the green symbol *bei Grün*, 5
greengrocer *der Gemüsehändler, -*, 7
grey *grau*, 11; the color grey *das Grau*, 11
group *die Gruppe, -n*, 10
guessing game *das Ratespiel, -e*, 9
guest room *das Gästezimmer, -*, 6
guitar *die Gitarre, -n*, 3
gymnastics *Gymnastik*, 3; to do gymnastics *Gymnastik machen*, 3

H

half *halb*, 7; half a pound of butter *ein halbes Pfund Butter*, 7
hamburger *der Hamburger, -*, 9
handsome *gut aussehen*, 6; he is handsome *er sieht gut aus*, 6
happy *froh*, 9; happy . . . *herzliche Glückwünsche zum . . .*, 11
hate *hassen*, 10
have *haben*, 11; I have it! *ich hab's!* 11; what do you have? *was gibt es alles?* 9
have to *müssen*, 10
he *er*, 2
head *der Kopf, ⸚e*, 7; a head of lettuce *ein Kopf Salat*, 7
heavyset *vollschlank*, 6
hello! *hallo!; Tag!; guten Tag!* 1; *Gruetzi!* (Swiss), 7
help: may I help you? *was darf es sein?* 11; yes, may I help you? *ja, bitte?* 11
her *ihr, ihre*, 9
here *hier*, 2; here comes *da kommt*, 2; here you are! *bitte!* 5
hey, . . . *du, . . .*, 2
hi! *grüss dich!; hallo!; Tag!* 1
high school *die Oberschule, -n*, 2; he goes to high school *er geht auf die Oberschule*, 2
his *sein, seine*, 5, 9
history *Geschichte*, 2
hm *tja*, 3
hobby *das Hobby, -s*, 3
hockey *Hockey*, 3
home: at home *zu Hause*, 10; to come home *nach Hause kommen*, 7; you'd better stay home *bleibt lieber zu Hause!* 7
homework *die Hausaufgaben* (pl), 2; he's doing homework *er macht Hausaufgaben*, 2
horror film *der Horrorfilm, -e*, 10
hot *heiss*, 7
house *das Haus, ⸚er*, 6
how *wie*, 1; and how! *und wie!* 9; how long? *wie lange?* 5; how many? *wieviel?* 6; how much? *wieviel?* 5; how much are . . .? *was kosten . . .?* 2; how much is . . .? *was kostet . . .?* 2; how often? *wie oft?* 3; how old are you? *wie alt bist du?* 1
hungry: to be hungry *Hunger haben*, 7; I'm hungry as a bear! *ich habe einen Bärenhunger!* 9

I

ice cream *das Eis*, 7
ice hockey *Eishockey*, 3
idea *die Idee, -n*, 9; I have no idea *keine Ahnung!* 7; idea for a gift *die Geschenkidee, -n*, 11
if *ob*, 5; *wenn*, 10
imaginative *phantasievoll*, 10
in *in*, 2; in the *im*, 5; they're in the ninth grade *sie gehen in die neunte Klasse*, 2
information *die Auskunft*, 5
inhabitant *der Einwohner, -*, 7
instrument *das Instrument, -e*, 3
interest *das Interesse, -n*, 10
interesting *interessant*, 3
interviewer *der Interviewer, -*, 3
into *in*, 5
invite *einladen*, 9
is: he is *er ist*, 1; she is *sie ist*, 1
it *er*, 2; *sie*, 2; *es*, 2
its *sein, seine*, 9

J

January *der Januar*, 11; in January *im Januar*, 11
joke *der Witz, -e*, 9
juice: apple juice *der Apfelsaft, ⸚e*, 9
July *der Juli*, 11
June *der Juni*, 11
just: I'll just ask . . . *ich frag' mal . . .*, 5; let's ask *fragen wir mal!* 10

K

kilogram *das Kilo = Kilogramm*, 7; 1 kilogram of tomatoes *1 kg Tomaten*, 7
kilometer *der Kilometer, -*, 5
kind: what kind of (a) *was für*, 10
kitchen *die Küche, -n*, 6
knapsack *der Rucksack, ⸚e*, 6
know *kennen*, 6; *wissen*, 7; I don't know *ich weiss nicht*, 2; I don't know yet *ich weiss noch nicht*, 11

L

land *landen*, 5
landmark *das Wahrzeichen, -*, 7
last: last night *gestern abend*, 10
later *später*, 9; a little later *etwas später*, 9
Latin *Latein*, 2
lazy: to lie around, be lazy *faulenzen*, 3
left *links*, 5; on the left *links*, 5
lemon soda *die Limonade, -n*, 9; *die Limo, -s*, 9
lettuce *der Salat, -e*, 7; a head of lettuce *ein Kopf Salat*, 7
lift *abheben*, 5; you lift the receiver *du hebst den Hörer ab*, 5
light *hell*, 6
like *mögen*, 10; *gern mögen*, 10; to like (to do) *gern (machen)*, 3; to like (to do) most of all *am liebsten (machen)*, 3; to not like (to do) *nicht gern (machen)*, 3; how do you like . . .?

wie findest du . . .? 3; would like to *möchten,* 5; yes, I'd like that *ja, gern,* 6
like *wie,* 5
likeable *sympathisch,* 6
listen (to) *hören,* 3; listen! *hör zu!* 9
liter *der Liter,* 7; a liter of milk *ein Liter Milch,* 7
live *wohnen,* 5; I live in Vienna *ich bin in Wien zu Hause,* 7
living room *das Wohnzimmer, -,* 6
locker *das Schliessfach, ¨er,* 5
look *schauen,* 5; to look in the newspaper *in die Zeitung schauen,* 10; look! *schau!* 2; *schau mal!* 2; to look (like) *aussehen,* 6; to look good *gut aussehen,* 6
look for *suchen,* 5
lose *verlieren,* 3
lot: a lot *viel,* 3
love story *der Liebesfilm, -e,* 10
luck: good luck! *viel Glück!* 2

M

mall: pedestrian mall *die Fussgängerzone, -n,* 7
many *viele,* 6
March *der März,* 11
mark *die Note, -n,* 2; *die Mark,* 2; German mark *Deutsche Mark (die D-Mark),* 5
math *Mathe,* 2
math teacher *der Mathematiklehrer, -,* 2
matter: what's the matter? *was ist los?* 7
May *der Mai,* 11
maybe *vielleicht,* 7
me? *ich?* 1; me too *ich auch,* 3
meat *das Fleisch,* 7; chopped meat *das Hackfleisch,* 7
meet *kennenlernen,* 6; you're going to meet a lot of people *du lernst viele Leute kennen,* 6
mention: don't mention it *nichts zu danken,* 6
merry *lustig,* 6; Merry Christmas *fröhliche Weihnachten,* 11
mile *die Meile, -n,* 5
milk *die Milch,* 7
million *die Million, -en,* 7; thanks a million! *tausend Dank!* 6
mineral water *das Mineralwasser,* 7
minute: wait a minute! *Moment mal!* 2
miserable *miserabel,* 10
Miss *Fräulein,* 1
missing: to be missing *fehlen,* 5
modern *modern,* 6
mom *die Mutti, -s,* 7
Monday *der Montag, -e,* 2; on Monday *am Montag,* 2
money *das Geld,* 5; German money *das deutsche Geld,* 5
monitor *der Monitor,* 5
month *der Monat, -e,* 3; (times) a month *im Monat,* 3
moped *das Moped, -s,* 2; by moped *mit dem Moped,* 2
more *mehr,* 6; once more *noch einmal,* 5; still more *noch mehr,* 6
most: to like (to do) most of all *am liebsten (machen),* 3
mostly *meistens,* 3
mother *die Mutter, ¨,* 5
Mother's Day *der Muttertag,* 11; for Mother's Day *zum Muttertag,* 11
movie *der Film, -e,* 9
movies *das Kino, -s,* 10; to go to the movies *ins Kino gehen,* 10
Mr. *Herr,* 1
Mrs. *Frau,* 1
much *viel,* 3
Munich *München,* 1
museum *das Museum, Museen,* 7
music *die Musik,* 2
music cassette *die Musikkassette, -n,* 3
must *müssen,* 10
mustard *der Senf,* 7
my *mein, meine,* 6

N

name *der Name, -n,* 2; his name is *er heisst,* 1; my name is *ich heisse,* 1; her name is *sie heisst,* 1; what's . . . name? *wie heisst . . .?* 1; is your name . . .? *heisst du . . .?* 1
name day *der Namenstag, -e,* 11; for (your) name day *zum Namenstag,* 11
nature film *der Naturfilm, -e,* 10
need *brauchen,* 5
never *nie,* 3
newspaper *die Zeitung, -en,* 10
nice *nett,* 6; *sympathisch,* 6; *schön,* 6; nice that you're here *schön, dass du da bist,* 6; not nice *unsympathisch,* 6
night: last night *gestern abend,* 10
nine *neun,* 1; nine-thirty *halb zehn,* 2
ninth grade *die neunte Klasse,* 2
no *nein,* 1; *kein, keine,* 9
nonsense! *Unsinn!* 2; *Quatsch!* 10
not *nicht,* 2; to not like (to do) *nicht gern (machen),* 3; not any *kein, keine,* 9
note *der Zettel, -,* 6
notebook *das Heft, -e,* 2
nothing *nichts,* 5
novel *der Roman, -e,* 3
November *der November,* 11
now *jetzt,* 2; now and then *ab und zu,* 7
number *die Zahl, -en,* 1; the numbers from zero to twenty *die Zahlen von null bis zwanzig,* 1; the numbers from 5 to 60 *die Zahlen von 5 bis 60,* 2

O

occupied *besetzt,* 5
October *der Oktober,* 11
of *von,* 6; a quarter of nine *Viertel vor neun,* 2; of course! *na klar!* 3; *natürlich!* 9
off *frei;* he has off, he has no school *er hat frei,* 2; off to *auf nach,* 5
official *der Beamte, -n,* 5
often *oft,* 3; how often? *wie oft?* 3
oh: oh, well *na ja,* 10
okay *O.K.,* 7; *gut,* 7; okay? *ja?* 10
old *alt,* 1
on *weiter,* 5; *auf,* 6
once *einmal,* 3
one *eins,* 2; (the grade of) one *eine Eins,* 2; *man,* 10
only *nur,* 2
opera *die Oper, -n,* 7; to go to the opera *in die Oper gehen,* 7
opinion: to have the opinion about *finden,* 3; *meinen,* 11
or *oder,* 1
our *unser, unsere,* 9
out *aus,* 2; school is out *die Schule ist aus,* 2; out of order *(der Apparat) geht nicht,* 5
over *aus,* 2; school is over *die Schule ist aus,* 2; over there *da drüben,* 2
overcast *bewölkt*

P

pants *die Hose, -n,* 11
pardon: I beg your pardon? *wie bitte?* 1
party *die Party, -s,* 6
passport *der Pass, ¨e,* 5; passport control *die Passkontrolle,* 5
passport case *die Brieftasche, -n,* 11
past: five past nine *fünf nach neun,* 2
pedestrian *der Fussgänger, -,* 7
pedestrian mall *die Fussgängerzone, -n,* 7
pen (ballpoint) *der Kuli, -s,* 2
pencil *der Bleistift, -e,* 2
penny *der Pfennig, -e,* 5
people *die Leute* (pl), 6; people in general *man,* 10
perfume *das Parfüm, -s,* 11
phone *der Apparat, -e,* 5; the phone is out of order *der Apparat geht nicht,* 5
phone booth *die Telefonzelle, -n,* 5
physics *Physik,* 2
pick up *holen,* 5
piece: a five-mark piece *ein fünf-Mark-Stück,* 5
pizza *die Pizza, -s,* 7
plan *planen,* 5
plane *die Maschine, -n,* 5
plans: to have plans *etwas vorhaben,* 9
play *spielen,* 3
playing cards *die Spielkarten* (pl), 5; *Kartenspielen,* 3
please *bitte,* 2
pleasure: my pleasure! *gern geschehen!* 5
pocket calculator *der Taschenrechner, -,* 2
poor: poor Peter! *armer Peter!* 6
post office *die Post,* 5
poster *das Poster, -,* 2
potato salad *der Kartoffelsalat, -e,* 9
pound *das Pfund,* 7; two pounds of sugar *zwei Pfund Zucker,* 7

prefer *lieber,* 3; to prefer (to do) *lieber (machen),* 3
present *das Geschenk, -e,* 5
pretty *hübsch; schön,* 6; she is pretty *sie sieht gut aus,* 6
punctual *pünktlich,* 5
pupil *der Schüler, -,* 3
put *stecken,* 5

Q

quarter: a quarter after nine *Viertel nach neun,* 2
quartz watch *die Quarzuhr, -en,* 11
quick *schnell,* 7
quiet! *Ruhe!* 9

R

radio *das Radio, -s,* 11
rain *der Regen,* 7; it's raining *es regnet,* 7
raincoat *der Regenmantel, ⸚,* 7
rather *lieber,* 3; I'd rather play soccer *ich spiele lieber Fussball,* 3
read *lesen,* 3; what do you read? *was liest du?* 3
really *wirklich,* 5; really? *wirklich? 3;* really great! *ganz prima!* 9
receive *bekommen,* 6
receiver (phone) *der Hörer, -,* 5; you lift the receiver *du hebst den Hörer ab,* 5
recess *die Pause, -n,* 2
record *die Platte, -n,* 9
record player *der Plattenspieler, -,* 9
red *rot,* 11; in red *in Rot,* 11; the color red *das Rot,* 11
relative *der Verwandte, -n,* 5
religion *Religion,* 2
reporter *der Reporter, -* (m), 10; *die Reporterin, -nen* (f), 10
restaurant *das Restaurant, -s,* 5
restroom *die Toilette, -n,* 5
ride *fahren,* 10
right *rechts,* 5; on the right *rechts,* 5; right away *gleich,* 9; that's right! *stimmt!* 3; to be right *recht haben,* 6
ring *klingeln,* 9; the phone rings *es klingelt,* 9
rock concert *das Rockkonzert, -e,* 10
roll *die Semmel, -n,* 7
room *das Zimmer, -,* 6

S

sad *traurig,* 7
sail *segeln,* 3
sailing *Segeln,* 3
sale: on sale *im Angebot,* 11
salesperson *die Verkäuferin, -nen,* 2
same: it's all the same to me *das ist mir gleich,* 10
Saturday *der Samstag, -e,* 3; *der Sonnabend, -e,* 2; on Saturday *am Sonnabend,* 2; (on) Saturdays *sonnabends,* 2
sausage *die Wurst, ⸚e,* 7; fried sausage *die Bratwurst, ⸚e,* 7
say *sagen,* 5; say, . . . *sag, . . .,* 11
scarf *das Halstuch, ⸚er,* 11
schedule: class schedule *der Stundenplan, ⸚e,* 2
schmaltzy *schmalzig,* 10
science-fiction film *der Science-fiction-Film, -e,* 10
school *die Schule, -n,* 2; high school *die Oberschule, -n,* 2; he goes to high school *er geht auf die Oberschule,* 2; how do you get to school? *wie kommst du in die Schule?* 2
school supplies *die Schulsachen* (pl), 2
see *sehen,* 6; oh, I see! *ach so!* 5; see you later! *bis dann!* 1; see you soon! *bis gleich!* 5
seldom *selten,* 3
sensational *sensationell,* 10
September *der September,* 11
she *sie; es,* 2
shine *scheinen,* 7
shirt *das Hemd, -en,* 11
shoe *der Schuh, -e,* 11
shopping: to go shopping *einkaufen gehen,* 7
shopping list *der Einkaufszettel, -,* 7
short *klein,* 6
should *sollen,* 7; what on earth should I give my father? *was schenke ich bloss meinem Vater?* 11
show *zeigen,* 6; I'll show it to you *ich zeig' es dir,* 6
sight *die Sehenswürdigkeit, -en,* 7
sing *singen,* 10
singer *der Sänger, -,* 10
sister *die Schwester, -n,* 6; brothers and sisters *die Geschwister* (pl), 6
ski: I go skiing *ich laufe Schi,* 3
slim *schlank,* 6
slip (of paper) *der Zettel, -,* 6
small *klein,* 6
snack bar *die Imbiss-Stube, -n,* 7
so *so,* 2; so long! *tschüs! tschau!* 2; so what?! *na und?* 9
soccer *Fussball,* 3
something *etwas,* 5
sometimes *manchmal,* 3
soon *bald,* 11; see you soon! *bis gleich!* 5
sore *sauer,* 3
so-so *so lala,* 10
soup *die Suppe, -n,* 9
speak: (Nedel) speaking *hier (Nedel),* 5
spend (time) *verbringen,* 10
spite: in spite of *trotzdem,* 7
spring *das Frühjahr,* 3; in the spring *im Frühjahr,* 3
sport *der Sport,* 3; sports *der Sport,* 3; to participate in a sport, to do sports *Sport machen,* 3
sports event *die Sportveranstaltung, -en,* 10
squash *Squash,* 10
stamp *die Briefmarke, -n,* 3
start *anfangen,* 10
stay *bleiben,* 5
stick *stecken,* 5
still *noch,* 5; still more *noch mehr,* 6
straight: straight ahead *geradeaus,* 5
strawberry punch *die Erdbeerbowle, -n,* 9
street *die Strasse, -n,* 7; on Prinzregenten Street *in der Prinzregentenstrasse,* 7
streetcar *die Strassenbahn, -en,* 2; by streetcar *mit der Strassenbahn,* 2
stroll: stroll through the city *der Stadtbummel, -,* 10; to take a stroll through the city *einen Stadtbummel machen,* 10
student *der Schüler, -,* 3
stupid *blöd,* 2; *dumm,* 10
subject *das Fach, ⸚er,* 2
suburb *der Vorort, -e,* 7
sugar *der Zucker,* 7
suit: that suits me fine *das passt prima,* 9
summer *der Sommer, -,* 3; in the summer *im Sommer,* 3
sun *die Sonne,* 7
Sunday *der Sonntag, -e,* 3; on Sunday *am Sonntag,* 3
sunny *sonnig,* 7
super! *super!* 3
supermarket *der Supermarkt, ⸚e,* 7
supposed to *sollen,* 7
sweater *der Pulli, -s,* 11
swim *schwimmen,* 3
Switzerland *die Schweiz,* 1; from Switzerland *aus der Schweiz,* 1; in Switzerland *in der Schweiz,* 7

T

take *nehmen,* 9
talk *sprechen,* 9; Karin would like to talk to you *die Karin möchte dich sprechen,* 9
tall *gross,* 6
taste *schmecken,* 7; how does it taste? *wie schmeckt's?* 7; that's a matter of taste *das ist Geschmackssache,* 6
teacher *der Lehrer, -* (m), 1; *die Lehrerin, -nen* (f), 1; German teacher *der Deutschlehrer, -,* 1
telephone *das Telefon, -e,* 5; to telephone, make a phone call *telefonieren,* 5
telephone receiver *der Hörer, -,* 5
telephoning *Telefonieren,* 5
tell *erzählen,* 9
teller *der Bankangestellte, -n,* 5
tennis *Tennis,* 3
terrible *furchtbar,* 9
terrific! *Spitze!* 3
test *die Klassenarbeit, -en,* 2
thank *danken,* 5; thank goodness! *Gott sei Dank!* 5; thank you *danke,* 2
thanks *danke,* 2; fine, thanks *gut, danke,* 10; thanks a lot! *vielen Dank!* 6; thanks a million! *tausend Dank!* 6
that *das,* 1; that comes to *das sind,* 5; that's . . . *das ist . . .* 1; *dass,* 6
the *der, die, das,* 1

theater *das Theater, -,* 10; to go to the theater *ins Theater gehen,* 10
their *ihr, ihre,* 9
then *dann,* 2; now and then *ab und zu,* 7
there *da, dort,* 2; over there *da drüben, dort drüben,* 2; there is, there are *es gibt,* 5; up there *dort oben,* 7; we'll be there *wir sind da,* 5; we're here *wir sind da,* 6
these *dies-,* 11; these are *das sind,* 6
they *sie,* 2
think *finden,* 3; *meinen,* 6; *glauben,* 10; do you think so? *findest du? meinst du?* 6; don't you think so? *meinst du nicht?* 6; I don't think so *das finde ich nicht,* 3; I think so *ich glaube, ja,* 11; what do you think? *was meinst du?* 11; what do you think about . . .? *wie findest du . . .?* 3
this *dies-,* 11
thousand *tausend,* 6
three *drei,* 3; three times *dreimal,* 3
through *durch,* 5
Thursday *der Donnerstag,* 2; on Thursday *am Donnerstag,* 2
ticket (plane) *das Flugticket, -s,* 5
tie *die Krawatte, -n,* 11
time *die Zeit, -en,* 5; at what time? *um wieviel Uhr?* 9; free time *die Freizeit,* 3; in your free time *in deiner Freizeit,* 3; on time *pünktlich,* 5; what time is it? *wie spät ist es?*
times: three times *dreimal,* 3; four times *viermal,* 3
to *nach; zu,* 5; off to *auf nach,* 5
today *heute,* 2
together *zusammen,* 10
toilet *die Toilette, -n,* 5
tomato *die Tomate, -n,* 7
tomorrow *morgen,* 5
too *zu,* 10; me too *ich auch,* 3
tower *der Turm, ¨e,* 7
train *die Bahn,* 5; by train *mit der Bahn,* 5
travel bag *die Reisetasche, -n,* 5
travel book *das Reisebuch, ¨er,* 11
travel guide *der Reiseführer, -,* 5
traveler *der Reisende, -n,* 5
traveler's check *der Reisescheck, -s,* 5
trip *die Reise, -n,* 5
true! *stimmt!* 3; not true! that's not so! *stimmt nicht!* 3
try *versuchen,* 5; *probieren,* 7; why don't you try . . . *probier doch mal . . .* 7
T-shirt *das T-Shirt, -s,* 11
Tuesday *der Dienstag,* 2; on Tuesday *am Dienstag,* 2
twice *zweimal,* 3

U

umbrella *der Regenschirm, -e,* 7
uncle *der Onkel, -,* 6
understand *verstehen,* 9
unfortunately *leider,* 7; I'm sorry, I don't know *ich weiss es leider nicht,* 7
unpack *auspacken,* 6; he unpacks his backpack *er packt den Rucksack aus,* 6
unpleasant *unsympathisch,* 6
up: up there *dort oben,* 7; what's up? *was gibt's?* 9
upstairs *oben,* 6
usually *gewöhnlich,* 11

V

vacation *die Ferien* (pl), 5; have a nice vacation! *schöne Ferien!* 5; to go on vacation *Ferien machen,* 5
vegetable *das Gemüse,* 7
very *sehr,* 6
video recorder *der Video-Recorder, -,* 9
Vienna *Wien,* 1
village *das Dorf, ¨er,* 7
visit *besuchen,* 3
visitor *der Besucher, -,* 7

W

wait: wait a minute! *Moment mal!* 2
waiting room *die Wartehalle, -n,* 5
Walkman *der Walkman,* 5
wallet *das Portemonnaie, -s,* 11
want *wollen,* 10
war film *der Kriegsfilm, -e,* 10
warm *warm,* 7
watch *die Uhr, -en,* 11; wristwatch *die Armbanduhr, -en,* 11
we *wir,* 2
weather *das Wetter,* 7
weather report *der Wetterbericht, -e,* 7
Wednesday *der Mittwoch,* 2; on Wednesday *am Mittwoch,* 2
week *die Woche, -n,* 5; (times) a week *in der Woche,* 3
weekend *das Wochenende, -n,* 3; on the weekend *am Wochenende,* 3
welcome: welcome to . . .! *Willkommen in . . .!* 6; you're welcome *bitte,* 2; *bitte sehr,* 5; *bitte schön,* 6
well *na,* 2; *gut,* 9; well, okay *na gut,* 7; well then *so,* 6; *na, dann,* 9; *also,* 10; well, yes *nun ja,* 10
western *der Western, -,* 10
what? *was?* 2; *welche?* 2; what?! *was?!* 3
when? *wann?* 2; *wenn?* 10
where? *wo?* 2; from where? *woher?* 1; to where? *wohin?* 5; where are you from? *woher bist du?* 1
whether *ob,* 5
which *welch-,* 10
white *weiss,* 11; the color white *das Weiss,* 11
who? *wer?* 1; who's that? *wer ist das?* 1
whom? *wen?* 5
why? *warum?* 10
win *gewinnen,* 3
winter *der Winter, -,* 3; in the winter *im Winter,* 3
with *mit,* 7
worry: don't worry *keine Sorge,* 7
wow! *Mensch!* 6
wristwatch *die Armbanduhr, -en,* 11

Y

year *das Jahr, -e,* 1; thirteen years old *dreizehn Jahre alt,* 1; (times) a year *im Jahr,* 3
yellow *gelb,* 11; the color yellow *das Gelb,* 11
yes *ja,* 1
yet: not yet *noch nicht,* 11; I don't know yet *ich weiss noch nicht,* 11
yogurt *der Joghurt,* 7
you *du,* 1; *Sie* (formal), 1; *ihr, Sie* (pl), 2; (in general) *man,* 10; it's you! *du bist's!* 5
young people *die Jugend; die Jugendlichen* (pl), 10
your *dein, deine* (sing), 6; *euer, eure* (pl), 9; *Ihr, Ihre* (formal), 9
youth *die Jugend,* 10

V

vase *die Vase, -n,* 11

GRAMMAR INDEX

ABBREVIATIONS

acc	*accusative*	nom	*nominative*
comm	*command*	pers	*person*
conv past	*conversational past*	plur	*plural*
dat	*dative*	prep	*preposition*
def	*definition*	pres	*present*
def art	*definite article*	pron	*pronoun(s)*
dir obj	*direct object*	ques	*question(s)*
indef art	*indefinite article*	sep pref	*separable prefix*
indir obj	*indirect object*	sing	*singular*
inf	*infinitive*	subj	*subject*
interr	*interrogative*		

15: (c)Elizabeth Opalenik/Stock Market; (b)Julius Fekete/Stock Market; **16:** (t)Courtesy *Beitung und Herold;* (b) Culver; **17:** Bettmann Archive; **18:** (l)Culver; (c) Culver; (r)German Information Center; **22:** (t)Maggie Steber/Stock Boston; (b)German Information Center; **23:** (tl)Dagmar Fabricius/Stock Boston; (tr)Ted Horowitz/Stock Market; (c) Courtesy of CMA–German Agricultural Marketing Board; (2nd from b)Courtesy Mercedes-Benz; (b)Courtesy Braun; **24:** (tl)Paolo Koch/Photo Researchers; (tr)Joachim Messerschmidt/Leo de Wys; (cl)Gabe Palmer/Stock Market; (cr)Rick Browne/Stock Boston; (bl)Arthur Grace/Stock Boston; (br)Gabe Palmer/Stock Market; **25:** (tr)Tomas Sennett/Magnum; (c)Brownie Harris/Stock Market; (bl)Chris Sorensen/Stock Market; (br)Homer Sykes/Woodfin Camp; **34:** (tr)Abbott/Leo de Wys; (2nd row l)Ted Horowitz/Stock Market; (3rd row l)Robin Schwartz/International Stock Photo; (b, 3rd from l)Nancy Brown/Image Bank; (b, 2nd from r)Gabe Palmer/Stock Market; (br)S. Niedorf/ Image Bank; **38:** (cl)Abbott/Leo de Wys; (cr)Ted Horowitz/Stock Market; **53:** Shostal Associates; **70:** (br)Ted Horowitz/Stock Market; **95:** (tl)Clyde Smith/Peter Arnold; (c)Werner Müller/Peter Arnold; (tr)Werner Müller/Peter Arnold; (bl)Jon Feingersh/ Stock Market; (br)Tom King/Image Bank; **104:** (br)© World Copyright 1986 by Rolf Kauka and Erich Pabel Verlag GmbH; **119:** (t)*Max und Moritz,* the complete edition, by Wilhelm Busch. Pestalozzi Verlag; (cl)© 1966 and 1952 Walt Disney Productions. Deutsche Übersetzung: © 1970 Walt Disney Productions. Erschienen im Delphin Verlag, Stuttgart and Zurich; (c)© Dargaud Editeur 1969; (cr)*Der Struwwelpeter,* the complete edition, by Dr. Heinr. Hoffman. Pestalozzi Verlag; **125:** (t)Joachim Messerschmidt/Leo de Wys; **127:** (cl)Wolfgang Kunz/Bilderberg; **128:** (cr)Steve Vidler/Leo de Wys; (b)Porterfield/Chickering/Photo Researchers; **129:** (tl)Milan Horacek/Bilderberg; (tr)Milan Horacek/Bilderberg; (bl)Walter Schmidt/Peter Arnold; (br)Dagmar Fabricius/Stock Boston; **134:** Lufthansa Airlines; **135:** (tr)Lufthansa Airlines; (bl)Lufthansa Airlines; **143:** Lufthansa Airlines; **144:** (t)Lufthansa Airlines; **145** (r)Volker Corell; **158:** Lufthansa Airlines; **168:** (tc)Lawrence Fried/Image Bank; (tr)Lawrence Fried/Image Bank; (cr)Nancy Brown/Image Bank; **191:** (b)Culver; **210:** (bl)Porges/Peter Arnold; (bc)Lothar Reupert/Image Bank; (br)Lisl Dennis/Image Bank; **229:** Thomas Höpker/ Woodfin Camp; (insert)Thomas Höpker/Anne Hamann; **230:** (tl oval)Thomas Höpker/ Anne Hamann; (tr)Jim Cartier/Photo Researchers; (cl) J. Kappelmeyer/Leo de Wys; (cr)Rudi Meisel/Visum/Woodfin Camp; (b)Yada Claassen/Stock Boston; **231:** (tl)Thomas Höpker/Anne Hamann; (tr)Tom McHugh/Photo Researchers; (cl)Thomas Höpker/Anne Hamann; (cr)Thomas Höpker/Anne Hamann; (b)Tom McHugh/Photo Researchers; **232:** (cr)Fred McKinney/Stock Market; (b)Vera Bradshaw/Photo Researchers; **233:** (t)Cornell Capa/Magnum; (tr insert)Thomas Höpker/ Anne Hamann; (cr)Thomas Höpker/Anne Hamann; (bl)John Mason/Stock Market; (br)Claudia Parks/Stock Market; **234:** (t)Dallas & John Heaton/Click Chicago; (cl)Claudia Parks/Stock Market; (cr)Swiss National Tourist Office; (b)Swiss National Tourist Office; **235:** (tl)Fred Mayer/Anne Hamann; (tr circle)Cottom Coulson/Woodfin Camp; (cl)Fred Mayer/Anne Hamann; (cr)Paolo Koch/Photo Researchers; (b)Fred Mayer/Anne Hamann; **236:** (t)J. Mahl/Leo de Wys; (t insert)James Sugar/Photo Researchers; (cr)Weiss-Rapho/Photo Researchers; (b)Ossi Baumeister/Anne Hamann; **240:** (t)George Ancona/International Stock Photo; **243:** (bl)Ted Horowitz/Stock Market; (bc)Abbott/Leo de Wys; (br)Jonas/Leo de Wys; **247:** (bl)Jonas/Leo de Wys; **248:** (l)Peter Russell Clemens/International Stock Photo; **255:** (cl)Peter Russell Clemens/International Stock Photo; **256** (tl)Peter Russell Clemens/International Stock Photo; **281:** (tr)Museum of Modern Art Film Stills Library; (cl)Kobal Collection; (center)Globe Photos; (cr)Kobal Collection; (bl)Kobal Collection; (bc)Kobal Collection; (br)Kobal Collection; **285:** (t)Globe Photos; (c)Kobal Collection; (b)Universal Pictures; **296:** D. Fineman/Sygma; **297:** T. Westenberger/Sygma; **298:** (1)Reporta/New Eyes: (r)Gurlitt/ Gamma-Liason; **299:** (l)Gamma-Liason; (r)Lothar Lange/New Eyes; **313:** (b)K. McCunnall/Leo de Wys; **333:** (t)Owen Franken/Stock Boston; (c oval)Francisco Hidalgo/Image Bank; (bl)Michael Rosenfeld/Image Bank; (br)Horst Schäfer/Peter Arnold; **334:** (tl)H. Gritscher/Peter Arnold; (tr)H. Gritscher/Peter Arnold; (bl)Wolfgang Kunz/Bilderberg; (br)Horst Schäfer/Peter Arnold; **335:** (tl)Horst Schäfer/Peter Arnold; (tr)Horst Schäfer/Peter Arnold; (b)Horst Schäfer/Peter Arnold; **336:** (t)Hans Madej/ Bilderberg; (cr)Michael Engler/Bilderberg; **337:** (t)J. Messerschmidt/Leo de Wys; (b)F. Damm/Leo de Wys; **338:** (t)F. Damm/Leo de Wys; (tl insert)Horst Schäfer/Peter Arnold; (c)Owen Franken/Stock Boston; (b)F. P. Wartenberg/New Eyes; **339:** (tl)Silvestris GmbH; (tr)Horst Schäfer/Peter Arnold; (c 2nd from b)Grotty/New Eyes; **340:** (tl)L. Freed/Magnum; (tr)Volker Corell; (c)Silvestris GmbH.

ART CREDITS: Bert Dodson **164, 165, 324, 325, 326** Eldon Doty **321** Don Dyen **36, 42, 45, 50, 51, 78, 84, 94, 101, 106, 111, 140, 157, 181, 187, 215, 252, 261, 305** Tonia Hampson **205, 206, 207, 208, 209, 266, 267** Diane Dawson Hearn **192, 193** Steven Schindler **39, 40, 79, 89, 97, 98, 107, 108, 182, 183, 274** Lauren Simeone **64, 66, 67, 81, 97, 142, 171, 185, 258, 276, 290, 302, 303, 306, 307, 308, 311, 312, 313, 314, 315, 316, 317, 319, 320, 321, 331**

A 7
B 8
C 9
D 0
E 1
F 2
G 3
H 4
I 5
J 6